# Answers to Objections

# ANSWERS
## TO OBJECTIONS

AN EXAMINATION OF THE MAJOR OBJECTIONS RAISED
AGAINST THE TEACHINGS OF SEVENTH-DAY ADVENTISTS

*(Revised and Greatly Enlarged)*

**BY**
## FRANCIS D. NICHOL

**Foreword by W. H. Branson**

**TEACH Services, Inc.**
P U B L I S H I N G
www.TEACHServices.com • (800) 367-1844

## Facsimile Reproduction

As this book played a formative role in the development of Christian thought, the publisher feels that this book, with its candor and depth, still holds significance for the church today. Therefore, the publisher has chosen to reproduce this historical classic from an original copy. Frequent variations in the quality of the print are unavoidable due to the condition of the original. Thus the print may look darker or lighter or appear to missing detail, more in some places than in others.

Copyright © 1932, 1947, 1952 Review and Herald Publishing Association
Copyright © 2005, 2014 TEACH Services, Inc.
ISBN-13: 978-1-4796-0205-6
Library of Congress Control Number: 2004111586

Published by

TEACH Services, Inc.
P U B L I S H I N G
www.TEACHServices.com • (800) 367-1844

## DEDICATION

*To That Valiant Company in the Advent
Movement, Both Ministerial and Lay, Who
Seek to Present to Men the Truth of God
With Convincing and Convicting Power,
This Book Is Prayerfully Dedicated*

# CONTENTS

## PART I

### Section I: Law

7

# CONTENTS

24. When we as Sundaykeepers declare that the ten-commandment law was abolished at the cross, Adventists try to embarrass us by asking us if we believe it is all right in the Christian Era to steal or kill or do any other of the heinous deeds prohibited by the Decalogue. We do not. We believe that God has great moral principles that have governed the universe from all eternity and will continue to govern it to all eternity. The Decalogue was simply a partial reflection of these principles. The principles remain, but the Decalogue is gone. Hence the Sabbath is gone. ................................................................ 138

25. The fourth commandment in the Decalogue is not inherently a moral precept, but the other nine are self-evidently moral commands. "All moral principles are discoverable by the light of nature" or reason, but the necessity of keeping the seventh day is not thus discoverable. For example, all men naturally know that it is wrong to steal, kill, commit adultery, et cetera, but no one would thus know that a particular day had been set apart as holy. That required a direct revelation from God. Hence the Sabbath command is not moral. Furthermore, there is nothing inherently holy in the seventh day of the week. Hence "it would never have been wrong to work on the seventh day unless God had given a command to rest on it." ................................................................ 141

26. "The Sabbath was not a day of special religious worship. . . . In God's plan, the keeping of the seventh day on the part of His earthly people was to be an external form, or rite; the performance of a definitely prescribed ceremony, stipulating the cessation of all work on a given day, or a day of complete *physical* rest. Only when connected with the annual feasts was it observed as a day of religious significance." All this proves that the seventh-day Sabbath was simply one of the ceremonial sabbaths. All those sabbaths, in common with every other ceremonial statute, were abolished at the cross. .................... 150

27. That the fourth command of the Decalogue is ceremonial, but the other nine are moral, "is clearly proved by the fact that Jesus, according to the strictest Sabbatarians of His day, broke the fourth commandment and was criticized by them for doing so. Furthermore, Jesus distinctly says, 'The priests in the temple profane the Sabbath, and are blameless.' [Matt. 12:5.] Would He have dared to say this if the fourth commandment were

# CONTENTS

# CONTENTS

# CONTENTS

ANSWERS TO OBJECTIONS

16

# CONTENTS

17

# CONTENTS

**Section V: Sanctuary and Atonement**

19

# CONTENTS

ingman and are blind to the fact that the very stability of the country is endangered by the godless course of millions who give no day in the week to God. It seems that they are more concerned to protect themselves against persecution than to give support either to the workingman or to the moral uplift of the country. .................... 429

## PART II

### Section I: Science and the Advent Faith

### Section II: The Law and Legalism

### Section III: The Sabbath and the Weekly Cycle

### Section IV: The Second Advent

# ANSWERS TO OBJECTIONS

# FOREWORD

## By W. H. Branson

IN BRINGING out a revised and enlarged edition of this work, the author has rendered a signal service to the cause of God, further strengthening the hands of those whose lives are dedicated to the proclamation and defense of present truth.

The history of the Christian church is one of conflict. The enemy of truth and righteousness has always tried to minimize obedience to the commandments of God and to pervert the true teachings of the Bible. Wherever the pure gospel has been preached, opposition has made itself felt. The struggle has continued through the centuries in different forms. In these closing days of time, when the dragon with increased fury is warring against the remnant who seek to uphold the integrity of God's eternal law, there is need as never before that the champions of truth stand fast in defense of the faith. The Christian witness is called upon today to present a positive message, hewn out of the Word of God, a message that will stand in the evil day of satanic delusion and will leave men and women established in the Christian verities.

This volume gives a clear-cut, convincing answer to the objections most frequently raised by critics of the doctrines held by the Seventh-day Adventist Church. The objection is frankly set forth and the answer fully given in such a way as to win the confidence of the reader in the integrity of the presentation. Sources of information and authority not ordinarily available to the minister engaged in general church work are brought forward to clarify the logic of the statements made.

Throughout their entire history Seventh-day Adventists have stood for certain distinct doctrines, some of which differ rather sharply from the teaching of other Christian bodies. Because of our insistence upon the Scriptural authenticity of these unpopular teachings, we have naturally found it frequently necessary to defend our positions against those who would by careless or faulty interpretation seek to sweep away the distinctive tenets of our faith. Those pioneers of the church who laid so truly and well the foundation upon which we now build, were able to do so only by arduous study and fervent prayer. But their work has survived. Every assault has further demonstrated the impregnability of our fundamental doctrinal positions. This does not mean, however, that we are now immune to attack or that we can safely ignore the criticisms of the present day. There is no discharge in the war we are called upon to wage in defense of the faith. With meekness and fear, and yet with an unalterable resolution, we are constantly to be ready with an answer for the hope within us, and so much the more as we "see the day approaching."

With hearty approval, therefore, we commend this book to every gospel worker. It will prove a ready helper in meeting both the attacks of the theological critic and the sincere questions of the perplexed inquirer. It will without doubt win honored acceptance as a valuable contribution to the literature written in defense of the Holy Scriptures and the doctrines of the Advent faith.

# To the Reader of This Book

IT IS much more delightful to revel in the fragrance and beauty of the flowers in a garden than to busy oneself removing cutworms from the plants. Few of us even wish to discuss such unpleasant things, much less to deal with them. Why talk of them when we may talk of flowers? But unless we remove the cutworms we shall not long be able to enjoy the flowers.

This simple illustration provides the reason for this book. It is written to meet false doctrine and thus to help ensure that the flowers of truth may continue to bloom and disseminate their heavenly fragrance to the children of men.

Perhaps some devout individual may reply that the illustration does not fit. He does not wish to think that enemies lurk in the garden of God. At least he feels that God will care for His own, and that the plants of the Lord, with their roots deep in the soil of eternal truth, can safely withstand all attacks. Therefore we should devote our time wholly to enjoying the flowers and to inviting the wayfarer to enter the heavenly garden and enjoy them with us.

The troubled history of the Christian church reveals the fallacy of such thinking. Even in the earliest, most divinely vigorous period of Christianity, the apostles felt it necessary to deal with threatening doctrinal dangers. John, whose writings breathe the spirit of love, warned, in his epistles, against the deadly Docetic heresy then developing, that Christ was but an apparition. (See 1 John 1:1-3; 4:2, 3.) He also warned against the heretical idea that a Christian is beyond sin, and the equally heretical idea that we do not need to keep God's commandments. The person who sets forth such a view, said John, "is a liar, and the truth is not in him." 1 John 2:4. He discusses the matter at length to prove *why* such teachings are false.

Paul told the Corinthian church: "I determined not to know any thing among you, save Jesus Christ, and him crucified." 1 Cor. 2:2. And some would use that isolated declaration to support the contention that the gospel minister should take no notice of false teachings or opposition. How unwarranted a conclusion can be drawn from a text when it is isolated from its whole context!

Paul's epistles are generally tightly reasoned presentations of truth, with a negative as well as a positive aspect. Indeed he preached Christ crucified. But he realized that unless the deadly heresy of Jewish legalism was exposed and refuted, the preaching of Christ would profit nothing. That is why his epistles deal so repeatedly and lengthily with that heresy. Nor was it the only doctrinal error that he exposed and refuted. Note, for example, his extended and militant argument against the false teaching that "there is no resurrection of the dead." 1 Cor. 15:12. One cannot read his writings without exclaiming: "If Paul was not God's lawyer, pray tell what was he!"

Nor was this great apostle content simply to carry on militantly himself. He exhorted others to do likewise. To Timothy he wrote: "Fight the good fight of faith." "Hold fast the form of sound words, which thou hast heard of me." 1 Tim. 6:12; 2 Tim. 1:13. To the elders of the church at Ephesus he told of the "grievous wolves" that would "enter in among" them, "not sparing the flock," and of those in their own midst who would "arise, speaking perverse things, to draw away disciples after them." Then he added immediately: "Therefore watch, and remember, that by the space of three years I ceased not to warn every one night and day with tears." Acts 20:29-31. When you "warn" you warn *against*. And this inevitably involves a negative action, justified however by its results, the protecting of the believer from false doctrine.

Jude wrote: "Beloved, when I gave all diligence to write unto you of the common salvation, it was needful for me to write unto you, and exhort you that ye should earnestly contend for the faith which was once delivered unto the saints." Jude 3. The whole of his brief letter warns against and exposes "certain men" who had "crept in unawares" and were corrupting morals and "denying" basic Christian doctrine.

Peter warned the church of "false teachers among you, who privily shall bring in damnable heresies." 2 Peter 2:1. Then he proceeds to devote most of his epistle to an examination and refutation of those heresies.

The written record of these resolute, militant men of God seems not to support the idea that we should concentrate exclusively on enjoying the flowers, because forsooth the hardy plants of truth need no protecting care from God's husbandmen.

During the Reformation period its advocates had to do more than focus on the positive truth of righteousness by faith, and related doctrines. They had to deal with strong and specious arguments brought forth by Rome's most subtle protagonists.

In the Advent awakening of the early 1840's William Miller and his associates were not permitted to deal exclusively with the glorious, positive truth of the personal soon coming of Christ. They had to spend time refuting the plausible arguments of popular ministers who sought, among other things, to prove from Scripture that world conversion preceded Christ's Advent. The literature of the 1844 movement is filled with the vigorous, cogent reasoning of the Advent leaders as they exposed error and exalted truth.

When the Seventh-day Adventist movement developed, immediately afterward there began to come from our press special tracts and pamphlets and books answering the claims of those who contended that Sunday is taught in the Scriptures, that immortality of soul is the possession of men, that the law of God is abolished, and other false doctrines.

All this was inevitable. The presentation of any belief or doctrine, religious or otherwise, is in two parts: setting forth evidence for the belief, and answering those who bring forth arguments for a contrary belief.

Now, the initial period of militant advocacy of belief, and the refutation of false teachings, has almost always been followed by quieter times. A religious movement brought forth amid controversy and opposition discovers in time that it has secured a measure of standing among men. Then comes the temptation to stress less earnestly the distinctive truths that brought the movement into existence. It was this policy that caused early Christianity to merge with paganism and various Protestant churches ultimately to lose their distinctiveness. Peace appeals as strongly to the warrior on the religious battlefield as it does to the literal soldier. The mistake that the spiritual warrior makes is in thinking that in this world, so dominated by evil, he can ever hope to conclude an honorable peace that will leave the kingdom of God safe from all future attacks. There is no discharge in the warfare until God declares, "It is done."

I am fully aware that the religious temper of the times is against emphasizing, much less fighting for, distinctive beliefs. It is not supposed to be good taste. It delays the much-desired union of all churches. Certainly if the churches wish above all else to unite, they must play down their differences in theology. But by the same token, if a church wishes to maintain its identity and to justify its separate existence, it must be ready to give a reason for the hope and the doctrines that it holds, and this inevitably includes meeting the assaults of those who would seek to undermine its hope and its doctrines.

There is one point above all others that distinguishes this Advent movement, the firm belief that God raised it up to preach a distinctive message, and to call on all men to join it in readiness for the day of God. If we sincerely act upon this belief, we must be prepared to meet opposition, an opposition which we have prophetic reason to know will become more active and more bitter as the end draws near. Let us never forget that our announced objective is the completing of the great sixteenth-century Protestant Reformation. That Reformation owes its very name to the militant protest made against false teachings though, of course, Prot-

TO THE READER OF THIS BOOK

estantism stands for a great body of positive truths. We belie
the great name Protestant when we no longer are concerned to
protest that which is opposed to truth.

As members of the Advent movement we should be forever
warned of the danger of buying peace with the currency of compromise as we note what has happened to most of Protestantism
today. At the opening of the twentieth century a great number
of the Christian ministry were still firm believers in the historic
doctrines of Christianity, beginning with the doctrine of creation.
But an active, persuasive, and well-educated group of clergy were
presenting the case for evolution and related rationalistic ideas.
It was evident that their theories were opposed to the long-established doctrines of Christianity. And how did they seek to pierce
this defensive doctrinal wall? By the simple expedient of minimizing the importance of doctrine and affirming that Christianity is
really a matter of the spirit, a beautiful fellowship with God as our
Father and with all men as brothers, and that everything else is
incidental. Hence, if science has great discoveries for us, let us
make the doctrines fit the discoveries. Which is another way of
saying, Let us abandon the doctrines.

And that is precisely what has happened in most churches.
True, there was a fierce war waged for a time, coming to something
of a climax in the 1920's. After that the majority of church leaders who had fought for orthodoxy gradually gave up, their will
to fight having been sapped by the highly promoted notion that
peace and harmony are more important than any doctrine. And
so today most preachers discourse on the love of God, idealistic
living, right attitudes of mind, the brotherhood of man, and the
like. The great Bible doctrines of creation, sin, and salvation, and
other cardinal tenets that have ever constituted the framework
of the Christian edifice—these are now rarely heard in Modernist churches, which constitute the great majority of churches.

But the day that the Advent movement fails to put emphasis
on doctrine, that day we have lost the justification for our existence. We have a definite doctrine to present on the Second Advent,

else we lose the goal and the objective that should be ours. We have a definite doctrine to preach on creation, else we remove the foundation for the Sabbath. We have a definite doctrine to preach on sin and salvation, else we make meaningless our teaching on the sanctuary. We have a definite doctrine to preach on the nature of man, else we take all point out of our preaching on the resurrection and life only in Christ and our warning against the final delusions of spiritism. And thus we might go on enumerating. If ever there was a movement built on clear-cut beliefs, beliefs interlocked like the girders of a building, it is the Advent movement. We minimize these beliefs only at the peril of destroying the building. On the other hand, if we put emphasis on these beliefs, we must be prepared to meet opposition and contrary views.

However, someone may still inquire incredulously: Ought we not to follow Nehemiah's example in regard to the adversaries of truth? "I am doing a great work, so that I cannot come down." Neh. 6:3. I subscribe to Nehemiah's words. It is easy to fall into unnecessary controversy. Certainly we ought always to keep on building the walls of Jerusalem rather than go down into the valley to hold a conference with Sanballat and Tobiah.

But Nehemiah is the last man of God in all the Bible who ought to be quoted in behalf of inaction, where the adversaries of the Lord are concerned. When Sanballat and Tobiah sent their threats against the wall-builders Nehemiah kept his men working, to be sure, but only half of them, and they with only one hand, for "the other hand held a weapon." The remainder of his men he armed with swords and spears and instructed them to guard the walls with their lives. Certainly the walls would not have been constructed if men had not continued to labor. But with equal certainty we may say that those walls might never have been built if there had not been militant men with flashing swords and spears guarding the laborers. It was the gleam of the swords on the ramparts that gave heart to the builders. (See Neh. 4:16-18.) Unquestionably, we should never go down into the valley seeking controversy, but when adversaries attack the citadel of truth on which this

Advent movement stands, we should, in the name of the Lord God of hosts, be prepared to defend that citadel. To provide arms for the defense is the purpose of this book.

And now, lest this all sound too militant, let me quickly add that there are different ways to fight for the faith. We need to make certain that we fight the good fight in harmony with the principles of heaven. Only thus will we bring strength to the Advent movement and glory to God's name. A few primary rules, if followed carefully, will enable the soldier of Christ to conform to those principles. These rules apply to a discussion on the public platform, through the press, in the parlor, or over the back fence.

1. *Impute good faith and sincerity to the one with whom you are disputing.* Sincerity may be possessed even by one who sets forth the most preposterous opinion.

2. *Keep calm.* If you cannot fight for the faith without displaying a rise of temperature, do not fight. Stay by the stuff, and let others of more equable disposition, or those who have gained the victory over anger, carry on the active warfare for the faith.

3. *Be very sparing of strong language.* There are doubtless times when such language may be in order, but those occasions, I believe, are rare. We are not often called to stand, like Elijah, on Mount Carmel. Because we are sure in our hearts that the truth and the evidence are on our side we can well afford to be not only calm and cool but kind in our language. The spectators, if there be any, will measure our argument, at least in part, by our form of speech, even if the one with whom we are differing does not.

4. *Reveal a spirit of great seriousness.* Let it be evident that your contending for your religious views is not to satisfy a desire for wrangling or controversy, but is prompted by a solemn conviction that the beliefs you hold are of most serious importance.

5. *Appeal to the heart as well as to the head.* It is one thing to convince a man; it is another thing to convict him, and create in his soul a desire to obey the truths you have set forth. It is not simply a question of what to say, but how to say it, if you would bring conviction. As the discussion progresses seek increasingly to

lift it above the level of a mere question of facts and evidence to the plane of the relation that the facts bear to the hearer's heart and eternal destiny. If we are really to help a man, we must do more than close his mouth; we must open his heart to receive the truth we have so earnestly been endeavoring to prove.

Now a word concerning the history of this book. It was first published in 1932, and contained 254 pages. In 1947 a portion of the book, then out of print, with considerable new matter, was published under the title *Reasons for Our Faith.* Some material from this latter book, now also out of print, with certain additional matter from the 1932 volume, plus much new matter, has been combined to make this present volume. Probably more than half of the contents is material never before published in book form. Part I deals exclusively with specific objections to Adventist teachings. Part II provides certain added material in answer to various charges and more fully sets forth the evidence in behalf of certain doctrines.

In most instances the objections considered have come to me through the years in letters from our ministers and lay workers who have stated that these were objections they frequently met. Sometimes these workers have sent in marked copies of anti-Adventist leaflets and booklets, which, they explain, have been widely circulated in the area where they are holding an evangelistic meeting. Sometimes the exact words of such printed matter are used in this book. Quotation marks indicate such use. Thus the objections considered are not academic, but practical. In answering them I have attempted to avoid the barren procedure of dealing merely with the negative; rather, I have endeavored to present the positive Bible truth on each question.

This book is sent forth with a desire, not to create needless dispute, but to aid you as you seek to carry out the Scriptural injunction to "earnestly contend for the faith which was once delivered unto the saints."

*Washington, D.C., August, 1952.*

# Part I

# IN SIX SECTIONS

# Section I

# LAW

## Objections 1 to 19

The reader is also referred
to Part 2, Section II, pages 493-542,
"The Law and Legalism"

# Objection 1

Adventists quote much from the Old Testament in proof of their doctrines, particularly the law and the Sabbath. Christians find their guidance and doctrines in the New Testament.

We do quote much from the Old Testament. We also quote much from the New. Actually we make no distinction in authority between the Old and the New Testament, and for the very reason that we are Christians. We believe that the whole Bible, from Genesis to Revelation, is inspired of God and thus rightly the guide for our lives.

Some people, when they discuss the law and the Sabbath, seek to set up a contrast or even conflict between the Old and the New Testament, as though the former were of little or no value and quite superseded by the latter. This false contrast lies at the root of much of the erroneous reasoning that marks the arguments of those who contend that the law and the Sabbath were abolished at the cross.

The "Bible" of the apostles was what is now known as the Old Testament. The first writings of these earliest Christian ministers did not begin to come from their pens until twenty, thirty, and more years after the ascension of Christ. Nor were there printing presses and fast-mail service quickly to distribute these writings. Only slowly did they gain circulation. It is wholly reasonable to believe that during the first century of the Christian Era the term *the Scriptures,* mentioned repeatedly in the New Testament, was largely understood to mean what we call the Old Testament.

Christ admonished the Jews to "search the scriptures; for in them ye think ye have eternal life: and they are they which testify of me." John 5:39. And then He added, "Had ye believed Moses, ye would have believed me: for he wrote of me. But if ye believe not his writings, how shall ye believe my words?" Verses 46, 47

37

The reason the disciples did not understand the events of crucifixion week was that they did not rightly understand the Scriptures, the Old Testament. (See Luke 24:27.) On His resurrection day He showed them how His death and resurrection were a fulfillment of prophecy: "Then opened he their understanding, that they might understand the scriptures." Luke 24:45. Christ knew nothing of the doctrine of discounting the Old Testament.

Nor did the apostles give any hint that they discounted the Old Testament in favor of some writings they were soon to produce. Paul wrote to Timothy: "From a child thou hast known the holy scriptures, which are able to make thee wise unto salvation through faith which is in Christ Jesus. All scripture is given by inspiration of God, and is profitable for doctrine, for reproof, for correction, for instruction in righteousness: that the man of God may be perfect, throughly furnished unto all good works." 2 Tim. 3:15-17. Could the New Testament accomplish more than this!

Both Christ and the apostles repeatedly cited the Old Testament in confirmation of their teachings. To Satan, Christ said, "It is written," and thrice quoted the Old Testament. (See Matt. 4:4-10.) He chided the scribes and Pharisees by quoting the fifth commandment, from the book of Exodus, and by quoting the words of Isaiah. (See Matt. 15:1-9.) See also Christ's conversation with the rich young ruler and with the lawyer. (Matt. 19:16-19; Luke 10:25-28.) Prominent in these references to the Old Testament are the quotations from the Ten Commandments!

How did Paul prove that all men, Jews and Gentiles, were guilty before God and thus in need of the salvation offered through Christ? By quoting from the Old Testament. (See Rom. 3:9-18.) And how did he know that he himself was a sinner before God and in need of the gospel? By calling to mind what was written in the Old Testament, specifically what was written in the Ten Commandments. (See Rom. 7:7.) To the church at Rome Paul commanded: "Owe no man any thing, but to love one another: for he that loveth another hath fulfilled the law." Rom. 13:8. And did he profess to be setting forth a new code, which was the result of a new revelation then given to him? No, he quotes the Old Testament, and specifically the Ten Commandments. (See verses 9, 10.) And how did Paul support his appeal to children to obey their parents? By quoting from the Old Testament, specifically the Ten Commandments. (See Eph. 6:1-3.)

As James develops his argument against having "respect to persons," does he set forth new laws? No, he quotes the Old Testament, focusing on citations from the Ten Commandments. (See James 2:8-12.)

And what proof did Peter offer in support of his declaration that we should be "holy"? "Because it is written, Be ye holy; for I am holy." 1 Peter 1:16. His proof is a quotation from Leviticus 11:44.

The Scriptures, from Genesis to Revelation, are one whole. The source of the Old and the New Testament is the same: the inspiration of the Spirit of God. Their objective is the same: to unfold the plan of God, to reveal Christ, to warn against sin, and to present God's holy standard of right. Someone long ago well observed: The New Testament is concealed in the Old, the Old Testament is revealed in the New. We can best understand the promise in the last book of the Bible, of a re-created, a new, earth and a verdant tree of life, when we turn to the first book of the Bible that describes the good earth, with its original tree of life, that came forth from God's hand when He first created this world. We best grasp the meaning of the cross, and Christ's words, "I, if I be lifted up from the earth, will draw all men unto me," when we read the Genesis account of man's fall.

We should never forget that the very titles "Old Testament" and "New Testament" are man-made titles. Bible writers do not thus divide the Scriptures. Both Testaments deal with old and new in the drama of sin and salvation. The Old Testament presents the promise of a new earth and a new covenant, as well as picturing man's iniquities from earliest days. The New Testament discusses at length the "old man" of sin and the ancient problem of man's rebellion, as well as describing the "new man" in Christ Jesus and the glories of a world to come.

The interrelationship of Old Testament to New, the dependence of one on the other, has ever been understood by our adversary the devil. That is why he long ago began his attacks on the Bible by seeking to undermine the historicity and authenticity of the Old Testament. It was at this point that higher criticism of the Bible began. And with the Old destroyed, the New soon collapses for lack of historical foundation and meaning. It is understandable that Modernists should be found minimizing the spiritual authority and significance of the Old Testament. But what is inexplicable is the attitude of some who consider themselves Fundamentalists of the Fundamentalists in regard to the Old Testament. Why should they seek to tear in two the seamless garment of Scripture? Why should they set forth the doctrine that a holy command of God in the Old Testament must wait for restatement in the New before it has authority in the Christian Era, when the record is clear that the New Testament writers quoted from the Old, not to inform their readers that the particular passage from the Old was still binding, but to provide corroborative proof that their newly uttered New Testament declarations agreed with the Old and thus were also binding. In other words, the apostles, who reminded their readers that the "holy men of God" in "old time" "spake as they were moved by the Holy Ghost," wished those readers to see that they, the apostles, spoke by the same Holy Ghost. (2 Peter 1:21.) Hence they repeatedly cited in support of their admonitions and doctrinal reasoning the words of those "holy men" who wrote the Old Testament.

It is true that a ceremonial ritual described in the Old Testament expired, by limitation, at the cross, for then the shadow met reality. And the New Testament writers specifically state that those rites, as set forth in a series of ceremonial laws, had come to an end. But that fact in no way makes the Old Testament inferior to the New or justifies the contention that the New supplants the Old.

# Objection 2

**Adventists seek to prove that there are two laws described in the Bible, one moral, the other ceremonial. But there is only one law.**

The logic of the objection is this: There is but one law; the Bible speaks clearly of a law abolished; therefore, the Ten Commandments were abolished, including, necessarily, the fourth, on which Adventists build their case for the Sabbath.

So much false reasoning has been reared on this one-law doctrine that it must be considered at length.

The word "law" is used in the Bible in a number of ways. In the phrase, "the law and the prophets," the word "law" rather uniformly means the books of Moses, because in his writings the laws of God are specially set forth. The word "law" is sometimes used without reference to any particular code, as a collective term to describe any and all laws. Again, the word "law" is often employed to designate a particular code, for example, the moral law, or the ceremonial law, as we shall seek to show.

To contend that every time the Bible uses the word "law" it means the same code would be as reasonable as to contend that every time the Bible uses the word "day" it means the same period of time. The facts are that "day" may mean (1) the light part of the twenty-four-hour cycle, as day in contrast with night, or (2) the whole twenty-four-hour period, as seven days in a week, or (3) an indefinite period of time, as "now is the day of salvation." What would we think of the man who reasoned that because certain texts in the Bible speak of the ending of the day, therefore the day of salvation has necessarily ended?

The Bible does say that "the law" was "abolished" by Christ. (See Eph. 2:15.) But Paul, who wrote that statement, also declares: "Do we, then, make void the law through faith? God forbid: yea, we establish the law." Rom. 3:31. The contrast between the state-

41

ments is sharpened when attention is called to the fact that Paul used the same Greek root for the words here translated "abolished" and "make void." That root, *katargeo*, means "to make inoperative," "to cause to cease," "to do away with," "annul," "abolish." But did the inspired writer, Paul, say to one church that "the law" is "abolished," and then to another church exclaim, "God forbid," at the very thought that "the law" is abolished, and refer to the same law in each instance? Obviously Paul must be speaking of two different laws. These two texts are sufficient in themselves to expose the fallacy of the argument that the Bible speaks only of one law.

The first formal recording of any codes of divine laws for man was at the time of the Exodus. Then it was that God, who had chosen a people for His name, set them on their way to the Promised Land. The former centuries possessed no Scriptures, for none of the sixty-six books of the Bible had been written. Through Moses God began to give to men a written revelation to guide them, and from his day onward, with one striking exception, the words of God for man, including His laws for man, have been penned by human agents, the prophets. That one exception was a code of laws that God spoke to men with His own voice. Sacred history records no other sermon ever preached by God to man amid the supernatural, flaming glory that surrounds the eternal God. Referring to this lone majestic instance, Moses declared to Israel:

"For ask now of the days that are past, which were before thee, since the day that God created man upon the earth, and ask from the one side of heaven unto the other, whether there hath been any such thing as this great thing is, or hath been heard like it? Did ever people hear the voice of God speaking out of the midst of the fire, as thou hast heard, and live?" Deut. 4:32, 33.

And when God had spoken the code, the "ten commandments," the record declares, "He added no more." (See Deut. 4:13; 5:22.) The sermon was finished, it was a complete whole, there was nothing more that God desired to add. Then He wrote down the sermon with His own hand on "two tables of stone." (Deut. 5:22.) On no other document in the history of man has the hand of God ever been inscribed. "The tables were the work of God, and the writing was the writing of God, graven upon the tables." Ex. 32:16. And what God wrote on those tables of stone He described as "a law." (See Ex. 24:12.)

Then follows another dramatic moment, a sequel to the giving and the writing of this "law." Moses started down from the mount with the two tables in his hands. He was bringing to Israel the permanent record of that awesome sermon by the God of heaven. His indignation at the sight of Israelites worshiping the golden calf caused him to dash the stones to earth and break them, a symbol of their breaking of the divine code.

Did the Lord then command Moses to write a copy of the code to take the place of the broken tables? No. The Lord wrote the Ten Commandments a second time on new tables of stone. A most distinctive code, indeed, that God Himself should twice write it on stone. He entrusted to His prophets many vital messages for men, but the Ten Commandments He wrote Himself.

The focal point, the most holy object of the religious service instituted by God for the Israelites, was the ark of the covenant, above which hovered the holy light of the presence of God. When, in the journeyings of the Israelites, the ark was to be moved, none were to touch it lest they die. And in that most sacred of the sacred objects of the sanctuary Moses was instructed to place the tables of stone. (Deut. 10:5.) Nor was any other code of laws placed within that sacred ark. "There was nothing in the ark save the two tables of stone, which Moses put there at Horeb." 1 Kings 8:9.

Again, this code of laws was distinguished as the basis of a covenant between God and the Israelites. Those who oppose the Scriptural doctrine of the perpetuity of the moral law, which Adventists believe, have sought to support their view with this fact—see objection 5—but what they have overlooked is this: The very fact that the ten-commandment law is described as uniquely the basis of a covenant, proves once more that the Decalogue is a distinct code, not to be confused with any other. Said Moses to Israel: God "declared unto you his covenant, which he commanded you to perform, even ten commandments; and he wrote them upon two tables of stone." Deut. 4:13.

Let us summarize these historical facts concerning the giving of the ten-commandment law:

1. God spoke the law with His own voice in the hearing of all Israel—He gave no other law in that way. "He added no more."

2. God wrote the ten-commandment law with His own finger —the only law that He ever wrote out for man.

3. God wrote the law on stone, and Himself prepared the stone —the only law of Bible record that was ever thus written.

4. God sent Moses down from the mount in the sight of all Israel, bearing the two tables of stone that contained only the Ten Commandments.

5. God Himself rewrote the law after Moses had broken the first tables.

6. God instructed Moses to place the tables within the ark of the covenant—the only law thus honored.

7. God declared that the ten-commandment law was "his covenant"—the only law thus described.

Yet objectors profess to be unable to find in the Bible any grounds for believing that the ten-commandment law is a distinct code of laws, not to be confused with any other code. We would ask: If they could have dictated the manner of the giving of this law, and had wished to provide convincing proof that it was a law set apart, what procedure could they possibly have followed that would have set it apart more fully or more dramatically?

But the ten-commandment law was not the only one formally set forth by God at Sinai. There was a code of laws, known as ceremonial laws, that gave the rules for the religious ritual that the Jews should follow; for example, their sacrifices and offerings, their annual feast days, the duties of the priesthood. The book of Leviticus is filled with these laws. There were also civil laws to govern the Jews as a nation, such as laws on marriage, divorce, slave holding, property. (See Exodus 21.) To the extent that the dim spiritual understanding and willingness of the Israelites permitted, the Lord caused these civil statutes to reflect the perfect ideal expressed in the ten-commandment law. The statute on slave holding is an illustration of the adaptation of moral principle to the low spiritual state of a people. Of the divorce statute Christ declared: "Moses because of the hardness of your hearts suffered you to put away your wives: but from the beginning it was not so." Matt. 19:8. (See Mark 10:4-6.)

But these ceremonial and civil laws were not given by God directly to the hosts of Israel. As to how God made known these laws, who wrote them, and where they were deposited, the Scriptures are clear:

1. After stating that the Lord wrote the Ten Commandments "upon two tables of stone," Moses adds immediately: "And the Lord commanded me at that time to teach you statutes and judgments." Deut. 4:13, 14. A later Bible writer sets forth the same distinction: "Neither will I make the feet of Israel move any more out of the land which I gave their fathers: only if they will observe to do according to all that I have commanded them, and according to all the law that my servant Moses commanded them." 2 Kings 21:8.

In recalling the events of Sinai, Nehemiah, in addressing the Lord, also speaks of the fact that certain laws were spoken by God and others were given to Israel through Moses: "Thou camest down also upon mount Sinai, and speakest with them from heaven, and gavest them right judgments, and true laws, good statutes and commandments: and madest known unto them thy holy sabbath, and commandedst them precepts, statutes, and laws, by the hand of Moses thy servant." Neh. 9:13, 14.

2. "Moses wrote this law." Deut. 31:9.

3. "And it came to pass, when Moses had made an end of writing the words of this law in a book, until they were finished, that Moses commanded the Levites, which bare the ark of the covenant of the Lord, saying, Take this book of the law, and put it in

the side of the ark of the covenant of the Lord your God, that it may be there for a witness against thee." Deut. 31:24-26. The words: "Put it in the side of the ark," might seem to suggest that this book was placed within the ark. But that would make it contradict the already quoted words of Scripture, that the Decalogue was the only law placed therein. The Revised Version reads: "Put it by the side of the ark." With this translation of the Hebrew, commentators agree.

Because of the fact that the ceremonial law, and also the civil statutes, were written down by Moses, and by him given to the people, they are generally described in the Bible as "the law of Moses." See, for example:

1. 2 Chron. 23:18. Priests to offer burnt offerings, "as it is written in the law of Moses."

2. 2 Chron. 30:16. Priests conducting Passover "according to the law of Moses."

3. Ezra 3:2. Building of an altar for burnt offerings "as it is written in the law of Moses."

4. Dan. 9:13. The destruction of Jerusalem had come "as it is written in the law of Moses."

5. Malachi 4:4. "Remember ye the law of Moses my servant, which I commanded unto him in Horeb [Sinai] for all Israel."

The New Testament also reveals, in many of its references to law, the same distinction between the ten-commandment law and the code of laws given through Moses. Note the following references to the law of rites and ceremonies, sometimes described as the "law of Moses," and sometimes simply as "the law":

1. "If a man on the sabbath day receive circumcision, that the law of Moses should not be broken." John 7:23.

2. "But there rose up certain of the sect of the Pharisees which believed, saying, That it was needful to circumcise them, and to command them to keep the law of Moses." Acts 15:5. Later in the chapter, when the claim of these Pharisees is restated, it is abbreviated thus: "Ye must be circumcised, and keep the law."

Verse 24. This well illustrates how a New Testament writer may use the nonqualifying phrase, "the law," and yet mean a very specific law, in this instance, "the law of Moses." The context is generally sufficient to make clear what law is intended. Certainly if circumcision is under discussion in the New Testament—and it is often the bone of contention—it is sufficient to refer to the code of laws enjoining circumcision, simply as "the law"; that is, the law of rites and ceremonies given by Moses.

3. "The law of commandments contained in ordinances." Eph. 2:15.

4. "The sons of Levi, who receive the office of the priesthood, have a commandment to take tithes of the people according to the law." Heb. 7:5.

5. "For the priesthood being changed, there is made of necessity a change also of the law." Verse 12.

6. "For the law maketh men high priests which have infirmity." Verse 28.

7. "There are priests that offer gifts according to the law." Heb. 8:4.

8. "And almost all things are by the law purged with blood." Heb. 9:22.

9. "For the law having a shadow of good things to come, and not the very image of the things, can never with those sacrifices which they offered year by year continually make the comers thereunto perfect." Heb. 10:1.

The ten-commandment law gives no instruction or information on burnt offerings, the Passover, the building of an altar, the judgments that would come on Jerusalem because of disobedience, circumcision, the order of the priesthood. But the Bible repeatedly reveals that there is a "law" that does give such instruction. That law is the ceremonial law, described in the Bible as the "law of Moses."

It is true that "the law of Moses" was also the law of God, because God was the author of all that Moses wrote. Hence it is not strange that a Bible writer should, at least occasionally, describe this law of Moses as "the law of the Lord," though such instances are few. See, for example, Luke 2:22, 23, where both phrases are used to describe the same law. *However, nowhere in the Bible is the ten-commandment law called the law of Moses.*

Note, now, some representative New Testament references to another law, which does not deal with rites and ceremonies, but with moral questions, the ten-commandment law, which is also referred to, at times, as simply the commandments:

1. "If thou wilt enter into life, keep the commandments." Matt. 19:17. Then Christ immediately names several of the ten commands.

2. "And they returned, and prepared spices and ointments; and rested the sabbath day according to the commandment." Luke 23:56.

3. "I had not known sin, but by the law: for I had not known lust, except the law had said, Thou shalt not covet." Rom. 7:7.

4. "For whosoever shall keep the whole law, and yet offend in one point, he is guilty of all. For he that said, Do not commit adultery, said also, Do not kill. Now if thou commit no adultery, yet if thou kill, thou art become a transgressor of the law. So speak ye, and so do, as they that shall be judged by the law of liberty." James 2:10-12.

5. "Whosoever committeth sin transgresseth also the law: for sin is the transgression of the law." 1 John 3:4. What law? Certainly no one in the Christian Era believes that a failure to obey the law regarding rites and ceremonies is sin. Yet John warns us that transgressing "the law" is sin. He did not feel it necessary to explain what "law" he meant. How eloquently that argues that there was a certain law, known to all John's readers, that was the moral rule of life. What confusion and consternation his words would have created among the first-century Christians if they had been laboring under the impression that there was but *one* law, a law that was a mixture of ceremonial and moral precepts! And that transgression of that law in the Christian Era is sin!

In conclusion, let us summarize certain of the contrasting

# LAW

statements made in the Bible concerning the moral and the ceremonial codes of laws:

## The Moral Law

1. Spoken by God Himself. Ex. 20:1, 22.
2. Was written by God. Ex. 31:18; 32:16.
3. On stones. Ex. 31:18.
4. Handed by God, its writer, to Moses. Ex. 31:18.
5. Deposited by Moses "in the ark." Deut. 10:5.
6. Deals with moral precepts. Ex. 20:3-17.

7. Reveals sin. Rom. 7:7.

8. Breaking of "the law" is "sin." 1 John 3:4.

9. Should "keep the whole law." James 2:10.

10. Because we "shall be judged" by this law. James 2:12.
11. The Christian who keeps this law is "blessed in his deed." James 1:25.
12. "The perfect law of liberty." James 1:25. (Cf. James 2:12.)
13. Paul said, "I delight in the law of God." Rom. 7:22. (Cf. verse 7.)

14. Established by faith in Christ. Rom. 3:31.
15. Christ was to "magnify the law and make it honourable." Isa. 42:21.
16. "We know that the law is spiritual." Rom. 7:14. (Cf. verse 7.)

## The Ceremonial Law

1. Spoken by Moses. Ex. 24:3.

2. Written by Moses. Ex. 24:4; Deut. 31:9.
3. In a book. Ex. 24:4, 7; Deut. 31:24.
4. Handed by Moses, its writer, to Levites. Deut. 31:25, 26.
5. Deposited by the Levites "by the side of the ark." Deut. 31:26, A.R.V.
6. Deals with ceremonial, ritual matters. (See parts of Exodus, Leviticus, Numbers, Deuteronomy.)
7. Prescribes offerings for sins. (See book of Leviticus.)
8. No sin in breaking, for now "abolished." Eph. 2:15. ("Where no law is, there is no transgression." Rom. 4:15.)
9. Apostles gave "no such commandment" to "keep the law." Acts 15:24.
10. Not to be judged by it. Col. 2:16.
11. The Christian who keeps this law is not blessed. (See, for example, Gal. 5:1-6.)
12. The Christian who keeps this law loses his liberty. Gal. 5:1, 3.
13. Paul called this law a "yoke of bondage." Gal. 5:1. (See Acts 15:10.)
14. Abolished by Christ. Eph. 2:15.
15. Blotted "out the handwriting of ordinances that was against us." Col. 2:14.
16. "The law of a carnal commandment." Heb. 7:16.

These and other comparisons that might be made reveal beyond all controversy that the Bible presents two laws. To conclude otherwise would be to say that the Bible presents a hopeless series of contradictions.

We grant that there are certain references to "the law," particularly in Paul's writings, where the context fails to make wholly clear which law is intended. In some instances it seems evident that neither law is singled out, but only the principle of law, in contrast to grace, is under consideration. But these facts provide no proof that there is only one law. Because there are obscure or difficult texts in the Bible does not mean that we cannot be sure of the meaning of the clear and the simple texts. And those easily understood texts should protect us from drawing false conclusions from the difficult ones.

Reference to the two laws in terms of the centuries before Moses will also aid us in maintaining a clear distinction between them. Though we may rightly focus on the Exodus as the great time of the giving of the law, both moral and ceremonial, we should not conclude that the time before Moses was a period of no law, at least of no Decalogue. This point we shall examine more fully under objection 3. We need only remark here that the Ten Commandments existed in Eden. Also the first tender shoots of the ceremonial vine, which was to grow large at the Exodus, made their appearance in the form of the simple sacrificial services of our first parents after sin entered.

Who has not had the experience of looking at a towering tree and marveling at its heavy and varied foliage, only to discover on closer scrutiny that a vine is entwined around the tree and that what appeared to be one is really two. Though a far look at a high branch, especially if it is swaying in the breeze, may fail to reveal this fact, an examination of the trunk near the roots, where the vine first makes contact with the tree, leaves no doubt that there are two.

Now the Decalogue might be likened to a stately tree, with ten stalwart branches, that our first parents found flourishing in the

Garden of Eden. After their fall a vine of ceremonial law was planted close by, watered by the blood of animal sacrifices. For centuries the vine grew little if any. Then at the time of the Exodus it suddenly assumed a definite form and grew large. The tree did not need the vine in order to live, but the vine was wholly dependent on the tree. In later centuries men inclined always toward cultivating the vine rather than the tree, until the foliage of the vine well-nigh hid the tree and threatened to choke it. It is therefore easy to understand why some Christian people today, looking at the Biblical word picture of that tree, with its clinging vine, should fail to see that the two are not one. Particularly is this true if the winds of theological discussion are swaying the branches. But as with a literal tree, there need be no uncertainty in the matter if attention is focused, not on the topmost limbs, but on the trunk and roots. To speak literally, an examination of the origins of the two laws, and the formal giving of them at the Exodus, leaves no possible doubt that there were two.

Nor can Adventists claim any special Biblical vision in discerning that there are two, not one. From the days of the Protestant Reformation onward the great church bodies have clearly seen this and recorded the fact in their creeds and confessions of faith! See page 493 for extracts from the creeds, et cetera. The claim that there is but one law has gained currency today among a certain segment of Christians in a fervent endeavor to meet the force of the Sabbath evidence now so vigorously and widely being presented by Adventists. In the following pages we shall examine several arguments against the law that owe their appearance of strength to this one-law theory.

# Objection 3

## The Ten Commandments did not exist before the time of Moses.

The average reader will probably remark that inasmuch as we live *since* the time of Moses, the law applies to us, and we are therefore not concerned. as to just when the law was given. Very true, and we might dismiss the matter right here were it not for the fact that the objector is endeavoring to build a plausible argument on this objection. If we grant that the world moved along safely for centuries before Moses without the Ten Commandments, then we have halfway prepared ourselves to believe the next objection, namely, that the law was abolished at the cross. Surely if godly men like Enoch and Abraham needed not the Ten Commandments, why should Christians?

Therefore, because of the subtle reasoning built upon it, we must give some attention to this claim that the Ten Commandments did not exist before Moses.

Right on the face of it this is an unbelievable claim. The Decalogue commands men not to make idols, for example, not to take God's name in vain, not to kill, steal, or commit adultery. Could we possibly bring ourselves to believe that such a code of laws was not in force before Moses? There are some things too incredible to warrant belief, and this is one of them.

Nor, indeed, do any of the leading denominations thus believe. There is no point on which the great branches of the Christian church agree more cordially than that the Ten Commandments were in force from the beginning of the world. (See page 493 for quotations from church creeds on the law of God.)

The plausible core of the objection before us is the assumption that those who sinned before Moses' day could not possibly have been transgressors of the Decalogue, because it had not yet been given. Here is the argument:

"Angels 'sinned' (2 Peter 2:4), but they did not violate the law of Sinai, for it was not given until thousands of years after they fell—and they were not under it anyway. Adam 'sinned' long before that law was given (see Romans 5:12-14); Cain sinned (Gen. 4:7); the Sodomites were 'sinners' (Gen. 13:13), and vexed Lot with their 'unlawful deeds' (2 Peter 2:8). Surely none of these violated 'the law,' which was not given till Moses."

But the conclusion does not necessarily follow that because the ten precepts of the Decalogue were not audibly proclaimed before Sinai, or written down before that date, therefore those precepts were not in existence before that time. Analogy to human laws reveals how unwarranted such a conclusion is. For long centuries England has had what is known as "the common law," which law is an integral part of the whole system of English, and later, American, jurisprudence. But only slowly was the common law codified and placed in written form. For centuries many of the statutes of this common law were passed on from one generation to another with little or no written reference. But even unschooled yeomen had had passed on to them by their fathers enough of the common law to make them oftentimes embarrassingly acquainted with their primary rights under the law. There was no particular moment in English history when the common law was all transcribed in a book and proclaimed by the king as the law of the land. And even if there had been such a moment in England's legal history, what would we think of the person, who, looking back on the event, declared that previous to that great legal proclamation such criminals as troubled England never violated this law? Pray tell, what other law did those criminals violate in the days before England had a written legal code for all men to see and read?

No, history teaches us that a law need not be formally proclaimed or written in a book in order to be in force.

Even so with the moral laws of God for man. When Adam and Eve were created they were perfect and served God with a whole heart. Hence we properly conclude that they had the law of God written in their hearts. God also talked to them. For a lifetime of nearly a thousand years they were permitted to pass on the divine instruction they had received. Neither they nor their children needed a code written on parchment or stone. Paul well says that "the law is not made for a righteous man," that is, the law as it is ordinarily understood, a formally announced code duly written down. The law is written on the righteous man's heart.

After Adam's sin men soon began a rapid descent into the pit of corruption, as Paul describes it. (See Romans 1.) Could they excuse their evil deeds on the ground that they were not aware of any law that they had violated? No. Paul emphatically declares that they were "without excuse." (Verse 20.) But how could they be without excuse unless they still retained some knowledge of God's holy requirements and laws? Our accountability for our sins is in terms of our knowledge. (See John 15:22.) Paul enlarges on the matter by explaining that when the "Gentiles, which have not the law [that is, have no written law, no Holy Scriptures containing the moral code], do by nature the things contained in the law, these, having not the law, are a law unto themselves: which shew the work of the law written in their hearts, their conscience also bearing witness." Rom. 2:14, 15.

We believe there is only one reasonable conclusion from these facts: Though men early fell away from God, the knowledge of Him did not immediately or completely fade from their minds, nor was the divine code, originally written on the hearts of their first parents, Adam and Eve, suddenly erased. The troublesome light of conscience, even though the rays grew dim, ever and anon illumined the dim but heavenly outlines upon the heart. As the Revised Standard Version translates the passage: "They show that what the law requires is written on their hearts, while their conscience also bears witness and their conflicting thoughts accuse or perhaps excuse them on that day when, according to my gospel, God judges the secrets of men by Christ Jesus."

Unless we hold that the world before Moses knew sufficiently of the law of God to understand the moral import of their acts, we shall be charging God with injustice in destroying them for their evil deeds. The only possible way for the objector to avoid the embarrassing force of this fact is to contend that though men who lived before Moses knew nothing of the Ten Commandments, they did have a knowledge of certain eternal moral principles of heaven. If this reasoning has any validity, it must reside in the assumption that these eternal moral principles—left undefined by the objector—were different from the Ten Commandments. Only thus can it be held that the Ten Commandments are not eternal.

But what principles are more eternally moral than those of the Ten Commandments? And how could God be just in condemning the ancients for deeds that we can describe as sinful only by their nonconformity to the Ten Commandments, if indeed these commandments were not yet in force? Furthermore, if all the sinful deeds of devils and ancient men can be judged and condemned in terms of the Ten Commandments, what need is there to invoke some wholly undefined, unrevealed, moral principles in order to deal with the moral rebellion of those who lived long ago?

And can their deeds be condemned as sinful in terms of the Ten Commandments? Yes. The Bible says that Satan was "a murderer from the beginning," and also "a liar." John 8:44. The Ten Commandments deal with his deeds. He also sought to set himself up in the place of God. Here is a violation of the first commandment. Adam and Eve most certainly coveted the forbidden fruit, else they would not have reached for it when God had expressly told them that it was not theirs to have. They both coveted and stole. And the Ten Commandments cover those evil deeds. Cain killed his brother. The Ten Commandments are adequate to judge him. The Sodomites were distinguished by their lustfulness. Christ revealed that the seventh commandment covers both the impure thought and the impure act, and they were guilty of both.

But we are not left to the processes of deduction—conclusive though they be—in order to reach the conclusion that the Ten Commandments were in force before Sinai. The Bible writers have much to say about sin and sinners. And how do they define sin? "Sin is the transgression of the law," says John. (1 John 3:4.) And Paul observes: "Where no law is, there is no transgression," "for by the law is the knowledge of sin." Rom. 4:15; 3:20. We are left in no possible doubt as to what law is intended, for Paul adds, "I had not known sin, but by the law: for I had not known lust, except the law had said, Thou shalt not covet." Rom. 7:7. And what law says, "Thou shalt not covet"? The ten-commandment law.

When James spoke of those who "commit sin, and are convinced of the law as transgressors," he also left no doubt as to which law he meant. It is the law that says, "Do not commit adultery," and, "Do not kill." James 2:9-11.

There are those who say, and we quote their words, that "sin is a disregard for *some* law, but not necessarily the so-called 'moral law,' or the Ten Commandments." But that is not what Paul and James say. We do not see how they could more clearly have stated that the breaking of a certain law is sin and that that law is the ten-commandment law.

Furthermore, the objectors forget to tell us what law John means—1 John 3:4—if he does not mean the Decalogue. They do not know, for the Bible throws no light on *"some* law" morally binding on men other than the Decalogue. And the objectors as well as we are dependent on the revelations of Scripture. The same was true of those who lived in John's day. Hence, how incredible that he should define sin—that awful thing that keeps men out of heaven—as the "transgression of the law," without defining what law he meant, if indeed he meant some other law than Paul and James meant when they wrote of sin! The very fact that John offered no explanatory comment as to what law he meant, is the strongest proof possible that he meant the law which his readers, who by now had read Paul and James, understood as "the law," the Decalogue.

A favorite text of those who seek to prove that the Decalogue was unknown before Sinai is Moses' statement: "The Lord made not this covenant with our fathers, but with us, even us, who are all of us here alive this day." Deut. 5:3.

The argument runs thus: God declares that the Ten Commandments are His covenant. Moses is here speaking of this covenant and declares it was not made with the fathers before Sinai, therefore the Ten Commandments were not given, in fact were unknown, before that time.

What strange beliefs we would have to hold if we came to this conclusion! In the immediately preceding chapter Moses refers to this covenant and warns Israel: "Take heed unto yourselves, lest ye forget the covenant of the Lord your God, which he made with you, and make you a graven image, or the likeness of any thing, which the Lord thy God hath forbidden thee." Deut. 4:23. Are we to conclude that none of God's children before Sinai knew that it was wrong to make graven images? We can hardly believe anyone will answer yes. But the prohibition of images is the second command of the ten. Hence those who lived before Sinai must have known of the Decalogue. That is the only conclusion we can reach.

Then what does Moses mean in Deuteronomy 5:3? We think that the simplest explanation is that he viewed the gathered hosts at Sinai as the birth of the chosen nation that God had promised Abraham would spring from him. Through Moses, God told Israel that if they would be obedient to His covenant, "ye shall be unto me a kingdom of priests, and an holy nation." Ex. 19:6. Not until Sinai was it thus possible literally to make a covenant with the "nation" or "kingdom" of the Jews. It is also true that not until Sinai was there any formal proclamation of the Decalogue. The fathers before Sinai had never heard God speak His law to them as Israel had. And it was the law thus proclaimed that was the basis of the covenant. Hence in a very real sense the covenant made with Israel at Sinai had never been made before.

Commentators differ in their endeavor to clarify this text. Adam Clarke seeks to do so with the addition of parenthetical words, thus:

"The Lord made not this covenant with our fathers (only) but with us (also)."

Jamieson, Fausset, and Brown observe:

"The meaning is, 'not with our fathers' only, 'but with us' also, assuming it to be 'a covenant' of grace; or 'not with our fathers' at all, if the reference is to the peculiar establishment of the covenant of Sinai; a law was not given to them as to us, nor was the covenant ratified in the same public manner, and by the same solemn sanctions. Or, finally, 'not with our fathers' who died in the wilderness, in consequence of their rebellion, and to whom God did not give the rewards promised only to the faithful; but 'with us,' who alone, strictly speaking, shall enjoy the benefits of this covenant by entering on the possession of the promised land."

(For comment on the claim that because there is a new covenant, therefore the Decalogue is abolished, see objection 5.)

But says the objector finally: "If the decalogue was in existence before Moses, how is it that it was first proclaimed and first written down at Sinai?" Such a question reveals a forgetfulness of history. We might as appropriately question whether *any* of the moral instruction of the Holy Bible is really binding on us, seeing that none of it was written before Moses. The simple facts are that by the time of Moses and the children of Israel the knowledge of God and His laws had become so blurred in men's minds that it became necessary that a written revelation be given to the world. Coming directly out of Egyptian darkness, the Israelites were in special need of clear-cut declarations on the great moral precepts. For this reason God with His own finger carved in the everlasting stone the Ten Commandments. No one need then be in doubt. The changing moral conceptions of those Israelites could ever be corrected by the unchanging words graven in the stone.

# Objection 4

"The very wording of the Sinaitic law proves that it was designed only for the Jews. The Decalogue is introduced thus: 'I am the Lord thy God, which have brought *thee* . . . out of the house of bondage' (Ex. 20:2). To whom is that applicable? Only to the Israelite nation, of course." See also Deuteronomy 4:8, Romans 9:4, and similar passages, which state specifically that the law was given only to the Israelites.

We would ask: To whom else could the Lord have given the Ten Commandments? To the Egyptians, the Philistines, the Amalekites, the Hittites, the Jebusites, or any other of the many pagan peoples that cursed the earth with their unholy presence? No, you say. God could not make a revelation of Himself to any people until that people were of a mind and heart to hear Him. God found in Abraham and his descendants such a people. Accordingly He gave to them a revelation of His will and ways. Yes, He spoke exclusively that great day at Sinai to a literal people called Israelites, who had been delivered from a literal bondage in Egypt. But, we inquire again: To whom else could He have spoken?

We would further inquire: To whom was God speaking when He gave His great messages through Isaiah, Jeremiah, Daniel, and all the mighty prophets of Old Testament times? The answer is, To the Israelites. The inspired messages that constitute the Old Testament were addressed almost wholly to the Jews, and the prophets who delivered the messages were Jews. But does any lover of the Bible wish to suggest that therefore the beautiful messages of salvation in Isaiah, for example, which are so often addressed directly to Jerusalem, are not also addressed to us? We doubt not that many a Christian minister has taken for his text these typical words from Isaiah: "Cry aloud, spare not, lift up thy voice like a trumpet, and shew my people their transgression, and the house of Jacob their sins." Isa. 58:1. But no listener in the pew is troubled or confused or informs the preacher that the text is addressed to Jews, not Gentiles.

And who are the writers of the New Testament? With one possible exception they are all Jews. To whom did Christ address virtually all that He said while on earth? To the Jews. To whom is the Epistle to the Hebrews addressed? Obviously, to Jews. To whom is the Epistle of James addressed? "To the twelve tribes which are scattered abroad." James 1:1. But does any Christian have difficulty with these facts, or feel that any portions of the New Testament are not really for him? No.

In the objection before us, Romans 9:4 is cited. It reads as follows: "Who are Israelites; to whom pertaineth the adoption, and the glory, and the covenants, and the giving of the law, and the service of God, and the promises." Evidently it is offered as proof because it says that "the giving of the law" was to them. But it says more than that. The "covenants" also were given to them. Note the plural. Both the old and the new covenant! The new covenant is made with the "house of Israel, and with the house of Judah." (Jer. 31:31; Heb. 8:8.) But does any Christian believe that the new covenant is confined to the believing Jew? No. We all claim a part in it and believe that the new covenant promise is intended for us as well, even though the announcement of it is addressed directly, and apparently exclusively, to the Jews.

The words of Moses in Deuteronomy 4:8 are also cited. They read as follows: "And what nation is there so great, that hath statutes and judgments so righteous as all this law, which I set before you this day?" We would simply say that this statement is a good commentary on Romans 9:4. And we have found that this verse in Romans proves more than the objector desires. Another inspired comment on Deuteronomy 4:8 is the statement of Christ: "Salvation is of the Jews." John 4:22. But has any Christian despised salvation because of this fact?

We must never forget that the revelations and admonitions of the Scriptures are not given in a vacuum. Almost always they are placed in the context of historical events and flesh-and-blood people. The sermon on the mount has as literally a rocky platform as the address from Sinai. And the multitudes addressed in that sermon were as definitely Jewish as the hosts gathered before Sinai. Often God took occasion in giving a revelation, or invoking a certain course of conduct, to refer to some actual experience through which the listeners had passed. That is one of the marks of Bible revelations. But that fact in itself never troubles any of us, nor prevents us from believing that those counsels of God's Word apply to us as well.

Now, inasmuch as God worked mighty miracles to draw out of the turbulent sea of paganism a people for Himself, how appropriate that He should place His eternal revelation to them in the context of the immediate experience that they had miraculously passed through. Thus they might be prompted to give that revelation maximum weight in their minds and be most diligent in obeying it. Furthermore, that historical context provides a setting that we today, who are also flesh and blood, can understand, and, understanding, be likewise prompted to greater obedience to God. Well does the Bible commentator Murphy observe on Exodus 20:2:

"This [deliverance out of Egypt] in the manner of Scripture and of Providence is the earnest and the guarantee of their deliverance from all other and greater kinds of bondage. The present is the type of a grander future. We must descend the stream of revelation to the New Testament before we fathom the depths of this greatest deliverance."—JAMES G. MURPHY, *Commentary on the Book of Exodus.*

Any display of God's mercy and deliverance to His children at any moment in earth's history is a reason why those living at that time and those who read of the account in all subsequent ages should serve Him with their whole heart and obey His holy will.

# Objection 5

The Bible says that the Ten Commandments are the covenant that God made with Israel at Sinai, that is, the old covenant. (See Deut. 4:13.) This covenant has been abolished, and we live under the new covenant. Therefore we have nothing to do with the Ten Commandments.

The text reads thus: "And he [the Lord] declared unto you his covenant, which he commanded you to perform, even ten commandments; and he wrote them upon two tables of stone." Deut. 4:13.

The key word here is "covenant," translated from the Hebrew word *berith,* which may be translated "compact," "league," "covenant." Now, these terms have as their most essential feature the idea of agreement between two or more parties. Webster's Dictionary thus defines "covenant": "An agreement between two or more persons or parties." We normally think of a covenant as an agreement made. And appropriately we find various references to God's covenant with the Israelites of the Exodus, couched in this very language. For example, "The Lord our God made a covenant with us in Horeb." Deut. 5:2. "The tables of the covenant which the Lord made with you." Deut. 9:9.

Then why should Moses describe the Ten Commandments themselves as the covenant? For the same reason that Moses should say to the Israelites, "And I took your sin, the calf which ye had made, and burnt it." Deut. 9:21. Strictly speaking, the sin was their turning to a false god, an action of their rebellious will, but the calf was that concerning which the sin was committed. Likewise, though the covenant was "made" by the action of the will of the Israelites in response to God (see Ex. 19:5-8), the Ten Commandments were that concerning which the covenant was made. Our English language employs this same figure of speech. Webster says further on "covenant": "A solemn compact between members of a church to maintain its faith, discipline, etc.; also, the document recording such a compact."

When the Israelites came to Sinai the Lord said to them through Moses: "Now therefore, if ye will obey my voice indeed, and keep my covenant, then ye shall be a peculiar treasure unto me above all people: for all the earth is mine: and ye shall be unto me a kingdom of priests, and an holy nation. These are the words which thou shalt speak unto the children of Israel." Ex. 19:5, 6. The response of the Israelites was agreement: "And all the people answered together, and said, All that the Lord hath spoken we will do. And Moses returned the words of the people unto the Lord." Verse 8.

Then follows in the next chapter the proclaiming of the Ten Commandments by the voice of God. This is followed, in the next three chapters, by a summary of civil statutes, which show the application of the Decalogue's principles, and by an even briefer summary of certain ceremonial requirements that the Lord gave to the people through Moses. Then in chapter 24 we read that Moses "told the people all the words of the Lord," and again the people responded, "All the words which the Lord hath said will we do." Verse 3. "And Moses wrote all the words of the Lord. . . . And he took the book of the covenant, and read in the audience of the people: and they said, All that the Lord hath said will we do, and be obedient." Verses 4-7. Then Moses took the blood of certain sacrificial animals and "sprinkled it on the people, and said, Behold the blood of the covenant, which the Lord hath made with you concerning all these words." Verse 8.

Here the record explicitly states, not that the words of the proclaimed statutes and judgments and laws were the covenant, but that the covenant was made "concerning all these words."

Refer back for a moment to objection 2, on the two laws. Here two comments may properly be interjected:

1. The fact that Moses wrote a copy of the Ten Commandments in this "book of the covenant" does not minimize the force

of the distinguishing fact that God wrote the Decalogue with His own hand on tables of stone. A copy implies an original. Endless copies of the Ten Commandments have been made. The Israelites had simply heard the Decalogue as God spoke it. They promised to be obedient. Moses, in giving them a copy to see in a book, made doubly certain that they fully realized what they were covenanting to do. God Himself had not yet transferred the words of the Decalogue to stone. The distinction between the earthy touch of Moses' hand and the divine hand of God and the sharp distinction between the varied laws in the book and the one supreme moral law are sharply emphasized a few verses further on: "And the Lord said unto Moses, Come up to me into the mount, and be there: and I will give thee tables of stone, and a law, and commandments which I have written; that thou mayest teach them." Verse 12.

2. The fact that statutes and judgments and certain ceremonial precepts in addition to the Ten Commandments were included in the covenant does not make them all one law or confuse their distinctive features one whit. The essence of the covenant, the agreement, between God and the Israelites was that they would obey Him. This meant that they would faithfully keep not only the Ten Commandments but also the civil statutes, which were to govern them as a nation, and the ceremonial precepts, which dictated the religious ritual by which they expressed their desire for forgiveness for transgressions of the moral laws.

However, the very fact that the civil statutes were simply an extension of the Decalogue's principles, and the ceremonial precepts simply set forth the means by which the Israelites were to express their sincere desire for freedom from sins committed against the moral code, fully justified the Biblical description of the Decalogue as that concerning which the covenant was made. The civil statutes and ceremonial laws were accessory to the Decalogue; they owed their existence and meaning to it, but it was not dependent on them.

With these facts in mind we are able to understand a whole

series of statements concerning the "covenant" that is found in the Bible record following the Exodus experience. Five facts stand out sharply as we trace the record of this covenant through the Old Testament:

1. The frequent references to it by one after another of the prophets.

2. The sorry fact that Israel so repeatedly broke it.

3. The repeated combining of the statement that the people broke the covenant, with the statement that they had violated various commands of the Decalogue, the latter fact explaining the former.

4. The reminding of Israel that sacrifices were not a substitute for obedience, and the essentially minor status that the Lord gave to the ceremonial ritual.

5. The promise of a new covenant.

Anyone who reads the Bible attentively will surely agree with these five statements. Moses warned Israel against transgressing the covenant by serving "other gods." (Deut: 17:2, 3.) The Lord revealed to Moses that after his death Israel would "go a whoring after the gods of the strangers of the land, . . . and will forsake me, and break my covenant which I have made with them." Deut. 31:16. When Joshua was dying he warned of the day when Israel would transgress the covenant by serving "other gods." (Joshua 23:16.) A judgment was pronounced upon Solomon because he had gone after "other gods" and had not kept "my covenant." (1 Kings 11:11.) In the last years of the kings of Israel the inspired writer recounted their long years of turning repeatedly to heathen gods and rejecting God's covenant. (See 2 Kings 17:7-23.) Jeremiah was instructed by the Lord to tell the "men of Judah" in their dark hour of national disaster that they had failed to keep the covenant He had made with their fathers at Sinai, "saying, Obey my voice, and do them, according to all which I command you: so shall ye be my people, and I will be your God." But "they went after other gods to serve them." Jer. 11:4, 10. Hosea declares: "The Lord hath a controversy with the inhabitants of the land, because there is no truth, nor mercy, nor knowledge of God in the land. By swearing, and lying, and killing, and stealing, and committing adultery, they break out, and blood toucheth blood." Hosea 4:1, 2. And he goes on to add a little later in his description: "They have transgressed my covenant." Hosea 8:1.

Despite their almost constant turning away from God's moral precepts, they did not always turn from the ceremonial laws of sacrifices, burnt offerings, feast days, and the like. They evidently, at times, glorified these ceremonies while transgressing the Ten Commandments, as though the ritual that was intended of God to give expression to their sorrow for sin—transgression of His law—could serve as a substitute for obedience. It is this fact that explains some striking passages in the Old Testament and reveals still further the sharp contrast between the ceremonial laws and the moral laws.

Through Hosea the Lord said to the morally corrupt "inhabitants of the land": "For I desired mercy, and not sacrifice; and the knowledge of God more than burnt offerings. But they like men have transgressed the covenant." Hosea 6:6, 7. It is true that the Israelites sometimes forgot even the ritual of their religious services. But that, evidently, was not at the heart of their apostasy. Long after they had "transgressed the covenant" by their moral corruption they were still carrying on a ceremonial service in obedience to the ceremonial law, as if the outward forms were a proper substitute for heart obedience to God's moral requirements. That is why the Lord, through Hosea, pronounced this judgment: "I will also cause all her mirth to cease, her feast days, her new moons, and her sabbaths, and all her solemn feasts." Hosea 2:11. A reference to the ceremonial law reveals that all the special days here listed are found in that code.

In similar language the Lord inquires through Isaiah, "To what purpose is the multitude of your sacrifices unto me?" Isa. 1:11. He describes their offerings as "vain oblations." "Incense is an abomination unto me; the new moons and sabbaths, the calling of assemblies, I cannot away with; it is iniquity." And why was this whole ceremonial service of offerings and special holy days so abhorrent to God? Because their carrying on of this ceremonial service was hypocritical. The sacrifices, the Passover sabbath, Day of Atonement sabbath, and essentially all the ceremonial ritual were intended of God to provide an expression of repentance for violations of the moral code and a desire for cleansing from sin. But the Israelites were set in evil ways and had no heart desire to reform. "Your hands are full of blood." Verse 15. After pleading with them to turn from their corrupt ways, the Lord declares, "If ye be willing and obedient, ye shall eat the good of the land." Verse 19. Here is the echo of the covenant agreement made at Sinai.

Jeremiah presents a similar description of the violation of God's moral code by rebellious Israel: "Will ye steal, murder, and commit adultery, and swear falsely, and burn incense unto Baal, and walk after other gods whom ye know not; and come and stand before me in this house, which is called by my name, and say, We are delivered to do all these abominations?" Jer. 7:9, 10. Then follows this declaration that shows perhaps more sharply than any other in this series of passages the clear distinction between moral and ceremonial laws: "Thus saith the Lord of hosts, the God of Israel; Put your burnt offerings unto your sacrifices, and eat flesh. For I spake not unto your fathers, nor commanded them in the day that I brought them out of the land of Egypt, concerning burnt offerings or sacrifices: but this thing commanded I them, saying, Obey my voice, and I will be your God, and ye shall be my people: and walk ye in all the ways that I have commanded you, that it may be well unto you." Verses 21-23.

But did not the Lord give commandments at Sinai concerning offerings? Bible commentators believe that the only way to resolve the apparent contradiction is by interpreting this passage in Jeremiah to mean that by comparison with the glory and primacy of the moral code given at Sinai, the ceremonial statutes pale into insignificance. To borrow the words of the learned commentator, Lange, on this passage:

# ANSWERS TO OBJECTIONS

"Thus those commentators are right who find here this meaning, that the whole of the enactments relating to sacrifices do not enter into consideration in comparison with the importance of the moral Law."

It is doubtless in this same sense that we may understand those scriptures that equate the covenant with the Ten Commandments (Deut. 4:13), even though certain ceremonial laws and civil statutes were also involved (Ex. 24:3-8). As earlier stated, the civil statutes were only an extension of, and the ceremonial laws only an accessory to, the moral code.

Now, in this long, dismal record of Israel's backsliding, where lay the trouble? Were the terms of the covenant at fault? Nowhere do the prophets suggest that the Ten Commandments were either inequitable or deficient. Had God failed in His part of the agreement? No. The trouble was with the Israelites, who failed to live up to their promise to be obedient to God's voice, His holy law. They were stiffnecked, hard of heart, rebellious. Christ could say to His Father, "I delight to do thy will, O my God: yea, thy law is within my heart." Ps. 40:8. But not so with the children of Israel. "Their heart went after their idols." Eze. 20:16. "The sin of Judah . . . is graven upon the table of their heart." Jer. 17:1.

The children of Israel had promised at Sinai, "All that the Lord hath spoken we will do." Ex. 19:8. But they knew not how deceitful were their hearts, how weak their will and their spirit. It is in this setting that we are able to appreciate the promise of the new covenant as foretold through Jeremiah: "Behold, the days come, saith the Lord, that I will make a new covenant with the house of Israel, and with the house of Judah: not according to the covenant that I made with their fathers in the day that I took them by the hand to bring them out of the land of Egypt; which my covenant they brake, although I was an husband unto them, saith the Lord: but this shall be the covenant that I will make with the house of Israel; after those days, saith the Lord, I will put my law in their inward parts, and write it in their hearts; and will be their God, and they shall be my people." Jer. 31:31-33.

The promise of the new covenant is not a forecast of an era

when grace would supplant law, but of a time when the law of God would be written in men's hearts by the grace of God acting upon those hearts. So far from God's law being abolished, it is enshrined within those who have received a new heart. Now, if there is only one law, as some contend, then the new covenant, under which all of us declare we may live today, calls for the writing upon our hearts, not only of God's moral precepts, but of all the ceremonial statutes also! The logic that requires this conclusion is unanswerable—if there is only one law. Could better proof be offered that there must be more than one law?

The writer of Hebrews, in referring to this passage in Jeremiah, makes clear that the trouble with the old covenant lay, not with the law, but with the people. The Lord found "fault with them." (Heb. 8:8.)

In the same connection we read concerning the new covenant, that Christ "is the mediator of a better covenant, which was established upon better promises." Verse 6.

The first covenant broke down on the faulty promises of the Israelites. The second covenant is built upon the divine promise of God to change our hearts.

The first covenant was ratified at Sinai by the shedding of the blood of sacrificial animals. (Ex. 24:5-8.) The second covenant was ratified at Calvary by the shedding of the blood of Jesus Christ. (Heb. 9:12, 23.)

The mediator of the first covenant was Moses. (Ex. 19:3-8; 24:3-8.) The mediator of the second covenant is Christ. (Heb. 8:6.)

Under the first covenant the worshiper brought his offering to an earthly priest, who ministered at an earthly sanctuary, which ministry could not of itself "make him that did the service perfect, as pertaining to the conscience." Heb. 9:9. Why? Because this earthly sanctuary service "stood only in meats and drinks, and divers washings, and carnal ordinances, imposed on them until the time of reformation." Verse 10. Only as the worshiper looked by faith beyond the animal sacrifices to the sacrifice of Christ, the promised Messiah, could he receive genuine spiritual blessing and forgiveness of sins. And because it was possible for a child of God in the days preceding Christ's first advent to exercise true faith and to look beyond, the new covenant experience could be his.

Under the new covenant we appropriate by faith the offering made by the Lamb of God, coming boldly to the throne of grace and into the presence of our great High Priest. We look back to Calvary and upward to heaven. (Heb. 9:11-15, 24-26; 10:19-22.)

It was foretold of Christ that He would "cause the sacrifice and the oblation to cease." Dan. 9:27. No longer was there any occasion for the slaying of animals. Hence the ceremonial laws regarding all such offerings expired by limitation. There were no longer to be earthly priests drawn from a certain tribe and according to a certain law of the ceremonial code. Hence we read, "For the priesthood being changed, there is made of necessity a change also of the law." Heb. 7:12. The Levitical priesthood was changed, abolished, and so was the law that governed the selection and the ministry of that priesthood. Yet under the new covenant God promises, "I will put my law in their inward parts, and write it in their hearts." Jer. 31:33. How evident that we are dealing with a wholly different law from that mentioned in Hebrews 7:12.

To sum up the matter in briefest form, note these comparisons and contrasts between the two covenants:

| Old Covenant | New Covenant |
|---|---|
| 1. Parties to covenant: God and Israel. | 1. Parties to covenant: God and Israel. |
| 2. Mediator: Moses. | 2. Mediator: Christ. |
| 3. Based on mutual promises of God and Israel. | 3. Based on God's promise and our acceptance of promise by faith. |
| 4. Text of covenant: Ten Commandments. | 4. Text of covenant: Ten Commandments. |
| 5. Written: On tables of stone. | 5. Written: In the believer's heart. |
| 6. Ratified at Sinai. | 6. Ratified at Calvary. |
| 7. By the shedding of blood of animals. | 7. By the shedding of the blood of Christ. |
| 8. Its ministration: In terms of an endless number of animal sacrifices, whose blood was ministered by earthly priests in earthly sanctuary. | 8. Its ministration: In terms of one sacrifice by Christ, our High Priest, who now ministers His shed blood in heavenly sanctuary. |

# LAW

Not a change in the terms of the covenant, the Ten Commandments, but a change in the *location* of these commandments, this is the essence of the difference between the two covenants. And the effecting of this change requires Christ and His divine sacrifice. In other words, to live under the new covenant is to live by the faith of the Son of God, who loved us and gave Himself for us. Faith and obedience to God's commandments go hand in hand. How significant in this connection is the description of those who will finally be awaiting the return of Christ: "Here are they that keep the commandments of God, and the faith of Jesus." Rev. 14:12.

Yes, and how significant is Paul's statement that the "carnal mind," which distinguished rebellious Israel, is "not subject to the law of God, neither indeed can be." Rom. 8:7. Also his statement of what has taken place for "them which are in Christ Jesus": "For what the law could not do, in that it was weak through the flesh, God sending his own Son in the likeness of sinful flesh, and for sin, condemned sin in the flesh: that the righteousness of the law might be fulfilled in us ["that the just requirement of the law might be fulfilled in us." R.S.V.], who walk not after the flesh, but after the Spirit." Rom. 8:3, 4.

The weakness is not in God's holy law but in us who are too weak of ourselves to give obedience. When we are changed by the gospel from carnal to spiritual, then the law can be written in our hearts. The person who says that he has nothing to do with the law because he lives under the new covenant, reveals instead that he has nothing to do with the new covenant, for the new covenant believer has the law engraved on his heart.

71

# Objection 6

Paul states that the "ministration of death, written and engraven in stones" was "done away." Therefore the ten-commandment law, which was written on the tables of stone, has been done away. (See 2 Cor. 3:5-11.)

Let us see what Paul really did say. The introduction to the passage before us finds Paul declaring to the Corinthian brethren: "Ye are our epistle written in our hearts, known and read of all men: forasmuch as ye are manifestly declared to be the epistle of Christ ministered by us, written not with ink, but with the Spirit of the living God; not in tables of stone, but in fleshy tables of the heart." 2 Cor. 3:2, 3.

Here is the key to interpret the words that follow. His figure of speech is patently borrowed from the Scriptural contrast between the old and the new covenant, "Tables of stone" contrasted with "tables of the heart," "ink" contrasted with "the Spirit of the living God." These Corinthians, he said, were "ministered by us."

By an easy transition Paul moves into a discussion of the two covenants by adding immediately that Christ "also hath made us able ministers of the new testament [covenant]; not of the letter, but of the spirit: for the letter killeth, but the spirit giveth life." (The word "testament" in this and almost all other instances in the New Testament does not have the meaning of a "will" as made by a testator in anticipation of death, but of covenant, and is so translated in the Revised Version.)

We might close the discussion right here, for our examination of the two covenants revealed clearly that the ratifying of the new covenant did not mean the abolishing of the Ten Commandments. However, let us proceed.

"But if the ministration of death, written and engraven in stones, was glorious, so that the children of Israel could not sted-

72

fastly behold the face of Moses for the glory of his countenance; which glory was to be done away: how shall not the ministration of the spirit be rather glorious? For if the ministration of condemnation be glory, much more doth the ministration of righteousness exceed in glory. For even that which was made glorious had no glory in this respect, by reason of the glory that excelleth. For if that which is done away was glorious, much more that which remaineth is glorious. Seeing then that we have such hope, we use great plainness of speech: and not as Moses, which put a vail over his face, that the children of Israel could not stedfastly look to the end of that which is abolished." Verses 7-13.

Here is a series of contrasts, intended not so much to belittle the old dispensation as to glorify the new. It was ever Paul's studied endeavor to prove that Christ and His ministry are the blazing glory beside which the spiritual glory of the former times seems pale. This argument by contrast particularly marks the book of Hebrews, which was written for the Jewish believers, who, until they accepted Christ, had thought that the glory of Sinai and the ministration of the divine law under the Jewish priests and rulers were the last word in heavenly glory. The contrasts that Paul seeks to make are essentially the same as the contrasts between the old and new covenants:

1. "The ministration of death" versus "the ministration of the spirit."

2. "Ministration of condemnation" versus "ministration of righteousness."

3. "Letter killeth" versus "spirit giveth life."

4. "Was glorious" versus "exceed in glory."

5. "Done away" versus "remaineth."

Numbers one and two are simply variant expressions. The questions before us are therefore:

1. What are these two ministrations?

2. What is meant by "letter" and "spirit"?

3. What is this relative "glory"?

4. What was "done away" and what "remaineth"?

The objector quickly answers: The "ministration of death" was that which was "written and engraven in stones," and is plainly the Ten Commandments. But not so quickly. Is it correct to speak of a "ministration" and a "law" as synonymous? No. It is correct to speak of the "ministration" or, as we would say, the administering of a law. The administering of the law is the means by which it is put in operation, and is not to be confused with the law itself. Therefore, "the ministration of death," or "the ministration of condemnation," refers to the ministration, or the administering, of the law that was "written and engraven in stones."

By a simple figure of speech the law is called "death" and "condemnation." On a certain occasion in Elisha's day the sons of the prophets gathered with him around a "great pot" in which had been cooking certain "wild gourds." Evidently the gourds were poisonous, for one of those eating cried out: "There is death in the pot." (See 2 Kings 4:38-40.) He meant, of course, that there was something in the pot that would *cause* death, and substituting *cause* for *effect*, he cried out as he did.

Paul had earlier said to the Corinthians, "The sting of death is sin; and the strength of sin is the law." 1 Cor. 15:56. That is, if it were not for the law of God, which condemns those who violate it, there would be no sin, and hence no death in penalty for sin, "for where no law is, there is no transgression." Rom. 4:15. Thinking on this fact and the contrasting fact that "the law is holy, . . . and just, and good," caused Paul to inquire: "Was then that which is good made death unto me?" Here he speaks of the law as "death." Now, how does Paul say that we escape from this "ministration of death," this "ministration of condemnation"? By abolishing the law of God? Listen to his words:

"There is therefore now no condemnation to them which are in Christ Jesus, who walk not after the flesh, but after the Spirit. For the law of the Spirit of life in Christ Jesus hath made me free from the law of sin and death. For what the law could not do, in that it was weak through the flesh, God sending his own Son in the likeness of sinful flesh, and for sin, condemned sin in the flesh:

74

that the righteousness of the law might be fulfilled in us, who walk not after the flesh, but after the Spirit." Rom. 8:1-4.

We escape from "condemnation" through Jesus Christ, who changes our hearts so that "the righteousness of the law might be fulfilled in us." Paul describes this changed state as walking "after the Spirit," and adds, that "to be spiritually minded is *life* and peace." Verses 5, 6.

Here is a state of "condemnation" and "death" changed to one of "no condemnation" but rather "life." In other words, a ministration of condemnation and death exchanged for a ministration of the spirit and life. How evident that we are here discussing the two covenants. And how evident also that Paul's words in Romans 8 parallel his words in 2 Corinthians 3. That is the plain teaching of the Scripture.

The cold letter of the law as it appeared on the stone tables had no life-giving power. It could only point accusingly at every man, for all have sinned and come short of the glory of God. An administration of the law based on its letter alone results only in death for violators. But an administration of it based on the forgiveness possible through the action of God's Spirit on the heart results in life. The contrast between "letter" and "spirit" does not mean a contrast between an age of law and an age of freedom from all law. As we have already noted, when God's Spirit is in control, the law's requirements are carried out in our hearts.

What, now, of the "glory" mentioned by Paul? He plainly speaks of the relative glory of two ministrations. The justice and righteousness of God shone forth in awesome, even terrifying glory on Mount Sinai as He proclaimed His law. He stood there as a consuming fire. But how much greater the glory of God that bathed the earth with its life-giving rays when Christ came down to "save his people from their sins." Matt. 1:21. Here was the glory of justice and mercy combined, for in dying for our sins—our "transgression of the law"—Christ revealed how God at one and the same time could "be just, and the justifier of him which believeth in Jesus." Rom. 3:26.

# ANSWERS TO OBJECTIONS

This brings us to the last question: What was "done away" and what "remaineth"? The question is really already answered. The glory attendant upon the giving of the law is so greatly excelled by the glory attendant upon the saving of men from its violation that Paul could appropriately speak of the first as "glorious" and the second as "the glory that excelleth." But right here Paul weaves in an incident in connection with the giving of the law at Sinai to illustrate a point that he wishes to make in the verses that immediately follow this disputed passage. When Moses came down from the mount with the tables of stone in his hands, "the skin of his face shone; and they were afraid to come nigh him." So Moses "put a vail on his face" while he spoke to the Israelites. (See Ex. 34:29-35.)

Paul refers to this: "The children of Israel could not stedfastly behold the face of Moses for the glory of his countenance; which glory was to be done away." 2 Cor. 3:7. He refers to this again in verse 11, saying it was "done away," and then again in verse 13 in these words: "And not as Moses, which put a vail over his face, that the children of Israel could not stedfastly look to the end of that which is abolished."

It was the *glory* of the former ministration, now ended, and not the law administered, that was "done away," "abolished," even, as by historical analogy, Paul reminds them that it was the glory on Moses' face that was "done away." The record declares that the veil was on Moses' face, not on the tables of stone, that it was his face that shone and not the tables of stone, and that it was the glory on his face that faded, not the luster that ever surrounds the divinely written Decalogue.

Well do Jamieson, Fausset, and Brown, in their Bible commentary, make this general observation in their comments on 2 Corinthians 3:

"Still the moral law of the ten commandments, being written by the finger of God, is as obligatory now as ever; but put more on the Gospel spirit of 'love,' than on the letter of a servile obedience, and in a deeper and fuller spirituality (Matthew 5.17-48; Romans 13.9)."

# Objection 7

**Paul's allegory on the two covenants in Galatians 4 proves that we have nothing to do with law in the Christian dispensation.**

In the fourth chapter of Galatians, Paul recounts that Abraham had two sons. After relating the incidents of the birth of Ishmael to the bondwoman Hagar and the birth of Isaac to the free woman Sarah, the first "born after the flesh," the second "by promise," Paul declares:

"Which things are an allegory: for these are the two covenants; the one from the mount Sinai, which gendereth to bondage, which is Agar. For this Agar is mount Sinai in Arabia, and answereth to Jerusalem which now is, and is in bondage with her children. But Jerusalem which is above is free, which is the mother of us all." Gal. 4:24-26.

God had promised Abraham a son. He believed the promise, and the Lord "counted it to him for righteousness." Gen. 15:6. This promise was of vast significance to Abraham, for God had also promised him: "In thy seed [Christ] shall all the nations of the earth be blessed." Gen. 26:4. (See Gen. 12:3.) But his faith and that of his long-childless wife, Sarah, evidently waned. She encouraged him to take Hagar to wife and thus raise up seed. But the Lord told him that Ishmael, who was born of that union, was not the fulfillment of the divine promise of a son and that that promise would yet be fulfilled.

Adapting this historical incident to the current experience of the Galatian Christians, who were trying to secure Heaven's promised salvation by their own works—"ye observe days, and months, and times, and years," Gal. 4:10—he declares that here is an "allegory," a figurative description of "the two covenants."

In the allegory Hagar stands for Sinai. She was a bondwoman, and her children would therefore be in the same state of slavery.

77

She also stands for "Jerusalem which now is, and is in bondage with her children." From Mount Sinai came the old covenant. How can it be said that the old covenant "gendereth to bondage"? All Bible commentators, along with the apostle Peter, agree that our brother Paul wrote some things hard to be understood, and the book of Galatians illustrates that fact. But we believe that in two ways the old covenant might be regarded as leading into bondage.

1. The ceremonial ritual of numerous sacrifices, feast days, and the like, by which the Israelites were to express their desire for freedom from sin—the transgression of the moral law—tended to become more and more an intolerable burden upon them as the rabbis constantly refined and multiplied the ritual. At the Jerusalem council the early Christian leaders first considered in a formal way the contention of certain Jews who declared "that it was needful to circumcise them [the Gentile converts], and to command them to keep the law of Moses." Acts 15:5. To this contention Peter replied, "Now therefore why tempt ye God, to put a yoke upon the neck of the disciples, which neither our fathers nor we were able to bear?" Verse 10.

This question seems to parallel the one that Paul asks the Galatians: "But now, after that ye have known God, or rather are known of God, how turn ye again to the weak and beggarly elements, whereunto ye desire again to be in bondage? Ye observe days, and months, and times, and years." Gal. 4:9, 10.

Obviously here is a "bondage" that suffices to provide a reasonable interpretation of Paul's words about the Sinaitic covenant gendering to bondage. The *Pulpit Commentary* well observes on Galatians 4:25:

"The religious life of Judaism consisted of a servile obedience to a letter Law of ceremonialism, interpreted by the rabbins with an infinity of hair-splitting rules, the exact observance of which was bound upon the conscience of its votaries as of the essence of true piety."

2. The moral law, central to the old as well as the new covenant, can be considered as bringing a man into bondage if that man seeks to keep the law in his own strength. "The law worketh

wrath," says Paul. Rom. 4:15. Why? Paul explains: "I was alive without the law once: but when the commandment came, sin revived, and I died." Rom. 7:9. And when a man is dead in sin is he a freeman? Again Paul speaks: "Know ye not, that to whom ye yield yourselves servants to obey, his servants ye are to whom ye obey; whether of sin unto death, or of obedience unto righteousness?" Rom. 6:16.

Now, how could those of whom Paul was speaking—"Jerusalem which now is, . . . with her children"—hope to escape from their bondage? The answer is, By moving from the old over to the new covenant.

By contrast to those "in bondage" Paul, in his allegory, declares that "Jerusalem which is above is free, which is the mother of us all." In Hebrews, Paul employs this figure also: "For ye are not come unto the mount [Sinai] that might be touched, and that burned with fire, . . . but ye are come unto mount Sion, and unto the city of the living God, the heavenly Jerusalem, and to an innumerable company of angels, to the general assembly and church of the firstborn, which are written in heaven, and to God the Judge of all, and to the spirits of just men made perfect, and to Jesus the mediator of the new covenant, and to the blood of sprinkling, that speaketh better things than that of Abel." Heb. 12:18-24.

Without going into a detailed examination of figures of speech, which would carry us beyond the range of the particular question at issue—the perpetuity of the Decalogue—we may simply say that Paul here turns to describe the state of those who are under "the new covenant." We have already found that under the new covenant God's law is written in our hearts. In this very passage in Hebrews, Paul makes clear, by a series of contrasts and comparisons, that obedience to the voice of God is still of pre-eminent importance:

| | |
|---|---|
| 1. "Not come unto the mount [Sinai]." | 1. "Come unto mount Sion . . . the heavenly Jerusalem." |
| 2. "That burned with fire." | 2. "Our God is a consuming fire." |
| 3. [To Moses the mediator of the old covenant.] | 3. "To Jesus the mediator of the new covenant." |

4. "And the voice of words." [The voice of God, commanding obedience.]

4. "See that ye refuse not him that speaketh."

5. "If they escaped not who refused him that spake on earth."

5. "Much more shall not we escape, if we turn away from him that speaketh from heaven."

6. [To the blood of sprinkling of animal sacrifices, even as "Abel" offered long before.]

6. "To the blood of sprinkling, that speaketh better things than that of Abel." [The blood of Christ.]

7. "Whose voice then shook the earth."

7. "Yet once more I shake not the earth only, but also heaven."

Because we come under the new covenant by our act of faith in accepting the promise of God to write His law in our hearts, we are no longer "by nature the children of wrath, even as others" (Eph. 2:3), but the children of promise. The figure is apt. We become children of God by the sacrifice of our Lord, and by accepting through faith God's promise of a new covenant relationship. Isaac also was a child of promise, an answer to an act of faith on Abraham's part. Blending the two ideas, Paul really comes to the climax of his allegory with these words: "Now we, brethren, as Isaac was, are the children of promise." Abraham's act of faith in believing God's promise was counted unto him for righteousness. Our act of faith in believing God's promise is counted unto us for righteousness. That is the way we acquire true righteousness, new-covenant righteousness.

And why did the Lord make His promise to Abraham? "Because that Abraham obeyed my voice, and kept my charge, my commandments, my statutes, and my laws." Gen. 26:5.

And how are those described who are literally waiting to be taken to "Jerusalem which is above"? "Here are they that keep the commandments of God, and the faith of Jesus." Rev. 14:12.

No, Paul's words in Galatians do not teach freedom from the law of God. They teach freedom from bondage to sin, freedom from transgression of the law of God, through Jesus Christ and the new covenant relationship.

# Objection 8

Paul declares that we are not under the law, but under grace. (Rom. 6:14.) The law was given by Moses, but grace and truth came by Jesus Christ. (John 1:17.) Paul also declares that "Christ is the end of the law for righteousness to every one that believeth." Rom. 10:4. These texts prove that the law was abolished by Christ.

There is no conflict between law and grace, or between law and gospel. A simple definition or two will help us out in this matter. By "law" we mean God's standard of right and wrong—the yardstick by which we can tell whether we have fallen short of God's requirements. The word "gospel" means good news—good news of salvation from sin. (See Matt. 1:21.) And the Bible defines sin as any violation of the divine law. (See 1 John 3:4.) So, then, the gospel is the good news of God's plan to save us from breaking His holy law. Thus instead of law and gospel being in opposition, they are in close fellowship. And the very existence of the gospel proves that the law is still in force, for what would be the point in preaching the good news of salvation from breaking the law if the law were no longer in force? A man cannot break that which does not exist.

Let us now read, in its setting, the key text in this discussion: "Sin shall not have dominion over you: for ye are not under the law, but under grace. What then? shall we sin, because we are not under the law, but under grace? God forbid." Rom. 6:14, 15. We discover immediately that whatever else Paul wishes us to understand by this passage, he does not want us to think that the reign of grace frees us from obedience to the law, "What then?" says he; "shall we sin," that is, break the law, "because we are not under the law, but under grace? God forbid."

The very next verse makes clear that Paul here uses the phrase "under the law" to mean "under its condemnation," and "under

81

grace" to mean "living under the plan that God has offered of salvation from the bondage of sin." For Paul follows right on to say: "Know ye not, that to whom ye yield yourselves servants to obey, his servants ye are to whom ye obey; whether of sin unto death, or of obedience unto righteousness? . . . Being then made free from sin, ye became the servants of righteousness." Verses 16-18.

The contrast is between servants "of sin" and servants "of obedience unto righteousness." What is it that gives strength to sin? It is the law, says Paul. (See 1 Cor. 15:56.) The fact that the law exists and pronounces a death penalty for evildoing and evil living is what gives to sin its power over those who indulge in unlawful acts. The law does not lay its strong hand on the man who does not violate it. Its strength is felt only by the lawbreaker.

Paul says sin is no longer to hold us in its grip, because we are living under, or have accepted, God's plan of grace, which gives us a power that breaks the grip of sin. Thus instead of being servants of sin, we become servants of "obedience unto righteousness." And what is righteousness? It is rightdoing, right living—a state of heart the very opposite of sinfulness or lawlessness. Paul in a later chapter tells how the grace of the gospel of Jesus Christ brings righteousness to us, and how this righteousness is directly related to the law. We read: "What the law could not do, in that it was weak through the flesh, God sending his own Son in the likeness of sinful flesh, and for sin, condemned sin in the flesh: that the *righteousness of the law* might be fulfilled in *us,* who walk not after the flesh, but after the Spirit." Rom. 8:3, 4.

Paul deals with the same problem in Galatians 3:24, 25: "Wherefore the law was our schoolmaster to bring us unto Christ, that we might be justified by faith. But after that faith is come, we are no longer under a schoolmaster."

The law can show us our sinfulness and bring to us such conviction of sin that we shall be driven to Christ, who can free us from our sins. When we receive Christ we are no longer under the domination—the condemnation—of the law. But we are not freed from obedience to God's law, for in accepting Christ we receive divine power for obedience to that law, as is explained in the passage just quoted from Romans 8. Thus Galatians 3:24, 25 gives no support to the claim that the law is abolished.

How plain and simple it is, then, that when we accept God's Son and the grace He offers, we do not turn our back on the law! Rather, we find that the "righteousness of the law" is "fulfilled in us." Instead of being sinners, breakers of God's law, we find that we are obedient to it.

In the light of these facts there is no difficulty in the text: "The law was given by Moses, but grace and truth came by Jesus Christ." John 1:17. While Moses served a very great purpose in the plan of God—for through him God gave to the world the written form of the moral code—yet through Christ came divine grace, without which the law cannot truly be kept.

The man who accepts Christ no longer strives to *obtain* righteousness by keeping the law. Upon his acceptance of Christ, the Saviour's righteousness is imputed to him. Says Paul: "Now the righteousness of God without [or, *apart from*] the law is manifested being *witnessed by* the law and the prophets; even the righteousness of God which is by faith of Jesus Christ unto all and upon all them that believe." Rom. 3:21, 22. Because "the righteousness of God" can be obtained *apart* from the law, Paul can well declare: "Christ is the end of the law of righteousness to every one that believeth." Rom. 10:4. To everyone who *believes* on Him, Christ brings to an absolute end the *use* of the law as a means of *obtaining* righteousness. Or, again, we may understand that word "end" as meaning the objective or purpose. Christ was the objective the law had in view; for the purpose of the law is to cause men so to realize their sinfulness, their unrighteousness, that they will go to Christ for His righteousness, which not only is imputed in justification but is actually imparted in the daily living, as is clearly taught in Galatians 2:20. This use of the word "end" is found in James 5:11 and 1 Timothy 1:5.

Both law and grace came from heaven. How happy are we as Christians that we are not called upon to reject one in order to have the other! By the power of God's grace we no longer dwell under the condemnation of the law, but are in Him raised up to the lofty plane of complete obedience to this divine code.

Well do Jamieson, Fausset, and Brown, in their Bible commentary, make this observation in a note at the close of their comments on Romans 6:

"The fundamental principle of Gospel-obedience is as original as it is divinely rational; that 'we are set free from the law in order to keep it, and are brought graciously under servitude to the law in order to be free' (v. 14, 15, 18). So long as we know no principle of obedience but the terrors of the law, which condemns all the breakers of it, and knows nothing whatever of grace, either to pardon the guilty or to purify the stained, we are shut up under a moral impossibility of genuine and acceptable obedience: whereas when Grace lifts us out of this state, and through union to a righteous Surety, brings us into a state of conscious reconciliation, and loving surrender of heart to a God of salvation, we immediately feel the glorious *liberty to be holy*, and the assurance that 'Sin shall not have dominion over us' is as sweet to our renewed tastes and aspirations as the ground of it is felt to be firm, 'because we are not under the Law, but under Grace.'"

# Objection 9

**Luke 16:16 proves that Christians have nothing to do with law.**

Luke 16:16 reads as follows: "The law and the prophets were until John: since that time the kingdom of God is preached, and every man presseth into it." Place beside this the parallel passage in Matthew 11:13: "For all the prophets and the law prophesied until John."

The word "were" in Luke 16:16 is a supplied word. Luke simply wrote: "The law and the prophets, until John." If the translators had compared his words with those of Matthew, they would have seen that Luke did not mean that the law and the prophets ended in John's day, but that they "prophesied" until that day. The difference is very great and provides the key to the meaning of the passage under discussion.

The phrase, "the prophets and the law," or more commonly, "the law and the prophets," is used often in the Bible to describe the writings of Moses plus the writings of the other Old Testament prophets. The writings of Moses were so distinguished by the codes of laws there recorded that they very understandably were often described as "the law," in contrast to the writings of the other prophets. That fact in itself really removes this objection from consideration, for neither Luke nor Matthew is really discussing the ten-commandment law.

But what did these two gospel writers mean? The context gives the answer. Skepticism of the mission and character both of Christ and of John the Baptist marked many of the Jews. They insisted that they believed Moses and all the prophets. Christ sought repeatedly to make clear to them that He was the one foretold by the prophets, and likewise His forerunner, John the Baptist, was foretold, and that now the kingdom of God was being preached unto them.

# ANSWERS TO OBJECTIONS

When Christ began His public ministry He declared, "The time is fulfilled, and the kingdom of God is at hand." Mark 1:15. The prophets had foretold the coming of the Messiah. Christ announced that those prophecies were now fulfilled.

To the skeptical Jews, who failed to see in Christ the fulfillment of these prophecies, He declared: "Do not think that I will accuse you to the Father: there is one that accuseth you, even Moses, in whom ye trust. For had ye believed Moses, ye would have believed me: for he wrote of me. But if ye believe not his writings, how shall ye believe my words?" John 5:45-47.

When Philip found Nathanael and sought to bring him the thrilling news that the promised Messiah had come, he said, "We have found him, of whom Moses in the law, and the prophets, did write, Jesus of Nazareth." John 1:45.

When Christ was resurrected from the dead He came that same day to the troubled, bewildered disciples and inquired, "Why are ye troubled? and why do thoughts arise in your hearts?" Luke 24:38. Then He reminded them that what had happened to Him on that fateful week end was what the prophets had foretold—"that all things must be fulfilled, which were written in the law of Moses, and in the prophets, and in the psalms, concerning me." Verse 44.

Paul declared that his mission in life was "witnessing both to small and great, saying none other things than those which the prophets and Moses did say should come." Acts 26:22.

Hence it is evident that the prophesying of Moses and the other prophets was one of the prime proofs offered by Christ and the apostles in support of the claim that the Messiah had come. Prophets prophesy "until" the time when their prophecies meet fulfillment, after that prophecy becomes history. Thus our Lord, in declaring that the "prophets and the law prophesied until John," was simply announcing that "the time is fulfilled, and the kingdom of God is at hand." He was not implying that either Moses or the prophets were now abolished, much less that the ten-commandment law had come to an end.

86

# Objection 10

Romans 7:1-7 proves that the law is done away. Under the figure of marriage Paul explains that we are "delivered from the law," that, indeed, the law is dead.

What is Paul discussing in this chapter? The same general subject that he is discussing in the chapters immediately preceding and following—the subject of the carnal man, the slave of sin, who is unable to save himself, and who must find salvation through the grace of God as revealed in Jesus Christ.

Paul sets down the premise: "The law hath dominion over a man as long as he liveth." Rom. 7:1. In various ways in this epistle he shows that the sinner, because he has transgressed God's law, is under the dominion of sin. In other words, our old sinful nature, which Paul describes as "the old man," has dominion over us. It is because of this that Paul declared, of his former state: "For what I would, that do I not; but what I hate, that do I." Verse 15. "The strength of sin is the law." 1 Cor. 15:56. Once we have become transgressors of the moral law, which knows no revocation, and demands judgment upon the violator, we cannot gain freedom, for we have no power within ourselves to escape from the domination of sin.

Now, how do we escape from "the old man," that holds us in servitude? By the death of this "old man," that is, by our conversion, for at conversion our old nature is crucified. "Knowing this, that our old man is crucified with him [Christ], that the body of sin might be destroyed, that henceforth we should not serve sin." Rom. 6:6. But there is not only the death of "the old man," there is also the birth of "the new man." "Therefore we are buried with him by baptism into death: that like as Christ was raised up from the dead by the glory of the Father, even so we also should walk in newness of life." Verse 4. Paul refers to this changed state of the Christian when he says, "Lie not one to another, seeing that ye have put off the old man with his deeds; and have put on the new man, which is renewed in knowledge after the image of him that created him." Col. 3:9, 10. Because Christ's followers have put off "the old man" and put on "the new man," Paul says we should reckon ourselves "to be dead indeed unto sin, but alive unto God through Jesus Christ." Rom. 6:11.

It is to illustrate this transition from the domination of sin to the rule of righteousness that Paul employs the figure of marriage. There are four principal parts to the figure he uses: a woman, her first husband, her second husband, the law of marriage.

"The woman which hath an husband is bound by the law to her husband so long as he liveth; but if the husband be dead, she is loosed from the law of her husband. . . . If her husband be dead, she is free from that law; so that she is no adulteress, though she be married to another man." Rom. 7:2, 3.

The first and most important point in this illustration, from which Paul proceeds at once to draw his lesson, is this: He is not speaking of the death of the law, but of the death of a husband. In fact, there would be no point to his illustration if the law were dead, for in that event, there would be nothing to hold the wife to either husband, and any discussion of adultery would be pointless. How could there possibly be adultery, which is transgression of a precept of God's law, if the law containing the prohibition against adultery were dead? The marriage law is not abolished in a country because a husband dies. It remains on the statute books to govern all who are married or who seek to marry.

Now follows Paul's application of the figure to the life of the man who has turned from sin to righteousness:

"Wherefore, my brethren, ye also are become dead to the law by the body of Christ; that ye should be married to another, even to him who is raised from the dead, that we should bring forth fruit unto God." Verse 4.

We have been crucified with Christ, His crucified body vicariously ours. All the condemnatory claim that the law had upon our "old man" ends with the death of that "man." Now we are free from its condemnation and can be married to Christ. We can put on "the new man."

Well do Jamieson, Fausset, and Brown, in their Bible commentary, remark on this passage:

> "It is we that are 'crucified with Christ,' and not the law. This death dissolves our marriage obligation to the law, leaving us at liberty to contract a new relation—to be joined to the Risen One, in order to spiritual fruitfulness, to the glory of God. . . . Believers are here viewed as having a double life—the old sin-condemned life, which they lay down with Christ, and the new life of acceptance and holiness to which they rise with their Surety and Head."—Comment on Romans 7:4.

Because of this new union we "bring forth fruit unto God," whereas, "when we were in the flesh, the motions of sins, which were by the law, did work in our members to bring forth fruit unto death." Verse 5. In other words, while we were under the dominion of sin, the only fruitage of our actions could be further condemnation and renewed certainty of death, and all because the law of God was in force against us and giving "strength" to sin.

To prevent his readers from thinking that the trouble was with the law rather than with sinful man, Paul immediately adds: "What shall we say then? Is the law sin? God forbid. Nay, I had not known sin, but by the law: for I had not known lust, except the law had said, Thou shalt not covet. . . . For sin, taking occasion by the commandment, deceived me, and by it slew me." Verses 7-11. The wages of sin—that is, the wages of law breaking—is death. That is why Paul says, "The commandment, which was ordained to life, I found to be unto death." Verse 10. Then to make doubly sure that no one would conclude that anything in his argument was intended to throw discredit on God's law, he declares, "Wherefore the law is holy, and the commandment holy, and just, and good." Verse 12. The trouble, he emphasizes once more, is with sinful man: "For we know that the law is spiritual: but I am carnal, sold under sin." Verse 14.

Paul comes to the climax of his argument in the opening verses of the next chapter. He explains that God "sending his own Son in the likeness of sinful flesh, and for sin, condemned sin in the flesh: that the righteousness of the law ["the just requirement of the law," R.S.V.] might be fulfilled in us, who walk not after the flesh, but after the Spirit." Rom. 8:3, 4. Christ's death made possible our salvation, which in turn results, not in the death of the law, but in the implanting of that law in our hearts. Thus we are enabled to "bring forth fruit unto God."

Returning, now, to the figure of marriage, let us adapt a little Paul's illustration, and summarize his argument: Even the most perfect marriage law cannot make a marriage a success. Hence the failure of a marriage is no reason for repealing the law. All that the marriage law can do is to set a standard for marriage. If the standard is violated, the violators are condemned, but the law remains. Thus with God's moral law. It sets a standard for our lives. If we violate that standard, we stand condemned, but God's law remains. The trouble is not with the law, which is "spiritual," but with us who are "carnal, sold under sin." "Because the carnal mind is enmity against God: for it is not subject to the law of God, neither indeed can be." Verse 7. While we are "sold under sin," that is, enslaved by it, we are under the domination of "the old man." That domination is broken by the death of the "old man" and the putting on of the "new man." In our former state the law pointed only a condemning finger at us. In our redeemed state the "righteousness of the law" is "fulfilled in us," for the law is written in our hearts.

We do not know how Paul could have been more explicit in the matter. And it is in the setting of the whole context that we examine the only clause in the passage that appears to make Paul teach the abolition of the law. Romans 7:6 reads, "But now we are delivered from the law, that being dead wherein we were held." If Paul here teaches the death of the law, he not only confuses the figure of speech he has been using, but also squarely contradicts the very literal statements he has made in the same context. He has spoken of the death of a husband, and by application of the figure, our death. In the fourth verse he speaks of our becoming "dead to the law." Does he turn around in the sixth verse to tell us that it is the law that is dead? We do not wish to charge Paul with such confused reasoning.

There are two ways of relieving the apparent contradiction and confusion.

1. By explaining the clause, "that being dead wherein we were held," as referring to the sinful nature, "the old man" that has had dominion over us. Sin, operating through our sinful nature, is what "held" us. (See verses 24, 25.)

2. By taking the position that the clause, "that being dead wherein we were held," which is the reading in the so-called Authorized Version, is not the correct reading. Later versions, which draw from further and sometimes older manuscripts, give a translation that is consonant with Paul's whole argument. For example, the American Standard Version—generally called the Revised Version—gives the clause thus: "having died to that wherein we were held." The Revised Standard Version gives it thus: "dead to that which held us captive." On this point Jamieson, Fausset, and Brown remark:

"It is now universally agreed that the true reading here is, 'being dead to that wherein we were held.' The received reading [of the Authorized Version] has no authority whatever, and is inconsistent with the strain of the argument; for the death spoken of, as we have seen, is not the *law's* but ours, through union with the crucified Saviour."—Comment on Romans 7:6.

# Objection 11

**Ephesians 2:14, 15 and Colossians 2:14, 16 prove that the law was abolished at the cross.**

Very true. But which law? Under objection 2 we found that the Bible speaks of more than one law, and that these two texts describe the ceremonial law. Strictly speaking, we might therefore throw out the so-called proof before us without further discussion. But so plausibly are these texts set forth by many that we shall here examine them further.

We found that "where no law is, there is no transgression," and that specifically the law that makes sin known to us is the one containing the command against coveting—the Decalogue. (See Rom. 4:15; 7:7.) The simple proof that there was sin long before Moses' time established for us the fact that the law must have been in existence before then.

It is evident that by the very same process of reasoning we can quickly discover whether the law existed after Christ's time. Did sin exist after the cross? Most certainly. The apostles went out to preach to sinners after Christ's return to heaven. The New Testament has as much to say about sin and sinners as has the Old. "But sin is not imputed when there is no law." Rom. 5:13.

Thus it is as clear as a spring morning that the Decalogue is as surely in existence *after* Christ as it was *before* Moses. No Christian would admit that in the centuries before Christ men lived by a higher moral standard than we, for certainly there could not be a more exalted code than the Ten Commandments. How could we longer contend that in the Christian dispensation men were brought up to a higher moral plane if we say at the same time that in this dispensation men are freed from the highest conceivable code, the Ten Commandments?

We are therefore prepared to believe, even before we examine the texts quoted by the objector, that they cannot possibly teach what he claims. The texts declare: "He [Christ] is our peace, who hath made both one, and hath broken down the middle wall of partition between us; having abolished in his flesh the enmity, even the *law of commandments contained in ordinances;* for to make in himself of twain one new man, so making peace." Eph. 2:14, 15. "Blotting out the handwriting of *ordinances* that was against us, which was contrary to us, and took it out of the way, nailing it to his cross. . . . Let no man therefore judge you in meat, or in drink, or in respect of an holy day, or of a new moon, or of the sabbath days." Col. 2:14, 16.

What do we generally mean by "ordinances" when we speak religiously? The Standard dictionary thus defines the word: "A religious rite or ceremony as ordained or established by divine or by ecclesiastical authority; as, the ordinance of the Lord's supper." We found that the Jewish church before Christ had certain ordinances, even as we since Christ's time have ordinances, such as the Lord's supper and baptism. Only they had many more. They had special rites and ceremonies, like the Passover and various holy days and meat offerings and drink offerings, et cetera. We read, for example, "This is the ordinance of the passover." Ex. 12:43. When these are referred to in the New Testament, the same language is used, for example: "Meats and drinks, and divers washings, and carnal ordinances." Heb. 9:10.

We also found that there were various laws and commandments stating just how these ordinances should be carried out. These were all written down by Moses in a book, and are generally described by Bible writers as the law of Moses, or the ceremonial law, which is not to be confused with the ten-commandment law. How evident, then, that the law which Paul here says is "abolished" and blotted out, does not include the Ten Commandments.

The book of Hebrews contains the best explanation of the relation of the ancient Jewish ceremonies to the work of Christ. Incidentally, this book is generally regarded as having been written by Paul, the author of the two texts we are considering in the objection before us. In it we read of "the law having a shadow of good things to come." Heb. 10:1. Plainly the writer means the *ceremonial* law, first, because the *moral* law could not be described as a "shadow" of something "to come," for it deals with eternal principles; second, the writer says "the law" there spoken of deals with "burnt offerings and offering for sin," et cetera. Verse 8.

All the offerings under the Jewish service were intended to shadow forth the good things of the gospel, when Christ, the great sacrifice, should be offered up. When that one great, perfect sacrifice for sins was made, there was no longer need of imperfect shadows. Christ "offered one sacrifice for sins for ever." Verse 12. The laws and ordinances commanding the offerings of sacrifices, of meat and drink offerings, of annual holy days, like the Passover, were all abolished at the cross. Shadow met reality.

In view of this we have no difficulty in understanding what Paul refers to when he speaks of the "law of commandments contained in ordinances," and the "handwriting of ordinances," in the two texts we are examining. He means simply the *ceremonial* law. He makes this doubly clear by saying in the succeeding verses that because these "ordinances" are abolished we are no longer under obligation as to offerings of meat or drink, and certain holy days, which "are a shadow of things to come." The comparison with the language of the book of Hebrews is exact.

This conclusion is made doubly evident by the following facts:

1. Contrast Paul's words concerning meats and drinks, et cetera, with the words of the Ten Commandments. Those commands deal with great and soul-shaking matters, such as idolatry, blasphemy, lying, stealing, adultery.

To illustrate the contrast, let us imagine that a certain country repealed all its traffic laws. Would it not be almost humorously obvious for a government official to declare solemnly that *now* no one may judge you for parking overtime, or failing to have your car inspected, when actually no one may judge you even for driving a hundred miles an hour through town and endangering a thousand lives. And so on the highway toward heaven. If actually in the Christian Era travelers are suddenly freed from "the law," including the Ten Commandments, how unbecomingly irrelevant for an inspired guide to inform them that *now* no one may judge them on relatively minor matters, as "meat" or "drink," when actually no one may longer judge them on such mighty matters as killing or stealing. Or why should a guide feel it impressive or important to announce that the travelers need no longer be concerned with holy days when actually, if the Decalogue is a part of the blotted-out law, they may, with impunity, commit the sacrilege of blasphemy and idolatry? And with sacrilege permitted, what possible significance could a holy day have anyway?

On the other hand, if a certain country repealed only those traffic laws that dealt with such minor, and often burdensome, matters as parking, how understandable for an official to make the announcement that no one may *now* be judged in the matter of parking. Likewise, if the government of heaven has repealed only the ritualistic laws on meats and drinks, et cetera, how appropriate and relevant Paul's words become.

2. The law mentioned in these two texts is said to have been abolished by the death of Christ. If the Decalogue is a part of that law, then God sent His Son to shed His blood to repeal, among other things, the formerly divine ban on idolatry, profanity, murder, and all the other evils denounced in the Decalogue. What a monstrous idea!

3. Again, this abolished law is said to be "against us," "contrary to us." Will anyone be so presumptuous as to say that the Ten Commandments are "against us," "contrary to us"?

So far from these texts teaching that the ten-commandment law is abolished, they do not even mention it.

(See objection 29, for a further discussion of the Colossian passage as it relates specifically to the Sabbath command.)

# Objection 12

Through Moses, God gave commandments to His people. Fifteen hundred years later Christ also gave commandments. Adventists fail to make a distinction between God's law, which was abolished at Calvary, and Christ's commandments that bind the Christian. Hence Adventists mistakenly contend that the Ten Commandments and Christ's commandments are the same and equally binding.

Here is a new and rather breath-taking idea: It is a mark of legalism to keep the Father's commandments, but a mark of grace to keep the Son's! The substance of most of the contentions against the law that we have had to consider is this: The Christian has nothing to do with the law, meaning, the ten-commandment law. Now we are informed that the Christian has much to do with law; in fact, he must give obedience to many commandments, for a number of references are given to prove that Christ set forth a list of new commandments.

The references given are largely from the record of Christ's sermon on the mount, beginning with Matthew 5:29. The reader, of course, is familiar with Christ's commands in this notable sermon. We need not enumerate them here. Suffice it to summarize them by saying that they deal with a variety of human relationships and are really an exposition of what we call the golden rule. In fact, the golden rule is given as a kind of climax to this sermon. (See Matt. 7:12.) And strangely enough, this very reference is given, among others, to prove that Christ set up a new code of laws that were to supersede those given by God in an earlier era. But let us read the text:

"Therefore all things whatsoever ye would that men should do to you, do ye even so to them: for this is the law and the prophets." Matt. 7:12.

Christ emphatically declares that the golden rule is but the epitome of the "law and the prophets." As just stated, His various commands given in this sermon on the mount are summarized in the golden rule. Hence, His allegedly new commands are simply an exposition of the "law and the prophets." This understanding of the matter is in harmony with the classic Protestant view of the Scriptures; namely, that the New Testament is infolded in the Old and the Old Testament is unfolded in the New. (See the discussion on this point under objection 1.)

That Christ was indeed commenting upon and expanding very specifically God's ten-commandment law is evident in various of the references given by the objector as proof that Christ set up new commandments to supplant those of His Father. Take this reference: "And he said unto them, Take heed, and beware of covetousness: for a man's life consisteth not in the abundance of the things which he possesseth." Luke 12:15.

Many of the allegedly new commands of Christ are most evidently an expansion of this tenth precept of the Decalogue.

Or take this reference, which for some reason is not given by the objector: "Ye have heard that it was said by them of old time, Thou shalt not commit adultery: but I say unto you, That whosoever looketh on a woman to lust after her hath committed adultery with her already in his heart." Matt. 5:27, 28.

Is Christ here freeing us from the seventh precept of God's ten-commandment law, and setting up a new law? The idea would be blasphemous. Instead, He is showing how broad is the import of that command.

Christ did not set aside God's law; instead, He magnified it. And this is what the prophet Isaiah foretold of Him: "The Lord is well pleased for his righteousness' sake; he will magnify the law, and make it honourable." Isa. 42:21. The well-known *Pulpit Commentary* observes on this text:

"He will magnify the Law; rather, *to magnify the Law*—to set it forth in its greatness and its glory before his people. It is not the original giving of the Law at Sinai only that is meant, but also its constant inculcation by a long series of prophets. Israel's experience (ver. 20) had included all this; but they had not profited by the instruction addressed to them."

# ANSWERS TO OBJECTIONS

We have looked in vain, among the references offered by the objector as proof that Christ gave commandments to supersede the law of God, for the words of our Lord to the rich young ruler, who had asked what he should do to "have eternal life": "If thou wilt enter into life, keep the commandments." Matt. 19:16, 17. And did Christ here set forth a new set of commandments? Surely here was the time to do it, for the eternal life of a human soul was at stake. But when the young man asked Christ to be specific as to "which" commandment, our Lord recited a number of the commands found in the Decalogue, and ended with the summarizing command: "Thou shalt love thy neighbour as thyself." And this last command, be it noted, is not new; it is quoted from Leviticus 19:18.

What further evidence need be offered than this to prove that no new commandment from Christ was necessary to salvation.

This passage provides also a most excellent proof that apparently new commandments from Christ are but an amplification of principles set down in the commands long before given by God. When the young man declared that he had kept all these commands from his youth up, and inquired, "What lack I yet?" Christ told him to go and sell all that he had and give to the poor and "follow me." This command to sell was simply an exposition of the tenth precept of the Decalogue and a commentary on Luke 12:15. And would anyone think of contending that the command, "Follow me," meant that the youth should turn his back on God's holy law?

We have Christ's own words, expressed over and over, that He did not come to set up new laws, but only to set forth what had been given unto Him of His Father. Note these typical references—which the objector failed to include in his presentation:

"For I have not spoken of myself; but the Father which sent me, he gave me a commandment, what I should say, and what I should speak. And I know that his commandment is life everlasting: whatsoever I speak therefore, even as the Father said unto me, so I speak." John 12:49, 50.

"He that loveth me not keepeth not my sayings: and the word

which ye hear is not mine, but the Father's which sent me." John 14:24. (See also John 7:16; 8:28.)

These passages harmonize perfectly with Christ's declaration: "I and my Father are one." John 10:30.

They also dispose of the claim that the apostles set forth new commandments that took the place of the law of God. Would the apostles do something that even Christ would not do? When Christ sent forth His disciples on the great task of carrying the gospel to all men, He declared that they were to teach men "to observe all things whatsoever I have commanded you." Matt. 28:20. And Christ declared, "The Father which sent me, he gave me a commandment, what I should say." John 12:49.

That the Father and Son are united in this matter of commandments is further revealed by the fact that Christ was present when the Israelites were in the wilderness, where they received the ten-commandment law. (See Neh. 9:11-15 and 1 Cor. 10:1-4.)

Not three lawgivers, the Father, the Son, and the apostles, but one only. That is what these texts teach. They agree perfectly with the words of James: "There is one lawgiver." James 4:12.

Need we no longer keep God's commandments, but only Christ's? The texts before us give the clear answer. For good measure let us add two more. The saints of God in the last days of earth's history are thus twice described:

1. "The remnant . . . , which keep the commandments of God, and have the testimony of Jesus." Rev. 12:17.

2. "They that keep the commandments of God, and the faith of Jesus." Rev. 14:12.

In fact, the Bible knows of only two classes of people—those who keep God's law and those who do not. Those described as "saints" (Rev. 14:12) are subject to His law. Those who are not are thus described by Paul: "The carnal mind is enmity against God: for it is not subject to the law of God, neither indeed can be." Rom. 8:7.

(For a discussion of a closely related line of reasoning see objection 13.)

99

# Objection 13

The only command that we need to keep now is Christ's new commandment to love one another, for He declared that we should keep His commandments even as He had kept His Father's commandments. And does not the Bible say that love is the fulfilling of the law?

It is quite true that Christ said, "A new commandment I give unto you, That ye love one another; as I have loved you, that ye also love one another." John 13:34. Would the objector want to reason from this that all other commandments are abolished? The text does not allow such a conclusion. Christ did not say that we should keep His commandments in the *place* of His Father's commandments. It would be rebellion for the Son to free us from the Father's laws and set up new ones in their place. Christ's purpose was not to destroy the great moral teachings and laws that had been given in former centuries. In His sermon on the mount He declared: "Think not that I am come to destroy the law, or the prophets: I am not come to destroy, but to fulfil. For verily I say unto you, Till heaven and earth pass, one jot or one tittle shall in no wise pass from the law, till all be fulfilled." Matt. 5:17, 18.

And when we read further in that wonderful sermon, we find Christ telling His hearers that they were viewing various commandments of the Decalogue in too narrow a sense. Instead of abolishing or even restricting His Father's commandments, Christ *magnified* them.

Thus in His commandment to the disciples concerning love, Christ wanted them to view love in a more magnified, a more holy sense than formerly. He wanted them to love one another, not as the world interprets love—selfishly or even merely sentimentally. By His life Christ had set before them an example of what true, unselfish love really is, such love as had never before been witnessed on the earth. In this sense His commandment might be described as new. It charged them, not simply "that ye love one another," but "that ye love one another, *as I have loved you.*" John 15:12. Strictly speaking, we have here simply one more evidence of how Christ magnified His Father's laws.

But what of the statement that love is the fulfilling of the law? The objector often expands this by saying that Christ declared that all we are to do is to love God with all our heart and our neighbor as ourselves. Let us read exactly what the Bible does say on this matter.

"Then one of them, which was a lawyer, asked him a question, tempting him, and saying, Master, which is the great commandment in the law? Jesus said unto him, Thou shalt love the Lord thy God with all thy heart, and with all thy soul, and with all thy mind. This is the first and great commandment. And the second is like unto it, Thou shalt love thy neighbour as thyself. On these two commandments hang all the law and the prophets." Matt. 22:35-40.

Christ was here setting forth no new doctrine. On the contrary, He was answering the specific question, "Which is the great commandment *in the law?*" His answer is almost an exact quotation from the Old Testament. (See Deut. 6:5; Lev. 19:18.) In other words, the two great commandments to love God and to love our neighbor belong definitely to Old Testament times. Now then, if these two commandments take the place of the Ten Commandments, why were the Ten Commandments ever given? But the very Israelites who listened to the exhortation to love God and their neighbor also listened to the clear-cut command to obey the ten precepts of the Decalogue.

No, these two commandments on love do not take the place of any other law. Instead, Christ declared that *"on* these two commandments *hang all* the law and the prophets." How evidently wrong, then, to make these two commandments hang *by themselves,* and cut off everything else. This is contrary to the teaching of Christ.

According to the Bible you cannot separate love from law. "By this we know that we love the children of God, when we love God, and keep his commandments. For this is the love of God, that we keep his commandments: and his commandments are not grievous." 1 John 5:2, 3. Thus reads the Good Book. If we truly love our fellow man, we will not steal his goods or lie about him or kill him. Indeed, we will not do any of the things prohibited by God's commandments. And if we truly love God, we will not bow down to false gods, or take God's name in vain, or use for our own purpose His holy Sabbath day. In other words, if we love God and our fellow men, we will not willfully break any of the Ten Commandments. Thus is love the fulfilling of the law. Instead of love's being a substitute for law, it is the one power that brings forth true obedience to God's commandments. The Bible warns us against those who say they know and love God but refuse to keep His commandments. (See 1 John 2:4.) Such love is counterfeit.

# Objection 14

Seventh-day Adventists are constantly preaching that men should obey God's commandments, keep the law, as if that were the sum and substance of true religion and a passport to heaven. But the Christian has nothing to do with law; he lives wholly by the grace of God, which is made available to him through faith in the gospel of Jesus Christ. Thus, and thus only, can any man be right with God and be in readiness for heaven.

We freely admit that we preach that men should obey God's commandments. We also preach with equal vigor that a man's only hope of heaven is through the grace of God made available in the gospel. There is no conflict between the two declarations, as we shall seek to show. Note, first, these similar declarations regarding obedience, as set forth in the Old and the New Testament:

### Old Testament

"And the Lord God commanded the man, saying, Of every tree of the garden thou mayest freely eat: but of the tree of the knowledge of good and evil, thou shalt not eat of it: for in the day that thou eatest thereof thou shalt surely die." Gen. 2:16, 17.

"I will perform the oath which I sware unto Abraham thy father; . . . because that Abraham obeyed my voice, and kept my charge, my commandments, my statutes, and my laws." Gen. 26:3-5.

"Now therefore, if ye will obey my voice indeed, and keep my covenant, then ye shall be a peculiar treasure unto me above all people: for all the earth is mine." Ex. 19:5.

"Thou shalt love thy neighbour as thyself." Lev. 19:18.

"And Samuel said, Hath the Lord

### New Testament

"Whosoever therefore shall break one of these least commandments, and shall teach men so, he shall be called the least in the kingdom of heaven: but whosoever shall do and teach them, the same shall be called great in the kingdom of heaven." Matt. 5:19.

"Why do ye also transgress the commandment of God by your tradition?" Matt. 15:3.

"If thou wilt enter into life, keep the commandments." Matt. 19:17.

"In vain do they worship me, teaching for doctrines the commandments of men. For laying aside the commandment of God, ye hold the tradition of men." Mark 7:7, 8.

"He that hath my commandments, and keepeth them, he it is that loveth me." John 14:21.

as great delight in burnt offerings and sacrifices, as in obeying the voice of the Lord? Behold, to obey is better than sacrifice, and to hearken than the fat of rams." 1 Sam. 15:22.

"Turn ye from your evil ways, and keep my commandments and my statutes, according to all the law which I commanded your fathers, and which I sent to you by my servants the prophets." 2 Kings 17:13.

"But this thing commanded I them, saying, Obey my voice, and I will be your God, and ye shall be my people: and walk ye in all the ways that I have commanded you, that it may be well unto you." Jer. 7:23.

"For I earnestly protested unto your fathers in the day that I brought them up out of the land of Egypt, even unto this day, rising early and protesting, saying, Obey my voice." Jer. 11:7.

"The great and dreadful God, keeping the covenant and mercy to them that love him, and to them that keep his commandments." Dan 9:4.

"For this, Thou shalt not commit adultery, Thou shalt not kill, Thou shalt not steal, Thou shalt not bear false witness, Thou shalt not covet; and if there be any other commandment, it is briefly comprehended in this saying, namely, Thou shalt love thy neighbour as thyself." Rom. 13:9.

"But whoso looketh into the perfect law of liberty, and continueth therein, he being not a forgetful hearer, but a doer of the work, this man shall be blessed in his deed." "So speak ye, and so do, as they that shall be judged by the law of liberty." James 1:25; 2:12.

"By this we know that we love the children of God, when we love God, and keep his commandments. For this is the love of God, that we keep his commandments: and his commandments are not grievous." 1 John 5:2, 3.

"Here is the patience of the saints: here are they that keep the commandments of God, and the faith of Jesus." Rev. 14:12.

Note now the similar declarations of the Old and the New Testament concerning the grace of God that is made available through faith in the gospel of Jesus Christ. Because of the fact that the experiences of certain Old Testament worthies are revealed to us through the comments of New Testament writers, the column entitled "Old Testament Times" will contain a number of New Testament texts:

### Old Testament Times

"And I will put enmity between thee and the woman, and between thy seed and her seed; it shall bruise thy head, and thou shalt bruise his heel." Gen. 3:15.

"By faith Abel offered unto God a

### New Testament Times

"And she shall bring forth a son, and thou shalt call his name JESUS: for he shall save his people from their sins." Matt. 1:21.

"And saying, The time is fulfilled, and the kingdom of God is at hand:

more excellent sacrifice than Cain, by which he obtained witness that he was righteous, God testifying of his gifts: and by it he being dead yet speaketh." Heb. 11:4.

"By faith Noah, being warned of God of things not seen as yet, moved with fear, prepared an ark to the saving of his house; by the which he condemned the world, and became heir of the righteousness which is by faith." Heb. 11:7.

"And in thy seed shall all the nations of the earth be blessed; because thou hast obeyed my voice." Gen. 22:18.

"For if Abraham were justified by works, he hath whereof to glory; but not before God. For what saith the scripture? Abraham believed God, and it was counted unto him for righteousness. Now to him that worketh is the reward not reckoned of grace, but of debt. But to him that worketh not, but believeth on him that justifieth the ungodly, his faith is counted for righteousness. Even as David also describeth the blessedness of the man, unto whom God imputeth righteousness without works, saying, Blessed are they whose iniquities are forgiven, and whose sins are covered. Blessed is the man to whom the Lord will not impute sin." "Therefore it is of faith, that it might be by grace; to the end the promise might be sure to all the seed; not to that only which is of the law, but to that also which is of the faith of Abraham; who is the father of us all." Rom. 4:2-8, 16.

"For this commandment which I command thee this day, it is not hidden from thee, neither is it far off. It is not in heaven, that thou shouldest say, Who shall go up for us

repent ye, and believe the gospel." Mark 1:15.

"The next day John seeth Jesus coming unto him, and saith, Behold the Lamb of God, which taketh away the sin of the world." John 1:29.

"Then Peter said unto them, Repent, and be baptized every one of you in the name of Jesus Christ for the remission of sins, and ye shall receive the gift of the Holy Ghost." Acts 2:38.

"Ye are the children of the prophets, and of the covenant which God made with our fathers, saying unto Abraham, And in thy seed shall all the kindreds of the earth be blessed." "Neither is there salvation in any other: for there is none other name under heaven given among men, whereby we must be saved." Acts 3:25; 4:12.

"And brought them out, and said, Sirs, what must I do to be saved? And they said, Believe on the Lord Jesus Christ, and thou shalt be saved, and thy house." Acts 16:30, 31.

"For I am not ashamed of the gospel of Christ: for it is the power of God unto salvation to every one that believeth; to the Jew first, and also to the Greek." Rom. 1:16.

"But now the righteousness of God without the law is manifested, being witnessed by the law and the prophets; even the righteousness of God which is by faith of Jesus Christ unto all and upon all them that believe: for there is no difference." Rom. 3:21, 22.

"Therefore being justified by faith, we have peace with God through our Lord Jesus Christ: by whom also we have access by faith into this grace wherein we stand, and rejoice in hope to heaven, and bring it unto us, that we may hear it, and do it? Neither is it beyond the sea, that thou shouldest say, Who shall go over the sea for us, and bring it unto us, that we may hear it, and do it? But the word is very nigh unto thee, in thy mouth, and in thy heart, that thou mayest do it." Deut. 30:11-14. (Paul quotes this passage in .Deuteronomy, prefacing it thus: "The righteousness which is of faith speaketh on this wise." See Rom. 10:6.)

"Have mercy upon me, O God, according to thy lovingkindness: according unto the multitude of thy tender mercies blot out my transgressions. Wash me throughly from mine iniquity, and cleanse me from my sin." "Create in me a clean heart, O God; and renew a right spirit within me." "For thou desirest not sacrifice; else would I give it: thou delightest not in burnt offering. The sacrifices of God are a broken spirit: a broken and a contrite heart, O God, thou wilt not despise." Ps. 51:1, 2, 10, 16, 17.

of the glory of God." Rom. 5:1, 2.

"But by the grace of God I am what I am." 1 Cor. 15:10.

"But God, who is rich in mercy, for his great love wherewith he loved us, even when we were dead in sins, hath quickened us together with Christ, (by grace ye are saved;) and hath raised us up together, and made us sit together in heavenly places in Christ Jesus: that in the ages to come he might shew the exceeding riches of his grace in his kindness toward us through Christ Jesus. For by grace are ye saved through faith; and that not of yourselves: it is the gift of God: not of works, lest any man should boast." Eph. 2:4-9.

"For the grace of God that bringeth salvation hath appeared to all men." Titus 2:11.

"And the Spirit and the bride say, Come. And let him that heareth say, Come. And let him that is athirst come. And whosoever will, let him take the water of life freely." Rev. 22:17.

Here are the evident conclusions we must reach from studying these passages on obedience and grace in the Old and the New Testament:

1. Throughout all the history of this earth God has had but one rule for those who desire to be His children and thus qualify for heaven, and that rule is, obedience to His commands.

2. Likewise throughout all history there has been but one means by which men can be cleansed of the sin of their past disobedience and be enabled to give true obedience in the future; namely, the grace and power of God, which are made available through faith in the gospel.

Answers to a few questions will help to make these conclusions even more evident.

## LAW

1. How did sin begin in the human race? *Answer:* By man's failure in the Garden of Eden to give obedience to God's will, His holy command.

2. Where is God's will most concisely expressed? *Answer:* In His holy law, the Ten Commandments.

3. What is the attitude of rebellious men toward His law? *Answer:* "Because the carnal mind is enmity against God: for it is not subject to the law of God, neither indeed can be." Rom. 8:7.

4. How is sin defined in the Bible? *Answer:* "Sin is the transgression of the law." 1 John 3:4.

5. How many of us are sinners? *Answer:* "All have sinned, and come short of the glory of God." Rom. 3:23.

6. Then how do we stand in relation to God? *Answer:* "Guilty before God." Rom. 3:19.

7. Can a man remove his guilt for *past* sins, and thus stand justified before God, by faithful obedience to God's law in the *future? Answer:* "By the deeds of the law there shall no flesh be justified in his sight." Rom. 3:20.

8. What is the purpose of the law in relation to a guilty man? *Answer:* "By the law is the knowledge of sin." Verse 20. "For where no law is, there is no transgression." Rom. 4:15.

9. What is the gospel? *Answer:* The good news that Christ has come to die for our sins and to offer to men the grace of God. (Matt. 1:21; 2 Cor. 5:18-21.)

10. What is grace? *Answer:* The unmerited favor of God displayed toward man in saving and preserving him.

11. How is the grace of God toward guilty man displayed? *Answer:* (1) By offering him a means by which he may be freed from the guilt of his past sins. (2) By taking away his "carnal mind" and stony heart, which are "enmity against God" and "not subject to the law of God," and giving him a new heart and mind that delight to do the will of God. (Rom. 8:7; Heb. 8:10.)

12. How is man freed from the guilt of past sins? *Answer:* "Ye know that he [Christ] was manifested to take away our sins." 1 John 3:5. "Being justified freely by his grace through the redemp-

tion that is in Christ Jesus: . . . for the remission of sins that are past." Rom. 3:24, 25.

13. How does the guilty man avail himself of this proffered cleansing? *Answer:* By simple faith in Christ. "That whosoever believeth in him should not perish, but have everlasting life." John 3:16.

14. At the moment of accepting Christ by faith what takes place for repentant sinners? *Answer:* There is fulfilled for them the promise of the new covenant: "I will put my laws into their mind, and write them in their hearts: and I will be to them a God, and they shall be to me a people." Heb. 8:10.

15. With God's laws thus written in our minds and hearts how do we relate ourselves to its holy requirements, its claim on our obedience? *Answer:* Christ "condemned sin in the flesh: that the righteousness of the law ["the just requirement of the law," R.S.V.] might be fulfilled in us, who walk not after the flesh, but after the Spirit." Rom. 8:3, 4.

16. How else is this miraculous new life of the pardoned sinner described? *Answer:* "I am crucified with Christ: nevertheless I live; yet not I, but Christ liveth in me: and the life which I now live in the flesh I live by the faith of the Son of God, who loved me, and gave himself for me." Gal. 2:20.

17. Now if Christ is the one who lives out His life through us, what will be our relation to God's law? *Answer:* The same relation to it that Christ bore.

18. What was Christ's relation to God's law? *Answer:* "I delight to do thy will, O my God: yea, thy law is within my heart." Ps. 40:8.

19. How does the pardoned sinner reveal that he is no longer at enmity against God, but that he truly loves Him? *Answer:* By obedience to God, which is the opposite of rebellion against Him. "For this is the love of God, that we keep his commandments." 1 John 5:3.

20. How may we summarize the contrast between the sinner and the pardoned child of God? *Answer:* In this way:

# LAW

| The Sinner | The Pardoned Child of God |
|---|---|
| 1. "Enmity against God." | 1. In harmony with God. |
| 2. "Has a carnal mind." Minds the things of the flesh. | 2. Walks "not after the flesh, but after the spirit." |
| 3. "Not subject to the law of God." | 3. God's law in his mind and heart. |
| 4. Controlled by Satan (Rom. 6:16), who originated all rebellion. | 4. Christ lives in him, and Christ has His Father's law in His heart. |

How evident, then, that there is no conflict between law and grace; between obedience to God's holy law, which is the true mark of the child of God, and salvation from sin through God's grace displayed in the atoning sacrifice of Christ. We are saved from sin, lawbreaking, that we might live a life of obedience, law keeping. No sinner will enter heaven. The "saints" standing in readiness for Christ's Second Advent are distinguished in two vital ways: They (1) keep "the commandments of God" and (2) "the faith of Jesus." (Rev. 14:12.) Adventists, who seek to prepare their hearts and the hearts of others for the Second Advent, preach that men should "keep the commandments of God" and possess "the faith of Jesus." Thus law and grace are combined. And it is *because* "the faith of Jesus" is kept that "the commandments of God" can be kept.

# Objection 15

**Why preach the law when no one can be saved by obeying it? Furthermore, man is morally unable to keep the commandments.**

This objection is really only a variant of objections already answered. But because the no-law argument is made to appear so plausible under different guises, let us examine this objection.

We agree with the objector that no one can be saved by keeping the law, and that man is morally unable to keep it. But we do not agree with the conclusion he would have us draw from these facts; namely, that the law was abolished at the cross. What would we say to the man who should argue that mirrors ought to be abolished as worthless because no one can obtain beauty by looking into them? Why, we would say that it is not the business of a mirror to make people beautiful, that no one ever made any such claims for mirrors. The function of the mirror is to provide us with a means of knowing whether we look as we ought. And when we have discovered how we look, we can take appropriate means for remedying the imperfections.

Even so with the law. The law was never intended to make man holy or pure or beautiful. Its task is not that of saving man from his sins and imperfections, but of providing him with a means of discovering just what his condition is. When he gazes at the law, with mind quickened by the convicting Spirit of God, he sees immediately where this moral defect or that mars the beauty of his soul, even as he discovers from gazing into a mirror just where this physical defect or that mars the beauty of his body.

And when men thus see their spiritual defects, and become conscious of their uncleanness, they are in a frame of mind to listen to a message that offers cleansing from their defilement. In other words, only when a man realizes that he is a sinner is he ready to listen to the gospel, which is the good news of salvation *from* sin.

It is by the law that we have the knowledge of sin. (See Rom. 3:20.) Therefore it is evident that only as the law is made known to men can they be brought into a frame of mind that will cause them to wish to hear and accept what the gospel offers them.

We would ask: If sinful man is *unable* to keep the law, and when he becomes a Christian he *need not* keep it, pray tell why was the law of God ever given? Shall we make a farce of God's law, and charge Heaven with proclaiming a code that was for thousands of years impossible of being kept, and that for the last two thousand years need not be kept?

We are puzzled to understand why the objection before us should be used to prove that the law was abolished at the *cross.* Men were no more morally able to keep God's holy law in the centuries before Christ than they have been in the centuries following. Nor could they in those years before Christ hope to obtain salvation through the law, for, as we have found, God has had only one way of saving men from the days of Adam down, and that is through the sacrifice of Christ. (See objection 14.) So, then, if the objection before us really proves anything against the law today, it proves it against the law in all past days, back to the beginning of man's sinful history. In other words, there would be no useful place for God's law at all in the whole history of the world.

The fact is, that instead of the law's being abolished for the Christian, there is really *no* true keeping of the law *except* by Christians. The divine code would be a dead letter in this world were it not for the Christians who obey it. By faith Christ comes into our hearts, and lives out in us the precepts of heaven. (See Eph. 3:20; Gal. 2:20; 1 Cor. 1:23, 24.) Thus, instead of God's law being wholly ignored and flouted in this rebellious world, there are found men and women upholding and establishing it in the only way a law can be upheld—by living in obedience to its claims. That is why Paul says, "Do we then make void the law through faith? God forbid: yea, we establish the law." Rom. 3:31. Our faith in Christ has not abolished but established the law.

111

# Objection 16

By preaching the law you endeavor to deprive Christians of the glorious liberty of the gospel.

Christ declared, "Every one that committeth sin is the bond-servant of sin." John 8:34, A.R.V. And what is sin? "Sin is the transgression of the law." 1 John 3:4. Therefore it is the man whose life is *not* in obedience to the law of God who is deprived of liberty. The righteous man willingly obeys God's law, and finds happiness in such obedience.

Law and liberty are not opposite words. You need not surrender one in order to have the other. True, there are men who stand up at street corners and declare that the only way to have real liberty is to abolish all laws. But as good citizens we do not take such talk seriously. Instead, we know that laws wisely made and well kept provide the only sure foundation for liberty in any country. In fact, someone has aptly remarked, "Obedience to law is liberty." And this phrase is often found inscribed on public buildings in the liberty-loving United States of America.

In any country the ones who find in law a curtailing of their liberty are those whose habits of life are in opposition to the law. The man who is accustomed to steal or to murder finds that the law checks the freedom of his actions very greatly.

If as citizens of this world we find liberty in obedience to man-made law, why, as citizens of the heavenly world, do we need God's law abolished in order to have liberty? Is it because the laws of heaven are unjust and deprive us of the freedom that ought right-fully to be ours? It were blasphemy to utter the thought.

The law of God prohibits making or worshiping idols. No man who calls himself a Christian can feel deprived of liberty by such a prohibition. The law also commands us not to take God's name in vain or to desecrate His holy Sabbath day. Does the child of

God want to be freed from these prohibitions? Likewise the law commands respect for parents, and prohibits killing, adultery, stealing, lying, and coveting. Certainly no follower of Christ will feel that these precepts deprive him of liberty.

Indeed, the Bible definitely speaks of God's holy law as "the law of liberty." (See James 2:10-12.) True, if the law is preached to men apart from the gospel—the saving power of God—the result will be only a feeling of condemnation on the part of the hearers. They will simply be brought to a realization of how guilty they are. But when the high code of heaven is presented in terms of God's promise to give us of His Divine Spirit to carry out the law's holy requirements, then the hearers can find happiness and liberty in such preaching; for "where the Spirit of the Lord is, there is liberty." 2 Cor. 3:17.

No one would ever have thought of bringing against Seventh-day Adventists the charge of depriving men of Christian liberty if it were not that we preach the law exactly as it reads in the Bible. Protestant denominations believe in the law and declare that obedience to it is necessary. (See page 493 for references to creeds.) They have believed so strongly that the Ten Commandments should be obeyed by all that they have persuaded legislatures in most of the so-called Christian countries to enact statutes for the observance of the fourth commandment, the Sabbath command, as they interpret it.

Just why we who invoke only the grace of God to enable men to obey the command to keep holy the seventh day, should be charged as legalists, while the hosts of Sundaykeepers who invoke the strong arm of the law in order to compel men to rest on the first day of the week, should claim to be the exponents of grace, is surely one of the strange contradictions in modern religion. Seventh-day Adventists have ever been vigorous opponents of the principle of approaching Sabbath rest from the legal standpoint, whereas Sundaykeeping preachers are the ones who have lobbied almost every legislative body in Christian lands into passing strong laws to enforce Sunday rest.

# ANSWERS TO OBJECTIONS

Just what is there about preaching first-day sacredness from the fourth commandment—as Protestant denominations, in general, do—that allows them to bask in the warmth of grace; whereas the preaching of seventh-day sacredness from the same fourth commandment consigns such preachers to the chill limbo of legalism? The explanation cannot possibly be found in the theory that we who preach seventh-day sacredness do so more sternly and rigorously than first-day preachers. Even a cursory acquaintance with Protestant history reveals that Sunday sacredness has quite generally been proclaimed with a severity that frightened into conformity the majority, and thrust into jail the remainder. If today there is a certain relaxation of this severity, it surely does not reflect any change of view toward the first day by Sundaykeeping *religious leaders*. They bemoan the laxity that has crept in.

When we declare that a certain definite day has been set apart as holy, we are frequently met with the argument that there is no difference in days in the Christian Era, that it is unreasonable to maintain that a special sacredness or significance attaches to a particular day in the cycle of the week. But evidently by the actions and statements of Sundaykeepers themselves there is a vast difference in days, so vast a difference that the keeping of one particular day means that you are shackled by legalism, and the keeping of another particular day means that you roam freely over the wide expanses of grace. Seventh-day Adventists never taught a sharper contrast in days than this.

Therefore the point at issue is not whether the Ten Commandments should be obeyed or not; virtually all Protestant creeds clearly teach obedience to the Decalogue. (See p. 493.) Nor is it a question of whether there is a wide difference in days. Protestants in general believe there is so mighty a difference as to justify civil laws and penalties to maintain the difference. The real question is this: Seeing that the Decalogue is in force, and seeing that there is a difference in days, which day is the right one, the seventh or the first? In the series of Sabbath objections beginning on page 123 a partial answer, at least, will be found.

# Objection 17

The Bible repeatedly and emphatically declares that no one can be justified by keeping the law. Hence to preach the keeping of the law is to preach another gospel. "Whosoever of you are justified by the law; ye are fallen from grace." Gal. 5:4.

In harmony with the Bible, Adventists repeatedly and emphatically declare that no one can be *justified* by keeping the law. (See objection 14.) The confused reasoning in the objection before us resides in the evidently mistaken idea of what the word "justified" means Scripturally. The evidence presented under objection 14 revealed that the divine act of justifying a sinner takes place at the moment he comes to God, repentant and in faith, to claim the offered pardon for sins that are past through the sacrifice of Christ. To teach that man can wipe out past guilt, that is, past disobedience to the law of God, by faithful keeping of that law in the future, is to flout the grace of God and to preach another gospel.

The very word "gospel" means good news—good news that a divine plan has been devised whereby sinful man may be purged of his guilt; that the Lamb of God that taketh away the sin of the world has been delivered for our offenses and raised again for our justification. (John 1:29; Rom. 4:25.)

This is clearly revealed in the words of the angels who spoke to Joseph and to the shepherds. Said the angel to Joseph, regarding Mary's son that was to be born: "And she shall bring forth a son, and thou shalt call his name Jesus: for he shall save his people from their sins." Matt. 1:21.

To the shepherds the angel declared: "Fear not: for, behold, I bring you good tidings of great joy, which shall be to all people. For unto you is born this day in the city of David a Saviour, which is Christ the Lord." Luke 2:10, 11.

## ANSWERS TO OBJECTIONS

When we preach the keeping of God's commandments we are not preaching a different gospel from the one just described. We are simply echoing the words of the apostle John: "For this is the love of God, that we keep his commandments: and his commandments are not grievous." 1 John 5:3. We are simply calling on the now justified child of God to live in obedience to God.

Paul, apparently, feared that some who read what he had written about men not being justified by the law might wrongly conclude that God's grace frees us from any obligation to keep the law. He states the matter thus: "What then? shall we sin, because we are not under the law [that is, not under the condemnation of the law], but under grace? God forbid." Paul, who knew, of course, that "sin is the transgression of the law," is really asking this: Shall we transgress the law because we are under grace? He answers, "God forbid." We simply echo his answer and call on men who are saved by grace to refrain from transgressing God's law in the future.

# Objection 18

**1 Timothy 1:9 proves that the Christian has nothing to do with the law, for we read there that "the law is not made for a righteous man."**

Let us read the whole passage: "Knowing this, that the law is not made for a righteous man, but for the lawless and disobedient, for the ungodly and for sinners, for unholy and profane, for murderers of fathers and murderers of mothers, for manslayers, for whoremongers, for them that defile themselves with mankind, for menstealers, for liars, for perjured persons, and if there be any other thing that is contrary to sound doctrine." 1 Tim. 1:9, 10.

The first fact that stands out from this Bible statement is that it says nothing about the law's being abolished in the Christian dispensation. Instead, it reveals that the law serves as definite a purpose in the Christian Era as in the centuries before Christ. The class of people against whom the law is directed—murderers, liars, et cetera—are found in every period of the world's history. Really there is no text in the Bible that proves more conclusively than does this one that the law was not done away at the cross.

The only way to attempt to offset this proof would be by contending that murderers and liars, for example, should obey the law, whereas Christians are free from it. To this strange conclusion would we be brought by following out the objector's logic.

But even that defense of the no-law position is unavailing. Can even the most devout among righteous men rightly claim that they never commit sin? No. Even the greatest saints have had to claim repeatedly the comforting promise: "If any man sin, we have an advocate with the Father, Jesus Christ the righteous." 1 John 2:1. But the same apostle who wrote that promise also wrote, "Sin is the transgression of the law." 1 John 3:4. Therefore, every time we confess our sins, we confess that God's law is still binding and that we desire to be obedient to it. Then, as we again place our hand in the hand of God and walk in righteousness, we are not brought into conflict with the law, for "the law is not made for a righteous man."

There is really nothing hard to understand about this text. It is a simple statement concerning the purpose of law that every judge or legislator or layman would agree to today in matters civil as well as religious. For whom are our criminal laws laid down? For the law-abiding citizen? No, for the lawless, you say. That is right. But is the law-abiding citizen therefore freed from the requirements of the statute books? No.

The same is true concerning God's law. It is directed against the lawless, not against the righteous, who are law-abiding citizens of the kingdom of God. But are the citizens of the heavenly kingdom therefore freed from the requirements of that divine code? No.

Furthermore, good citizens in any government are not the ones who complain about the law. They have little occasion to complain. Their lives are in harmony with it. Even so in the spiritual realm. The man whose heart is right with God finds no occasion to fight the divine law or to tell others that it ought to be abolished. Instead, he says with the psalmist, "O how love I thy law! it is my meditation all the day." Ps. 119:97. And if he is overtaken in a fault and falls into sin, he does not excuse his sinful act by arguing that the law has no claim upon him. Rather he confesses his sin —his lawbreaking—and seeks, through divine grace, more faithfully to obey God.

# Objection 19

**Seventh-day Adventists teach that a man must keep the commandments in order to be saved.**

Again, we are confronted simply with a variant of objections already answered. But the present objection so tersely sets forth a mistaken idea regarding Adventist teaching that it is here examined as a separate objection.

To the rich young man who inquired of Christ, "Good Master, what good thing shall I do, that I may have eternal life?" Jesus replied, "If thou wilt enter into life, keep the commandments." Matt. 19:16, 17. The verses that follow show clearly that Christ referred specifically to the Ten Commandments.

It is surely unfortunate that so many Christians remember only one portion of the statements of Christ. They preach much about the passive side of Christianity—of accepting Jesus Christ as a Saviour. But there is an active side as well, for Christianity embraces much more than the saving of a man from his *past* sins. It has to do with his living a sinless life. There is for the Christian a *doing* of God's will, a *keeping* of God's commandments, and a certain *working out* of his own salvation. (See Matt. 7:21; Rev. 14:12; Phil. 2:12.)

Although we do *not* teach that a man keeps the commandments in order to be saved, we do emphatically teach that a man who *is* saved gives evidence of that salvation by keeping the commandments of God. It has been well remarked that although there is no salvation in keeping the law, there is awful condemnation in not keeping it.

Christianity does not free man from the claims of God's law, which he as a sinner has not been able to fulfill. If it did thus free him, Christianity would be but an opiate to his soul, leaving him in the same unfortunate state as before. No, Christianity is God's plan whereby man can obtain power to keep the laws of heaven. It is the divine scheme by which Christ lives and works within us. (See Gal. 2:20.)

We believe the words of Christ, "If thou wilt enter into life, keep the commandments," but we also believe that the *keeping* power is a gift from God. We confess that we of our own selves can do nothing, but we believe that we can do *all things* through Jesus Christ who strengthens us. (See Phil. 4:13.) We accept without reserve the words of our Lord: "I am the vine, ye are the branches: he that abideth in me, and I in him, the same bringeth forth much fruit: for without me ye can do nothing." John 15:5. Though we say with Paul, "Work out your own salvation," we immediately add, as does the apostle, "It is *God* which worketh in you both to will and to do of his good pleasure."

# Section II

# SABBATH

## Objections 20 to 55

The reader is also referred
to Part 2, Section III, pages 545-562,
"The Sabbath and the Weekly Cycle"

# Objection 20

Seventh-day Adventists declare that the seventh day of the week was set apart as a Sabbath by the blessing and sanctification of God at the creation of the world. They thus seek to prove that the Sabbath preceded the Jewish race and applies to all men. But Genesis, which contains the record of God's resting upon and blessing the Sabbath, was written by Moses two thousand five hundred years after creation, or about the time of the Exodus. Moses simply set down in that Genesis reference to the Sabbath a statement of what God actually did for the seventh day at Mount Sinai.

The first fact that here stands out clearly, and should be noted at the outset, is this: It is admitted that the Genesis record of the blessing of the Sabbath at creation carries with it a powerful argument in behalf of the universality of the Sabbath for all peoples in all ages.

The second fact is this: The objector poses as possessing a knowledge of Moses' literary procedures that is remarkable to say the least. How did he gain it? He has access to no other sources of knowledge than those known to all Bible students. And such students, including eminent commentators, have rather uniformly through the years held that Moses, in the book of Genesis, is giving a historical record of creation week when he mentions the blessing of the Sabbath day. And they have held this view despite the fact that they were Sundaykeepers. But, in all honesty, what else could they do but hold this view? Let us examine the facts.

1. What is the nature of the book of Genesis? It is plainly, from beginning to end, a book of history. It sets forth a brief narrative, in chronological order, of events from creation through to the death of Joseph. Therefore, in the absence of clear evidence to the contrary, we should consider the various parts of it, the accounts of what men said and did, and likewise the accounts of what God said and did, as being historical incidents occurring at the time

indicated in the narrative. The account of God's resting on the seventh day of creation week and blessing and sanctifying it fits as naturally into the historical sequence as do any other incidents mentioned in Genesis. There is nothing in the context to suggest differently.

2. The fact that the book of Genesis was written some twenty-five hundred years after creation has no bearing on the matter whatever. All books of history are written after the events described. And obviously any history book that essayed to record twenty-five hundred years of history would have to be written at least that long after the incidents of the first year took place. To say that a history writer projected back into the year one an event occurring in the year 2500, or thereabouts, is to make a statement that could be believed only if we were ready to charge the author with fraud and deception. We are not ready to do that with Moses.

3. But note the point at which the objector claims the record ceases to be historical and becomes a throwback from an incident that occurred twenty-five hundred years later. He carries the narrative through the creation week, including God's resting on the seventh day from all His work. (Gen. 2:2.) At this point, the objector declares, the break comes, and the immediately following words are a throwback: "And God blessed the seventh day, and sanctified it: because that in it he had rested from all his work which God created and made." Verse 3.

Now why should God rest? Not because He was weary. His resting, which is faithfully recorded by Moses, must have had a meaning. The next verse reveals the meaning. The resting was the reason for the blessing. He blessed and sanctified the seventh day "because that in it he had rested from all his work." Verse 3. And what reason is there for contending that God rested on the seventh day of creation week in order to provide the occasion for blessing it, and then waited twenty-five hundred years to pronounce the blessing? None whatever.

4. Let us note the instances of blessing that are recorded in the creation narrative:

# SABBATH

| Event | Blessing |
|---|---|
| **Fifth Day** | |
| "And God said, Let the waters bring forth abundantly." Gen. 1:20. | "And God blessed them, saying, Be fruitful, and multiply." Verse 22. |
| **Sixth Day** | |
| "And God said, Let the earth bring forth the living creature. . . . Let us make man in our image." Gen. 1:24-26. | "And God blessed them, and God said unto them, Be fruitful, and multiply." Verse 28. |
| **Seventh Day** | |
| "And he rested on the seventh day from all his work which he had made." Gen. 2:2. | "And God blessed the seventh day, and sanctified it." Verse 3. |

The objector is willing to agree that the blessings upon the acts of the fifth and sixth days follow immediately the incidents described. Parallel literary construction and the complete absence of any suggestion of a break in narration require him to agree that the blessing of the seventh day follows immediately upon the incident of God's resting on that day.

5. Note also the parallel constructions, so far as tense is concerned, that are found in the fourth commandment itself. Here the Lord is speaking to Israel:

a. "In six days the Lord *made* heaven and earth."

b. "And *rested* the seventh day."

c. "Wherefore the Lord *blessed* the sabbath day, and *hallowed* it."

Note the four verbs, all in the past tense: "made," "rested," "blessed," and "hallowed."

It is this consistent past tense that gives maximum force to the word "remember," that introduces this command. The obvious meaning of the verb "remember" is to call to mind a past event or experience of some kind. Israel was commanded to "remember the sabbath day, to keep it holy," and why? Because God was *now* going to bless it? No, but because God *had* blessed it.

With these facts before him the reader should have no difficulty in deciding the question in controversy.

# Objection 21

Exodus 16:29 and Nehemiah 9:13, 14 prove that the Sabbath was not given until Israel left Egypt. The very silence of the Scriptures regarding anyone's keeping it before that time is strong corroborative proof.

Two claims are here made: First, that the Sabbath was instituted in a Jewish setting. This claim is intended to prepare the way for the next, that the Sabbath was made *only* for the Jews.

Exodus 16:29 and Nehemiah 9:13, 14, whatever they state, are supposed to neutralize the statement in Genesis 2:2, 3 and quite expunge it from the record. But does one Scriptural statement do that to another? No. When one text appears to contradict another we may be sure that we have made a mistake in our interpretation of one or the other of the texts. We have already seen—objection 20—that Genesis 2:2, 3 stands firmly as a testimony that God rested on the seventh day of the first week of time and then and there blessed it. Thus we are prepared at the outset to believe that whatever Exodus 16:29 and Nehemiah 9:13, 14 teach, they do not teach contrary to Genesis 2:2, 3.

Exodus 16:29 is part of the narrative of the giving of the manna, which was to be collected each day for the six working days, with twice as much to be collected the sixth day, because God gave no manna on the seventh day. But some of the Israelites, contrary to God's command, went out on the Sabbath day to collect it. This caused the Lord to inquire of Moses: "How long refuse ye to keep my commandments and my laws? See, for that the Lord hath given you the sabbath, therefore he giveth you on the sixth day the bread of two days." Ex. 16:28, 29.

Nehemiah, long afterward, recalls what God did for Israel in bringing them out of captivity, declaring in part: "Thou camest down also upon mount Sinai, and spakest with them from heaven, and gavest them right judgments, and true laws, good statutes and commandments: and madest known unto them thy holy sabbath, and commandedst them precepts, statutes, and laws, by the hand of Moses thy servant." Neh. 9:13, 14.

These passages deal with essentially the same incidents and are so similar in construction that they may be considered together. Let us note certain phrases:

1. "The Lord hath given you the sabbath." Ex. 16:29.

2. "Gavest them right judgments, and true laws, good statutes and commandments." Neh. 9:13.

3. "Madest known unto them thy holy sabbath." Neh. 9:14.

We believe that the answer to the objection before us is found clearly revealed in the second of these three phrases. If, as claimed, the construction of the first and the third phrase requires the conclusion that the Sabbath law did not exist before the Exodus, then the construction of the second phrase requires us to conclude that the wide range of statutes, laws, and commandments that were formally stated at Sinai did not formerly exist. Therefore, not only would it have been no sin to work on the seventh day, previous to the Exodus, but it would have been no sin, previous to Sinai, to have done any of the things prohibited by the various laws and commandments which God "gavest them" at that time.

But no one will claim that it would have been right to do the latter, for he agrees that nine of the Ten Commandments are an expression of eternal moral principles. When, at Sinai, God commanded, "Thou shalt not commit adultery," it might be said, in one sense of the word, that He then *gave* Israel the law against immorality. It was the first formal proclamation of that principle to the newly formed nation that stood in need, at the outset, of a clearly expressed code of laws. But no one believes for a moment that previous to the giving of that law against adultery from the flaming mount, there was no divine ban on adultery and therefore no sin in indulging in immoral acts.

Even so with the Sabbath law. It, along with the other great precepts of the Decalogue, and many other statutes, was formally made known to Israel as they began their national life. The long darkness of Egypt had quite blurred their understanding of God's will. Now by the light of the pillar of fire God made clear to them all His requirements, including the Sabbath.

God declares, "I made myself known unto them [the Israelites], in bringing them forth out of the land of Egypt." Eze. 20:9. Would the objector reason from this text that God did not exist before the Exodus? No. Then why contend that the Sabbath did not exist before that time simply because God then made it known to Israel? The facts are that the knowledge both of God and of the Sabbath had largely faded from the minds of the Israelites during their long Egyptian bondage.

Only a word need be said in reply to the claim based on the fact that the Scriptures are silent about anyone's keeping the Sabbath before the Exodus. The few pages of the Bible that precede the account of the Exodus cover some twenty-five hundred years. Obviously, only a few high lights of the long record could be penned. Chiefly, Moses sought to provide a running narrative to connect creation with the events that followed the fall of man, on down through the Flood, the call of Abraham, the rise of Israel, and their exodus from Egypt. Little is mentioned of the religious activities in which men engaged during those twenty-five hundred years. To present this silence of Scripture as a proof against the seventh-day Sabbath is to rely on an exceedingly weak argument.

Those who promote the importance of Sunday generally include in their reasoning that man needs a recurring day of worship each week, nor do they set any bounds of time or place on that claim. Hence those who lived before the Exodus were in need of such a recurring day. Seeing they were, would God fail to provide for that need? Indeed, did He not do that very thing when, at creation, He set apart for a holy use the seventh day? And do we need to find a specific mention of their keeping that day before we reasonably conclude that holy men like Enoch, Noah, and Abraham kept that holy day? In fact, what other conclusion would be reasonable?

# Objection 22

The Sabbath is Jewish. It was given only to the Jews and was part of the old covenant that was made only with the Jews. Further, Deuteronomy 5:15 states explicitly that God commanded the Jews to keep the Sabbath as a memorial of their deliverance from Egypt. Therefore it has no meaning for us who are Gentile Christians.

This reasoning goes over much the same ground covered by the claim that the law given at Sinai was intended only for the Jews. See under objection 4, where evidence is presented to show that the whole Bible was written by Jews, much of it directly addressed to Jews, that both old and new covenants were made with the "house of Israel," and that Christ Himself declared that "salvation is of the Jews." Yet all Protestantism turns to the Bible, both the Old and the New Testament, for spiritual guidance. We all claim a right to the new covenant relationship, and we all preach that "salvation" which Christ declared "is of the Jews," is for every man in every land.

We would ask this simple question, Why is the seventh day of the week more Jewish than the first day of the week? The Westminster Confession, which is the clearest expression of the Protestant view on the sacredness of a weekly rest day, declares that the Sabbath "from the beginning of the world till the resurrection of Christ, was the last day of the week." That is a period of at least four thousand years. Yet for the first half of this long period there were no Jews. Did the seventh day of the week suddenly acquire a different character and quality at Sinai as God was leading His chosen people from Egypt to the Promised Land?

Someone may venture to say yes, and to support his answer by reference to those Old Testament declarations that the Sabbath was a distinguishing mark and a sign between God and the children of Israel. But if this answer proves anything, it proves too much, for the very same Old Testament records which thus describe the Sabbath reveal to us also that God describes Himself as being in a very peculiar and distinctive way the God of Abraham, Isaac, and Jacob. Why should not the Lord enjoin the Sabbath of the Lord upon the Lord's own people?

The reason that the observance was confined to the Jews in the last part of that four-thousand-year period before Christ was that no other people on the face of the earth were true followers of God. They were pagans and heathen. Of course the Sabbath was closely associated with the Jews during the time of their national history; and as we have noted, so was everything else of the revealed will of God, including all the prophets of God and all the writings that make up the Holy Word.

"But," someone may reply, "the Bible does not say anywhere that the Saviour and salvation were to be confined to the Jews." Very true. Neither do we read anywhere that the Sabbath was to be confined to the Jews. On the contrary, we have very specific declarations of Scripture to show that the Sabbath was intended of God to have a worldwide application. Let us enumerate a few of these:

1. The Sabbath commandment itself specifically declares that not only were the Jews to rest but also the stranger that was within their gates. (See Ex. 20:10.) The strangers were those not of the family of Israel; they might belong to any other race or people or nation.

2. Christ declared that "the sabbath was made for man." Mark 2:27. He did not say "Jew," but "man," and there is no justification for confining the meaning of the word "man" to the Jews. If we should thus confine the word, we would soon come into great difficulty. We read that Christ is "the true light, which lighteth every *man* that cometh into the world." John 1:9. Did Christ bring light only to such men as are Jews? Furthermore, the Sabbath was given so that men might have the blessing of rest and the worship of their Creator. Why should God desire that only a small fraction of His created beings—for the Jews have ever been a very small

part of the world's population—should partake of the happiness of rest and worship?

3. How could the Sabbath have been given only to the Jews, when it was made at creation, which was long before the days of Abraham, the father of the Jewish race? (See Gen. 2:2, 3.)

4. The prophet Isaiah, speaking of the closing days of earth's history, when God's "salvation is near to come," talks of the blessing that will come upon "the son of the stranger" that "keepeth the Sabbath." (See Isa. 56:1-8.)

5. Finally, in the new earth, where there will be people of every race and nation, the Sabbath will be kept. (See Isa. 66:22, 23.)

Now what of Deuteronomy 5:15, which is said to prove that the Sabbath was given only to the Jews? The text reads as follows: "Remember that thou wast a servant in the land of Egypt, and that the Lord thy God brought thee out thence through a mighty hand and by a stretched-out arm: therefore the Lord thy God commanded thee to keep the sabbath day."

Note the setting of this text. The fifth chapter of Deuteronomy consists of a summing up by Moses, with appropriate comments, of the great event at Sinai forty years before, when God spoke the Ten Commandments. That Moses was not attempting to repeat verbatim the commandments, but rather to urge the *keeping* of these well-known precepts, is shown by verse 12, where he says "Keep the sabbath day to sanctify it, *as the Lord thy God hath commanded thee.*"

Therefore the first point to note is that this recital of the commandments in Deuteronomy cannot be taken as a substitute for the form of the commandments found in Exodus 20. In Exodus we find the record of the commands as God spoke them, and to this record Moses specifically referred Israel when he urged them, "Keep the sabbath day to sanctify it, as the Lord thy God hath commanded thee." And whatever *reasons* or *appeals* are presented by Moses must be considered as an *addition* to, and *not* as a substitute for, the reasons given by God when He originally spoke the commandments.

God declared that the seventh day is the Sabbath on which all should rest, because "in six days the Lord made heaven and earth, . . . and rested the seventh day." And He added, "*Wherefore* the Lord blessed the sabbath day, and hallowed it." Ex. 20:11.

Let us look again at the context of Deuteronomy 5. Moses proceeds with his paraphrase of the Sabbath command, and closes the fourteenth verse—which describes how servants as well as masters were to rest—by adding: "That thy manservant and thy maidservant may rest as well as thou." Then follows immediately verse 15, which reminds the Israelites of how they were servants in Egypt, et cetera.

What is the natural conclusion, then, for us to reach? Simply this, that Moses was giving an *added* reason for the keeping of the Sabbath commandment, especially that feature of it which had to do with the servants' resting.

This, we say, is the *natural* conclusion to be reached. It becomes the *inevitable* conclusion when certain parallel passages are quoted.

A little further on Moses gives instruction as to the treatment of a servant, and how, after he had served six years, he should be released in the seventh and sent away with liberal provisions from the flocks and herds of the master. "And," added Moses, "thou shalt remember that thou wast a bondman in the land of Egypt, and the Lord thy God redeemed thee: *therefore* I command thee this thing to day." Deut. 15:15. Shall we conclude that liberality and love toward servants are a command originating at the Exodus, that all who lived before that time might deal grudgingly with their servants without incurring God's displeasure, and that only Jews are required by God to display such kindness toward servants?

Again, let us read a more detailed command: "Ye shall do no unrighteousness in judgment, in meteyard, in weight, or in measure. Just balances, just weights, a just ephah, and a just hin, shall ye have: I am the Lord your God, which brought you out of the land of Egypt. *Therefore* shall ye observe all my statutes, and all my judgments, and do them: I am the Lord." Lev. 19:35-37. Shall we take this verse by itself and build up the argument that the command to deal justly in the various affairs of life originated with the Exodus, that previous to that a man might shortchange his neighbor with impunity, and that only Jews are required by God to refrain from shortchanging anyone?

Or take this further statement: "I am the Lord that bringeth you up out of the land of Egypt, to be your God: ye shall *therefore* be holy, for I am holy." Lev. 11:45. Are we to conclude from this that the command to "be holy" is intended only for literal Israel, who were brought "up out of the land of Egypt"? We believe that even the most vigorous opponent of the Sabbath would hesitate to endorse such an idea. But if both holiness and Sabbathkeeping have a certain relationship to deliverance from Egyptian bondage, and yet we agree that all men should be holy, we surely cannot use Egypt as an excuse for violating the Sabbath.

In the light of these passages, and others that might be given, how evident it is that the fact of their Egyptian bondage, when they were treated unkindly and unjustly, was cited by Moses simply as an *added* reason why they, now that the Lord had graciously delivered them from such conditions, should deal justly and lovingly with others! The law of just dealings with others, especially with those in an unfortunate condition, has been binding on men from the beginning of the world; but it took on added force and obligation when applied to those who had been so lately compelled to work as slaves in Egypt.

Instead of weakening the Sabbath command, Deuteronomy 5:15 simply serves to show how exceeding broad is the command, and how God intended the Sabbath to prove a source of refreshment and blessing even to servants.

# Objection 23

In Exodus 31:14 we read that Sabbath violators were to be stoned to death. Do you believe the same penalty should be enforced today? If you say that the penalty feature of the Sabbath law is done away, then you have really declared the Sabbath abolished, for a law has no force if there is no penalty provided for its violation.

Again, in Exodus 35:3 we read that no fires were to be kindled on the Sabbath. If you believe the Sabbath law is still in force, why do you kindle fires on that day?

Exodus 31:14 reads, "Ye shall keep the sabbath therefore; for it is holy unto you: every one that defileth it shall surely be put to death: for whosoever doeth any work therein, that soul shall be cut off from among his people."

If the reader will turn to Deuteronomy 13:6, 10; 21:18, 21; 22:21-28, and all of Leviticus 20, he will read there a whole series of injunctions concerning the putting to death of persons who were idolaters, who were rebellious to their parents, who committed adultery or were guilty of incest, who cursed father or mother—in fact, who violated any part of the moral code. Indeed, someone has estimated that no less than nine of the Ten Commandments are specifically mentioned in connection with the penalty of death for their violation.

Now we would ask the Sabbath objector: Do you believe that the idolater, for example, ought to be put to death, or the son who curses his father? Of course you answer no. Then, according to your logic, if you believe that this penalty should not be enforced today, you evidently believe that it is no longer wrong to be an idolater, for example, or for a son to curse his father. But such a conclusion would obviously be monstrous, to say nothing of being unreasonable. Yet it would be no more unreasonable than the contention that because present-day Sabbathkeepers do not believe Sabbathbreakers should be put to death, therefore the Sabbath law is abolished. This kind of reasoning proves too much, and thus proves nothing.

We agree that if a law has no penalty, it has no force. But it does not follow that because we do not believe in stoning people, therefore we believe there will be no punishment for those who violate the Sabbath or any other part of the law of God.

The only difference between the ancient Jewish order of things and ours today is as regards the *time* of punishment and the executor of the punishment. When God was the direct ruler, He saw fit to have an immediate punishment inflicted. Now the evildoer must look forward to the last great day of judgment. (See Heb. 10:26-29.)

Therefore let not the Sabbathbreaker feel at ease in his mind simply because God has not suddenly brought judgment upon him for his violation of the fourth precept of the Decalogue, which declares that the seventh day is the Sabbath of the Lord thy God, Creator of heaven and earth.

The story is told of a certain godless man who found special delight in flaunting his disobedience of the Sabbath command. He lived in a locality where the other farmers near him were devout Sabbathkeepers. When October came and he harvested his crop, he found that he had even more in his barn than his neighbors.

Meeting the Sabbathkeeping minister on the street one day, he gloatingly mentioned this fact. The minister's only reply was: "God does not always make a full settlement in October." No better answer could have been given.

The faithful Sabbathkeeper awaits the day of final judgment to receive his full reward for obedience to God, the Creator of the whole earth. And likewise, the Sabbath violator must await that last great day of accounting in order to receive the final reward for his failure to obey the explicit command of God. The violation of the law of God is sin, the Scriptures inform us (1 John 3:4), and the wages of sin is death (Rom. 6:23). Is that not sufficient penalty?

What of the command against kindling fires on the Sabbath? Exodus 35:3 reads, "Ye shall kindle no fire throughout your habitations upon the sabbath day." Our answer, briefly, is this:

1. The prohibition against kindling a fire is not part of the fourth commandment of the Decalogue. And it is the precepts of the Decalogue that we consider moral and thus eternally binding.

2. There were many civil as well as ceremonial statutes given to Israel that had limited duration. For example, there were civil statutes that declared how a slave should be treated. (See Ex. 21:1-11.) The Sabbath objector finds in these statutes on the holding of slaves, for example, no justification for slavery today. Instead, he agrees with the Sabbathkeeper that many of the statutes given to Israel through Moses were an adaptation of great moral principles to the degree of moral understanding of the Israelites, or to particular situations that existed locally. Therein lies the basic distinction between the moral commands of the Decalogue given to Israel directly by God on Sinai, and the host of other statutes given through Moses.

Now if the Sabbath objector feels free to discard the statute on the care of slaves while holding that nine of the ten commands of the Decalogue are still in force, are we not equally reasonable in discarding the statute against kindling fires on the Sabbath while holding that all ten commands of the Decalogue are still in force?

3. It is not even certain, from the context, that the command to the Jews against Sabbath fires was intended to apply to other than their wilderness journeying. The command comes as a preface to a series of commands concerning the erection of the tabernacle, which commands had life only so long as the tabernacle was under construction, and then died by limitation. The Jews themselves have never been agreed on whether the prohibition against Sabbath fires extended beyond the wilderness period.

In the wilderness the temperature was rather generally warm, hence fire would hardly be needed to protect against sickness. The Israelites were instructed to bake and seethe on the sixth day such of the manna as they desired to eat in that form on the Sabbath day. Hence there was no need to kindle a fire for cooking on that day.

Again, to "kindle" a fire in those times meant to engage in very real and extended labor. As the *Pulpit Commentary* in its comments on Exodus 35:3 observes:

"The kindling of fire in early times involved considerable labour. It was ordinarily effected by rubbing two sticks together, or twisting one round rapidly between the two palms in a depression upon a board. Fire only came after a long time. Moreover, as in the warm climate of Arabia and Palestine artificial warmth was not needed, fire could only have been kindled there for cooking purposes, which involved further unnecessary work. . . . The Jews generally view the precept as having had only a temporary force."

In the light of these facts, how could the prohibition against kindling fires raise any possible doubt as to the moral quality and permanency of the fourth command of the Decalogue?

# Objection 24

When we as Sundaykeepers declare that the ten-commandment law was abolished at the cross, Adventists try to embarrass us by asking us if we believe it is all right in the Christian Era to steal or kill or do any other of the heinous deeds prohibited by the Decalogue. We do not. We believe that God has great moral principles that have governed the universe from all eternity and will continue to govern it to all eternity. The Decalogue was simply a partial reflection of these principles. The principles remain, but the Decalogue is gone. Hence the Sabbath is gone.

How does the objector know that God has had these great moral principles from eternity? Does he have access to heavenly information that we do not have? No! Christianity is a revealed religion. It does not rest on the philosophical speculations of wise men, but on a revelation from God, and that revelation is contained in a written record called the Bible. What we may deduce from viewing God's creation, or from communing with our own spirit, must ever be corrected by what we read in the Book. That is the historic Protestant position.

No, the objector has no authoritative source of information that we do not possess. That is why he fails to give us any information as to what these "moral principles" are. He carefully leaves them undefined and undescribed. He is wholly warranted in affirming that God has had "moral principles" in force through all eternity. Reason and common sense assure us that a universe governed by a holy God must certainly be controlled by "moral principles," or more exactly, moral laws, for Christian theology always speaks of the universe as being divinely governed by moral *laws*. But neither reason nor common sense can define with certainty just what is comprehended in those laws. We repeat, only by a study of the revealed will of God in the Bible can we know for certain what those laws are.

We do know from the Bible that when God first called out a people for His own name He delivered to them in His own handwriting Ten Commandments, or laws, which were to be the moral basis of their government. Now, we would ask the objector whether he believes that any of these ten commands were part of the eternal moral laws. We can imagine his quickly agreeing that at least nine were—the commands against false gods, making idols, blasphemy, killing, adultery, stealing, lying, covetousness, and the command to honor our parents. Thus by the admission of the objector himself, when God saw fit to reveal to men His eternal moral laws, He gave to them the Decalogue, nine tenths of which consisted of eternal moral laws.

God's speaking from Sinai simply made those eternal moral laws audible to men. And His writing them out simply made them visually evident. Thus men might both hear and see and thus know for certain those eternal moral laws that should govern their lives. To say that the Decalogue was simply a "reflection" of eternal moral laws, as though it were a shadowy image and not the enduring reality, is to confuse simple truth by subtle words. We might as appropriately say that God's voice that spoke the Decalogue, and His hand that wrote it, were merely a shadowy reflection of Himself. The commands of the Decalogue were as truly a projection of the eternal moral laws into the realm of men as the divine hand and voice were a projection of God into our mortal realm. Thus it would be as irrational to speak of destroying the Decalogue while preserving the eternal moral laws as it would be to speak of destroying the divine voice and hand while preserving God.

Therefore, when someone declares that the Decalogue was abolished at Calvary he is, in strict logic, really asserting that God's eternal moral laws, or at least nine of them, were then abolished. In other words, after God had supernaturally revealed nine of His eternal moral laws to men and had exhorted them repeatedly through the prophets to be obedient, He suddenly abolished these nine eternal moral laws at Calvary. That is what the objector really declares. Yet he feels that it is grossly unfair for us to conclude that the logic of his declaration permits him to lie and steal and kill, and so on.

We do not believe that those who declare that the Decalogue has been abolished really think that they may now kill and steal. We simply affirm that the premises from which they reason logically lead to that conclusion, and that the defenses they erect against the conclusion will not stand up. We seek to show, not that their moral standards are bad, but simply that their logic is, and most evidently so because of the bad premise on which it rests and the bad conclusion to which it leads.

And how do the advocates of this abolition doctrine seek to avoid this obvious conclusion? By a variety of arguments, some of which have already been considered. For example, that in the Christian Era we are fulfilling the law if we have love to God and man, and that such love will not permit us to bow down to idols or lie or steal, et cetera. But does love, which has ever existed, make unnecessary the eternal moral laws which, he admits, have ever existed? No, love simply gives us spiritual discernment to see and a heart tender to obey these moral laws. Furthermore, the prime importance of love to God and man is revealed in the Old Testament. Yet there was a need for the Ten Commandments in Old Testament times. Why not also in our times?

The objector's primary reasons for claiming that the abolition of the Decalogue permits him to break the fourth commandment, but does not permit him to break the other nine, are these:

1. The fourth commandment alone, of the ten, was ceremonial, and with all the other ceremonies, expired at Calvary. Therefore we are not required to keep it.

2. The other nine commandments, because they are moral, were re-enacted by the apostles, and thus are binding on us.

Though these two contentions are really parts of the objection before us, and must be answered before a full reply is provided, they also carry us into new areas of discussion. Hence they will be examined separately in the following pages.

# Objection 25

The fourth commandment in the Decalogue is not inherently a moral precept, but the other nine are self-evidently moral commands. "All moral principles are discoverable by the light of nature" or reason, but the necessity of keeping the seventh day is not thus discoverable. For example, all men naturally know that it is wrong to steal, kill, commit adultery, et cetera, but no one would thus know that a particular day had been set apart as holy. That required a direct revelation from God. Hence the Sabbath command is not moral. Furthermore, there is nothing inherently holy in the seventh day of the week. Hence "it would never have been wrong to work on the seventh day unless God had given a command to rest on it."

The most direct reply may be presented in terms of answers to the following three key questions:

**First Question**

Do all men *naturally know* that it is wrong to steal, commit adultery, worship idols, or violate any other of the nine commands that the objector certainly agrees are moral?

This question obviously challenges the very foundation on which the whole objection before us rests. Fortunately, a clear and sure answer can be given. Let us start with the first commandment. This command not only forbids polytheism but also requires that we worship one certain God, the true God. Do all men naturally know that it is wrong to worship more than one god? Or do they naturally know who the true God is? The answer to both questions is no. Though most men of all races and ages have felt that they should worship some god or gods there never has been agreement as to which god or gods should be worshiped.

Says Paul, "For after that in the wisdom of God the world by wisdom knew not God, it pleased God by the foolishness of preaching to save them that believe." 1 Cor. 1:21. His sermon on Mars' Hill is an exhibit of such preaching. And how did Paul know the true God? By the revelations given to him and by his study of that revelation called the Scriptures.

The one true God is pure and holy, and though just, is merciful. The gods of the nations have been anything but holy, and their mercy at best has been capricious. Now, the first commandment calls on us to worship the one true God. Hence we must know His nature and holy requirements if we are truly to obey that command. But only revelation can provide that knowledge.

Let us take the second commandment. Do men know by reason or nature that it is wrong to make a likeness of God or of any creature and use it as an object of religious worship? No. The history of almost all mankind is a history of idol worship. Indeed, Roman Catholics declare that there is nothing sinful in making images and bowing down before them. And how do we as Protestants seek to show the evil of idols, either Catholic or heathen? Do we rest our case on reason and nature? No. On revelation.

Take the third commandment. The reason why we see force and meaning in the prohibition against taking God's name in vain is that revelation presents to us a picture of a most pure and holy God to whom we owe all and to whom we must someday give an account. But the heathen, even the most enlightened Greeks, who possessed no revelation, thought of their gods as altogether like themselves, lustful, depraved, vindictive, even murderous. Would it have seemed reasonable to a Greek to believe that there was anything wrong in taking lightly the name of any of his gods?

Let us turn to a commandment that deals with man's relation to his fellow man and see whether reason and nature prove sufficient here. We who are Christians are shocked at the thought of adultery in any of its evil manifestations. And when we send missionaries to far lands we seek to turn men from this evil, along with all other evils. But these missionaries do not make their appeal on the basis of reason and nature. They would be ridiculed if they did. That is the testimony of many who have preached to non-Christian peoples. Instead, they preach morality and chastity in terms of a revelation from God and a command of God.

But why lengthen the survey of the nine commands that the objector admits are moral? We believe that reason and nature play some part in giving us a knowledge of right and wrong, of God and the judgment, so that men are without excuse. But how limited a part they play is sadly revealed in the long, sinful history of man. We believe that the inhabitants of Sodom and Gomorrah had enough knowledge of God and right and wrong to be morally accountable and justly entitled to the fiery destruction that descended upon them. But our Lord declared that it would be more tolerable in the day of judgment for Sodom and Gomorrah than for those cities that refused to receive the message that His disciples would bring to them. And why? Because the disciples would bring to them a revelation from God, received through Jesus Christ. Said Christ, "If I had not come and spoken unto them, they had not had sin: but now they have no cloke [margin, "excuse"] for their sin." John 15:22.

How clear it is that a divine revelation is needed, not simply in regard to the fourth commandment, but in regard to the others also! Thus the very foundation on which this impressive objection has been reared, disappears. Strictly speaking, it should not be necessary for us to deal further with this objection. But let us look briefly at the other questions involved.

**Second Question**

What are the proofs that Seventh-day Adventists can offer to support their claim that the fourth commandment is moral rather than ceremonial, and thus eternally binding like the other nine?

We answer:

1. "Moral duties and precepts are such as grow out of the attributes of God. Creative power is the distinguishing attribute of the living God, and the Sabbath grew directly out of the exercise of this attribute in the creation of the world." *

---

* This and other non-Biblical quotations in this series of proofs that the Sabbath command is a moral one are taken from the pamphlet *The Morality of the Sabbath*, written in 1875 by none other than D. M. Canright. His later defection from the Seventh-day Adventist Church no more invalidates these proofs than does the defection of a minister from the Christian religion invalidate the reasons he formerly presented in behalf of Christianity. Rather, they stand as an indictment of the man's defection.

2. The second reason follows closely on the first: "Man's moral duty to love and obey God rests chiefly upon the fact that the Lord created all things, which fact the Sabbath was given to commemorate."

3. "Man's nature, physically and mentally, requires just such a day of rest as the Sabbath precept provides, and hence, like all moral precepts, it provides for a natural and universal want of the race."

4. "Man's moral and spiritual well-being requires just what the Sabbath precept provides, and hence it is moral."

Proofs three and four are identical with those used by ardent Sunday law advocates, except that when they say "Sabbath" they mean "Sunday." They present medical and scientific evidence to show that those who take a day of rest at regular intervals of about one week can better carry on their work during the next week. They also point to religious history which shows that in so-called Christian lands where a weekly day of worship has not been faithfully observed, religious life wanes.

Thus it is a well-established fact that Sunday leaders in Protestantism see a moral quality in the fourth commandment as certainly as Seventh-day Adventists do. Their contention is that the command is partly moral and partly ceremonial. The moral part, say they, is the command to keep holy one day in seven; the ceremonial part, the particular day that was set apart. They must claim that part of it is moral in order to enforce Sunday; they must claim that part of it is ceremonial in order to justify their changing the day of worship.

In taking this position they overlook the following facts:

*a.* As has already been shown, the moral quality of the Sabbath command resides not simply in the physical, mental, and spiritual needs of man. Most primarily the moral quality springs from the relation of the command to the creative act of God.

*b.* The creative act displayed itself in a certain time sequence, six days in which God labored and the seventh day on which He rested.

*c.* "God blessed the seventh day, and sanctified it: because that in it he had rested from all his work." Gen. 2:3.

*d.* The very reason offered in the fourth commandment as to why men should keep the Sabbath is this historical fact of creation and God's resting on the last day of creation week. "The seventh day is the sabbath: . . . for in six days the Lord made heaven and earth . . . : wherefore the Lord blessed the sabbath day, and hallowed it." Ex. 20:10, 11.

How could language make more clear that a particular day is involved in the Sabbath command? And that that day memorializes a specific historical event? Or how could language make more clear that the sanctifying of this particular weekly rest day springs from the fact that this specific historical event occurred on that day, the seventh day?

The "wherefore" in the Sabbath command refers back to this incident and to the particular day God blessed. Remove the "wherefore," and the reason for the Sabbath command disappears. But that is exactly what Sunday advocates do when they invoke the Sabbath command in favor of one day's rest in seven but discard the reason for a weekly holy day. When they contend that the weekly rest-day feature of the command is moral, but the seventh-day feature is ceremonial, and hence of relatively minor importance, they are in the curious position of asserting that a great moral principle enunciated in the Decalogue rests upon a ceremonial, and thus relatively minor, act of God.

5. "The Sabbath precept, like all moral precepts, applies equally well to all nations, in all countries, and at all times." This follows from the fact that recurring periods of physical rest and similar periods of religious exercise are as much needed by one people as another, in all climes and in all ages.

6. "The Sabbath precept guards the right of property the same as the eighth commandment does; and hence, like that, is moral." The Lord divided the seven-day week into two parts, six days man might use as he desired in honest labor, the seventh God reserved. "The seventh day is the sabbath of the Lord thy God." Ex. 20:10.

ANSWERS TO OBJECTIONS

The Lord speaks of the Sabbath as "my holy day." (Isa. 58:13.) It is as morally wrong to steal from God the holy time that belongs to Him as it is to steal from our neighbor some possession that is his. Hence the command that prohibits such stealing from God is a moral command.

7. "Marriage is a moral institution. The Sabbatic institution, being made at the same time, by the same authority, for the same persons, and in a similar manner, is also moral for the same reason."

Only those who are ready to contend that marriage rests, not on a moral, but on a ceremonial, law, should logically contend that the Sabbath rests simply on a ceremonial law. It is in this setting that we better see how unreasonable is the argument that although the Sabbath institution is moral, because all men naturally know that rest is needed, the particular day mentioned in the Sabbath command is ceremonial, because men do not naturally know the day on which we should rest. No Christian would be impressed with the argument that though the marriage institution is moral, because men naturally know that marriage is needful, the monogamous feature of it is simply ceremonial, because men do not naturally know that a man should have only one wife. We would respond that even if men do not know this naturally, they do know it by revelation, and then we would cite God's act in Eden in uniting one man and one woman, and His declaring that "they twain shall be one flesh." We would not consider it necessary to do more than this to prove the moral quality of monogamy, that one joined to one is right, but one joined to two or more is not. Christians believe that God's act and declaration can give a moral quality even to arithmetic.

By precisely the same reasoning we may dispose of the argument about the ceremonial quality of that part of the Sabbath law that speaks of a particular day.

8. One of the most distinguishing marks of the various ceremonial laws in the Bible is that they were all given *after* man sinned, were made necessary in some way or other by man's sinful

146

state, and expire by limitation while man is still on this present world. (The ceremonial statutes given to the ancient Jews expired at the cross; the ceremonial rites of Christians—for example, the Lord's supper—expire at the Second Advent.) That is not true of the Sabbath, which was given to sinless Adam and Eve in Eden, and will be kept by the redeemed in Eden restored. (See Isa. 66:23.)

9. The very fact that God placed the Sabbath command in the heart of the Decalogue, known to all Christians as the moral law, is in itself the most convincing proof that that command is moral. God confined His audible lawgiving to ten commands; He confined His writing to ten commands. How unreasonable to believe that with brevity so distinguishing a mark of this code, with weighty and eternally moral precepts on both sides of it, God should insert in the midst a ceremonial statute that was to expire at Christ's first advent! But we are not required to entertain so unreasonable an idea. The series of proofs here given reveal beyond all reasonable doubt that the fourth commandment is moral.

**Third Question**

What of the claim that "it never would have been wrong to work on the seventh day unless God had given a command to rest in it"? The objector here most evidently seeks to prove that the Sabbath is a ceremonial statute, which owes its authority, not to any inherent moral quality, but to an arbitrary command of God. The point is really covered in what has already been presented. But two observations more may help to reveal fully the fallacy of the objection.

1. Through the ages there have been those who preached and practiced free love. Even in nineteenth-century America some societies formed of people that claimed kinship with Christians, advocated free love and thus the abandonment of marriage. Now, how would the Sabbath objector answer such a free-love advocate who contended that it never would have been wrong to practice free love if God had not commanded that there should be marriage,

with twain as one? We think we hear him responding immediately and with vigor: "What more do we need than God's command to determine what is right or wrong?" Nor would he countenance for a moment the argument that seeing men do not know naturally that monogamy is right, therefore the Christian rule of monogamy is arbitrary and may be abandoned by those who desire greater freedom. Even so with the Sabbath command.

2. We earlier noted that one of the reasons for the Sabbath command was to guard property rights. The seventh day belongs to God. It was because God set apart the day as His own, with blessing and sanctification, that He commanded men to regard it as different from other days, to rest from their own toil on that day, and to keep it holy. Hence the objector is forgetful of the historical facts and sequence when he declares that "it never would have been wrong to work on the seventh day unless God had given a command to rest in it."

The wrongness of using the day for secular interests resides in the fact that the Sabbath is God's holy day. The command springs from that fact. It is therefore not an arbitrary command, but a moral one growing out of the nature of the seventh day, the sanctified possession of God.

There is something very strange about the claim that the Sabbath command is ceremonial. Those who set it forth generally are devout Sundaykeepers who deplore the widespread profanation of Sunday and often seek to secure civil legislation to protect it, even as their spiritual fathers in past generations did. They quite uniformly hold that the keeping of Sunday is a moral matter, certainly not ceremonial, though they can cite no command of Scripture in support of this belief, no action of God in blessing or sanctifying the day. They must fall back on the fourth commandment, albeit with alterations and a sixteenth-century new interpretation, in order to make out the appearance of a case for the moral quality of Sundaykeeping. (See page 545 for the historical evidence in support of this statement.) Yet we who keep the Sabbath are declared to be resting our case on a ceremonial law, though we appeal to the same fourth commandment, and in the exact form that God gave it.

All this surely adds up to the conclusion that the real controversy is not over whether a weekly rest day is a moral requirement of God—the Sabbath institution soon begins to disintegrate unless it is so viewed—but which day of the week the fourth commandment calls on us to keep, the seventh or the first?

(See objection 38 for a discussion of this point. See also objections 26 and 27 for a discussion of other aspects of the claim that the Sabbath is ceremonial.)

# Objection 26

"The Sabbath was not a day of special religious worship. . . . In God's plan, the keeping of the seventh day on the part of His earthly people was to be an external form, or rite; the performance of a definitely prescribed ceremony, stipulating the cessation of all work on a given day, or a day of complete *physical* rest. Only when connected with the annual feasts was it observed as a day of religious significance." All this proves that the seventh-day Sabbath was simply one of the ceremonial sabbaths. All those sabbaths, in common with every other ceremonial statute, were abolished at the cross.

By two unwarranted claims this objection seeks to drop the seventh-day Sabbath down to the level of the ceremonial sabbaths, which were blotted out at the cross. Let us consider them in order:

## First False Claim

The seventh-day Sabbath was merely an "external form," which called simply for "complete *physical* rest." Hence it could not be that essentially spiritual, morally binding, holy day that Seventh-day Adventists declare that it is.

It is difficult to understand how anyone acquainted with the Bible would make this statement. Let the Bible provide the refutation.

The creation of the Sabbath reveals that it is distinguished in two ways: (1) by God's resting on it, and (2) by His blessing and sanctifying it. And as earlier stated, to sanctify means to set apart for a holy use.

When the Lord sought first to impress on the new nation of Israel the significance of the Sabbath, which had doubtless been forgotten by many during their Egyptian bondage, He caused manna to fall for the six working days, and then withheld it on the seventh. The Israelites were to gather extra on the sixth day, and to rest on the seventh. When they came to the first Friday and found that they were able to gather twice as much as on preceding

150

days, Moses said to them, "This is that which the Lord hath said, To morrow is the rest of the holy sabbath." Ex. 16:23. The Sabbath presented was not only as a day of "complete *physical* rest" but also as "the *holy* sabbath."

When Nehemiah long afterward referred to the formal giving of the Decalogue on Mount Sinai he declared that God there made known unto them His *"holy* sabbath." (Neh. 9:14.)

Nehemiah found certain Jews working on the Sabbath and buying wares on that day. With indignation at this threat to the life of the nation, now rising from its long captivity, he cried out:

"What evil thing is this that ye do, and *profane* the sabbath day? Did not your fathers thus, and did not our God bring all this evil upon us, and upon this city? yet ye bring more wrath upon Israel by profaning the sabbath." Neh. 13:17, 18.

It is only holy things that are capable of being profaned. How strange to Nehemiah's ears would have sounded the words of those who today try to dismiss the Sabbath as merely an "external form" that dealt only with "physical rest." Would God, who bore so long with the most grievous iniquities of Israel, have uprooted the Jewish nation and sent it into captivity because of a failure to keep a merely "external form, or rite"?

The Lord, through Isaiah, offers a special blessing to those who truly keep the Sabbath:

"If thou turn away thy foot from the sabbath, from doing thy pleasure on my holy day; and call the sabbath a delight, the holy of the Lord, honourable; and shalt honour him, not doing thine own ways, nor finding thine own pleasure, nor speaking thine own words: then shalt thou delight thyself in the Lord; and I will cause thee to ride upon the high places of the earth, and feed thee with the heritage of Jacob thy father: for the mouth of the Lord hath spoken it." Isa. 58:13, 14.

### Second False Claim

The seventh-day Sabbath acquired a "religious significance" "only when connected with the annual feasts." Hence it owed its religious or spiritual quality to its connection with obviously ceremonial, annual sabbaths. And can that which is blessed—in this case, given "religious significance"—be on a higher level than that which blesses it? All this proves that the seventh-day Sabbath was simply one of the ceremonial sabbaths.

But we have discovered that the seventh-day Sabbath has an inherent holiness given to it by God in Eden. There were no annual feast days with which it might possibly be "connected" until twenty-five hundred years later. When the manna was first given, Moses described the seventh day as "the *holy* sabbath," though no annual feasts, with which it might be "connected," had yet been given. When God announced the Sabbath as a part of the Decalogue, it could be described as His *"holy* sabbath," wrote Nehemiah. But the giving of the Decalogue preceded the setting forth of the laws that created the annual feast days. We found nothing in the context of the passages in Genesis, Exodus, Nehemiah, or Isaiah which speak of God's holy Sabbath, that gives any suggestion that it needed to be "connected" with any annual feast in order to possess holiness.

Strictly speaking, we need not, therefore, spend time in discussing annual feasts. However, an examination of them really adds further proof that they are essentially different from the seventh-day Sabbath. From Leviticus 23 we learn that there were seven annual sabbaths:

1. The fifteenth day of the first month of the Jewish year, the first day of the Feast of Unleavened Bread, known also as the Passover sabbath.

2. The twenty-first day of the first month, the last day of the Feast of Unleavened Bread.

3. The fiftieth day from "the morrow after the" fifteenth of the first month, known later as Pentecost.

4. The first day of the seventh month, called "a memorial of blowing of trumpets."

5. The tenth day of the seventh month, known as the Day of Atonement.

6. The fifteenth day of the seventh month, the first day of the Feast of Tabernacles.

7. The twenty-second day of the seventh month, the last day of the Feast of Tabernacles.

These annual convocations were properly called "sabbaths," for the Hebrew word *shabath,* from which our English "sabbath" is translated in the Old Testament, simply means "rest." And on those annual sabbaths the people rested from their labors. But the mere fact that these annual holy days are called "sabbaths" does not in itself warrant placing them in the same class with the seventh-day Sabbath. Both are rest days, to be sure, but that does not mean that they are of the same character or standing. In terms of the Hebrew language, we could properly describe a modern holiday as a "sabbath," a rest day; we could also describe a Christian Era holy day as a "sabbath." But how foolish would be the person who decided, therefore, that holidays and holy days are of the same nature, and thus stand or fall together, simply because both are rest days, or "sabbaths," according to the Hebrew. Though they have one point in common, namely, rest, their dissimilarities are many. Thus with the annual sabbaths and the seventh-day Sabbath. Their dissimilarities are many and great. Let us note them:

**Seventh-day (Decalogue) Sabbath**

1. Made at the creation of the world. Gen. 2:2, 3.

2. Memorialized an event at beginning of time, the creation, before there was a Jewish people.

3. Intended ever to turn men's minds back to creation. Ex. 20:8-11.

**Annual (Ceremonial) Sabbaths**

1. Made at Sinai, about twenty-five hundred years after creation. Leviticus 23.

2. Memorialized events in current Jewish history. For example, Feast of Tabernacles. Lev. 23:43.

3. Intended to turn men's minds ever forward to cross, etc. "A shadow of things to come." Col. 2:17. For example, "Christ our passover is sacrificed for us." 1 Cor. 5:7.

4. God rested on the seventh-day Sabbath and specifically blessed and sanctified it. Gen. 2:2, 3.

4. God did not rest on these days, nor set them apart with distinctive blessing or sanctification.

5. Commemorates a world that had come forth perfect from Creator's hand.

5. Commemorates and foreshadows events in a world plagued with sin.

6. Tied to weekly cycle, and the same day of the week always.

6. Tied to the Jewish calendar, and thus a different day of week each time celebrated.

7. Could be kept anywhere in world, because weekly cycle operates free of all calendars.

7. Could be known and kept only where Jewish calendar in existence.

8. Kept every week.

8. Kept only once a year.

9. "Made *for* man." Mark 2:27.

9. A part of that ceremonial ritual which was "against us." Col. 2:14.

10. Will continue beyond this world. Isa. 66:23.

10. Abolished, taken "out of the way," at Christ's crucifixion. Col. 2:14.

Though it is true that all things that pertain to the service of God at any time have a certain holy quality, and though, in the present instance, these annual sabbaths had some features in common with the seventh-day Sabbath, the dissimilarities are so real and so great as to leave no doubt that the former should not be confused with the latter.

When the Lord instructed Moses concerning the annual feasts, known as "holy convocations," which revolved around the seven annual sabbaths, He declared in conclusion, "These are the feasts of the Lord, which ye shall proclaim to be holy convocations . . . : *beside* the sabbaths of the Lord." Lev. 23:37, 38.

Thus are we instructed by God Himself that the annual sabbaths are apart from, and in addition to, "the sabbaths of the Lord."

As the Bible commentary by Jamieson, Fausset, and Brown well observes:

"Leviticus 23, 38 expressly distinguishes 'the sabbath of the Lord' from the other sabbaths."—Comment on Col. 2:16.

# Objection 27

That the fourth command of the Decalogue is ceremonial, but the other nine are moral, "is clearly proved by the fact that Jesus, according to the strictest Sabbatarians of His day, broke the fourth commandment and was criticized by them for doing so. Furthermore, Jesus distinctly says, 'The priests in the temple profane the sabbath, and are blameless.' [Matt. 12:5.] Would He have dared to say this if the fourth commandment were a moral law? Could the seventh commandment, or any other of the ten except the fourth, be broken by the priests, and the fact that they were broken in the temple make them blameless?"

We would like to ask two questions:

1. If Christ broke the fourth commandment, then why did He say, "I have kept my Father's commandments"? John 15:10.

2. The Sabbath objector says that "the law"—and he insists that all laws both moral and ceremonial are comprehended in that term—was in force until the cross. Then if Christ broke the Sabbath commandment, was He not a sinner? There is only one answer. But we know that Christ did no sin; therefore there must be something wrong with the reasoning in the objection before us.

What proof is offered that Jesus "broke the fourth commandment"? An inspired declaration of Holy Writ? No, only the charge of the "strictest Sabbatarians of His day."

On a certain Sabbath day, while our Lord was in a synagogue, there came before Him a man with a withered hand. Divining that Christ might plan to heal the cripple, some "strict Sabbatarians" asked the Master: "Is it lawful to heal on the sabbath days? that they might accuse him. And he said unto them, What man shall there be among you, that shall have one sheep, and if it fall into a pit on the sabbath day, will he not lay hold on it, and lift it out? How much then is a man better than a sheep? Wherefore it is lawful to do well on the sabbath days." Matt. 12:10-12. Whereupon He immediately healed the cripple. "Then the Pharisees went out, and held a council against him, how they might destroy him." Verse 14.

Another instance of Christ's healing on the Sabbath is recorded in John 5:2-18. In verse 18 we read that the judgment of the Jews was that Christ "had broken the sabbath."

Here we see the charge of the "strictest Sabbatarians" in its Scriptural setting. Yet the Sabbath objector evidently considers this charge to be sufficient ground for saying that Christ "broke the fourth commandment." Incredible!

We believe the incident of the healing of the crippled man proves the very opposite of what some people allege it does, as the following questions will reveal:

1. If Christ considered the fourth commandment simply ceremonial, was this not an excellent opportunity for Him to discourse upon the distinction between ceremonial and moral precepts? Present-day Sabbath opposers surely would have done so, for here they argue that very point, insisting that it was proper to break the fourth commandment, because it was ceremonial, but that it would have been sin to break any other of the ten, because they were moral. But Christ did not use any such reasoning.

2. Note the question asked of Christ: "Is it lawful to heal on the sabbath days?" When the Samaritan woman at the well asked Christ where men should worship, a question that through the long past years had had genuine importance, He dismissed it summarily by informing her that the time was at hand when the question no longer had significance. If Christ was soon to abolish the Sabbath law on the cross, would we not expect Him to dismiss, in similar fashion, the question the "strictest Sabbatarians" had posed? Instead, He gave no hint of impending abolition, but replied, "It is lawful to do well on the sabbath days."

There is no suggestion that He considered He was breaking the Sabbath. Instead, He was interpreting its true meaning. Nor is there anything in His interpretation, or His miraculous action that followed, that warrants the conclusion that the Sabbath rests on a ceremonial law. It is always lawful to "do well" in relation to moral laws.

But it is alleged that the Sabbath is ceremonial because Christ declared that the priests "profane the sabbath, and are blameless." His reference to the priests was simply offered in illustration of His statement that "it is lawful to do well on the sabbath days." Christ's adversaries were contending that He and His disciples profaned the Sabbath by engaging in some form of work on the Sabbath. He reminded them that the priests also worked on the Sabbath, and were blameless. Even the "strictest Sabbatarians" would agree that what the priests did on the Sabbath, in harmony with "the law," was "lawful," even though the priests each Sabbath had to engage in the work of slaying and offering sacrifices.

Christ's use of the word "profane" must be understood in the context of the controversy. His reasoning appears to be this: If His and His disciples' deeds were profanation of the Sabbath, then by the same token the deeds of the priests were profanation. To contend that Christ really meant that the priests, whose Sabbath deeds of sacrificing were done in harmony with the law, did, in truth, desecrate the Sabbath, would lead to an impossible conclusion. Christ would really be saying that God gave a holy law to guard the sacredness of the Sabbath and then gave to Moses another law that resulted weekly in the desecration of the Sabbath! Those who wish to, may hold this conclusion. We do not.

The Sabbath commandment, like the other commands in the Decalogue, is relatively brief. It sets down the principle that men should refrain from all their own labors on the seventh day. But the God who gave the law also revealed—for example, through other laws given to Moses, and through Christ's words—just how the Sabbath command should be understood and how it is related to other aspects of life. But that does not warrant the conclusion that the Sabbath command was therefore ceremonial. Commands that the Sabbath objector admits are moral, sometimes need interpretation to enable a person to know how to carry out the real intent of those commands under differing circumstances. For example, the fifth commandment makes the unqualified statement that children should honor their parents. And in Oriental lands that would be understood in a most far-reaching sense. But what if the parents were heathen, a situation that began to present itself when Christianity was preached to the Roman world? Paul, who quotes the opening words of the command, prefaces it with this obvious interpretation: "Children obey your parents *in the Lord:* for this is right." Eph. 6:1. That permitted them to disobey the command of a heathen parent if that command was contrary to the standards of Christ.

The eighth commandment reads, "Thou shalt not steal." Was ever a command more unquestionably moral! But is it possible that what man might consider a violation of that command, God might not? Evidently, for Moses was instructed to tell the people that a person going through someone else's field could satisfy his hunger by eating to the full, though he must not carry anything away. (See Deut. 23:24, 25.) Did a hungry person by eating his neighbor's grapes thus flout, or profane, the law against stealing? No. Why? Because the God who gave the law declared that such eating was in harmony with the law, the "strictest" honesty advocates notwithstanding. The same is true of the Sabbath command. Neither Christ nor the priests violated or vitiated the Sabbath command, because the God who gave the command also declared that the work of the priests and the work of Christ were "lawful" on that day.

The Sabbath objector may take his choice: either assert that the fourth command is ceremonial, which logically calls for the eighth command to be considered ceremonial also; or admit that the eighth is moral, which logically calls for the fourth to be also. But he is already on record as affirming that all the commands of the Decalogue are moral, except the fourth. Consistency calls for him to include it also.

# Objection 28

Though the Ten Commandments were abolished at the cross, nine of them were re-enacted in the New Testament, and thus are binding on Christians, but the fourth command was not; hence we are not obligated to keep it.

Two fallacies underlie this reasoning:

1. People often speak of the Old Testament in the same breath with the old covenant, and of the New Testament in the same breath with the new covenant. The almost unconscious effect upon both speaker and hearer is a minimizing of the Old Testament to the point of considering it nonessential and quite superseded by the New. And if there is coupled with this the view that the Ten Commandments are the old covenant, the way is paved for the kind of reasoning set forth in the objection now before us. But we have already shown (objection 5) that the Ten Commandments are not the old covenant, and that the New Testament in no way supersedes the Old (objection 1). When we keep clearly in mind that both the Old and the New Testament are our inspired guides, much of the force of this objection disappears.

2. The claim is that the Ten Commandments were abolished at the cross, but as already noted (objections 24, 25) those who make this claim admit that nine of the ten commands state eternal moral principles or laws. He therefore finds himself in the curious position of declaring that eternal things can be abolished. At least this is the point to which his reasoning leads him. Does he hesitate to admit this? Then we would ask him: How can you abolish the ten-commandment law unless you abolish the ten precepts that constitute it? There is only one answer to this question, as the objector himself evidently realizes, for he speaks of the re-enactment of nine of the ten. His dilemma is this: He must needs abolish the Decalogue in order to do away with the Sabbath

command, which is in the heart of it. But abolishing the Decalogue creates moral chaos, so he must promptly re-enact nine of the precepts. It is this that necessitates the incredible conclusion that eternal moral principles, or laws, were abolished, and then, equally incredible, re-enacted.

Now there are two things to remember about these eternal moral laws that constitute the nine commands:

1. They cover virtually the whole range of moral conduct.

2. Because they are eternal moral principles they are an expression of the very nature of God Himself, as Christian theologians have ever held, and govern all moral beings in the universe.

In the light of these undebatable facts the claim that the Decalogue was abolished at the cross takes on a monstrous, even sacrilegious, quality. When Christ died on the cross was the moral nature of God changed? It is sacrilege to ask the question. But so long as God is unchanged in nature the moral principles radiating from His nature remain unchanged. So long as God's nature abhors lying, stealing, killing, adultery, covetousness, false gods, et cetera, so long will the universe to its farthest corners be controlled by moral laws against these evil deeds. But we are told that the Decalogue was abolished at the cross, which, if words mean anything, means that the prohibitions of that holy code, the "Thou shalt not's" have disappeared. Now, either these precepts were abolished, or they were not. There is no middle ground. For example, either the sixth command, which prohibits murder, was abolished, or it was not. And so with the other commands.

The objector hopes to avert the appalling conclusions that inevitably flow from the logic of his position by hurrying out for inspection his re-enactment theory. The casual onlooker may feel that probably all is well, for does not the re-enactment thus preserve the continuity of moral law in the universe? Yes, if we might think of the re-enactment as we would think of the changing of gears in an automobile traveling the highway. But to make this kind of comparison is to violate both language and history. The idea of gear shifting, with forward motion continuing, has nothing in common with the thought of abolishment. Furthermore, the figure of gear shifting implies essentially no time interval in the transition. But it is this point of time interval that brings to light the most incredible feature of this whole re-enactment theory.

The apostles, from whose New Testament writings certain lines are quoted to prove the re-enactment of nine of the ten commands, did not pen their inspired manuscripts until twenty, thirty, forty, and more years after the cross! This simple historical fact leads to the fantastic conclusion that the whole world, if not the whole universe, was free from the great moral laws for this period of time. For example, when we inquire of the objector if he believes it proper to kill, steal, lie, et cetera, seeing that the Decalogue is abolished, he replies no, and informs us that the New Testament has re-enacted laws against these. Then he will probably quote Romans 13:9, where there is certainly found explicit prohibition of these crimes. But there is general agreement that Paul wrote Romans about the year A.D. 58. What about the time in between that year and the year of the crucifixion?

But there is a further dilemma that confronts those who present the re-enactment theory. They seem hard pressed to find in the New Testament explicit restatements of all the nine commands. So they generally draw, in part, from Christ's words in the four Gospels. But those words were uttered *before* His crucifixion! We cannot speak of re-enacting a law before it is abolished. Nor can the objector consistently contend at one time that the cross marks the dividing point between the old and the new, with all things becoming new at the resurrection, and at another time offer Christ's words *before* His crucifixion as exhibits of the new, re-enacted law.

Nor is this all the perplexity that confronts those who set forth this re-enactment theory. They are really not able to find in the New Testament a clear and sufficiently detailed restatement of the second commandment. We must turn to the words of the Decalogue if we, as Protestants, are to bring a wholly convincing indictment against Rome for the images in Catholic churches.

This is strange, indeed, if the re-enacted law should be wholly adequate for every situation in the Christian Era! Will the objector have the hardihood to affirm that the great God, in writing out the words of the second command, was needlessly detailed; or that, in inspiring New Testament writers, He failed to have them be as specific as is needed? Either conclusion would be sacrilegious. We need accept neither.

As earlier set forth in the discussion on the equal authority of the Old and the New Testament (objection 1), the New Testament writers give no suggestion that they are enacting a new code, or giving us a new revelation in the sense of superseding a former revelation in any area of our spiritual life. They quote many passages from the Old Testament in illustration of what they are presenting, and sometimes those quotations are from the Decalogue. At times the quotations are brief; at other times, more extended. That explains why the precepts of the Decalogue are not generally found in exactly the same form or so detailed as in the Old Testament. Why should they need to repeat verbatim? They constantly referred their readers to the Scriptures, which at that time meant the Old Testament, and in the Old Testament could be found the more detailed and explicit statement of the precept to which the apostle made reference.

In the light of these facts there is no point to the contention that the fourth command is not re-enacted in the New Testament.

But to remove the last shadow of plausibility from the objection let it be said in conclusion that the New Testament is not silent regarding the fourth command. On the contrary the references to it are as plentiful as to any other command. Note the following:

1. Our Lord declared, "The sabbath was made for man." Mark 2:27. Mark, in writing down these words of our Lord years after the cross, felt no necessity to qualify His words with the comment that the Sabbath was made for man only until the cross. In the absence of that comment what would Mark's readers naturally deduce from that statement by Christ? Obviously, that the words of our Lord still stand, and that the Sabbath remains. Yes,

the writers of the New Testament were silent at times regarding the Sabbath, but not the kind of silence that the objector refers to.

2. Matthew records what Christ said as to certain things being lawful on the Sabbath day. (Matt. 12:12.) Now if the Sabbath law were abolished at the cross, how important that Matthew should add immediately a comment to explain to the early Christians who might read his writings in some far corner of the world, that the whole discussion of the lawfulness of this or that on the Sabbath day is merely a bit of history, for the Sabbath law was abolished shortly after Christ made His statement! In the absence of that comment Matthew's readers would naturally conclude that they should be careful to see that they followed Christ's counsel on the matter of the Sabbath.

3. When Christ described to His disciples the destruction that was to come on Jerusalem, and told them that they were to flee when the Roman armies drew near, He added, "But pray ye that your flight be not in the winter, neither on the sabbath day." Matt. 24:20. The destruction occurred in A.D. 70. For almost forty years they were to pray that they might be spared fleeing on the Sabbath. But if the Sabbath were abolished at the cross, what point would there be in this? The force of this question is so great that some have sought to weaken it by declaring that on the Sabbath the gates of Jerusalem would be shut. But Christ, who knew all the future, knew that in A.D. 70 the Jews *would* go out to battle the Romans on the Sabbath. (See Josephus, *Jewish Wars,* book 2, chap. 19.) Further, the command to flee is addressed to "them which be in Judaea." (Matt. 24:16.) Judea was not surrounded with walls and gates. Yet *they* in Judea were to pray that *their* flight should not be on the Sabbath day! Could evidence be clearer that Christ viewed the Sabbath day as different from other days?

When we read Christ's counsel to His disciples to pray regarding the Sabbath, and when we couple with that His words regarding certain things being lawful on the Sabbath, with both statements being recorded by Matthew decades after the Christian Era had begun, should we not conclude that the Sabbath law is binding for Christians? Matthew says nothing to stop us from drawing this logical conclusion.

It is hard to speak restrainedly of so fantastic a proposition as that the Decalogue was abolished at the cross and then nine of its precepts were later re-enacted. Perhaps some reader, fully persuaded of the folly of such a view, may inquire in bewilderment: Is it really true that the great body of Protestant leaders through the years have believed and taught so incredible a doctrine? The answer is no. The classic position of Protestantism, as we have earlier stated, is that the Decalogue is the eternally binding rule of life for all men in all ages, and that only the ceremonial statutes were done away. (See page 493.) Those who set forth the Decalogue-abolition doctrine, with its re-enactment corollary, have forgotten for the moment the historic Protestant position regarding the Decalogue.

(For discussion of one New Testament reference to the Sabbath that might seem to support the claim that it was abolished at the cross, see objection 29.)

# Objection 29

**Paul specifically declares, in Colossians 2:14-17, that the Sabbath is abolished.**

The passage reads as follows: "Blotting out the handwriting of ordinances that was against us, which was contrary to us, and took it out of the way, nailing it to his cross; and having spoiled principalities and powers, he made a shew of them openly, triumphing over them in it. Let no man therefore judge you in meat, or in drink, or in respect of an holyday, or of the new moon, or of the sabbath days: which are a shadow of things to come; but the body is of Christ."

Under objection 2 we learned that there are two laws, one moral, the other ceremonial, and that it was only the latter that was abolished by Christ. Under objection 11 we learned that Paul, in Colossians 2:14-17, is speaking of the ceremonial law. Under objection 26 we learned that the ceremonial law had certain annual sabbaths. Hence we may properly conclude that Paul, in the passage before us, is not even referring to the seventh-day Sabbath.

If Paul here was referring to the weekly Sabbath of the Decalogue, then the only conclusion to reach would be that in the Christian Era there is no weekly holy day of rest. And does Christendom, in general, believe that? No. The sternly enforced Sunday laws of the different Christian lands in all the generations past, provide militant, embarrassing, even shameful, proof that the general belief is that a weekly holy day is proper, right, and Scriptural. And in many instances Sunday advocates have employed as first proof in defense of that belief, the fact that the Decalogue commands a weekly holy day. The very fact that they have read "first day of the week" into the command only proves the more eloquently that they believe that the obligation to keep a weekly holy day must be found in the fourth command of the Decalogue.

Though Seventh-day Adventists have consistently denounced Sunday laws as an infringement of conscience, they have gladly conceded that in general those who enacted these laws acted in good faith, and in harmony with what they thought the Bible commanded. But the Sabbath objector, unless he claims he has just discovered the true meaning of Paul's words that eluded all his Sundaykeeping forebears, must charge those forebears with rank hypocrisy and of flying in the face of Scripture. Paul says, "Let no man therefore judge you . . . in respect of an holyday, . . . or of the sabbath days." But Sunday laws judge men in respect of a holy day, a sabbath day, and with a vengeance.

No, Christendom in general has never believed that Paul's declaration wiped out every distinction in days and that in the Christian Era a person may, with complete spiritual immunity, refrain from considering any day holy. True, some theologians, as certain Bible commentaries reveal, have thought they found in Paul's words the justification for turning their back on the seventh-day Sabbath, but they have always hastened to add that in the Christian Era we have a new sabbath. But that is playing fast and loose with Paul's words. He does not even intimate that a new holy day is to be substituted. He speaks only of the abolition of certain holy days. Hence, honest reasoning demands that if we are obligated to keep a holy day in the Christian Era, that obligation must be found in a law that is above and beyond the range of Paul's declaration. And that law is the Decalogue, which Paul did not have under discussion in this passage in Colossians.

That Paul was not discussing the Sabbath of the Decalogue is freely admitted by some of the best of Bible commentators, and with their comments we close this discussion:

Says the Methodist, Adam Clarke, in comment on Colossians 2:16:

"There is no intimation here that the *Sabbath* was done away, or that its moral use was superseded, by the introduction of Christianity."

Jamieson, Fausset, and Brown, in their comment on this text, note first that the annual sabbaths "have come to an end with the Jewish services to which they belonged." Then they add immediately:

"The weekly sabbath rests on a more permanent foundation, having been instituted in Paradise to commemorate the completion of creation in six days."

Albert Barnes, eminent Presbyterian Bible commentator, observes:

"There is no evidence from this passage [Col. 2:16] that he [Paul] would teach that there was no obligation to observe *any* holy time, for there is not the slightest reason to believe that he meant to teach that one of the ten commandments had ceased to be binding on mankind. . . . He had his eye on the great number of days which were observed by the Hebrews as festivals, as a part of their ceremonial and typical law, and not to the *moral* law, or the ten commandments. No part of the moral law—no one of the ten commandments could be spoken of as '*a shadow* of good things to come.' These commandments are, from the nature of moral law, of perpetual and universal application."

# Objection 30

**"The word 'Sabbath' occurs some sixty times in the New Testament. In every case except one, the Adventists admit that the weekly Sabbath is meant. In the one case, however, where the word, in the Greek, is the same (Col. 2:16), they insist that it means something different. Why is this so? Is it not because they know that this one verse . . . completely shatters all their arguments for Sabbathkeeping by Christians?"**

The eminent Bible commentators quoted at the close of the preceding objection "admit that the weekly Sabbath is meant" in some fifty-nine instances, as reference to their comments on those texts reveals, but they likewise declare that this sixtieth instance deals with the annual sabbaths! Yet they have no interest in proving anything in behalf of the seventh-day Sabbath. We quoted *Sundaykeeping* commentators!

It is no secret that the Greek word translated "sabbath" in the New Testament means simply "rest" and in itself gives no indication as to what *kind* of rest or what *day* of rest. The Greek-speaking Christians gave the right meaning to the word by the context in which they found it, even as we do with many words. To repeat an illustration earlier given: The word "day" requires a context to make certain the period of time meant. We may mean the light part of the twenty-four hours; we may mean the whole twenty-four hours; or we may mean an indefinite period, as "this is a great day and age we are living in." Now, simply because a writer uses the word "day" fifty-nine times to mean twenty-four hours, provides no proof in itself that his sixtieth use of the word must mean the same time period! Context must decide. If a writer, for example, said that "the day ended as the western horizon glowed red with the reflected light of a setting sun," the context of red sky and setting sun would be sufficient to determine that he was not using the word "day" to mean twenty-four hours, but only the

168

daylight part of it. The writer's fifty-nine or five hundred and fifty-nine previous uses of the word to mean twenty-four hours would not affect our conclusion that here was an instance where only the daylight part of the day was meant.

Actually the facts in the case before us call for the very opposite conclusion from that which the Sabbath opposer seeks to establish. He admits that some fifty-nine other references to "sabbath" in the New Testament speak of the seventh-day Sabbath. None of these references even suggest that the Sabbath had lost, was in process of losing, or was going to lose any of the sanctity that had thus far distinguished it. Hence, if the New Testament teaches Sabbath abolition, that teaching must be found in this lone sixtieth reference.

We do not recall at the moment that anyone has seriously attempted to find a reason for Sabbath abolition in any of the other fifty-nine references. Sabbath opposers confine themselves to this sixtieth reference to "sabbath" in Colossians 2:16 and frankly rely on "this one verse" "completely" to shatter all the Adventist "arguments for Sabbathkeeping by Christians."

That is a very great weight to place on one text, but it is enlightening to know that the discussion of the word "sabbath" in the New Testament can be narrowed down to this. If this text does really thus teach Sabbath abolition, what a shock must have come to the Christian believers scattered over the Roman Empire as the Colossian letter slowly made its way, in the form of handwritten duplicates, to the different churches. We might imagine their saying something on this order: "We have read the Scriptures from Moses to Malachi, and we find there a command to keep holy the seventh-day Sabbath of the Decalogue. We have read numerous references to the Sabbath in the writings of the apostles, but they have given no hint that the Sabbath was abolished at the cross. Why have they failed to do this in all their fifty-nine references to it?"

But would those early Christians have found it necessary to raise such a question? No. They had read in the writings of the apostles that the ceremonial rites and services of the Jews were abolished by Christ, and they knew, as almost anyone in the Roman Empire knew, that those services included regulations on meats and drinks and various feasts, new moons, and annual sabbaths. Therefore, when they read in the Colossian letter that the ritual of meats and drinks, new moons, sabbaths, et cetera, was abolished what would they naturally conclude, in view of the context, were the sabbaths Paul meant? Honestly, now, what *would* be their conclusion? The same conclusion we would reach after we had read in a book fifty-nine references to "day" as meaning twenty-four hours, and then read the sixtieth reference to "day" in the context of red sky and setting sun. They would conclude that a *different* time period was meant, that Paul was speaking of *annual* sabbaths.

# Objection 31

Many who were converted to Christianity in apostolic times came out of heathenism and lived in countries where Sabbathkeeping was unknown. "It would have been necessary to enjoin them as to the particular day they should observe. But the New Testament is absolutely silent on the point." If the Sabbath is still in force, why was it not mentioned in Christ's reply to the rich young ruler (Matt. 19:17-27), or in the gospel commission (Matt. 28:19), or on the day of Pentecost (Acts 2), or in the decision of the council at Jerusalem (Acts 15)?

This is simply a variant form of a claim made in connection with a number of objections. The churchman who in false zeal opposes the Sabbath, also generally believes most ardently that the first day of the week holds a spiritually unique place in the week. He sees vast import in the fact that the New Testament writers nowhere reissue a command in behalf of the Sabbath. But he sees nothing impressive or damaging in the fact that both the Old and the New Testament writers are silent about a command in behalf of Sunday. The complete silence of *all* the Scriptures concerning a Sunday command sounds more impressive to him in *behalf* of *Sunday* than the awesome thunder of Sinai, echoing down through the pages of Holy Writ, sounds in *behalf* of the *Sabbath*. One is almost tempted to believe that the objector's repeated insistence that the New Testament issues no new command for the Sabbath is for the purpose of drawing attention away from the fact that the Bible, from Genesis to Revelation, is completely silent about a command for Sunday.

But what about those converts from heathenism who needed instruction as to a weekly holy day? Undoubtedly they did need instruction. Hence if Sunday were the day to keep holy, where is the record of apostolic instruction on it? Except for 1 Corinthians 16:1-3, which instructs the Corinthians to lay by some funds on the first day of the week for a future offering for the poor at Jerusalem, there is no suggestion as to anything of any kind, secular or religious, that the apostles ever asked any Christian church to do or not to do on the first day of the week. (See under objection 42 for a discussion of 1 Corinthians 16:1-3.) This is strange indeed. No command, no instruction! One searches the New Testament in vain, not simply for a Sunday command, but for any formula of service, any suggestion of holiness to the day, any counsel on the proper program of living for that day. The point bears repeating: The churches raised up among the heathen would never have stumbled onto the idea of Sunday sacredness in any form from reading what the apostles wrote.

But what of the seventh-day Sabbath? They would have read fifty-nine references to it, and those references pictured it as the weekly day of worship, when Paul and others might most often have preached. They would have read Luke's description of it as "the sabbath day according to the commandment." Luke 23:56. Most of these fifty-nine references are almost casual; that is, they take for granted that their hearers are conversant with the Sabbath. But how would those Christian converts from heathenism have been conversant with the Sabbath unless they had been instructed concerning it?

Paul said near the close of his ministry that he had preached "none other things than those which the prophets and Moses did say should come." Acts 26:22. In that he followed the course outlined by our resurrected Lord who, "beginning at Moses and all the prophets," expounded "in all the scriptures the things concerning himself." Luke 24:27. The disciples who thus listened saw there the pattern for their preaching. The Scriptures they expounded, of course, were what we call the Old Testament.

Now, in order for Paul or the other apostles to teach the Old Testament, they would need to carry it with them. And as they won converts would they do less than exhort them to read those Scriptures? This conclusion is irresistible. Christianity has always been the religion of the Book, a revealed religion. We need hardly

172

add that when those converts read the Scriptures they would certainly find the Sabbath right in the heart of the Decalogue. Therefore they would most certainly know of it and would understand the fifty-nine references to it in the New Testament. Why should the apostles need to reissue a Sabbath command? In the light of all this the argument based on the silence of the New Testament in the matter of a new command becomes pointless.

But in view of the fact that the converts from heathenism would naturally conclude from the Scriptures that the Sabbath should be kept holy, how strange is the silence of the apostles about the matter of the abolition of it, if as the Sabbath objector contends, they actually did preach its abolition.

Paul told the elders of the church of Ephesus that he had "kept back nothing that was profitable." Acts 20:20. But where in his letter to the Ephesians does he inform them that the seventh-day Sabbath of the Decalogue is abolished? He does speak of the abolition of certain "commandments contained in ordinances." Eph. 2:15. But we have found that he was not speaking of the Decalogue. (See under objection 11.) He "kept back nothing that was profitable" to any church he raised up. But in all the letters he wrote to those churches there is only *one* reference in *one* letter to the abolition of certain "sabbath days," and we have found that he was there speaking of annual sabbaths. (See under objection 29.)

We do find Paul's writings bristling with discussions of the ceremonial ritual that God gave to Israel at Sinai. The heart of the controversy between him and the Judaizing leaders was the rite of circumcision. He declared repeatedly that circumcision was not needful, that it was done away in the Christian Era. Because of this Jewish mobs tried to kill him.

Lay alongside this the fact that the Jews were perhaps even more fanatically attached to the Sabbath than they were to circumcision. They were ready to kill Christ simply because He healed a man on the Sabbath.

Hence, if Paul or the other apostles had gone about declaring that the Sabbath was abolished, even as they declared that circumcision was, would not a furor have been raised, and would not something of that furor have echoed through the pages of the New Testament, even as the circumcision controversy did? But we look in vain for it. Of the total of some sixty times that the word "sabbath" is used in the New Testament, only one, we repeat, declares that certain "sabbath days" are abolished. And the only instances where the word "sabbath" is used in the setting of controversy are those in the Gospels, where Christ sought, not to show that the Sabbath was abolished, but to show what was "lawful" to do on that day. Again we see that the silence of the apostles, instead of being an argument against the Sabbath, is rather a powerful argument that the apostles never spoke against it.

In the light of these facts it is hardly necessary to examine in any detail the specific texts cited in the objection. We are supposed to conclude that because the Sabbath command is not mentioned in these texts, therefore it is not in force in the Christian Era. By the same logic we should therefore conclude that if any other of the Ten Commandments are not mentioned in these texts, they likewise are not in force. In Matthew 19:17-27 the commandment against idolatry, for example, is not mentioned. Shall we conclude that it is no longer binding? In the gospel commission, Matthew 28:19, none of the commandments are mentioned. On the day of Pentecost Peter preached a great sermon, Acts 2:14-40, but he mentions *none* of the commandments. At the Jerusalem council the apostles gave this order: "That ye abstain from meats offered to idols and from blood, and from things strangled, and from fornication: from which if ye keep yourselves, ye shall do well. Fare ye well." Acts 15:29. Not many commandments mentioned here either.

Now the Sabbath objector agrees that nine of the Ten Commandments are binding in the Christian Era, even though he cannot find those nine all listed in these texts. Why may not we be permitted to believe that the fourth is also binding, even though it is not mentioned in these texts?

174

# Objection 32

**If Paul were living, he would offer the same condemnation of Seventh-day Adventists that he did of the Galatians. (See Gal. 4:9, 10.)**

The passage in Galatians reads as follows: "But now, after that ye have known God, or rather are known of God, how turn ye again to the weak and beggarly elements, whereunto ye desire again to be in bondage? Ye observe days, and months, and times, and years."

We have earlier found (under objection 7) that the yoke of bondage was the endless series of ceremonial rites, particularly in view of the fact that those rites had been heavily encrusted with rabbinical refinements and additions. It is evident that Paul is not here speaking of the moral law, for it deals only with one day, the seventh-day Sabbath. He must be speaking of the ceremonial law, for only there do we find commands on how to "observe days, and months, and times, and years."

How could Paul possibly say that the seventh-day Sabbath was one of "the weak and beggarly elements," and that the keeping of it would bring men into "bondage"? Paul was the man who instructed Timothy that "all scripture is given by inspiration of God, and is profitable for doctrine, for reproof, for correction, for instruction in righteousness." 2 Tim. 3:16. Therefore Paul would be guided in his appraisal of the Sabbath by the prophets' appraisal of it. Isaiah, for example, declares that the Lord calls the Sabbath "my holy day," and then appeals to us to call it "a delight, the holy of the Lord, honourable." Isa. 58:13.

Christ died on the cross to redeem men from sin and to sanctify them, to blot out from this world everything that relates to sin, and to restore this world to its original Edenic glory. But why would Christ seek to abolish the Sabbath, which came forth blessed and sanctified from God's hand in the sinless beauty of

Eden, was held before God's people as the sign of His sanctifying power, was commended to the "sons of the stranger" (Isa. 56:6), as well as to the Jews, and will be kept in Eden restored? Sabbath objectors make no serious attempt to face squarely this question.

There is another question we would ask: If Paul would indict those who keep the Sabbath, why would he not also indict those who keep Sunday? Is there not as much the keeping of a day in the one case as in the other?

But let us take the matter a little further. Paul's indictment is against those who "observe" a variety of days and seasons, and so on. Seventh-day Adventists are marked by the fact that they do not observe a variety of holy days or seasons, for example, Good Friday or Easter, though we attach vast significance to the death and resurrection of our Lord. We keep only one day holy. Plainly Paul would not indict us along with the Galatians.

We wonder, however, what he might say if he could speak today to the Sundaykeeping world that is giving ever-increasing attention to a variety of religious days and seasons. One current Protestant paper, under the title "The Increasing Observing of Lent," remarks: "Lent has a most important place in the calendar of the Roman Catholic, the Greek Catholic, the Episcopalian, and the Lutheran Churches," and then goes on to add that "in our churches there is an increasing acknowledgment of Lent." Another Protestant paper is not content simply to promote the observance of Sunday, Good Friday, Easter, Christmas, and Lent, but wishes to add another. It regrets that "Ascension Day has not bulked more largely in Christian thought and the calendar of the churches." The editorial states what it believes the observance of Christmas has done for men, and likewise the observance of Easter and other days, and goes on from this to argue that the observance of Ascension Day would further enrich the spiritual life of Christians.

This is the same kind of reasoning that governed the theologians of the Middle Ages when they were adding one holy day after another, and building the structure of the Catholic Church that is so sweepingly indicted by God's prophets. But we are not quoting from a medieval Catholic writer but from an editorial in a twentieth-century Protestant paper, the *Christian Statesman*. This is the official organ of the National Reform Association, which so earnestly strives to obtain rigid Sunday laws throughout the whole United States, and which declares that it speaks for a great percentage of the Protestant bodies of the country!

If Paul's words have a present-day application, we leave the unbiased reader to judge as to which group would be indicted, Seventh-day Adventists or the great Sundaykeeping Protestant bodies?

In view of the fact that Adventists are often considered defective in their Christianity because they do not observe Good Friday, Easter, the Lenten season, or any special days or seasons, we would ask: Why should Adventists be indicted for failing to observe a variety of days and seasons, and at the same time be indicted by Paul as being guilty of that very thing?

# Objection 33

The Old Testament prophets foretold that the time was coming when the Sabbath would be done away. (See, for example, Hosea 2:11.) In Amos 8:5 the question is asked, "When will the sabbath be gone?" The prophet answers that this would take place when the sun went down at noon and the earth was darkened in a clear day. (Amos 8:9.) The earth was thus darkened when Jesus was crucified. Hence the Sabbath came to an end at the cross.

To the credit of Sunday advocates it should be said at the outset that this objection is not frequently presented against the Sabbath. Hosea 2:11 reads as follows: "I will also cause all her mirth to cease, her feast days, her new moons, and her sabbaths, and all her solemn feasts." Place alongside this the word of the Lord through Isaiah: "To what purpose is the multitude of your sacrifices unto me? saith the Lord: I am full of the burnt offerings of rams, and the fat of fed beasts; and I delight not in the blood of bullocks, or of lambs, or of he goats. When ye come to appear before me, who hath required this at your hand, to tread my courts? Bring no more vain oblations; incense is an abomination unto me; the new moons and sabbaths, the calling of assemblies, I cannot away with; it is iniquity, even the solemn meeting. Your new moons and your appointed feasts my soul hateth: they are a trouble unto me; I am weary to bear them. And when ye spread forth your hands, I will hide mine eyes from you: yea, when ye make many prayers, I will not hear: your hands are full of blood. Wash you, make you clean; put away the evil of your doings from before mine eyes; cease to do evil. . . . If ye be willing and obedient, ye shall eat the good of the land." Isa. 1:11-19.

Here is a picture of backslidden Israel given over to idolatry and every evil, yet observing the forms of the ritual of days and seasons given to them at Sinai. Thus they made mockery of divinely ordained services. In return God declared that fearful judgments were to come upon them. No more would they engage in a round of services; no more would mirth or the sound of gladness be heard in the land. The very "trees" and "vines" were to be destroyed. (Hosea 2:12.) God would shut His eyes from seeing them and His ears from hearing them.

And when were these fearful prophecies uttered? Well in advance of the destruction of the kingdom of Israel, with its capital in Samaria, and the taking into Babylonian captivity of the kingdom of Judah, with its capital at Jerusalem. In that fearful destruction and captivity Bible commentators find adequate fulfillment of these prophecies. But these judgments came on Judah and Israel several centuries *before* the cross. Thus the Sabbath objector would have the Sabbath ending more than half a millennium too soon to fit his theory that at the cross the Sabbath ended and Sunday took its place.

Not the abolition of the Sabbath, or of any religious service for that matter, is foretold by these texts, but rather the abolition of a rebellious nation.

Now, what of the question asked in Amos 8:5? The passage, including the immediately preceding verse, reads thus: "Hear this, O ye that swallow up the needy, even to make the poor of the land to fail, saying, When will the new moon be gone, that we may sell corn? and the sabbath, that we may set forth wheat, making the ephah small, and the shekel great, and falsifying the balances by deceit?"

Nothing was allowed to be sold on the Sabbath. Greedy, godless merchants desired to take up their traffic as soon as possible again. So they inquired as to when the Sabbath would be gone. To say that such a question is directed toward the prophet Amos or that the questioners desire to know when the Sabbath will be abolished, is to say something patently without foundation and contrary to the evident facts.

And what of the claim that Amos predicted the darkening of the sky at the crucifixion of Christ? Immediately after he has described the greed and iniquity of the Israelites, Amos tells of the judgments that are to come on them: "And it shall come to pass in that day, saith the Lord God, that I will cause the sun to go down at noon, and I will darken the earth in the clear day: and I will turn your feasts into mourning, and all your songs into lamentation." Verses 9, 10.

Let Amos interpret his own words. Three chapters earlier he discusses these same judgments and says, "Woe unto you that desire the day of the Lord! to what end is it for you? the day of the Lord is darkness, and not light. . . . Shall not the day of the Lord be darkness, and not light? even very dark, and no brightness in it? I hate, I despise your feast days, and I will not smell in your solemn assemblies." "Therefore will I cause you to go into captivity beyond Damascus, saith the Lord, whose name is The God of hosts." Amos 5:18-21, 27.

It is evident that this darkening of the sun was a synonym for the blackness of God's judgment, and the sun's going down at noon on a clear day, a figurative way of describing the suddenness and unexpectedness of that awful judgment. And this judgment, this sudden blackness, that was to envelop Israel was their being led "into captivity beyond Damascus." That judgment fell on the kingdom of Israel about seven hundred years before the cross.

When Nehemiah, long afterward, gathered a remnant of the Israelites that had been taken captive into Babylon, and sought to restore Jerusalem, one of the things he endeavored most valiantly to do was to revive the true keeping of the Sabbath. (See Neh. 13:15-22.)

# Objection 34

The psalmist prophesied that there would be a new day of worship. (See Ps. 118:22-24.) The "day" mentioned in Psalms 118:24 can refer only to Sunday, the day on which Christ became the headstone of the corner.

Psalms 118:22-24 reads as follows: "The stone which the builders refused is become the head stone of the corner. This is the Lord's doing; it is marvellous in our eyes. This is the day which the Lord hath made; we will rejoice and be glad in it."

The objector's line of reasoning is this: (1) Christ became "the head stone of the corner" by the act of rising from the grave. (2) He rose on Sunday. (3) The statement, "This is the day which the Lord hath made," applies to a twenty-four-hour day, and the day referred to is Sunday. (4) Therefore, "we will rejoice and be glad" on Sunday by keeping it as God's holy day.

But nowhere does the Bible say that Christ became the "head stone of the corner" by the act of rising from the dead. In the New Testament, Christ is frequently referred to as "the chief corner stone" (Eph. 2:20; 1 Peter 2:6) and as "the head of the body, the church" (Col. 1:18). But these references do not narrow down to any one act of Christ's life, or to any moment of time, His acquiring of this title of headship. The context of Colossians 1:18 would indicate that if any one act is focused upon, it is the death of Christ, which occurred on the sixth day of the week.

It is true that the reference to Christ as "the head over all things to the church," in Ephesians 1:22, is found in a context that mentions the resurrection of Christ. But a reading of the context from verse 18 to verse 23 shows that Paul is discussing a whole series of important events in connection with Christ, events which are given in sequence, with no warrant for concluding that they are to be understood as having occurred on the same day. We

181

read that God (a) "raised him from the dead," (b) "set him at his own right hand in the heavenly places," (c) "put all things under his feet," and (d) "gave him to be the head over all things to the church."

An examination of Paul's further writings indicates clearly that Christ's sitting at God's "right hand" is in His capacity as our High Priest: "We have such an high priest, who is set on the right hand of the throne of the Majesty in the heavens; a minister of the sanctuary, and of the true tabernacle, which the Lord pitched, and not man." Heb. 8:1, 2. Certainly Christ did not enter on His work of ministry that Sunday morning He rose. He was with His disciples on earth for forty days after His resurrection.

Further, the phrase, "put all things under his feet," brings to our mind another passage of Paul's, in which he says of Christ: "But this man, after he had offered one sacrifice for sins for ever, sat down on the right hand of God; from *henceforth expecting till* his enemies be made his footstool." Heb. 10:12, 13.

Without taking the matter further, it is evident that Paul's statement in Ephesians 1:22, concerning Christ's headship of the church, does not warrant the conclusion that the acquiring of His headship took place on the Sunday of the resurrection. On the contrary, the related passages in Hebrews would rather indicate it involved a sequence of events over a period of time.

Sometimes another text is quoted by the advocates of this Sunday theory who seek to prove that Christ became the chief cornerstone precisely on the first day of the week, the resurrection Sunday. That text reads, "Jesus Christ our Lord, which was made of the seed of David according to the flesh; and declared to be the Son of God with power, according to the spirit of holiness, by the resurrection from the dead." Rom. 1:3, 4. That passage parallels the one in Ephesians that we have just analyzed, particularly Ephesians 1:19, 20. Hence it gives no further proof in support of the theory.

Any theory that depends for its strength on focusing everything on one act of Christ's life, to the exclusion of all other acts, may rightly be viewed with suspicion. Christ's great plan for the salvation of man depends on a whole series of momentous events. The incarnation was an event of vast significance; without it there would have been no plan of salvation. The crucifixion holds a similar position, for without the shedding of blood there is no remission of sins. The resurrection is likewise of vast importance; for if Christ is not raised, then we who die in Christ must perish. Finally, the Second Advent is imperative to the success of the plan of salvation; for it is then that Christ comes "without sin unto salvation" to fulfill His promise "that where I am, there ye may be also." (Heb. 9:28; John 14:3.) It is then that He becomes King of kings and Lord of lords and sees all His enemies put down under His feet.

Only the tremendous urge to load the first day of the week with sufficient sanctity to command reverence for it, can explain the theological reasoning of those who seek to convey the impression that everything of significance for the salvation of man occurred on the resurrection morning. The Bible conveys no such impression. True, the Scriptures give profound meaning to the opened tomb; but they also give similar meaning to Bethlehem's manger, Calvary's cross, and the rolling back of the heavens at the last day to reveal the face of our Lord.

So much for the part of the argument that would narrow down the fulfillment of Psalms 118:22 to a certain twenty-four-hour day, the resurrection day. Let us now inquire as to what the psalmist meant when he said, "This is the day which the Lord hath made; we will rejoice and be glad in it."

An examination of the verses that immediately precede and follow the passage under consideration reveals that the psalmist is here concerned with the broad subject of salvation. Verse 21 reads thus, "I will praise thee: for thou hast heard me, and art become my salvation." Verse 25 reads, "Save now, I beseech thee, O Lord: O Lord, I beseech thee, send now prosperity."

Compare with this the New Testament comment by Peter: "This is the stone which was set at nought of you builders, which is become the head of the corner. Neither is there salvation in any other." Acts 4:11, 12.

The natural conclusion, therefore, concerning the statement, "This is the day which the Lord hath made," is that the psalmist is speaking of the day of salvation that would be ushered in most definitely by the Advent of our Lord as the Saviour of men. The Bible frequently uses the word "day" to describe an indefinite period of time. For example, we read of the "day of the Lord," the "day of judgment." We know these cover very much more than a twenty-four-hour period. Likewise, the Bible speaks of the "day of salvation." In Isaiah's prophetic writings we read, "Thus saith the Lord, In an acceptable time have I heard thee, and in a day of salvation have I helped thee." Isa. 49:8.

Note, now, Paul's comment on this prophetic declaration as he addresses the church at Corinth. After quoting a portion of Isaiah 49:8, the apostle affirms, "Behold, now is the accepted time; behold, now is the day of salvation." 2 Cor. 6:2. According to the apostle Paul, the "day of salvation," of which the prophets had written, was "now," when he was writing to the church at Corinth, many years after the day of the resurrection. It is evident that he understood the "day" to refer to the whole period of God's grace, which was to continue on until the close of man's probation.

In a discussion with the unbelieving Jews, Christ spoke of those who were the servants of sin, and of how they could be saved from sin: "If the Son therefore shall make you free, ye shall be free indeed." John 8:36. The Jews did not understand this divine plan of salvation, and scornfully declared that they were Abraham's children and were never in bondage to anyone. Then Christ replied, "Your father Abraham rejoiced to see my day: and he saw it, and was glad." Verse 56. Abraham, with prophetic eye, looked forward to the very time when Christ would stand before men to offer salvation to them, and Abraham "rejoiced." Quite evidently the "day of salvation" began before the resurrection.

Now let us view together the statement by the psalmist and the statement concerning Abraham, remembering that the psalmist

184

and our spiritual father Abraham both looked forward to the coming of the Messiah:

"This is the day which the Lord hath made; we will rejoice and be glad in it." Ps. 118:24.

"Your father Abraham rejoiced to see my day: and he saw it, and was glad." John 8:56.

The parallel is perfect. We need not search further to discover the meaning of the psalmist's words.

As stated in the opening paragraph, some earnest Sunday advocates, hard pressed for a Bible command to keep holy the first day of the week, fasten on this passage in the Psalms, and declare that the Bible commands us to "rejoice and be glad" on Sunday. The Bible reveals that Abraham "rejoiced" and "was glad" in relation to the "day" of which the psalmist spoke. Is there any Sunday advocate so courageous as to affirm that Abraham kept Sunday? What more need be said?

# Objection 35

Noted astronomers have discovered that our world is twenty-four hours behind the rest of the universe in point of time. The Bible record of Joshua's long day—twenty-three hours and twenty minutes—and of the turning back of the sun forty minutes in Hezekiah's day, accounts for this twenty-four hours. Hence both Jews and Seventh-day Adventists are wrong about the time of the Sabbath. Our blessed Lord brought the Sabbath and the first day of the week together, merging them into the glorious day on which He arose from the dead, the day we celebrate as the Sabbath.

Briefly, the answer to this remarkable objection is as follows:

1. It proves too much, which is the most fatal weakness of any piece of reasoning. According to it the Sabbath and Sunday were merged long before the resurrection. They were virtually merged at the time of Joshua, with a forty-minute refinement at the time of Hezekiah. That is another way of saying that the Jews actually kept Sunday. And if that be so, then certainly most Christians today are not keeping either the Sabbath or Sunday, for they are keeping the day that follows immediately after the day held sacred by Jews.

2. Is it reasonable to believe that God would answer the prayer of His servant Joshua in such a manner as to confuse the reckoning of time so that it would be difficult, if not impossible, to give obedience to the Sabbath law? Sundaykeepers today ring the changes on what they describe as the legalistic quality of the Jewish dispensation, declaring that everything was governed then by rigid law in contrast to our present period of grace. And they never fail to remind us that the Sabbath law was so exacting in those times that a man could be put to death for breaking that law.

But now, behold, we are asked to conclude that Moses had scarcely gone to his rest before the Lord worked a miracle through Joshua that broke the cycle of time and certainly gave to the

Sabbath an elasticity that has never revealed itself in the Christian Era. At least no one has ever claimed that the sun has been made to stand still in the Christian age.

We read of Nehemiah's holy jealousy for God's day that led him to close the gates of Jerusalem as it began to grow dark on the eve of the Sabbath. What a fine opportunity that would have been for his opponents to remind him that only a short while before, in the days of Hezekiah, there was a difference of forty minutes in the arrival of the Sabbath, and that therefore it was quite an elastic affair anyway, and no one should be exercised about the matter. But we find no record of anything like this occurring in the dispute between Nehemiah and those who were breaking the Sabbath. We do find references there and elsewhere throughout the Old Testament that discuss the divine obligation of the Sabbath and the penalties that would descend upon the disobedient. Neither Nehemiah nor any other of the inspired writers were aware of shifting time. Their messages all breathe the conviction that the Sabbath is a fixed day, the reckoning of which can be easily computed, so definite indeed that the guilty have no excuse, and should justly suffer dire punishment.

3. The closing verses of the twenty-third chapter of Luke and the opening verse of the twenty-fourth chapter forever settle the question of the relationship of a certain day to the Sabbath command. Christians generally are in agreement that Christ was crucified on Friday, and that He rose on Sunday. The day in between is described as "the sabbath day according to the commandment." The language is simple and explicit. Anyone who reads the Sabbath commandment and wishes to free himself from all uncertainties of theological discussion has only to read this passage in Luke.

We need not be astronomers, we need not have a knowledge of all past time, or be able to settle all the dark questions about chronology, in order to be clear concerning the Sabbath commandment. Luke, who along with the other Gospel writers gave us the inspired record of the Saviour on which our Christian religion depends, informs us that there is a certain day which is "the sabbath day according to the commandment." It is the day following this that Sundaykeepers revere. Luke knew nothing about a merging of days because of Joshua and Hezekiah. The day that Christ lay in the grave is "the sabbath day according to the commandment," and the next day is described simply as "the first day of the week."

4. However, someone may inquire at this point, "But what are you going to do about the Bible record concerning Joshua and Hezekiah?" We don't believe we need to do anything about the record. We are very willing to let it stand, and we believe it. We insist only that all the rest of the record in the Bible also be permitted to stand, such as the references that have been cited. The Bible is always its own best interpreter. If, despite amazing and baffling miracles, we still find God's prophets commanding obedience to a definite holy day, and Luke informing us that the seventh day of the week is the Sabbath day according to the commandment, then we are in no darkness whatever as to how to give explicit obedience to God's command. The shadow on Hezekiah's sundial was never intended to cast a shadow on the Sabbath, nor did God work a bright miracle to help an ancient warrior in fighting the battles of the Lord so that modern warriors might find weapons to aid them in their fight against God's Sabbath command. What an irony if the additional light given on that eventful day of battle long ago should throw darkness ever afterward on the Sabbath, indeed, should give us neither a definitely defined Sabbath day nor a clear-cut Sunday, but something that was forty minutes from being either until Hezekiah's day.

5. It is always a favorite strategy in debate to claim that eminent scientists are on your side. Perhaps some astronomer has worked out certain cycles back through the millenniums that lead him to conclude there is a difference of twenty-four hours in time between our world and the rest of the universe. We say "perhaps," for we have never heard of such a discovery. But what of it? We do not have to travel into interstellar space to find a difference

in reckoning. We can cross the Pacific and find a difference of twenty-four hours. Yet no matter on what side of the Pacific a man lives, there seems to be no difficulty in keeping the accurate reckoning of time down through the centuries. In fact, Sunday-keepers in Australia are just as certain that they are keeping the correct first day of the week in cycles of seven from the resurrection day as are those in the mother country, England. Indeed, in both countries the certainty is so great that Sunday laws have been enacted to enforce observance of the day. It is bad enough for Sabbath opponents to attempt to lose the seventh-day Sabbath by traveling around the world, though they never lose Sunday, but what is to be said for the man who seeks to carry us into the uncharted reaches of interstellar space in order to lose God's holy day?

However, we would say right here that for anyone to make a sweeping claim as to the exact relationship in time of our solar system to all the rest of the universe is to make a claim that cannot be substantiated.

6. Finally, it should be remembered that the Bible way of reckoning days is from sunset to sunset. Therefore, the lengthening out of the day in some miraculous way in Joshua's time would not break the cycle of seven in counting days according to Bible reckoning. After all, we are dealing with a Bible institution and not with a question of chronometers or stop watches or even astronomers. We need not explore the mystery of the long day in Joshua's time in order to be sure that we keep the correct time in relation to God's holy Sabbath day.

# Objection 36

**The Sabbath day is abolished, because Paul says that it is all right to consider every day alike in the Christian Era. (See Rom. 14:5.)**

Let us give, first, the passage mentioned, in its context: "Him that is weak in the faith receive ye, but not to doubtful disputations. For one believeth that he may eat all things: another, who is weak, eateth herbs. Let not him that eateth despise him that eateth not; and let not him which eateth not judge him that eateth: for God hath received him. Who art thou that judgest another man's servant? to his own master he standeth or falleth. Yea, he shall be holden up: for God is able to make him stand. One man esteemeth one day above another: another esteemeth every day alike. Let every man be fully persuaded in his own mind. He that regardeth the day, regardeth it unto the Lord; and he that regardeth not the day, to the Lord he doth not regard it. He that eateth, eateth to the Lord, for he giveth God thanks; and he that eateth not, to the Lord he eateth not, and giveth God thanks." Rom. 14:1-6.

Further in the chapter Paul refers to the matter of drink as well as food. (See verses 17, 21.)

Here is a discussion of meats and drinks and various holy days, and Paul's counsel is that no believer should "judge" any other believer in such matters. How strikingly similar is all this to Paul's counsel to the Colossians: "Let no man therefore judge you in meat, or in drink, or in respect of an holyday, or of the new moon, or of the sabbath days." Col. 2:16. But we found (objection 29) that Paul was speaking to the Colossians about the ceremonial law, which dealt with meats and drinks and a variety of holy days, and not at all with the moral law and its seventh-day Sabbath.

But let us look a little more closely at the passage in Romans: "Him that is weak in the faith." What faith? The faith of the gospel of Christ, which teaches that we receive pardon from all our sins and acceptance by our Lord without the works of the law. Some coming in from Jewry, who had long been immersed in the ritual of the ceremonial law, seemed not to have a faith quite strong enough at the outset to grasp fully the truth that we are saved wholly by the grace of God, without any good deed on our part. Others who had stronger faith, or who were Gentiles, and thus never devotees of the ceremonial law, were tempted to judge critically those whose faith was weak and who thus continued to make certain ceremonial distinctions in meats and drinks and holy days. Paul counseled against this critical attitude.

The crux of the passage, of course, is this statement: "One man esteemeth one day above another: another esteemeth every day alike. Let every man be fully persuaded in his own mind." And the key phrase is, "every day alike." The reasoning of the Sabbath objector might be summarized thus: Does not "every day" mean all seven days in the week? And if a believer considers all days "alike," does not that mean he attaches no special sacredness to any day? And does not Paul rebuke those who would pass critical judgment on the believers who thus viewed "every day alike"?

The reader has doubtless noted that some words in the Bible are italicized. The word "alike" is one such word. Now, the italicizing of a word indicates that it is not a translation of a word written by the Bible writer, but a word supplied by the translator in his endeavor best to express what *he* thinks is the meaning of the original writing. This is done in all translations and is inevitable. The scrupulously conscientious Bible translators indicated the instances when they thus supplied a word to round out what they considered was the thought in a text. We have no way of knowing whether Paul, if he were alive and could speak to us in English, would use the word "alike" to round out his sentence. Hence, the very fact that no argument can rightly be built on the single word "alike" reduces at once a great part of the plausibility of the objector's series of questions.

But he will probably still inquire confidently: Does not "every day" mean all seven days in the week? And he may add for good measure: Do not the Scriptures mean just what they say? What he forgets is that though the Bible writers were inspired, they used human language to convey their heavenly instruction. And human language is a very inexact and constantly changing medium for expressing thoughts. We must remember also that all languages have idioms, those singular combinations of words that often defy translation. For example, we may say in colloquial English that certain facts "center around this point." But how can they both "center" and yet be "around"? We understand perfectly what is meant, but we also admit that strictly speaking we cannot make sense out of the phrase if we look at each word separately.

Christ told His disciples that He would "be killed, and after three days rise again." Mark 8:31. The Sabbath objector might plausibly ask: Does not *"after* three days" mean just that? In other words, does it not mean at least the fourth day, or perhaps later? But wait! The Bible also informs us that Christ told His disciples that He must "be killed, and be raised again the third day." Matt. 16:21. Why should not the Sabbath objector now ask: Does not "the third day" mean just that? Only as we concede that the phrase "after three days" was an ancient Jewish idiom that meant to them the equivalent of "third day" can we harmonize the two passages.

Now to borrow our English idiom, the question before us centers around this point of the proper understanding of a Bible phrase. If we carefully compare scripture with scripture, both as to constructions of phrases and as to doctrines taught, we shall have no more trouble over the Bible's literary forms than over those in any other book.

To the Sabbath objector who insists that "every day" in Romans means all the days of the week, we would direct this question: Does the phrase "every day" in Exodus mean all the days of the week? In Exodus 16 is the record of the giving of the manna. The Lord through Moses instructed the Israelites to "go out and gather a certain rate every day." Verse 4. But when the sixth day came they were told to gather a double portion, because on the seventh day they would find none in the field. (Verses 22-26.) But some forgot, or were unmindful, and went out to gather on the seventh day. For this God rebuked them, "How long refuse ye to keep my commandments and my laws?" Verses 27, 28. There is no record that any Israelite replied, "Every day" means every day in the week, and therefore I thought it proper to consider the seventh day just like every other day. Evidently they had not heard of the modern "every day" argument against the Sabbath!

Exodus 16:14 clearly reveals that the word "every" may be understood to have a qualified meaning at times in the Bible. We must read the context and compare scripture with scripture to discover whether there are possible qualifications. The same is true of the word "all." Paul said, "All things are lawful unto me." 1 Cor. 6:12. A libertine, who isolated that statement from all other scripture, might possibly seek to prove thereby that his wastrel life and scandalous deeds were altogether "lawful." But we protest that Paul's statement shall be kept in the context of all scripture. And when we do so we have no trouble with the passage. We understand it to mean that Paul considered that all things within the scope of God's holy law, and the Christian practices of life growing out of it, were lawful to him. It was needful for him to make the all-embracing statement in order to give greatest force to the qualifying words that immediately followed: "But all things are not expedient."

If we view Paul's words in Romans in terms of these simple rules of Bible study, we shall see their true meaning. "Every day" meant every one of the days that were regarded as holy under the *ceremonial* law, which is the law obviously under discussion here. Why should Paul need to interject that he did not mean to include the seventh day, when the seventh-day Sabbath was not part of the controversy before him. Nowhere in all Paul's writings is the seventh-day Sabbath the subject of controversy!

# ANSWERS TO OBJECTIONS

We close with a comment on Romans 14:5 by two commentators. First from the Methodist commentator Adam Clarke:

"Perhaps the word *hemera, day,* is here taken for *time, festival,* and such like, in which sense it is frequently used. Reference is made here to the *Jewish institutions,* and especially their *festivals;* such as the *passover, pentecost, feast of tabernacles, new moons, jubilee,* etc. . . . The converted *Gentile esteemeth every day*—considers that all *time* is the Lord's, and that each day should be devoted to the glory of God; and that those festivals are not binding on him.

"We [the translators] add here *alike,* and make the text say what I am sure was never intended, viz. that there is no distinction of days, not even of the Sabbath: and that every Christian is at liberty to consider even this day to be holy or not holy, as he happens to be persuaded in his own mind."

Second, from the commentary by Jamieson, Fausset, and Brown, so highly regarded in Fundamentalist circles:

"From this passage about the observance of days, ALFORD unhappily infers that such language could not have been used if the *sabbath-law* had been in force under the Gospel in any form. Certainly it could not, if the sabbath were merely one of the Jewish festival days: but it will not do to take this for granted merely because it was observed *under* the Mosaic economy. And certainly if the sabbath was more ancient than Judaism; if, even under Judaism, it was enshrined amongst the eternal sanctities of the Decalogue, uttered, as no other parts of Judaism were, amidst the terrors of Sinai; and if the Lawgiver Himself said of it when on earth, 'The Son of man is Lord *even of the sabbath day*' (see Mark 2.28)—it will be hard to show that the apostle must have meant it to be ranked by his readers amongst those vanished Jewish festival days, which only 'weakness' could imagine to be still in force—a weakness which those who had more light ought, out of love, merely to bear with."

If the Sabbath objector still demurs at the thought of letting words and phrases be understood in certain contexts and according to current usage, we would ask him this question in closing: Do you understand the phrase, "every day clothes" to mean clothes worn *every* day in the week, that is, *all* seven days of the week? If not, why seek to build an anti-Sabbath argument out of "every day" in Romans 14:5?

# Objection 37

The days of creation were not literal, twenty-four-hour days, but long indefinite periods, millions of years in length. Therefore Seventh-day Adventists are not warranted in using the creation story of Genesis 1 as an argument for the holiness of the literal seventh day of the weekly cycle.

If the person setting forth this view is an evolutionist, and thus does not believe that Genesis gives a dependable historical record, there is no point in our trying to provide here an answer. We would need, first, to compass the wide question of the truth of evolution and the dependability of the Bible, and that would carry us far beyond the compass of this book. But such reasoning is sometimes presented by Christian people who believe the Bible. To such, we direct our answer.

The way the matter is stated one might think that Adventists, late in earth's history, thought they discovered a valid connection between creation week and the specific seventh-day Sabbath. The facts are that we found that connection by reading the straightforward narrative in Genesis and the simple declaration of the fourth commandment. "In six days the Lord made heaven and earth, the sea, and all that in them is, and rested the seventh day: wherefore the Lord blessed the sabbath day, and hallowed it." Ex. 20:11.

Certainly when God spoke those words to Israel they understood Him to mean that the seventh day of the weekly cycle had been blessed, for it was that particular day in the cycle they were called upon to honor. Indeed, there would have been no point to the command that they should work six days and keep the seventh day of the week, in memory of creation, if creation had not taken place on that same pattern—six days God labored and the seventh day He rested. To make the days of creation long periods is to spoil the parallel that God, not the Adventists, set up between the creation incidents and the weekly cycle of human activity and rest.

This Sabbath objection goes too far. No matter how hard most Sunday advocates seek to prove that the Sabbath is not binding in the Christian Era, they quite uniformly agree that it was binding in the days before Christ. But the objection before us, if true, could have been used by all the good men before the first advent, and hence there would have been no seventh-day Sabbath in all earth's history!

How anyone who accepts the Bible record as true history could think of the creation days as long, indefinite periods, millions of years in length, we cannot understand. Adam was created on the sixth day. He lived only 930 years. Long before those years were totaled he had been driven from the Garden of Eden, and in his sinful state had reared a family. According to the objection, Adam must have lived his whole life within the span of that sixth "day," for 930 is but a small segment of a period that is measured in millions of years. But when God had rested the seventh day and looked back over the week, He blessed that day as a climax to a perfect work. Therefore, no sin had yet entered to mar the earth. How, then, could Adam, who lived sinlessly at least beyond the end of creation week, have lived a grand total of only 930 years, when he had to live through a fraction of the sixth and all of the seventh day of creation, and yet those days were millions of years long?

The whole creation account is written as a simple narrative. There is nothing in the record to suggest that words should not be understood in their ordinary meanings. To each day of that first week there is "the evening and the morning." Indeed, that is how each day is marked off. But "evening" and "morning" belong to twenty-four-hour days, not to long, indefinite periods of millions of years.

On the third day grass, herbs, trees, and other vegetation were brought forth. Now these all require sunlight if they are to thrive. According to the creation narrative the sun appeared the next day. Does that mean millions of years later? If so, then we are confronted with a more amazing miracle than Genesis has been thought to contain—the plant kingdom flourishing for ages without sunlight!

Of the fourth day we read, "And God made two great lights; the greater light to rule the day, and the lesser light to rule the night." Gen. 1:16. Here, obviously, the words "day" and "night" are being used as we use them today. From the beginning of the fourth day the day and night were thus ruled. But according to the record, the length of that fourth day, and of succeeding days, is the same as that for each of the first three days: "The evening and the morning were the fourth day." Verse 19. Hence the question that the objector should answer is this: If on the fourth day and onward "the evening and the morning" mean an ordinary day measured by sun and moon, why should the identical phrase used earlier in the narrative regarding the first three days mean something entirely different? Was part of creation week a long, indefinite period, and the remainder ordinary days?

But why carry the discussion further? For the man who believes that Genesis is history, there can be no doubt that the creation days are literal days. And the "seventh day" is as literal as the others. Some who do not wish to keep that day holy would fain lose it amid the billowing mists of indefinite geological ages. We prefer to believe the straightforward historical narrative, so eloquently summarized by God Himself in the fourth commandment: "In six days the Lord made heaven and earth, . . . and rested the seventh day."

# Objection 38

The phrase, "the seventh day," in the fourth commandment, means simply one day in seven. Therefore I am keeping the spirit of the Sabbath law so long as I keep one day in seven. And is not Sunday one day in seven?

There are some very real reasons why "the seventh day" means a specific day, not simply one day in seven:

1. Those who believe the Bible speak of creation *week* and view the series of events that then occurred as setting in motion the unique time cycle, the seven-day week. Was the Sabbath simply one day in seven in that first week? No, it was the specific seventh day of that week. Why would it become less specific in succeeding weeks and years and centuries?

2. The Sabbath memorializes a certain historical event, the completion of the creation of this world. Memorial days, if they are to have significance, must be anchored to definite points of time. They are intended to recall a particular day or a particular moment of past history. For example, to Americans "the Fourth" means, not the fourth of any month, but the Fourth of July. And why? Because on a certain fourth of July long ago a certain event took place. By law that particular day is set apart in memory of the Declaration of Independence. Now, what would we think of the man who reasoned that "the Fourth" means simply the fourth day of any month, that he can therefore choose some other "fourth" on which to remember some other historical event, and still be keeping the law that sets apart "the Fourth" as a special day for the nation?

But there are Sunday advocates, devout and sincere men, who contend that they are obedient to the fourth commandment, which calls for the keeping of the *seventh* day of the week in honor of the *creation*, when they keep the *first* day of the week in honor of the *resurrection!*

# SABBATH

It is true that the fourth commandment does not say "the seventh day *of the week*" was blessed and sanctified by God as the Sabbath, but simply that "the seventh day" was. Sabbath objectors seek to make capital of this, declaring that the phrase "the seventh day" may therefore justifiably be construed to mean simply one day in seven. But that God intended the phrase, "the seventh day," in the commandment to mean the seventh day of the week will be increasingly evident as we proceed.

3. The Sabbath command refers back to the creation week, and it is in the historical setting of that week that the phrase "the seventh day" of the commandment must therefore be understood. God did not simply rest one day in seven in the creation week. He rested on *the seventh* day of that *week.*

4. No day was so solemnly set before Israel by the prophets of God as the weekly Sabbath day. When certain Israelites went out to gather manna on "the seventh day" they were rebuked. When one of them gathered sticks on the Sabbath day he was stoned. When certain of those who had returned from the Babylonian captivity tried to carry on commerce on the Sabbath they were denounced. Neither Sunday advocate nor Sabbathkeeper today has any doubt in his mind that those Old Testament instances of Sabbathbreaking had to do with a specific day, the seventh day of the week. But the prophets could point only to the fourth commandment to support their fervent admonition to keep holy this certain specific seventh day of the week. Therefore we must conclude that these inspired men of God understood "the seventh day" in the commandment to mean the specific seventh day of the week. And would anyone wish to challenge the ability of the prophets rightly to interpret the meaning of God's commands? Indeed, is it not part of the holy work of God's prophets to make absolutely clear to our finite minds the meaning of His holy commands?

5. Christendom in general believes that our Lord lay in the tomb on the seventh day *of the week.* And how does Luke describe that day? "The sabbath day according to the commandment." Luke

23:56. That one inspired statement is sufficient in itself to settle the question as to what the commandment means when it says that "the seventh day is the Sabbath." It means the seventh day of the week.

6. As already noted, no one has any doubt but that those who lived before Christ were required by God's holy commandment to keep the seventh day of the week. In other words, "the seventh day" in the command unquestionably meant the specific seventh day of the week. Then, what rational ground can be found for claiming that when Christ came, the plain and specific meaning of the commandment suddenly became vague and nonspecific, and now means merely one day in seven? No one at the time of Christ or for almost sixteen hundred years afterward ever thought of making so astounding a claim. Until the year A.D. 1595, Christians, as certainly as the Jews, understood "the seventh day" in the commandment to mean the seventh day of the week. (See page 545 for historical proof.) So far from having any foundation in Scripture, this one-day-in-seven theory was not even heard of until fifteen hundred years after the last of the apostles had gone to his grave.

7. The very phrase "the *seventh* day" makes evident that a particular day, not merely one day in seven, is meant. If we told a friend that we lived in the seventh house in a certain block, what would we think if he began at the first house on the block and knocked at each door until he came to the seventh, explaining at each front door that he was trying to find an old friend who had told him he lived in the seventh house in the block, and that that meant, of course, that he lived in any one of the seven houses? What *would* we think? Yes, and what would our neighbors think of the sort of friends we had?

8. Through the long generations ardent Sunday advocates have succeeded in having placed on the law books of most Christian lands a statute requiring at least nominal observance of Sunday. Often the prime argument in favor of such a law has been that God commands the keeping of a weekly day of rest. The only

command to which they could point was, of course, the fourth command of the Decalogue. If they were reminded that the fourth command calls for honoring the seventh day, not the first, they could escape embarrassment only by replying that the fourth commandment simply means one day in seven. It never occurred to them that if the Bible commands merely that one day in seven be kept holy, they were presumptuous, to say nothing of being inconsistent, in seeking to require all men to rest on a certain specific day. But church history, even down to our very time, grimly records that such Sunday advocates, though they have been willing to let "the seventh day" in God's law mean any day in the week, have been ready to imprison the man who should thus interpret "the first day" in their Sunday law!

Now a word regarding the matter of keeping the spirit of the law. The Bible has much to say about the letter and the spirit, and some have obtained the mistaken idea that the spirit of a law means less than the letter of it, at least as regards divine law, and very particularly as regards God's Sabbath law. It is difficult to understand how such an idea could obtain credence. Perhaps it is due to the fact that the word "spirit" conveys to some minds the thought of vague apparitions, airy, elusive, and shadowy, and that therefore the keeping of the spirit of a law means obeying something that is only a vague and shadowy resemblance of that law.

Nothing could be further from the truth in the matter. When we speak of keeping the "spirit of the law"—and the phrase is not uncommon in our everyday language—we mean keeping that law in its fullest and deepest sense. For example, take the eight-hour labor law found in many States today. An employer may keep the letter of that law, and yet slave-drive his employees so as to get from them in eight hours as much work as he formerly got in nine or ten. We say he has failed to keep the spirit of the law.

Do we mean that if such an employer had kept the spirit of that law, he would have been freed from the letter of it, which definitely declares that eight hours is the maximum that an employee can be required to work in one day? Why, no, of course not. In other words, the keeping of the spirit of a law requires much *more* of a man than the mere keeping of the letter of it.

The Bible provides us with some choice illustrations of how this principle applies to the law of God. In the sermon on the mount Christ explained that the command "Thou shalt not kill" involved much more than refraining from committing actual violence against some person. The man who hates his brother is a murderer. In other words, the spirit of that divine law against killing demands that he shall not hate any man. But there is no one so irrational as to say that in keeping the spirit of this law we are thereby released from obeying the letter of it. What a horrible thought!

How evident that those who keep the spirit of a law go far beyond the letter of it, not by disregarding the letter, but by seeing in the letter a far greater depth of meaning.

# Objection 39

Seventh-day Adventists insist that a particular seventh day, coming down through from creation in cycles of seven, is the day God blessed and therefore the day that all should keep as the Sabbath. But no one now knows what that day is. Besides, calendar changes have confused the reckoning.

Before we take seriously this objection we would like to ask the objector a question: Why do you keep Sunday? If you answer as Sundaykeepers have routinely answered through the centuries, you will say, Because Christ rose on the first day of the week. Indeed, we have never heard any other answer ever given. Then we would ask, Are you sure that you and your spiritual ancestors have been keeping the particular first day of the week that has come down in cycles of seven from the resurrection Sunday? You can hardly answer no, for that would be a dreadful indictment of all your Sundaykeeping forebears who generally succeeded in having men sent to jail if they failed to give due reverence to Sunday. If you answer yes, then what becomes of your contention that time has been lost? Did the first day of the week come down safely through the centuries, but not the seventh day?

Strictly speaking we need not take the discussion further. It should be time enough for us to examine seriously this question of lost or scrambled time when Sunday advocates are ready to admit that they are not sure they are really keeping the first day of the week. But so generally is the lost-time theory brought forth, when all other arguments against the Sabbath are lost, that we should probably give some attention to it.

What proof is offered that time has been lost? None whatever. We are simply supposed to believe that in the long ago everybody woke up one morning and decided that Monday was Tuesday, or something like that. Or perhaps that when the calendar was changed the days of the week became confused.

Of course we do not have a history that tells us all that has happened since creation. But we do know that when we come down to the time of Christ's crucifixion "the sabbath day according to the commandment" was definitely known, and that that day was the day between crucifixion Friday and resurrection Sunday, the seventh day of the weekly cycle. That makes unnecessary our peering into the vistas of time before Christ.

And what of the centuries since Christ? Have calendar changes confused our reckoning of weeks? Fortunately we need be in no doubt. Here are the facts: There has been one change in the calendar since New Testament times, from the Julian to the Gregorian calendar, under which we live today. The change to the new calendar was first made in Spain, Portugal, and Italy in A.D. 1582, under an edict of Pope Gregory XIII. It is for this reason that our present calendar is known as the Gregorian calendar. The correction of the calendar in changing from the old to the new called for the dropping out of ten days from the month of October. The result was that October, 1582, in such countries as made the change at that time, appeared as shown below:

| A.D. 1582 | | OCTOBER | | | | A.D. 1582 |
|---|---|---|---|---|---|---|
| SUN. | MON. | TUE. | WED. | THU. | FRI. | SAT. |
| | 1 | 2 | 3 | 4 | 15 | 16 |
| 17 | 18 | 19 | 20 | 21 | 22 | 23 |
| 24 | 25 | 26 | 27 | 28 | 29 | 30 |
| 31 | | | | | | |

Thursday, the fourth of October, was followed immediately by Friday, the fifteenth. The result was that although certain *days* were removed from the *month*, the order of the days of the *week* was not interfered with. And it is the cycle of the *week* that measures off the Sabbath days for us. As the years passed by, the other nations gradually changed to the Gregorian from the Julian calendar, as the former one was called. And every nation, in making the change, employed the same rule of dropping out days from the month without touching the order of the days of the week.

But the case is even stronger than this. Not only was the week not tampered with in the revision of the calendar, but even the *idea* of breaking the weekly cycle in any way was not *thought* of. Speaking of the variety of plans suggested for the correction of the calendar, the *Catholic Encyclopedia* says, "Every imaginable proposition was made; only one idea was never mentioned, viz., the abandonment of the seven-day week."—Volume 9, p. 251.

Why should time be lost? Who would want to lose it? Civilization and commerce have existed all down through the centuries, and can we not believe that those who lived before us were quite as able to keep count of the days as we? Surely all wisdom and knowledge is not confined to the present century. Furthermore, the accurate keeping of time records is a vital necessity in religious worship, both for Christians and for Jews. Christianity and Judaism have come down through all the centuries since Bible times. They are probably the most definite links binding us to ancient times.

Would it be conceivable that all Christian peoples and Jews would lose the reckoning of the weeks, which would involve confusion for *all* their holy days? And if such a thought be conceivable, could we possibly bring ourselves to believe that *all* the Christians in every part of the world and *all* the Jews in every part of the world would lose exactly the same amount of time? To such incredible lengths must one go in order to maintain the idea that time has been lost!

Look at the question from still another angle. Ask the astronomer whether time has been lost, or whether the weekly cycle has been tampered with. He will tell you simply no.

There is no uncertainty whatever in tracing back the weeks to Bible times; and when we reach there we read that the "sabbath was past" when the "first day of the week"—the resurrection morn —arrived. (Mark 16:1, 2.) If you wait until Sunday to rest and worship, you have missed the Sabbath, for the Word of God declares it is "past."

(See page 553 for a further treatment of this question.)

# Objection 40

Seventh-day Adventists declare that the Sabbath was intended for all men in all lands. But it is evident that it was intended only for the Jews in the little land of Palestine. How could anyone keep the definite seventh-day Sabbath up in the Arctic circle, where there is six months day then six months night? Or how would a person keep track of the order of the days of the week in traveling around the world, for you lose a day if you travel in one direction and gain a day if you travel in the other direction?

Arctic explorers keep a reckoning of the days and weeks and report in their diaries what they did on certain specific days. They tell us that in that strange and almost uninhabited part of the earth it is possible to tell the passing of the days, during the months that the sun is above the horizon, by the changing positions of the sun, and during the months that the sun is below the horizon, by the twilight at noon.

If a Sabbathkeeper should find himself up in that weird world of ice and had any fear that he had lost his reckoning of the weeks, he need only go to a mission conducted for the Eskimos by some Sundaykeeping church and compare his reckoning with theirs! They would keep a reckoning, of course, in order to know when the first day of the week arrived!

And what of the problem of traveling around the world in relation to keeping a correct reckoning of the weeks? Do we really lose or gain a day? Here are the simple facts:

The so-called dropping or adding of a day in circling the earth is only an apparent and not a real loss or gain. Otherwise the most astounding things could happen. For example, twins could cease being twins by the simple expedient of traveling in opposite directions around the world—one gaining a day and the other losing a day! And if one gained and the other lost a day, that would mean that one of the twins was really two days older than the other—and all as the result of one trip around in opposite directions. But what if they were both sea captains, and the route of their respective boats caused them to keep going around the world in opposite directions! Would it not be only a matter of time until one of them would be so many days older than the other that he would be really old enough to be the father rather than the brother?

"How preposterous!" you say. We agree. But that is exactly what would happen if it were true that a person could *really* lose or gain a day by traveling eastward or westward around the world.

The objector will probably now say: "Well, even if you don't really lose or gain days in traveling, the facts are that the people in one part of the world cannot keep the Sabbath at the same moment of time as the people in other parts of the world, because, for example, the people in Europe begin their day several hours earlier than we in America. What are you going to do about that?"

We don't intend to do anything about it. There is no need. The Sabbath commandment says nothing about keeping the Sabbath at the same moment of time everywhere over the earth. It simply commands us to keep "the seventh day." And does not the seventh day arrive everywhere over the earth? It does.

Furthermore, we showed in our examination of the lost-time theory that no time has been lost; that, on the contrary, the cycles of the weeks have come down to us in unbroken succession through the centuries, so that we can be certain as to which is the seventh day of the week. And of course that means we can be as certain in Hong Kong or Cairo as in Washington or London, for the cycles have come down just as faithfully in one place as another.

When we reach any country in our travels we find all the people there—scientists and laymen, Jews, Christians, and infidels —in perfect agreement as to the days of the week. Indeed, this is probably one of the few facts of everyday life in which such a mixed group are in agreement. Ask them separately or collectively, and they will all give the same answer as to when the seventh day of the week arrives.

Then how simple is God's command to keep "the seventh day"!

# Objection 41

The Sabbath was changed from Saturday to Sunday at the time of Christ's resurrection. One of the strong proofs of this is the fact that Christ, after His resurrection, always met with His disciples on that day. A further proof is the fact that the Holy Spirit was poured upon the disciples on Sunday.

Who changed the day? We are asked to believe that Christ did so. But on so important a matter as a weekly holy day we cannot be content simply to presume. We do not have to presume as to the holiness of the seventh day of the week. We have a clear command, often repeated through the writings of the prophets, so that no one might be in doubt, and those who are inclined to forgetfulness might ever be reminded. That is the picture up to the time of Christ. But we look in vain for a command for Sunday-keeping in the New Testament. What warrant have we for believing that suddenly after the time of Christ men would no longer need to be given a clear command as regards the keeping of a holy day, or to be reminded of that command from time to time? What warrant is there for thinking that the followers of God in the Christian Era would just naturally conclude from a combination of circumstances that two most important events had taken place: (1) The explicit command of God to keep the seventh day had been revoked; and (2) a new command, for the keeping of the first day, was now in force?

Only one text in the New Testament speaks of the abolition of "sabbath days" (Col. 2:16), but we have found that this text is not speaking of the weekly Sabbath, as eminent Sundaykeeping Bible commentators admit. (See under objection 29.) And, as just stated, no text in the New Testament contains a command for Sunday. Yet despite all this, we are asked to believe that the seventh-day Sabbath was abolished at the cross and that Sunday took its place as the weekly holy day!

# SABBATH

We shall find, in examining this objection, and the ones immediately following that the case for Sunday sacredness in the New Testament is built on surmises, deductions from shaky premises, and wishful thinking. Let the facts speak for themselves.

We are asked to believe (1) that after the resurrection Christ always met with His disciples on Sunday, and (2) that that provides unanswerable proof that Christ changed the weekly holy day from the seventh to the first day of the week.

Only six texts in the New Testament mention the first day of the week in connection with Christ's life: Matthew 28:1; Mark 16:2, 9; Luke 24:1; John 20:1, 19. (John 20:26 is often thought to refer to Sunday, and will be discussed a little later on.)

These four Gospel writers penned their narratives anywhere from twenty or thirty years up to nearly seventy years after the ascension of Christ. These and other New Testament writers all speak of the seventh day as "the sabbath," with no suggestion that this weekly holy day had been abolished or was in process of being abolished. Now, we shall discover that when they speak of the first day of the week they fail to suggest, even, that it had acquired, or was in process of acquiring, any sanctity. Strange, indeed, if as Sunday advocates so confidently declare, Sunday began to be regarded as the Christian holy day immediately after the resurrection.

From a study of the six texts before us the following facts come to light:

1. Each time Sunday is called simply "the first day of the week." No title of holiness or a title that even suggests holiness is employed.

2. There is no statement by Christ in connection with His meetings with the disciples, either in these texts or in the context, that even suggests that special significance should henceforth be attached to the first day of the week.

3. The reason why the disciples were all in one place on the resurrection day was not because they were holding a religious service to institute Sunday worship, but because they were in "fear of the Jews." (John 20:19.)

4. Three of the four Gospel writers plainly state that the Sabbath had ended when the first day of the week began.

5. Evidently, then, the true significance that attaches to the mention of the first day of the week in the resurrection record is the evident desire of the Gospel writers to give an accurate history of the events surrounding the crucifixion and to show that Christ's declaration that He would be raised on the third day was fulfilled.

In addition to His meetings with the disciples and certain women on the resurrection day, as mentioned in the six "first day" texts, what other visits, which state the *time* of His visit, are recorded? There are two:

1. The day of the ascension, which occurred "forty days" after the resurrection. (See Acts 1:3, 9.) Obviously, if resurrection day is Sunday, Ascension Day must be Thursday. Those churches that honor Ascension Day do so on a Thursday.

2. A meeting held a week after the resurrection day. The time is thus given: "And after eight days again his disciples were within, and Thomas with them: then came Jesus, the doors being shut, and stood in the midst, and said, Peace be unto you." John 20:26. Learned theologians generally hold that "after eight days" is a Jewish idiom for a week. Thus this is a meeting of Christ with His disciples on the second Sunday after His resurrection.

Accepting this view, we find evidence, then, of Christ's meeting with His disciples on only two Sundays. The first Sunday meeting obviously proves nothing—why should He wait beyond the resurrection to meet His disciples. Hence all the evidence for Christ's changing the day of worship that is to be drawn from His meetings with the disciples must be drawn from this second appearance. Perhaps Jamieson, Fausset, and Brown, in their Bible commentary, present the case for Sunday as favorably as possible:

"They [the disciples] probably met every day during the preceding week, but their Lord designedly reserved His second appearance amongst them till the recurrence of His resurrection-day, that He might thus inaugurate the delightful sanctities of THE LORD'S DAY." —Comment on John 20:26.

SABBATH

Here is an admission that the disciples were not singling out Sunday for a meeting. That is a most important admission. In fact, the record gives no suggestion of any meeting. If this twenty-sixth verse is compared with the nineteenth verse, we most naturally would conclude that the disciples were continuing together behind closed doors simply for protection. They feared to be out on the streets. But the text gives no hint that Jesus specially "reserved His second appearance amongst them" until Sunday, and that He did so to "inaugurate" the Lord's day. What phrase or words in the text even suggests such an idea? None whatever.

But the text does hint, at least, as to the reason why He appeared at this particular time, but that reason has nothing to do with Sunday sacredness. We read, "And after eight days again his disciples were within, and *Thomas with them."* John specifically mentions Thomas' absence from the upper room on the resurrection Sunday, and his consequent incredulity. (John 20:24-26.) He may even have been absent for a number of days after the resurrection. But this day he was "with them" in the upper room. So far as John's record discloses, the purpose of Christ's visit "after eight days" was to talk to Thomas. Naturally He chose a time when Thomas was "with them." Beyond that, nothing can be reasonably deduced from the record. Thus the Sunday-inaugurating significance of this meeting "after eight days" disappears.

Of course it is true that He did meet with them at other times, but these were undated. Perhaps the Sabbath objector will wish to affirm—though without possible proof—that such meetings were on Sunday. If so, then let us examine the account of "the third time" that Christ met His disciples after His resurrection. (See John 21:1-14.) The disciples were fishing! Evidently they considered fishing proper on that day, whatever it was. Nor does the record even suggest that Christ rebuked them for it. Instead, He instructed them how to catch fish! We do not recall that Sunday advocates discuss this "third time that Jesus shewed himself to his disciples, after that he was risen from the dead." They focus, instead, on His first appearance to the disciples, which proves to

211

be explainable in terms of His desire immediately to reassure them of His resurrection; and on His second appearance, which is explainable as a visit made because Thomas was present. They focus on no other appearances, for there are none other that can possibly be fixed as on Sunday, or that can be strained to support in any way the theory that Christ inaugurated Sunday worship.

What of the proof for Sunday sacredness that is supposed to reside in the fact that the Holy Spirit was poured upon the disciples on the day of Pentecost? We will pass by the fact that some Sundaykeeping theologians are not even certain that Pentecost fell on Sunday that year, though that fact is obviously weakening to the Sunday argument. We think Pentecost *did* come on Sunday that year, but we would never discover that fact from the Biblical record of the outpouring of the Spirit. No mention is even made as to which day of the week is involved. The record informs us only that "when the day of Pentecost was fully come" the outpouring of the Divine Spirit took place. (Acts 2:1.) Surely, if the apostolic writer saw in this outpouring any significance for Sundaykeeping, he would have at least disclosed the fact that the event took place on the first day of the week, even if he did not take time to comment on the sacredness of Sunday that is supposed to follow from the divine outpouring.

But the objector may reply: Everyone reading the book of Acts knew that Pentecost was on Sunday that year, and could thus draw his own conclusions as to the relationship between the divine outpouring and the first day of the week. If this reply means anything, it means that so far from Acts 2:1 being an inspired reference to Sunday sacredness, or even a mention of the day of the week involved, the reader must rely on his own knowledge of the facts and draw therefrom his own deductions. That is surely a long way from a "Thus saith the Lord" for Sunday.

But would every reader of the book of Acts know that Pentecost came on Sunday that year? Luke wrote Acts about A.D. 63, or some thirty years after the Pentecostal event. The annual Jewish festivals, of which Pentecost was one, came on different days of the week each year, even as, for example, our Armistice Day does. But does everyone today, a generation after World War I, who reads of the Armistice, November 11, 1918, know what day of the week it came on? No. Even so with the day of Pentecost in the year our Lord ascended. The reader of Acts, which was written a generation after Christ, would no more be aware of the day of the week involved in that great Pentecost than we would be aware of the day of the week on which the 1918 Armistice came.

The very words of Luke reveal that he desires the reader to note the fact, not that the Holy Spirit was poured out on a certain day of the week, but that it was poured out "when the day of Pentecost was fully come." Do we not find an evident explanation for the timing of the incident in the fact that certain events in connection with Christ's first advent were the fulfillment of certain typical services of the Jews. "Christ our passover" (1 Cor. 5:7) fulfilled the typical Passover service and was sacrificed on the very day that the Passover lamb was slain, the fourteenth day of the first month (Ex. 12:1-6). The offering of the first fruits on the sixteenth day of the first month met its fulfillment in Christ's resurrection on that day, the first fruits of them that sleep. (Lev. 23:5-11; 1 Cor. 15:20-23.) Then "when the day of Pentecost was fully come," a further typical service evidently met its fulfillment. (Lev. 23:15-21.) If we are to deduce anything from the timing of the Holy Spirit's outpouring, it is this: Luke is seeking to show that Christ is the great antitype of the Jewish services. At least, no further deduction seems at all warranted by the text of the narrative.

# Objection 42

From earliest apostolic days Christians kept Sunday in honor of Christ's resurrection. This is clearly revealed in two scriptures, Acts 20:7 and 1 Corinthians 16:2.

We have already learned (objection 41) that there is no Scriptural foundation for the statement that "from earliest apostolic days Christians kept Sunday," because there is no proof that Christ instituted Sunday worship on the resurrection day or during any time that He appeared to His disciples in the forty days before His ascension. Nor is there anything in the Scriptures to show that during that forty-day period the apostles gave any kind of veneration to Sunday.

Therefore, if there is Biblical proof that the apostles kept Sunday, it must be found some decades later in the two texts cited in this objection, and in one further text to be considered in the next objection. Strange, is it not, that a practice so revolutionary as the keeping of a new weekly holy day, by Jewish Christians as well as Gentile, and thus the abandonment of the seventh-day Sabbath, should not have been the subject of extended and repeated discussion in the writings of the apostles? When they said that circumcision was no longer necessary, a hurricane was let loose, and the wind of that controversy blows strongly through the pages of the New Testament. But we are asked to believe that they told the Christian converts that the Sabbath need no longer be kept, and yet no tempest ensued, at least nothing important enough to find mention in the New Testament! Yet the Jews were fanatically zealous about the Sabbath! Here is a most singular situation.

In the light of these facts we have a right to be suspicious of the Sunday claim that is based on the two texts cited. And remember, they are the only two in the Bible that mention the first day of the week subsequent to the resurrection day. The first one reads thus:

"Upon the first day of the week, when the disciples came together to break bread, Paul preached unto them, ready to depart [from Troas] on the morrow; and continued his speech until midnight." Acts 20:7. This text is part of a running narrative describing various incidents of Paul's homeward trip to Jerusalem at the close of his third missionary journey. The whole story requires two chapters. Let us examine first the statement about breaking bread. In Acts 2:46 we read that the disciples continued "*daily* with one accord in the temple, and breaking bread from house to house, did eat their meat with gladness and singleness of 'heart." If a communion service is implied by "break bread," in Acts 20:7, it proves nothing distinctive for this particular day in Acts, because the disciples broke bread, "*daily.*"

Notice that no holy title is used for this day. It is simply called "the first day of the week." Therefore, on what are we to base an argument for Sunday sacredness? Apparently simply on the fact that a religious meeting was held that day. In other words, the logic is as follows:

1. The holding of a meeting on a certain day is proof that that day is holy.

2. Paul held a meeting on the first day of the week.

3. Therefore Sunday is a holy day.

Thus stripped of all surplus language, the argument for Sunday that is supposed to reside in Acts 20:7 stands revealed in its true weakness. When we read the whole story of the journey we find that Paul preached in various places along the way as he traveled to Jerusalem. Were all these sermons timed to come on Sunday?

Look at the last half of the twentieth chapter, which gives a summary of what was probably one of the most important sermons Paul preached on this trip—at least, it is the only one that is described in detail. An examination of the context, especially verse 15, would indicate that it was probably preached on a Wednesday, certainly not on a Sunday. Therefore shall we conclude that Wednesday is a holy day? That would be the conclusion we could reach from the logic set forth in behalf of Sunday sacredness in this chapter. Really, the logic would force us to conclude that Paul made almost every day of the week holy by this one journey, so many were the services he conducted along the way. No, it takes more than the preaching of a sermon to make a day holy, or to reverse the divine command that "the seventh day is the sabbath of the Lord thy God."

When the exact time of the Troas meeting is noted, this passage in Acts 20 becomes even less convincing as a proof for Sunday, if that could be possible. The service was held at night, for "there were many lights in the upper chamber, where they were gathered together." Verse 8. The record declares also that Paul "continued his speech until midnight," the reason being that he had to "depart on the morrow." Verse 7. His speech continued past midnight, "even till break of day," and "so he departed." Verse 11. The accompanying narrative reveals that Paul had to make a trip across a peninsula from Troas, where he had left his boat, to Assos, where he would embark again.

It is a well-known fact that the Bible reckons days from sunset to sunset, not from midnight to midnight, as we do today. (See Gen. 1:5, 8, 13, 19, 23, 31; Lev. 23:32.) Therefore the dark part of that "first day of the week" was what we would describe as Saturday night. Conybeare and Howson, in their authoritative work, *Life and Epistles of the Apostle Paul*, write as follows concerning the time of the meeting:

"It was the evening which succeeded the Jewish sabbath. On the Sunday morning the vessel was about to sail."—Page 520 (1-vol. ed.).

Thus we see that Paul held a Saturday night meeting, and started off on his long journey Sunday morning. We do not see Sundaykeepers today attaching any sacredness to Saturday night, yet they wish to rely upon this record of a Saturday night meeting as a proof of Sunday sacredness. It was only because Paul preached a very long sermon that this meeting even stretched over into what Sundaykeepers regard as their holy day.

Paul abode at Troas "seven days." Verse 6. Then on Saturday night, the beginning of "the first day of the week," he "preached unto them, ready to depart on the morrow." There is no good reason to believe that Paul refrained from preaching during the "seven days," and then because "the first day of the week" had come, held a service. The account of his journeys reveals that he preached constantly. In this case we are specifically told why he preached: Because he was "ready to depart on the morrow." In other words, he took advantage of a last opportunity to speak to them, "when the disciples came together to break bread," even to preaching "till break of day." Verse 11. If the record proves anything, it proves that this first-day meeting was held, not because of a usual religious custom, but because of an unusual travel situation.

In the light of the *whole* narrative of Paul's journey the mention of "the first day of the week" is most simply explained as one of several mentions of time to give the reader a general picture of the time involved in that journey. Note these references:

1. "Abode [in Greece] three months." Acts 20:3.
2. "Sailed away from Philippi after the days of unleavened bread." Verse 6.
3. Came "to Troas in five days." Verse 6.
4. "Where we abode seven days." Verse 6.
5. "And upon the first day of the week." Verse 7.
6. "Ready to depart on the morrow." Verse 7.
7. "The next day over against Chios." Verse 15.
8. "The next day we arrived at Samos." Verse 15.
9. "The next day we came to Miletus." Verse 15.
10. "Hasted . . . to be at Jerusalem the day of Pentecost." Verse 16.
11. "The day following unto Rhodes." Acts 21:1.
12. Tarried at Tyre "seven days." Verse 4.
13. "And when we had accomplished those days." Verse 5.

14. "Abode with them [at Ptolemais] one day." Verse 7.

15. "The next day we . . . departed, and came to Caesarea." Verse 8.

16. "Tarried there many days." Verse 10.

17. "After those days we . . . went up to Jerusalem." Verse 15.

Dr. Augustus Neander, one of the most eminent of church historians, and a Sundaykeeper, remarks thus concerning the proof for Sunday sacredness that is supposed to be found in Acts 20:7.

"The passage is not entirely convincing, because the impending departure of the apostle may have united the little Church in a brotherly parting-meal, on occasion of which the apostle delivered his last address, although there was no particular celebration of a Sunday in the case."—*The History of the Christian Religion and Church*, translated by Henry John Rose (1831), vol. 1, p. 337.

If this "passage is not entirely convincing" to a Sundaykeeping church historian, it should hardly be expected to prove convincing to a Sabbathkeeper who rests his belief on the overwhelmingly convincing command of God: "The seventh day is the sabbath of the Lord."

For a Sunday advocate to declare that he looks to Acts 20:7 for proof of Sunday sacredness is only to reveal how weak is the case for Sunday in the Scriptures.

The second of the two "first day" texts before us reads thus: "Now concerning the collection for the saints, as I have given order to the churches of Galatia, even so do ye. Upon the first day of the week let every one of you lay by him in store, as God hath prospered him, that there be no gatherings when I come." 1 Cor. 16:1, 2. We are supposed to find here a picture of a religious service when a company is gathered together, and the offering is being taken up. The reasoning, of course, is that if a service was held on Sunday, that proves Sunday is sacred, and, by inference, that the Sabbath of the Decalogue has been abolished.

This is a very great deal to attempt to find in one text, especially when the text will not permit of the deductions drawn from it. Instead of describing a church offering, where the communicants pass over their gifts to a deacon, the record says that each one was to "lay by him in store." The most recent and most widely accepted version of the Scriptures translates the text thus: "On the first day of every week, each of you is to put something aside and save, as he may prosper, so that contributions need not be made when I come." R.S.V. In other words, when the first day of the week had come, each one was to decide from the last week's earnings how much he wanted to set aside for the special collection that Paul was going to take to the poor at Jerusalem, and lay it by in a special place apart from the other money of the house. This was an act of bookkeeping rather than an act of worship.

That this is the correct understanding of this passage is admitted by scholarly Sundaykeeping theologians, whose desire to translate the Scriptures accurately exceeds their desire to find proofs for Sunday. Take, for example, the typical comment that is found in *The Cambridge Bible for Schools and Colleges,* a commentary on the Scriptures, published by the Cambridge University Press, and edited by Church of England clergymen. Speaking of this text, the commentator declares that, as to the practice of Christians to meet on the first day of the week, "we cannot infer it from this passage." Then follows his comment on the phrase "lay by him"—

"i.e., at home, not in the assembly, as is generally supposed. . . . He [Paul] speaks of a custom in his time of placing a small box by the bedside into which an offering was to be put whenever prayer was made."—*The First Epistle to the Corinthians,* edited by J. J. Lias, p. 164.

Certainly it requires much more than the fact that the disciples were gathered together in fear in their abode on the first day of the week, or that Paul preached one sermon on that day, or that he commanded the Corinthians to set aside some money in their homes the first of each week—much more than this, we say, to give any believer in the Bible a reason for violating one of the precepts of the eternal Decalogue, which declares that "the seventh day is the sabbath of the Lord thy God."

# Objection 43

The apostle John calls Sunday the "Lord's day," and declares that he was "in the Spirit" on that day. This proves that Sunday is the sacred weekly rest day of the Christian church and that the Sabbath has been abolished.

The claim is based on Revelation 1:10: "I was in the Spirit on the Lord's day, and heard behind me a great voice, as of a trumpet."

Significantly, those who make this claim feel it necessary to abolish the Sabbath in order to find a place for Sunday worship. Naturally so, for the Bible provides for only *one* weekly holy day, and Sunday advocates have rather uniformly sought to provide some kind of Bible foundation for Sunday. But even if John meant "Sunday" by "Lord's day," that would provide no proof that the fourth commandment of the Decalogue had been abolished or even changed. Let that fact be clear at the outset.

Now, how do Sabbath opposers attempt to prove that this text refers to Sunday? In this fashion: They declare that the phrase "Lord's day," as a synonym for Sunday, began to be used by church fathers in their writings very soon after John's death, and that therefore he used the phrase in the same sense.

What are the facts? Briefly these: There have come down to us today certain writings attributed to various martyrs and other church fathers who lived in the generations immediately following that of the apostles. Church historians declare that many of these writings are spurious, and of those that are genuine, most have been so garbled or so added to by later writers that it is almost impossible to know what portion was written by the original author. And the very fact that an author's words were often garbled, coupled with the fact that some of these earliest fathers employed unusual, if not incoherent, literary constructions, has caused learned translators to be in great uncertainty as to the true meaning of many passages in those writings. The church historian Augustus Neander thus sums up the problem of their value:

"The writings of the so-called apostolic Fathers have unhappily, for the most part, come down to us in a condition very little worthy of confidence, partly because under the name of these men, so highly venerated in the church, writings were early forged for the purpose of giving authority to particular opinions or principles; and partly because their own writings which were extant, became interpolated in subservience to a Jewish hierarchical interest, which aimed to crush the free spirit of the gospel."—*General History of the Christian Religion and Church* (1854), vol. 1, Appendix, sec. 4, p. 657.

In view of these facts the reader can immediately see how undependable is any argument based on *what* the apostolic fathers are supposed to have said or *when* they are supposed to have said it. Only if we shut our eyes to the spurious element, with the uncertainty as to date that grows out of it, and only if we are ready to add a little wishful thinking to our translation of certain garbled and incoherent passages, can we unquestioningly accept the claim that the phrase "Lord's day" began to be used by the church fathers shortly after John's death. We believe that there is no clear, undebatable use of that phrase in any writings of the fathers until near the end of the second century. (See page 773 for historical proof of this statement.) And if that be true, the argument for Sunday based on John's use of the phrase stretches out so thin—for it must stretch out over nearly a century—that it cannot carry the weight of argument suspended on it.

But so plausible can even a garbled, doubtful passage sound to those who need the support it provides that, despite the damaging evidence here presented, there will still remain in many minds at least a halfway feeling that the phrase was actually used by church fathers to describe Sunday within a generation or so of John's day. Furthermore, so intriguing is the fact that John uses a phrase that is later used to describe Sunday that those same minds will naturally lean toward the conclusion that probably, after all, John likewise used the phrase to describe Sunday. Besides the emotional weakness that afflicts that kind of conclusion, there is a glaring fallacy that invalidates it, the fallacy of concluding that because a word has a certain meaning at one time it has identically the same meaning at an earlier time. This is one of the worst fallacies into which a person can fall in reading writings of a former day. Because in the writings of a second-century father the phrase "Lord's day" meant Sunday, it does not therefore follow that in the writings of John the phrase meant Sunday. Words change and even reverse their meanings, and sometimes in an amazingly short period.

Until the seventeenth century the word "Sabbath" had rather uniformly been used by Christian speakers and writers to describe the seventh day of the week. But in the British Isles, in that century, there was a great Puritan revival of religion, which focused on an endeavor to secure better observance of Sunday. Sunday was declared to be commanded in the Decalogue, with simply a change from the seventh to the first day of the week. (See page 545 for historical proof.) In order to make their language consistent with this view the Puritanical reformers began to call Sunday "Sabbath." In almost one generation the change was made, so far as a large segment of the population was concerned, and the term "Sabbath" for "Sunday" has come down to our day.

Take the word "Sabbatarian." For long years, even to the opening of the twentieth century, the term was used to describe a Sunday advocate who believed that Sunday should be rigorously kept, generally with the aid of civil legislation. Today "Sabbatarian" is used to describe a *Seventh-day* Adventist, who keeps a different day and who is opposed to civil laws for Sabbathkeeping. Here again is a complete reversal of meaning, and in a rather short space of time.

Or take another change in word values, more startling as to difference in meaning and as to speed of change. As late as the 1840's in America the word "spiritualist" meant a person who spiritualized away the literal meaning of Scripture, or one who had very spiritual views. But in less than ten years the word began to be used to describe those who had taken up with the Hydesville rappings of 1848, which started the modern cult of spiritism.

SABBATH

All one needs to do is to examine an unabridged dictionary to find an endless list of such changes in meanings of words. And after such an examination he will be hopelessly suspicious of any argument that would seek to read back into the words of a man who wrote at one time the meaning given to those words by men who wrote at a later time. Why conclude, on the reading of a "spiritualist" in a theological journal in 1840, that a believer in departed spirits is there described? Or why conclude on reading in a newspaper of the 1890's that a group of "Sabbatarians" held a meeting that therefore a company of Seventh-day Adventists were in session? Or why conclude from reading John's statement on the "Lord's day," written about A.D. 90, that he was "in the Spirit" on Sunday?

We may properly understand a writer's words in the light of the meaning that those words have had *up to* the time he wrote. But we cannot safely read back into his words a meaning acquired by those words in *later* years.

Now, as noted, John wrote the Revelation about the year A.D. 90. Up to that time had the Bible writers ever used the term "Lord's day" to describe Sunday? No. They uniformly described Sunday simply as "the first day of the week." Even more striking is the fact that John himself, in his Gospel, which, it is generally agreed, was written some years *after* the Revelation, still calls Sunday by the same colorless phrase as the other Bible writers used, "the first day of the week."

There is only one day described in the Bible that could lay claim to being the "Lord's day," and that is the Sabbath. The Decalogue describes it as "the sabbath of the *Lord*." Ex. 20:10. Isaiah tells us to call this day "the holy of the *Lord*." Isa. 58:13. Christ described Himself as "*Lord* also of the sabbath." Mark 2:28. John had heard the Saviour utter these words. He knew also the words of the Decalogue and the words of Isaiah. How reasonable, then, to conclude that he meant the Sabbath when he said "*Lord's* day."

Of course someone may contend that if John used "Lord's

day" for Sabbath in the Revelation, he would naturally use it also in his Gospel. But instead he there uses the customary term "sabbath." We grant that we do not know just why he used "Lord's day" this one time. Evidence has been presented to show only (1) that the Sabbath objector's interpretation of "Lord's day" in Revelation 1:10 will not stand scrutiny, and (2) that the only reasonable interpretation of his words is that he meant "Sabbath."

However, the history of John's day offers an interesting suggestion as to why he used "Lord's day" for Sabbath in the book of Revelation. Christianity was coming into ever greater and greater conflict with pagan Rome. The Caesars were often deified, and Christians were sometimes called on to offer incense to them, or forfeit their lives. There were emperor days, such as the emperor's birthday, which took on a religious quality because of the blending of state and church. The day when a Caesar visited a certain city was ever afterward a holiday in that city and known, by translation, as a worshipful day, a day worthy of worship. The emperor Domitian was "accustomed to call himself and to be called 'Lord and God.'"—PHILIP SCHAFF, *History of the Christian Church* (8th ed., 1903), vol. 2, p. 44.

Now, John, who had been banished to Patmos almost certainly during Domitian's reign, was specially favored with revelations of Christ's coming kingdom and glory, as Patmos lighted up for him with the glory of his Lord. This Lord he described as "King of kings, and Lord of lords." And how meaningful that title was for the persecuted Christians who, at the cost of their lives, refused to acknowledge Caesar as "Lord and God." In Revelation 1:10 John introduces his first revelation of Christ's glory. In view of the Christian conflicts with Rome, how natural for him, if that first vision was on the Sabbath, to declare that he "was in the Spirit on the Lord's day," the day of the true Lord, whose proof of Lordship is His Creatorship, which the Sabbath memorializes. (See Rev. 4:11; 10:6; 14:7.)

# Objection 44

"Pages of authentic statements, selected from the writings of primitive Christian authors, could be quoted in proof of the fact that the first day of the week . . . was continuously observed as a day of Divine worship from the Saviour's resurrection on through the succeeding early centuries of the present dispensation." But despite this evidence "Seventh-day Adventists teach (supposedly by 'inspiration') that the change came in with Constantine, the first so-called 'Christian emperor' of Rome, 'in the early part of the fourth century.' (See *The Great Controversy*, p. 53.) And by the same authority, they, contradicting themselves, also teach that 'the Pope changed [the Sabbath] from the seventh to the first day of the week.' (See *Early Writings of Mrs. White*, p. 33, edition of 1916.)"

We have already discovered that no passage of Scripture can be found to support the claim that Christians kept Sunday. The "primitive Christian authors," beyond the apostles, provide no undebatable proof of veneration for Sunday earlier than the second century. (See page 773 for historical proof.) It is generally held that virtually all the apostles had gone to martyrs' graves by A.D. 70. But we must wait at least forty or fifty years beyond this date before we find written evidence worthy of any serious consideration that Christians were giving any special regard to Sunday. And even some of the evidence would be seriously challenged by church historians as highly doubtful in regard to authorship and date and possible exact meaning.

What the average reader does not know, and the Sabbath objector is glad to forget, is that in the years immediately after the death of the apostles many pagan ideas and customs began to infiltrate the church. Speaking to the elders of the church at Ephesus, about the year A.D. 60, Paul warned: "Take heed therefore unto yourselves, and to all the flock, over the which the Holy Ghost hath made you overseers, to feed the church of God, which he hath purchased with his own blood. For I know this, that after my departing shall grievous wolves enter in among you, not sparing the flock. Also of your own selves shall men arise, speaking perverse things, to draw away disciples after them." Acts 20:28-30.

A few years earlier he had written to the Thessalonian church of a "falling away" from the faith that was to come and that would result in the exaltation of the "man of sin." This "mystery of iniquity," he added, "doth already work." (2 Thess. 2:3-7.)

Most Protestant theologians through the centuries have regarded this as a prophecy of the growth of the Papacy, the great Roman Catholic power.

In his general comments on this whole prophetic passage in 2 Thessalonians, the Bible commentator Adam Clarke, though uncertain in his own mind on various points, adds immediately:

"The general run of *Protestant* writers understand the whole as referring to the *popes* and *Church* of *Rome,* or the whole system of the *papacy.*"

Then he summarizes at length the comments of Bishop Newton, one of the most eminent of Anglican writers on prophecy, remarking that "the principal part of modern commentators follow his steps. He applies the whole to the *Romish Church.*" And here is what Newton, as quoted by Clarke, says in part:

"*The mystery of iniquity was already working* [in Paul's day]; the seeds of corruption were sown, but they were not grown up to maturity."

"The foundations of popery were laid in the apostle's days."

Protestant historians are generally agreed that the roots of Roman Catholicism run down at least to the second century.

The eminent church historian Philip Schaff, declares:

"The first example of the exercise of a sort of papal authority is found towards the close of the first century in the letter of the Roman bishop Clement (d. 102) to the bereaved and distracted church of Corinth."—*History of the Christian Church* (8th ed., 1903), vol. 2, p. 157.

"He [Clement] speaks in a tone of authority to a sister church of apostolic foundation, and thus reveals the easy and as yet innocent beginning of the papacy."—*Ibid.*, p. 646.

Paul died a martyr at Rome about A.D. 68. Clement, bishop of Rome, was a disciple of Paul and died A.D. 102. Schaff describes "the interval between Clement and Paul" as a "transition from the apostolic to the apocryphal, from faith to superstition."—*Ibid.*

The Sabbath objector speaks warmly of "primitive Christian authors," who are alleged to have provided such good proof for Sundaykeeping in the early church. But what is here revealed of the early beginnings of the Papacy casts a heavy shadow of suspicion over these "authors." Clement, bishop of Rome, was one of the earliest, though he did not write on the question of Sunday! Of the so-called fathers of the church who lived in the two centuries immediately following the apostles Schaff says:

"We seek in vain among them for the evangelical doctrines of the exclusive authority of the Scriptures, justification by faith alone, the universal priesthood of the laity; and we find instead as early as the second century a high estimate of ecclesiastical traditions, meritorious and even overmeritorious works, and strong sacerdotal, sacramentarian, ritualistic, and ascetic tendencies, which gradually matured in the Greek and Roman types of catholicity."—*Ibid.*, p. 628.

We have learned (under objection 43) that we cannot even be sure, when we read the so-called apostolic fathers—those "primitive Christian authors"—that we are actually reading what they said rather than what some later forger introduced into their writings.

Schaff quotes a "distinguished writer" as declaring that when we move from the inspired writings of the New Testament to the uninspired writings of the fathers, it is like passing, " 'by a single step,' " from the verdant confines of " 'an Eastern city in the desert' " out " 'into a barren waste.' " (*Ibid.*, p. 636.)

Into this "barren waste" the Sabbath objector would lead us for proof of Sundaykeeping! Even if we can be sure of what the fathers said on the matter, what value is their testimony that the church, so far as their limited knowledge of a little part of it was concerned, was already following the practice of Sundaykeeping? The church historians just cited disclose that the roots of various false teachings, even of all Romanism, run back to the days of those earliest fathers.

Now, because these various false teachings and practices, when crystallized by custom and the centuries, finally culminated in the Papacy, it is natural to speak of these different errors as having been brought into the Christian church by Rome, which is equivalent to saying that they were brought in by the popes. We have found that Sundaykeeping is not apostolic, not Scriptural; therefore it is one of those un-Scriptural teachings that came in later, which teachings finally constituted the Roman Catholic system of doctrine. Hence Mrs. E. G. White, speaking for Seventh-day Adventists, made no historical mistake in saying that the Pope changed the day of worship. Nor is there any conflict between that statement and her other statement, that Constantine "issued a decree making Sunday a public festival throughout the Roman empire."—*The Great Controversy*, p. 53. Mrs. White does not say that "the change" from the Sabbath to Sunday "came in with Constantine," as the Sabbath objector declares, but simply that he issued a certain Sunday law, which is a statement of historical fact.

It is true that the church historians we have quoted—all of them Sundaykeepers—believe that Sunday had the sanction of apostolic custom, even if not of apostolic command. And the only real argument they offer, in the complete absence of Scriptural command or proof of an apostolic Sundaykeeping custom, is this: Surely we would not find Sunday veneration so widespread in the second century unless it had had apostolic sanction. What these historians forget for the moment is this: They have just told us of endless false doctrines and practices rampant in the second century, and supported by the writings of the fathers. Did all these evil things have apostolic sanction? They further forget for the moment that the same plausible argument they use to prove apostolic beginnings for Sunday worship, Rome uses to prove apostolic authority for numerous of her un-Biblical teachings and practices. The argument is as good in one instance as in the other. And, need we add, it is worthless in either instance. Not in "the barren wastes" of post-Biblical times and writers can we find safe places for our feet. If we would walk in the path of truth, we must keep on the highway of the Scriptures, hand in hand with our Lord and His holy apostles.

If it still seems incredible to any reader that so great an apostasy could set in within the brief compass of, say, half a century—from the last part of the first century through the early part of the second century—let him note a modern parallel. In the latter part of the nineteenth century most of the Christian ministry could be described as Fundamentalist in belief, though subtle evolution teachings were quietly beginning to receive a sympathetic hearing from some. But by the end of the first quarter of the twentieth century a revolutionary change in religious belief, known as Modernism, had occurred in the major branches of Christendom. Such basic terms as the deity of Christ, the atonement of Christ, the inspiration of Scripture, had vastly changed in meaning.

How unwarranted a future church historian would be in reasoning that because early in the twentieth century church leaders in general held certain Modernist beliefs, therefore those views must likewise have been held in the nineteenth century; that indeed the great church leaders of the nineteenth century must have thus taught their pupils! The evidence before us regarding the first and second centuries leads us to conclude that historians are equally unwarranted in reasoning that because certain beliefs were held in the second century, therefore they must have been held in the first, indeed, promoted by the apostles. Why blacken the reputation of those holy men?

# Objection 45

**The resurrection is the greatest event in the history of Christianity; therefore we keep Sunday. Sabbathkeepers are not Christians, because they do not commemorate the great event of Christ's rising from the dead.**

Even if we agree that the resurrection is the greatest event in the history of Christianity, it does not therefore follow that the Sabbath of the Decalogue should be abolished and Sunday worship be substituted in its place. But who are we frail mortals that we should make our own decision as to which is the greatest event in the history of God's dealings with His people? The Bible has never made a pronouncement on this question. Furthermore, who are we to say how a holy event in Christ's life shall be commemorated? If human beings must decide which is the greatest event and how it should be kept in mind, then Sunday sacredness, which grows out of that decision, rests upon a human foundation.

All that would be needed in order to change the day of worship would be for Christians to agree that some other event is the greatest in Christianity's history. And might not a very good case be made out for the crucifixion as being the most notable event, for then the world witnessed the supreme example of unselfish love—the Son of God giving His life for a rebellious world? Or might not a plausible case be built up for the notable event of Christ's birth, when the universe witnessed the amazing scene of God made manifest in the flesh?

Christianity without the crucifixion of Christ would be meaningless. The same is true of the miraculous birth. How, then, can we say dogmatically which is the greatest event in the history of Christianity?

How could we prove wrong the man who declared the crucifixion, for example, to be the greatest event? And if, in harmony with that declaration, he proceeded to keep Friday, how could we say he was not as consistent as the Sundaykeeper, who attempts to build his holy day on his own private view as to which is the most important event in the history of Christianity?

The logic of all this brings us to the conclusion that a man might keep any one of several days, depending altogether upon his appraisal of notable events, and still be a good Christian. Apparently the only day a Christian must not keep holy is the seventh day of the week. The Sabbathkeeper is to have leveled against him the charge that he is not a Christian, because he does not honor the event that the Sundaykeeper has decided should be honored, or rather because he does not honor it in the *way* the Sundaykeeper has decided it should be honored.

But Sabbathkeepers do remember the fact of our Lord's resurrection and its meaning to the Christian, for we carry out faithfully the ordinance of baptism, which is intended of God to keep bright in our minds both the death and the resurrection of Christ. (See Rom. 6:3-5.) And we baptize by immersion, which enables us Scripturally and most vividly to remember that Christ was buried and rose again.

The Sundaykeeper, by instituting a certain *day* in remembrance of the resurrection, makes quite pointless, if not wholly meaningless, the institution of baptism, which *God* intended should recall that event. Perhaps that is why most churches have reduced the rite of baptism to the sprinkling of a few drops of water, a procedure that conveys no idea whatever of "baptism into death," or of rising again to walk in newness of life.

# Objection 46

**Seventh-day Adventists make a great point out of the fact that the Sabbath memorializes creation. But we are not so much concerned with creation as with redemption, which is greater. Therefore we keep Sunday, the great memorial of our redemption.**

This objection has much in common with the immediately preceding one, and all that is said there in reply is pertinent here. But the reasoning is here carried a little further; in fact, a great deal further, as will immediately be evident.

Not only is the Bible an inspired book; it is a historical book. Indeed, much of the inspired counsel in that book is presented in a historical framework. Or to use a figure of speech, the Bible is a tall, imposing edifice. The foundation rests in the Garden of Eden, the glittering pinnacle points to Eden restored. The various stories, or levels, of the building represent the different centuries in which God's revelations have been given to men. A great dividing point between foundation and pinnacle is that level where God was revealed in His Son to save men on the cross.

All rests on the foundation; destroy that and the whole structure of revelation loses symmetry and beauty and is ready to fall.

To speak literally, all the Bible writers build their messages on the assumption, implied or expressed, that, as recorded in Genesis, man was created and placed in Eden and then fell from his holy estate into sin, which fall is the explanation of all the tragedy of the world. The burden of the prophets in the Old Testament is to present a heavenly plan of salvation whereby man may be lifted up again, redeemed and restored to Eden. The burden of the apostles in the New Testament is to announce that what the prophets forecast regarding a Saviour had been fulfilled and that men should believe on His name. The last book of the Bible pictures us returned to the blissful abode of Eden.

232

But what if the Genesis record of man's beginning is a fable? Can that which rests on a fable have more substance or value than the fable? No. The whole Bible loses its rugged historical character, loses much of its meaning and literality, if the Genesis record of creation is a fable. Obviously, a person's belief as to the origin of man and of this world is tremendously important. That is why the evolution theory, so largely accepted today in place of the Genesis creation account, has such a religious significance.

When the evolution theory was first gaining acceptance, Joseph Le Conte, a university professor, wrote a book entitled *Evolution and Its Relation to Religious Thought,* in which he set forth the relation of this new theory to religious belief:

"Its truth or falseness, its acceptance or rejection, is no trifling matter, affecting only one small corner of the thought-realm. On the contrary, it affects profoundly the foundations of philosophy, and therefore the whole domain of thought. It determines the whole attitude of the mind toward Nature and God."—Pages 3, 4.

Just how the evolution theory affects the "attitude of the mind toward Nature and God" is tersely set forth by a spokesman for Bible-deriding skeptics who, significantly, were among the first to accept the theory:

"But—no Adam, no fall; no fall, no atonement; no atonement, no Saviour. Accepting evolution, how can we believe in a fall? *When did man fall; was it before he ceased to be a monkey, or after? . . . And if there never was a fall, why should there be any atonement?"* —ROBERT BLATCHFORD, *God and My Neighbor,* p. 159.

The relation of belief in the first chapter of Genesis to belief in all the rest of the Bible was vividly brought·out by a writer early in the twentieth century:

"When we found that . . . Adam was not made directly from dust, and Eve from his rib, and that the tower of Babel was not the occasion of the diversification of languages, we had gone too far to stop. The process of criticism had to go on from Genesis to Revelation, with no fear of the curse at the end of the last chapter. It could not stop with Moses and Isaiah; it had to include Matthew and John and Paul. Every one of them had to be sifted; they had already ceased to be taken as unquestioned, final authorities, for plenary inspiration had followed verbal inspiration just as soon as the first chapter of Genesis had ceased to be taken as true history."—New York *Independent,* June 24, 1909.

How evident, then, that the Genesis creation account is the foundation of the whole edifice of the Bible revelation. And how evident that when men forget, or deny, creation they open their minds to endless untruthful, unholy theories as to their origin and destiny. The awful account of the descent of men into the pit of pagan idolatry and immorality, as given in Romans 1, would never have had to be written if they had kept ever before their minds the holy record of their origin at the hands of the one and only true God, who is of too pure eyes to behold iniquity. The evolution theory of our day could never have gained acceptance if men had believed in and kept bright in their minds the creation account of Genesis. In other words, there never would have been a departure from the true God, and the whole plan of salvation portrayed in the Bible would ever have had maximum meaning for men if they had not forgotten, and ultimately disbelieved, the heavenly account of their beginnings in Eden.

How important, then, above all else that we should remember creation! How strange if God should not have made careful provision for the keeping of it in mind! But He did make provision. He created a memorial to that opening event of our history. He set that memorial at the very beginning of man's journey. (Gen. 2:2, 3), and when He delivered His one audible, brief address to His people salvaged out of Egyptian idolatry and vice, He called upon them to "remember the sabbath day to keep it holy." They were to remember each week that "in six days the Lord made heaven and earth, the sea, and all that in them is."

Remembering creation, they would remember the God of creation. And remembering the God of creation as holy, and who created their first parents holy, they would constantly see in the Sabbath a sign and a pledge that the God whom they served could sanctify them, make them holy, by creating in them new hearts and right spirits. (See Ex. 31:13; Ps. 51:10.)

Remembering creation, with its beauty and purity and perfection, they would be led to look forward with earnest and contrite eagerness to the coming of Christ, who, by His death and resurrection, would make possible their release from sin and death and their restoration to Eden.

The Sabbath command is part of that great code of laws that is the foundation of morality, and memorializes an event that is the foundation of the whole historical revelation of God's ways toward man. Without the creation truth memorialized by the Sabbath the cross has no foundation and the resurrection no meaning. That is evident.

It is by keeping creation in mind that we give maximum meaning to the cross and the resurrection. And that is but another way of saying that by keeping the Sabbath, the memorial of creation, we place under the cross and the resurrection a sure and solid foundation and give to them their true force and meaning. We keep the Sabbath because we wish to give greatest glory to God the Father and to His Son, through whom He created all things. We keep the Sabbath because we wish to give greatest glory to the Book of God, which rests upon the foundation of Genesis. We keep the Sabbath because we wish to witness before all men that we are on the side of God against the great apostasy that has developed in the Christian church because of evolution.

In the light of these facts how pointless, yes, how foolish, seem the major indictments brought against our Sabbathkeeping! In keeping the Sabbath we are not Jews, we are not legalists, we are creationists! And, as already made clear, a creationist is one who stands solidly for the Scriptures against all apostasy.

With religious bodies on every side of us split asunder by the evolution theory, if not wholly committed to it, Seventh-day Adventists stand solidly for the Genesis account of creation and for the inspiration of the whole Book of God. How could we ever believe in evolution when each week we take a whole day solemnly to "remember" God's awesome act of creation—to "remember the sabbath day to keep it holy"?

# Objection 47

The phrase "the first day of the week" in Matthew 28:1 should be translated "the first of the sabbaths," or "one of the sabbaths." This proper translation indicates that the apostle spoke of the resurrection Sunday as the first of a new order of sabbaths.

The basic premise of the contention regarding the translation in question is that the Greek word *sabbaton* translated "week" in Matthew 28:1 and parallel passages should never be thus translated, that instead it should always be rendered "Sabbath." *Sabbaton* occurs in the New Testament sixty-eight times, and is translated "Sabbath" fifty-nine times, and "week" nine times. These nine references are Matthew 28:1; Mark 16:2, 9; Luke 18:12; 24:1; John 20:1, 19; Acts 20:7; 1 Corinthians 16:2.

To the English reader it may come as a surprise that both *week* and *Sabbath* should be translated from the same word in the Greek. It is this fact that gives plausibility to the Sabbath objector's claim. But that two different time periods should be described by the same term is not peculiar to the Greek. In English, as earlier noted, we describe the twelve-hour period, the twenty-four-hour period, and even a vague, indefinite period by the same word, *day.* The context determines the time limit of the word *day;* so also with *sabbaton.*

Happily, this matter of the two meanings for *sabbaton* is not in dispute. All Greek scholars, Jewish and Christian, are in agreement as to the correctness of translating *sabbaton* by "week." The following authoritative statements are typical:

### Authorities Agree as to Double Value of Sabbaton

"WEEK (Hebrew 'shabua',' plural 'shabu'im,' 'shabu'ot'; . . . New Testament Greek, *sabbaton, sabbata*): A division of time comprising seven days, thus explaining the Hebrew name."—*The Jewish Encyclopedia*, vol. 12, p. 481, art. "Week."

# SABBATH

"The expression *hebdomas* [a Greek word for "week"] is not found in the New Testament, but rather *sabbaton* (e.g., Luke 18:12) or *sabbata* (e.g., Matt. 28:1), used, however, in the sense of it."—*Schaff-Herzog Encyclopedia of Religious Knowledge* (ed. 1891), vol. 4, p. 2484, art. "Week."

"Of the two Hebrew names for 'week' one is derived from the number seven, and the other is identical with 'Sabbath,' the day which completes the Jewish week. The New Testament takes over the latter word, and makes a Greek noun of it."—*Hastings' Bible Dictionary* (ed. 1924), p. 936, art. "Time."

"The Hebrew *shabhua'*, used in the Old Testament for 'week,' is derived from *shebha'*, the word for 'seven.' As the seventh day was a day of rest, or *Sabbath* (Hebrew, *shabbath*), this word came to be used for 'week,' as appears in the New Testament (*shabbaton, -ta*), indicating the period from Sabbath to Sabbath (Matt. 28:1). The same usage is implied in the Old Testament (Lev. 23:15; 25:8)."—*The International Standard Bible Encyclopedia* (ed. 1915), vol. 5, p. 2982, art. "Time."

"The plural *sabbata* . . . means a week as well as a Sabbath or Sabbaths (comp. Mark 16:2; Luke 24:1; John 20:1, 19; and Matt. 28:1). . . . *Sabbata* in the second clause [of Matt. 28:1] certainly means 'week' and not the Sabbath day."—JOHN PETER LANGE, *A Commentary on the Holy Scriptures*, translated by Philip Schaff, Comments on Matthew 28:1.

Luke 18:12, which is one of the nine texts in which *sabbaton* is translated "week," is a choice illustration of where *sabbaton* must be translated "week" in order to make sense. The Pharisee declared in his prayer, "I fast twice in the week [*sabbatou*]." It would have been pointless for him to say that he fasted twice in the Sabbath. There would be no mark of distinction in refraining from eating between breakfast and dinner and between dinner and supper. Doubtless even the publican did that. Only when *sabbatou* in this text is translated "week" does it make sense.

The Sabbath objector tries diligently to break the force of this passage by declaring that Luke 18:12 should read, "I fast two sabbaths," that is, two of the fixed sabbaths in the year. But the Greek will not permit this. The word *dis*, translated "twice," is an adverb, and cannot properly be translated "two." The word *sabbatou,* translated "week," is in the *singular* number, which is never translated by the plural form "sabbaths" in our English Bible.

The second part of the objector's contention is based on the fact that in the Greek the word *day* is not found in the phrase "first day of the week." This phrase in Matthew 28:1, is in the original, *mian sabbatōn.* Concerning its proper translation, eminent theologians and Greek scholars of Sundaykeeping denominations have written. As far back as the year 1899 the claim for Sunday that was built upon this revised translation of *mian sabbatōn* was exploded by a scholarly Sundaykeeper, as the following quotation reveals:

"This widely heralded Klondike discovery as to *mian sabbatōn* turns out to be only the glitter of fool's gold. It rests upon the profoundest ignoring or ignorance of a law of syntax fundamental to inflected speech, and especially of the usage and influence of the Aramaic tongue, which was the vernacular of Jesus and His apostles. Must syntax die that the Sabbath [Sunday] may live?

"Let these affirmations [of the theory] be traversed: '4. No Greek word for "day" occurs in any of the passages [that is, in Matthew 28:1 and parallel passages].' Made for simple readers of English, that statement lacks candor. Said word is there, latent, to a much greater degree than it is in our phrase, 'The twenty-fifth of the month.' Upon being asked, 'The twenty-fifth what?' the veriest child instantly replies, 'Day.' But stronger yet is the case in hand. The adjectival word *mian* is in the feminine gender, and an immutable law requires adjective modifiers to agree with their nouns in gender. *Sabbatōn* is of the neuter gender, and out of the question. What feminine Greek word is latent in this phrase, and yet so patent as to reflect upon this adjectival numeral its feminine hue? Plainly the feminine word *hēmera,* 'day,' as analogously it is found in Mark 14:12, *prōtē hēmera tōn azumōn,* 'the first day of unleavened bread.' Boldly to aver that 'no Greek word for "day" occurs in any of the passages,' is to blind the simple English reader to the fact that an inflected language, by its numerous genders and cases, can indicate the presence and force of latent words to an extent undreamed of in English. . . .

"As a vital or corroboratory part of any argument for the sanctifying of the Lord's day, this travestied exegesis, instead of being a monumental discovery, is but a monumental blunder. Thereby our foes will have us in derision.

> "Tell it not in Gath,
> Publish it not in the streets of Battle Creek,*
> Lest the daughters of the Sabbatarians rejoice,
> Lest the daughters of the Saturdarians triumph."

—DR. WILBUR FLETCHER STEELE, "Must Syntax Die That the Sabbath May Live?" in the *Methodist Review* (New York), May-June, 1899.

In 1931 this question of *mian sabbatōn* was raised by an inquirer in *The Expositor,* a widely circulated preachers' journal. At that time *The Expositor* ran a question-and-answer feature entitled "Expositions," by Prof. A. T. Robertson, D.D., one of the most eminent of modern Greek scholars, and the author of a number of works on Biblical Greek, including an exhaustive grammar. For years Professor Robertson held the chair of New Testament interpretation at the Southern Baptist Theological Seminary, Louisville, Kentucky. The question and answer are as follows:

"DEAR DR. ROBERTSON: Can it be proven, beyond doubt, that 'the first day of the week' is the proper rendition of '*mia sabbatōn*' (Matt. 28:1; Mark 16:2; Luke 24:1; John 20:1, 19; Acts 20:7; and 1 Cor. 16:2), instead of '*one of the sabbaths,*' as Mr. Knoch's Concordant Version reads? The Concordant Version reads 'first Sabbath' (Mark 16:9) instead of the first day of the week.'

> "J. D. PHILLIPS,
> "Editor of *The Truth,*
> "Littlefield, Tex."

After offering certain caustic comments on the Concordant Version, Dr. Robertson proceeds with his answer:

"Now about the case of *sabbatōn* in the New Testament. It is the singular, the transliteration of the Hebrew word *Shabbath,* which was used for the seventh day of the week, as in John 5:9. The plural, *sabbata,* is a transliteration of the Aramaic *shabbatha.* Curiously enough, the Jews used the plural form in two ways. One way was for a single Sabbath, like the singular *sabbaton.* So in Josephus. (We

---

* At the time this was written the Seventh-day Adventist headquarters were in Battle Creek, Michigan.

have *tēn hebdomēn Sabbata caloumen.* We call the seventh day Sabbath.) Precisely this usage occurs in the New Testament, as in Luke 4:16, 'on the Sabbath day,' *en tē hēmera tōn Sabbatōn.* So also Acts 13:14; 16:13, just like Exodus 20:8; 35:3, etc. So also in Matthew 12:1; 5:10-12, *tois sabbasin,* on the Sabbath, though plural, Mark 1:21; Luke 4:31, etc. But the word *sabbaton,* in the singular, was used also for the week which began [ended*] with the Sabbath. So in Mark 16:9 we have *prōi prōtē sabbatou,* early on the first day of the week. Here *prōi* is an adverb, but *prōtē* is a feminine adjective, locative, singular, agreeing with *hēmera* (day) understood, while *sabbatou* is neuter gender, genitive, singular, so that it is impossible to render this 'early on the first Sabbath.' See also Luke 18:12. But the plural *sabbata* is also used for the week, as in Luke 24:1. In the preceding verse the singular occurs, *to sabbaton,* 'they spent the Sabbath.' The very next words in verse 1 are, *tē de mia tōn sabbatōn,* 'on the first day of the week.' There we have *mia* used as an ordinal like *prōtē,* as is common in the *Koinē.* The same use of both *mia* for 'first' and the plural *sabbatōn* for 'week,' we find in Matthew 28:1; Mark 16:2; John 20:1, 19; Acts 20:7."—*The Expositor,* August, 1931.

Since Sundaykeeping theologians so thoroughly expose the false-translation argument for Sunday, it is hardly necessary to add anything more.

---

NOTE.—Right on this point of dealing with arguments against the truth which opponents construct out of a claim that certain passages in the Scriptures should be rendered differently from what they are, a brief word might not be amiss. With our lay members becoming more and more active in presenting the truth to the world, this type of objection has to be met by them increasingly. They may not have had the privilege of studying the original languages, or may not have available the standard commentaries which, in most cases, reveal the unreasonableness of quibbles built on the claim that some different translation should be given than that found in the well-known versions.

What, then, is the layman to do when he is confronted with such an argument? Become confused and withdraw from the field? Not at all. Instead, he should reply briefly that the translations of the Bible into the English language, the King James Version, and later the Revised, are the product of the united endeavors of a large group of the most learned Greek scholars ever gathered together, and that he sees

---

* "Began" should read "ended." See correction of this typographical error by Dr. Robertson in *The Expositor,* October, 1931.

no reason for making a drastic change in their translation simply because some lone man of the present day, who has no linguistic standing, declares that there ought to be a change.

That is about all the answer that is needed. It is a sound and substantial one, and will appeal to the reason of any unprejudiced person who hears it. Of course, this does not mean that a clearer understanding of a Bible passage cannot sometimes be obtained by reference to the original language, as is well illustrated in the matter of the original terms for *soul* and *spirit*. But calling attention to the original words and the possible alternate translation allowed by the lexicons is an altogether different thing from manufacturing translations that violate the primary rules of the original languages.

# Objection 48

**Seventh-day Adventists say that everyone who keeps Sunday has the mark of the beast. Such a teaching places under God's condemnation all other Christian people and dooms forever all Sunday-keeping Christians who died before Seventh-day Adventists began to preach. By teaching that a person cannot be saved unless he keeps the Sabbath, Seventh-day Adventists make Sabbathkeeping the means of salvation instead of Christ.**

Seventh-day Adventists do not say that everyone who keeps Sunday has the mark of the beast. Hence we do not place anyone, dead or alive, under condemnation. Note this authoritative statement from the writings of the best recognized of Adventist writers, Ellen G. White:

"Christians of past generations observed the Sunday, supposing that in so doing they were keeping the Bible Sabbath; and there are now true Christians in every church, not excepting the Roman Catholic Communion, who honestly believe that Sunday is the Sabbath of divine appointment. God accepts their sincerity of purpose and their integrity before Him. But when Sunday observance shall be enforced by law, and the world shall be enlightened concerning the obligation of the true Sabbath, then whoever shall transgress the command of God, to obey a precept which has no higher authority than that of Rome, will thereby honor popery above God. He is paying homage to Rome, and to the power which enforces the institution ordained by Rome. He is worshiping the beast and his image. As men then reject the institution which God has declared to be the sign of His authority, and honor in its stead that which Rome has chosen as the token of her supremacy, they will thereby accept the sign of allegiance to Rome— 'the mark of the beast.' And it is not until the issue is thus plainly set before the people, and they are brought to choose between the commandments of God and the commandments of men, that those who continue in transgression will receive 'the mark of the beast.' " —*The Great Controversy*, p. 449.

Take this further word from the pen of Mrs. White:

# SABBATH

"No one has yet received the mark of the beast. The testing time has not yet come. There are true Christians in every church, not excepting the Roman Catholic communion. None are condemned until they have had the light and have seen the obligation of the fourth commandment. But when the decree shall go forth enforcing the counterfeit sabbath, and the loud cry of the third angel shall warn men against the worship of the beast and his image, the line will be clearly drawn between the false and the true. Then those who still continue in transgression will receive the mark of the beast."—*Evangelism*, pp. 234, 235.

Paul said to the ancient, idolatrous Athenians, "The times of this ignorance God winked at; but now commandeth all men every where to repent." Acts 17:30. It is not what we do ignorantly that brings God's condemnation, but what we do willfully after we have a clear knowledge of the truth. "Therefore to him that knoweth to do good, and doeth it not, to him it is sin." James 4:17. God sent the Advent movement into the world, not to condemn the world, but to preach the truth. We have no desire to judge any man. Judgment belongs to God.

In view of this fact it is not an accurate statement of our position to say that we hold that a person cannot be saved unless he keeps the seventh-day Sabbath. Here is our position: Only those will be saved who, having been redeemed by the grace of Christ, walk in obedience to all the light that God sheds on their way. Surely no Christian will question that position. The Bible says that "the path of the just is as the shining light, that shineth more and more unto the perfect day." Prov. 4:18. Peter calls on Christian believers to "add to your faith" a long list of Christian graces. (See 2 Peter 1:5-7.) So long as we continue to walk in the light and add graces and Christian practices as they are revealed by that light, we grow in grace, and continue on the road to heaven.

When we willfully refuse to go forward in the path because some requirement God reveals to us seems hard to obey, we reject Heaven's light. When we do this do we not immediately jeopardize our hope of salvation, and must we not change from rejection to acceptance of that further light before it can be said of us again that we are truly saved? Of the Jews who refused to accept the light that Christ brought, He declared, "If I had not come and spoken unto them, they had not had sin: but now they have no cloke [margin, "excuse"] for their sin." John 15:22.

In far lands missionaries of the various churches preach Christ crucified, presenting the love of God and the atoning sacrifice of Christ. They preach to savage races of men who have brazenly and perhaps without a twinge of conscience been violating the whole range of the Ten Commandments. As the natives are touched by God's Spirit and express their sincere desire to accept Christ's proffered salvation, what do the missionaries do? They explain to the natives that Christ offers them salvation as a free gift, but that if they desire to be true children of God, they will give evidence of this by walking in the path that God has revealed. In other words, the missionaries will say to them, as Paul said to the Ephesians: "Let him that stole steal no more." Eph. 4:28. They will speak of turning not only from stealing but from the other violations of the Decalogue—murder, adultery, lying, idolatry, et cetera. They will probably add that no liar or thief or murderer or idolater will ever enter the kingdom of God.

This, in substance, is what missionaries of all faiths say day after day as they bring men to God. But we have never heard anyone charge that they are thus substituting obedience to the Ten Commandments for the grace of God. Then, why should Adventists be accused of substituting Sabbathkeeping for the grace of God simply because our appeal to men to walk by grace in the way of truth includes a presentation of *all* the Ten Commandments, for the Sabbath command is one of the ten? We do not say, for we do not believe, that keeping the Sabbath command, or any other of the Ten Commandments, gives a man entrance to heaven. Entrance will ever be only through the grace of God received by faith. But we do say that the man who willfully breaks any of God's commandments, which includes the fourth, shuts the doors of heaven against himself. No willful sinner will enter its portals.

# Objection 49

I don't believe that a God of love would keep men out of heaven just because of a day. I think Seventh-day Adventists put too much emphasis on a certain day that should be kept holy.

The answer to this is largely found in the answer to the immediately preceding objection. We wish to ask the objector this question: Do you think God is particular? To reply that you do not think that God *is* particular, is to free yourself not only from obedience to the fourth command but from obedience to every other command as well. By what process of reasoning should we conclude that God is particular about nine of the commands but not about the fourth?

God gave the command that men should keep "the seventh day." Did He really mean that, or may we just keep any day we choose, or none at all if that pleases us more? In language more terse and blunt: Does God really mean what He says?

In the early days of Jewish history God instructed the priests that when they ministered in the sanctuary they should not use "strange fire," that is, common fire, but that they should always draw from the holy flame that burned continually on the altar. It may be very plausibly argued that all fire is alike, even as one might argue that all days are alike, and conclude that God would really not care if His command concerning the particular kind of fire was not obeyed. Evidently two priests—Nadab and Abihu— acted on this theory for they employed strange fire in offering incense before the Lord. And what was the result? "There went out fire from the Lord, and devoured them, and they died before the Lord." Lev. 10:2.

The context shows that this judgment came upon them because they had failed to obey the command to put a "difference between holy and unholy." Verse 10.

How remarkable is the parallel! The Sabbath commandment is intended to put a difference between the holy and the unholy in days. "Remember the sabbath day, to keep it *holy*." Is God less particular about His holy day than He was about the holy fire that He gave to the Israelites?

Take another illustration: The children of Israel were forbidden to touch the ark of God or "any holy thing." (See Num. 4:15, 20.) The command was very simply worded, so that all could understand. But once when the ark was being moved over rough ground, a man by the name of Uzzah "put forth his hand to the ark of God, and took hold of it; for the oxen shook it." 2 Sam. 6:6. Uzzah doubtless reasoned that the command against touching the ark did not apply in such a circumstance. But what are the facts? "The anger of the Lord was kindled against Uzzah; and God smote him there." Verse 7. Was the Lord particular? Did He mean just what He said? And shall we say that God is less particular today than in former years? Is He not the same yesterday, today, and forever? Indeed, were not these experiences of the ancient Israelites written for our admonition, that we might profit by their mistakes? If God punished a man for laying his hand upon the holy ark, will He condone the man who lays violent hands upon the Sabbath day, moving it about to suit his own convenience?

The Israelites, so the record leads us to conclude, thought that the Lord was surely not so particular as to bring a judgment upon them if they failed in such a small matter as keeping a particular day holy. But the Good Book informs us that the destruction of Solomon's Temple and the carrying away captive of the people from the land of Canaan was a direct judgment on them for their desecration of the Sabbath. (See Jer. 17:21-27; 2 Chron. 36:17-21; Neh. 13:17, 18; Eze. 22:26.) Now if God drove His chosen people *out* of the *literal* land of Canaan for their disregard of the day He had commanded them to keep holy, how unreasonable to think He will *admit* men to the *heavenly* Canaan if they willfully disregard that holy day.

# Objection 50

**The Sabbath cannot save anyone. Why not preach Christ instead?**

The answers to the two objections immediately preceding are largely the answer to the one before us. The weakness of this one becomes clearly evident by simply expanding it to its logical limits. The statement is made that the Sabbath cannot save anyone; in other words, that Sabbathkeeping can never win for man a place in heaven. But it is also true that the mere keeping of any other commandment of the Decalogue will not purchase entrance into heaven. Shall we therefore conclude that it is unnecessary for a minister to preach on the third commandment, for example, or the fifth, with their stern declarations concerning the reverencing of God's name and the honoring of one's father and mother? No, you say, by all means preach out boldly on these, for profanity is heard on every side, and honor to parents has been too much forgotten by the youth today.

Well then, if it is not only proper but highly important to preach about the third and the fifth commandment, how can you say that we should not preach the fourth commandment? And when we think of the wholesale violation of that fourth commandment—as widespread surely as the violation of the third or the fifth—the candid reader will immediately realize that the preaching of the Sabbath commandment is not only proper but highly important. It is for this reason that we raise our voice so clearly regarding the Sabbath.

We have stated that no one can purchase entry into heaven by Sabbathkeeping, and have shown that such a statement proves nothing against the Sabbath. But we would take the matter a little further. Simply because it is true that the keeping of any or all of the commandments cannot ensure our entrance into heaven, is it therefore true that the *failure* to keep the commandments will not prevent us from entering that blessed abode? No, you say, the person who willfully violates the commandments cannot enter heaven. Abstaining from murder will not ensure our entrance, but the violation of that command will certainly keep us out. Refraining from stealing or from adultery will not assure us entrance, but certainly the breaking of those commandments clearly debars us.

Well then, does not the most obvious analogy cause us to conclude that although Sabbathkeeping cannot secure us admission into heaven, Sabbathbreaking will certainly *prevent* our entrance? And if it is possible for a man so to relate himself to the Sabbath, or to any other commandment in the Decalogue, that his entrance to heaven is impossible, is it not very important that the minister of the gospel preach on those commandments, the Sabbath commandment included?

But let us go still further. The inference we are supposed to draw is that the preaching of Christ is something wholly different from preaching the obligations of God's holy law—that the two have nothing in common. Some have gone so far as to declare that the very idea of law is in opposition to the gospel of Christ. But such views cannot stand a moment's investigation, as we have already discovered. Two texts of Scripture are sufficient to reveal the close relationship between the law and the gospel. Christ said to His disciples, "If ye love me, keep my commandments." John 14:15. Thus if we would preach the doctrine of love to Christ, we must include an exhortation to obey the commandments. Obedience is the fruit of love. Or, take this other text in the book of Revelation: "Here are they that keep the commandments of God, and the faith of Jesus." Rev. 14:12. This is a description of the true children of God in the closing days of earth's history. How closely related is their faith in Christ and their obedience to God's commandments!

The reason why some men do not want to hear the Sabbath preached is that it troubles their consciences, and they feel condemned before God as violators of His law. It is not the preaching that is wrong, but their lives.

# Objection 51

**I have the baptism of the Holy Spirit, and the Holy Spirit has given me to understand that I do not have to keep the Sabbath.**

This statement reflects the teaching of a certain religious organization that believes it possesses the gift of the Holy Spirit in a way different from all other Christians. The members believe themselves guided very directly by this Spirit in matters of doctrine. Now, it is true that the Bible says much about the presence of the Spirit in the lives of Christians, but the Good Book also warns against the presence of another kind of spirit that will lead men away from truth. The mere fact that one is possessed by a supernatural power does not prove that that power is the Holy Spirit of God.

The Bible instructs us to "try the spirits." (1 John 4:1.) It does not say we should try a Bible doctrine by the spirits, but that we should try the spirits by the Bible doctrine. Otherwise how could we tell what sort of spirit was possessing us? The prophet Isaiah warns against being under the influence of certain "spirits," and provides a means whereby we may know whether a spirit is of God. His words are plain, and easily understood: "To the law and to the testimony: if they speak not according to this word, it is because there is no light in them." Isa. 8:20. Then if a spirit does not speak in harmony with the law, that spirit does not belong to the kingdom of light but to the kingdom of darkness.

This one inspired statement ought to be sufficient. When a spirit declares that the Sabbath, which is part of the law—indeed, is found right in the heart of the law—need not be kept, what are we to conclude? Is not the answer evident? Such a spirit speaks not in accordance with the teachings of God's Word; on the contrary, it speaks against them.

The book of Revelation pronounces a dire woe against anyone

who should add to or take from the words of the prophecy in the book. (See Rev. 22:18, 19.) One statement in that book describes the people of God as "they that keep the commandments of God, and the faith of Jesus." Rev. 14:12. A spirit that informs a man he need not keep the Sabbath commandment is really attempting to change the inspired description of God's children to read, "Here are they that keep nine of the commandments of God, but do not have to keep the fourth commandment."

By such an act this spirit comes under the last fearful woe found in God's Book. (See Rev. 22:18, 19.) And what kind of spirits are they that stand under the condemnation of God? Certainly not heavenly spirits. A spirit sent from God does not diverge from God's Word. Said Christ to His disciples, "When he, the Spirit of truth, is come, he will guide you into all truth: for he shall not speak of himself; but whatsoever he shall hear, that shall he speak: and he will shew you things to come." John 16:13. The Spirit of God brings to the believer only that which has been heard in the courts of heaven. And violation of any of God's commandments is never advocated in heaven, that is, not since the day that Satan and his evil spirits were cast out.

We read that one of the duties of the Spirit of God is to "reprove the world of sin." Verse 8. And what is sin? Transgression of the law. (See 1 John 3:4.) But the spirit we are here investigating would not be reproving sin, but condoning it, by telling men that they may transgress one of the commandments —the fourth.

Therefore when a spirit declares that the Sabbath need not be kept, we may properly conclude that we should immediately free ourselves, not from the Sabbath, but from that spirit. The Sabbath has stood the test of the ages; its credentials are signed by God Himself. No, the Sabbath is not on trial. Try the *spirits!*

# Objection 52

**We should keep all days holy in the Christian dispensation. But inasmuch as the law of the land has marked out a certain day—Sunday—as the particular day of rest, we should obey the law of the land, and keep Sunday.**

This Sabbath objection grows out of a predicament. Different groups in the Sundaykeeping ranks of Christendom have different ways of trying to avoid the straight command of God to keep holy "the seventh day." One group, frank enough to admit that the New Testament contains no command to transfer the Sabbath to Sunday, has attempted to escape the Sabbath obligation by declaring that in the Christian dispensation all days are alike holy, and because of this there need not be given to the Sabbath day any particular veneration over any other day.

Those who claimed merely that all days were holy thought that they were solving the difficulty in simple fashion. But in actual practice their solution did not work so well. If all days are holy, then one day is no better than another, and why should we do special honor to any day by centering our religious services on that day? Thus men could reason. In other words, the whole idea of the Sabbath would vanish out of the minds of men because it had lost its definiteness.

But how was definiteness to be introduced without surrendering the whole argument? Why, by the simple expedient of invoking the scripture that declares we should be subject to civil government, and then calling attention to the fact that there is a civil statute requiring rest from labor on a certain day in the week, Sunday. Thus by a wide detour this group of Sundaykeepers reach their desired day without apparently laying themselves open to the troublesome necessity of trying to prove that the day was changed to Sunday by the New Testament writers—a theological feat that they have observed other Sundaykeepers unable to accomplish.

It is hard to know just where to begin in answering such a fallacy as this, for every main statement of it is incorrect. Take the claim that all days are alike holy. Is it not asking a little too much of the Sabbath defender to expect him to meet the Sunday challenger from two opposite sides at the same time? Must we be expected to demolish with one stroke the claim that the Sabbath was transferred to the first day of the week and the contention that it was transferred to all the seven days of the week? Might we not be pardoned for demanding that Sundaykeepers first agree among themselves as to just *what* claim they will make for Sunday before asking a Sabbathkeeper to answer them?

But let us examine the claim that we should keep a certain day because the government so decrees. True, the Bible says we should be subject to the civil power. But where do we read that we should guide our religious lives by the statutes of civil government? (Rather, we read the contrary. Acts 5:29.) If we ought so to guide ourselves, then our religion would change whenever we moved to a new land, and one so unfortunate as to live in a pagan land would find himself keeping holy certain days set apart for pagan gods. Into what desperate situations does false logic bring us!

But let us take the matter a little further. How do we happen to have Sunday laws on the statute books of various so-called Christian governments? Because certain militant Sundaykeepers who believed the Sabbath had been definitely changed to the first day of the week persuaded legislatures to enact a law setting aside that particular day. And now, incredible though it be, those who declare that *all* days are alike holy come urging *Sunday* sacredness because of a civil statute that was passed at the behest of those who declare that the Sabbath was transferred to the first day of the week.

Could paradox be greater? Is it really possible to tell just what such people believe?

# Objection 53

**If Saturday is the right Sabbath, why do not more leading men believe it? If what you preach about the Sabbath is true, why wasn't it discovered before?**

Is it not common knowledge that when Christianity began in the world the people of that day, both Jews and Greeks, had much to say about its being a *new* doctrine? When Christ rebuked an evil spirit, commanding it to come out of a man, the people "were all amazed, insomuch that they questioned among themselves, saying, What thing is this? what new doctrine is this?" Mark 1:27. When Paul came to Athens and began to preach Christianity, the people inquired, "May we know what this new doctrine, whereof thou speakest, is?" Acts 17:19. Various other passages might be given, showing that the teachings of Christianity were considered new and strange.

Come down to the time of the Reformation in the sixteenth century. Who does not know that the most common argument against the Reformers was that their teachings were new? The argument was about in the form of the objection we are considering: If what you Reformers say is true, how is it that these doctrines were not discovered before?

But did such charges against Christ and the apostles and the Reformers prove that their teachings were not of God? No. Doctrines must be judged by a different standard from that.

But what of this charge of newness made against Christianity and the Reformation? When Christ or His disciples were confronted with the charge, they always denied it, declaring that they did not preach new, strange doctrines, but that, on the contrary, as Paul affirmed, they preached "none other things than those which the prophets and Moses did say should come." Acts 26:22. When the charge was made against the Reformers, they proceeded to show from the Bible that the doctrines they preached were not

253

new but very ancient. And, further, they could show that all down through the centuries there had been a few faithful children of God who had known and preached those doctrines.

As we read history we still marvel at the charges made against Christ and the Reformers, and wonder why men should have been so slow to discern truths that now seem so evident. But the fact that they were so slow is an indictment of *them* and *not* of the doctrines they failed to see.

The relation of these facts to the question before us is clear. With Christ and the disciples and the Reformers we would say that the Sabbath doctrine is not new; it is as old as creation, and has been known and kept by godly men through all the centuries. Granted that this Sabbath truth was almost completely suppressed for centuries, and did not burst forth again until relatively modern times, is it not a fact that the truth of righteousness by faith was almost wholly lost for more than a thousand years, and did not burst forth again until the sixteenth century?

Now a word as to why more "leading men" do not believe this Sabbath truth. What of the "leading men" in the days of Christ, and of the Reformation? Who does not know that it was "the common people" who heard Christ gladly; that His disciples were ordinary people, such as fishermen? And who does not know that the "big men" of Christ's time endeavored to argue people out of accepting Christ by inquiring, "Have any of the rulers or of the Pharisees believed on him?" John 7:48. What was it that Paul declared to the early believers? "Ye see your calling, brethren, how that not many wise men after the flesh, not many mighty, not many noble, are called." 1 Cor. 1:26. And in Luther's day what about all the "leading men"? All the church dignitaries were spending their time trying to catch him to burn him.

True, we believe that God has among the so-called "big men" many honest hearts, and that from their ranks will finally be drawn strong believers in the Sabbath. But though none such should accept, the seventh day would still be the Sabbath of the Lord, for no man is big enough to change God's commandments.

# Objection 54

**If I should keep the Sabbath, all my friends and neighbors would ridicule me.**

What if they do ridicule you? Surely you do not govern all your acts by what your neighbors may think or say about you. Ridicule is generally the price men have had to pay for holding any sort of idea different from the majority. We would not have many of our great inventions today if men like Bell and Edison and others had refused to adopt some new mechanical idea simply because people would ridicule them. For this very reason it often takes courage to be an inventor. But you say that it is worth the price. Very true. And is it not worth the price of ridicule to be a Christian and to be assured of the rewards promised to those who obey God? That is the real question involved.

The Bible does not attempt to hide the fact that those who obey God will often suffer reproach and be falsely accused, and that divisions will come even between members of a family, to say nothing of neighbors. Said Christ: "Suppose ye that I am come to give peace on earth? I tell you, Nay; but rather division: for from henceforth there shall be five in one house divided, three against two, and two against three. The father shall be divided against the son, and the son against the father; the mother against the daughter, and the daughter against the mother; the mother in law against her daughter in law, and the daughter in law against her mother in law." Luke 12:51-53.

If you are haunted by the fear that people will ridicule you if you do what God commands, read the lives of God's loyal men of the past, who suffered much more than ridicule for the cause of right. You will receive a new idea of values, and will begin to realize that the ridicule of men means little. Read what that mighty man Paul wrote from his dungeon cell to Timothy: "Be not thou therefore ashamed of the testimony of our Lord, nor of me his prisoner: but be thou partaker of the afflictions of the gospel according to the power of God." 2 Tim. 1:8.

And why did Paul feel no shame, no humiliation, over his imprisonment and over his being subjected to the taunts of the Roman soldiers? "I am not ashamed," he said; "for I know whom I have believed, and am persuaded that he is able to keep that which I have committed unto him against that day." Verse 12. "I have fought a good fight, I have finished my course, I have kept the faith: henceforth there is laid up for me a crown of righteousness, which the Lord, the righteous judge, shall give me at that day: and not to me only, but unto all them also that love his appearing." 2 Tim. 4:7, 8.

That was the secret of Paul's disdain of ridicule, shame, and reproach. He looked beyond the brief present to the eternal future, with its rewards. And to those who fix their eyes on that better land of the future the Good Book declares, "They desire a better country, that is, an heavenly: wherefore God is not ashamed to be called their God: for he hath prepared for them a city." Heb. 11:16.

There should be coupled with this the solemn words of Christ: "Whosoever therefore shall be ashamed of me and of my words in this adulterous and sinful generation; of him also shall the Son of man be ashamed, when he cometh in the glory of his Father with the holy angels." Mark 8:38.

Would you rather be on good terms with your neighbors than with God? Would you rather do what *they think* is right, or what *God says* is right? Would you not rather have your neighbors ashamed of you in this day than to have Christ ashamed of you in the last great day? What is your answer to solemn questions like these?

# Objection 55

**If I keep the seventh-day Sabbath, I won't be able to make a living.**

Is this really a proper objection to raise against a commandment of God? Should we decide first whether we will profit financially by following God's voice before we obey? What a different story the Bible would tell us of the great men of old if they had all stopped to reason out whether it would pay them to serve God! Men of God are of different mettle.

What if you cannot make a living; you can make a dying. Nor would you be the first one who has been called on to pay with his life for serving God. The history of the children of God is one long record of martyrdom. There have always been men who would rather die than disobey God. It calls for courage and bravery to serve Heaven.

However, God does not often require the supreme sacrifice in order to serve Him. You say you could not make a living. How do you know? Did God tell you that you would starve to death, or was it just a temptation from the devil to keep you from making the right decision? No, you could not have read any such thought in the Bible, for Christ declares: "Wherefore, if God so clothe the grass of the field, which to day is, and to morrow is cast into the oven, shall he not much more clothe you, O ye of little faith? Therefore take no thought, saying, What shall we eat? or, What shall we drink? or, Wherewithal shall we be clothed? (for after all these things do the Gentiles seek:) for your heavenly Father knoweth that ye have need of all these things. But seek ye first the kingdom of God, and his righteousness; and all these things shall be added unto you." Matt. 6:30-33. And David in his old age wrote, "I have been young, and now am old; yet have I not seen the righteous forsaken, nor his seed begging bread." Ps. 37:25.

God still lives, and loves those who show their love for Him by obeying His commandments. Why not have faith in Him, and believe that He will enable you to make a living if you keep the Sabbath?

There are many thousands of men and women throughout the world who have displayed just that sort of faith in God, and have stepped out to keep the Sabbath. And has God failed them? He has not. True, some of them have had their faith tested for a time before they were able to find employment as Sabbathkeepers. But they have not starved. The testimony of a million Sabbath-keepers disproves completely the objection we are here examining.

To those who fear they cannot obey God and make a living, I would say: If you really think that God would desert you if you turned to serve Him, you need a new idea of God rather than of the Sabbath. But if you believe that God will fulfill His promise to provide for those who obey His commandments, and that even if He tests your faith you would rather die than disobey Him, then your course is clear—keep the Sabbath.

# Section III

# SECOND ADVENT

# Objections 56 to 68

The reader is also referred to
Part 2, Section IV, pages 565 to 632,
"The Second Advent"

# Objection 56

The Seventh-day Adventist Church sprang from the religious movement of the 1840's, known as Millerism, which set a time for the coming of Christ. Such a historical background reveals how irrational and unworthy of serious consideration that church is.

The charge is not that we set a time but that our spiritual ancestors did. Let that fact be clear in introduction. Seventh-day Adventists throughout the entire history of this body have not only *not* set a time for the Advent, but have emphatically declared, in the words of Christ: "Of that day and hour knoweth no man." Any critic who has read our literature knows this fact. Hence the charge against us is framed in terms of our predecessors, our spiritual background. This is said, not in any attempt to avoid the fact that the Millerites set time in 1844, but simply to place the whole matter in proper historical perspective.

Note these facts: The Millerite movement of the early 1840's was essentially an interchurch movement; ministers and members of various churches were known as Millerites. Further, the movement was the expression of a quickened interest in those various portions of Scripture, especially the prophecies, which present the subject of the Second Advent. Finally, any religious body that might have arisen as a result of that quickening of Scripture study on the Advent should rightly be judged by the creed that governs that body rather than by the views of the loosely knit Millerite movement, which focused on one great doctrine.

However, this does not mean that we prefer to forget about the events of the 1840's. Far from it. Because we here emphasize the fact that Seventh-day Adventist doctrines should not be confused with the views of Millerism, we do not mean that there was something so sadly embarrassing, even fanatical, about the Millerite time-setting incident in 1844 that we wish to stand completely apart from all who joined in that movement. Not at all. The following six facts will put Millerite time setting in a wholly different light from that long thrown upon it by those who have framed the objection before us:

## Fact Number 1

Though time setting is a theological mistake, it is a mistake no more grave than that committed by eminent theologians on other questions of Christian doctrine or practice. For example, the Scriptures declare that God is long-suffering, not willing that any should perish, but that all should come to repentance. Yet Calvin, and all who have followed him, have shut their eyes to this most explicit statement, and declared that some are predestined to salvation and some to reprobation. After attending the Synod of Dort, which dogmatized on predestination and its evil corollary, reprobation, the Anglican bishops declared that it was unwise to discuss reprobation, because it tended to desperation rather than edification!

No worse indictment could ever have been made against time setting. But here is the difference: Theologians have lost their tempers discussing predestination, but they have not lost their reputations. Their mistaken conclusions have been too mysterious, dealing, as they have, with the divine decrees concerning the end of man. But those who mistakenly concluded they had solved the mystery of the divine time decree concerning the end of the world have been held up to ridicule. And this despite the fact that they may have discussed their subject with sweet harmony and brought edification rather than desperation to those who accepted their theology. Strange, indeed.

## Fact Number 2

It is far better for a follower of Christ to seek to learn as much as he can regarding the coming of his Lord than to be found with that company whom Christ rebukes for saying, "My Lord delayeth his coming." Of all the mistakes that a Christ-loving student of the

Scriptures could make, time setting might reasonably be described as the most pardonable.

**Fact Number 3**

But much more weighty than the question of the relative gravity of the mistake of time setting is the fact that time setting was not of the essence of the Advent message preached by Miller and his associates. The proof of this statement is unequivocal. When the first advent conference was held (Boston, October 13, 14, 1840) there was published a statement addressed "to all that in every place call upon the name of Jesus Christ our Lord, both theirs and ours." This statement declared that the purpose of the meeting was to "revive and restore" the "ancient faith" held by the "first Christians, the primitive ages of the church, and the profoundly learned and intelligent Reformers," regarding the personal coming of Christ. Then follows this paragraph:

"Though in some of the less important views of this momentous subject we are not ourselves agreed, particularly in regard to fixing the year of Christ's second advent, yet we are unanimously agreed and established in this all-absorbing point, that the coming of the Lord to judge the world is now specially 'nigh at hand.' "—*The First Report of the General Conference of Christians Expecting the Advent of Our Lord Jesus Christ*, sec. "Proceedings of the Conference," p. 12.

The chairman of that first conference, Henry Dana Ward, and the secretary, Henry Jones, both went on record as opposed to setting a time.

At a conference that opened on May 24, 1842, in Boston, a resolution was passed to the effect that there were weighty reasons for expecting the end in 1843. But the proceedings go on to declare that a person need not subscribe to this time element, he need only subscribe to the belief that the personal Advent of Christ is the next great event of prophetic history in order to be a member of the conference and in good standing. (See *Signs of the Times*, June 1, 1842, p. 69.)

In the spring of 1844 the editor of *The Advent Herald*, leading Millerite weekly, argued for the adoption of the name Adventist as a title for the movement because "it marks the real ground of difference between us and the great body of our opponents." He clarifies his statement thus:

"We are fully aware that they [the opponents] have endeavored to keep the question of time before the public as the obnoxious and heretical point, (and we fully believe the time to be as distinctly revealed as any other part of the subject. On that account we have defended it, and thus it has become so prominent,) still that is not, nor has it ever been, the only, or the main question in dispute. In fact, there is a greater difference between us and our opposers on the *nature of the events* predicted, than upon the interpretation of the prophetic periods [of time], or their termination."—*The Advent Herald*, March 20, 1844, p. 53.

So far as the setting of a definite *day* for the Advent is concerned, namely, October 22, 1844, the record is clear that Miller, Himes, and other principal leaders did not accept this definite date until in October. This did not make them any the less parties to the time-setting error, but it provides clear proof in support of the proposition that a definite date for the Advent was not of the essence of the Millerite movement. Even to the last some prominent Millerite preachers held to the Scripture that the day and hour could not be known. Miller himself, who on October 6 finally accepted the definite date, veered from it on October 21, as his letter to Dr. I. O. Orr, shortly afterward, reveals. This letter, in Miller's handwriting, gives, among other things, details of the days just preceding the expected Advent on the tenth day of the seventh Jewish month, that is, October 22. We quote:

"The ninth day [of the seventh month, that is October 21] was very remarkable. We held a meeting all day, and our place of worship was crowded to overflowing with anxious souls apparently. In the evening I told some of my brethren Christ would not come on the morrow. Why not? said they. Because He can not come in an hour they think not, nor as a snare."—Manuscript Letter, Dec. 13, 1844.

In other words, Miller evidently wished to say that if Christ came on a day known in advance, He would not truly be coming, as the Scriptures declare He will, in an hour when men think not, and as a snare. This revelation of Miller's thinking on the eve of the expected Advent may be viewed by cynical critics merely as proof that he did not know what he thought on the matter. To all others, we believe, this letter to Dr. Orr shows that Miller, the leader of the Advent movement in 1844, could calmly doubt the possibility of knowing the day of Christ's coming without in any way questioning the spiritual, prophetic significance of the movement of which he was the leader.

**Fact Number 4**

Time setting did not vitiate the basic principles of prophetic interpretation on which Millerism rested, and on which interpretation they built their message. This conclusion follows almost certainly from the fact that time setting was not of the essence of Millerism and that some prominent leaders were not believers in a definite date for the Advent. The Millerites based all their interpretation of the great time prophecies on the principle that a day stands for a year. They therefore saw in those prophecies great measuring rods to span the centuries and to give a clue to God's final plans for this earth. They saw in certain great prophecies the work of the Papacy described. In all this the Millerites were but following in the steps of most eminent theologians of former centuries. It was on the strength of these views of prophecy and related Bible statements regarding the Second Advent that the Millerites based their belief that the Advent of Christ might soon be expected, and that His coming was to be literal and personal. The time-setting feature simply brought into sharper focus the "when" of the Advent, but did not invalidate the basic Millerite preaching concerning this climactic event.

**Fact Number 5**

Some of the very theologians who joined in the ridicule of Millerism in the early 1840's were themselves time setters. The proof of this is undebatable. One minister, in the closing chapter of his book which sought to expose Miller's views, declared:

"If any reliance can be placed on the inference, that the historical events to which we have adverted, are subjects of prophecy, then the Millennium will commence at the close of the nineteenth or the early part of the twentieth century."—W. H. COFFIN, *The Millennium of the Church,* pp. 81, 82.

Wrote another widely quoted theological opponent in the closing chapter of his work on Millerism:

"If, therefore, we could ascertain the precise date of *the commencement* of the 1260 years, during which the Papal Antichrist is to continue, there would be no difficulty in fixing the year of his downfall, which is either to be contemporaneous with the commencement of the millennium, or else to precede this glorious era by a very few years. [Then follows a discussion of possible dates.] . . . My own opinion is in favor of the last, viz.: A.D. 2015."—JOHN DOWLING, *An Exposition of the Prophecies,* pp. 190, 191.

These opponents drew from Bible prophecies their conclusions as to time. If they were less certain as to the date of the grand climax, it was due, not to any hesitancy to believe that such a date might be discovered, but simply that they had not been able to fix upon it with finality. Yet these men were nowhere the objects of derision. No one accused them of fanaticism. Why? We think there is but one answer to this question: They did not predict that on a certain date the world would come to a fiery end by the supernatural appearing of Christ in judgment, but that the world would enter a millennial era in which all would know the Lord from the least to the greatest. It was not the *time* but the event that was really at issue. We do not truly understand the real issue between the 1844 Adventists and their opponents until we understand that the controversy centered on the *event* to take place. Not time setting but the event predicted by the Millerites seemed ridiculous to the world.

## Fact Number 6

We can truthfully declare that Seventh-day Adventists have never set a time for the Lord to come, although we admit freely, and without the slightest embarrassment, that we grew out of the soil of Millerism. This is the natural conclusion from the evidence here presented. All Protestants boast that they are spiritual descendants of the sixteenth-century Reformers without thereby meaning that they are to be held accountable for every view or teaching that may have been promulgated by the Reformers, particularly if such a teaching is clearly not of the essence of the Reformation message. Furthermore, the Reformation, at the outset, was a loose-knit movement. Afterward came the clearly defined Lutheran and Calvinistic bodies. Each grew directly out of the soil of the Reformation, but each may rightly contend that it is to be held strictly accountable only for those doctrines and practices that have been believed and practiced since its church organization and authority was established. Even so with Seventh-day Adventists in relation to Millerism and time setting.

# Objection 57

The Millerite, or Second Advent movement, out of which Seventh-day Adventism sprang, was tainted with weird fanatical actions such as the wearing of ascension robes by the deluded followers of Miller who sat on housetops and haystacks to await the coming of Christ. Multitudes were made insane by the fanatical preaching. The fanaticism was rampant both before and after 1844. This proves that God was not in the movement that brought forth Seventh-day Adventism.

For practical purposes let us divide the answer into two parts.

1. What are the facts regarding the Millerite movement up to the date when the second coming of Christ was expected on October 22, 1844?

We deny, in whole, the two most commonly framed charges, that ascension robes were worn and that multitudes were made insane by the Millerite preaching. Further, we deny virtually in whole a wide array of other charges of fanaticism. It has never been possible for any religious movement to escape wholly from the charge of fanatical acts, for no movement can prevent at least a few unstable persons from entering its ranks and taking its name.

The proof in support of this sweeping denial is found in the book *The Midnight Cry*.* There the original sources are quoted on every important point of Millerite history, including the question of fanaticism, up to the end of the Millerite movement proper.

2. What are the facts regarding the Millerite movement *after* 1844?

So long as the movement had united leadership, more or less official publications, and frequent general conferences, the spirit and temper of the movement could be quite accurately determined. An erratic or fanatical individual or group stood out in sharp contrast to the main body, and the spokesmen for the movement

---

* Published in 1944 by the Review and Herald Publishing Association, Washington 12, D.C. For book reviews, which contain the admissions of scholarly reviewers that the charges against the Millerites have been clearly refuted, see Appendix F, page 836.

could record their disapproval of anything irrational in conduct. Such declarations of disapproval were sometimes necessary, for there are always unstable and fanatical spirits that seek to attach themselves to any new religious movement.

After 1844, when the movement broke up, there was no longer a well-defined and unified company called Millerites, who could unitedly denounce and expel any fanatical spirits who might seek to parade under the name of Millerite or Adventist.

All the while a hostile world was ready to accept and broadcast any story, no matter how fanciful, regarding anyone who had espoused the Advent teachings. The marvel is, not that charges of fanaticism have come down to us regarding the Millerites in the period immediately following 1844, but that there are not more such stories.

However, if the following six facts are kept in mind, an unprejudiced person will have no difficulty in deciding that Seventh-day Adventists—and for that matter, Adventists in general —should not be blackened by such stories.

1. The most plausible stories so widely circulated about the Millerites up to October 22, 1844, have been proved wholly groundless in most instances and grossly exaggerated in the few remaining instances. Why give any more weight to stories told about these people after 1844? Did the storytellers suddenly become more veracious in 1845 and in the years following?

2. The great body of Millerites stand revealed, from a scrutiny of their writings and their conduct up to the end of 1844, as quiet, circumspect people, earnest Christians drawn from many churches. Is it reasonable to believe that they suddenly changed their essential nature and broke forth on every side in fanatical excesses?

3. Such isolated instances of fanaticism as actually occurred after 1844 received only vigorous condemnation from such leadership as did exist, whether among the first-day Adventists or among those who later took the name Seventh-day Adventists.

4. In this twilight period from 1845 to the early 1850's there was no real organization known as Seventh-day Adventists. There

was literally only a handful of the former Millerite thousands who added to their doctrine of the imminence of the Advent, the doctrine of the Sabbath and the sanctuary. Sometimes a small church group of Adventists would consist only in part of those who had added these two doctrines to their beliefs. Among the troubled and bewildered Millerites traveled prominently three persons who were the pioneers of the Seventh-day Adventist Church: Joseph Bates, James White, and Ellen G. White. They encouraged steadfastness in the faith of the Advent and presented the further truths of the Sabbath and the sanctuary. Slowly there began to emerge the form of what is now known as the Seventh-day Adventist Church.

That these three pioneers met fanaticism at times is clearly recorded in their writings. That they denounced it unsparingly is also recorded. Undoubtedly some who were fanatically inclined were turned from their folly and became stable members of the then-developing Sabbathkeeping Advent movement. But that proves only the power of the movement to subdue turbulent spirits. In other words, it proves that Seventh-day Adventism is an antidote for fanaticism.

5. The three who pioneered in the Seventh-day Adventist movement were with it for many years. They continued to preach the same basic views on religious living throughout all their public life. Hence it is proper to conclude that the more or less well-defined Seventh-day Adventist Church in the 1860's and 1870's, when these three pioneers were still the dominant figures, was constituted of people with essentially the same beliefs and the same ideas of propriety in religious life as were held by those who accepted and followed the teachings and counsel of these pioneers in earlier days. And when we examine the bona fide church records of the 1860's and 1870's what do we find? Anything that warrants the conclusion that Seventh-day Adventists were given to fanatical religious excesses at that time? The answer is emphatically, No! Indeed, the Seventh-day Adventist Church through the hundred years of its history has been singularly free of fanaticism and has

ever denounced any variety of it that might rear its head. That is a simple, undebatable fact. It would be strange, indeed, if a movement that has had such a record consistently throughout all its history should have flowed forth from the springs of fanatical excess! Is it possible that we have here the reversal of a hitherto unchallenged dictum that a river cannot rise higher than its source?

6. Quite uniformly the charges of fanaticism on the part of Seventh-day Adventists in the years immediately following 1844 have been both vague and general. Obviously it is impossible to answer conclusively an indictment that fails to state names, places, and dates.

However, in 1944, a full century after the alleged fanaticism, an avowed critic published a specific charge of rank fanaticism on the part of "the S.D.A." pioneers in the post-1844 days. In *The Gathering Call,* edited and published by E. S. Ballenger, appeared this charge:

"We affirm without fear of successful contradiction that the S.D.A. pioneers crossed bridges on their hands and knees, to show their humility, and that they also crawled under tables, and under old-fashioned stoves to exhibit their humility. It is also a fact that the pioneers used to kiss each other's feet. In their general gatherings, they used to crowd all the men into one room, and each man would put his foot out from under his covers while the man at the head of the line would go down the line and kiss the foot of each one of his brethren; then the next one would follow until everybody had kissed all the others' feet. *These things were practiced, not by ignorant laymen but by such men as J. N. Andrews.*" (Emphasis his.)

Here was an opportunity finally to run to earth the vague stories about fanaticism among "S.D.A. pioneers," for here specific instances of fanaticism were mentioned. The charges were unequivocally presented as "a fact" and prefaced with the impressive declaration: "We affirm without fear of successful contradiction." Here, indeed, was a chance to make a test case of stories of fanaticism on the part of Seventh-day Adventists.

Dr. J. N. Andrews, the grandson of J. N. Andrews, engaged in correspondence with Ballenger regarding these charges. The correspondence was placed in my hands. In that correspondence Ballenger admitted that he based his charge wholly on a statement allegedly made to him by Oswald Stowell somewhere between the years 1905 and 1912, when Stowell was "not far from 80 years of age." In this correspondence Ballenger admitted that Stowell did not say that Andrews kissed the feet of the brethren, but that others, whom Ballenger was unable to name, did so. Ballenger stated that there was no one else living who heard Stowell tell this story!

This correspondence was published in an article entitled "Dead Men Tell No Tales," in *The Ministry*, May, 1944. This article noted that Oswald Stowell, the alleged source of the story, was a very old man at the time he was said to have told this story, and that the one now retelling it was also very old. Further, that the story had to do with something supposed to have happened a hundred years ago. A story so good as this surely would not have been kept quiet by Stowell—a long-time Seventh-day Adventist who had lived in Adventist communities all his life—until his last days. Yet no one had heard this story before, not even the grandson of J. N. Andrews. A daughter of Stowell's, Mrs. Parker Smith, who had heard from her father's lips many times the narrative of the early days, had never heard it! Her letter, so stating, was also published.

In his reply in *The Gathering Call*, July-August, 1944, Ballenger discussed for eight vehement, adjective-packed pages everything from Adventist preachers' morals to their theology. All this filled space, but was transparently irrelevant in answer to the demand for better evidence for his charge of fanaticism. In fact, Ballenger affected surprise that anyone should take seriously one of the "trivial things" he had brought against Adventists.

Now, men who wish to be taken seriously are not in the habit of prefacing "trivial" charges with the impressive words, "We affirm without fear of successful contradiction." Perhaps he, in common with other critics who hurl the charge of fanaticism, considers it a "trivial" thing to make long-dead good men look ridiculous. It appears now that the only thing "trivial" about his charge was the evidence he submitted in support of it.

Thus ended the attempt to pin down what is probably the most specific story ever set forth by an Adventist critic regarding alleged fanatical excesses on the part of "S.D.A. leaders" in that twilight period immediately following 1844.

In view of the facts here presented, honest objectors who have voiced this charge of fanaticism, thinking it could be historically proved, will, of course, no longer do so!

# Objection 58

Seventh-day Adventists say that they constitute a prophetic movement raised up by God to preach His last message to the world. At
the same time they admit that their movement sprang from the soil
of Millerism, whose leaders taught that Christ would come in 1844.
Is God the leader of a movement that preached error at the outset
and suffered great disappointment and confusion as a result of that
error?

If we had no record of God's dealings with man other than in
1844 we might be embarrassed by this question. But we have the
Scriptural record, which was written aforetime for our learning.
When the disciples went over Palestine to announce that the kingdom of God was at hand, both they and their hearers understood
that Christ was about to set up His kingdom. How fervently the
multitudes believed this is revealed by their exultant shouts as
He rode into Jerusalem: "Hosanna to the son of David: Blessed is
he that cometh in the name of the Lord." Matt. 21:9.

What is more significant in the present connection is that the
Bible records no rebuke from our Lord, no word to correct their
mistaken ideas. The only comment is that of the apostle who
chronicled the story. He declared that this triumphal march fulfilled the prophecy: "Tell ye the daughter of Sion, Behold, thy
King cometh unto thee, meek, and sitting upon an ass, and a colt
the foal of an ass." Matt. 21:5. But neither the multitude, who
doubtless had this prophecy in mind, nor the apostles, who were
debating as to who should have the highest place in the kingdom,
realized that the King riding in apparent triumph was soon to
suffer the ignominy of the cross.

It is true that Christ spoke to His disciples of His coming death,
but it is equally true that the disciples did not really grasp what
He meant. There can be no possible doubt of this. The two
disciples on the way to Emmaus confided to their incognito Lord:

"We trusted that it had been he which should have redeemed Israel." Luke 24:21. And Christ responded: "O fools, and slow of heart to believe all that the prophets have spoken: ought not Christ to have suffered these things, and to enter into his glory? And beginning at Moses and all the prophets, he expounded unto them in all the Scriptures the things concerning himself." Luke 24:25-27.

How completely those disciples were disappointed! How completely disillusioned! Their distress was heightened by the fact that they would stand exposed before the world as the disciples and promoters of a deceiver. Those were their feelings when He was lifted up on a cross instead of a throne. The Adventists who in October 22, 1844, had expected Christ to come to rule the world could not possibly have suffered greater disappointment.

If the reasoning of Seventh-day Adventist critics is correct, God was not in the movement represented by the apostles, the seventy, and all who proclaimed, The kingdom of God is at hand. But it would be sacrilege to say that God was not with the apostles and all who proclaimed the glad news of the kingdom. We are amazed at their spiritual dullness, their failure to see the approaching cross, their inability to understand "all that the prophets" had written. But we do not doubt for a moment the divine call of the apostles, nor the divine character of the message they preached. When they preached that the kingdom of God was at hand, they preached the Word of God, but they did not properly understand what they preached. Religious history presents no more striking case of misunderstanding of the message on the part of the messengers, and no more appalling disappointment as a climax, than that of the apostles and all who joined with them. But what is more impressive in this connection is that history provides no other instance of a religious movement so definitely and directly led of God.

In view of all this how pointless is the question in the objection before us!

# Objection 59

**The Millerites thought they found in Daniel 8:13, 14 the proof that Christ would come on October 22, 1844. After their disappointment some of them, the founders of Seventh-day Adventism, sought to maintain their claim that God was leading them by inventing a new interpretation to Daniel 8:13, 14, which enabled them to maintain that the prophecy was indeed fulfilled in 1844, but by an event that took place in heaven. Hence Seventh-day Adventism was born of a dilemma.**

We need not here turn aside to discuss the validity of the Seventh-day Adventist interpretation of Daniel 8:13, 14. That is presented at length in our denominational literature. We confine ourselves to the dilemma feature.

Even if we desired, we could not make an exclusive claim to a dilemma origin. The Catholic Church might plausibly describe Protestantism in similar fashion. Luther had to admit the awful fact of sin and the imperative need of redemption. But he refused to admit that the penances and good works set down by the church were effective as redemptive agencies. So he solved the dilemma by "inventing" a new formula for salvation; he declared that it was effected wholly through a work done by Christ in heaven above and that we accept it by faith.

Infidels often declare that the Christian church is the result of a dilemma. Their reasoning runs like this: The disciples had to admit they were mistaken, for Christ did not establish His kingdom on earth as they had anticipated. They refused to admit that they had been deceived as to their Lord. So they revised their preaching and invented the story that He had arisen and ascended and was ministering for us in heaven above, from which He would return to set up His kingdom.

Other illustrations might be given from the religious world, but these suffice to show that the charge of a dilemma origin does not necessarily prove anything. The strict logic of such a charge demands that a person or a movement at the outset must have either the whole truth or none of it, that it is not possible to have part of the truth at the outset and to gain the remainder in the school of disappointing experience. When the matter is stated in this form the unreasonableness of the charge becomes evident. Our critics, along with the rest of us, will have to admit that they have learned new truths at times as a result of disappointing experiences, even dilemmas, that have confronted them. And if these critics believe that God is guiding their lives, they will also have to admit, along with the rest of us, that some of the dilemmas have clearly been permitted by God, if not ordained of Him, for their spiritual good.

# Objection 60

**For several years after the 1844 disappointment Seventh-day Adventists believed that probation had closed for the world. Was God leading a movement that believed so un-Scriptural a teaching as that?**

The answer to objection 58 is almost a sufficient answer to this. The parallel there drawn between Christ's disciples and the Adventists can be extended to cover the question before us. The Bible states explicitly that the disciples, particularly Peter, thought at first that their message of salvation was only for the Jews. So, far from including the Gentiles in their preaching, they did not think it proper even to sit down and eat with them. Peter had to be given a vision on the housetop in order to prepare him to go down to the house of the centurion. When he returned from that visit he told the brethren at Jerusalem how the Holy Spirit had been poured upon those gathered at the centurion's home, and added, "Forasmuch then as God gave them the like gift as he did unto us, who believed on the Lord Jesus Christ; what was I, that I could withstand God?" Acts 11:17. "When they [the apostles and Jewish believers at Jerusalem] heard these things, they held their peace, and glorified God, saying, Then hath God also to the Gentiles granted repentance unto life." Verse 18.

Only slowly did the Jewish believers in Christ come to sense fully the sublime truth that the gospel was to be preached to all men, even to the uttermost parts of the earth. We marvel at their original, exclusive ideas on salvation, and particularly at the fact that the apostles themselves were as exclusive as any. But it never occurs to any of us, even to the critics of Adventism, to question the leadership of God in the apostolic church. Their idea of exclusive salvation for the Jews was un-Scriptural we declare, but God was leading them, nevertheless. Why should it be considered a thing incredible that God also was leading the Advent movement at the beginning, even though they held for a little time that probation for the world had closed? Is it any worse to believe that the door of mercy has closed on men than to believe that it never was opened to them?

If the apostolic church had failed to enlarge its vision and correct its narrow view, then might a real indictment be brought against the Christian church as the stronghold of un-Christian exclusivism. Likewise, if our spiritual ancestors of the 1840's had continued to hold that probation had closed for the world, then might a real indictment be brought against Seventh-day Adventists. But in neither case was the erroneous doctrine retained. In both instances the Divine Spirit, whose task it is to lead God's children into all truth, soon led them to see the truth regarding the worldwide scope of the plan of salvation.

It is not really relevant to the present argument to show just how our Adventist forebears quickly began to enlarge their view so that by the early 1850's—a decade before the formal organization of the Seventh-day Adventist Church—the erroneous doctrine was fully corrected.* We need only establish the fact that they did speedily correct it under the illumination of the Divine Spirit.

---

* For an extended discussion of this matter see the author's *Ellen G. White and Her Critics*, pp. 161-252, and 598-615.

# Objection 61

**Christ's second coming is not literal but spiritual. He comes to the Christian at conversion or at death.**

There is a sense in which Christ comes to us at conversion. When we accept Him He comes into our hearts by His Spirit and guides our lives. The spiritual experience of the Spirit's coming into the lives of the apostles was dependent on Christ's going away. Said the Master, "If I go not away, the Comforter ["which is the Holy Ghost"] will not come unto you; but if I depart, I will send him unto you." John 16:7; 14:26. Therefore this experience of spiritual fellowship with Christ through His Spirit is so far from being the second coming of Christ that the fellowship is dependent on Christ's going "away."

When Christ spoke of His going away, He told His disciples that it was for the purpose of preparing a place for them. Then He added, "I will come again, and receive you unto myself; that where I am, there ye may be also." (See John 14:1-3.) Now certainly Christ did not come to take the disciples away to the heavenly land on the day of Pentecost, when the Holy Spirit came upon them. Yet when Christ comes again, an outstanding feature will be the receiving of believers unto Himself.

Said Paul to the Philippians, who were converted and had begun to walk the Christian way: "Being confident of this very thing, that he which hath begun a good work in you will perform it until the day of Jesus Christ." Phil. 1:6. He spoke to the Thessalonians in similar vein when he declared to them, "Ye turned to God from idols to serve the living and true God; and to wait for his Son from heaven." 1 Thess. 1:9, 10. In both instances the people addressed by Paul were converted, and in both instances they were instructed to look forward, "to wait" for the coming of Christ "from heaven, whom he raised from the dead, even Jesus." Paul certainly did not believe that the coming of Christ was at conversion, but rather that conversion prepared us for the glorious *future* event of the coming of a personal Being who had been raised from the dead.

When Christ came the first time, His advent was literal. He was a real being among men. Even after His resurrection He said to His disciples, "Behold my hands and my feet, that it is I myself: handle me, and see." Luke 24:39. What ground is there for concluding that His Second Advent will be less real? If He came literally the first time, are we not naturally to conclude, unless there is clear evidence to the contrary, that He will come literally at the Second Advent?

Not only is there no Bible evidence to the contrary; there is specific evidence in support of this conclusion that His Second Advent will be literal. When Christ ascended, two heavenly messengers said to the disciples, "This *same* Jesus, which is taken up from you into heaven, shall so come in like manner as ye have seen him go into heaven." Acts 1:11. Couple with this the statement of Paul: "The Lord *himself* shall descend from heaven." 1 Thess. 4:16. Not simply a spiritual influence will come again, but "this *same* Jesus, which is taken up from you into heaven." Not even a heavenly representative, literal and real as such a representative might be, but "the Lord *himself* shall descend from heaven." Thus reads the scripture.

We read also that when Christ comes, the brilliance of that coming lights the whole heavens, and its blinding glory causes the wicked to flee in terror. Further, we read that when Christ comes, the dead are raised to life, and these, accompanied by the living righteous, are caught up to meet the Lord in the air. (See Matt. 24:27; Rev. 6:14-17; John 5:28, 29; 1 Thess. 4:15-18.)

Only when a person is ready to spiritualize away the most literal and obvious value of words can he support the idea that the second coming of Christ is spiritual not literal. But when words are deprived of their most natural meaning, then there is removed the whole basis of discussion as to what the Bible teaches.

# ANSWERS TO OBJECTIONS

The very evidence that establishes the fact that the coming of Christ is literal, and that it is not to be confused with conversion, establishes also the fact that the coming cannot be at death. The wicked do not flee in terror at the death of a righteous man, nor are the righteous raised from the dead at death; yet the fleeing of the wicked and the raising of the righteous will characterize the Second Advent.

The Advent of Christ will be so real that "every eye shall see him, and they also which pierced him." Rev. 1:7.

# Objection 62

**It is revolting to the Christian idea of love to believe that Christ will come as a destroyer and wreak vengeance on the world.**

It seems strange that this objection should be presented, because almost without exception it comes from those who hold the quite widely accepted doctrine that the wicked go at death into hell-fire, there to stay through the ceaseless ages of eternity. If it seems to the objector more in harmony with the Christian idea of love to believe in never-ending torment as the portion of the wicked, rather than speedy destruction in connection with the Second Advent of Christ, then we must simply confess our inability to follow such reasoning, and close the discussion. But with the matter set forth in this definite way, we doubt very much whether the objector, or anyone else, would think of affirming that greater love is indicated by the ceaseless tortures of hell than by the consuming of the wicked in connection with the Second Advent.

Everyone who holds to the primary doctrine that there is a difference between right and wrong, and that there is a judgment day when God will reward men according to their deeds, must believe that there is a punishment for the wicked as well as a reward for the righteous. This is too evident for dispute by any believer in the Bible.

The believers in the literal Second Advent of Christ certainly are not unique in holding that the wicked will suffer. Surely the consuming fires of the Second Advent could burn no more fiercely than those pictured in the hell-fire of the creeds of many denominations. How can it conceivably be argued that it is in harmony with the Christian idea of love to take the wicked to some *distant* place for punishment by eternal torment; while it is revolting to the Christian idea of love to punish them by death right *here* on the earth, where their sins have been committed?

God does not take any pleasure in the death of the wicked. (See Eze. 18:32.) It is not because God hates men that He finally destroys the wicked. There is simply no other alternative left if He is to blot out sin from the universe. Sin is something found only in connection with moral beings, possessed of free will. The germs of sin can thrive only as they burrow deep into the very mind and heart. Thus the destruction of sin necessitates the destruction of those who are determined to hold on to their sins.

God has ever been of too pure eyes to behold iniquity. It has never been possible for sinful man to gaze upon the face of God. It is the pure in heart who will finally see God. When Moses in the mount sought to see God's face his plea was denied. The Lord placed him in a "cleft of the rock," that he might be hid from the divine glory as God passed by. (See Exodus 33 and 34.)

From this we may learn a spiritual lesson. We as poor sinners may also be hid in the cleft of the rock, the rock Christ Jesus. The opportunity is offered to all to avail themselves of this protection. When hid in Christ our sins are forgiven; His holy life covers us. We thus stand unafraid in the day when the glory of God is revealed from heaven at the Second Advent. The same awful brilliance envelops all, the righteous as well as the wicked. The difference is that the righteous are protected by the covering of Christ's righteousness, while the wicked stand spiritually naked. They must cry for the literal rocks to fall on them, and hide them from the face of Him that sitteth on the throne. They have brought death upon themselves by the course they have willfully taken throughout their lives.

# Objection 63

We should spend more time helping people to make this a better world rather than stir them up about another world, as is the case when the Second Advent doctrine is preached.

All will agree that this world would be a much better place if sickness could be removed; and that our earth would be almost ideal if we could banish from men's hearts selfishness, jealousy, hatred, and lust.

But does the preaching to men to make ready for another world prevent us in any way from dealing with the first of these two basic troubles, that of sickness? No, assuredly not. Christ spent much of His time ministering to the sick, and yet He preached to the people: "Lay not up for yourselves treasures upon earth, . . . but lay up for yourselves treasures in heaven: . . . for where your treasure is, there will your heart be also." Matt. 6:19-21.

Christ commissioned His disciples to go out and heal the sick. This they did, but they also made the doctrine of the Second Advent, the preparing of men for heaven, the central feature of their preaching. And it is a simple matter of record that Seventh-day Adventists, who make the Second Advent so distinctive a feature of their preaching, are at the same time ministering to the sick through a chain of sanitariums and dispensaries in every continent.

In view of the objection before us, this is really a remarkable fact. Yet it is not remarkable, but rather the natural result of belief in the Advent doctrine. The love of Christ that comes into the hearts of those who believe that He will come again, causes them to spend their time and means in aiding the sick.

In preaching that Christ, who had ascended, would come again, the disciples made this present world a better one in which to live, not only by healing the sick, but also by helping the poor. Those who accepted the preaching and who had money, willingly gave it into a general fund, so that those who were poor might not suffer. (See Acts 4:32-37.) What untold hunger and want·might be relieved if that same spirit controlled the Christian church at large today!

And what of the relation of the vices of men's hearts to the doctrine of the Second Advent? Certainly all the schemes that the wise of this world have devised, have failed to provide any solution for the steadily growing problem of crime and moral corruption. Does the objector wish us to spend our time on some crime commission or social research committee rather than on the preaching of the Advent? If so, which committee would he suggest, and what proof would he offer that our time would be well spent?

Men can devise ways of chaining the body but not of changing the heart, and the prisoner goes forth from the jail ready to repeat his offense, or to commit a worse one. The fear of the law may hold back a wicked man from the outward act of violence, but he is nevertheless a criminal at heart, and awaits only the favorable opportunity to carry out his evil desires.

But when the mighty doctrine of the personal, literal return of Christ is preached to men, there is brought home to their sin-dulled senses with a vividness not otherwise possible the tremendous fact that they must someday meet God face to face and give an account for their deeds. And that mighty truth may prove the means, under God, of arousing them to cry out for spiritual help, that they may be ready for that day. If the objector is willing to grant that religion has *any* message for man, then.he must grant that the message of accountability to God, as set forth in the doctrine of the Advent, is one of the most powerful that can ever be brought to the human heart.

Every man who accepts the Advent doctrine and lives in the hope of meeting Christ face to face has ever within his heart the mightiest incentive to holy living. "Every man that hath this hope in him purifieth himself, even as he is pure." 1 John 3:3. And the man whose heart is purified is a good citizen. The more such people there are in the world, the better place it is to live in.

# Objection 64

Christ Himself said that He would come as a thief in the night. The apostle Paul made a similar statement. Seventh-day Adventists are therefore unwarranted in claiming that they can know something definite as to the time of Christ's coming.

We agree that it is not possible for us to know exactly when Christ will come. Throughout our whole history as a distinct religious body we have accepted literally the words of Christ concerning the time of His coming: "Of that day and hour knoweth no man." "Watch therefore: for ye know not what hour your Lord doth come." Matt. 24:36, 42. Christ immediately follows with an allusion to a thief's unexpected coming.

But we do not confine our belief regarding the Advent to these two statements by Christ. We believe *all* that He said. We accept *all* the Bible. Christ did not confine His statements about the Advent to the two texts quoted. Those texts are part of a long discourse on the subject. That discourse was prompted by the question asked by His disciples, who knew He would soon leave them and who naturally wondered when He would return: "What shall be the sign of thy coming, and of the end of the world?" Matt. 24:3. The first and perhaps most significant fact to be noted in Christ's reply is this: He did not even suggest that their question was out of order.

Christ most evidently thought the question so much in order that He proceeded at length to answer it. He described various signs that were to occur both in the heavens and in the earth, and then added: "Now learn a parable of the fig tree; When his branch is yet tender, and putteth forth leaves, ye know that summer is nigh: so likewise ye, when ye shall see all these things, know that it is near, even at the doors." Verses 32, 33.

The tender leaves on the trees in early spring provide us clear proof that summer is near, but do not enable us to say precisely when summer will arrive. By this simple illustration Christ harmonized His two statements, the one which declares that we may know when the Advent is near, with the statement that "of that day and hour knoweth no man."

It is true that Paul says Christ's coming will be wholly unexpected—even like a thief's coming—to a class who will be mistakenly forecasting "peace and safety." (1 Thess. 5:3.) Thus lulled to sleep with a false sense of security they will be overtaken by "sudden destruction," Paul adds. But what of those to whom Paul is writing, who know "the times and the seasons"? Listen to his words: "But ye, brethren, are not in darkness, that that day should overtake you as a thief. Ye are all the children of light, and the children of the day: we are not of the night, nor of darkness. Therefore let us not sleep, as do others; but let us watch and be sober." Verses 4-6.

And how may we know "the times and the seasons"? By studying the prophecies of the Book of God. When the prophet Daniel stood before the Babylonian king, Nebuchadnezzar, who had been troubled over the question of "what should come to pass hereafter," he said to the monarch, "There is a God in heaven that revealeth secrets, and maketh known to the king Nebuchadnezzar what shall be in the latter days." Dan. 2:28, 29. The whole book of Daniel is filled with prophecies regarding Christ's coming in glory.

When Christ answered the disciples' question regarding the time of the end of the world, He referred to a prediction made "by Daniel the prophet," and added, "whoso readeth, let him understand." Matt. 24:15.

The opening chapter of the Revelation contains this blessing: "Blessed is he that readeth, and they that hear the words of this prophecy, and keep those things which are written therein: for the time is at hand." Rev. 1:3.

To say that nothing can be known about the time of Christ's coming is to fly in the face of these and similar texts and to affirm that the God of the prophets has concealed from them any information concerning the climactic event of earth's history.

# Objection 65

One of the best proofs that no one can tell whether Christ will come tomorrow or a thousand years from now is the fact that the apostles thought He would come in their day. But they were all mistaken. So will Seventh-day Adventists be.

It is true that the apostles set before the believers as the one important event of the future the Second Advent of Christ. He was the center and circumference of their preaching. Looking back, they saw Christ crucified and then raised from the dead. Looking upward, they saw Christ ministering as the great High Priest for men. Looking forward, they saw Christ coming in the clouds of heaven. Earthly events did not enter into their reckoning. All was in terms of the relation of Christ to them—what He had done for them, what He was doing for them, and how He would finally come to receive them unto Himself. The very fact that they fixed their thoughts so completely on this one future event might easily cause the superficial reader of the Bible to conclude that the apostles all believed and taught that Christ would return in their day. But this would be unwarranted.

There are a few specific statements that, considered alone, might lead to that conclusion. Let us take the most typical one as an example.

Paul, in his first epistle to the Thessalonians, speaks of the dead who are raised and of those who "are alive and remain unto the coming of the Lord." 1 Thess. 4:15. Not only do objectors today conclude from this that the apostles expected the coming of the Lord in their day, but apparently some of the Thessalonians thought that Paul intended for them to understand that the day of Christ was right upon them.

But such an interpretation of Paul's words is unwarranted, for in his second epistle to them he took occasion to correct such an impression, declaring, "Be not soon shaken in mind, or be troubled, neither by spirit, nor by word, nor by *letter as from us,* as that the day of Christ is at hand." 2 Thess. 2:2. Then he proceeds to assure them that that day would not come until after a certain great prophecy was fulfilled, and that this prophecy could not be fulfilled "except there come a falling away first." Verse 3. Paul told the elders of Ephesus that this falling away would come after his "departing," that is, after his death. (See Acts 20:28-30; 2 Tim. 4:7, 8.)

To his spiritual son, Timothy, he wrote from his death cell at Rome: "The things that thou hast heard of me among many witnesses, the same commit thou to faithful men, who shall be able to teach others also." 2 Tim. 2:2. How evident it is that Paul looked forward to events quite beyond the span of his life.

If we always remember that the inspired writings of the Bible were not simply for those who first read them but also for us, Paul's statement in 1 Thessalonians 4:15, and similar statements by other apostles, will not prove perplexing.

To some of the apostles God may not have seen fit to give so explicit an understanding of the events that must precede the Second Advent as He did to Paul, for example, in which case they might most properly urge the believers to be always in a state of readiness for Christ's return.

In Old Testament times the prophets frequently did not understand the prophecies they uttered. It was left for those who lived near the time of their fulfillment to obtain the real understanding of them. Thus Peter explained to the New Testament church. (See 1 Peter 1:9-12.) And he reminded them, "We have also a more sure word of prophecy; whereunto ye do well that ye take heed, as unto a light that shineth in a dark place, until the day dawn." 2 Peter 1:19.

The apostle John himself may have understood little of the prophecies contained in the Revelation, yet by inspiration he declared, "Blessed is he that readeth, and they that hear the words of this prophecy." Rev. 1:3.

# SECOND ADVENT

As already stated, we freely agree that God may not have given to all the apostles a knowledge of the future. But this admission does not require us to conclude that nothing can be known about the Second Advent. We, looking back to the first century of the Christian Era, wonder why all the Jews were not ready to receive Christ, so plain were the prophecies concerning the manner and time of His advent. There were a few back there who did study the prophecies, and when the time drew near, God graciously revealed more fully their meaning to these searchers for truth. If we today are in an attitude of searching the prophecies rather than of scoffing at them, is it not possible that God may open their meaning to us more fully? And thus we may learn something very definite regarding the Second Advent.

We agree no *man* "can tell whether Christ will come tomorrow or a thousand years from now." But prophecy can and does. We would ask the objector: Have you studied these inspired writings? Have you obeyed the injunction of Christ Himself to read and to understand the prophecies of Daniel? (See Matt. 24:15.) Have you studied Christ's own prophecy of His return? (See Matthew 24 and Luke 21.) Are you one of those who can claim the blessing because you have read, prayerfully and diligently, the book of Revelation? (See Rev. 1:3.) Until then, why declare that nothing can be known about the Second Advent? The Bible reveals plainly that in all past ages God has always told men when a great event was near at hand. "Surely the Lord God will do nothing, but he revealeth his secret unto his servants the prophets." Amos 3:7. Are you ready to contend that God has changed His plan toward men, and will not give us any knowledge of the coming of an event that surpasses in grandeur all events that have ever occurred?

The Bible contains whole books devoted to a prophetic discussion of the Second Advent of Christ in relation to great prophetic periods and historical incidents. Shall we ignore these portions of Holy Writ? Shall we say they are meaningless? If not, then should we not study them, and will they not give us light on this great subject of the nearness of the Second Advent?

# Objection 66

By preaching the soon coming of Christ, Seventh-day Adventists are falsely creating hope and excitement. Misguided people through the centuries have repeatedly thought His coming was at hand. That fact is best illustrated by the excitement that spread throughout Europe in A.D. 1000, when multitudes waited in fanatical fervor for Christ's coming.

One of the most common substitutes for logic and evidence is ridicule and scorn. There are many persons calling themselves Christians who think it a mark of superior religious understanding to heap ridicule on the whole doctrine of the literal soon coming of Christ. Such persons are sure not only that those who preach this doctrine are misguided visionaries but also that those who give ear to the preaching most certainly become ludicrous fanatics. To prove their point beyond any debate, they make the sweeping statement, found in this objection, that the centuries, most notably the year A.D. 1000, have witnessed deplorable incidents of fanatical excitement regarding this doctrine.

The facts are that during the long, and generally dark, centuries the great masses of the people were grossly ignorant of the Scriptures and thus unaware, even, of what its inspired pages say on the Second Advent. True, there were at times scholars who, from their study of the Bible, expressed certain views as to the nearness of the Advent. But such views were generally expressed in language not too exact. Nor did these views, except in rare instances, have any currency beyond the walls of a monastery, the usual abode of theological scholars in medieval times.

The story that Europe witnessed wild excitement in anticipation of the Advent as the year 1000 drew near is a groundless legend. How critics of the doctrine of Christ's coming have loved to believe it! Their love for it has been as strong as their love for the story that the Millerites in the year 1844 draped themselves in ascension robes in fanatical Advent expectancy. In fact these two stories have been the chief "proofs" that the preaching of Christ's soon coming can result only in false hope and fanatical excitement. The wild stories about what allegedly happened in A.D. 1844 have been disposed of. (See objection 57.) The stories about the year A.D. 1000 can as certainly be exploded. For those who wish to examine a summary of the evidence that exposes these stories, we suggest that they read the article "The Year 1000 and the Antecedents of the Crusades," by George Lincoln Burr, in the *American Historical Review,* April, 1901, pages 429-439. (This journal is the official organ of the American Historical Society.) After summarizing some of the investigations of eminent nine-teenth-century historians who have examined the events of the year A.D. 1000 Burr observes:

"In fine, then, the sole contemporary evidence for a panic of terror at the year 1000 proved to be a statement that forty years earlier one Paris preacher named it as the date of the end of the world—a preacher whose prophecy was at once refuted, and, for aught we can learn, at once forgotten."—Page 434.

Still further on in his article Burr quotes approvingly these words of one of the historians who has investigated the legend:

" 'The terrors of the year 1000 are only a legend and a myth.' " —Page 435.

It would be far more accurate to say that all through the centuries the vast majority of Christians have had little interest in the doctrine of the personal second coming of Christ. The reasons are two:

1. All through the Dark Ages and virtually up to Reformation times only the clergy and a few intellectuals had copies of the Scriptures. Hence Christians at large could hardly become particularly concerned about the doctrine. That was the long period of papal dominance in religious thought.

2. In the eighteenth century certain Protestant leaders began to teach, and their view has been increasingly accepted, that the coming of Christ will be spiritual, invisible, the coming of the

Divine Spirit into human hearts, gradually to turn all men to righteousness. Hence there would be no occasion for anyone to look forward with intense feeling to a certain climactic moment ahead. (See objection 61 for a discussion of the claim that Christ's coming is a spiritual one.)

It would also be equally accurate to say that the long centuries fail to support any general charge that those who have believed in the doctrine of Christ's personal appearing have deported themselves in an irrational, fanatical fashion.

# Objection 67

Seventh-day Adventists declare that the great meteoric shower of November 13, 1833, was a fulfillment of the prophecy that the stars shall fall from heaven as one of the signs of the nearness of Christ's coming. But we need not seek some supernatural, miraculous explanation of this starry event. Astronomers inform us that whirling in space is a great swarm of meteorites, known as the Leonids, which are probably the shattered remains of a comet. These Leonids come within the orbit of our earth about every thirty-three years. There were showers in 1866 and 1899, though very small, because, as the astronomers explain, the planet Jupiter deflected the meteoritic group from the direct path of the earth. Probably this or a similar reason explains the absence of a star shower in 1933.

The prime fallacy underlying this reasoning is the assumption that because a phenomenon has been explained, it has been explained *away*. Is a stupendous act of God in the operation of His universe any the less so because poor finite men have been able to discover something of the plan that the Infinite has employed?

A devout astronomer once exclaimed, as he charted the course of the stars, that he was thinking God's thoughts after Him. But did that make those thoughts any the less divine?

We describe as egotistical the man who, after examining the product of some inventive wizard, declares that he could have invented such a device, and that there is really nothing to it. But what shall we say of the man who, after discovering a little of the plan that God has used in the performance of some marvelous act, scoffingly declares that there is nothing remarkable about it, that it is merely a "natural phenomenon"! We do not discount an inventor's production because he has called to his aid some simple, natural law, as has been the case in most inventions. On the contrary, we consider it a mark of the superior mind to be able to see the possibilities of such a simple law and to harness it to such wonderful ends. And shall we not as reasonably conclude that a phenomenon in the heavens, in which "natural" laws have been called into service, proves eloquently the superiority of the Mind that produced it?

If God has seen fit to permit His divinely appointed laws of motion to operate so that a comet should be shattered and some of its parts scattered like flaming stars over our earth, what is man that he should impiously contend that some other method should have been employed; or that inasmuch as he can explain something of the laws that operated in producing the starry sign, he will reject it as being no sign? And if God, once having produced that phenomenon should allow the wreckage of the comet to remain in our path, so that at recurring intervals until the final end we should be reminded of the great sign that earlier occurred, why should a man perversely declare he will therefore see in it no sign at all?

But let us look at the matter from another angle. When Christ gave that wonderful prophecy marking out the high points along the centuries between His first and second advents, He foreknew just what would take place in the earth and in the heavens. He foresaw, for example, that as the centuries wore along, the world would be filled with war, but that at the same time there would be great plans for peace. Foreknowing that this would be the state just before His return, He declared that when we see such conditions we may know that the end is near. The contention that this paradoxical war-and-peace condition is the "natural" result of forces that have played upon human nature in recent times does not in any way invalidate the paradox as a sign. Only God could foreknow that these particular forces would be working upon men's hearts in a certain particular way two thousand years later. And the taking place of such war-and-peace scenes at the very time when other prophecies declare that the "time of the end" is at hand, provides the proof that He who foretold it was divine and that His promise to return will be fulfilled.

Likewise, Christ foresaw that in the time shortly before His return a great cluster of meteoric fragments would cross the earth's path, thus producing what would be described as a shower of falling stars. Foreknowing this, why should He not declare that when we see this sight we may know the end is near? What could be more easily understood by mankind than such a sight as this?

If a foreknowledge of conditions upon the earth is a proof of Christ's divinity, how much more so a foreknowledge of events in the heavens? The fact is that after counseling His followers to "understand" the book of Daniel, which made specific predictions as to the time of the end, Christ declared calmly that when *that* "time" arrived there would be a great falling of stars. Almost exactly eighteen hundred years before its occurrence the Son of man foretold an event that the wisest of the sons of men could not foretell by a single day.

And He foretold this striking heavenly event in relation to a great group of signs that would take place in the earth and in the heavens, for when we read *His* prophecy in connection with those He inspired Daniel and John to give, we discover a whole galaxy of signs that were to take place within a very limited and clearly marked period. The spectacular star shower of November 13, 1833, stands securely as a sign, for only the God who orders the courses of the stars could have caused that mighty shower to descend at exactly the right hour to blend with the other parts of a multicolored divinely predicted picture.

# Objection 68

The whole idea that Christ will appear in flaming glory in the heavens, suddenly to change the present order of nature, destroying the wicked, and taking the righteous to heaven, belongs to the age of superstition. We who live in this modern era know that all this is incredible and contrary to the laws of nature.

It is perhaps profitless to attempt to answer this, because those who make such declarations are so confident they know just what is credible and just how the laws of nature must always operate, that it is hard for them to consider any line of reasoning that might challenge their viewpoint. But for the benefit of those who are willing to believe the Advent doctrine, but who are awed or confused by declarations like the above, we offer some observations in reply.

First, we would ask: What solution to the long tragedy of a disordered and dying world does the objector offer? Until recent years he would probably respond with easy assurance that the world is gradually getting better, because there is operating throughout the universe a great law of progress, and thus ultimately all will be well. If he were a religious man, he would add that this improvement was taking place as a result of the slow but steady work of the Spirit of God on the hearts of men.

But this theory that the world is gradually getting better has suffered a mortal blow. The guns of two world wars, capped with the atomic bomb, have quite shattered it. Even that great host of ministers who formerly declared most confidently that we were headed for the millennium have quite completely lost their confidence. Ask them what solution they now have for the world's tragedy, what way through to a new earth wherein dwelleth righteousness, and they almost invariably begin to speak in vague and shadowy language of a divine solution of the tragedy of our world *beyond history*. But they do not explain what they mean by that phrase; it is rather new and strange to them.

If you ask nonreligious men what their present solution of the world problem is, they will probably look at you in astonishment. Their expression reveals that they are amazed you should expect them to have an answer. They forget how recently they were sure they had the answer—because they were sure they knew just how the laws of nature must operate!

To the objector we would say: You admit, as we all must do, that you don't know how nature's laws operate in relation to the betterment of the world. Then how can you any longer assert confidently that the coming of Christ is contrary to nature's laws? Why confess ignorance on the former and claim sure knowledge on the latter?

But perhaps you fall back on the general statement that the whole idea of the supernatural appearing of Christ to bring an end to the present world is unreasonable, incredible. Then let us ask you another question: If you believe in a God—as most men do—does it seem reasonable to you that God would permit this tragic world of ours, where the innocent so often suffer at the hands of the guilty, and where tragedy and death stalk the steps of all men, to continue on in this state forever? We think you will naturally answer no.

That no gives us a point in common. If we both believe in God, and thus both agree that it is reasonable to believe that He will bring this present tragic world to an end, we come right around again to the question: How do you believe He will do this? You have admitted that you do not know, that your former idea that the world was steadily moving upward by some vast law of progress, must now be abandoned, or at best, viewed with deep suspicion. In other words, for all you are able to say or to know of the mysteries of nature's laws or of the ways of God to man, this world of ours might roll on in blood and tears forever. You have nothing to protect you from despair save your belief that a good God will surely not permit a bad world to go on forever.

# ANSWERS TO OBJECTIONS

But if you rest your hope, even if vaguely and uncertainly, on God, are you not thereby injecting the supernatural into the affairs of this world which, according to your objection, is fully in the control of natural laws? Most obviously so. And if the supernatural is admitted, are you going to presume to say just how God may be permitted to bring on the closing act in the drama of the world's tragedy? Is the divine Lawgiver the slave of the laws He has made?

Again, if we all think it reasonable for God to bring an end to injustice and cruelty, is it not also most reasonable that He, as the divine Judge, should call all men to His judgment bar and openly mete out penalties and rewards? Should not those who stand before the eternal bar be permitted, in fairness, to meet their Judge face to face?

But all this simply leads us to the doctrine of the personal second coming of Christ.

Again: Does not a belief in God, who will bring righteous judgment at last to all men, carry with it the belief that this God, in fairness to all, would provide men with some revelation of His will that they might know how to order their steps aright against the great day of judgment? The answer surely must be yes.

But to answer yes is really to admit that the Bible is the Book of God, for that is the book that believers in the true God have ever understood to be the revelation of His will. And when we open its pages we find clearly taught the great doctrine of an end to this wicked world and the creation of a better one. There we find explicit declarations that at the climax of earth's history, when God will mete out judgment, Christ will come in flaming glory, bringing joy and translation to the righteous, and terror and death to the wicked. (See, for example, 1 Thess. 4:16, 17; 2 Thess. 1:7-10; Rev. 1:7.) In that awful and climactic moment it will not occur to any of the children of men to protest the event because it is contrary to the laws of nature! They will be standing before the God of nature!

(For an extended discussion of related questions, see pages 449-489.)

Section IV

MORTAL MAN

Objections 69 to 92

# Objection 69

When Christ was transfigured there appeared with Him on the mount "Moses and Elias talking with him." (See Matt. 17:3.) The fact that Moses was there proves that man is an immortal soul, for Moses died and was buried at the time of the Exodus.

There are two ways to view this transfiguration incident: as a vision or as a literal event. If we view it as a vision, then the objection before us is pointless, for in vision a prophet may have presented to him a picture of men and events without either the men or the events being at that moment actually before him. But if we view the incident as literal, which we believe it was, then the objection is equally pointless, for the transfiguration narrative says nothing about an immaterial spirit, or soul, called Moses hovering beside Christ. Instead we read that Christ was present, and beside Him, "Moses and Elias." We know that Christ was real —"the Word was made flesh." We know that Elias was translated bodily to heaven. Therefore we may rightly presume that he was real. And there is nothing in the account to suggest that Moses was any less real. We repeat, for it is of the essence of the question before us, that the account does not say that Moses' *spirit* was there, but that *Moses* was.

Further, the disciples most evidently must have considered Moses to be as truly real as the other two, for Peter wished to build three tabernacles, "one for thee, and one for Moses, and one for Elias." Verse 4. Tabernacles are not built for immaterial spirits.

In his well-known Bible commentary, Adam Clarke, a Methodist scholar, and a believer in the immortal soul doctrine, makes this clear comment on Matthew 17:3:

"Elijah came from heaven in the same body which he had upon earth, for he was *translated,* and did not see death, 2 Kings ii.11. And the body of Moses was probably raised again, as a pledge of the *resurrection;* and as Christ is to come to judge the *quick* and the *dead,* for we shall not all *die*, but all shall be *changed*, 1 Cor. xv.51, he probably gave the full representation of this in the person of Moses, who *died*, and was thus raised to life, (or appeared now as he shall appear when raised from the dead in the last day,) and in the person of Elijah, who never *tasted death*. Both their bodies exhibit the same appearance, to show that the bodies of glorified saints are the same, whether the person had been *translated*, or whether he had *died*."

The very presence of Moses on the mount of transfiguration, which Clarke explains in terms of Moses' resurrection, may help us to understand the real meaning of the rather obscure passage in Jude: "Yet Michael the archangel, when contending with the devil he disputed about the body of Moses, durst not bring against him a railing accusation, but said, The Lord rebuke thee." Jude 9.

The transfiguration record provides support, not for the doctrine of immortal souls, freed from the shell of a body, but for the doctrine of the resurrection.

# Objection 70

Christ said, "Fear not them which kill the body, but are not able to kill the soul: but rather fear him which is able to destroy both soul and body in hell." Matt. 10:28. This proves that the soul and the body are two distinctly different things, that the body can be destroyed and the soul remain, and therefore, that the soul is a separate entity that lives on forever after the body is dead.

Those who teach the immortal-soul doctrine teach not only that the souls of the righteous live on but that the souls of the wicked do also. They teach that though the body is destroyed, the soul is not. But this text explicitly declares that it is possible "to destroy *both* soul and body in hell," in other words, that it is possible "to kill the soul." Surely this is the last text in the world that the immortal-soul advocate should offer to support his belief.

But the believer in the immortality of the soul will remind us that at least the text makes clear that the body is one thing and the soul another, and therefore the soul should be considered a separate entity. The word here translated "soul" is from the Greek word *psuche;* indeed, this is true in every instance where the word "soul" is found in the New Testament in the King James Version of the Bible. But there are almost as many instances where *psuche* is translated "life." The translators, who were not inspired, *but who were believers in an immortal soul,* varied their translation of *psuche* according to their best understanding and inevitably through the eyes of their theology. We do not question their honesty, only their accuracy.

Note the following words of Christ as translated in this King James Version: "For whosoever will save his life [*psuche*] shall lose it: and whosoever will lose his life [*psuche*] for my sake shall find it. For what is a man profited, if he shall gain the whole world, and lose his own soul [*psuche*]? or what shall a man give in exchange for his soul [*psuche*]?" Matt. 16:25, 26.

Obviously the translators could not translate *psuche* in the twenty-fifth verse as "soul" without creating a theological dilemma of the first order. In the twenty-sixth verse "lose his own *psuche*" obviously means lose it in the judgment fires that devour the damned. But in the twenty-fifth verse Christ states that it is possible for a man to *"lose his psuche"* for His [Christ's] sake! The translators solved the dilemma and saved their immortal-soul doctrine by translating *psuche* as "life" in the twenty-fifth verse and as "soul" in the twenty-sixth. We might add that the translators of the American Standard Version (commonly known as the Revised Version) and the translators of the Revised Standard Version, both translate *psuche* as "life" in the twenty-sixth as well as in the twenty-fifth verse.

Coming back now to Matthew 10:28: "Fear not them which kill the body, but are not able to kill the soul [*psuche*]: but rather fear him which is able to destroy both soul [*psuche*] and body in hell." When the word "life" is substituted for "soul," as it may most properly be, any semblance of an argument for the immortal-soul doctrine disappears. Indeed, the text becomes one of the strongest in support of the doctrine that the day is coming when the wicked will have the very life within them destroyed; and if that does not mean final annihilation, we do not know how that meaning could be conveyed in words.

# Objection 71

Paul says, "For which cause we faint not; but though our outward man perish, yet the inward man is renewed day by day." 2 Cor. 4:16. This proves that the real man, the soul, is something different from the body, and flourishes despite the perishing of the body.

Believers in the immortal-soul doctrine seem to feel that if a Bible writer speaks of a contrast between one part of man and another, between the body and the spirit (or soul), that proves unquestionably the truth of their doctrine. But we also believe there is a difference between body and spirit, or between body and soul. We are to glorify God in our body and in our spirit, the Scriptures declare. We simply insist that the Scriptures nowhere say that the soul, or spirit, is a distinct, a separate, immortal entity encased within a shell, the body.

Paul wrote to the Corinthian church about his being "absent in body but present in spirit." 1 Cor. 5:3. Would anyone have the hardihood to say that Paul wishes us to understand that he left his body one place and flitted away to another place, Corinth? Then why seek to discover the immortal-soul doctrine in his words: "Though our outward man perish, yet the inward man is renewed day by day"?

In several passages Paul speaks, in variant language, of this "inward man." To the Ephesians he wrote, "That he [Christ] would grant you, according to the riches of his glory, to be strengthened with might by his Spirit in the inner man; that Christ may dwell in your hearts by faith." Eph. 3:16, 17. Again he writes, "Ye have put off the old man with his deeds; and have put on the new man, which is renewed in knowledge after the image of him that created him." Col. 3:9, 10.

It is evident that the "inward man," or "inner man," is, in the case of the Christian, known as the "new man." And what is this "new man"? The new nature, the new heart and spirit, that comes to us when, on accepting Christ, our "old man," or old nature, is crucified. As Paul declares, "I am crucified with Christ: nevertheless I live; yet not I, but Christ liveth in me: and the life which I now live in the flesh I live by the faith of the Son of God, who loved me, and gave himself for me." Gal. 2:20. The "inward man" is renewed daily by the presence of the indwelling Christ who causes us to grow constantly in spiritual stature even though the body may be wasting away.

So far from proving the immortal-soul doctrine, 2 Corinthians 4:16 is not even discussing the subject of immortality.

# Objection 72

When Stephen was martyred he prayed, "Lord Jesus, receive my spirit." Acts 7:59. Christ on the cross said, "Father, into thy hands I commend my spirit." Luke 23:46. This proves that at death the real man, that immortal entity called the "spirit," departs from the body.

The word here translated "spirit" is from the Greek word *pneuma*, which is true of virtually every use of "spirit" in the New Testament. The primary meaning of *pneuma* is "wind, air," and because life is associated so inextricably with the air we breathe, *pneuma* may also mean "life." There is nothing in the word *pneuma* that suggests an immaterial, conscious entity.

Stephen did not pray, "Receive *me*." This is most significant, for surely in this prayer the real man is speaking, not just the shell, the body. If Stephen believed that the righteous go to heaven at death, we should rightly expect him to pray, "Receive *me* up into glory." But Stephen, the animate being, still conscious, though dying, committed something to Christ, his *pneuma*, his life.

Stephen knew that his life was a gift from God. He would say, as did Job, "The breath of the Almighty hath given me life." Job 33:4. This great gift was about to leave him, and he wished to commit to the keeping of God that which he could no longer retain. He believed the truth, later penned by Paul: "Your life is hid with Christ in God. When Christ, who is our life, shall appear, then shall ye also appear with him in glory." Col. 3:3, 4. Stephen knew that at the resurrection day he again would receive life, *immortal* life.

Much of what has just been said regarding Stephen's words applies, most evidently, to Christ's words also. He commended to the keeping of His Father the life He was about to lay down for the sins of the world. On the resurrection morning the angel of God called Him forth from Joseph's new tomb, to take up once more that life He had voluntarily laid down.

# Objection 73

Hebrews 12:23 proves that man has a spirit, which is the real man, and that with this spirit we shall have fellowship in our perfected state. In other words, this text proves that disembodied spirits dwell in celestial bliss.

The passage in its context reads as follows: "But ye are come unto Mount Sion, and unto the city of the living God, the heavenly Jerusalem, and to an innumerable company of angels, to the general assembly and church of the firstborn, which are written in heaven, and to God the Judge of all, and to the spirits of just men made perfect, and to Jesus the mediator of the new covenant, and to the blood of sprinkling, that speaketh better things than that of Abel." Heb. 12:22-24.

The writer of Hebrews, who, it is believed, was Paul, is here contrasting the state of the Christian under the new covenant with the state of the self-confident, and soon rebellious, Israelites under the old covenant. The contrast begins with the eighteenth verse: "For ye are not come unto the mount [Sinai] that might be touched, and that burned with fire, nor unto blackness, and darkness, and tempest." "But ye are come unto mount Sion." Verse 22.

We should remember first that the prime purpose of this whole book of Hebrews is to show the superiority of the new covenant relationship over the old, the superiority of Christ's sacrifice and ministration for the believer over that of the Mosaic priests for the Jews. Hence, in the passage before us we may rightly presume that Paul is making another of his contrasting statements, and that in verses 22 and 23 he is describing a company on this earth, not in heaven. Paul would hardly be guilty of laboring so evident a point as that heaven is superior to earth. But to the Hebrews it was necessary often to remind them that though the Mosaic dispensation was glorious, even awesome and magnificent, when considered in the setting of God's presence at Sinai, nevertheless the Christian dispensation was more glorious. That he is describing a company of Christians in the Christian Era, and not a company in heaven, is further revealed by the fact that he says, "Ye are come . . . to Jesus the mediator of the new covenant." To those who finally reach heaven Christ is no longer the priestly mediator of any covenant. The saved in heaven will not be in need of a mediator.

Though the language is in part figurative, it is not difficult to see that Paul is describing the state of the believer in Christ in this world. Note the following:

1. "Ye are come unto mount Sion, and unto the city of the living God, the heavenly Jerusalem." Compare with this Peter's words: "To whom coming, as unto a living stone, disallowed indeed of men, but chosen of God, and precious, ye also, as lively stones, are built up a spiritual house, an holy priesthood, to offer up spiritual sacrifices, acceptable to God by Jesus Christ. Wherefore also it is contained in the scripture, Behold, I lay in Sion a chief corner stone, elect, precious: and he that believeth on him shall not be confounded." 1 Peter 2:4-6.

2. "To an innumerable company of angels." When we are drawn into the circle of heaven we draw near to the angels. Also, when we become children of God His holy angels minister to us. (See Heb. 1:14.)

3. "To the general assembly and church of the firstborn, which are written in heaven." Christ set up His church in the world, and to that we come when we accept Him.

4. "And to God the Judge of all." Compare with this other statements by Paul: "Let us therefore come boldly unto the throne of grace."Heb. 4:16. "Wherefore he is able also to save them to the uttermost that come unto God by him." Heb. 7:25.

Without taking the parallels further it is evident that Paul is describing the life of the Christian here in this world. Distinguishing features of that life are the fellowships he has with—

## ANSWERS TO OBJECTIONS

1. "An innumerable company of angels."
2. "The general assembly and church of the firstborn."
3. "God the Judge of all."
4. "The spirits of just men made perfect."
5. "Jesus the mediator of the new covenant."

Now, while we are on earth, attending church, communing with God and our Saviour Jesus, with what kind of "men" do we associate? Disembodied spirits? No. Then what does the phrase "The spirits of just men" mean? We believe that the most simple explanation, one wholly consistent with Scripture, is that Paul is telling us that the Christian communes with his fellow Christian on the spiritual level. Our meeting with other Christians is not on a carnal, earthy plane, as was true of the pagans at the time Paul wrote.

This contrast between flesh and spirit is frequently made by Paul. For example, his words to the Romans: "For they that are after the flesh do mind the things of the flesh; but they that are after the Spirit the things of the Spirit. For to be carnally minded is death; but to be spiritually minded is life and peace. Because the carnal mind is enmity against God: for it is not subject to the law of God, neither indeed can be. So then they that are in the flesh cannot please God." Rom. 8:5-8.

Christ said, "That which is born of the flesh is flesh; and that which is born of the Spirit is spirit. Marvel not that I said unto thee, Ye must be born again." John 3:6, 7.

Paul and Christ are both speaking of the converted man who is still walking this earth in flesh and blood. But in contrast to "flesh," which is a synonym for our sin-contaminated nature, they use the word "spirit" as a general term to describe the "born again" man who has a spiritual nature and who is controlled by the Spirit of God. But there is nothing airy, ghostly, immaterial, about this "born again" man, even though it is said of him: "That which is born of the Spirit is spirit." He sits in a pew in the church on the Sabbath day!

312

It is true that the majority of Bible commentators, looking at this difficult passage—and they all admit that verses 22 to 24 are somewhat difficult—through the eyes of their immortal-soul doctrine, understand verse 23 to refer to departed saints. That is what makes so significant the admissions, by some of them, that this verse refers to Christians living in this present world. Jamieson, Fausset, and Brown, in their comment on this text, remark:

"*Spirit* and *spirits* are used of *a man* or *men in the body, under the influence of the spirit* the opposite of *flesh.* (John 3.6.)"

Adam Clarke, Methodist commentator, remarks on this text:

"*The spirits of the just men made perfect,* or the *righteous perfect,* are the full grown Christians; those who are justified by the blood and sanctified by the Spirit of Christ. Being *come* to such, implies that spiritual union which the disciples of Christ have with each other, and which they possess how far soever separate; for they are *all joined in one spirit,* Eph. ii.18; they are *in the unity of the spirit,* Eph. iv.3, 4; and of *one soul.* Acts iv.32."

# Objection 74

Paul makes it clear that it was possible for him to be "out of the body." This proves that the real man is an immaterial soul, or spirit, that is independent of the body. (See 2 Cor. 12:2, 3.)

The passage, in its context, reads thus: "It is not expedient for me doubtless to glory. I will come to visions and revelations of the Lord. I knew a man in Christ above fourteen years ago, (whether in the body, I cannot tell; or whether out of the body, I cannot tell: God knoweth;) such an one caught up to the third heaven. And I knew such a man, (whether in the body, or out of the body, I cannot tell: God knoweth;) how that he was caught up into paradise, and heard unspeakable words, which it is not lawful for a man to utter." 2 Cor. 12:1-4.

The first fact that we wish to make clear is this: According to the believers in the immortal-soul doctrine, the departure of the soul from the body takes place at the instant of death, that indeed such a departure must result in death to the body. Indeed, two of their proof texts are supposed to support this very contention that death marks the departure of the soul: "And it came to pass, as her soul was in departing (for she died)." Gen. 35:18. "And the soul of the child came into him again, and he revived." 1 Kings 17:22. (See objection 81 for a study of these texts.)

Hence, following such reasoning, if Paul was "out of the body," he died! But is any believer in soul immortality really willing to admit that Paul is saying that he does not know whether or not he died at a certain time "above fourteen years ago"? And, of course, if he died, then he must have been afterward raised, or rather his body must have been raised, when he returned from "the third heaven." Here, indeed, would be something most remarkable for Paul to write about, but he makes no allusion anywhere in his writings to his having died and been resurrected.

Obviously, there must be something wrong with an interpretation of Paul's words that would produce so startling a conclusion.

But we are not required to follow any such reasoning. Paul is speaking of "visions and revelations." What he saw and heard was so real and vivid that he was not certain but that God might actually have transported him to heaven for the brief period of the revelation. And yet he would not affirm it as a fact. Obviously, the other alternative was that he had simply seen a vision and heard in that vision the revelation which it was "not lawful" for him to repeat. But if he was not literally taken to heaven in body, he seemed to be there nevertheless, and naturally he might describe that state as being "out of the body." Indeed, how better could one express the thought of being in a far-off place without literally going there?

In writing to the Colossian church Paul uses this very same kind of language: "For though I be absent in the flesh, yet am I with you in the spirit, joying and beholding your order, and the stedfastness of your faith in Christ." Col. 2:5.

We have no trouble understanding these words of Paul. No one finds in them any proof of an immortal, airy entity called a soul. In fact, we may write to a friend with whom it will not be possible for us to be on a certain important occasion: "I'll be with you in spirit." But none of us, including the objector, believes that when we speak thus we mean that an immortal entity within us will flit away at a certain time to be with the friend. Then why should anyone think that Paul in 2 Corinthians 12:2, 3 is teaching the doctrine of disembodied spirits?

# Objection 75

The apostle Paul says that at the second coming of Christ God will bring with Him from heaven those who have fallen asleep in Jesus. (See 1 Thess. 4:14.) This proves that the righteous go to heaven at death instead of lying in the grave until the Second Advent.

The text reads as follows: "For if we believe that Jesus died and rose again, even so them also which sleep in Jesus will God bring with him." 1 Thess. 4:14. In the verses immediately preceding and following, Paul discusses two groups: (1) "them which are asleep" and (2) "we which are alive and remain unto the coming of the Lord." In his discussion he sought to accomplish five things:

1. Assure them that they need not "sorrow" as the pagans about them did, "which have no hope." Verse 13.

2. Inform them that the living saints would not "prevent [precede] them which are asleep" as regards being taken to glory. Verse 15.

3. Inform them how "them which are asleep" will be awakened; namely, "the trump of God" shall cause them to "rise." Verse 16.

4. Inform them what happens immediately following the resurrection: The living saints are "caught up together with them [the resurrected saints] in the clouds, to meet the Lord in the air." Verse 17.

5. Inform them of the state of the living and resurrected saints subsequent to meeting their Lord: "And so shall we ever be with the Lord." Verse 17.

Now if the righteous dead are to *"rise"* at a future resurrection date, and together with the living saints then go heavenward to dwell forever with the Lord, how can Paul possibly be declaring in verse 14 that the righteous dead come *down* from heaven at the great resurrection day? The only way the believer in soul immortality can harmonize his interpretation of verse 14 with the related verses is to declare that the souls of the saints ascended heavenward at death and that these souls come down with the Lord at the resurrection day to receive their resurrected bodies.

The prime weakness in this explanation is that it assumes what is to be proved. The objector submits this passage in Thessalonians to prove the immortal-soul doctrine, and then proceeds to *assume* that there is such a thing as an immaterial entity, an immortal soul, in order to escape from a hopeless conflict between verse 14, as interpreted by him, and the succeeding verses!

But his assumption can easily be shown to be not even plausible. Here is how the righteous dead are described:

Verse 13: "Them which are asleep."

Verse 14: "Them also which sleep in Jesus."

Verse 16: "The dead in Christ."

By what rule of language is it proper to say that in verse 14 Paul is speaking only of the souls of the saints, whereas in verses 13 and 16 he is speaking only of their bodies?

Most evidently the interpretation given to verse 14 must be wrong. What is Paul there seeking to establish? To assure the believers that the resurrection was a certainty. The certainty of the resurrection was the key point that the apostles stressed in their preaching. First, the certainty that Christ was raised from the dead, and then because of that, the certainty that we also will be freed from the prison house of death. Listen to Paul argue the case:

"And if Christ be not risen, then is our preaching vain, and your faith is also vain. Yea, and we are found false witnesses of God; because we have testified of God that he raised up Christ: whom he raised not up, if so be that the dead rise not. For if the dead rise not, then is not Christ raised: and if Christ be not raised, your faith is vain; ye are yet in your sins. Then they also which are fallen asleep in Christ are perished. . . . But now is Christ risen from the dead, and become the firstfruits of them that slept. . . . But every man in his own order: Christ the firstfruits; afterward they that are Christ's at his coming." 1 Cor. 15:14-23.

His reasoning sums up thus: Unless we believe that Christ rose from the grave we have no hope of a resurrection. Christ rose as the firstfruits from the grave, and "afterward they that are Christ's" will be raised "at his coming."

In his letter to the Hebrews, Paul thus describes God: "The God of peace, that brought again from the dead our Lord Jesus." Heb. 13:20.

In the light of these and related passages we have no difficulty in finding an interpretation for 1 Thessalonians 4:14 that harmonizes with the whole context of that chapter and with Paul's whole argument elsewhere regarding the resurrection. The verse is in two parts:

1. "For if we believe that Jesus died and rose again."

2. "Even so them also which sleep in Jesus will God bring with him."

Paul is here simply presenting the case for the certainty of our resurrection on the ground that Christ was raised. Now it was God "that brought again from the dead our Lord Jesus." "Even so" "will God bring with him [Jesus]" from the grave "them also which sleep in Jesus." "Christ the firstfruits; afterward they that are Christ's at his coming."

It becomes plain, therefore, that Paul teaches in 1 Thessalonians 4:14, not the immortal-soul doctrine, but the great doctrine of the resurrection.

# Objection 76

We agree that those who died in Old Testament days remained unconscious in their graves, as the Old Testament Scriptures prove. (See, for example, Eccl. 9:5, 6, 10.) But when Christ came He declared that "whosoever liveth and believeth in me shall never die." John 11:26. This proves that in the New Testament times those who believe in Christ do not die, but go direct to heaven. In support of this conclusion is Paul's declaration that Christ "abolished death" (2 Tim. 1:10), also the repeated statements of Scripture that the Christian now possesses everlasting life.

Well may the objector admit that the Old Testament worthies did not go to their heavenly reward at death, but lie silent yet in the grave. The Scriptural evidence is overwhelming. On the day of Pentecost, Peter said to the multitude: "Men and brethren, let me freely speak unto you of the patriarch David, that he is both dead and buried, and his sepulchre is with us unto this day." "For David is not ascended into the heavens." Acts 2:29, 34.

But this admission regarding these good men of Old Testament days is fatal to the whole case for the immortal-soul doctrine. Why do most Christian people believe that a Christian goes to heaven at death? Because they believe that there resides within man an immortal soul, and that the soul of the man who is a Christian must of course go to heaven at the time the man's body goes to the grave. Then, we would ask: Did righteous men begin to have immortal souls *only* at the beginning of the Christian Era? We have never heard that idea set forth seriously by any exponent of the immortal-soul doctrine. But if men have always had immortal souls, then what happened to the souls of the holy men of Old Testament times when they died? It is really a denial of the whole immortal-soul doctrine to say that the souls of those ancient worthies stayed in the grave! An immortal, *conscious* entity, the real man, lying in the dust for ages! That idea passes credulity, no one really believes it.

We think that some definite position should be taken by the objector, for how can we hope to give an answer unless we really know what he affirms. If he takes the position that the Old Testament worthies did have immortal souls, which is the standard teaching in almost all Christendom, then he really denies that position by his admission that these worthies "remained unconscious in their graves." But if he affirms that those worthies did not have immortal souls, then the heavy burden of proof rests on him to present clear Scriptural proof that Christ, when He came to earth, gave to believers from that time onward immortal souls, so that instead of remaining "unconscious in their graves" they go directly to heaven at death. Apparently he takes this latter position, and offers in proof of his position John 11:26.

Before we examine specifically this text we wish, first, to show that the Bible makes no distinction between the state in death of Old Testament and New Testament holy men. Note this parallel:

| Old Testament Saints | New Testament Saints |
| --- | --- |
| "And these [holy men of Old Testament times] all, having obtained a good report through faith, received not the promise: God having provided some better thing for us, that they without us should not be made perfect." Heb. 11:39, 40. | "We which are alive and remain unto the coming of the Lord shall not prevent [precede] them which are asleep. For the Lord himself shall descend from heaven with a shout . . . : and the dead in Christ shall rise first: then we which are alive and remain shall be caught up together with them in the clouds, to meet the Lord in the air." 1 Thess. 4:15-17. |

As regards the Old Testament saints, they must await a future date for their reward, and that date is when all God's elect are ready. We are to be given our reward together.

When Paul writes to the Thessalonian church "concerning them which are asleep," that they "sorrow not, even as others which have no hope" (1 Thess. 4:13), he was discussing New Testament saints who had died. He does not here teach that their fellow believers who had died—"are asleep"—had gone to meet their Lord. On the contrary, he sought to make clear to them that the righteous living at the last great day would not precede to glory those who "are asleep." We are to go to our reward together. Which is exactly what Paul, in Hebrews, teaches regarding the Old Testament saints in relation to the New Testament ones!

Thus we conclude that there is no difference between Old and New Testament saints as regards the time when they go to heaven. We find reinforcement of this conclusion in the words of John, who thus speaks of Christians in the last days of earth's history: "Blessed are the dead which die in the Lord from henceforth: Yea, saith the Spirit, that they may rest from their labours; and their works do follow them." Rev. 14:13. Hence we come inevitably to the conclusion that whatever Christ was seeking to teach in John 11:26, He was not seeking to tell His followers that beginning then, they, in contrast to the ancient worthies, would escape death, would possess an immortal soul, and thus would go to heaven at death.

Then what was He seeking to tell Martha when He said to her, "Whosoever liveth and believeth in me shall never die"? This is not a lone passage. We find Him saying to the Jews, "If a man keep my saying, he shall never see death." John 8:51.

We believe that the explanation is this: When God first placed man on the earth He warned him against the tree of the knowledge of good and evil, and said, "In the day that thou eatest thereof thou shalt surely die." Gen. 2:17. Some have wondered how that judgment was fulfilled, inasmuch as Adam lived on for centuries after he ate the forbidden fruit. But the reasonable answer is that on the day Adam ate the fruit he came under the condemnation of death. His fate was there irrevocably fixed. Thus in the sight of God, who thinks rather of the ultimate end than of the relatively transient period before judgment is executed, Adam could be considered dead the moment he ate.

It is in this sense that we understand Paul's words, for example, where he tells the Colossian church that before they accepted Christ they were "dead" in their "sins." (Col. 2:13.) Also his words descriptive of a dissolute woman: "She that liveth in pleasure is dead while she liveth." 1 Tim. 5:6.

Contrast with these and similar texts the words of our Lord: "He that heareth my word, and believeth on him that sent me, hath everlasting life, and shall not come into condemnation; but is passed from death unto life." John 5:24. Note also the words of John: "We know that we have passed from death unto life, because we love the brethren. He that loveth not his brother abideth in death." 1 John 3:14. Then take the words of Paul: "For to be carnally minded is death; but to be spiritually minded is life and peace." Rom. 8:6.

How evident that the Bible writers consider man as being in one or the other of two states, lost or saved, and that moving from one state to the other is passing "from death unto life."

Add to these Scriptural facts another: The Bible speaks of two deaths and two resurrections. We read the promise: "He that overcometh shall not be hurt of the second death." Rev. 2:11. "Blessed and holy is he that hath part in the first resurrection: on such the second death hath no power." Rev. 20:6. But this is simply another way of saying that the first death does have power, even over the righteous. The "second death" is the death suffered by those who are cast "into the lake which burneth with fire and brimstone." Rev. 21:8.

The first death brings all men into graves in the earth, where all sleep until they are resurrected at the end of time, the righteous in the first resurrection, the wicked in the second. Christ describes the first as the "resurrection of *life,*" the second, as the "resurrection of *damnation.*" Obviously, then, the first death is as it were a "sleep," for there is a certain and sure awakening. (See Dan. 12:2.) But not so with the second death, which brings wicked men into the lake of fire, that burns them up so that there is left of them "neither root nor branch." (Mal. 4:1.)

That is why the Bible, in speaking of the righteous of all ages, declares, "Blessed and holy is he that hath part in the first resurrection." Such persons "die in the Lord" (Rev. 14:13), they "sleep in Jesus" (1 Thess. 4:14), and come forth in the first resurrection to dwell forevermore with their Lord.

But the wicked, "dead in trespasses and sins" (Eph. 2:1), dwell under "condemnation" of death (John 5:24); they are dead even while they live (1 Tim. 5:6); they go down into Christless graves, rise in the resurrection to receive judgment, and go down in the "second death" (Rev. 21:8).

When we see Christ's statement in John 11:26 in this setting we have no difficulty in understanding it. We do not have to give His words a strained interpretation. We do not have to make ourselves believe the plainly un-Scriptural idea that there is a difference between Old and New Testament saints. We do not have to reject the evidence of our senses and claim that when the Christian goes down into the grave he really goes to heaven. We simply understand Christ to mean that those who accept His proffered salvation are freed from the penalty of death that hangs over all men and will never suffer that "second death," which is death in the ultimate sense of the word, for there is no return from it. Indeed, the "second death" is the opposite of eternal life, which is the gift given to the Christian. Of the one who has eternal life, or everlasting life, it can be said that the "second death" has no power over him.

Christ declared to the unbelieving Jews, "Ye will not come to me, that ye might have life." John 5:40. But the Christian has accepted Christ, who is the life, into his heart. That is why he has everlasting life abiding in him. When the Christian dies he commends to God his life, as did the martyr Stephen, then sleeps in Jesus against the day of the "resurrection of life." Such a one never truly sees or experiences death. He experiences only a little time of sleep.

Adam Clarke, Methodist theologian, in his commentary, says this in comment on the phrase "shall never die":

*"Shall not die for ever.* Though he die a temporal death, he shall not continue under its power for ever; but shall have a resurrection to life eternal."

In the light of the foregoing, Paul's statement that Christ "abolished death" (2 Tim. 1:10) may most naturally be understood to mean this: Christ, having risen from the grave, has the victory over death, and has provided thereby absolute assurance that it will be abolished. Paul makes clear that the actual abolition of death awaits the second coming of Christ, when the righteous dead are raised. Then it is that "death is swallowed up in victory." 1 Cor. 15:54.

Compare with Paul's words John's description of the final consuming fires that are to burn up every trace of sin: "And death and hell were cast into the lake of fire." Rev. 20:14. Then, and not until then, will death truly be "abolished." Christ's resurrection made certain the abolition of death, even as it made certain the resurrection of all who have died in Christ. But even as the resurrection of the righteous awaits the end of the world, even so the abolition of death awaits that great hour.

# Objection 77

In Matthew 22:32 Christ declares that He is not the God of the dead but of the living. Yet He said, "I am the God of Abraham, and the God of Isaac, and the God of Jacob." This proves that the souls of these patriarchs, who died long ago, are really alive in heaven.

Let us look at this passage of Scripture in its context. We read that there came to Christ "the Sadducees, which say that there is no resurrection." Matt. 22:23. Mark introduces the incident in exactly the same language. (Mark 12:18.) Luke says, "The Sadducees, which deny that there is any resurrection." Luke 20:27. Hence we may properly conclude that the only point at issue in the discussion that the Sadducees raised on this occasion was whether or not there was to be a resurrection.

That this was the one point at issue is made even more clear by the hypothetical case that the Sadducees described and the question they asked. They cited Moses' command that if a man's brother die without children, he should marry the widow and raise up seed to his brother. Now, said they, a man died, his brother married the widow, then the brother died, and another brother married the widow, and so on through seven brothers, with the seventh finally dying, and afterward the woman dying. Then comes the Sadducees' question: "Therefore in the resurrection whose wife shall she be of the seven? for they all had her." Matt. 22:28.

The Sadducees, who affirmed their belief in Moses and their disbelief in the resurrection, apparently thought that they had asked an unanswerable question and therefore had proved incredible the idea of a resurrection. Christ dissolved the dilemma by declaring, "In the resurrection they neither marry, nor are given in marriage." Verse 30. Note that the discussion continues to focus on a certain future event, "the resurrection."

# ANSWERS TO OBJECTIONS

Now, strictly speaking, though Christ had dissolved the dilemma, He had not thereby given a Scriptural proof that there is to be a resurrection, which was the real point at issue, for the Sadducees, as fervently as the Pharisees, affirmed their belief in the books of Moses. Hence Christ proceeds immediately to offer proof that the dead will be raised: "But as touching the resurrection of the dead, have ye not read that which was spoken unto you by God, saying, I am the God of Abraham, and the God of Isaac, and the God of Jacob? God is not the God of the dead, but of the living." Matt. 22:31, 32. Mark introduces Christ's proof with similar language: "And as touching the dead, that they rise." Mark 12:26. Luke records, "Now that the dead are raised, even Moses shewed." Luke 20:37.

But for some reason the believers in the immortal-soul doctrine believe that "Moses shewed" and that Christ quoted Moses to show, not that "the dead are raised," but that their immortal souls have *never* died! There have always been those who believed that at death an airy entity leaves the body, who did not therefore believe that there would ever be a bodily resurrection. Belief in the one does not logically necessitate belief in the other. Hence, if Christ simply proved that Abraham, Isaac, and Jacob were then living as immortal souls in bliss, He did not thereby prove that there would be a resurrection.

But, as we have seen, the question at issue was, Will there be a resurrection? Did Christ answer the question? Did He prove that there would be a resurrection? It surely gives small honor to our Lord to reason that He did not, when He expressly declared that His reference to Abraham, Isaac, and Jacob was intended to prove "that the dead are raised." We prefer to conclude that the Lord proved His point rather than that the immortal-soul advocates have proved theirs! We cannot conclude that both have!

Only one question remains for examination: If "God is not the God of the dead, but of the living," then must not Abraham, Isaac, and Jacob be living? The answer is found in the discussion of the preceding objection (No. 76). Indeed, that objection, so confidently brought forward to show that when Christ came an undying quality was given to Christians, is really the refutation of the whole objection before us. Under objection 76 evidence was presented to show that the believer in God has "passed from death unto life" and that therefore God does not regard his sleep in the grave as eternal, but only as a little interval between the earthly life and the heavenly.

That God does speak in terms of the assured future as though it were already present, is clearly stated by Paul: "God, who quickeneth the dead, and calleth those things which be not as though they were." Rom. 4:17. This statement is made in relation to Abraham! Again, take Paul's words regarding all Christians: "For none of us liveth to himself, and no man dieth to himself. For whether we live, we live unto the Lord; and whether we die, we die unto the Lord: whether we live therefore, or die, we are the Lord's. For to this end Christ both died, and rose, and revived, that he might be Lord both of the dead and living." Rom. 14:7-9. And why are we still "the Lord's," even though we die? Because we "sleep in Jesus," and the "dead in Christ shall rise" in the "resurrection of life." (1 Thess. 4:14, 16; John 5:29.)

Only as we understand the matter in this way do we avoid a conflict between two texts of Scripture: (1) "God is not the God of the dead," and Christ is (2) "Lord both of the dead and living." In the first Christ is speaking to the Sadducees, who held that all men, good as well as bad, suffered eternal extinction at death. In the second Paul is speaking of those who have died in "the Lord," and who thus simply "sleep" for a little while till they are called forth at the resurrection of life. God is indeed the God of all who thus have died.

# Objection 78

**Ecclesiastes 12:7 proves that there is a conscious, immortal entity that leaves the body at death. (See also Eccl. 3:21.)**

Ecclesiastes 12:7 reads, "Then shall the dust return to the earth as it was: and the spirit shall return unto God who gave it." This text speaks of the dissolution of man at death. We cannot accept the belief that this "spirit" is a conscious entity that is released at death and soars away, because:

1. If this "spirit" is a conscious entity when it *"returns"* to God, then it was a conscious entity when it *came* from God. The construction of the text demands this, for it gives us the specific statement that the dust returns to the earth "as it was," and unless otherwise stated, it would follow that the spirit returns as *it* was. In fact, for the believer in immortal souls to declare that the "spirit" needed lodgment within the so-called shell of the body to possess consciousness, would be to surrender the whole argument.

Now, the Bible teaches the pre-existence of Christ before He was born in Bethlehem. But the view stated in the objection before us would demand the astounding conclusion that all the members of the human family, as spirits, had an existence before they were born on this earth. This makes good Mormon theology, with its unseen world of spirits waiting for human bodies in order to find abodes on this earth. But it is to be doubted whether any orthodox Christian could bring himself to accept this view.

2. If the "spirit" which returns to God is a conscious entity, and thus the real man, then all men, whether good or bad, go to God at death. Are all to have the same destination? If it be said that the wicked go to God simply to receive judgment, we would reply that the Bible states definitely that the judgment is still a future event. (See Matt. 25:31-46; Rev. 22:12.)

3. Of the creation of man we read, "The Spirit of God hath made me, and the breath of the Almighty hath given me life."

328

Job 33:4. Job thus describes his state of being alive: "All the while my breath is in me, and the spirit of God is in my nostrils." Job 27:3. The act of dying is set forth in these words: "If he [God] set his heart upon man, if he gather unto himself his spirit and his breath; all flesh shall perish together, and man shall turn again unto dust." Job 34:14, 15. The spirit returns because it came from God and because God gathers it to Himself.

The whole cycle indicates nowhere a conscious entity, exercising a free will to go to God. On the contrary, the Bible declares that God gathers "unto himself *his* spirit." If this returning spirit is the real man, then we would be forced to believe that certain pagan religions are right when they teach that man is but a manifestation of the Divine Spirit, and at death is absorbed again into that one great Spirit. We cannot accept this pagan view, which means that we cannot accept the view set forth in the objection based on Ecclesiastes 12:7.

The answer to this objection is really an answer also to the objection based on Ecclesiastes 3:21, which reads as follows: "Who knoweth the spirit of man that goeth upward, and the spirit of the beast that goeth downward to the earth?" Because this text says that man's spirit goes upward and the beast's downward at death, we are supposed to conclude that therefore man, in contrast to the beast, has an immortal soul, or spirit, that soars heavenward at death.

But such reasoning requires that at death all men go "upward" to heaven. We have always understood that those who believe in the immortality of the soul teach that at death the wicked go "downward" to hell. This text proves more than they wish it to prove. If Solomon is here teaching that the "spirit of man" means an immortal entity, the real man, then he is teaching that all men will be saved. But that doctrine, called universalism, has ever been considered by both Protestants and Catholics as rank heresy.

Furthermore, to reason that this text proves man's immortality because it seems to contrast the "spirit of man" with the "spirit of the beast," is to make Solomon contradict himself. In the immediately preceding verses he explicitly states that as regards their destination at death, there is no difference between man and beast: "For that which befalleth the sons of men befalleth beasts; even one thing befalleth them: as one dieth, so dieth the other; yea, *they have all one breath;* so that a man hath no preeminence above a beast: for all is vanity. All go unto one place; all are of the dust, and all turn to dust again." Eccl. 3:19, 20.

Solomon says that "they have all one breath." The Hebrew word here translated "breath" is *ruach.* The word "spirit" that is used twice in the twenty-first verse—"the spirit of man," "the spirit of the beast"—is also from this same Hebrew word *ruach.*

The objector may now remark that Solomon is therefore contradicting himself. In verses 19 and 20 he argues that "a man hath no preeminence above a beast," and then in verse 21 he declares that man's spirit goes upward, in contrast to the beast's, which proves that man does have a pre-eminence.

But whenever, in Scripture, there is an apparent contradiction, we need to look a little deeper, and perhaps to compare the translation that we commonly use with other translations. Since our common version of the Scriptures, known as the King James Version, was translated in A.D. 1611 many more old manuscripts of the Bible have been discovered, which help us in many instances better to understand what a Bible writer is saying. Thus with the passage before us. In the American Standard Version, commonly known as the Revised Version, verse 21 reads, "Who knoweth the spirit of man, whether it goeth upward, and the spirit of the beast, whether it goeth downward to the earth?"

This translation of Solomon's words in verse 21 permits complete harmony with what he has declared in the preceding verses. And with this question in verse 21 placed in the setting of the preceding verses, it is evident that Solomon does not intend the reader to understand that there is any difference in the destination of the spirit (*ruach*) of man and beast. His question simply constitutes a challenge to anyone to provide proof, if he can, that there is a difference in destination.

And why should there be any difference? All life comes from God, no matter whether that life is displayed in man or in the humblest animal. That is sound Christian doctrine. At death the life, which is a gift from God, returns to God. This follows logically from the preceding statement. Where believers in the immortal-soul doctrine find themselves in perplexity is that they define the word "spirit" (*ruach*), when it is used in relation to man, as an immortal entity, the real man; but when the word "spirit" (*ruach*) is used in relation to beasts, they are content to define it abstractly as the principle of life, the breath of life. They must make this arbitrary distinction in definition, else one of two dilemmas confronts them: (1) Either man and beasts both have within them an immortal entity, (2) or neither man nor beasts are possessed of such an entity.

Seventh-day Adventists find no necessity of making arbitrary differences in definition of a word. We see in such a passage as Ecclesiastes 3:19-21 a simple statement that life from God is given to all, man and beasts, and that at death that life returns to God. We do not need to invent a difference in definitions for "spirit" (*ruach*) in order to preserve a clear difference between man and beasts. We believe that man was made in "the image of God," which the beasts were not. We believe that man has a moral nature, which the beasts have not. We believe that man may have communion with God, which the beasts cannot. We believe that man will answer at a final judgment day for all his deeds, which the beasts will not. Finally, we believe that man may ultimately be translated to dwell with God in an earth made new, which the beasts will not. But we believe that this is possible for man, not because of an immortal entity within him, but because of a resurrection from the dead.

# Objection 79

That the righteous dead go to heaven immediately at death, and that man therefore possesses an immortal spirit, is evident from Paul's statement in 2 Corinthians 5:8. (See also 2 Peter 1:14.)

The passage in its context reads as follows: "For we know that if our earthly house of this tabernacle were dissolved, we have a building of God, an house not made with hands, eternal in the heavens. For in this we groan, earnestly desiring to be clothed upon with our house which is from heaven: if so be that being clothed we shall not be found naked. For we that are in this tabernacle do groan, being burdened: not for that we would be unclothed, but clothed upon, that mortality might be swallowed up of life. Now he that hath wrought us for the selfsame thing is God, who also hath given unto us the earnest of the Spirit. Therefore we are always confident, knowing that, whilst we are at home in the body, we are absent from the Lord: (for we walk by faith, not by sight:) we are confident, I say, and willing rather to be absent from the body, and to be present with the Lord. Wherefore we labour, that, whether present or absent, we may be accepted of him." 2 Cor. 5:1-9.

Paul here deals with three possible states:

1. "Our earthly house." "At home in the body." "Absent from the Lord." This house can be "dissolved." "In this we groan."
2. "Unclothed." "Naked."
3. "A building of God." "House not made with hands, eternal in the heavens." "Our house which is from heaven." "Clothed upon." "Present with the Lord." "Absent from the body."

If the "earthly house" means our present, mortal body, as all agree, then unless there is clear proof to the contrary, it would logically follow that our heavenly house is the immortal body. And thus by a process of elimination the "unclothed," "naked," state can mean none other than that state of dissolution known as death.

We are assured of the desired third state because we have "the earnest [pledge] of the Spirit." Verse 5. But how will God's Spirit finally ensure our reaching this desired state? Paul answers, "If the Spirit of him that raised up Jesus from the dead dwell in you, he that raised up Christ from the dead shall also *quicken your mortal bodies* by his Spirit that dwelleth in you." Rom. 8:11.

The learned Dr. H. C. G. Moule well says:

"That same Spirit, who, by uniting us to Christ, made actual our redemption, shall surely, in ways to us unknown, carry the process to its glorious crown, and be somehow the Efficient Cause of 'the redemption of our body.' "—*The Expositor's Bible,* comment on Romans 8:11.

Now, if the fulfilling to us of that pledge of the Spirit is the change that takes place in our "mortal bodies" at the resurrection, then we must conclude that the change to the third state, that of being "clothed upon" with the heavenly house, comes at the resurrection, and is the change in our bodies from mortal to immortal.

Paul declares further: "We know that the whole creation groaneth and travaileth in pain together until now. And not only they, but ourselves also, which have the firstfruits of the Spirit, even we ourselves groan within ourselves, waiting for the adoption, to wit, the redemption of our body." Rom. 8:22, 23. That he is here dealing with the same problem as in 2 Corinthians 5 is evident:

| Romans 8:22, 23 | 2 Corinthians 5:1-8 |
|---|---|
| "Groan within ourselves." | "We groan." |
| "Firstfruits of the Spirit." | "Earnest of the Spirit." |
| "Waiting for." | "Earnestly desiring." |
| "Redemption of our body." | "Clothed upon" with heavenly house. |

Thus we conclude again that the change from the "earthly house" to the "house which is from heaven" is an event that involves the "redemption of our body," which "redemption," all agree, occurs at the resurrection day. (See also Phil. 3:20, 21.)

The apostle states that he longs to be "clothed upon" with the heavenly house, *"that mortality might be swallowed up of life,"* or, as the American Revised Version states it, "that what is mortal may be swallowed up of life." 2 Cor. 5:4. In other words, "what is mortal" loses its mortality by this change.

According to the immortal-soul doctrine, "what is mortal" is the body only, which at death dissolves in the grave; but the soul simply continues on in its immortal state, freed from the mortal body. But Paul longs to be "clothed" with the heavenly house, "that what is mortal may be swallowed up of life." Thus by their own tenets the immortal-soul advocates must agree that Paul in this passage is not dealing with an experience that takes place at death. We might therefore close the discussion at this point.

In his first letter to the Corinthians, Paul declared, "We shall not all sleep, but we shall all be changed." When? "At the last trump." And what will take place? "The dead shall be raised incorruptible, and we shall be changed." And what will result from this? *"When* this corruptible *shall have* put on incorruption, and this mortal *shall have* put on immortality, *then* shall be brought to pass the saying that is written, *Death is swallowed up in victory."* 1 Cor. 15:51-54. This last phrase parallels the language in 2 Corinthians 5: "What is mortal [or subject to death] may be swallowed up of life." The swallowing up of death, or mortality, is still a future event.

That Paul expected to be "clothed upon" with the heavenly house at the resurrection day is the certain conclusion from all his statements. Being "present with the Lord" is contingent upon being "clothed" with the heavenly house. Therefore the being "present with the Lord" awaits the resurrection day. How beautifully this agrees with the apostle's statement to the Thessalonians, that at the *resurrection* we are caught up "to meet the Lord," and "so shall we ever be *with the Lord."* 1 Thess. 4:17.

If it seems strange to some that Paul should speak of putting off one "house" and putting on another when he meant simply the change in his body from mortal to immortal, we would remind them that he uses a similar figure of speech when describing the change that takes place in the heart at conversion. He declares that we should "put off . . . the old man," and "put on the new man." (Eph. 4:22-24.)

The fact that Paul coupled together the being freed from the earthly house and the being clothed upon with the heavenly does not prove that he expected an *immediate* transfer from one to the other. He makes specific reference to an "unclothed," a "naked," state. On the question of immediate transfer, the reader is referred to the discussion of Philippians 1:21-23 under objection 83.

With propriety might Paul "groan" for the day when he could put off this mortal body, with all the evils suggested by it, and could put on, be "clothed upon" with, the promised immortal body, in which body he would be ready "to meet" and to "ever be with the Lord."

In the light of the foregoing we need not spend much time on 2 Peter 1:14, which is also mentioned by the objector. The passage in its context reads as follows: "Yea, I think it meet, as long as I am in this tabernacle, to stir you up by putting you in remembrance; knowing that shortly I must put off this my tabernacle, even as our Lord Jesus Christ hath shewed me. Moreover I will endeavor that ye may be able after my decease to have these things always in remembrance." 2 Peter 1:13-15.

The reasoning of the immortal-soul advocate here runs about as follows: Peter said that he dwelt in a tabernacle, and that *"I must put off this my* tabernacle." Therefore, this proves that Peter had an immortal soul, indicated by the "I" and "my," and that he, looking at his body, his tabernacle, thought of it as something apart from himself.

We are all agreed that Peter refers to his death when he speaks of putting "off this tabernacle." Christ spoke to him as to his death: "When *thou* wast young, *thou* girdest thyself, and walkedst whither *thou* wouldest: but when *thou* shalt be old, *thou* shalt stretch forth *thy* hands, and another shall gird *thee,* and carry *thee* whither *thou* wouldest not. This spake he, signifying by what death he [Peter] should glorify God." John 21:18, 19.

Notice that here Christ does not make a distinction between Peter and his "tabernacle," as though they were two, and separate. And John, in recording this forecast of Peter's martyrdom, speaks of the "death *he* should die." Not Peter's "tabernacle" dying, but "he" dying. This agrees with Peter's own words: "After *my* decease." We agree with the objector that the "I" and the "my" of verse 14 refer to Peter. But is it not equally evident that the "my" of verse 15 also refers to Peter? Yes. But in this verse Peter says, "My *decease.*" When Peter is allowed to speak for himself, the apparent case for the immortal-soul doctrine disappears—immortal entities do not suffer decease.

# Objection 80

**Man is made in the image of God; God is immortal; therefore man is immortal.**

Why should only one of God's attributes, that of immortality, be singled out for comparison? God is all-powerful. Does it therefore follow that man, made in the image of God, is also all-powerful? God is all-wise. Is man therefore possessed of boundless wisdom, because made in God's image?

The Bible uses the word "immortality" only five times, and the word "immortal" only once. In this lone instance the term is applied to God: "Eternal, immortal, invisible, the only wise God." 1 Tim. 1:17. The five references that contain the word "immortality" are as follows:

1. Romans 2:7. In this text the Christian is exhorted to "seek" for immortality. Why should he seek for it if he already possesses it? In this same book of Romans, Paul quotes the prophet Elijah as saying of his enemies, "They seek my life." We understand from this that the prophet's enemies did not yet have his life in their hands. Therefore, when we are exhorted to seek for immortality, for a life that knows no end, we must conclude that we do not now possess such a life.

2. 2 Timothy 1:10. Here we learn that Christ "brought life and immortality to light through the gospel." The only deduction from this is that so far from immortality's being a natural possession of all men, it is one of the good things made possible through the gospel. Paul wrote, "The gift of God is eternal life through Jesus Christ." Rom. 6:23. Why would we need this gift if we already had undying souls?

3. 1 Corinthians 15:53. This passage tells when we shall receive immortality. The time is "at the last trump." Then "this mortal must put on immortality." Why should the apostle Paul

speak of our putting on immortality at a future date if we already possess it?

4. 1 Corinthians 15:54. This verse simply adds the thought that when "this mortal shall have put on immortality, then shall be brought to pass the saying that is written, Death is swallowed up in victory."

5. 1 Timothy 6:16. Here we learn that God "only hath immortality." This final text settles the matter as conclusively as words could possibly do, and explains fully why we are exhorted to "seek" immortality, and why we are told that immortality is something that is to be "put on" "at the last trump."

Not only do we learn from these texts that we do not have immortality, but also we are told that God alone has it.

There are other texts which contain in the original Greek the same word that is translated "immortal" or "immortality" in the six texts we have just considered. But these additional texts do not require us to change our conclusion; on the contrary they strengthen it. Take, for example, Romans 1:23, where Paul, speaking of the idolatrous action of the heathen, says that they "changed the glory of the uncorruptible [immortal] God into an image made like to corruptible [mortal] man." In the Greek, the word here translated "uncorruptible" is the same as that rendered "immortal" in 1 Timothy 1:17: "Eternal, *immortal,* invisible, the only wise God." The Expositor's Bible translates the passage thus: "Transmuted the glory of the immortal God in a semblance of the likeness of mortal man." The uncorruptible, the immortal God is sharply contrasted with corruptible, mortal man.

We read in John 5:26 that the "Father hath life in himself," and that He hath "given to the Son to have life in himself." But nowhere do we read that God gave to human beings to have life in themselves. That is why the Bible never speaks of man as immortal.

# Objection 81

The Bible describes the death of Rachel by saying that "her soul was in departing." Gen. 35:18. (See also 1 Kings 17:21, 22.)

The reference from First Kings deals with the account of a child that died, and of how the prophet Elijah prayed: "O Lord my God, I pray thee, let this child's soul come into him again. And the Lord heard the voice of Elijah; and the soul of the child came into him again, and he revived."

These accounts of the child and of Rachel may be examined together. The explanation of one is obviously the explanation of the other.

The claim is that the "soul" that departed was the real person that soared away at death, leaving behind only the shell, the body; in other words, that really Rachel and the child departed. But such a view does not fit with the Bible description of the child's death. Elijah did not pray that the child return and re-enter his body, but "let this child's soul come into *him* again." "And the soul of the child came into *him* again, and *he* revived." The next sentence says that "Elijah took the child, and brought *him* down out of the chamber," and gave him to his mother. The lifeless form is called "the child," or "him," and the revived boy being led by the prophet to his mother is described in exactly the same language. This complete failure of the Bible writer to use any difference in language in referring to the child before and after the resurrection miracle is but typical of Bible writers throughout.

For example, take the Lord's statement to Adam: "In the sweat of thy face shalt thou eat bread." Gen. 3:19. We all agree that God is addressing Adam. The personal pronoun "thou" could have no other meaning. But the whole sentence reads thus: "In the sweat of thy face shalt *thou* eat bread, till *thou* return unto the ground; for out of it wast *thou* taken: for dust *thou* art, and unto dust shalt *thou* return."

# ANSWERS TO OBJECTIONS

What rule of language permits the pronoun "thou" to have its correct personal meaning in the first part of a sentence and a different, an impersonal, value in the remainder of the sentence? If the Lord, as we believe, really wished to inform Adam that he, not merely the so-called shell of a body, would return to the ground, could any plainer language have been used? Now if, in order to support a belief, it is necessary to give personal and impersonal values to one and the same pronoun when addressed to a single person in a single sentence, there must be something the matter with that belief. If we who teach that man is mortal and lies in the grave till the resurrection, are not to be permitted to use the ordinary rules of language and the most obvious meaning of words in presenting our view from the Bible, then of course we have no basis for discussion.

Perhaps believers in natural immortality think we are attempting to build too much of a case on the use of pronouns. But suppose the Lord had said to Adam, "In the sweat of thy face shalt thou eat bread, until thou return unto me." How triumphantly would they have reminded us that "thou" is a personal pronoun, and that therefore Adam was to return to God at death! Then surely we may be pardoned for calling attention to the fact that the Lord said the very opposite; namely, *"thou* return unto the *ground."*

Turning again, now, to Elijah and the child: If "he" and "him" mean neither he nor him in one half of the story, then this much only is certain, that personality can depart from personal pronouns. If when the child died, *he* really departed, why should the prophet pray that his "soul come into *him* again"? If at death *he* never really died, but simply departed, why should the record describe this miracle of resurrection by declaring that *"he* revived"? We despair of attempting to settle this question if personality elusively departs from personal pronouns at the ready convenience of the believers in natural immortality.

Now, what was this "soul" that departed and which, in the case of the child, came back again? The word "soul" here and in the case of Rachel, is a translation of the Hebrew word *nephesh*. Gesenius, generally considered the greatest of Hebrew lexicographers, gives the following as the primary meaning of the word: "1. Breath." (See Job 41:21, where *nephesh* is translated "breath.")

We surely need not offer any apology for employing the primary definition given to a word by one of the most learned of Hebrew scholars. And when we do this, the whole matter becomes simple. When Elijah prayed, "the soul [*nephesh*, breath] . . . came into him again." Thus translated, the text finds a parallel in the account of the child's death in an earlier verse: "His sickness was so sore, that there was *no breath* left in him." Verse 17. The fact that "breath" in verse 17 is from a different Hebrew word, does not affect the comparison, seeing that both Hebrew words may properly mean "breath."

When we examine the account of this child's soul (*nephesh*) in terms of the original Hebrew word, we make still another interesting discovery. This word *nephesh* is translated "life" in the following passage from the creation story: "To every beast of the earth, and to every fowl of the air, and to everything that creepeth upon the earth, wherein there is life [*nephesh*], I have given every green herb for meat." Gen. 1:30. In the margin of the Bible the translators give "a living soul" as a variant rendering for *nephesh*, "life." If the *nephesh* within the child proves that he is an undying soul, then it proves the same for the beasts, the fowls, and even the creeping things.

Speaking personally, we would rather "seek" for the immortality the Bible promises the righteous at the second coming of Jesus, than to rest in the belief that this choice possession is already ours simply because there is within us something (a *nephesh*) that is also found in the beast of the field. (See page 379 for a further treatment of the word "soul.")

# Objection 82

**Revelation 6:9, 10 proves that the souls of the righteous dead are in heaven.**

This passage of Scripture reads thus: "When He had opened the fifth seal, I saw under the altar the souls of them that were slain for the word of God, and for the testimony which they held: and they cried with a loud voice, saying, How long, O Lord, holy and true, dost thou not judge and avenge our blood on them that dwell on the earth?"

It is at least interesting to note, by way of introduction, that the believers in natural immortality here endeavor to prove their position by reference to the book of Revelation. Almost without exception they declare that Revelation is too mystical to be understood, whenever Seventh-day Adventists appeal to this book in support of doctrine. Does Revelation suddenly become plain and understandable when it is thought to support the belief of those who teach immortality? Do they wish in this lone passage to give a literal meaning to the words of this symbolic, prophetic book? Evidently so, for their whole argument depends for its plausibility on a literal interpretation of the texts before us. We therefore wish to ask them certain questions to discover whether they are really willing to maintain that this is a literal passage.

If the souls of the righteous soar away at death to enter immediately into eternal happiness in the presence of God, how is it that the most worthy of these, the martyrs, should be confined under an altar? Is this a particularly ideal location? Apparently not, for these souls seem to be in distress.

Why should they need to cry for vengeance on their persecutors, who had for centuries carried on these persecutions? The immortal-soul doctrine teaches that the wicked, at death, go immediately into the flames of hell. Surely the martyrs would not wish for any more terrible vengeance than this.

The believers in natural immortality contend vigorously that Christ's story of the rich man and Lazarus should be understood literally, and not as a parable. We shall consider this story later; but we raise one query in the present connection: If heaven and hell are so near together that the good man Lazarus could actually hear from the rich man's own lips the details of his suffering, why should the martyrs need to cry for vengeance? Are we to understand that these souls were not satisfied with the sights and sounds of torture and agony which, according to popular theology, greeted their eyes and ears as they looked over into hell?

But why continue the questions further? Indeed, why should we be asked to meet this passage of Scripture at all, when various of the most learned theologians declare that the passage should not be viewed literally? For example, Albert Barnes, the well-known Presbyterian commentator, affirms:

"We are not to suppose that this *literally* occurred, and that John actually saw the souls of the martyrs beneath the altars, for the whole representation is symbolical; nor are we to suppose that the injured and the wronged in heaven actually pray for vengeance; . . . but it may be fairly inferred from this that there will be *as real* a remembrance of the wrongs of the persecuted, the injured, and the oppressed, *as if* such prayer were offered there; and that the oppressor has as much to dread from the divine vengeance *as if* those whom he has injured should cry in heaven to the God who answers prayer. . . . Every persecutor should dread the death of the persecuted *as if* he went to heaven to plead against him."—Comments on Revelation 6:10. (Italics his.)

Of course, in fairness to Barnes, we would make clear that he is a believer in soul immortality and consciousness in death, that indeed he even believes that in some fashion this passage in Revelation provides proof of that doctrine. But this does not in any way invalidate his clear-cut admission that the passage should be viewed figuratively, not literally. That is all we wish to establish from his testimony. Just how he can make this admission, and yet believe that the passage supports soul immortality, he does not explain.

Adam Clarke, the Methodist scholar, says:

# ANSWERS TO OBJECTIONS

"Their *blood*, like that of Abel, cried for vengeance. . . . We sometimes say, *Blood cries for blood.*"—Comments on Revelation 6:9, 10. (Italics his.)

The limits of space do not permit us to discuss here the symbolical value of these texts, which form part of a very important prophecy in the Revelation. Nor is it indeed necessary, for having shown that the language is not to be understood literally, we have removed the whole basis of the argument. Even literal souls are almost too airy and vaporous for the advocates of the immortal-soul doctrine to describe or picture very satisfactorily. It would be asking too much to expect them to maintain their side of a discussion with nothing more substantial to present than symbolical souls under a symbolical altar uttering symbolical cries.

# Objection 83

Paul declared that when he died he would go immediately to be with Christ. (See Phil. 1:21-23.)

The passage reads thus: "For to me to live is Christ, and to die is gain. But if I live in the flesh, this is the fruit of my labour: yet what I shall choose I wot not. For I am in a strait betwixt two, having a desire to depart, and to be with Christ; which is far better." Phil. 1:21-23.

If there were no other text in the Bible that dealt with the question of the final reward of the righteous, the reader might be pardoned for concluding that Paul expected, immediately at death, to enter heaven. This much we freely grant. But we would add at once that if a lone phrase in some one text of Scripture is to be viewed by itself, the Bible would seem to teach salvation by works, prayers for the dead, and other doctrines that Protestants consider un-Scriptural.

We cannot agree with the interpretation of Paul's words as given in the objection before us. Why? Because it would make the apostle contradict himself. Paul wrote much on the subject of being with Christ. Let us examine at least a part of his writings before drawing a conclusion concerning this passage.

In another of his letters Paul goes into details as to the time when the righteous will go to "be with the Lord": "The Lord himself shall descend from heaven with a shout, with the voice of the Archangel, and with the trump of God: and the dead in Christ shall rise first: then we which are alive and remain shall be caught up together with them in the clouds, to meet the Lord in the air: and so shall we ever be with the Lord. Wherefore comfort one another with these words." 1 Thess. 4:16-18.

It is impossible to think that Paul believed that the righteous go to be with the Lord at death, since he specifically told the Thessalonians that the righteous, both the living and those raised from the dead, go "together" to "be with the Lord" at the Second Advent. He declared that he was writing them so that they would not be "ignorant." It is incredible that he would leave them in ignorance as to being with Christ at death, if he thus believed. In fact, he told them the very opposite—that the righteous dead do not go to be with the Lord at death, but await the resurrection morn. If he believed that we go to be with the Lord at death, why did he fail to mention this fact when he was writing specifically to "comfort" them? He exhorted them to find their "comfort" in a future event—the resurrection.

Those ministers today who believe in immortal souls, "comfort" the bereaved with the assurance that the loved one has already gone to be with the Lord, and they declare that we who hold a contrary view deprive a sorrowing one of the greatest comfort possible. Do they therefore indict Paul also?

Again, if Paul believed that the righteous go to God at death, why did he tell the Corinthian church that the change from mortality to immortality will not take place until the "last trump"? (See 1 Cor. 15:51-54.)

Or why did he tell the Colossians that when Christ appears "*then* shall ye also appear with him in glory"? Col. 3:4.

Or why should he have said, as the time of his own "departure," by the executioner's sword, drew near, "Henceforth there is laid up for me a crown of righteousness, which the Lord, the righteous Judge, shall give me *at that day:* and not to me only, but unto all them also that love his appearing"? 2 Tim. 4:8.

Yes, and why should Christ Himself tell His disciples that they would once more be with Him when He fulfilled His promise: "I will come again, and receive you unto myself"?

Yes, why should Christ have focused the attention of the troubled disciples wholly on His Second Advent if it were really true that all of them would go to be with their Lord immediately at death?

These, and other passages we could quote, are in hopeless contradiction to the interpretation placed on the words of Paul in the objection before us. Are we to conclude, therefore, that Scripture contradicts itself? No. Paul in his statement to the Philippians does not say *when* he expects to be with Christ. He states briefly his weariness of life's struggle, his desire to rest from the conflict, if that would cause Christ to be "magnified." But to this veteran apostle, who had so constantly preached the glorious return of Christ as the one great event beyond the grave, the falling asleep in death was immediately connected with what would occur at the awakening of the resurrection—the being "caught up" "to meet the Lord."

It is not an unusual thing for a Bible writer to couple together events that are separated by a long span of time. The Bible does not generally go into details, but concerns itself with setting forth the really important points of God's dealing with man along the course of the centuries. For example, Isaiah 61:1, 2, contains a prophecy of the work that Christ would do at His first advent. In Luke 4:17-19 is the account of Christ's reading this prophecy to the people, and informing them: "This day is this scripture fulfilled in your ears." Verse 21. But a close examination will reveal that Christ did not read all the prophecy from Isaiah, though apparently it is one connected statement. He ended with the phrase: "To proclaim the acceptable year of the Lord." But the very next phrase in the sentence is: "And the day of vengeance of our God." He did not read this, because it was not yet to be fulfilled. This passage in Isaiah does not even suggest that a period of time intervenes between this phrase and the ones preceding. But other Bible passages indicate this fact clearly, and it is by examining all these other passages that we learn how to understand a brief, compressed prophecy like that of Isaiah 61.

Or take the prophecy of the Second Advent as given in 2 Peter 3:3-13. If no other Bible passage was compared with this one, the conclusion might easily be reached that the Second Advent of Christ results immediately in the destruction of this earth by fire. Yet when we compare 2 Peter 3 with Revelation 20, we learn that a thousand years intervene between the Second Advent and the fiery destruction of this earth. Peter was giving only a brief summary of the outstanding events impending. He passed immediately from the great fact of the Second Advent over to the next great act in the drama of God's dealing with this earth, its destruction by fire. But with Peter's prophecy, as with that of Isaiah, there is no need for confusion if we follow the Bible plan of comparing scripture with scripture to fill in the details.

Now if Peter could place in one sentence (2 Peter 3:10) two great events separated by a thousand years, and Isaiah could couple in another sentence (Isa. 61:2) two mighty events separated by a period of time, why should it be thought strange if Paul followed this plan, and coupled together in one sentence (Phil. 1:23) the sad event of dying with the glorious event of being "with Christ" at the Second Advent? In the other passages we have quoted from Paul, the death of the Christian is directly connected with the resurrection at Christ's Advent, events which we know are separated by a long span of time. Therefore the mere fact of the coupling together of the event of dying with the event of being with the Lord, does not necessarily mean that these two events are immediately related. And when we follow the Bible rule of comparing scripture with scripture, we discover that the two events are widely separated.

# Objection 84

During the time between His crucifixion and His resurrection Christ went and preached to the spirits in prison. (1 Peter 3:18-20.) This proves that there is an immaterial spirit, the real person, which departs from the body at death.

The passage reads thus: "Christ also hath once suffered for sins, . . . being put to death in the flesh, but quickened by the Spirit: by which also he went and preached unto the spirits in prison; which sometime were disobedient, when once the long-suffering of God waited in the days of Noah, while the ark was a preparing, wherein few, that is, eight souls were saved by water."

We wonder why Protestant believers in the immortality of the soul should quote this passage. If it gives them aid and comfort on this one doctrine, it thereby gives them great discomfort on two other doctrines, or rather heresies, according to orthodox Protestantism—purgatory and a second probation. If Christ went to preach to certain sinners after their death, the clear inference is that a second chance, or probation, was being extended to them. And if there was this second probation, then the place of torture in which they were confined was one from which there was escape, and that is perilously close to the idea of purgatory.

Furthermore, if Christ at His crucifixion really preached to lost spirits, why did He single out only the spirits of those who were "disobedient" "in the days of Noah"? Were none others entitled to a second chance? Away with an interpretation of Peter's words that would make him support such heresies!

Peter teaches the very opposite of the second-probation doctrine, declaring that the preaching took place "when once [or, at the time when] the longsuffering of God waited in the days of Noah." The phrase, "which sometime were disobedient," is simply an interjected explanatory statement. If the passage is read without this phrase, the time of the preaching can easily be seen: "He went

349

and preached unto the spirits in prison . . . *when* once the long-suffering of God waited in the days of Noah."

But how did Christ go to preach to these people? The text says, "By *which* also he went and preached." Now the "which" refers back to "the Spirit." Thus Peter is declaring that it was by the agency of "the Spirit" that Christ preached to these "spirits in prison" in the days of Noah.

Christ told His disciples that it was the Spirit that would "reprove the world of sin" (see John 16:7-9), and that they were therefore to wait until they were endued with the Spirit before they started out to preach. When the disciples brought conviction to sinners in the Christian Era, the real source of the preaching was the indwelling Spirit of God.

Now was there a preacher of God in antediluvian days through whom the Spirit could preach to men? Yes, Peter tells us that Noah was "a preacher of righteousness." (2 Peter 2:5.) In the inspired account of God's plan to destroy the earth by a flood, we read, "The Lord said, *My Spirit* shall not always strive [or, plead] with man, for that he also is flesh: yet his days shall be an hundred and twenty years." Gen. 6:3. Then follows the account of God's calling Noah to make ready for the Flood. In other words, God's Spirit preached to these antediluvians through Noah, "a preacher of righteousness," waiting, in His long-suffering, a hundred and twenty years before finally destroying them.

But why should these people be said to be "in prison"? The Bible describes those who are in the darkness of sin as being "prisoners" and as being in a "prison house." And, specifically, the prophet Isaiah declares that the work of Christ, with "the Spirit of the Lord God" upon Him, was "the opening of the prison to them that are bound." (See Isa. 42:7; 61:1; cf. Luke 4:18-21.) The work of the Spirit in antediluvian times was evidently the same as in the time of Christ—the preaching to those who are prisoners of sin, offering them a way of escape.

Only one query remains. It will be asked why these people to whom Noah preached were called "spirits" if they were men alive on the earth. We will let an eminent commentator, Dr. Adam Clarke, answer this. The fact that he is a believer in the immortal-soul doctrine makes his testimony on this passage particularly valuable. After declaring that the phrase, "he went and preached," should be understood to mean, "by the ministry of Noah," he remarks:

"The word *pneumasi, spirits,* is supposed to render this view of the subject improbable, because this must mean *disembodied* spirits; but this certainly does not follow; for *the spirits of just men made perfect,* Heb. 12:23, certainly means *righteous men,* and men *still in the church militant;* and the *Father of spirits,* Heb. 12:9, means *men still in the body;* and *the God of the spirits of all flesh,* Num. 16:22 and 27:16, means *men, not in a disembodied state."*—Comments on 1 Peter 3:19. (Italics his.)

Another learned commentator, Dr. J. Rawson Lumby, in The Expositor's Bible, remarks that during the earlier centuries, which was the period when the Catholic religion, with its belief in purgatory, was dominant, the passage was interpreted to mean that Christ went to preach to souls in hell.

"But at the time of the Reformation the chief authorities expounded them [these words of Peter's] of the preaching of Christ's Spirit through the ministry of the patriarch [Noah]."—Comments on 1 Peter 3:17-22.

Dr. John Pearson, in his *Exposition of the Creed,* a classic Church of England work, observes:

"It is certain then that Christ did preach unto those persons which in the days of Noah were disobedient, all that time 'the long-suffering of God waited,' and, consequently, so long as repentance was offered. And it is as certain that He never preached to them after they died." —Page 166.

Why should we be asked to explain this passage in harmony with our views when eminent theologians, who believe in the immortality of the soul, admit that the immortal-soul doctrine is not here taught?

# Objection 85

**Christ told the thief on the cross that he would be with Him that day in Paradise. (See Luke 23:43.)**

The text reads thus: "Jesus said unto him, Verily I say unto thee, To day shalt thou be with me in paradise."

Believers in the doctrine of immortal souls, or spirits, boldly bring forth 1 Peter 3:18-20 in an attempt to prove that when Christ died on the cross He went down to preach to certain lost souls in hell. But that claim is no sooner proved to be groundless than they confront us with this text in Luke 23:43, and inform us that when Christ died on the cross He went immediately to Paradise. We believe that Christ did not go to Paradise that crucifixion Friday, and for the following reasons:

If the reader will compare Revelation 2:7 with Revelation 22:1, 2, he will see that Paradise is where the "throne of God" is. Therefore, if Christ had gone to Paradise that Friday afternoon, He would have gone into the very presence of God. But Christ Himself, on the resurrection morning, declared to Mary, as she fell at His feet to worship Him, "Touch me not; for I am *not yet ascended* to my Father: but go to my brethren, and say unto them, I ascend unto my Father, and your Father; and to my God, and your God." John 20:17. How perfectly this statement of Christ's agrees with the words of the angel to the women at the tomb: "Come, see the place where the *Lord* lay." Matt. 28:6. He had lain in the tomb, that was why He said on the resurrection morning, "I am *not yet* ascended to my Father."

Are we therefore to be placed in the embarrassing position of attempting to decide whether to accept the statements made to the women by Christ and the angel on Sunday morning, or the statement made by Christ to the thief on Friday afternoon? No, Christ did not contradict Himself. Note the punctuation of Luke 23:43. Then remember that the punctuation in the Bible is quite modern.

The early manuscripts of the Bible not only did not use the comma, which is the particular punctuation mark in this sentence, but they actually ran the words right together in the line. Our translators used their best judgment in placing punctuation marks, but their work was certainly not inspired. Therefore we need not be held to these marks made by translators only about four hundred years ago, when we are endeavoring to determine the intent of the writers of nineteen hundred years ago.

The change of a comma may make a great difference in the meaning. If you write, "The teacher says my boy is no good," you mean one thing. But you mean something quite different if you add two commas, thus: "The teacher, says my boy, is no good." The words are the same, but the meaning is different. Now if the translators, who did such excellent work in general, had placed the comma in Luke 23:43 after "to day" instead of after "thee," we would not be confronted with an apparently hopeless contradiction. Christ's words could then properly be understood thus: Verily I say unto thee today (this day when it seems that I am deserted of God and man and am dying as a common criminal), Thou *shalt* be with Me in Paradise. Instead of being deprived of meaning, the words "to day" take on a real significance.

A similar sentence construction is found in the writings of the prophet Zechariah: "Turn you to the strong hold, ye prisoners of hope: even to day do I declare that I will render double unto thee." Zech. 9:12. The context shows that the rendering "double" was not to take place on that very "to day," but was a future event. It is evident that "to day" qualifies "declare." Even so in Luke 23:43, if "to day" be allowed to qualify "say," which is not only proper grammar, but a parallel to the language of Zechariah, there is no contradiction between the message to the thief and that to Mary. And, we should add, there is no conscious entity soaring away to Paradise that sad Friday afternoon.

# Objection 86

How do you harmonize with your belief in the unconsciousness of man in death the Bible account of the witch of Endor, who brought forth Samuel to talk with King Saul? (See 1 Sam. 28:7-19.)

Saul commanded his servants, "Seek me a woman that hath a familiar spirit, that I may go to her, and inquire of her." Verse 7. They found such a woman at Endor. The woman inquires, "Whom shall I *bring up* unto thee? And he [Saul] said, *Bring me up* Samuel." Verse 11. A moment later the woman declared, "I saw gods *ascending out of the earth.* . . . An old man *cometh up;* and he is covered with a mantle." Verses 13, 14. "And Samuel said to Saul, Why hast thou disquieted me, to *bring me up?* . . . Moreover the Lord will also deliver Israel with thee into the hands of the Philistines: and *to morrow shalt thou and thy sons be with me.*" Verses 15-19.

This narrative says nothing about the prophet Samuel's coming down from heaven for this occasion. Saul uses the words, *"bring up."* The witch uses the same and similar expressions, "bring up," "ascending out of the earth," "cometh up." And to Samuel are attributed equivalent words, "bring me up." If anyone might claim this weird, tragic story, it would be we who believe that when the dead return to this earth they come "up" "out of the earth." But in seeking evidence regarding the state of man in death, we do not consider it safe to rely on the events and conversations of a devil-infested, God-condemned séance. However, inasmuch as the believers in the immortality of the soul appeal to this séance, we would inquire: How do you harmonize all these statements with *your* belief. You believe that the righteous dead are *up* in heaven, not *down* in "the earth." Can "ascending out of the earth" mean descending out of heaven?

Again, the narrative thus describes "Samuel": "An old man . . . covered with a mantle." Is this the way an immortal spirit

354

would appear? Does it actually take on a body? If so, where does it obtain the body? If it be answered that there was a resurrection, we would reply that such a confession spoils the whole case, for we believe that the dead may be raised. But we do not believe that the devil has power to raise the dead, and certainly God was not at the bidding of this witch, who was under the divine death edict for practicing sorcery. (See Lev. 20:27; Deut. 18:10, 11.)

Now the record tells us later that Saul climaxed his sinful course by committing suicide. (See 1 Sam. 31:4.) But "Samuel," foretelling Saul's death, declares, "To morrow shalt thou and thy sons be *with me.*" Pray tell, where did Samuel dwell, if the suicide Saul was to be with him? Really, we marvel that those who believe the doctrine of natural immortality ever bring up this Bible story, for by so doing they "bring up" Samuel from the "earth" when, according to their view, he is supposed to be in heaven; and they have the wicked Saul going to "be with" the holy Samuel, when this royal suicide is supposed, instead, to go to hell.

But why does the story speak of "Samuel" if he was not really there? The record does not say that *Saul* saw "Samuel," for when the witch cried out, he inquired, "What sawest *thou?*" And a moment later, "What form is he of?" If Samuel had really been there, why would not Saul have seen him? Were only the hag's eyes keen enough to discern "an old man . . . covered with a mantle"? We read that "Saul perceived that it was Samuel." The word "perceived" is from a different Hebrew word than "saw." The meaning is that Saul understood, or concluded, as a result of the description given by the witch, that Samuel was present.

The witch practiced a deception on Saul. She, deceived also by the devil, probably thought she saw Samuel. Saul, in turn, accepted her explanation. The Bible narrative then simply describes this spiritualistic séance in terms of the suppositions of the witch and of Saul. This is a literary rule known as the *language of appearance.* When the story says "Samuel," we may understand it to mean simply that devil-generated apparition that doubtless appeared, and which they *supposed* was Samuel.

# Objection 87

**Christ's story of the rich man and Lazarus proves the immortality of the soul. (See Luke 16:19-31.)**

This story says nothing about immortal souls leaving the body at death. Instead, the rich man after he died had "eyes" and a "tongue," that is, very real bodily parts. He asked that Lazarus "dip the tip of his finger in water." If the narrative is to be taken literally, then the good and bad at death do not soar away as intangible spirits, but go to their rewards as real beings with bodily parts. Yet how could they go there bodily, seeing that their bodies had been buried in the grave?

Again, if this is a literal account, then heaven and hell are near enough for a conversation to be held between the inhabitants of the two places—a rather undesirable situation, to say the least. If the believers in natural immortality claim that this is a literal picture of the geography of heaven and hell, then they must surrender the text concerning the "souls under the altar" crying for vengeance against their persecutors. (See Rev. 6:9-11.) Both passages cannot be literal. If the righteous can actually see the wicked in torture, why should they need to cry to God for vengeance?

When the rich man pleaded that Lazarus be sent back to earth to warn others against hell, Abraham replied, "They have Moses and the prophets; let them hear them." And "if they hear not Moses and the prophets, neither will they be persuaded, though one *rose from the dead.*" Luke 16:29, 31. Thus the narrative nowhere speaks of disembodied spirits, not even in the matter of returning to warn men. Instead, return is in terms of rising "from the dead."

To avoid believing that spirits have bodies and that heaven and hell are really near enough for conversations, does the objector now wish to view this story simply as a parable? Then we would remind him that theologians with one accord agree that doctrines ought not to be built upon parables or allegories. A parable, like other illustrations, is generally used to make vivid one particular point. To attempt to build doctrines on every part of the story would generally result in absurdity, if not utter contradiction. Certainly to try to find in the illustration a proof for a belief the very opposite of that held by the speaker or writer, would violate the most primary rule governing illustrations. We affirm that the objector, by using this parable to prove that men receive their rewards at death, would cause Christ to contradict Himself.

Elsewhere Christ states definitely the time when the righteous receive their reward and the wicked are cast into the consuming fire: "*When* the Son of man shall come in his glory, . . . and before him shall be gathered all nations: . . . *then* shall the King say unto them on his right hand, Come, ye blessed of my Father, inherit the kingdom. . . . *Then* shall he say also unto them on the left hand, Depart from me, ye cursed, into everlasting fire." Matt. 25:31-41.

There is no need that one return to give warning regarding the fate beyond the grave, because the living "have Moses and the prophets; let them hear them." We, the living, are therefore surely justified in understanding the parable in harmony with what the prophets have said. Malachi, for example, states that "the day *cometh*" (it is a future event) when the wicked are to suffer the torments of consuming fire. (See Mal. 4:1-3.) The Old Testament writers are very emphatic in stating that the dead, righteous and wicked alike, lie silent and unconscious in the grave until the resurrection day. (See Job 14:12-15, 20, 21; 17:13; 19:25-27; Ps. 115:17; Eccl. 9:3-6, 10.)

Thus to declare the story a parable or an allegory, gives the objector no more support than if he declared it to be literal, unless he wishes to maintain the impossible claim that a particular point in a figurative story should be taken literally, even though there is thus created a direct contradiction of the literal statements of "Moses and the prophets" and Christ (in Matthew 25).

We believe that the story is a parable, which was the usual method Christ employed in His teaching, even though here, as in various other instances, He does not specifically so state. We therefore seek to find just what lesson Christ was trying to teach, and do not attempt to make the parable prove anything more than this. Evidently Christ was wishing to rebuke the Pharisees, "who were covetous." Luke 16:14. They, indeed many of the Jews, thought that riches were a sign of God's favor, and poverty of His displeasure. Christ drove home the one primary lesson, that the reward awaiting the covetous rich, who have naught but crumbs for the poor, was the very opposite of what the Jews believed.

This is what the parable is intended to teach. It would be as consistent for us to contend that Christ taught here also that the righteous literally go to "Abraham's bosom," and that heaven and hell are within speaking distance, as that He taught that the reward comes immediately at death. Christ guarded against the drawing of unwarranted conclusions from this lesson He was teaching the Jews by placing it in the setting of a story. He doubly guarded it by declaring in closing that "Moses and the prophets" should be the guide to the living as regards their fate beyond death. Yes, He triply guarded it by definitely describing the return of anyone from the dead in terms of a resurrection.

By employing the language of allegory He could very properly have the unconscious dead carry on a conversation without necessitating the conclusion that the dead are conscious. Elsewhere in the Bible we find the vivid parable of the trees going "forth on a time to anoint a king over them," and of the conversation carried on between them. (See Judges 9:7-15; also 2 Kings 14:9.) Why not attempt to prove by this parable that trees talk and that they have kings? No, you say, that would be trying to make it prove more than was intended by the speaker. We agree. The same rule holds for the parable of the rich man and Lazarus.

# Objection 88

The Bible speaks of "everlasting punishment" (Matt. 25:46) for the wicked, and of "everlasting fire" (verse 41) in which they will burn, and of their being "tormented day and night for ever and ever" (Rev. 20:10). This proves the immortality of the soul.

The words translated "everlasting" and "for ever" do not necessarily mean *never ending*. These terms, when found in the New Testament, come from the Greek noun *aiōn*, or from the adjective *aiōnios* derived from this noun. When we examine various Scripture texts containing *aiōn*, we discover at once how impossible it would be to attempt to make this Greek root always mean an *endless* period. We read in Matthew 13:39 and elsewhere of "the *end* of the world [*aiōn*]." How could there be an "end" to something if it were endless? (Here is an illustration of where *aiōn* might be translated "age," the "world" being viewed in its aspect of time. In Colossians 1:26 *aiōn* is thus translated.) We read of Christ that He has been exalted above "every name that is named, not only in *this* world [*aiōn*], but also in *that which is to come.*" Eph. 1:21. We read of "this *present* world [*aiōn*]." 2 Tim. 4:10. Thus again we see that an *aiōn* can have an *end*, for this present *aiōn* is to be followed by another and a different one. The Bible speaks of what "God ordained *before* the world [*aiōn*]." 1 Cor. 2:7.

Of Christ we read also, "Thou art a priest for ever [*aiōn*]." Heb. 5:6. Here "for ever," or *aiōn*, clearly means this present age, for all theologians agree that Christ's work as a priest comes to an *end* when sin has been blotted out. (The work of a priest is to deal with sin. See Heb. 2:17 and 5:1.)

Paul, writing to Philemon regarding the return of his servant Onesimus, said, "Thou shouldst receive [have, A.R.V.] him for ever [*aiōnios*], . . . both in the flesh, and in the Lord." Philemon 15, 16. (Here we have the adjective that is derived from *aiōn*.)

# ANSWERS TO OBJECTIONS

H. C. G. Moule, in that scholarly commentary, *The Cambridge Bible for Schools and Colleges,* remarks on this text:

"The adjective tends to mark *duration as long as the nature of the subject allows.* And by usage it has a close connection with things spiritual. 'Forever' here thus imports both natural and spiritual permanence of restoration; *'forever'* on earth, and then hereafter; a final return to Philemon's home, with a prospect of heaven in Philemon's company."

We need not here raise the question as to whether Moule has altogether correctly measured Paul's words. We inquire simply: How could Philemon have Onesimus " 'for ever' *on earth,* and *then* hereafter," unless the earthly "for ever" had an end to it?

We read of "Sodom and Gomorrah, and the cities about them . . . suffering the vengeance of eternal [*aiōnios*] fire." Jude 7. Are those cities, set ablaze long ago as a divine judgment, still burning? No; their ruins are quite submerged by the Dead Sea. The Bible itself specifically states that God turned "the cities of Sodom and Gomorrah into ashes." 2 Peter 2:6. Now the fate of these cities is declared to be a warning to all wicked men of the fate that impends for them. Therefore if the *"aiōnios* fire" of that long ago judgment turned into ashes those upon whom it preyed, and then died down of itself, we may properly conclude that the *"aiōnios* fire" of the last day will do likewise.

When we turn to the Old Testament we discover that "everlasting" and "for ever" sometimes signify a very limited time. We shall quote texts in which these two terms are translated from the Hebrew word *olam,* because *olam* is the equivalent of the Greek *aiōn.*

The Passover was to be kept "for ever [*olam*]." Ex. 12:24. But it ended with the cross. (See Heb. 9:24-26.) Aaron and his sons were to offer incense "for ever [*olam*]" (1 Chron. 23:13), and to have an "everlasting [*olam*] priesthood." Ex. 40:15. But this priesthood, with its offerings of incense, ended at the cross. (See Heb. 7:11-14.) A servant who desired to stay with his master, was to serve him "for ever [*olam*]." (See Ex. 21:1-6.) How could a servant serve a master to endless time? Will there be masters and servants in the world to come? Jonah, describing his watery experience, said, "The earth with her bars was about me for ever [*olam*]." Jonah 2:6. Yet this "for ever" was only "three days and three nights" long. Jonah 1:17. Rather a short "for ever." Because Gehazi practiced deceit, Elisha declared, "The leprosy therefore of Naaman shall cleave unto thee [Gehazi], and unto thy seed for ever [*olam*]." 2 Kings 5:27. Should we conclude, therefore, that Gehazi's family would never end, and that thus leprosy would be perpetuated for all time to come?

Thus by the acid test of actual usage we discover that in a number of cases *aiōn, aiōnios,* and *olam* have a very limited time value.*

What Bible usage thus reveals, Greek scholars confirm. For example, Liddell and Scott's Greek Lexicon, a standard work, gives the following as the principal meanings of *aiōn:*

"A space or period of time, especially a lifetime, life. . . . Also one's time of life, age: the age of man. . . . 2. A long space of time, eternity. . . . 3. Later, a space of time clearly defined and marked out, an era, age, . . . this present life, this world."

Alexander Cruden, in his concordance, which for many years was the one great concordance in the English language, remarks under the word "eternal":

"The words eternal, everlasting, forever, are *sometimes* taken for a long time, and are not always to be understood strictly."

The learned Archbishop Trench, in his authoritative work, *Synonyms of the New Testament,* remarks concerning the primary sense of *aiōn:*

"In its primary, it signifies time, short or long, in its unbroken

---

* The agreement in meaning between *olam* and *aiōn* is revealed in two ways:
1. The Septuagint, the ancient Greek translation of the Old Testament, always translates *olam* by *aiōn*. (See *A Greek and English Lexicon*, by Edward Robinson, under the word *aiōn*.)
2. The New Testament writers, in quoting an Old Testament passage, or using an Old Testament phrase, where *olam* is used, translate it by *aiōn*, or by the adjectival form, *aiōnios*. Note the following quotations:
Hebrews 1:8, "for ever and ever [*aiōn*]," quoting Psalms 45:6, "for ever and ever [*olam*]."
Hebrews 5:6; 6:20; 7:17, 21, "for ever [*aiōn*]," quoting Psalms 110:4, "for ever [*olam*]."
1 Peter 1:25, "for ever [*aiōn*]," quoting Isaiah 40:8, "for ever [*olam*]."
Hebrews 13:20, "everlasting [*aiōnios*]," as in Genesis 17:19, "everlasting [*olam*]."
2 Peter 1:11, "everlasting [*aiōnios*]," as in Psalms 145:13, "everlasting [*olam*]."

duration; oftentimes in classical Greek the duration of human life."
—Pages 208, 209.

During recent years many discoveries have been made of Greek writings of the first century A.D. These writings, called *papyri*, enable us to know just how the Greek was written and just what meanings belonged to words at the very time when the New Testament authors wrote. The Greek scholars J. H. Moulton and George Milligan, in their monumental work entitled *The Vocabulary of the Greek Testament*, cite various instances in the *papyri* where *aiōn* is equivalent simply to the "period of life" of a person. Under *"aiōnios"* they make the following statement in summing up the evidence as to its usage by the first century Greek-speaking people of the Roman Empire:

"In general, the word depicts that of which the horizon is not in view, whether the horizon be at an infinite distance, . . . or whether it lies no farther than the *span of Cæsar's life*." (Italics ours.)

Now, having proved from the Bible and from Greek scholars that *aiōn* and *olam* are elastic terms, and oftentimes mean only a very limited period, we have removed the very basis on which rests the objection before us. But our case is even stronger when we note the rule that commentators give for measuring the time involved in *aiōn* or *olam* in any text.

Adam Clarke, in commenting on Gehazi's leprosy (2 Kings 5:27), remarks:

"The *forever* implies as long as any of his [Gehazi's] posterity should remain. This is the import of the word *le-olam*. It takes in the whole extent or duration of the thing to which it is applied. The *forever* of Gehazi was till his posterity became extinct."

This agrees with the statement found in the quotation given earlier from Moule on Philemon 15:

"The adjective [*aiōnios*] tends to mark duration as long as the nature of the subject allows."

Therefore, we should first decide whether a "subject" is so

constituted that he can live endlessly before we decide that hell-fire will continue endlessly. Now note the statement made in the well-known commentary by J. P. Lange:

"The bodies and souls of the wicked will suffer *as long as they are capable of suffering,* which, *since they are immortal,* will . . . be forever."—Comment on Jude 7. (Italics ours.)

The scholarly theologians do not attempt, as does the objector, to prove that souls are immortal because the judgment fires burn for an *aiōn.* On the contrary, knowing that the time value of *aiōn, aiōnios,* and *olam* must be determined by the "nature of the subject" involved, these scholars conclude that the fire will burn endlessly because they believe that the souls of the wicked "are immortal." But the claim that the soul is immortal is the very point to be proved.

The Bible nowhere declares that the soul is immortal. (See answer to objection 80.) On the contrary, the Bible uses words that clearly convey the thought that in the case of the wicked the "nature of the subject" demands the conclusion that complete and speedy annihilation will take place. The wicked are described as "chaff," "stubble," "wax," "fat," et cetera. (See Matt. 3:12; Mal. 4:1; Ps. 68:2; 37:20.) We are told explicitly that the fire "shall burn them up" and "shall leave them neither root nor branch," so that "they shall be ashes under the soles" of the feet of the righteous. Mal. 4:1-3.

Now, while we can thus correctly conclude that the "everlasting" torment of the wicked is but a limited period, we can at the same time logically conclude that the "everlasting" reward of the righteous is an unending one, for we are explicitly told that the righteous "put on immortality" at the Advent of Christ. (See 1 Cor. 15:51-55.) Thus the "nature of the subject" being immortal, the "everlasting" is correctly understood as meaning *endless.*

# Objection 89

The Bible repeatedly speaks of hell and hell-fire, and of the wicked going down into hell when they die. This proves the conscious state of the dead.

The simple way to answer this objection is to examine the use of the word "hell" throughout the Bible. In the Old Testament, "hell" is always translated from the Hebrew word *sheol,* which means simply "the unseen state." (See Young's Analytical Concordance.) The idea of fire or punishment is not found in the word. We read, "Then Jonah prayed unto the Lord his God out of the fish's belly, . . . out of the belly of hell [*sheol*] cried I." Jonah 2:1, 2. It would be difficult to imagine anything akin to fire in connection with a cold sea monster. The marginal reading of this text gives "the grave" as the translation of hell, or *sheol.*

*Sheol* is very frequently translated "grave." Both good and bad go there. "What man is he that liveth, and shall not see death? shall he deliver his soul from the hand of the grave [*sheol*]?" Ps. 89:48. The godly man Job said, "If I wait, the grave [*sheol*] is mine house." Job 17:13. The psalmist wrote, "The wicked shall be turned into hell [*sheol*]." Ps. 9:17.

In the New Testament the word "hell" * is translated from the three following Greek words:

1. Once from the root *tartaros,* which means "a dark abyss." (See Liddell and Scott's Greek Lexicon.) This word is used in connection with the casting out of the evil angels from heaven down into "darkness." There is no idea of fire or torment in the word. The passage specifically declares that these angels are *"reserved* unto judgment." It is a *future* event. (See 2 Peter 2:4; Rev. 12:7-10.)

---

* Following are the New Testament references where the word "hell" is used:
1. From *tartaros,* 2 Peter 2:4.
2. From *hades,* Matt. 11:23; 16:18; Luke 10:15; 16:23; Acts 2:27, 31; Rev. 1:18; 6:8; 20:13, 14.
3. From *Gehenna,* Matt. 5:22, 29, 30; 10:28; 18:9; 23:15, 33; Mark 9:43, 45, 47; Luke 12:5; James 3:6.

2. Ten times from *hades,* which means "the nether world, the grave, death." (See Liddell and Scott's Greek Lexicon.) *Hades* describes the same place as *sheol.* This is evident from these two facts:

*a.* The Septuagint, the ancient Greek translation of the Old Testament, almost without exception, uses *hades* as the translation of *sheol.*

*b.* In quoting the Old Testament prophecy regarding Christ: "Thou wilt not leave my soul in hell [*sheol*]," the New Testament writer gives, "hell [*hades*]." (See Ps. 16:10; Acts 2:27.)

When the word "hell," translated from *hades,* appears in the New Testament, the reader should not understand it to mean the exclusive abode of the wicked or a place of fire and brimstone, because:

*a.* The primary definition of *hades,* as already noted, does not demand such an understanding of the word.

*b.* We have shown that the Old Testament speaks of the righteous as well as the wicked going down to *sheol.* We have also shown that *hades* describes the same place or state. Did the ancient patriarchs go down into a place of flames?

*c.* The New Testament speaks of Christ's being in *hades.* (See Acts 2:27.) In order to be consistent, most of those who believe in the doctrine of disembodied souls and present-burning hell-fire, feel forced to interpret this text in Acts to mean that Christ's disembodied soul went *down* into hell-fire when He died on the cross, though at other times they endeavor to prove from Luke 23:43, 46 that Christ went *up* to God when He died. Both positions certainly cannot be right. The fact is that neither is correct.

Under objection 85, we showed that Luke 23:43 is wrongly interpreted. The interpretation of Acts 2:27 is equally false. As Christ died He cried out, "It is finished." His dying completed His suffering to save mankind. The erroneous ideas held by most theologians as to hell and *hades* have caused them their perplexity when reading this text in Acts. They cannot understand why Christ should descend into hell-fire.

Though a believer in soul immortality, Albert Barnes, the eminent Presbyterian commentator, boldly disposes of the difficulty by discarding in this text the lurid value which theology has given to the word *hades*. He remarks: "The Greek word hades means literally a place devoid of light, a dark, obscure abode." In view of this he explains Acts 2:27 thus: "The meaning is simply, *Thou wilt not leave Me* AMONG THE DEAD." (Emphasis his.) Incidentally he reminds his readers that the original word for soul may be understood to mean "the individual himself." That is why Barnes renders "My soul" by "Me."

Thus we may view Acts 2:27 as proving that *hades* means simply the abode of the dead, even though righteous, and thus in no way connected with fire or torment.

We conclude thus also from 1 Corinthians 15:55, where the word "grave" is a translation of *hades*, and describes that over which the righteous are finally victorious at the resurrection. Incidentally, 1 Corinthians 15:55 is a quotation from the Old Testament (Hosea 13:14), where we find the equivalent word *sheol* employed.

In one other text the translators of the King James Version indicated that "hell" may properly be translated by "grave." In Revelation 20:13, where "hell" is given in the text, the marginal reading is "the grave."

d. The Greek scholars who made the American Revised Version, sensing doubtless that our word "hell" has come to mean a place of fire and torment, did not use it to translate the Greek term *hades*. Instead, they simply transferred the Greek word *hades* right into the English. They use the word "hell" to translate a different Greek word, one which we will examine in a moment.

e. Moulton and Milligan, eminent Greek scholars, give this bit of information: "The word [*hades*] is common on tombstones in Asia Minor."—*The Vocabulary of the Greek Testament,* under "Hades."

We need hardly remark that the bereaved in Greek-speaking Asia Minor would surely not use the word *hades* on tombstones if it meant what English-speaking people mean by the word "hell." *

3. Twelve times from *Gehenna* (or, as it is sometimes transliterated, *Geenna*). This is the Greek equivalent of the Hebrew word *Hinnom*, the name of a valley near Jerusalem "used as a place to cast carcasses of animals and malefactors, which were consumed by fire constantly kept up." (See Liddell and Scott's Greek Lexicon.) Thus *Gehenna* is the only one of those words translated "hell" in the Bible, that has any idea of fire or torment resident in it.

Now in connection with the twelve times *Gehenna* is used two facts stand out:

1. The "body" as well as the soul is said to be "cast into hell." Twice is the phrase used, "the whole body." (See Matt. 5:29, 30; 10:28.)

2. In not one of the twelve instances does the text tell *when* the wicked will be "cast into hell." The fiery judgment is simply described as a *future* event. This takes the whole point out of the objection before us.

However, these two facts contain evidence that this future event does not follow *immediately* after death. The "whole body" is not cast into the flames at death, and there is no suggestion in the texts that the "soul" is cast in at one time and the "body" at another. The immortal-soul doctrine, by defining "soul" as the real man and the body as but a fleshly prison house, really asks us to believe that the real man goes immediately at death to hell-fire, and then at some distant future date God raises the body, which has turned to dust, and consigns it to the fires. We avoid such an irrational and un-Scriptural conclusion by understanding the phrase "soul and body" to mean the whole person, viewed

---

* The only place in the Bible where fire or torment is coupled with *hades* is in Luke 16:23. This is in the parable of the rich man and Lazarus, which we have already examined. It is an accepted rule in theology that doctrines should not be based upon parables. It is even more questionable to attempt to discover the real meaning of a word by the setting in which it is placed in a parable or allegory.

physically and mentally in his entirety, "the whole body." But when are persons cast bodily into the judgment fires? At the last great judgment day, when the wicked dead who have been raised, and who have been judged guilty, are "cast into the lake of fire." (See Rev. 20:11-15.)

Note that the wicked are here said to be "cast into" the fire, as though to describe the act of hurling an object into the flames. Note, further, the interesting fact, which is surely more than a mere coincidence in words, that the very same word "cast" (even in the original Greek) is repeatedly used in the various *Gehenna* texts. In no less than six of these texts we read, *"Cast into* hell [*Gehenna*]." (See also Matt. 25:31, 41, as to the time when the wicked are consigned to the judgment flames.)

From all the foregoing we reach the conclusion that the Bible does not support the idea that the wicked go at death into the flames of hell, but that the day when the impenitent objects of God's wrath are "cast into *Gehenna*" is still in the future.

# Objection 90

The Bible says that hell-fire will not be quenched and that "their worm dieth not." (See Mark 9:43-48 and Isa. 66:24.) This proves the immortality of the soul.

Even if we should agree that *unquenched* means endlessly burning, we would not find it necessary to accept the doctrine that at death an immortal soul is freed from man and lives apart from the body. These texts do not speak of disembodied souls, or spirits, burning. The Bible paints a picture of literal, wicked men at the judgment day being "cast into the lake of fire." (See Revelation 20.) Christ speaks of the "whole body" being "cast into hell." (Matt. 5:29, 30.) If it be replied that the body would be destroyed by the flames, and therefore only the spirit would be left, we ask for the Bible proof that spirits, or souls, are impervious to fire. Christ declared we should "fear him which is able to destroy *both* soul and body in hell." Matt. 10:28. If "destroy" means *consume* as regards the "body," we demand very clear proof if we are expected to believe that "destroy" means to *leave unconsumed* as regards the "soul." A failure to produce such proof really takes the whole point out of the objection based on Mark 9 and Isaiah 66.

In Mark 9:43-48 Christ quite evidently refers to the same judgment fires as those described in Isaiah 66:24, where we read: "They [the righteous] shall go forth, and look upon the carcasses ["dead bodies," A.R.V.] of the men that have transgressed against me; for their worm shall not die, neither shall their fire be quenched." We are told in so many words that the agencies of "worm" and "fire" are working, *not* upon disembodied spirits, but upon bodies, *dead* bodies.

The word "hell" used in Mark 9:43-48 is from the Greek word *Gehenna.* This term, as we have learned (see objection 89), is the Greek equivalent of the Hebrew word *Hinnom,* the name of a valley near Jerusalem, "used as a place to cast carcasses of animals and malefactors, which were consumed by fire constantly kept up." (See Liddell and Scott's Greek Lexicon.)

Christ here uses this Valley of Hinnom to teach His hearers the fate that awaits the wicked. Certainly the Jews who heard His words could not possibly have obtained any idea of wicked, disembodied souls endlessly suffering. They saw in Hinnom dead bodies being devoured by flames, or if the flames did not reach them, then by worms, those ever-present agents of destruction and disintegration. The fact that the fires of Gehenna were ever kept burning, were "not quenched," was the surest proof that whatever was cast into them would be entirely consumed. To declare that if a fire keeps ever burning, then whatever is cast into it keeps ever living, is to go contrary both to the evidence of our senses and to the testimony of Scripture.

The question may now be asked: If whatever is cast into this fire is completely consumed, why will the fire always be kept burning? The answer is, It will not. A city-wide conflagration once enveloped Chicago. If we should describe that fire by saying that the flames could not be quenched, would you conclude that Chicago was still burning? No, you would simply understand that the fire raged until it had devoured everything within reach. Common knowledge makes unnecessary the additional statement that the fire itself then died down.

It is this natural sense of the word "quench" that we find used in the Bible. The Lord through Jeremiah declared to the ancient Jews, "If you will not hearken unto me, . . . then will I kindle a fire in the gates thereof [of Jerusalem], and it shall devour the palaces of Jerusalem, and it shall not be quenched." Jer. 17:27. (In the Septuagint the very same Greek root is here used for "quenched" as in Mark 9.) In 2 Chronicles 36:19-21 we read of the literal fulfillment of this prophecy when the Babylonians put the torch to the city. Is that fire still burning? Are those Jewish "palaces" ever consuming, but never quite consumed? How preposterous, you say. Then why should anyone wish to take Christ's statement in Mark 9 and force from it the conclusion that the judgment fire will never end; and then build upon this the conclusion that the wicked will ever be consuming, but never quite consumed; and then finally rear upon this the conclusion that therefore the wicked have immortal souls?

Each and every one of these conclusions is unwarranted by logic and contrary to Scripture. The Bible nowhere says that souls are immortal, but declares that "the soul that sinneth, it shall die." Eze. 18:4. The Bible nowhere says that the wicked will ever be consuming; instead it declares that they will become "ashes." Mal. 4:3. The Bible does not say that the judgment fires will burn endlessly, for we read that these fires are due to God's setting ablaze this wicked earth, and that following this conflagration He creates "a new earth." (See 2 Peter 3:7-13 and Revelation 20 and 21.) There must therefore be an end to the fire, else this earth could not be re-created. In other words, the very promise of God to give us a new earth wherein dwelleth righteousness is contingent upon there being an end to the judgment fires.

# Objection 91

**The doctrine that a Christian at death goes down into the grave, there to lie unconscious until the resurrection day, is a gloomy belief.**

Even if we granted that the doctrine is gloomy, this would not be any proof that it is false. The question is not whether a doctrine appears gloomy or bright to our way of thinking, but whether it is taught in the Bible. Certainly the objector will agree that the doctrine of never-ending torment for the wicked is even worse than gloomy, yet it does not occur to him that the doctrine is therefore proved false. No, our feelings and fancies are hardly a safe guide in making any final decisions on questions of doctrine.

But we do not grant the charge made in this objection. It is more sentimental than sound. What does a sleeping man know of the passage of time, or of his condition in sleep? Likewise, what do those who "sleep in the dust of the earth" (Dan. 12:2) know of the passing of millenniums, or of the fact that the earth is their couch? Their return to consciousness at the voice of Christ, is the signal for them to "come forth." John 5:28, 29. And as the righteous, raised from the dead, look back over the centuries of their "sleep," the whole period will seem but a moment; and as they look forward to an endless eternity, their period of unconsciousness will seem even less than a moment.

We repeat, the charge is more sentimental than sound; and sentiment, when not re-enforced with Scripture, is not a valid objection. But we go further, and say that the charge is not even sentimentally sound. The minister who becomes eloquent in describing the happiness of Mr. Brown's departed son, finds his tongue cleaving to the roof of his mouth when he attempts to preach the funeral sermon for the late lamented son of Mr. Jones, who died in a drunken debauch. Mr. Brown is always cheered by the thought that his beloved son is enjoying the happiness of heaven, while Mr. Jones is ever haunted with the belief that his equally beloved, though wayward, son is suffering constantly the unspeakable tortures of hell. Yet the state of mind of both fathers is the result of the same doctrine! If the matter is to be decided on sentiment, then we insist that Mr. Jones as well as Mr. Brown be asked to answer the question: Is the doctrine of "soul sleeping" more gloomy than that of the immortality of the soul?

Or view the matter from another standpoint. Let us say that the godly Mr. Jones dies and that the wayward son lives. According to the immortality doctrine, a departed father gone to glory can see what his children are doing, can even hover near them as a spirit. Would heaven be any place of happiness for Mr. Jones as he gazed down upon the course his wastrel son was following? The father's state would be even more distressing in heaven than on earth, for while on earth he could possibly do something by counsel and example to reform his son, but in heaven he could only helplessly watch this child of his heart move steadily on to destruction. And then, when the son finally dies, the father's anguish is only intensified by the thought that this erring son has been transferred from earth to the endless tortures of hell-fire. All this logically follows from the doctrine of the immortality of the soul.

In view of this, we marvel that an objection based on sentiment should ever be raised against the doctrine called "soul sleeping." We freely grant that any thought of death and the grave is tinged with sorrow and gloom, for death and the grave are enemies in God's universe. But is the sadness really lessened for the human family by belief in the immortal-soul doctrine? No, the very opposite. We believe that both the Bible and sentiment agree in favor of the doctrine of unconsciousness in the grave until the resurrection day.

# Objection 92

**The Adventist doctrine that when a man dies he lies silent and unconscious in the grave until the resurrection day is un-Scriptural, illogical, and gross, as compared with the doctrine held by Christians in general that the real man is an immortal soul that departs from the body at death.**

Much of this objection, at least as it touches the question of the Scriptural character of the Adventist doctrine, has already been covered in the preceding pages. But the form in which the objection is framed invites a comparison of the two doctrines regarding the nature of man. Note these distinguishing marks of the immortal-soul doctrine:

1. This doctrine demands that we believe there dwells within us an entity possessed of personality, yet without weight or discernible dimensions. Indeed, this tenet logically requires us to believe that this entity is the real man, for the body is viewed as but a shell, a temporary prison. This calls for a stretch of faith beyond the reach of many otherwise devout men, especially among those who make up the ranks of the learned and scientific. In the attempt to prove the existence of this alleged entity, the Christian theologian and philosopher have had to rely on certain vague scriptures and metaphysical deductions. To many minds such "proof" has failed to offset the testimony of the senses and the fundamental laws of science, for the senses can discern no such entity, and the most definitely established of nature's laws find no place for a "something" without weight or dimensions.

2. This belief that man, the real man, is but an airy soul, without weight, and so minute that ten thousand could dance on the point of a cambric needle, as the older theologians declared, takes the reality out of the future life. Tangibility cannot be given to the term *heaven*, for consistency demands that vaporous, invisible beings dwell in a place of the same nature. This doctrine

374

makes heaven appear as an airy abode of attenuated spirits, who apparently, because it would be illogical to think of their doing anything more substantial, are pictured as endlessly flitting about to the accompaniment of harps. Such a conception of heaven has gone far to quench the longing of many to reach that blessed abode, for the human mind is so constituted that it must think in terms of something more substantial than this vaporous picture of heaven presents.

3. This doctrine makes an ever-burning hell a logical necessity; for if man is inherently immortal, then the wicked as well as the righteous will live through the ceaseless ages of eternity. Blood-curdling are the sermons this belief has produced. Granted that the average minister today does not preach on the topic as was done in former times. His silence is only a confession of the hideousness of the doctrine that must be true if man is an immortal soul. Indeed, there has been a definite trend away from belief in any kind of retribution, because the average mind is unable to harmonize an ever-burning hell with the character of God. Thus there has come about a great loss in moral values, for a belief in punishment is as vital to a balanced view of religion as a belief in reward.

No other doctrine has ever brought such reproach upon the name of God and of Christianity. It is said that Robert Ingersoll after listening, when a boy, to an orthodox sermon on the kind of judgment God would mete out to sinners, exclaimed, "If that is God, I hate Him." The united arguments of all the Christian apologists who have attempted to harmonize this dogma with the universal and deep-seated belief in a loving God, fall far short of their goal. This is the dark spot in apologetics.

But there is still another problem that this eternal-hell doctrine presents. The Christian view of the universe requires that the completion of God's plan for the salvation of man and the conquest of evil should bring about the restoration of that state of universal holiness and happiness that existed at first. But if there be a hell, then we have, not the annihilation, but merely the segregation of evil. Now the policy of segregation is considered by Christians as a poor makeshift for an earthly government to employ in dealing with crime and criminals. Is it possible that such a procedure is ideal when employed by the government of heaven?

4. The doctrine of the immortality of the soul leaves no rational place for the resurrection of the body or for an executive judgment at the close of earthly history. While these two doctrines —the resurrection and the future judgment—are in the creeds of almost all denominations, they are inconsistent with the teaching that the body is merely a prison house from which the soul escapes at death, going directly to its reward. Why should the soul again be thrust into a "prison house" and why should there be held a judgment, seeing each soul receives judgment at death by being consigned either to heaven or to hell?

These questions suggest their own answer, and explain, at least in part, the almost complete absence of preaching on the subject of the resurrection.

5. This immortal-soul doctrine makes spiritism appear highly reasonable. The popular view, which pictures our departed loved ones as near us and deeply interested in our affairs, is but a step removed from spiritism, which simply adds the feature of communication. Thus instead of a wall's being reared against this cult, which virtually all ministers regard as evil, there is a door opened to it.

Beyond all controversy, there is something vitally the matter with orthodox belief regarding man and the future life. If the inspired maxim, "By their fruits ye shall know them," is still a safe rule, then this teaching stands condemned, for its fruits are theological confusion, spiritism, and infidelity.

The Bible doctrine that Seventh-day Adventists preach concerning man's nature dissolves the dilemmas and doctrinal difficulties that confront Christians who hold the immortal-soul theory, and in the very process of dissolving these difficulties this true Bible doctrine brings a new sense of reality and certainty to various important aspects of the Christian religion.

## MORTAL MAN

We do not have to teach the incredible doctrine that there exists within a man a "something" which is the real man, but which is not discernible to any of the senses, and is not answerable to any of the proved laws of science. We view the word *man* as signifying something very real and substantial. We do not wander off into the mazes of metaphysical discussion in an attempt to understand or explain how God could breathe into man's nostrils the breath of life, and man become a living soul; we simply affirm, on the strength of the Bible record, that body, soul, and spirit are all required to give existence and meaning to what the Bible refers to when it speaks of man in the most basic sense of that word.

Nor are we embarrassed by the charge that there is something gross in this conception of man. We believe that this charge reveals that Christendom is still infected in some degree with the Gnostic heresy that matter is essentially evil. It has been said that in Catholicism, Gnosticism gained half a victory. The monkish fervor that took hold of many in the early centuries of the church, and which reached a dramatic height in the body-mortifying asceticism of the pillar saints, was a natural fruitage of the pernicious idea that matter is essentially evil, and that the more the body is wasted away, the more the soul can flourish.

Monkish asceticism could never find logical rootage among Seventh-day Adventists. On the contrary, our view of man calls for us to give great care to these bodies of ours. We see a fullness of meaning in Paul's injunction: "Whether therefore ye eat, or drink, or whatsoever ye do, do all to the glory of God." 1 Cor. 10:31. And we, of all people, are best able to appreciate the apostle's declaration that our bodies are the temples of the Holy Ghost, and that if we defile these bodies, God will destroy us. Our doctrine of healthful living rests solidly and logically on the foundation of our doctrine regarding the nature of man.

Believing as we do regarding man, we do not have to describe the future state of the blessed as composed of a mixture of misty vapors and harp music. Our view of man calls for a real place of abode. That harmonizes with our understanding of the first creation of man as a perfect being which, by analogy, calls for equally literal as well as equally perfect beings to dwell on the earth made new.

Our view of the nature of man does not interfere in any way with the doctrine of final hell-fire. Indeed, if the real man is a literal being, then the place of punishment must surely be a literal place, and the punishment must be something very literal. But what our view of man as mortal does save us from is the teaching that hell's fires will never end. A literal fire burns to ashes literal beings, which fact harmonizes with the prophecy of Malachi 4:1-3. There is no immortal entity to resist eternally the flames. Our belief concerning the creation of this earth anew as the abode for literal, perfect beings requires of itself that there shall be an end to the fires of hell.

Obviously our doctrine of man's nature makes necessary a belief in the bodily resurrection from the grave. We can take most literally the declarations of Paul concerning the "redemption of our body," and his further statement that "when this corruptible shall have put on incorruption, and this mortal shall have put on immortality, then shall be brought to pass the saying that is written, Death is swallowed up in victory." We can also understand what the apostle means when, in concluding his account of the famous worthies, in the epistle to the Hebrews, he declares, "These all, having obtained a good report through faith, received not the promise: God having provided some better thing for us, that they without us should not be made perfect." Heb. 11:39, 40.

Finally, we have an ironclad argument against spiritism, with its materializations; Catholicism, with its supplications to long-dead saints and its prayers for the dead; and any ism that is built on the doctrine of the inherent immortality of the soul. In fact, those who accept the Bible view that man lies silent in the grave until the resurrection are the only ones who can consistently oppose spiritism or return an answer to the perplexing inquiry of spiritists: "Why do Christian ministers oppose the investigations of spiritism,

MORTAL MAN

when our success would simply serve to establish one of the great doctrines of the Christian church—immortality?" With psychic activities increasing every year, this question will become an increasingly distressing one to those who hold to the so-called orthodox view of the soul.

## NOTE

### The Hebrew and Greek Words Translated "Soul" and "Spirit" and "Hell"*

An adequate and harmonious explanation of certain perplexing texts that deal with the nature of man requires a knowledge of the meaning of certain key words in the original languages. Hence this extended note.

### Soul in the Old Testament

In the Old Testament the word *soul* is used 473 times. There are three words in the Hebrew from which *soul* is translated:

1 time from *nedibah*.
1 time from *neshamah*.
471 times from *nephesh*.

These three terms are translated by the following words:

*Nedibah*
1 time, *soul*. Job 30:15. (The only use of *nedibah* in the Bible.)

*Neshamah*
17 times, *breath* (breathe, breatheth, breathed). For example: Gen. 2:7; 7:22; Deut. 20:16; Joshua 10:40; 11:11.
3 times, *blast*. 2 Sam. 22:16; Job 4:9; Ps. 18:15.
2 times, *spirit*. Job 26:4; Prov. 20:27.
1 time, *souls*. Isa. 57:16.
1 time, *inspiration*. Job 32:8.

*Nephesh*
471 times, *soul*. (Every text in Old Testament where *soul* is used, except Job 30:15 and Isaiah 57:16.)

---

* In one or two instances the figures given to indicate the specific number of times that a Hebrew or Greek term is translated by a certain English word, will vary, depending on which concordance is used as authority. The figures in this chapter have been obtained from a comparative study of The Englishman's Hebrew and Chaldee Concordance, The Englishman's Greek Concordance, Young's Analytical Concordance, and Strong's Exhaustive Concordance. However, the fact of interest is not so much the particular number of times that a certain term is translated by a particular English word, as the great *variety* of words by which the Hebrew or Greek term is rendered.

379

118 times, *life* (*life's, lives*). For example: Gen. 1:20, 30; 9:4; 1 Kings 19:14; Job 6:11; Ps. 38:12.

29 times, *person*. For example: Num. 31:19; 35:11, 15, 30; Deut. 27:25; Joshua 20:3, 9; 1 Sam. 22:22.

15 times, *mind*. For example: Deut. 18:6; Jer. 15:1.

15 times, *heart*. For example: Ex. 23:9; Prov. 23:7.

9 times, *creature*. Gen. 1:21, 24; 2:19; 9:10, 12, 15, 16; Lev. 11:46.

7 times, *body* (or, *dead body*). Lev. 21:11; Num. 6:6; 9:6, 7, 10; 19:13; Haggai 2:13.

5 times, *dead*. Lev. 19:28; 21:1; 22:4; Num. 5:2; 6:11.

4 times, *man* (*men*). Ex. 12:16; 2 Kings 12:4; 1 Chron. 5:21; Isa. 49:7.

3 times, *me*. Num. 23:10; Judges 16:30; 1 Kings 20:32.

3 times, *beast*. Lev. 24:18.

2 times, *ghost*. Job 11:20; Jer. 15:9.

1 time, *fish*. Isa. 19:10.

*Nephesh* is also translated one or more times as *we, he, thee, they, her, herself, him* (and other forms of the personal pronoun), and as *will, appetite, lust, thing, breath*, etc.

Two striking facts stand out in this study of the word *nephesh*:

1. The wide variety of uses to which the word is put.

2. The word is used to describe something that can be killed, and also to designate dead persons.

Note also the repeated statements as to a "living creature [*nephesh*]." The adjective *living*, would be superfluous if *nephesh* itself meant an immortal, never-dying entity.

## Soul in the New Testament

In the New Testament the word *soul* is used 58 times and is uniformly the translation of the Greek word *psuchē*. *Psuchē* is rendered by the following words in our English Bible:

58 times, *soul*.

40 times, *life*. For example: Mark 3:4; 10:45; Luke 6:9; 9:56; John 13:37; Rom. 11:3; Rev. 8:9; 12:11.

3 times, *mind*. Acts 14:2; Phil. 1:27; Heb. 12:3.

1 time, *heart*. Eph. 6:6.

1 time, *heartily* (literally, *from the soul*). Col. 3:23.

*Psuchē* is also used, once in John 10:24 and in 2 Corinthians 12:15, in idiomatic phrases that cannot be literally translated.

Note that the words *kill* and *destroy* are used several times in regard to *psuchē*.

**Spirit in the Old Testament**

In the Old Testament the word *spirit* is used 234 times. It is a translation of the following Hebrew words:

2 times from *neshamah*.

232 times from *ruach*.

These two terms are translated by the following words in our English Bible:

*Neshamah*

(See analysis earlier in note.)

*Ruach*

232 times, *spirit*. (With the exception of Job 26:4 and Prov. 20:27, which are from *neshamah*, *spirit* in the Old Testament is always from *ruach*.)

97 times, *wind*. (*Wind* in the Old Testament is always a translation of *ruach*.)

28 times, *breath*. For example: Gen. 6:17; 7:15, 22; Job 12:10; Ps. 104:29; 146:4; Eccl. 3:19.

8 times, *mind*. Gen. 26:35; Prov. 29:11; Eze. 11:5; 20:32; Dan. 5:20; Hab. 1:11.

4 times, *blast*. Ex. 15:8; 2 Kings 19:7; Isa. 25:4; 37:7.

*Ruach* is also translated one or more times by the following words: *anger, air, tempest, vain*.

**Spirit in the New Testament**

In the New Testament the word *spirit* is used 290 times. It is a translation of the following Greek words:

2 times from *phantasma*.

288 times from *pneuma*.

These two Greek words are translated by the following words in our English Bible:

*Phantasma*

2 times, *spirit*. Matt. 14:26; Mark 6:49. (These are the only uses of the word *phantasma* in the Bible.)

*Pneuma*

288 times, *spirit*. (With the exception of Matt. 14:26 and Mark 6:49, *spirit* in the New Testament is always a translation of *pneuma*.)

92 times, *ghost*. Matt. 27:50; John 19:30. (Also every instance where the word is used in the phrase "Holy Ghost.")

1 time, *life*. Rev. 13:15.

1 time, *wind*. John 3:18.

1 time, *spiritual*. 1 Cor. 14:12.

# ANSWERS TO OBJECTIONS

### Hell in the Old Testament

In the Old Testament the word *hell* is used 31 times, and is uniformly the translation of the Hebrew word *sheol*. *Sheol* is rendered by the following words in our English Bible:

31 times, *hell*.

31 times, *grave*. For example: Gen. 37:35; 1 Sam. 2:6; Job 7:9; Ps. 30:3; Eccl. 9:10; Isa. 38:18; Eze. 31:15; Hosea 13:14.

3 times, *pit*. Num. 16:30, 33; Job 17:16.

### Hell in the New Testament

In the New Testament the word *hell* is used 23 times. It is a translation of the following Greek words:

10 times from *hades*.

12 times from *gehenna*.

1 time from *tartaroō*.

These three Greek words are translated by the following words in our English Bible:

**Hades**

10 times, *hell*. Matt. 11:23; 16:18; Luke 10:15; 16:23; Acts 2:27, 31; Rev. 1:18; 6:8; 20:13, 14.

1 time, *grave*. 1 Cor. 15:55.

**Gehenna**

9 times, *hell*, as a noun. Matt. 5:29, 30; 10:28; 23:15, 33; Mark 9:43, 45; Luke 12:5; James 3:6.

3 times, *hell*, as an adjective. Matt. 5:22; 18:9; Mark 9:47.

**Tartaroo**

1 time, *hell*, 2 Peter 2:4. (The only use of *tartaroō* in the Bible.)

### Definitions of Hebrew Terms

The following definitions are from Gesenius. The edition of the Lexicon here used is one published in 1875 by John Wiley & Son, New York, the English translation being by Samuel P. Tregelles:

"NEDIBAH: *Nobility, a noble* and happy *condition.*"

"NESHAMAH: (1) *Breath, spirit.* (a) The Spirit of God imparting life and wisdom. (b) The spirit of man, *soul.* A *living creature.* . . .

" (2) *The panting* of those who are angry, used of the anger of God."

"NEPHESH: (1) *Breath.* . . .

" (2) The *soul, anima, puschē,* by which the body lives, the token of which life is drawing breath, . . . hence *life,* vital principle. Gen. 35:18; 1 Kings 17:21; Ex. 21:23. *The soul* is also said both to live (Gen. 12:13; Ps. 119:175); and to die (Judges 16:30); to be killed (Num.

31:19). . . . It is often used in phrases which relate either to the loss or to the preservation of life. . . .

" (3) *The mind,* as the seat of the sense, affections, and various emotions. . . .

" (4) Concretely, *animal,* that in which there is a soul or mind. . . .

" (5) It is sometimes *I, myself, thou, thyself."*

"RUACH: (1) *Spirit, breath.* (a) Breath of the mouth. . . . Hence used of anything quickly perishing. . . . Often used of the *vital spirit.* . . . (b) *Breath* of the nostrils, snuffing, snorting. . . . Hence *anger.* . . . (c) *Breath of air, air in motion,* i.e., *breeze.* . . .

" (2) *Psuchē anima, breath, life, the vital principle,* which shows itself in the breathing of the mouth and nostrils (see No. 1, a, b), whether of men or of beasts, Eccl. 3:21; 8:8; 12:7. . . .

" (3) *The rational mind* or *spirit.* (a) As the seat of the senses, affections, and emotions of various kinds. . . . (b) As to the mode of *thinking and acting.* . . . (c) *Of will and counsel.* . . . More rarely (d) it is applied to the *intellect.* . . .

" (4) *The Spirit of God."*

"SHEOL: A subterranean place, full of thick darkness (Job 10:21, 22), in which the shades of the dead are gathered together; . . . hell, purgatory, *limbus Patrum. . . . A hollow and subterranean place."*

### Definitions of Greek Terms

The following definitions are from Liddell and Scott's Greek Lexicon:

"PSUCHE: I. *Breath,* Latin, *anima,* especially as the sign of life, *life, spirit.* . . . II. *The soul* or *immortal part of man, as opposed to his body* or *perishable part,* in Homer only in the significance of *a departed soul, spirit, ghost:* he represents it as bodiless and not to be seized by mortal hands. . . . III. As the organ of *nous,* i.e., of thought and judgment, the *soul, mind, reason, understanding.* . . . IV. The *anima mundi,* or *living spirit,* which was supposed in the ancient philosophy to permeate all lands and the whole extent of the sea and high heaven."

"PHANTASMA: *An appearance, image, phantom, specter.* . . . *A vision, dream.* 2. Especially *an image presented to the mind by an object.* . . . 3. *A mere image, unreality."*

"PNEUMA: *Wind, air.* . . . 2. Especially like Latin *anima, the air we breathe, breath,* . . . also *breathing, respiration.* . . . 3. *Life,* . . . also *the spirit, a living being.* . . . 4. *A spirit, spiritual being,* [in] New Testament. 5. Metaphorically, *spirit,* i.e., *feeling."*

"HADES: The *nether* world. . . . *Place of departed spirits.* . . . *The grave, death.*"

"GEHENNA: The *valley of Hinnom,* which represented *the place of future punishment.*"

"TARTAROO: [A form of the noun Tartaros] *The nether world* generally."

## Comments on Definitions

It should be remembered that the foregoing definitions are largely illustrations of how the terms were used by classic Greek writers. Hence pagan conceptions are inevitably interwoven. In these definitions of both Hebrew and Greek words agree the other lexicographers.

There is nothing in the *primary* definitions of the terms for *soul* and *spirit* that demands or even warrants the thought of an immortal, undying entity, independent of the body. True, the second definition given for *psuchē* is the "immortal part of man," but the lexicographers are simply noting down one of the uses of *psuchē* by the classical Greeks, such as Homer, who were *pagans.* To attempt to settle a question of Christian theology by appealing to a definition based on the usage of a word by pagan writers would indeed be a strange procedure. By such a method we could find support for the pagan doctrine of pantheism in the fourth definition of *psuchē,* which, again, is simply an illustration of the usage of the word by *pagan* writers.

We grant that the pagans believed in disembodied souls, or spirits, and therefore, at times, used *psuchē* and other terms to express that belief. The question is simply this: Does the primary meaning of *psuchē,* or any other term translated "soul" or "spirit," necessitate belief in the immortal-entity idea? The answer is no. Then follows the companion question: Does the use of these terms by *Bible* writers —not pagan writers—warrant such belief? The answer is no.

There is nothing in the definition or usage of *sheol* that even implies a place of burning or torment. The same may be said of the terms *hades* and *tartaroō.* The pagans knew that the dead went somewhere, they knew not where, and the terms they frequently used to describe that unknown abode were *hades* and *tartaroō.* The term *gehenna* is really a proper noun, a transliteration of a Hebrew name for the burning place outside Jerusalem. We have here the literary figure of simile. The final judgment, or destruction, of the wicked is likened to the fires burning in the valley of Hinnom. The fires of Hinnom were not quenched; that was why they were certain to consume all that was cast into them.

# Section V

# SANCTUARY AND ATONEMENT

## Objections 93 to 98

The reader is also referred to
Part 2, Section VI, pages 715-755,
"The Sanctuary"

# Objection 93

Seventh-day Adventists do not believe in Christ's salvation offered to all men freely, because they preach that salvation is found in the keeping of the law. This false view of salvation is repeatedly stated in the writings of Mrs. E. G. White, who is regarded by them as an inspired spokesman.

Various aspects of this charge have been discussed already. We therefore shall confine our present answer to the claim that Mrs. White believed and taught that salvation is found, not in Christ, but in the law. We shall let her answer for herself, by quoting from an article she wrote in the year 1889:

## Mrs. White Speaks

One time when I was traveling in Oregon on a steamer, a number of persons collected upon the hurricane deck, just outside of my stateroom, the door of my room being open. A ——— minister was talking to them concerning the law. After a while he said: "Mrs. White is on board, and she is a great stickler for the law. She says that no one can be saved except through keeping the law. She places all our salvation on the perfect keeping of the law." After he had misrepresented me and the Seventh-day Adventists for some time, I went to him and said: "Elder B., Mrs. White is here to speak for herself. I have listened to your words, and will assure you that Mrs. White believes no such thing. There is no quality in law to save the transgressor. It was because the law was broken, and there was nothing but death before the sinner, that He who was equal with the Father, came to earth and took upon Him the garb of humanity. It was because of man's sin that Christ stepped down from the royal throne, laid aside His royal robe, and clothed His divinity with humanity. He came to bring to man moral power, to unite the fallen race with Himself, that through faith in Jesus Christ we may become partakers of the divine nature, and escape the corruptions that are in the world through lust. Says the apostle, 'Sin is the transgression of the law.' But Christ was manifested to take away sin, to save His people from their sins. The soul that believes in Christ may be cleansed from all defilement, and, through the grace of Christ, may be restored to divine favor.

"The law points to Christ, and every transgression of the law can be atoned for only by the blood of the Son of God. The law is like a mirror, to reveal to man his defects of character, but there is nothing in the law that will remedy the defects it points out. Paul declares: 'I have kept back nothing that was profitable unto you, but have showed you, and have taught you publicly, and from house to house, testifying both to the Jews and to the Greeks, repentance toward God, and faith toward our Lord Jesus Christ.' Why did he preach repentance toward God?—Because man had broken the law of God, and therefore was not in harmony with God. Why did he preach faith toward our Lord Jesus Christ?—Because Christ had died on Calvary, and had opened a fountain for sin and uncleanness for Judah and Jerusalem to wash in, and be cleansed. . . .

"The death of Christ is an unanswerable argument that demonstrates the unchangeable character of the law of God. If God could have changed one precept of His law, then Christ need not have died."

I said to the minister, "Did you ever hear me speak?" He answered that he had not. "In the thousands of pages I have written, have you ever read anything to the effect that I believe the law will save us?" He answered, "No." "Then why have you made the statements which you have? I hope you will not repeat them again."—MRS. E. G. WHITE in *Signs of the Times,* Sept. 23, 1889, p. 578, "The Unchangeable Character of the Law." (Footnote states that it was a sermon preached at Chicago, Illinois, April 9, 1889.)

**Comment on Mrs. White's Words**

Those who present the objection we are here considering will agree with us that if they were studying the Bible they would insist that the Bible writers be allowed to speak for themselves. We agree, insisting only that Mrs. White also be allowed to speak for herself. When she is thus permitted to speak, the whole objection before us disappears, for Seventh-day Adventists subscribe without reserve to what Mrs. White here says.

# Objection 94

"Seventh-day Adventists teach that, like all mankind, Christ was born with a 'sinful nature.'" This plainly indicates "that His heart, too, was 'deceitful above all things, and desperately wicked.'" In harmony with this they also "teach that Christ might have failed while on His mission to earth as man's Saviour—that He came into the world 'at the risk of failure and eternal loss.'" But the Bible repeatedly states that Christ was holy, that "he knew no sin," and that He would "not fail nor be discouraged."

Endless are the controversies that have raged through the centuries over the nature of Christ. This has been inevitable, for we are here confronted with a very great mystery. The Bible throws some light on different aspects of the mystery, but presents no formal discussion of it. Theologians who have focused on the texts that speak of Christ as the "Son of God" have been so dazzled with the divine glory revealed in those texts that they have often been blinded to other scriptures regarding Christ; whereas theologians who have focused on the texts that speak of Christ as the "Son of man" have sometimes been led to minimize the divinity of Christ.

The facts are that Christ walked among men as both human and divine. This is the historic teaching of Christianity. Inexplicable? Yes. And that is why we need to tread cautiously as we seek to reach conclusions regarding the relationship of Christ to the problem of sin and the sinful nature that men possess. Indeed, just what is comprehended by the term "sinful nature"? Protestants, from the earliest of Reformation times, have been unable to agree. But the objector seemingly has no difficulty whatever in the whole matter, and moves forward with dogmatic assurance through the mystery of the nature of Christ and the mystery of a sinful nature to the conclusion that Seventh-day Adventists are guilty of fearful heresy.

# ANSWERS TO OBJECTIONS

Adventists have never made a formal pronouncement on this matter in their statement of belief. The only pronouncement in our literature that could be considered as truly authoritative on this is what Mrs. E. G. White has written. The objector quotes the following from her book *The Desire of Ages*, page 24:

"As one of us, He [Jesus] was to give an example of obedience. For this He took upon Himself *our nature*, and passed through our experiences." (Italics supplied.)

Let us give this quotation in its larger setting, that we may see the force of her reasoning:

"Satan represents God's law of love as a law of selfishness. He declares that it is impossible for us to obey its precepts. The fall of our first parents, with all the woe that has resulted, he charges upon the Creator, leading men to look upon God as the author of sin, and suffering, and death. Jesus was to unveil this deception. As one of us He was to give an example of obedience. For this He took upon Himself our nature, and passed through our experiences. 'In all things it behooved Him to be made like unto His brethren.' If we had to bear anything which Jesus did not endure, then upon this point Satan would represent the power of God as insufficient for us. Therefore Jesus was 'in all points tempted like as we are.' He endured every trial to which we are subject. And He exercised in His own behalf no power that is not freely offered to us. As man, He met temptation, and overcame in the strength given Him from God. He says, 'I delight to do Thy will, O My God; yea, Thy law is within My heart.' As He went about doing good, and healing all who were afflicted by Satan, He made plain to men the character of God's law and the nature of His service. His life testifies that it is possible for us also to obey the law of God.

"By His humanity, Christ touched humanity; by His divinity, He lays hold upon the throne of God. As the Son of man, He gave us an example of obedience; as the Son of God, He gives us power to obey."

On page 49 of this same work Mrs. White declares:

"Into the world where Satan claimed dominion God permitted His Son to come, a helpless babe, subject to the weakness of humanity. He permitted Him to meet life's peril in common with every human soul, to fight the battle as every child of humanity must fight it, at the risk of failure and eternal loss."

This is Adventist belief. And we hold this belief because we feel it agrees with revelation and reason. Note the following:

1. Paul says that God sent "his own Son in the likeness of sinful flesh." Rom. 8:3.

2. Paul explains that Christ did not take "on him the nature of angels; but he took on him the seed of Abraham" (Heb. 2:16); that He partook of "flesh and blood" (verse 14).

3. Paul reinforces this immediately with this further statement: "In all things it behoved him [Christ] to be made like unto his brethren." Verse 17. Like us, not simply in some things, but "in all things." The Revised Standard Version says, "Like his brethren in every respect." Then He must have had a human nature as well as a divine. And is not our human nature capable of being tempted? If that were not a fact, then Paul's point would be lost in the next verse, for he immediately adds, "For in that he himself [Christ] hath suffered being tempted, he is able to succour them that are tempted."

4. Again, Paul says that Christ "was in all points tempted like as we are, yet without sin." Heb. 4:15. The Revised Standard Version reads, "In every respect has been tempted as we are, yet without sinning." How are we to understand Paul when he says that Christ was "tempted"? He answers by saying that Christ was "tempted like as we are."

The objector seeks to avoid the force of these passages by declaring that so far as Christ was concerned "tempted" simply meant "tried" or "tested." But the texts before us emphasize the fact that the nature of Christ's temptation was exactly the same as that which comes to mankind. True, these scriptures do note one difference—when Christ was tempted he did not sin. That cannot be said of mankind. To a greater or less degree we have all fallen before temptation. The text does not say that Christ could not sin, but that He did not sin. If in His human nature it was impossible for Him to sin, why did not Paul so reveal in these texts before us? It would have been a great revelation.

But, the objector declares, if Christ had a human nature that was capable of sin, in other words, a nature like ours, then He could not have escaped sin, for the Bible declares that the heart of man is "deceitful above all things, and desperately wicked." We accept fully the statement that man's heart is "deceitful" and full of sin. But that distinguishing mark of *fallen* mankind is not necessarily involved in the possession of a human nature that is capable of sin. Adam in Eden had a human nature, which from the first moment of his existence was capable of sin. But Adam in Eden was spotless until that day that he exercised his will in the wrong way and drew sin into his bosom.

It is an interesting fact that Paul specifically compares and contrasts Adam, whom he calls the "first man Adam," and Christ, whom he calls the "last Adam." (1 Cor. 15:45.) "For since by man came death, by man came also the resurrection of the dead. For as in Adam all die, even so in Christ shall all be made alive." Verses 21, 22. Does not this contrast and comparison suggest to us the way through this difficult problem? Our father Adam lost the battle with the tempter, not because he had a "desperately wicked" heart—he came from the Creator's hand perfect—but because he wrongly exercised his free will and drew wickedness into his heart. And we, his children, have followed in his steps. Christ, the "last Adam," won the battle with the tempter, and we, through His promised forgiveness and power, may also win. Adam could have won, but he lost. Christ could have lost, but He won. Therein lies the startling contrast.

And the contrast is heightened by the fact that Christ was born into the human family some four thousand years after sin's entry into our world, with all that that mysteriously involved of a weakening of body and mind in the fight against sin. A dyspeptic may become a saint, but his path upward is sorely beset. A nervously frail person may likewise attain to sainthood, but how great are his added handicaps! Neither need sin, neither can excuse his sin. But the victory of either over temptation stands out as a greater triumph of God's grace, as revealed in a God-empowered free will, than the victory of a person free of such maladies. It is in this sense that we may properly think of Christ's victory as gaining even added luster, by contrast to Adam's defeat. Christ won despite the fact that He took on Him "the likeness of sinful flesh," with all that that implies of the baleful and weakening effects of sin on the body and nervous system of man and its evil effects on his environment—"can there any good thing come out of Nazareth?"

In other words, Adventists believe that Christ, the "last Adam," possessed, on His human side, a nature like that of the "first man Adam," a nature free of any defiling taint of sin, but capable of responding to sin, and that that nature was handicapped by the debilitating effects of four thousand years of sin's inroads on man's body and nervous system and environment.

The objector feels that the only way to do honor to Christ and to protect Him from all taint of sin is to take the position that He could not sin. But what comfort and assurance of personal victory over sin can we find in a spotless Christ if His freedom from sin as He walked this earth was not truly a victory over temptation but an inability to sin? We would rightly stand in awe of such a Holy Being. But we could not see in Him one who was "made like unto his brethren" "in all things," one who being "tempted like as we are" "is able to succour" us when we are "tempted." These statements of Holy Writ become meaningless if Christ could not sin.

We feel that we do the greater honor to Christ, without charging Him with any taint of sin, by believing that though He could have exercised His free will to sin, He did not; that although He felt the full force of temptation, even as we must, He set His will on the side of His Father instead of yielding it to the devil. Temptation assailed Him but found no response in His heart. Said He, "The prince of this world cometh, and hath nothing in me." John 14:30. He "loved righteousness, and hated iniquity." Heb. 1:9. In that sense was He most truly "separate from sinners." Heb. 7:26. Unreservedly we accept the words of Holy Writ that Christ "knew no sin." 2 Cor. 5:21.

In holding this view of Christ Seventh-day Adventists agree essentially with the view expressed by various devout theologians through the years. Space limits permit reference only to a few of them:

In his well-known commentary Albert Barnes says on Hebrews 2:18 that the word "tempted" may mean that a person is subjected to "afflictions or sufferings," or that he is allowed "to fall into *temptation,* properly so called—where some strong inducement to evil is presented to the mind." Then he adds, "The Saviour was subjected to both these in as severe a form as was ever presented to men."

Henry Jones Ripley, a Baptist theologian and seminary professor of a century ago, wrote thus in his commentary on the book of Hebrews:

"Christ is said to have become in all essential respects like men; he was, consequently, liable to be tempted in all respects like them. Being on earth as truly a man as any of us, he was tempted as men are, by Satan, by his human adversaries, and by his professed friends. Temptations arose from his bodily nature, from his rational faculties, from his emotional susceptibilities, from his connections with his natural relatives. . . . Whatever difficult questions may be raised from the peculiarity of his being the Son of God while yet humbled to the level of humanity, we must not allow ourselves to lose the efficacy of the equally scriptural truth that he was like us, that he was really made liable to the frailties and temptations of which men have experience. . . . To be *tempted* is not a proof that we are sinners; sin consists in *yielding* to temptation."—*The Epistle to the Hebrews* (1868), p. 62.

J. C. Macaulay, sometime pastor of the Wheaton Bible church, Wheaton, Illinois, in his comment on the phrase "without sin," in Hebrews 4:15, says:

"That means more than that He did not sin by responding to the temptations. It means that the temptations left His sinlessness intact, unshaken, undisturbed. . . . He shared our natural weaknesses, and these were targets of the adversary, occasions of temptation, but never causes of sin."—*Devotional Studies in the Epistle to the Hebrews* (1948), p. 70.

# SANCTUARY AND ATONEMENT

Moses Stuart, an early nineteenth-century Congregational theologian and seminary professor, in his commentary on Hebrews, observes thus on Hebrews 4:15:

"He [Christ] possessed a nature truly human, ii.14, 17; he was therefore susceptible of being excited by the power of temptations, although he never yielded to them."—*A Commentary on the Epistle to the Hebrews* (4th ed., 1876), p. 336.

Brooke Foss Westcott, Anglican bishop, and one of the greatest of Greek scholars of the past generation, remarks thus in his comment on Hebrews 4:15:

"We may represent the truth to ourselves best by saying that Christ assumed humanity under the conditions of life belonging to man fallen, though not with sinful promptings from within."—*The Epistle to the Hebrews* (3d ed., 1903), p. 108.

William Porcher DuBose, a Protestant Episcopal divine and professor at the University of the South (Tennessee) at the turn of the century, wrote thus on the subject:

"I do not know how better to express the truth of the matter than to say, in what seems to me to be the explicit teaching of our Epistle [Hebrews], and of the New Testament generally, that our Lord's whole relation to sin in our behalf was identical with our own up to the point of His unique and exceptional personal action with reference to it. Left to our nature and ourselves it overcomes and slays all us: through God in Him He overcame and slew it. He did it not by His own will and power as man, but as man through an absolute dependence upon God. And He made both the omnipotent grace of God upon which He depended, and His own absolute dependence upon it, His perfect faith, available for us in our salvation. He re-enacts in us the victory over sin and death which was first enacted in Himself."— Quoted by A. Nairne in *The Epistle to the Hebrews*, Introduction, p. lxxviii. The Cambridge Bible for Schools and Colleges.

Dean F. W. Farrar, whose *Life of Christ* and other works have edified the devout through many years, declares, in his comment on Christ's temptation in the wilderness:

"Some, in a zeal at once intemperate and ignorant, have claimed for Him [Christ] not only an actual sinlessness, but a nature to which sin was divinely and miraculously impossible. What then? If His great conflict were a mere deceptive phantasmagoria, how can the narrative of it profit us? If *we* have to fight the battle clad in that armour of human free-will which has been hacked and riven about the bosom of our fathers by so many a cruel blow, what comfort is it to us if our great Captain fought not only victoriously, but without real danger; not only uninjured, but without even a possibility of wound? . . . They who would *thus* honour Him rob us of our living Christ, who was very man no less than very God. . . .

"Whether, then, it comes under the form of a pseudo-orthodoxy, false and pharisaical, and eager only to detect or condemn the supposed heresy of others; or whether it comes from the excess of a dishonouring reverence which has degenerated into the spirit of fear and bondage—let us beware of contradicting the express teaching of the scriptures, and, as regards this narrative [of the wilderness temptation], the express teaching of Christ Himself, by a supposition that He was not liable to real temptation."—*The Life of Christ* (1-vol. ed.), pp. 95, 96.

Much more might be quoted from the writings of devout and learned theologians of various religious bodies, but these should suffice to prove that the Adventist view of Christ in relation to temptation is not a strange, heretical teaching.

Now, a word regarding the reference to Isaiah's prophecy that Christ would "not fail nor be discouraged." This prophecy is quoted as proof that Christ, therefore, could not have risked eternal loss when He came to earth. A few questions should clear up this matter: Does not God know the end from the beginning? Yes! Hence He knows in advance that certain wicked men will continue in their wickedness and be destroyed. But does His foreknowledge take from them their free will and necessitate their destruction? We all answer no. Again, God knows in advance that certain righteous men will continue in their righteousness and be saved in the great day. But does that foreknowledge take from them their free will and their genuine temptations to sin and necessitate their salvation? Again we answer no. Certainly God foreknew that His Son would "not fail nor be discouraged," but that foreknowledge did not free our Lord and Saviour from temptation to sin.

Let us repeat in closing. The Adventist belief concerning Christ is that He was truly divine and truly human, that His human nature was subjected to the same temptations to sin that confront us, that He triumphed over temptation through the power given Him of His Father, and that He may most literally be described as "holy, harmless, undefiled." (Heb. 7:26.)

---

NOTE.—A word of counsel to some of our Adventist writers and speakers may be in order here. The incarnation is a very great mystery. We shall never fully understand how a Being could at once be both "Son of God" and "Son of man," thus possessing both a human and a divine nature. Likewise, the presence of sin in the universe is a very great mystery. We shall probably never understand fully the nature of sin, and hence probably never understand fully the meaning of the term "sinful flesh," which we and others often use without attempting to define it. When we speak of the taint of sin, the germs of sin, we should remember that we are using metaphorical language. Critics, especially those who see the Scriptures through Calvinistic eyes, read into the term "sinful flesh" something that Adventist theology does not require. Thus if we use the term "sinful flesh" in regard to Christ's human nature, as some of our writers have done, we lay ourselves open to misunderstanding. True, we mean by that term simply that Christ "took on him the seed of Abraham," and was made "in the likeness of sinful flesh," but critics are not willing to believe this.

Let us never forget that a Scriptural mystery is always most safely stated in the language of Scripture. Hence, when we must move amid the mists of a divine mystery we do well to stay within the protecting bounds of quotation marks. We need not move beyond in order to secure from that mystery its saving, sanctifying power. And staying thus within those bounds, we best protect the mystery from the ridicule of skeptics, the Adventist name from the attacks of critics, and ourselves from becoming lost in the mist.

# Objection 95

Christ is the center and circumference of salvation. Paul declared to the Corinthian church: "I determined not to know any thing among you, save Jesus Christ, and him crucified." 1 Cor. 2:2. But Seventh-day Adventists, in their emphasis on the law and the Sabbath, and other peculiar doctrines, markedly fail to give Christ that central, dominant position that true Christians give to Him.

We believe that our so-called "peculiar doctrines" uniquely and strikingly emphasize the primacy of Christ. Note these facts:

1. *Our doctrine on the law.* We teach that "sin is the transgression of the law," and that all mankind stands guilty and condemned before God, for the wages of sin is death. If God's law could have been abolished, man would no longer have been guilty of death, hence Christ's death would not have been necessary to our salvation, for He died to save us from condemnation and death. Thus the historical incident of His death on Calvary would have significance simply as a beautiful exhibit of a good man's dying for a noble ideal, and setting before us a noble example. That is indeed the very position that some Christians take. Such a position robs Christ's death of its awe-inspiring, saving quality.

But Seventh-day Adventists are forever protected from this Christ-dishonoring view. We hold that God's law is eternal. Hence a guilty sinner's only hope of escape from the death that that violated law demands is found in Christ, who died in his stead. Our very belief in the inexorable, eternal quality of God's law causes us ever to flee to Christ as our only hope of life. How could we give greater significance to Christ as all-important to our salvation?

2. *Our doctrine on the Sabbath.* As set forth elsewhere in this book (see under objections 45 and 46), the seventh-day Sabbath focuses the worshiper's mind on the great truth of the creation as set forth in Genesis. It is this truth that is so largely denied by

evolutionistic Christians today. Now, when we focus thus on this creative display of divine power, we are led to give greater honor to Christ, for God "created all things by Jesus Christ." Eph. 3:9. "For by him were all things created, that are in heaven, and that are in earth, visible and invisible, whether they be thrones, or dominions, or principalities, or powers: all things were created by him, and for him." Col. 1:16.

True Sabbathkeeping is a weekly honoring of Christ in His role as Creator. Thus honoring Him we are prepared to believe most literally and fully His promise to create in us new hearts and minds, indeed, to make us new creatures in Christ Jesus.

Because our minds are turned, weekly, to the thought of an originally perfect world, we are prepared to realize most fully how great was the fall of our first parents, and to take most literally the words of our Lord: "And I, if I be lifted up from the earth, will draw all men unto me." John 12:32. How could we make Christ more central in our beliefs?

3. *Our doctrine on the sanctuary.* We teach that the earthly sanctuary service, given to the Israelites by God through Moses, was a type of the heavenly service that was to be conducted for man's salvation. Thus we make vivid to men the reality of a sacrificial service and the shedding of blood for the remission of sins, a truth so largely forgotten or denied in Christendom today. We see in the earthly lambs slain a type of the "Lamb of God"; in the earthly Passover, a type of "Christ our passover," who is "sacrificed for us"; in the earthly priests, a type of Christ our high priest who ministers in heaven above for us. (See 1 Cor. 5:7; Heb. 8:1.) How could we more highly emphasize or honor Christ in our teachings?

4. *Our doctrine on the mortality of man.* We take literally the text that "the wages of sin is death"; that is, we believe literally that the sinner's ultimate doom is destruction, annihilation. This follows logically from our belief that man does not possess an immortal soul. Hence we are led most fully to exalt Christ as the *only* hope of life. We take literally His words: "I am come that

they might have life, and that they might have it more abundantly." John 10:10. We believe that "life and immortality" were brought "to light through the gospel" of our Lord, and in no other way. (2 Tim. 1:10.) How could we more highly honor Christ than by thus teaching?

5. *Our emphasis on prophecy.* Nothing more definitely distinguishes us as a denomination than our belief that the prophetic portions of the Bible are intended of God to be understood and to guide us on the road to heaven. It is in the books of Daniel and the Revelation, so frequently the basis of the sermons at our evangelistic meetings, that we find some of the most glorious passages descriptive of Christ's power and coming kingdom. We focus on the opening words of the Revelation: "The revelation of Jesus Christ, which God gave unto him, to shew unto his servants things which must shortly come to pass." Rev. 1:1. We turn the hearer's eyes upward to Christ walking amid the seven candlesticks (Rev. 1:13), to Christ "a Lamb as it had been slain" (Rev. 5:6), to Christ as "King of kings, and Lord of lords" (Rev. 19:16) coming to set up His everlasting kingdom.

When we preach from the prophetic book of Daniel we climax with the vision of the 2300 days of Daniel 8:14, which includes the seventy-weeks prophecy of Daniel 9:24-27. And it is this prophecy, so central to Adventist theology, that provides one of the most irrefutable proofs that the Christ of Bethlehem was indeed "Messiah the prince," whom "Moses and all the prophets" had foretold. How could we more highly honor Christ?

6. *Our doctrine on the personal Second Advent of Christ.* No teaching is more central in Adventist theology than this doctrine of the Advent. A person cannot long attend an Adventist series of evangelistic services without hearing this doctrine set forth. Indeed, no doctrine is more extensively discussed in such services. And the heart of that doctrine is best revealed in the words of the angels to the disciples on the occasion of Christ's ascension: "This same Jesus, which is taken up from you into heaven, shall so come in like manner as ye have seen him go into heaven."

Acts 1:11. When a person accepts the Adventist faith he is continually reminded of this great truth, as the numerous articles on the Second Advent in our church literature reveal. We are not deceived by the false teaching so long prevalent in Christendom, that the world is gradually improving, and that finally all will be millennial. Not in man's power of improvement, but in God's power to recreate this earth, do we as Adventists find our hope of the future. We rest that hope on the promise that "the Lord himself shall descend from heaven with a shout" and that then we, with the resurrected righteous, will be caught up "in the clouds, to meet the Lord in the air: and so shall we ever be with the Lord." 1 Thess. 4:16, 17. How could we more highly exalt Christ?

We have here considered briefly the relation of Christ to six of our most distinctive teachings. We charitably like to think that the objector has never really found time to examine closely our teachings.

# Objection 96

"Adventists teach that it is deceptive either to believe or to say that one who accepts Christ as his Redeemer is saved. Mrs. White declares: 'Those who accept the Saviour, however sincere their conversion, should never be taught to say or feel that they are saved. This is misleading' (*Christ's Object Lessons*, p. 155)." "The gospel teaches that believers 'are saved' by 'the preaching of the cross' (1 Cor. 1:18). It teaches that God 'hath saved us, and called us with an holy calling' (2 Tim. 1:9)." To say that a born-again soul does not have salvation as "a present possession" is to proclaim a false gospel. Adventists make salvation a matter of "crucify self," "prove worthy," "struggle." This proves again that they preach a false, a legalistic, gospel.

First let us give the statement from Mrs. White in its context that we may better see what she is really teaching. The quotation is found in the chapter "Two Worshipers," which discusses the Pharisee and the publican who went up to the Temple to pray. Mrs. White remarks on the danger of spiritual pride and self-sufficiency that leads a man to feel self-righteous. She then cites Peter: "In his early discipleship Peter thought himself strong. Like the Pharisee, in his own estimation he was 'not as other men are.'" He assured his Lord that though others might be offended, he would not be. But a little later his unrealized weakness revealed itself, and he denied his Lord with cursing. We quote:

"Peter's fall was not instantaneous, but gradual. Self-confidence led him to the belief that he was saved, and step after step was taken in the downward path, until he could deny his Master. Never can we safely put confidence in self, or feel, this side of heaven, that we are secure against temptation. Those who accept the Saviour, however sincere their conversion, should never be taught to say or to feel that they are saved. This is misleading. Every one should be taught to cherish hope and faith; but even when we give ourselves to Christ and know that He accepts us, we are not beyond the reach of temptation.

God's word declares, 'Many shall be purified, and made white, and tried.' Only he who endures the trial will receive the crown of life.

"Those who accept Christ, and in their first confidence say, I am saved, are in danger of trusting to themselves. They lose sight of their own weakness and their constant need of divine strength. They are unprepared for Satan's devices, and under temptation many, like Peter, fall into the very depths of sin. We are admonished, 'Let him that thinketh he standeth, take heed lest he fall.' Our only safety is in constant distrust of self, and dependence on Christ."—*Christ's Object Lessons*, p. 155.

It is evident that Mrs. White is here using the word "saved" to describe a mistaken idea of salvation held by some. She is not using the word in the sense that Paul employs it in 2 Timothy 1:9, which the objector quotes.

There is a sense in which the Christian may say that he has been saved. When we confess our guilt and turn to Christ, He forgives us, *saves* us out of our state of condemnation, and places our feet on the path to heaven. Adventists believe this wholeheartedly.

But through the long years of Christian history there have been those who held the un-Scriptural view that when Christ saves us from our past sins He immediately and forever lifts us into a kind of heaven on earth from which there is no possibility of our ever straying. Thus we are here and now and forever saved, saved, saved! At best, such a view of salvation has ever led men to spiritual pride—"God, I thank Thee, that I am not as other men are." At worst, it has led men in their blind spiritual self-sufficiency and false security to fall into most heinous sin.

It is this false conception of "saved" that Seventh-day Adventists, and Christian leaders in general through the long years, have denounced.

We accept all that the Bible says about our being saved here and now from past guilt and thus standing justified through the blood of Christ. But we accept also all that the Bible says about the dangers that beset us on the heavenly path upon which our feet have been placed, and of the need of constant watchfulness unto prayer if we are to reach the heavenly goal.

Paul is quoted to prove that salvation is a present accomplished fact for those who have given heed to the true gospel: "For the preaching of the cross is to them that perish foolishness; but unto us which are saved it is the power of God." 1 Cor. 1:18. But let Paul speak further in the same epistle: "Moreover, brethren, I declare unto you the gospel which I preached unto you, which also ye have received, and wherein ye stand; by which also ye are saved, if ye keep in memory what I preached unto you, unless ye have believed in vain." 1 Cor. 15:1, 2.

Adam Clarke says in comment on this text:

"Ye are now in a salvable state; and are saved from your Gentilism, and from your former sins. . . . Your future salvation, or being brought finally to glory, will now depend on your *faithfulness* to the grace that ye have received."

That is good Methodist doctrine on salvation. It is also good Adventist doctrine.

Jamieson, Fausset, and Brown, in their well-known Bible commentary, would have the phrase "ye are saved" (1 Cor. 15:2) read, "ye are being saved." So also Lange's great commentary. This is consistent with the Bible figure of the Christian traveling a road, strait and tortuous, who may ever claim the protection of the angels against the danger of falling off the path, but who can never say that temptation and danger are past until the end of the journey is reached. Thinking of the Christian under that figure we may rightly speak of him as in the process of "being saved." No load of guilt weighs him down. From that Christ has freed him. But he has not been freed from the risk of sin, which again would bring guilt to his soul. He may still turn to the one side or the other from the path.

It is in this setting that we see full force to the words Paul addressed to Timothy: "Take heed unto thyself, and unto the doctrine; continue in them: for in doing this thou shalt both save thyself, and them that hear thee." 1 Tim. 4:16. Here Paul is using the word "save" in the *future* tense. And the salvation is assured only if Timothy shall "continue" in a certain course.

Again, Paul says to Timothy: "Fight the good fight of faith, lay hold on eternal life, whereunto thou art also called, and hast professed a good profession before many witnesses." 1 Tim. 6:12.

To the church at Corinth, Paul wrote: "Know ye not that they which run in a race run all, but one receiveth the prize? So run, that ye may obtain. And every man that striveth for the mastery is temperate in all things. Now they do it to obtain a corruptible crown; but we an incorruptible. I therefore so run, not as uncertainly; so fight I, not as one that beateth the air: but I keep under my body, and bring it into subjection: lest that by any means, when I have preached to others, I myself should be a castaway." 1 Cor. 9:24-27.

Adventists have never said anything more vigorous about the struggle and the warfare of the Christian life than Paul here does. Indeed, what we say is drawn, in no small part, from such statements as these by the great apostle.

The Scriptures are also filled with exhortations to Christians to remain steadfast lest they fall by the way and lose their reward. Says Paul, "Let us hold fast the profession of our faith without wavering." Heb. 10:23. A little further on in the same chapter he appeals, "Cast not away therefore your confidence." Verse 35.

In the book of the Revelation is found a prophecy of the history of the Christian church from the time of Christ to the Second Advent, under seven divisions, or churches. At the conclusion of the message to each church a promise of heavenly reward is given, but the reward is specifically promised "to him that overcometh." (See Rev. 2:7, 11, 17, 26; 3:5, 12, 21.) To the first church (Ephesus) came the warning: "Remember therefore from whence thou art fallen, and repent, and do the first works; or else I will come unto thee quickly, and will remove thy candlestick out of his place." Rev. 2:5. To the third church (Pergamos) came the same warning, "Repent." (Verse 16.) Likewise to the seventh church (Laodicea). (Rev. 3:19.) To the fifth church (Sardis) came the appeal: "That which ye have already hold fast till I come." Rev. 2:25. To the sixth church (Philadelphia) came a similar appeal: "Hold that fast which thou hast, that no man take thy crown." Rev. 3:11.

How could a Bible writer make more clear the sobering truth that those who have been saved from their past sins and have taken the name of Christian may fall by the wayside? Note the appeal to those who have not fallen to "hold fast" lest they also fall. All this agrees with the admonition of Paul to the Corinthian church: "Let him that thinketh he standeth take heed lest he fall." 1 Cor. 10:12. How evident it is that salvation in the ultimate sense of the word is not the possession of the Christian until he has finished his course and has kept the faith to the end. Said Christ, "He that shall endure unto the end, the same shall be saved." Matt. 24:13.

Against two extremes in this matter of salvation Mrs. White warns: (1) Against the self-assured attitude that would tempt a once-saved man to feel that he is now beyond all danger, or at least is able of himself to overcome all temptation. This is the dangerous attitude discussed in the quotation from *Christ's Object Lessons*. (2) Against the attitude of fearfulness regarding salvation that is born of a consciousness of the weaknesses of self. As regards this opposite extreme she writes:

"We should not make self the center, and indulge anxiety and fear as to whether we shall be saved. All this turns the soul away from the Source of our strength. Commit the keeping of your soul to God, and trust in Him. Talk and think of Jesus. Let self be lost in Him. Put away all doubt; dismiss your fears. Say with the apostle Paul, 'I live; yet not I, but Christ liveth in me: and the life which I now live in the flesh I live by the faith of the Son of God, who loved me, and gave Himself for me.' Rest in God. He is able to keep that which you have committed to Him. If you will leave yourself in His hands, He will bring you off more than conqueror through Him that has loved you."—*Steps to Christ*, pp. 76, 77.

The strength of the objector's position is that he narrows down the discussion of salvation to one aspect of it, and in that restricted setting makes his case seem Scriptural. The strength of the Adventist position is that we accept fully and unreservedly *all* the aspects of the divine plan to save men out of this world.

# Objection 97

**Seventh-day Adventists reject the atonement of Christ. They make of no effect the death of the Saviour, because they believe that His atonement for sin was not completed on Calvary.**

Those who raise objections to Seventh-day Adventist doctrines almost invariably endeavor to find some statement from Mrs. White's works that appears to support their charges. They do so because, as they explain, all Adventists accept Mrs. White's statements on doctrine. In view of this we shall quote from her writings to show what we really do believe is the relation of Christ to the sinner.

In the book entitled *Steps to Christ* she wrote:

"Christ took upon Himself the guilt of the disobedient, and suffered in the sinner's stead."—Page 36.

Again:

"Christ must be revealed to the sinner as the Saviour dying for the sins of the world."—*Ibid.*, p. 30.

These are but representative; many equally strong statements might be quoted.

How well do the foregoing statements agree with the words of John the Baptist as to Christ: "Behold the Lamb of God, which taketh away the sin of the world." John 1:29. And how beautifully do they harmonize with the declaration of Peter, that Christ "bare our sins in his own body on the tree." 1 Peter 2:24.

We believe that the death of Christ provided a divine sacrifice sufficient to atone for the sins of the whole world. We believe, further, that when we confess our sins, God does then and there forgive them; and that unless we afterward turn away to a life of wickedness, this divine forgiveness is complete and final, so far as we are concerned. But we also hold that, in harmony with the Levitical type of the Day of Atonement (Leviticus 16), there is a great final day when God will formally blot out of existence the sins of all who "shall be *accounted* worthy to obtain that [heavenly] world." Luke 20:35. This final accounting must come at the very close of probation, for only when we have run our entire course and the records are complete could this act—which settles our destiny for eternity—take place. Therefore the great hour of God's judgment is the logical time for all accounts to be finally settled. In making such statements we but echo the words of Christ: "He that shall endure unto the *end,* the same shall be *saved.*" Matt. 24:13.

Denying the atonement of Christ is one thing, believing that the final disposition of sins is yet future is an altogether different thing. We do not deny the atonement; we differ with some other Christian people simply as to the *time* element involved in it. We believe unqualifiedly that our sins are forgiven and will be blotted out wholly and only by virtue of the atoning blood of Jesus Christ, which was shed on Calvary. No discussion as to the *time* involved in the divine transaction can blur the real question at issue; namely, whether or not Christ and *Christ only* makes atonement for us. We do not believe that our Saviour's precious atoning blood loses any of its efficacy merely as the result of the passage of time. That certain acts of Christ subsequent to Calvary are also necessary in the plan of salvation from sin is evident by reference to such texts as the following: Romans 4:25; 1 Corinthians 15:17; Hebrews 7:25.

Of those who charge us with teaching strange doctrines because we believe that Christ's work of atonement for sin was begun rather than completed on Calvary, we ask these questions: If complete and final atonement was made on the cross for *all* sins, then will not all be saved? for Paul says that He "died for all." Are we to understand you as being Universalists? "No," you say, "not all men will be saved." Well, then, are we to understand that you hold that Christ made complete atonement on the cross for only a limited few, and that His sacrifice was not world embracing, but only partial? That would be predestination in its worst form.

Adventists are free from the dilemma that such questions as these create. We believe that Christ on the cross *made provision* for the atonement for all sinners. Thus all who *will* may be saved. But we believe also that only those who "endure unto the end . . . shall be saved." Thus we escape, on the one hand, the false doctrine of Universalism; and on the other, the equally false doctrine of claiming full and final salvation for a man before he has endured "unto the end." Therefore if the saving of a man involves his deeds "unto the end," which must be true of the last man saved in the world, as well as of those of former generations, the final phase of Christ's saving work of atonement cannot be completed until the end.

# Objection 98

**Seventh-day Adventists make Satan their savior, sin bearer, and vicarious substitute.**

We believe, with all evangelical Protestants, that there is no other name given under heaven whereby we must be saved than the name of Jesus Christ. We qualify this in no way. Not until the plan of salvation is *completed* and the righteous have been saved for eternity through the atoning work of Christ does Satan enter into the picture. Our belief as to the relationship of Satan to our sins might perhaps be stated more or less exactly with the aid of an illustration:

A group of men have been arrested, tried, and convicted of certain crimes. A heavy fine is imposed upon them. They are in a hopeless state, for they are penniless. But their hopelessness is changed to joy: a rich philanthropist offers to pay their fine. They accept, and are freed. The case is apparently settled. But no; the court, continuing its investigation, discovers that a person of fiendish cunning has really dominated these poor men and has seduced them into their course of wrongdoing. He is captured, and judgment is meted out to him. He is made to pay a heavy fine—much heavier even than that from which the poor men have been freed by the gracious act of the philanthropist, for the court reasons that the fiend is doubly guilty.

We all consider that the court has acted rightly. No one would think for a moment that because the group of men have been freed, therefore the matter is necessarily closed. And because the fiend has to pay the penalty for the crimes of the group of men whose heavy fines have been paid by the philanthropist, no one feels any reflection is being cast upon the gift of the rich man. The penalty that was to have been meted out to that group was completely paid by the gift, yet the fiend must finally suffer for the same crimes, because he was primarily responsible for them.

# SANCTUARY AND ATONEMENT

This, in vague outline, and with the handicaps of analogy, illustrates our view as to the relation of Satan to our sins. We are guilty before God. We are penniless and in a hopeless state, but Christ paid the price necessary to set us free—not with silver or gold, but with the price of His own precious blood. He is the philanthropist—the lover of man—in our illustration. The penalty for our sins is fully paid, for His gift is all-sufficient. He makes full and complete atonement for us.

But the court of heaven determines that Satan, the archfiend, has been the real instigator of all sin, from the very day when he seduced our first mother, Eve. He is brought before the bar of justice, and indicted, not simply for his own sins, but for the primary responsibility for the sins of those who have been pardoned. It is as though our Advocate, having obtained our pardon, turns prosecuting attorney against our fiendish adversary, causing to return upon his own head the mischief and woe into which the now pardoned and saved sinners had been drawn during their lives.

Thus instead of viewing Satan in any sense as our savior from sin, our doctrine makes most vivid the fact that he is the author of sin. Instead of viewing him as one who was made "to be sin for us, who knew no sin," we view him as one who, being the primary instigator of all sin, is about to suffer the final judgments of God. (See page 715 for a discussion of the scapegoat and the atonement.)

# Section VI

# GENERAL OBJECTIONS

## Objections 99 to 109

# Objection 99

Seventh-day Adventists, perhaps even more than most other religious bodies, carry on a vigorous foreign-mission program. But why impose the Christian religion on the people of other countries? Why disturb and disrupt their program of living?

Strictly speaking, this is not an objection to Seventh-day Adventists as distinguished from other churches. Our answer, therefore, is a defense of Christian missions in general. The essence of the charge is that the missionary imposes his religion on the nationals of other lands. Now the word "impose" implies force or compulsion. There are numerous instances where trade and business agreements have been imposed on pagan people by civilized nations. In fact, most of the relationships of the great nations to pagan countries have been built upon some element of force, so that the word "impose" might very accurately be used.

It is in the realm of missions that we find the one shining exception to this grim policy of imposition. The story of missions is a story of lone men and women going out without the strength of a government behind them, generally without even the moral support of the whole church; for too often has the Christian church been lukewarm in its missionary program. These missionaries have gone out with nothing more compelling than a Book and the story contained in that Book. So far from being able to dominate pagan peoples and compel them to accept these new beliefs, missionaries too often have had to live in terror of their lives, indeed, not infrequently to sacrifice their lives.

The Christian missionary goes out, not to compel the heathen to accept new views, but, in the words of Paul, to "persuade men." He has been constrained by the love of Christ to go forth as an ambassador for Christ to beseech men to be reconciled to God. He goes forth to share with them a belief and a hope and a new life that have come to him. He is in the position of one who, having come upon some great good fortune, feels that he cannot selfishly keep it to himself, but must let others enjoy it with him. The missionary is one who, having received freedom from the guilt of sin and the divine promise of everlasting life, feels an irresistible longing to bring the story of pardon to others, that they also may walk in newness of life.

The missionary is one who, having learned the wonderful story that Christ died and rose again and now sits at the right hand of God to make intercession for us, feels compelled in his own heart to tell others this most glorious news. He goes forth, not to impose alien ideas upon heathen people, but to broadcast news, the good news of salvation, which good news is alien to no land. The gospel deals with sin, and sin is a worldwide malady.

That the proclaiming of such news should shake to the very foundations many social and national institutions and practices of pagan lands is only to be expected. There is a power that goes with the gospel, even the power of God.

If no mighty upheaval and betterment of life followed the preaching of the gospel, the skeptic would have the strongest argument in the world that the gospel is a lifeless theory. This very upheaval and betterment is the best proof of the divine vitality and worth of the message that the missionary preaches.

But there is a further point to be made in favor of missions today more than ever before. After two world wars most of mankind is filled with suspicions, hatreds, and jealousies. The world is falling apart under the pressure of these evil forces. The desperate need today is for a display of mutual trust and understanding, a brotherly feeling, a sense of kinship. That is the only kind of cement that can keep the tottering edifice of civilization from collapsing completely.

And what can produce this? The League of Nations tried and failed, and the United Nations seems not to be faring better. Great armaments and large standing armies cannot produce this mystic cement. But let the Christian missionary preach in any corner of the world, and what happens? Men and women begin to call each other "brother" and "sister" in Christ Jesus. And they think of other Christians in the faraway homeland of the missionary as brothers and sisters in the Lord. But you cannot truly think of a man as your brother and yet be suspicious of him and want to turn your house into an arsenal to guard against him.

True, so-called Christian nations have gone to war with other so-called Christian nations. But that sad fact does not prove false what we have just written. We are not talking about so-called Christianity. We are talking about the genuine article. Christ said, "By this shall all men know that ye are my disciples, if ye have love one toward another." Genuine Christianity is revealed in genuine love for others. And to the degree that the missionary brings to men in a far land the genuine manifestation of Christian love and teachings, to that degree he is binding the hearts of men together.

Thus the Christian missionary stands out as a great apostle of peace in a world that is already gravely threatened with a third world war. Never was there greater need of Christian missionaries. We are glad that the objector places Seventh-day Adventists in the forefront of mission work. We believe we are doing the will of God when we send out missionaries, for our Lord commanded His disciples, "Go ye into all the world, and preach the gospel to every creature." Mark 16:15.

# Objection 100

**It is clear there must be something wrong in the system itself, when so large a number of persons leave the Seventh-day Adventists.**

This objection was first raised, we believe, about the year 1890, by a man who left the Adventist ministry, at least present-day objectors credit these exact words to him. They apparently do not know that he, and others in those earlier days, confidently forecast that the Seventh-day Adventist Church would soon break to pieces and disintegrate! Note the world membership in the year 1890 and by decades following:

| | | |
|------|---------|---------|
| 1890 | 29,711  | members |
| 1900 | 75,767  | "       |
| 1910 | 104,526 | "       |
| 1920 | 185,450 | "       |
| 1930 | 314,253 | "       |
| 1940 | 504,752 | "       |
| 1950 | 756,712 | "       |

Yes, there are those who leave the Adventist Church. How does the objector know? We publish the facts in our statistical reports. Similar reports of all religious bodies contain figures showing apostasies! But we have never heard any Christian believer reason that there "must be something wrong in the system itself" when so many people leave the different Christian churches. What a host of people there are who will tell you that they once were members of such and such a church—including the church to which the objector belongs—but that they have dropped out.

There is nothing either strange or new about this situation. Christ gave the parable of the sower to fortify the heart of the Christian minister in this very matter of departures from the church. (See Matt. 13:18-23.) That parable forewarns the minister that only a fraction of those who accept the word will endure.

Paul wrote to Timothy regarding the failure of the believers to stand by him at his trial: "At my first answer no man stood with me, but all men forsook me: I pray God that it may not be laid to their charge." 2 Tim. 4:16. In that same epistle he said, "This thou knowest, that all they which are in Asia be turned away from me." 2 Tim. 1:15. We have yet to hear any Christian believer reasoning that this fact proved that "there must be something wrong" in the very "system" of doctrine that Paul preached.

Yes, there have been and there will continue to be defections from the Advent movement. Those who look at this movement dispassionately are impressed, not that some leave it, but that so many stay, seeing that its members are called upon to live in accordance with high and inflexible standards of conduct and are ever confronted with the economic handicap of no Saturday labor. Onlookers have often told us that we might gain and hold a host more members if we did not call upon them to abstain from liquor, tobacco, the theater, and other practices that we believe are contrary to Scriptural standards. But then, if we lowered the standards, we would lose the real justification for our existence. We solemnly and humbly believe that it is our business to call men to the highest standards of heaven and to show them that by God's enabling power they can order their lives by those standards, in readiness for the day when all men must meet God face to face.

The objector seeks to give added force to his argument by printing a little group of letters from former Adventists who say they left this church because they no longer accepted the denomination's view of Mrs. White, or the interpretation that she gives to various doctrines. But why should this necessarily prove that either the denomination or Mrs. White is false? That the gift of prophecy normally belongs in the church is evident from Scripture (see objection 109). That some should refuse to accept a prophet's instruction, while insisting that they believe what the ancient prophets have written, is also evident from Scripture. The Jews, at Christ's time, rejected Him while vowing fervent belief in what Moses had written!

# Objection 101

When Seventh-day Adventist ministers go into a community to hold a series of lectures, they conceal, at the first, their denominational connection. They thus hope to draw into their audience people who would never come if they knew that Seventh-day Adventists were conducting the meetings. This is a form of deception. There is something the matter with a religious body that is afraid to identify itself as soon as it begins to carry on any activity in a community.

This objection might sound more plausible were it not for certain passages of Scripture. One of the most striking facts that stand out in the Gospels is that Christ concealed His identity on a number of occasions. Note these texts, for example:

"And Jesus saith unto him, See thou tell no man; but go thy way, shew thyself to the priest, and offer the gift that Moses commanded, for a testimony unto them." Matt. 8:4.

"And their eyes were opened; and Jesus straitly charged them, saying, See that no man know it." Matt. 9:30.

"Then charged he his disciples that they should tell no man that he was Jesus the Christ." Matt. 16:20.

We have yet to hear any devout Christian expressing misgivings and doubts about the ministry of Christ or declaring that He was ashamed or afraid because He concealed His identity for a time. Evidently, then, this much at least may be established at the outset as being proved by these texts: Concealing one's identity is not in itself a proof that one is either ashamed or afraid. There may be honorable and altogether reasonable grounds for such concealment.

On Matthew 16:20, Adam Clarke well observes:

"The time for his [Christ's] full manifestation was not yet come; and he was not willing to provoke the Jewish malice, or the Roman envy, by permitting his disciples to announce him as the Saviour of a lost world. He chose rather to wait, till his resurrection and ascension had set this truth in the clearest light, and beyond the power of successful contradiction."

# GENERAL OBJECTIONS

To this explanation most theologians, we believe, would agree.

Christ would evidently have cut short His work if He had permitted a premature announcement that He was the Messiah, for "malice" and "envy" blind men to truth.

Those who are Christ's followers may rightly be permitted to use Him as their guide in all matters, including the matter of how best to promote the truth concerning His coming again to this earth. Now, it is a fact that during most of the history of the Seventh-day Adventist Church, the very word "Adventist" has conveyed to the minds of most people a picture of a deluded band of fanatics sitting on housetops in ascension robes awaiting the opening of the heavens. This story of ascension robes has become a part of American folklore and been embalmed in impressive encyclopedias. And the ascension robes story is only part of the fanciful picture that has come into the minds of many when they have heard the name "Adventist."

The ascension robes story is a myth, and ninety-nine per cent of the related stories are likewise myth—as has now been proved —but that has not prevented people from believing them. The net result has been that many people have seen Seventh-day Adventists only through the distorting mists of slanderous myths. This is nothing new in religious history; witness, for example, the early history of the Quakers and the Baptists.

It should not be difficult, therefore, for any reasonable person to see why Adventist ministers through the past years have sought first to cause people to see them simply as Christian preachers before announcing their Adventist connection. After all, we seek to be first, and before all else, Christian preachers of righteousness. Then we hope to build on that the timely messages from Bible prophecy that may be described in the words of the apostle Peter as "present truth" for these last days of earth's history.

It has undoubtedly been true in years past that Adventists could not have gotten a crowd out to hear them in certain cities, at least, if they had revealed their identity at the outset. But we think that that proves, not the weakness of the Adventist case, but the strength of distorted ideas founded on fanciful myths. The other side of the picture is that many people, after they have attended Adventist meetings for a time, frankly admit that they have changed their ideas about us and are glad that they first came to the meetings not knowing who was conducting them.

In more recent years our activities have become so much better known that in many places the former distorted picture has been largely corrected. Accordingly, we are increasingly following the plan of announcing at the outset the Adventist sponsorship of the public meetings. That is what we like to do, and what we hope erelong to be able to do everywhere. We are not ashamed of our Adventism, far from it. An Adventist colporteur selling one of our books was asked by a prospective customer as to his religious connections. "Madam," he replied, "I don't want to boast, but I'm a Seventh-day Adventist." No, we don't want to boast, we simply want to proclaim to the world a message that we earnestly believe should be given at this time. And if, in order to secure an initial hearing, we must at the first conceal the name, we do so for a brief period only with a view to a clear-cut announcement of our Adventist connections a little later in the meetings. Then those who have been coming may decline to come further, if they desire. They generally decide to stay!

Unhappily, as the literature of many objectors to Adventism reveals, it is *they* who have often been most active in spreading the distorting myths regarding us. And then they are wont to add, as though to prove conclusively their case against us, that we sometimes fail to reveal our Adventist connections at the outset of a series of evangelistic lectures! If they will help us to clear away completely the slanderous myths that folklore has often thrown around the name "Adventist," we will be most happy to preface every one of our public meetings with the announcement of its Adventist sponsorship! In the meantime we shall, in such instances and areas as the situation necessitates, follow the precedent set by our Lord's instruction to His disciples as regards the time of disclosing our name.

# Objection 102

Seventh-day Adventists hold fanatical views on health reform and vegetarianism, and by such teachings restrict the liberty that belongs to Christians. In fact, the very distinction they make as to what is right to eat and drink brings them under the condemnation of the Bible. (See Rom. 14:2; 1 Tim. 4:3.)

When this charge was first made it seemed to have some strength, and we were compelled to answer it alone. But today, after many years of research in medical lines, the scientist meets this accusation for us, and rather generally changes the word "fanatical" to "sane" and "scientific" as regards our views on liquor, tobacco, tea, coffee, et cetera. We hold that certain things that are called "food" are to a greater or less degree harmful to the body. Therefore we believe that they have no proper place in our diet. Paul exclaims, "What? know ye not that your body is the temple of the Holy Ghost which is in you, which ye have of God, and ye are not your own? for ye are bought with a price: therefore glorify God in your body." 1 Cor. 6:19, 20.

How a Christian can partake of a food or a drink that is in *any* way injurious and still obey the solemn command to "glorify God in your *body*," we do not know. The Bible declares that "if any man defile the temple of God, him shall God destroy." 1 Cor. 3:17.

Further: We are to cooperate with God in our habits and customs for the development of perfect Christian characters. It is a known fact that right habits of eating and drinking have much to do with a good disposition as well as with a sound constitution. Certairily the reverse holds good.

The apostle Peter clearly shows that there is a direct relation between food and holiness. When he writes, "Be ye holy in all manner of conversation ["living," A.R.V.]," he refers to the Old

Testament passage containing God's condemnation of unclean foods. (See 1 Peter 1:15, 16; Lev. 11:44-47.)

But it will be urged: Does not the Bible allow us to partake of certain meats termed "clean"? Yes, permission is given. But let us ask, What would you think of a man who, because it pleased his palate, made a part of his diet some herb that science has proved is injurious to the body, and who defended his dangerous dietary course by stating that the Bible said he might eat of any herb? (See Gen. 1:29.) You would probably answer him that this statement in Genesis must be considered in the light of the continual degeneracy taking place as the result of the curse resting upon the world. Thus with the eating of what was once termed in the Scripture "clean" meat. Furthermore, flesh food was not a part of the original diet of man. (Gen. 1:29.)

However, recognizing the fact that every man must be guided by his own conscience in all matters not explicitly enjoined in the Scriptures, the Seventh-day Adventist denomination does not make the eating of the "clean" meats a test of fellowship, but urges its members to study carefully the whole question of their diet in the light of Scripture and scientific findings, so that they will not in any particular "defile the temple of God."

While remembering the Biblical pronouncement that "the kingdom of God is not meat and drink," we do not fail to keep in mind the inspired command: "Whether therefore ye eat, or drink, or whatsoever ye do, do all to the glory of God." Rom. 14:17; 1 Cor. 10:31.

Endeavoring to obey this and similar admonitions has led Adventists, contrary to the desires of carnal appetite, to become abstemious in regard to what they eat and drink. We hold that such a course enables us more easily to obey the injunction, "Abstain from fleshly lusts, which war against the soul," and to follow the practice of Paul, who declared, "I keep under my body, and bring it into subjection." 1 Peter 2:11; 1 Cor. 9:27.

Reference is made to Romans 14:1-5. The text in its context reads as follows: "Him that is weak in the faith receive ye, but not to doubtful disputations. For one believeth that he may eat all things: another, who is weak, eateth herbs. Let not him that eateth despise him that eateth not; and let not him which eateth not judge him that eateth: for God hath received him. Who art thou that judgest another man's servant? to his own master he standeth or falleth. Yea, he shall be holden up: for God is able to make him stand. One man esteemeth one day above another: another esteemeth every day alike. Let every man be fully persuaded in his own mind."

Earlier (see objection 36) this passage was discussed as it relates to holy days. We there concluded that Paul is considering Jewish holy days and Jewish restrictions as to meats and drinks, though the matter of meats and drinks was not discussed. Jewish ceremonial ritual made various contacts with the diet of the Jews. There were days of fasting, for example. It is easy to see how some Jews who had just accepted Christianity might still feel to honor such days, and hence to refrain from food on those days or to obey other related ceremonial requirements. In writing to the Colossians, Paul says, "Let no man therefore judge you in meat, or in drink, or in respect of an holyday." Col. 2:16. Paul is not here discussing the dietetic question of the food value of things that might be eaten or drunk. He is concerned only to free Christians from such restrictions as grew out of ceremonial requirements or out of the false idea that men can gain salvation by a certain diet.

As various commentators bring out, the Jews who were dispersed abroad, as was true of those at Rome, could not be sure that what they bought in the market place was clean, according to Jewish standards; even "clean" meat might not be ceremonially clean. Hence some Jews might refrain from eating any meat at all.

Again, in the pagan cities of the Roman Empire it was often the case that meat was first offered to the idols, in a kind of dedication, and then placed on the market. Paul talks to the Corinthian church about this very matter. Some Christians were not able to eat such meat without trouble of conscience; others were not so troubled. This leads Paul to offer the same kind of counsel that he gives in Romans 14 regarding forbearance one of another. (See 1 Corinthians 8.) Indeed some commentators believe that 1 Corinthians 8 is really the explanation of Romans 14:1-5.

In the light of these facts what conceivable relation does Romans 14:2 have to Adventist health teachings? The difference between them is as wide as the difference between ceremonial and dietary reasons for eating or not eating certain foods.

Let us look, now, at 1 Timothy 4:3. This text in its context reads thus:

"Now the Spirit speaketh expressly, that in the latter times some shall depart from the faith, giving heed to seducing spirits, and doctrines of devils; speaking lies in hypocrisy; having their conscience seared with a hot iron; forbidding to marry, and commanding to abstain from meats, which God hath created to be received with thanksgiving of them which believe and know the truth. For every creature of God is good, and nothing to be refused, if it be received with thanksgiving: for it is sanctified by the word of God and prayer." 1 Tim. 4:1-5.

Bible commentators are agreed that this passage finds its primary fulfillment in the Gnostic and related heresies that were already beginning to take shape. And many Protestant commentators believe that the passage finds its further and rather complete fulfillment in the Roman Catholic Church. The proof in support of this belief is both plentiful and persuasive.

The Gnostics, who early made deep inroads into the Christian church, believed that matter is essentially evil and that the food we eat was not made by God but by an inferior deity. They denounced marriage as evil. The Manicheans, another early heretical sect, "held that wine sprang from the blood and gall of the devil." See Lange's commentary in comment on 1 Timothy 4:3.

Later, the Roman Catholic Church, over which, observes Harnack, Gnosticism gained half a victory, established celibacy of the clergy, and instituted prohibitions against meat at various times of the year.

Well might Paul warn against such heresy. To refrain from

certain meat or drink for the reasons given by the Gnostics and others would be to endorse their false teachings by one's very course of life. Neither we nor the objector could practice or promote abstinence from wine, for example, on the basis set forth by these apostates. But the objector's denunciation of the reasoning of the Gnostics or Manicheans would not make him any less a believer in temperance, and perhaps in dietary reform as well.

Even so with us, we join with Paul in denunciation of the heresies described in 1 Timothy 4:1-4, while still believing that it is better, on dietary grounds, to abstain from certain foods and drinks.

In closing, we should add that the word "meats" in 1 Timothy 4:3 is from the Greek word *broma,* which simply means food. In the old English phrase, "sit down to meat," we preserve the idea of "meat" simply as food. Hence, Paul's discussion does not focus on the question of flesh food versus a nonflesh diet. Instead, he is concerned to forewarn against heresies that would lead Christians to "abstain" from various "foods," not because of any valid dietary grounds, but because of false philosophical, pagan reasons. We think that if Paul were resurrected today, he would be more than a little startled to find his words of warning against the already developing Gnostic heresy being interpreted to apply to twentieth-century Seventh-day Adventist nutritional. views!

# Objection 103

**Seventh-day Adventists are proselyters.**

To this charge we plead "guilty," for the dictionary says that to proselyte is "to win over to a different opinion, belief, sect, or party," and that is our work. Christ Himself gave us that work in His command, "Go ye therefore, *and make disciples of all the nations,* baptizing them." Matt. 28:19, A.R.V. This proselyting was the work of Peter, James, and John, and the mighty evangelist Paul, and we but follow in their steps, continuing the work that they began. To the nominal believers in God the apostles preached that the Messiah of the Old Testament had come. They called upon the heathen to turn "from idols to serve the living and true God." 1 Thess. 1:9. They went to the uttermost parts of the earth in their God-given task of proselyting.

So with us. To the nominal believer we preach that the Christ of the Old and the New Testament, the Christ who came once to die for our sins, will soon return to this earth. We call upon the heathen to turn from their idols to the true God, and to prepare for the soon coming of His Son from heaven.

Everywhere we find men and women holding un-Scriptural beliefs regarding the great events that are just ahead, and failing to worship the Creator of the heavens and the earth, as He has commanded, on the Sabbath. (See Ex. 20:8-11; Rev. 14:6, 7.) If we remain true to God, we must use every Christian means possible to turn men from these wrong beliefs—to proselyte them. We are recreant in our duty to Heaven if we do otherwise. Where would the world be today if Luther and Calvin and others of the Reformers had not gone about preaching to men to turn from their former views on religion—proselyting them? Our task is to complete the work of these Reformers, and we are happy to follow their example and adopt their methods.

# Objection 104

In their opposition to Sunday laws Seventh-day Adventists reveal that they are callous to the needs of the workingman and are blind to the fact that the very stability of the country is endangered by the godless course of millions who give no day in the week to God. It seems that they are more concerned to protect themselves against persecution than to give support either to the workingman or to the moral uplift of the country.

One of the evident facts regarding our denomination is that it is composed, not of rich men, but of workingmen! Yet our whole membership are opposed to Sunday laws! Need more be said on this point?

The next evident fact is that we are far from blind to the moral state of the world. Our literature says much about the woeful state of morality and the godless condition of men. The difference between us and the Sunday law advocates is not in the relative degree of our eyesight but in the methods that we believe should be employed to cure the malady of godlessness. They would bring in the kingdom of God through the gateway of politics, and have our legislators save us from destruction. We would invoke the promised second coming of Christ to save the godly from this evil world, and as we wait for His soon coming we work with earnestness to turn men to God by the preaching of the gospel.

The third fact, which will become evident as we proceed, is that our opposition to Sunday legislation is not prompted by a selfish desire to save ourselves from possible persecution. We do not concede, of course, that there is anything necessarily selfish or evil in a person's invoking his constitutional rights to save himself from persecution. Even the great apostle Paul repeatedly invoked his Roman citizenship to save him from brutal treatment by his erstwhile brethren. Our reasons for opposition are these:

1. As students of prophecy we believe that the day is coming

when the principles of religious intolerance that marked the Dark Ages will be revived, that there will be in the very closing hours of this world's history a mighty religio-political combine that will endeavor to dominate the consciences of men. We believe it is our solemn duty to warn men against giving their support to it. Indeed, we have no alternative in the matter, seeing that Christ, through the prophet John, has commanded us to cry out against this movement, so that men may be saved from giving their support to such an evil program.

2. In connection with this warning message that we are commanded to give, we find the injunction to proclaim the great Sabbath message to the world, and what more auspicious occasion could be found for giving special publicity to the true Sabbath than when men are endeavoring to stir up the world in support of the false? In this way our opposition to Sunday laws becomes not a negative but a positive thing. We simply capitalize the occasions of great public interest in Sunday laws to proclaim more fully the true Sabbath message.

As the time of trouble begins, the people of God are to go forth to preach the Sabbath doctrine more fully and more convincingly than ever before. The agitation for Sunday legislation provides a choice illustration of how the wrath of man can be made to praise God; or, to state it in the most charitable form, how the endeavors of mistaken zealots can be made to serve a good purpose.

As a result of the widespread campaign that reformers have made through the public press and otherwise in recent years, there are probably more people who have become acquainted with the real facts on the Sabbath question than ever before, because every agitation by Sunday advocates has made newspaper and magazine editors even more than ready to publish matter giving the other side of the case. We would have been woefully remiss in our duty if we had failed to use these opportunities.

3. We believe that there are many sincere and earnest men in the ranks of Sunday-law advocates. In fact, we are willing to admit

that all of them are striving, according to their conception of the gospel, to advance the kingdom of God. But their sincerity does not make their course any the less wrong. If their program is carried out, and the strong arm of the law is drafted in their support, they will thus become persecutors.

We can conceive of no fate more tragic than that of a man whose misguided zeal for God finally causes him to become a persecutor of others who are striving to preach the gospel. Christ foretold such a tragedy as this when He declared that the time will come when he that "killeth you will think that he doeth God service." This divine forecast was fulfilled during the Middle Ages, and may be fulfilled again in the last days. In fact, at the very last there will be only two classes, the persecutors and the persecuted—those who give support to the great religio-political combine and those who, because of the opposing stand, are forbidden even to buy or to sell. Not to save ourselves from being persecuted, but to save others from being persecutors, is a chief reason for our stand against Sunday laws. We have endeavored in all our literature to make clear to the reformers the evil direction in which they are going, and it should ever be our zealous endeavor to do this in a spirit of charity and Christian love, making our attack on principles, not on persons.

4. The Scriptures plainly declare that we owe allegiance to the state, and should endeavor loyally and zealously to support it in the carrying out of its proper functions. (See Rom. 13:1-7; Matt. 22:16-21.) In this fact is to be found a valid reason for our outcry against the endeavors of reformers to combine the church with the state. Knowing as we do from history and prophecy that such a combine can work only to the detriment of the citizens and to the destruction of the free institutions of the country, we would surely fail to carry out the full meaning of the divine injunction to support the government if we failed to raise our voice in warning against such a menacing danger.

The truly loyal citizen is the man who possesses the moral courage to rise up and sound an alarm, even though he may be in the minority, and his numerous opponents may be the advocates of an apparently good program. And the one who thus sounds the alarm is in no wise violating the principle of the separation of church and state. Instead, he is arousing all men to the need of continuing inviolate that vital separation.

5. Finally, we oppose Sunday legislation because we would protect Christianity from the false conception of it that the masses of the people would have if proposed religious legislation were allowed to go unchallenged. One of the greatest handicaps under which the minister of the gospel labors is the feeling on the part of the man on the street that the church symbolizes an organization that is striving to force its views upon people. Surely there is a historical basis for such a feeling. And when the average individual, who is not a churchgoer, sees the endeavors of present-day militant church leaders to employ the power of the state, the antipathy toward the church is only intensified.

We are jealous to protect the Christian religion from this gross misconception. We would not be loyal to our divine Lord if we did not use every means possible to let men know that the gospel of Jesus Christ is not a gospel of force, and that He has commissioned His disciples to *invite* men to believe in Him. We would oppose with equal vigor any attempt to enforce the seventh-day Sabbath by law.

# Objection 105

Seventh-day Adventists, in their opposition to Sunday laws, show themselves to be in league with the disreputable elements of the country.

It does not follow that because two individuals or organizations oppose a measure they are actuated by the same motive. Indeed, they often have nothing in common. One man opposes unrestricted immigration because he conscientiously feels that only by restriction can the great mass of undesirables be kept out of the country. Another opposes the same measure for the selfish reason that he does not want to see any competition in the field of labor, for fear he will not be able to demand his own price for his work. How altogether different are the motives prompting these two men! Yet both are on the same side—the opposition—as to the measure.

Again: Some men favor unrestricted immigration, and for the reason that they wish the downtrodden of Europe to have a chance in this country, whereas others—certain unscrupulous employers —support such a measure because they feel that it will result in cheap labor for their factories. Philanthropist and profiteer on the same side. Strange? No, a most common occurrence. Do we accuse one of being in league with the other? No—that is, not if we have regard to the truthfulness of our statements and the correctness of our logic.

Thus it is with us and Sunday legislation. We oppose it because it is a violation of the principles of religious liberty. The disreputable elements oppose Sunday laws because such laws take away from them their most lucrative day for business. There is nothing in common between us. In drawing this sharp contrast between ourselves and the disreputable elements, we do not wish to convey the thought that all other opponents of Sunday laws besides ourselves belong to the disreputable group. There are

433

many citizens who for a variety of very proper reasons may oppose Sunday laws.

The stand taken by Seventh-day Adventists is that any business or institution that is sufficiently questionable to justify closing it on one day, should be closed every day in the week. Thus we are seven times more opposed to these evil elements than the most ardent Sunday law advocate with his one-day-a-week closing measure. Take, for example, our militant fight for prohibition through many years. When many church people seemed willing to compromise by seeking only a Sunday closing of saloons, we worked to have them shut up seven days in the week, 365 days in the year.

# Objection 106

We do not hold this position. In the writings of Mrs. E. G. White, whom our opponents so frequently declare is our chief exponent of doctrine, are found these words:

"Among the heathen are those who worship God ignorantly, those to whom the light is never brought by human instrumentality, yet they will not perish. Though ignorant of the written law of God, they have heard His voice speaking to them in nature, and have done the things that the law required. Their works are evidence that the Holy Spirit has touched their hearts, and they are recognized as the children of God."—*The Desire of Ages*, p. 638.

Could any utterance be more liberal? We doubt whether the objector would subscribe to such a pronouncement. He would hold that it was *too* liberal. But surely we cannot be at once too narrow and too broad in our teaching on this vital question. We cannot be expected to plead guilty to both charges. No. We plead innocent of both, and offer the following as being the teaching of Seventh-day Adventists on the matter of salvation.

We agree unreservedly with the inspired statement: "Believe on the Lord Jesus Christ, and thou shalt be saved." Acts 16:31. Yet no Christian would hold that in the Scriptures "saved" means no more than being relieved from the punishment for sin. That is, of course, all-important; but he who would be saved from the wages of sin must first of all be saved from the practice of sin, as promised, "He shall save his people from their sins" (Matt. 1:21); and again in Romans 8:1-4 it is declared, as summed up in verse 4, that Christ gave His life for man, "that the righteousness of the law might be fulfilled in us, who walk not after the flesh, but after the Spirit."

Conversion is more than a philosophical change of the mind;

it is, as declared in John 3:5-8, a new birth. The first assent of the mind, that recognition of the need of divine help, which prepares the way for conversion, must be followed by wholehearted yielding to the will of God under the transforming power of the Holy Spirit; this is the new birth declared by Christ to be absolutely essential to salvation.

And this must be followed by growth in grace and in "the knowledge of our Lord and Saviour Jesus Christ." 2 Peter 3:18. When we first believe, we are as babes; but as we feed upon God's Word we grow. As we see more clearly the righteous requirements of the Bible and accept them, we become stronger and stronger Christians. This growth is to continue. "He which hath begun a good work in you will perform it until the day of Jesus Christ." Phil. 1:6. So long as a Christian continues to grow, that is, to walk in harmony with the fuller light that the Bible seeks increasingly to bring to his heart and mind, he is on the road that leads to the kingdom of God.

# Objection 107

**Seventh-day Adventists are calamity howlers.**

This charge is only a half-truth, since an examination of our books and magazines will reveal the fact that almost all of the so-called calamity-howling paragraphs are in quotation marks. And those quotation marks are significant because they inclose the words of some well-known authority in the political, social, religious, educational, or economic world.

You may pick up a representative issue of our papers and read an article portraying the awful increase of crime among the youth of the nation. But you will find that the most doleful portions of it are merely excerpts from authentic and indisputable official records or from the published statements of some judge or leading educator who is an authority on the subject. You may read an article in our journals telling of the dark future before the world, but a close examination discloses that the picture is painted dark, not by our writer, but by the renowned world statesmen whom he quotes. Again, you may perhaps glance through one of our editorials, which brings forward the charge that material advancement is no criterion of moral progress, and that the marvelous scientific inventions of our age are but means to our destruction. But upon rereading, you observe that authoritative quotations form the background of the editorial.

Not to "howl" about calamities, but to give the Bible explanation of them, is our work. When statesmen, presidents, and prime ministers are declaring that there is something wrong with the world and that the future is dark with a nameless dread, it behooves every clear-thinking man to inquire, What do these things mean? To arouse men everywhere to a realization of the seriousness of the times in which we live, and then to give them the solution of the perplexing question, is our task. We endeavor to arouse by quoting from those who are authorities on world conditions; and then we strive, as a people with a message for this time, to prepare men for the climax that is ahead by turning the Bible searchlight on the problem.

In actual fact Adventists are sharply distinguished from the doleful-voiced world authorities, who see only darkness and destruction ahead. We see, through the eyes of Bible prophets, a bright world beyond, even a "new heavens and a new earth, wherein dwelleth righteousness."

Indeed, as the shadows deepen over the world, and men's hearts increasingly fail them for fear, only those who believe in the Second Advent of Christ can truly be joyful. The great men of the world reveal that they are powerless to grapple with the fearful problems that threaten to take all peace from the world. Only the Prince of Peace can provide a way of escape. That is why we preach Christ's coming. And that is why we are truly happy. If the objector would listen more attentively, he would discover that our emphasis is not on the calamities impending, but on the joyous delivery of the righteous out of those calamities.

# Objection 108

Seventh-day Adventism is a new ism, and holds new and un-Scriptural doctrines.

This charge is a half-truth; true as regards the length of time this denomination as such has existed, false as regards the nature of the doctrines it holds.

As to the newness of our denomination, we would state simply that if age is the criterion of relative religious worth, then the Catholic Church is on a much higher plane than all the Protestant churches, and Buddhism still higher than Catholicism. But what fallacious reasoning! As to our teaching new and un-Biblical doctrines, we would say: One of the chief characteristics of our doctrines is their antiquity; and for all of them we have a "Thus saith the Lord," as the copious Scriptural references in all our books and papers attest.

Take, for example, our teaching concerning the Sabbath. This doctrine was given at creation (Gen. 2:2, 3) and incorporated in the earliest Scriptural code of laws, the Decalogue, fifteen hundred years before Christ. (See Ex. 20:2-17.) In this connection it might be added that almost in the same breath most of our opponents charge us with teaching *new* doctrines and with holding to an *"old Jewish Sabbath."* How a dogma can be at once both new and old they do not explain.

In teaching the doctrine of the second coming of Christ, that "the Lord cometh with ten thousands of his saints, to execute judgment upon all," we repeat the words of Enoch, "the seventh from Adam." Jude 14, 15. The antiquity of that doctrine, therefore, is not open to question.

Our belief that a meatless diet is the ideal can hardly be termed new. Adam and Eve were given a vegetarian dietary, and by the Lord Himself. (See Gen. 1:29.)

ANSWERS TO OBJECTIONS

From primitive times God's people have had the blessing of prophets, and have believed in the principle of prophetic guidance. (See Gen. 20:7; Ex. 15:20.) We believe that the gift of prophecy still belongs to the church. Certainly there is nothing new about this doctrine.

We believe that Christians should pay tithe. But we refer to such men as Abraham and other most ancient worthies for our precedent. (See Gen. 14:20.)

Our doctrines of a personal devil, who is responsible for sin, of a creation by the fiat of Almighty God, of a literal Second Advent, and of a punishment by fire of all sinners are in harmony with the teachings of Bible writers thousands of years ago, and—mark this too!—they are in harmony with the teachings of the founders of most of the Protestant churches, as their creeds and confessions will testify. The evolution doctrine, which banishes creation and finds no room for the Advent; the view that sin is only imaginary, and that somehow all will finally be saved, *these* are new teachings. Yet they are given out from many Protestant pulpits today. Not Seventh-day Adventists, but popular preachers are the promulgators of new and un-Scriptural doctrines.

The reason for our existence as a denomination is not to give out new doctrines but to restate the old and proved ones and to "contend for the faith which was once delivered unto the saints." Jude 3. In doing so we realize that we must often teach contrary to the popular view. But if the extent of one's departure from accepted teaching is the measure of one's heresy, then the early apostles were the greatest heretics who ever lived. Indeed, they were accused by the nominal people of God of turning the "world upside down." (See Acts 17:5, 6.)

In giving to men the everlasting gospel and the messages of warning for this time, every Seventh-day Adventist is willing to face the charge of heresy, saying with the mighty evangelist Paul: "After the way which they call heresy, so worship I the God of my fathers, *believing all things which are written in the law and in the prophets.*" Acts 24:14.

# Objection 109

**Seventh-day Adventists have a prophet like many other of the modern isms, and they make of her writings a second Bible.**

The very way in which this charge is framed would lead the ordinary reader to the conclusion that because certain modern cults have as one of their characteristics the presence of prophets whose messages certainly do not come from God, therefore any denomination possessing a prophet must be in the same class with these isms. They would have us infer that the term "prophet" should always be coupled with "false." But is this necessarily true? Because there are false prophets, does it therefore follow that all prophets are false? Because there is counterfeit money, does it therefore follow that all money is counterfeit? Certainly not. Where there is counterfeit, there is also genuine; where there is false, there is also true.

In an age when such a distorted idea possesses the minds of almost all regarding the relation of prophecy to God's plan of salvation, it is necessary that the history of the doctrine be gone over briefly in order for us to obtain a correct conception of the issue at hand. Unenlightened on it, we shall surely fall into one of two grievous difficulties: either we shall take up with anything that possesses uncanny powers, or else we shall turn down everything that claims supernatural origin. To do the first is to become hopelessly lost; to do the second is to go contrary to the divine command, "Despise *not* prophesyings." 1 Thess. 5:20. Instead, we should pursue the middle course, and "try the spirits whether they are of God." 1 John 4:1.

All through the history of God's dealing with His people there have been prophets and prophetesses. From the days of Moses and Miriam, through the times of Deborah, Huldah, and Anna, a prophetess "of a great age" in the time of Christ, even to the last years of the apostolic period, when the four daughters of Philip the evangelist "did prophesy," God has seen fit to give His instruction to the church through the agency of men and women upon whom He has placed the Spirit of prophecy. (See Ex. 15:20; Judges 4:4; 2 Kings 22:14; Luke 2:36; Acts 21:8, 9.) Finally, the Bible tells us explicitly that the church in the closing days of its earthly history will possess this gift. (See Rev. 12:17; cf. Rev. 19:10.)

So necessary did Solomon regard the gift of prophecy that he wrote, "Where there is no vision, the people *perish*." Prov. 29:18. And there is no reason to believe that in these last days, when every kind of deception and heresy is abroad, when the very elect are in danger of being ensnared (see Matt. 24:24), the statement of Solomon should be any less applicable than in his day.

Further, it is clear that God has given instruction to His church through prophets without adding to the permanent body of Sacred Writings. Have we not many cases in the Scriptures where prophets gave messages, both written and verbal, which most certainly were inspired, but which form no part of the Bible? Assuredly. (See 2 Chron. 9:29; Acts 21:8, 9.)

With this foundation laid, we are prepared to draw the Scriptural conclusion that the presence of a prophet in the church need not necessarily be a sign that that denomination is false. On the contrary, it may be the best evidence possible that God is especially directing that movement. We may also conclude that one may be a true prophet of God, giving out inspired utterances without stating that which should be considered in any sense an addition to the great standard of truth, the Bible.

It is not within the scope of this short answer to prove that the writings of Mrs. E. G. White, whom we regard as having possessed the gift of prophecy, are of God. The writings themselves furnish the best proof of their divine origin. However, we do not therefore hold that these writings, though inspired, should be considered as a second Bible or an addition to it. In this we are consistent with our foregoing conclusions. "The written testimonies," it is explained in Mrs. White's published works, "are *not to give new light*, but to impress vividly upon the heart the truths of inspiration already revealed. Man's duty to God and to his fellow man *has been distinctly specified in God's word;* yet but few of you are obedient to the light given. *Additional truth is not brought out;* but God has through the Testimonies *simplified the great truths already given.*"—*Testimonies for the Church,* vol. 2, p. 605.

In closing, we desire to ask the objector two questions: If you hold that true prophets do not belong to this age, are you prepared to maintain the logical inference that God has acted partially, and has been more gracious to men in past ages than to us who live in this most perilous time of the church? But seeing that the scriptures cited in this chapter clearly show that the gift of prophecy belongs to, and will be found in, the true church in these days, how do you explain its absence from the church of which you are a member?

# Part II

## IN EIGHT SECTIONS

# Section I

# SCIENCE AND THE ADVENT FAITH

# CHAPTER 1

# A Reasonable Faith

OUR MODERN times have been distinguished above all else by the marvelous advances made in the field of natural science. Men have probed the far depths of space with telescopes and unraveled the mysteries of the infinitely small with microscopes. They have explored and exploded the atom. They have discovered and measured the laws that operate in many areas of nature. They have conquered innumerable diseases. All this modern men have done as a result of becoming better acquainted with certain of nature's laws.

Now, as scientists delved ever more deeply into the physical world, they thought they discovered that the laws of nature are unchangeable, invariable. For example, could they not forecast what the sun, moon, and stars would do in the future? And was this not because these heavenly bodies operated according to laws that change not? Thus, to many scientific minds the universe took on the quality of a machine, each part operating like a cog, and the whole going on endlessly without possibility of change, because for some reason the whole universe is constituted that way.

## A False Attempt at Harmony

Certain religionists, who came to be known as modernists, thought they ought to accept what seemed to be the sure results of scientific investigation. At the same time they wished to hold on to religion. They did this by reinterpreting all the historic Christian beliefs in such a way as to harmonize them with the scientific views.

This modernizing process started with the idea of God Himself. He began to be viewed more and more as a kind of impersonal force in the universe. That eased the tension that naturally exists between the idea of a personal God who doeth all things according to His good pleasure, and a universe operating according to a set of unchangeable laws that make it function like an impersonal machine. But what the harmonizers gained in relief from tension of ideas, they more than lost by the disappearance of the soul-satisfying belief in a personal God to whom we can pray.

The harmonizing, which began with God, had to go all the way through Christian beliefs. If the universe operates by unchangeable laws, and has always done so, then all the Bible miracles had to be explained away, because miracles are contrary to the known operation of natural laws. That included the creation, the virgin birth, the resurrection, and the ascension. The Bible accounts of creation and the virgin birth were labeled legends. The resurrection was spiritualized away, so that a kind of ghostly, spiritualized Christ moved about before the eyes of the disciples after that resurrection Sunday. The belief in a literal Second Advent of Christ disappeared, and for the same reason. Thus disappeared the most basic of Christian doctrines.

Now, it is evident that the application of such harmonizing methods to Adventist beliefs would do away with most of them. Certainly there is no place for the seventh-day Sabbath. Why keep a memorial of an event that really did not take place? There was no literal creation week with its seventh day set apart, say the harmonizers. And, of course, we could hardly be Adventists, because, as stated, there is no place for the literal Advent of Christ if one's views are modernist.

No wonder the Seventh-day Adventist Church views modernism and all the reasoning associated with it as a deadly foe to its faith and to all that this movement stands for. It is not that we are opposed to science. We have science departments in all our colleges, where the most modern principles of scientific study and research are not only accepted but applied. We believe in all the facts of science, in all that the test tube and the laboratory can disclose to us of the mysteries of nature. We differ with others not regarding the *facts* of science but regarding the *interpretation* that they place upon the facts.

It is right at this point that a difficulty arises for some in our ranks, particularly for those who have received a higher education in non-Adventist schools. They know that scientists have made great discoveries that have revolutionized the world and opened vast vistas before us. Naturally they view with awe the scientists who make such discoveries. And when they find these scientists interpreting, in a certain way, the facts revealed by test tube, microscope, or telescope, these Adventist youth are tempted to feel that that is the correct interpretation. But, if the scientists' interpretation *is* correct, then there must be something the matter with Seventh-day Adventist doctrine. Hence, there arises in the minds of some Adventists the temptation to feel that Seventh-day Adventism is archaic, out of date, in its views and beliefs. And that is a long step toward apostasy.

We may be thankful to God that there are not many of our members who have apostatized for this reason, but there are some, and doubtless there will be others in the future as the membership grows larger. Nor would we confine the danger to advanced schools. Wrong patterns of thought regarding God and the origin of our world may be formed in the grammar grades or in high school.

### How to Meet the Danger

It is far better for us to face the danger openly, and thus place ourselves definitely on guard. Our hope does not lie in putting an absolute ban on attendance at non-Adventist institutions. There are certain instances where it is absolutely necessary for some to attend for specialized training. Indeed, the church has no authority to enforce a ban, even if it wished to do so.

Our hope lies in pointing out clearly the dangers and in offering a better interpretation of the facts of science. The Advent movement has nothing to fear from facts, scientific or otherwise. We believe that the God whom we serve is the God who made all the universe, who established its laws. Hence, we ought to be the most ardent students of nature, exploring ever more fully its mysteries, and thus entering into the antechamber, as it were, of the great God whom we love and serve.

It is impossible to emphasize too much the primary point, that the facts of science and the interpretation placed upon the facts are two different things. It is a fact, for example, that the stars in their courses operate according to laws whose workings can be forecast. That is why we can have a nautical almanac to guide mariners. It is a fact that a planet of our own solar system maintains certain relationships to other planets and to the sun and moon. But it is an interpretation of the facts to declare that this proves that the universe is a machine, that there is no place for a God, and that if there is a God, He cannot change His laws without wrecking the universe.

Adventists, along with all conservative Christians, give a different interpretation to the facts. We see in these laws governing all the heavenly bodies so beautifully and efficiently, not simply great laws, but a great Lawgiver. Indeed, we consider it entirely an unreasonable attitude for one who has discovered that the universe conforms to law to argue that this proves there is no Lawgiver, no personal God.

Let us imagine, for a moment, that the universe is not orderly, that there is no evidence of any laws governing or coordinating heavenly bodies. Let us picture them, therefore, as going helter-skelter, in unpredictable fashion, so that astronomers break out in cold perspiration for fear that at any moment there will be a general smashup. We wonder what scientists would think of those who argued that such a universe gives evidence of a personal God, a directing mind. We think that when the astronomers were not wiping the cold perspiration from their brows, they would be laughing cynically.

But the scientists have not discovered a disorganized universe. They have found one moving with such intricate precision that they can find no better analogy than that of a machine to describe

A REASONABLE FAITH

the marvelously coordinated working of all the parts. Yet many scientists seem to forget that if the universe resembles a marvelous machine, then somewhere in the picture must stand a marvelous Inventor of the machine. Adventists accept all the facts of the amazingly machinelike precision of the universe, but insist on interpreting those facts in terms of the great Inventor of the machine. We go one step further—we insist that a marvelously intricate machine calls not only for an Inventor but for a Sustainer of it. No machine will run by itself, and the more intricate, the more in need of constant personal supervision.

Some scientists and those religious people who want to harmonize religion with science will declare vehemently that they believe in God, and perhaps they may even believe in a not-too-vague or vaporous God. But they insist that changing in any way the operation of the laws of nature would bring chaos into the universe, and for this reason it is irrational to believe in miracles. What such persons do not seem to realize is that here again they are setting forth, not a fact of science, but an interpretation of the facts. Science has only the most elementary knowledge of the mysteries of nature and of how the laws of nature operate. How do we know that God could not invoke some law of which we have no knowledge, which would hold in check a presently known law, without violating that law and without creating chaos in the universe?

### Reasoning Plausible but False

Let us take a simple illustration, drawn from the Middle Ages. At that time there were wise men who doubted the claims of some that the world is round. They were absolutely certain that if it really were round, no one could live on the underside of it. Was it not evident that such persons would be upside down, and therefore would fall off into space? Hold an orange in the air and place a midget doll on its feet on the underside. Is not the doll upside down? Release your hold. Does not the doll fall to the floor immediately? Probably in the history of human thought no piece of reasoning ever seemed more transparently clear and undebatable than this medieval argument that people could not live on the lower side of a round world. How impressively could they argue that the very idea was contrary to the most evident facts of life that could be tested.

What was the trouble with the reasoning of these medievalists? Simply this: They had not reckoned with the law of gravitation, a law at that time unknown. Gravitation is a mysterious force exerted by a body to draw other bodies toward it, with the strength of the drawing power in ratio to the size of the body. The world is very large in relation to man, and so man is held tightly to the earth, no matter where on the earth he may stand. The medieval wise men did not know that if this law of gravitation were not operating, men could as easily fall off into space on the "top" side of the earth as on the "under" side of it. What would there be to hinder them?

We laugh at those men of long ago. Their erstwhile convincing argument stands revealed today as wholly foolish, and for the simple reason that they were ignorant of one law of nature, the law of gravitation. The facts are that this medieval reasoning began to be abandoned even before the law of gravitation was formally set forth by Sir Isaac Newton in the seventeenth century. And why? Because sailors began to travel around the world without falling off. No argument, no matter how plausible, about men falling off the underside of the world could last very long against the testimony of men who had been "down under" and had not fallen off. In other words, the testimony of men who had been sustained and protected, as it were, on the mysterious trip around the world and brought safely home again proved that there must be a fallacy in the reasoning of the wise men, even though at first no one knew where the fallacy lay. Sir Isaac Newton, by formulating the law of gravity, simply explained *why* men do not fall off the "under" side of the world.

Strictly speaking, he did not explain the law of gravitation; he only described it. Neither he nor anyone else from his day onward has been able to explain the mystery of gravity. Great as has been the work of scientists, there have been real limitations to their work. They describe, sometimes in vague outline and sometimes in greater detail, the workings of the laws of nature; but they do not really explain these laws. And there is a world of difference in this.

If scientists cannot really explain the mystery of the great laws, such as gravity or electromagnetism, are they not on dangerous ground when they dogmatize regarding the character of these laws and the chaos that would follow if God should hold in check some law? Seeing that they cannot truly explain the mystery of the laws that they have discovered, how do they know but that some other law, of which they as yet know nothing, may not force them in time to provide us a somewhat different description of the presently known laws? Might not the discovery of some new law make a great deal of plausible scientific reasoning today seem as foolish as the medieval reasoning concerning the impossibility of people living on the "under" side of the world?

### Has the Crane Operator Brought Chaos?

As Christians we need not be overawed when some interpreter of the facts of science assures us, with a dogmatism never exceeded by a medieval theologian, that it is unreasonable to think of God's interfering with any of the laws of nature, that indeed any interference would cause chaos. Such a person should go out to a railroad yard and watch a mighty electromagnet, suspended from a crane, lift tons of scrap iron from the ground high into the air. The pieces of iron seem to fly upward toward the magnet, and then are carried still higher by the crane.

If we personified gravitation, we might imagine its crying out from the earth that violence was being done to it by the operator of the crane, that it was contrary to the laws of nature for objects to fly upward from the earth. But is not the crane operator employing a law of nature when he uses the electromagnet? And does chaos ensue because these two laws actually operate at times in a way to make one neutralize the other? Of course, the man who controls the electromagnetic crane might cause a minor chaos by using the force within his power in an irrational way. But that is something else. Reference will be made later to the factor of the lawless action of man's free will.

Now, we need not go out to the railroad yard in order to see a law of nature being suddenly held in check. All one needs to do is hold his hat in his hand. No, the illustration is not absurd, except as it shows the absurdity of those who argue that nature's laws cannot be interfered with except at the risk of chaos in the universe. The reason the hat does not fall to the floor is that another law is operating, a law which is the expression of the mind of the man who holds the hat. He does not wish it to fall to the floor, and he gives expression to his wish and will through the muscles of his hand.

Here is the will, the law, if you please, of the mind of a man, operating to hold in check another law—the law of gravitation. But did chaos follow as a result of the man's expressing his will in a way that prevented the law of gravity from operating on a particular object, the hat? No! In fact, the law of gravity was still operating while the hat was being held. It was simply that the law of the mind of the man, expressed through the muscles of his body, was stronger than the law of gravitation.

CHAPTER 2

# Miracles and Natural Law

THE ORDERLY operating of the laws of nature that so amazes both scientists and devout religionists, may be viewed simply as a revelation of the orderly way in which God carries on the activities of His universe. These laws are not a group of independent entities; they are but the expression of the will and the mind of God. It is God who is unchangeable. That is why the scientist, in viewing the laws of nature, sees in them absolute consistency and dependability.

But the God of nature, who is far more jealous than the scientist about order in His universe, is not the slave of His laws. How could a personal being be the slave of that which is simply an expression of His own will and mind? Can He not extend His hand, as it were, to invoke some law of which we may not know anything today, and thus stay the operation of various laws that the scientists have been so faithfully watching? Why is it so scientific and reasonable to believe that the God, whom we know so imperfectly, and whose laws we understand in such small part, must always confine Himself to an expression of His will and purposes in terms of those few partially known laws? And if a scientist agrees, as he does, that the law of gravitation is not violated and no chaos ensues when a man lifts an object from the floor, why should anyone say that it is contrary to scientific laws, and thus impossible to believe, for example, that God will lift men bodily out of this world by translation at the day of Christ's Second Advent?

Of course most modernists and some scientists will say at this point: "We are not contending for a moment that God could not lift men up, but simply that it is unreasonable to believe that He would, in view of all that we know of the way that the universe operates, and that therefore no credence should be placed in the Bible story of translation or of any other miracle."

## An Objection Examined

The idea is supposed to be unreasonable on two grounds: first, that God ought not to be viewed as relating Himself in such a personal, realistic fashion to man; second, that the day-by-day events in nature round about us, which include no acts of translation or of other miracles, provide a far stronger reason for believing that such an event will never take place, than the words of a prophet provide for believing that it will.

The only answer necessary on the first point is this: How do men know just what is reasonable for God to do? How do they know God so certainly? On the second point, it is necessary only to restate what has been said in a little different connection, that the limited knowledge we have of the laws of nature does not warrant the conclusion that an event different from what we now experience might not or could not take place. On the contrary, there is good reason for believing that some very unusual event ought to take place soon if either we or the modernists and scientists are to retain our faith in the most basic premise in the reasoning of all of us; namely, that there is order and system and law in the universe.

That brings us to another phase of the subject, the relation of the moral realm to the physical. This world of ours gives evidence that there are two kinds of laws operating: laws in the physical realm and laws in the moral. And of course we who believe in God naturally believe that both kinds of laws are an expression of one will and one mind. Now, no matter what may be a man's religious belief, he will certainly admit that the laws that operate in the moral realm are being outrageously violated on every side, violated more dangerously than ever before, and that such violation is a threat to the very life of this world and all upon it.

# MIRACLES AND NATURAL LAW

Nothing could better illustrate this fact and also the fact of the interaction of physical and moral law than the discoveries in the field of atomic energy. These discoveries are a crowning work of brilliant scientific minds. Great physical laws have been explored and exploited to produce the most terrifying thing ever to come from human hands, an atomic bomb. But the bomb was no sooner produced than we all discovered that its probable uses would gravely violate moral laws. Yes, moral laws can be violated, held in check, the same as physical laws, and by the same means, the operation of the mind and the will of man. The free will of man, which can operate counter to a natural law by lifting a hat from the ground, can also operate counter to a moral law by striking the owner of the hat to the ground.

## Atomic Bomb Emphasizes Key Fact

The atomic bomb today has simply brought into sharp focus a fact that should have been evident to all before; namely, that moral laws and physical laws are closely related; and that if the free will of man be allowed to operate indefinitely without any supernatural intervention, chaos certainly could ensue for our world. What is it we hear the scientists on every side saying today? Simply this: That unless we have some accepted controls for atomic power, unless we are all willing to obey some moral principles in regard to the use of this power, we shall blow ourselves and our world to pieces someday erelong.

Yes, contrary to the whole tenor and temper of the scientific world, which has always thought of all physical processes as measured and slow and predictable in their operation, scientists are the ones who today shout from the housetops about sudden, explosive events that will shatter the world, events that have no parallel in history. And they explain that these events, which normally would have been considered incredible, must now be viewed as possible because science has discovered how to use certain laws of nature that were not understood before.

Let us gather together the threads of these sorry facts, and see what pattern they produce. There are moral as well as physical laws. Man, exercising his free will, often goes contrary to the moral laws, producing every variety of tragedy. Today the possibility of tragedy is raised to the intensity of world explosion and oblivion for all of us. That explosion can be sudden and of a magnitude undreamed of in past generations. Beyond that point science is silent. Perhaps scientists consider it pointless to reason beyond the explosion!

But we must carry the matter a little further, for here lies a most important truth. If there is now the frightful probability that unless checked, man will exercise his free will, in relation to physical and moral laws, to produce chaos and annihilation; and if there be no other being in the universe who is free to exercise his will to stay man's hand, then what kind of universe do we have?

## The Mood of the Cynic

A cynic may wish to minimize the question by remarking, blithely or cynically, that our speck of a world is hardly significant in a vast universe. But, if beings on this world have a free will to exercise their knowledge to blow themselves and the world apart, may not the beings on all other worlds have as much knowledge as we and also free will? There is no valid scientific reason for giving a negative answer to this question. We would therefore expand the question and ask, with increased emphasis, What kind of universe do we have? The answer is ready: We have a universe that could become chaos, so far as inhabited worlds are concerned. And that chaos would result from the orderly operating of certain natural laws—laws that apply to the atom—and the disorderly operating of free moral agents in relation to moral laws.

But is this the kind of universe that the modernists have pictured as they have sought to harmonize religion with science? No matter how much they have been willing to sacrifice their religious beliefs to scientific dogmas, modernists have tried to retain the idea that there is order and plan and purpose in the universe. To surrender that elemental idea is to cut loose from everything sure and certain in one's thinking. To cut loose from that is to take all moral meaning out of life and all meaning out of religion.

There are those who do cut loose in this way. There are certain scientists and philosophers who boldly declare that the universe is a blind machine operating with no plan or purpose. Hence it is simply our misfortune if man becomes so wise and so wicked as to hasten us into oblivion via the atomic bomb. But those who thus declare are not quite consistent. The idea of progress, so firmly believed, until recently, by the whole educated world, including the cynics, is really a denial of the doctrine of a purposeless universe.

Now, proceeding on the premise that there is purpose and plan in the universe, must we not believe that there dwells somewhere in our universe an omnipotent being who is also possessed of free will to stay the hand of lawless beings who dwell in His universe? Unless we thus believe, how can we at one and the same time admit that finite beings can create chaos in the universe, and claim that there is plan and purpose to the universe?

### Why Consider Divine Intervention Impossible?

And why should it be thought a thing incredible and contrary to science for God to intervene suddenly to prevent the sudden destruction of our world at the hands of men who have violated the moral laws which proceed from the throne of God? Is there anything more incredible or irrational in the idea of the heavens suddenly opening for God to appear to stay the hand of those "which destroy the earth" (Rev. 11:18) than in the idea of the earth itself suddenly opening here, there, and elsewhere over its wretched extent, under the explosive forces released by the free will of sinful men? Does not the greatness of the impending tragedy of our world demand some great and unusual event?

There is no more breaking of the orderly operations of nature, as we have measured them through the years, by the sudden bathing of the world in the flaming light of the Second Advent, than by the sudden bathing of the world in the flaming light of atomic rays. Both are out of the common order. Only a few short years ago men would have been as ready to dismiss as fantastic and contrary to known laws the idea of an explosive, atomic cloud over our world, as the idea of the coming of Jesus Christ in the clouds of heaven.

## Contrast Between Advent and Atomic Explosion

Both ideas deal with a sudden and incredible event. But here their similarity ends. The atomic explosion takes meaning and purpose out of the drama of our world, its joys and sorrows, its hopes and fears. But the coming of Jesus Christ gives meaning and purpose to the drama. The Advent reveals that the God who is long-suffering and patient, who is waiting in the shadows to allow man a probationary period in which to exercise his free will, is suddenly doing His "strange work," invoking laws that He does not commonly invoke, in order to prevent man from finally tearing apart a world that God designed for a purpose. The literal Second Advent of Christ is our assurance that God will not allow sinful men to operate their free will beyond a certain point, that He will not allow the righteous forever to suffer with the wicked in this world.

Belief in the Bible and in its record of miracles does not demand, as modernists and most scientists charge, that the Christian believe that some magical event may be expected to happen at almost any moment, any day. The Bible picture of the miraculous relationship of God to man is one of specially selected moments in history, moments that are often far apart. The Scriptures are filled with records of long periods when history moved on in sadly routine fashion. One who reads the Bible with the thought of a great plan of God is impressed that the occasional miracles recorded serve a very special purpose. In other words, they reveal, not disorder and violation of laws, but special order and a vindication of the inviolability of God's greatest laws, His moral laws.

The Bible does not present, through its record of thousands of years, a long series of virgin births, resurrections, and ascensions.

There is only one virgin birth described in the whole history of the Bible. Why did the Bible prophets, who, according to modernists, thought only in terms of their day and thus believed in every variety of magical event, speak of only one virgin birth? Why did they narrow down all their amazing predictions to one Person? Why did they describe Him, and Him alone, as being God manifest in the flesh? They lived in a world dominated by the pagan idea that the gods were like men, that they cohabited with earthly beings, and thus were often manifest in the flesh. The pagans believed in a number of virgin births. How did the Bible prophets escape so completely from all these ideas that surrounded them on every side, and present to us only one glorious instance of a virgin birth?

The Christian who reads his Bible with a view to the sweep of the ages sees the recorded miracle of the virgin birth, of God manifest in the flesh, as one of those few special instances where God has broken through into history, as it were, and invoked laws not commonly set in operation in order to carry out some part of a great plan for the world.

The Christian who accepts the Bible picture of man views this world not as some orderly sphere where man is ever progressing upward, but as a world disorganized, torn apart by forces contrary to the will of God. He therefore sees in those rare moments of divine intervention in earthly history the occasions when God is seeking in a special way to give impetus to His plan to salvage something out of this disordered world and to bring ultimate order out of moral chaos.

We see in the miracles that cluster around the first advent of Christ simply so many special proofs given by God to validate the amazing claims made by His Son, claims which must be accepted by men if they are to be saved through Jesus Christ. Let wise men offer any more effective way for validating Christ's claims than those set forth in Scripture. Here was a Being who declared that He could save men from sin. How could He prove that He could accomplish this inner work for man?

When the rabbis questioned in their minds regarding His assurance to the impotent man that his sins were forgiven, Christ raised the question as to whether it is more difficult to say, Thy sins be forgiven thee, than to say, Rise up and walk. And then to prove to them that He could do that inner work that their eyes could not see, He did an outer work that they could see, a work which could be done by no mere human being. He caused the impotent man to rise to his feet and to go away rejoicing.

Likewise, we see in the occasional miracles performed by prophets of God the same purpose of validation of their claims to be speaking for God. There is reason and purpose in the miracles of the Bible, even though they transcend our understanding of physical laws. Their reason is to be found in their consistency with moral laws and in the purposes of God to bring moral order into this world.

As touching the initial miracle of the Bible, the creation of the world, why are modernists and others who reject the Genesis story so dogmatic about what could, or could not, have happened? Scientists cannot even define what life is, and yet there can be no beginning of creatures upon this earth, bird or beast or man, without life. And if life departs, all creatures turn to dust again.

True, scientists do know some definite things about life. They know that life cannot be considered in the abstract, as something floating mysteriously in the air. Life can be conceived of only in terms of a living creature. Whenever we see a living creature there is one scientific conclusion of which we can be sure; that is, that there was a living creature that preceded it. The presence of a living being at any time in past ages demands that we believe that there was a living being before it that gave to it life.

The rigid logic of all this demands, finally, that there be at least one eternal source of life, one Eternal Being. Conservative Christians follow that logic without any difficulty; in fact, they insist on it. Now, if in the beginning we picture one eternally living Being, how are we to explain the later existence of a variety of living beings on a world like ours, for example? There is only one truly logical explanation, and that is that the ever-living Being willed to share a portion of His life with them.

Paul declared to the Athenians that God giveth to all men life and breath and all things, and that in Him we live and move and have our being. We describe this act on the part of God, in imparting a portion of His life to what would otherwise be dead clay, as an act of creation. We confess we know not how God does it; we simply say that there is no other explanation of how there could be on this world, or any other world, that mysterious phenomenon, a living creature, dust of the earth molded and made animate.

Skeptics have tried to avoid the force of this logic, and in two ways. Some have tried to push the question of the origin of life out into the vast reaches of interstellar space by theorizing that some spark of life might have been brought to our world by a meteorite. But obviously they have not escaped the force of the logic of an Eternal Being. How did life begin on that other world from which the meteor came? Would the skeptic have an endless supply of meteors? And where would the first meteor and the first world get their life?

### A Second Attempt to Escape Great Truth

A second way of attempting to meet the force of this logic of an Eternal Being is by arguing that in some way not yet understood chemical action may have taken place, indeed, must have taken place long ago, changing specks of dead earth into living forms, which forms, of course, later evolved into most complex creatures. This theory flies in the face of all that we know about the laws of nature as they apply to the origin of living creatures; namely, that life comes only from a preceding living being. In other words, the skeptic would really produce a miracle, a chemical miracle. It is correct to use the word *miracle* concerning his theory, for his very definition of a *miracle* is that it is something out of the ordinary course of nature, something that indeed goes contrary to all that we know about the laws of nature.

The difference between the skeptic's chemical miracle and a Christian miracle is that the skeptic, who fortunately does not represent all scientists, believes in such a miracle to escape believing in a creator God; the Christian's miracles take place to confirm men's faith in such a God. There is also a second great difference: Most of the Christian miracles are attested by many witnesses and are recorded in a Book that breathes the very spirit of truth and veracity. The alleged chemical miracle of the origin of life has no witnesses. It has reality only in the speculative mind of the skeptic, or in the interpretation he gives to elusive and equivocal reactions that he secures in certain experimentation.

# CHAPTER 3

# The Evolution Theory Examined

REGARDING the origin of life, Thomas Huxley, who coined the word *agnostic,* and who called himself Darwin's bulldog, so ardent was his advocacy of Darwin's evolutionist theories, made this statement:

"Looking back through the prodigious vista of the past, I find no record of the commencement of life, and therefore I am devoid of any means of forming a definite conclusion as to the conditions of its appearance. Belief, in the scientific sense of the word, is a serious matter, and needs strong foundations. To say, therefore, in the admitted absence of evidence, that I have any belief as to the mode in which the existing forms of life have originated, would be using words in a wrong sense. But expectation is permissible where belief is not; and if it were given me to look beyond the abyss of geologically recorded time to the still more remote period when the earth was passing through physical and chemical conditions, which it can no more see again than a man can recall his infancy, I should expect to be a witness to the evolution of living protoplasm from not living matter. I should expect to see it appear under forms of great simplicity, endowed, like existing fungi, with the power of determining the formation of new protoplasm from such matters as ammonium carbonates, oxalates and tartrates, alkaline and earthy phosphates, and water, without the aid of light. That is the expectation to which analogical reasoning leads me; but I beg you once more to recollect that I have no right to call my opinion anything but an act of philosophical faith."—*Discourses Biological and Geological,* pp. 256, 257.

### "An Act of Philosophical Faith"

Note that his "act of philosophical faith" is defended on the ground that his "analogical reasoning leads" him to it. The very logic of the theory that he has accepted concerning all life on this world demands the conclusion which he confessedly reaches by faith! He realizes that the world, as we know it today, does not offer any exhibits of life beginning from lifeless matter, and that there is no scientific evidence for it. So Huxley, moving into the realm of philosophical speculation, speaks of a long past time "when the earth was passing through physical and chemical conditions, which it can no more see again than a man can recall his infancy." In other words, something might have happened back there that could not happen now, though he reasons in a preceding paragraph that the future developments of science may disclose how to work this miracle in our day.

If such reasoning be rational, then is the Christian's reasoning also. The logic of our view of the nature and origin of all things calls for a different kind of beginning from that which Huxley pictures, a creation as described by Moses. And we who believe the Bible meet the objection that nothing like it occurs today by declaring that a different set of factors operated at the beginning, which cannot be duplicated today. We can even go a step further with Huxley, the mentor of all evolutionist logicians, and declare that the marvelous advances of science may someday help us to understand a little more clearly how a world could be made out of nothing. On this point we shall speak later.

The Bible skeptic will doubtless declare that even if it be granted—and some of them would grant—that an ever-living God is the explanation of all life, the observable facts concerning man and other living beings prove that the world did not start full fledged as Moses declared in Genesis, but on the contrary very minute living beings finally evolved into all the varied forms we now know, including man. Though it would carry us too far afield to discuss here all the so-called evidences for evolution, a few brief observations may be made.

The great majority of people are under the impression that in the nineteenth century a man named Charles Darwin made certain discoveries of the secrets of nature, and that his publication of his findings in 1859 in his book *Origin of Species* suddenly forced all reasonable-minded men to discard the idea of creation and to accept the idea of a gradual evolution upward.

But is it true that all the intellectual world up to the time of Darwin were confirmed believers in creation and were forced by the weight of Darwin's evidence to change their minds? No. The facts on this point are clear and undebatable. We will let an eminent intellectual, an evolutionist, speak:

### Word of Eminent Intellectual

"It is still true that the idea of Evolution, of change, growth, and development, has been the most revolutionary notion in man's thought about himself and his world in the last hundred years. This transformation of the setting of human life did not come about suddenly, overnight, it does not date from the justly epoch-making publication of Darwin's *Origin of Species* in 1859. Rather that event symbolized the new attitude that had in many ways been making its progress in men's thinking since the middle of the preceding century. Darwin's book, in fact, stands to our present-day scientific synthesis much as Newton's *Principia* stood to the earlier mechanical synthesis, as the confident marshaling of evidence and the systematic formulation in strictly scientific terms of a view that had already been for some time gaining acceptance by the best intellects. Both the rationalistic thinkers of the Enlightenment, in their growing emphasis on progress, and the romantic reaction, in its singling out of a process of development in time as the fundamental fact in human experience, had paved the way for a successful biological formulation of Evolution. Only such a state of affairs can explain the almost instantaneous acceptance of Darwin's doctrine when it was put forth in 1859."—JOHN HERMAN RANDALL, JR., *The Making of the Modern Mind,* p. 461.

In other words, the great majority of intellectuals had for long years preceding Darwin come increasingly under the spell of the idea that there is some kind of law operating in the world, and perhaps in all the universe, that urges everything onward and upward, so that there must be, in the very nature of the case, inevitable progress. This idea of progress was not built on scientific findings, laboratory data, or anything akin to them. It was a philosophical idea, a speculation, a very cheerful speculation at that, an idea not hard to believe. Men had the will to believe it. In fact, by the middle of the nineteenth century a great majority of intellectuals considered this idea rather well established.

What Darwin did was simply to offer a theory as to *how* the progress took place in the world of plants and animals. He talked of natural selection and the survival of the fittest. His theory was that minute differences between creatures of the same species finally pyramided over the ages until there were distinctly different species. He theorized too that weak and inferior creatures were generally killed off while the fittest survived. Thus there would be explained not only ever-increasing species and kinds and classes but a constantly improving world of animals and plants.

### Darwin's Theory Plausible

Obviously there was no way for Darwin to prove his theory correct, for the demonstration of it demanded long ages. But it was plausible, because it seemed to explain the facts of nature. Darwin did not present his theory to a hostile world, as we have noted, but to a very receptive world, a world that was waiting and longing for just such a theory. It is certainly no mystery that the theory was rapidly accepted. True, there were ardent theologians who stood out against it, but they were an exception.

When men want to believe something there is only one result that can happen: They will believe it, even though the evidence in behalf of it is shadowy and shaky and shot through with guesses. But once men have accepted an idea, particularly an idea that determines their viewpoint on the world at large, they begin to see everything through the glasses of that idea. In some small way we all have this experience from time to time. We remark, "I see this matter in an entirely different light from what I did before."

When men accepted Darwin's theory of evolution, facts in the physical world that formerly had not seemed to provide any proof for evolution suddenly began to take shape as unanswerable arguments in support of it. Take for illustration a major argument for evolution that is built on the bodily structure of animals. It had been evident to men before the days of Darwin that certain animals are small and very simply constructed; some, a little more complex; others, still more; and so on, until we come to man, the most complex creature of all.

Now, it took no brilliant scientist to discover the fact of these different degrees of complexity in the structure of animals, but it seemed to take Darwinian spectacles to enable men suddenly to discover in this fact an awesome, unanswerable argument for evolution. Could not men *see* creatures evolving before their eyes, as it were? Here was a panorama of the ages. Long ago there were only simple, one-celled creatures; then creatures with backbones; and finally man with a mind, and with all his complex organs and functions. Of course, it was unfortunate that all the poor one-celled creatures did not evolve upward, but additional theories soon began to be spun on every side to explain why only a few select ones came upward, and why all the unselect ones were not killed off. This graduation of complexity in animal structures is typical of the alleged evidence for evolution.

Here is a choice illustration of the difference between facts and the interpretation of the facts. It is a fact that there are creatures of increasingly complex structure all the way up to man, but it is an interpretation of the facts to say that this difference in structure is due to evolution. Bible believers do not take issue with the facts; they accept them heartily. But they think that those facts reveal something entirely different; namely, the plan and purpose of a great mind to populate the world, not with creatures all of one kind or class or complexity, but with different kinds, all the way from minute creatures up to man.

### God Planned for Variety

Indeed, we believe it would be strange if the great God confined Himself to any particular type or class or structure in the animal kingdom. We believe He wished for variety and that one form of that variety was the difference in complexity of structure. We see no reason to believe, therefore, that the more complexly constructed creatures evolved from the simpler ones; we think that the plan for all of them came forth, during creation week, from the mind of God.

To repeat, the basic difference between facts and the interpretation of the facts explains why Bible believers can look upon the various so-called evidences for evolution and be unimpressed by them. We interpret the evidence differently. We do not see the world through Darwin's glasses. We have never believed that there is some law of progress driving the world and the universe forward and upward. That is why we have never been driven to accept evolution.

So much in comment on the commonly held idea that Charles Darwin, in the middle of the nineteenth century, made certain great scientific discoveries which were so clear and convincing that they suddenly caused all reasonable-minded men to accept the idea of progress and evolution.

Let us now turn to a brief comment on the second commonly held idea on this subject; namely, that all the scientific investigation and discovery since Darwin's day have provided only added proof in behalf of evolution and nothing that goes counter to it.

### No Clear Proof Discovered

The facts are that nothing has been discovered in the scientific world from Darwin's day onward that has provided any clear and sure proof in behalf of evolution. All the evidence is what is termed circumstantial. Innocent men have been hanged on this kind of evidence, because such evidence can most easily be distorted or falsely interpreted through prejudice and passion.

There are two areas to which evolutionists have turned increasingly for evidence in support of their theory. Let us look first in the area of genetics. Genetics is the science that treats of heredity and inheritance. This science has made marvelous advances in the few decades since it became a well-defined branch of modern learning. We now know something definite concerning the laws that operate in the field of heredity and inheritance. We can determine, in advance, certain remarkable variations that will take place in the numerous generations of a certain species of fruit fly for example, a creature much used in such experimental work.

But these variations that present themselves are simply manifestations of different potential variations that existed in the parents. In other words, the extent and range of variations that can display themselves are predetermined by varying qualities and characteristics resident in the germ cell of the parent. This much seems to be well established in the scientific world. But this provides no proof for evolution. If anything, it seems to argue against evolution, for the children and grandchildren and all later generations must be viewed as exhibits only of characteristics that always existed in the germ cell of their ancestors.

Evolutionists believe they find support for evolution in genetics on the assumption that though there is a predetermined number of variations that can display themselves down through the generations of a particular species, in time different groups of the descendants will, if isolated, stabilize certain markedly different kinds of variations. As a result, there will be no crossbreeding with the parent stock, and thus clearly distinct species will develop. From there on, of course, it takes only more time and more of the same reasoning to produce biological groups even more divergent than the species.

But this reasoning, though plausible, is plainly incapable of proof—that is, unless a person could watch these variants over a million or two years. The evolutionists are sure that their evolution theory is true, and therefore little variations must have become greater variations, with the end result just described. That the cold, well-established, scientific facts prove something very short of this does not too greatly disturb them.

Bible believers can accept enthusiastically all the laboratory findings in the field of genetics. We are not troubled at the thought that God placed within the first created dog, for example, more potential canine characteristics than could all be manifested in one dog. Certainly one dog could not have both short and long ears, both a shaggy coat and a short, clipped one, both long and short legs. There would have to be many dogs born in the generations to come to reveal all the variations. How marvelous of our God to place in the original germ cell of the first dog all these potential variations. We see nothing in this to conflict with the doctrine of creation, with its distinct types of life from the beginning.

## The Alleged Proofs From Fossils

Let us look now at the other area that is said to provide evidence for evolution—the rocks, the layers of earth called strata, with their fossils. It is no mere play on words to say that the rocks are viewed by evolutionists as the real foundation of their theory. The fossils found in the various strata of the earth are remains of creatures that lived in the dim past. Naturally they might be expected to shed some important light on the long-past history of living things. We cannot here turn aside to explore the broad expanses of the earth to survey all the geological and fossil evidence that allegedly supports evolution. Your attention is called simply to one main point in regard to this fossil evidence in an attempt to discover how valid is the claim that all the discoveries and investigations since Darwin have provided only increasing proof for evolution.

To see the force of this point, the reader should remember that the classic picture of evolutionary development is that of a tree. Believing that all forms of life on the world came from some single, simple form, evolutionists have pictured this simple form as the base, or lower part of the trunk of the tree. Out from this trunk soon began to spread branches of more diversified forms of life. In turn the branches subdivided into smaller branches, and these again into twigs, as the forms of life became ever more diversified. The topmost bough, of course, was man, with the monkeys swinging just below and a little to one side.

Thus the theory of evolution calls for connecting links all the way along. No twig or branch stands alone; it is connected in some well-defined way with other twigs and branches, and all, in turn, to the main trunk. But what does the fossil record reveal?

474

THE EVOLUTION THEORY EXAMINED

Here is perhaps the most perplexing problem that confronts the specialists in the field of ancient fossil forms—paleontologists, they are called. They have discovered that there are great gaps between the major forms, called phyla, and often great gaps between the more closely related forms. There is little or nothing in the fossil record to indicate that any forms of life ever existed to bridge these major gaps. Of course, paleontologists have always hoped that sometime, somewhere, fossils would be found out of which to make the much-needed bridges. But that hope has gradually faded as the strata of the world have come increasingly under study.

Occasionally an apologist for evolution is frank enough to admit that he is puzzled by these gaps, as he ought certainly to be. But most times the gaps, while admitted, are immediately bridged, to the satisfaction of the evolutionary writer, by a span of speculation as to why there should be bridges. The speculative span is strictly a suspension bridge, in that it rests upon no supports along the way! So long as the general theory of evolution holds, this kind of bridge holds. It is anchored at each end to a theory and not to objective facts.

## One Authority Confesses, in Part

One recent brilliant authority, writing on this problem, declares:

"The facts are that many species and genera, indeed the majority, do appear suddenly in the [fossil] record, differing sharply and in many ways from any earlier group, and that this appearance of discontinuity becomes more common the higher the level, until it is virtually universal as regards orders and all higher steps in the taxonomic hierarchy [that is, in the evolutionary tree].

"The face of the record thus does really suggest normal discontinuity at all levels, most particularly at high levels, and some paleontologists (e.g., Spath and Schindewolf) insist on taking the record at this face value. Others (e.g., Matthew and Osborn) discount this evidence completely and maintain that the breaks neither prove nor suggest that there is any normal mode of evolution other than that seen in continuously evolving and abundantly recorded groups. This essentially paleontological problem is also of crucial interest for all

475

other biologists, and, since there is such a conflict of opinion, non-paleontologists may choose either to believe the authority who agrees with their prejudices or to discard the evidence as worthless."—GEORGE GAYLORD SIMPSON, *Tempo and Mode in Evolution*, p. 99.

This learned author seeks to ease the problem by arguing the incompleteness of the study of the fossil record. In other words, we may not yet have found the bridges. But in this view of the problem he can hardly find much consolation, for he admits that when "the [fossil] record does happen to be good" it "rarely" shows "complete continuity" for any group higher than "species and genera." On the "higher levels," he goes on to admit, "essentially continuous transitional sequences [that is, bridges] are not merely rare, but are virtually absent."—*Ibid.*, p. 105.

He adds, almost immediately, that the "absence [of these bridges] is so nearly universal that it cannot, offhand, be imputed entirely to chance and does require some attempt at special explanation, as has been felt by most paleontologists."—*Ibid.*, p. 106.

Some of the difficulties in dealing with the problem are suggested by his remark that "listing of data as to the occurrence of possible ancestry involves subjective judgment as to what constitutes a 'possible ancestry,' and in some cases opinions differ radically."—*Ibid.*

In the next paragraph he makes the sweeping statement:

"This regular absence of transitional forms is not confined to mammals, but is an almost universal phenomenon, as has long been noted by paleontologists. It is true of almost all orders of all classes of animals. . . . It is apparently also true of analogous categories of plants."—*Ibid.*, p. 107.

### Speculation Substitutes for Facts

A few pages further on he observes:

"In the early days of evolutionary paleontology [fossil study] it was assumed that the major gaps would be filled in by further discoveries, and even, falsely, that some discoveries had already filled them. As it became more and more evident that the great gaps remained, despite wonderful progress in finding the members of lesser transitional groups and progressive lines, it was no longer satisfactory to impute this absence of objective data entirely to chance. The failure of paleontology to produce such evidence was so keenly felt that a few disillusioned naturalists even decided that the theory of organic evolution, or of general organic continuity of descent, was wrong, after all. . . .

"Disregarding such easily discouraged serious students and ignoring less worthy critics with emotional axes to grind [obviously, those who believe in creation], paleontologists have interpreted the systematic gaps in two ways. One school of thought maintains that the gaps have no meaning for evolution and are entirely a phenomenon of record [that is, the fossil record has either been destroyed or has simply not been found yet]. Another school maintains that transitional forms never existed."—*Ibid.,* p. 115.

The author here quoted thinks the answer lies somewhere between these two views, and spends pages in building what is described as a suspension bridge of speculations to span the gaps. In one short paragraph a certain speculation requires the use of "if" seven times. If a certain condition existed, and if another situation developed, and so on and on. Strictly speaking, there is nothing illogical in this. *If* knowledge does not exist, and *if* one is committed to a theory, and *if* grave objections to the theory arise, then speculation is the only way to explain its deficiencies. But how different all this sounds from the dogmatic declarations made by popular exponents of evolution that all the evidence is clearly in favor of evolution and that every year only adds strength to the argument. In the case of the rocks and the fossils, the stronghold of the evolution theory, the passing years have brought a major problem.

CHAPTER 4

# The Creation Doctrine Examined

A FEW scientists, fully persuaded that the gaps between major forms of life will never be closed by any possible further evidence to be discovered in the fossil world, have actually proposed a distinct variation from the historic idea of an evolutionary tree. They suggest that instead of one tree there have been many —in other words, that each of the major types of life, known as phyla, runs back through all the ages. Now, it is true that not many scientists accept this idea, because it runs counter to the basic idea of the unity of nature as historically understood by evolutionists. But the very fact that even a few reputable scientists feel that they must advocate this revised idea, reveals how distressing are the gaps in the fossil record.

Listen to an exponent of this revised idea, an eminent scientist of the United States National Museum:

"No matter how far back we go in the fossil record of previous animal life upon the earth we find no trace of any animal forms which are intermediate between the various major groups or phyla.

"This can only mean one thing. . . .

"If we are willing to accept the facts we must believe that there never were such intermediates, or in other words that these major groups have from the very first borne the same relation to each other that they bear today."—AUSTIN H. CLARK, *The New Evolution*, p. 189.

He immediately asks, and answers, an obvious question:

"Is this creationism? Not at all. All living things are derived from other living things. Furthermore, all types of animal life must be explained in terms of a primitive single cell. The seemingly simultaneous appearance of all the phyla or major groups of animals simply means that life at its very first beginnings developed at once and simultaneously from the primitive single cell in every possible direction, giving rise to some original form or forms in every phylum."

# THE CREATION DOCTRINE EXAMINED

We all agree that this is not creationism, but it has very much in common with the idea of creation. We Christians believe, in the words of this scientist, that the "major groups have from the very first borne the same relation to each other that they bear today." In other words, there has been a grove of trees, instead of one evolutionary tree the scientists from Darwin's day have pictured.

Why is not this idea really creationism? The author answers by declaring that these different principal forms "developed at once and simultaneously from the primitive single cell in every possible direction." He begins with a primitive single cell, which suddenly and simultaneously provides all the forms of life. Creationists begin with an eternally living Being, who suddenly and simultaneously brought into existence these various forms.

## The Key Question

Why does this scientist, who finds that the evidence demands belief that all the main forms of life have continued back to the "very first beginnings" of time, suddenly make all these forms converge "at once and simultaneously" into a "primitive single cell"? Here is the crux of the difference between us. His answer is simple and direct: "All types of animal life must be explained in terms of a primitive single cell." And why "must" they? Because of clear evidence that demands this? No! Then why? Simply because of the presuppositions that underlie the thinking of almost all the learned world today. Not to have the different forms of life converge into a "primitive single cell" would leave no other alternative than creationism. But creationism involves the supernatural, and that is ruled out by the very canons that govern all scientific study!

No, it is not true that all the scientific discoveries and research since the days of Darwin provide only added proof for evolution. We think that the contrary is the case.

Earlier it was stated that there is no clear proof for evolution, that the evidence presented is what is known as circumstantial evidence. And no scientist would admit that circumstantial evidence ought to decide the case if his own life were at stake in court. One historian of science, who seems more frank than most, says this concerning evidence for evolution:

"Evolution is perhaps unique among major scientific theories in that the appeal for its acceptance is not that there is evidence for it, but that any other proposed interpretation of the data is wholly incredible."—CHARLES SINGER, *A Short History of Science*, p. 387.

In other words, even after it is shown that the observable facts do not require a belief that the world has had an evolutionary history, a spokesman for that view frankly seeks to conclude the whole discussion simply by ruling out any counterview as "incredible."

And why is any other interpretation of the data incredible? Because the only one other interpretation that is set forth—the Genesis story of creation—is considered incredible. For illustration, there are before us the data represented by creatures of different complexity, from simple one-celled amoeba up to man. One interpretation of the data, already noted, is that there has been an evolutionary development upward. The other interpretation, and the only other one, is that God made all these different creatures originally with different degrees of complexity, and that the similarities found in them simply indicate that there is one master mind that planned the whole creation.

### Back to the Subject of Miracles

To the average scientific mind this latter interpretation of the data "is wholly incredible." Creation is a miracle; and, as earlier explained, the scientific mind has no place for miracles. Everything in nature must be explained in terms of the measured actions of the laws of nature as we see them operating today. That tenet of science is so basic, so firmly established, that the Mosaic account of creation is automatically ruled out as "wholly incredible."

This brings us again to the subject of miracles. It will be well to return to this area of discussion specifically in terms of the creation miracle. The Bible pictures our world as being made out of nothing; or, to use the Bible phrase, "the things which are seen were not made of things which do appear." Heb. 11:3. This idea is unacceptable to many who have held that matter can be neither created nor destroyed, but can only be changed in form. This is the first and chief indictment of the creation account. The second major objection made by scientists, who would be philosophers, is that Moses allows only a week for creation, and that this is a fantastically short period. Such speed violates the idea of the slow, measured actions of nature.

Strictly speaking, there is a real inconsistency in this whole scientific attitude of hostility toward the Bible account of creation. All genuine scientists will declare that they know nothing about the ultimate beginning of anything, that they are concerned only with measuring, analyzing, and predicting the functioning of natural laws, which they see in operation about them. In the very nature of the case scientists are incapable of speaking with any certainty regarding ultimate beginnings, as this is in the realm of philosophy and religion.

Nor can they validly claim that though they do not know anything of absolute beginnings, they can be sure that the creation story is false, because their theory of evolution rules out creation. We have found that the so-called evidence for evolution is circumstantial at best and contradictory at worst. And we have just noted the frank admission of one historian of science, who confesses that "the appeal for its [evolution's] acceptance is not that there is evidence for it, but that any other proposed interpretation of the data is wholly incredible."

In other words, as we have discovered, the only ground on which creation is ruled out is that it seems "incredible" to the scientifically trained mind, which seeks to make a method in knowledge the whole of knowledge. But when scientists have no clear evidence in support of their evolutionary belief, how can they objectively prove that a counter belief is "incredible"? If they cannot test the creation belief in a scientific laboratory or measure it with a literal yardstick, how can they determine its lack of credibility? The answer is obvious: They must test it in the laboratory of their presuppositions, and by the subjective yardstick of their personal sense of values. But when they thus proceed they are no longer scientists but philosophers. And that makes a world of difference. Which is more credible, the words of a Bible writer or the words of a philosopher? That question is not difficult to answer, providing one will allow a personal God in his thinking. It is only when the scientist becomes a philosopher, and begins to interpret nature's laws and phenomena by his own presuppositions, and perhaps even prejudices, that we find ourselves in conflict with him.

### Fashions in Thought

It should never be forgotten that scientists, like the rest of mankind, are creatures of their environment and their times. When they move outside the narrow limits of investigating and measuring the activities of nature, and begin to interpret or philosophize, their conclusions as to the credibility of any idea are certain to reflect, at least in part, the general viewpoint of the era in which they live. There are fashions in thought as in dress. And do we not all believe that the current fashion we see on the street is quite in order while the fashion reflected in the family album is "incredible"? Right here the words of a stimulating and respected English author apply:

"In order to understand a period it is necessary not so much to be acquainted with its more defined opinions as with the doctrines which are thought of not as doctrines, but as FACTS. (The moderns, for example, do not look for [on] their belief in *Progress* as an opinion, but merely as a recognition of fact.) There are certain doctrines which for a particular period seem not doctrines, but inevitable categories of the human mind. Men do not look on them merely as correct opinion, for they have become so much a part of the mind, and lie so far back, that they are never really conscious of them at all. They do not see them, but other things *through* them. It is these abstract ideas at the centre, the things which they take for granted, that characterise a period. There are in each period certain doctrines, a denial of which is looked on by the men of that period just as we might look on the assertion that two and two make five. It is these abstract things at the centre, these *doctrines* felt as *facts*, which are the source of all the other more material characteristics of a period."—T. E. HULME, *Speculations*, pp. 50, 51.

### Evolution Corresponds With Secular Mood

In this present age, or period, distinguished for its secular viewpoint and its complete lack of any consciousness of the super-natural, those doctrines that support this viewpoint—for example, the evolutionistic explanation of the world—are naturally consid-ered reasonable. All such doctrines are "felt as *facts*." No wonder, then, that the doctrine of creation is considered "incredible." But why should the scientist declare that Moses was mistaken simply because he described great happenings that are outside the ken and the experience of science? Appropriate here are the words of Prof. P. W. Bridgman, of Harvard, who wrote thus critically of the attitude of certain scientific men:

"It is difficult to conceive anything more scientifically bigoted than to postulate that all possible experience conforms to the same type as that with which we are already familiar, and therefore to demand that explanations use only elements familiar in everyday experience. Such an attitude bespeaks an unimaginativeness, a mental obtuseness and obstinacy which might be expected to have exhausted their pragmatic justification at a lower plane of mental activity."—*The Logic of Modern Physics*, pp. 46, 47.

### Atomic Research Illustrates Point

This learned professor is here indicting some of his fellow intellectuals for objecting to the idea of "action at a distance," in explanation of gravitation. But his words take on more force in these last few years since research in atomic energy has developed. Let us illustrate this statement by a quotation from the opening chapter of the official report on atomic energy that was published under the auspices of the War Department in 1945. In giving the background of the study in atomic energy, the writer opens his report thus:

"There are two principles that have been cornerstones of the structure of modern science. The first—that matter can be neither created nor destroyed but only altered in form—was enunciated in the eighteenth century and is familiar to every student of chemistry; it has led to the principle known as the law of conservation of mass. The second—that energy can be neither created nor destroyed but only altered in form—emerged in the nineteenth century and has ever since been the plague of inventors of perpetual-motion machines; it is known as the law of conservation of energy.

"These two principles have constantly guided and disciplined the development and application of science. For all practical purposes they were unaltered and separate until some five years ago [that is, till about 1940]. For most practical purposes they still are so, but it is now known that they are, in fact, two phases of a single principle for we have discovered that energy may sometimes be converted into matter and matter into energy."—Henry D. Smyth, *Atomic Energy for Military Purposes*, p. 1.

If even a short generation ago someone had declared that it is good science to believe that "energy may sometimes be converted into matter and matter into energy," scientists would have ridiculed him as heartily as they have ever ridiculed the believer in the Mosaic record of creation. Such a declaration would have challenged two laws of the scientific world, laws as sacred to some scientists as the Decalogue is to the Christian. But it was not until those two laws were breath-takingly revised that scientists were able to proceed with their amazing discoveries in the atomic field!

Might it not be possible that some of the theories concerning scientific laws that are supposed to make incredible the Mosaic story of creation need revision? In fact, the two purported laws that have been most often invoked to rule out the Mosaic account are the very laws mentioned in this quotation on atomic energy, the laws of the conservation of matter and energy. If "energy may sometimes be converted into matter and matter into energy," then why is it illogical to believe that the God of all energy, the Omnipotent One, might convert some of His limitless energy into matter? The Christian conception of God has always been that He is infinite in power, in energy.

# THE CREATION DOCTRINE EXAMINED

Christians grant that the idea that God can speak and suddenly divine energy congeals itself, as it were, into a whirling sphere of solid earth, is difficult to comprehend, but certainly no more difficult than some of the amazing ideas set forth by atomic scientists regarding matter and energy. Note the following statement by a scientist, who is endeavoring to describe what investigation in the microscopic field has revealed as to the interchange of matter and energy:

"The simple concepts of space and matter have suffered in the microscopic field in much the same way that they have suffered in the astronomical field. As the result of investigations in the field of the small particles it has become necessary to broaden our ideas as to the nature of matter. Cloud-chamber pictures have allowed us practically to see two particles of matter created in space from the energy contained in radiation."—CLAUDE WILLIAM HEAPS, "The Structure of the Universe," *Smithsonian Annual Report,* 1944, p. 178.

This scientific writer goes on immediately to state that this phenomenon of matter being created from energy, which he declared we can dimly see in its miscroscopic operations, might be illustrated on a larger, visible scale by this analogy: "An equivalent phenomenon would be for a quantity of sunshine, passing by an iron ball, to change suddenly into a couple of buckshot."

For a scientist soberly to set forth that kind of illustration to indicate what seems to be taking place in the microscopic realm is quite sufficient to take one's breath away. Even the story of creation seems no more breath taking. Both are views resulting from faith and not from the scientific process.

Of course, he hastens to add immediately regarding his analogy of sunshine and an iron ball:

"Needless to say, no one has ever seen anything like this happen. It is only when sizes become so small as to prevent direct observation that the event occurs. We may well say that something peculiar is going on in the microscopic field. Something is happening which is foreign to our ordinary experience."—*Ibid.,* pp. 178, 179.

His last sentence is really an understatement. Something is

happening that not only is "foreign to our ordinary experience" but that contradicts some of the most primary tenets on which so-called scientific thinking proceeded from the earliest days of the scientific era right up to the time of atomic investigation. Note this scientist's further statement:

"Matter and energy can now be thought of as practically synonymous. It thus becomes possible to make certain grand inferences with the object of saving the universe from running down. Millions of suns are slowly but surely converting their matter and their energy into radiation and this radiation is constantly escaping into infinity. Perhaps somewhere in space radiation may be changed back into matter. Perhaps the universe is engaged in a reversible cycle, instead of an irreversible one, as is commonly supposed."—*Ibid.*, p. 179.

"Perhaps"! Why not? At least some scientists have come to the point where they no longer dogmatically declare that this could not be so. On the contrary, we hear a scientist saying, "Perhaps somewhere in space radiation may be changed back into matter." Perhaps in time men may come to realize that it was only their limited knowledge that kept them from seeing how reasonable it is to believe that He from whose throne "proceed lightnings," can create matter at His will. The Bible Christian believes that the "somewhere in space" where matter is thus created, is the throne of God.

### A Gloomy Forecast

"Perhaps the universe is engaged in a reversible cycle, instead of an irreversible one, as is commonly supposed." The learned writer is here referring to the long-held belief in the scientific world that the universe is "running down," that the sun and the stars are burning out, and that matter is dissolving into radiation, and energy is being dissipated into empty space. In other words, the best that philosophically inclined scientists have been able to offer us for the future is that ultimately all the universe will be cold and dead. This is the fatal, futile end that science has been able to see for the universe as the result of reasoning along certain lines and in terms of their knowledge of the laws of nature.

# THE CREATION DOCTRINE EXAMINED

Now comes this broad and dazzling field of atomic investigation that rests on the premise that matter can become energy, and energy matter. From that premise flow conclusions in the scientific, philosophical, and religious realms that are absolutely revolutionary. And among these revolutionary conclusions is that "perhaps somewhere in space radiation may be changed back into matter. Perhaps the universe is engaged in a reversible cycle, instead of an irreversible one, as is commonly supposed."

Thus we see that the Bible idea of creation, of energy being transmuted in some mysterious way into matter, is an idea that must be held if we are to escape from the fatal, futile idea of a cold, black ending for the universe. In other words, the only way that we can give satisfying meaning to the universe is in terms of the idea behind the Mosaic story of creation, that there is a Source "somewhere in space" where matter can be brought into existence.

Now, if scientists speak of the possibility that matter, lost in radiation, may be restored somewhere in the universe, we can reasonably go one step further and speak of God's restoring this matter to the suns whence it was dissipated. Thus, we need not envision a universe dying out.

## Two Objections Re-examined

In the setting of the discoveries and admissions of science today let us look again at the two major objections that scientific men have raised against the creation story: (1) The Bible describes the world as being created out of nothing, so to speak. (2) Too short a time is allowed for so great a creation.

The first objection, we have noted, seems very weak and pointless today in view of the marvelous revelations of science regarding matter and energy.

The second objection begins to look pointless also. If there is one fact that stands out above all others in the atomic experimentation, it is that changes of matter to energy, or the reverse, can take place in a moment of time. In fact, time hardly seems to be a factor in the whole operation. Whoever dreamed a short generation ago that so much of change could take place in a moment of time! It is not quite so hard now to take literally the Bible description of God's act of instant creation: "He spake, and it was done; he commanded, and it stood fast."

No one can see energy; yet energy can become matter. Hence, we find new force in Paul's words: "Things which are seen were not made of things which do appear." The apostle seems to be more scientific than we realized. At least it is an interesting fact that a recent scientific writer concluded a series of articles on the subject of the latest developments in science with these very words from Paul. (See *Harper's Magazine*, June, 1948, article by Lincoln Barnett, "The Universe and Dr. Einstein.")

Thus we come to the end of this brief study of the question of whether a person can be a Seventh-day Adventist, and thus a believer in creation and other Bible miracles, and at the same time be truly scientific, and thus a believer in all the certainly established facts of science. The answer to that question is yes. We do not say that we face no perplexities whatever in interpreting the facts of nature—evolutionistic scientists face very real perplexities. We simply affirm that there is such overwhelming and increasing evidence of the harmony between the facts of science and the declarations of revelation, that we may confidently await further researches into the mysteries of nature to secure the added confirmations and harmony that may be needed.

### No Conflict Between Bible and Science

The Bible and science are not in conflict. The God of the Bible is the God of nature. Some scientists and certain religionists, called modernists, have made the grave mistake of trying to square the Bible with their limited knowledge of science and to make science deal with philosophical problems which are completely out of the realm of the scientific method. We who are Bible believers have ever taken the opposite course, of understanding the mysteries of nature by the light that shines from the Book of God. Certainly mistakes have been made by conservative Christians, for we are not infallible. However, our mistakes have not included the fantastic blunder of trying to harmonize the facts of nature with the revelation of the Bible by explaining away, or spiritualizing away, the reality of these facts.

But modernists and most scientists have sought to harmonize revelation with science by explaining away the very reality of portions of the Bible record as merely myth or legend. The net result of that was not a harmonization of the Bible and science but a prostitution of science by seeking to make it a philosophy that would destroy the Bible. Conservative Christians hold that the revelation of God in the Bible is the starting point of our understanding of God and nature, and that any tampering with that record, or indicting it as myth, makes a burlesque of the idea of harmonizing the Bible and science.

Seventh-day Adventists, who believe in the Bible, believe also in science. We seek to take the Bible declarations as simple statements of facts and history and moral instruction, to be understood literally, unless internal evidence reveals that some portion should be taken figuratively. We also look the facts of science in the face, grateful to God for every new discovery. We are believers in the great God who made heaven and earth, the sea and the fountains of water. We believe in His Holy Book and in the universe that He created. We see harmony and unity between the two, for we see them as proceeding from the one divine source, the Omnipotent God.

# Section II

# THE LAW AND LEGALISM

# CHAPTER 5

# The Law of God in Church Creeds

UNQUESTIONABLY, the point of greatest controversy between Seventh-day Adventists and their theological critics is with regard to the law of God. This is understandable, for if it can be proved that the law of God has been abolished, then the seventh-day Sabbath has been abolished also. On the contrary, if the law of God stands revealed as perpetual in its claim upon men, then the fourth commandment confronts us with its injunction to keep holy the "seventh day."

The chief argument of those who seek to prove that the Decalogue has been abolished is this: The Bible speaks of only one law, which includes moral and ceremonial precepts. The Bible also speaks of the law's being abolished at the cross Therefore the Decalogue has been abolished. Those who thus reason seek to give added force to their argument and to make Adventists appear to be the promoters of strange doctrine, by implying, when they do not explicitly state, that the idea that two laws are described in the Bible is a peculiarly Adventist doctrine. For example, one writer declares: "The place to find emphasis placed upon these supposed distinctions [between the moral and ceremonial laws] is in the lectures and printed matter of the Seventh-day Adventists. Their 'two laws' theory is based upon mere assumptions, incorrect applications of Scripture, and detached Biblical phrases extracted from their proper connections."

This statement has been widely quoted in the literature of critics. If it means anything, it means that Adventists are unique, in contrast to Christendom at large, in holding to the doctrine that the Bible sets forth two laws. The most charitable way to view this statement is to say that its author and its many fervent quoters have never carefully read the creeds of Christendom from Reformation days onward.

From Reformation times down to the definite organization of the main Protestant bodies, the confessions of faith and creeds of Protestantism have generally contained some statement concerning the law of God. An examination of these statements reveals that Protestantism in general believes three important facts concerning the law:

1. That the Decalogue is God's moral standard for Christians.
2. That there is a clear distinction between the Decalogue and the ceremonial and other laws of ancient Israel.
3. That obedience to the Decalogue is not to be construed as being contrary in any way to grace—that law and gospel belong together in the Christian life.

For some readers, two words in the following quotations may require explanation. The word *catholic,* written thus with a small *c* and coupled with the word *church* in the Protestant creeds, means the whole body of Christian believers. The word *catholic* simply means "universal." The word *symbol* is used as a synonym for *creed* or *confession.*

The text of these creedal statements and the quoted comments on them are those given in the authoritative source work by Philip Schaff, *The Creeds of Christendom.**

### The Waldensian Catechism

"The Waldensian Catechism . . . must have been written before 1500. . . . It consists of fifty-seven questions, . . . and as many answers. . . . It embodies the Apostles' Creed, the Lord's prayer, and the ten commandments. . . . Under the head of Faith we have a practical exposition of the Apostles' Creed and the ten commandments, showing their subjective bearing on a living faith."—Volume 1, pp. 572, 573.

*"9. What is living faith?*

---

* Three volumes, fourth edition, revised and enlarged. Harper and Brothers. The same edition is used where Schaff is given as the source of creedal statements in later chapters.

"It is faith active in love (as the apostle testifies, Gal. 5:6), that is, by keeping God's commandments. Living faith is to believe in God, that is, to love Him and to keep His commandments."—*Ibid.*, p. 575.

### The Confession of the Waldenses, A.D. 1655

"This confession belongs to the Calvinistic family. . . . It is still in force, or at least highly prized among the Waldenses in Italy. The occasion which called it forth entitles it to special consideration. It was prepared and issued in 1655, together with an appeal to Protestant nations, in consequence of one of the most cruel persecutions which Roman bigotry could inspire."—Volume 3, p. 757.

"We believe, . . .

"XXXIII. Finally, that we ought to receive the symbol of the apostles, the Lord's prayer, and the decalogue as fundamentals of our faith and our devotion."—*Ibid.*, p. 768.

### Luther's Small Catechism, A.D. 1529

Speaking of this catechism in connection with the Heidelberg and the Shorter Westminster Catechisms, Schaff says: "These are the three most popular and useful catechisms that Protestantism has produced." —Volume 1, p. 543. Part I is entitled "The Ten Commandments," consisting chiefly of a series of questions on each of the ten commandments in order. Then follow immediately the two questions and answers given below.

"What does God say about all these commandments?

"He says this:

" 'I the Lord thy God am a jealous God, visiting the iniquity of the fathers upon the children unto the third and fourth generation of them that hate Me, and showing mercy unto thousands of them that love Me and keep My commandments.'

"What does this mean?

"Answer:

"God threatens to punish all who transgress these commandments: we should, therefore, fear His anger, and do nothing against such commandments. But He promises grace and every blessing to all who keep them: we should, therefore, love and trust in Him, and gladly obey His commandments."—Volume 3, p. 77.

# ANSWERS TO OBJECTIONS

## The Heidelberg Catechism, A.D. 1563

"The Heidelberg Catechism was translated into all the European and many Asiatic languages. . . . It is stated that, next to the Bible, the 'Imitation of Christ,' by Thomas á Kempis, and Bunyan's 'Pilgrim's Progress,' no book has been more frequently translated, more widely circulated or used." "As a standard of public doctrine the Heidelberg Catechism is the most catholic and popular of all the Reformed symbols."—Volume 1, pp. 536, 540. Schaff adds that this "was the first catechism planted on American soil," and that it is "the honored symbol of the Dutch and German Reformed Churches in America."—*Ibid.*, p. 549.

"*Question 92.*—What is the law of God?

"*Answer.*—[The answer consists of a verbatim quotation of the Ten Commandments as given in Exodus 20:1-17.]

"*Ques. 93.*—How are these commandments divided?

"*Ans.*—Into two tables, the first of which teaches us, in four commandments, what duties we owe to God; the second, in six, what duties we owe to our neighbor."

[The next twenty questions, 94 to 113, deal with the significance of each of the Ten Commandments.]

"*Ques. 114.*—Can those who are converted to God keep these commandments perfectly?

"*Ans.*—No; but even the holiest men, while in this life, have only a small beginning of this obedience, yet so that with earnest purpose they begin to live, not only according to some but according to all the commandments of God.

"*Ques. 115.*—Why, then, doth God so strictly enjoin upon us the ten commandments, since in this life no one can keep them?

"*Ans.*—First, that all our life long we may learn more and more to know our sinful nature, and so the more earnestly seek forgiveness of sins and righteousness in Christ; secondly, that we may continually strive and beg from God the grace of the Holy Ghost, so as to become more and more changed into the image of God, till we attain finally to full perfection after this life."—Volume 3, pp. 340-349.

# THE LAW OF GOD IN CHURCH CREEDS

## The Form (or Formula) of Concord, A.D. 1577

"The last of the Lutheran Confessions." "The Formula of Concord is, next to the Augsburg Confession, the most important theological standard of the Lutheran Church, but differs from it as the *sectarian* symbol of Lutheranism, while the other is its *catholic* symbol."—Volume 1, pp. 258, 338. The object of this Formula was to bring harmony into Lutheranism after some thirty years of theological disputation. Among the many questions raised by various theologians was that of the proper relation of the law to the gospel. Schaff well observes in this connection: "Protestantism in its joyful enthusiasm for the freedom and all-sufficiency of the gospel, was strongly tempted to antinomianism [no-law-ism], but restrained by its moral force and the holy character of the gospel itself."—*Ibid.*, p. 277. The following quotation from the Formula of Concord shows how clearly and how vigorously the no-law doctrine was repudiated:

## ART. VI.—OF THE THIRD USE OF THE LAW

### "STATEMENT OF THE CONTROVERSY

"Since it is established that the law of God was given to men for three causes; first, that a certain external discipline might be preserved, and wild and intractable men might be restrained, as it were, by certain barriers; secondly, that by the law men might be brought to an acknowledgment of their sins; thirdly, that regenerate men, to all of whom, nevertheless, much of the flesh still cleaves, for that very reason may have some certain rule after which they may and ought to shape their life, etc., a controversy has arisen among some few theologians concerning the third use of the law, to wit: whether the law is to be inculcated upon the regenerate also, and its observation urged upon them or not? Some have judged that the law should be urged, others have denied it.

### "AFFIRMATIVE

*"The sound and godly doctrine concerning this controversy.*

"1. We believe, teach, and confess that although they who truly believe in Christ, and are sincerely converted to God, are through Christ set free from the curse and constraint of the law, they are not, nevertheless, on that account without law, inasmuch as the

497

Son of God redeemed them for the very reason that they might meditate on the law of God day and night, and continually exercise themselves in the keeping thereof (Ps. 1:2; 119:1 sqq.). For not even our first parents, even before the fall, lived wholly without law, which was certainly at that time graven on their hearts, because the Lord had created them after His own image. (Gen. 1:26 sq.; 2:16 sqq.; 3:3).

"2. We believe, teach, and confess that the preaching of the law should be urged not only upon those who have not faith in Christ, and do not yet repent, but also upon those who truly believe in Christ, are truly converted to God, and regenerated and are justified by faith. . . . [Sections 3 to 6 amplify the foregoing statement.]

"NEGATIVE

"*Rejection of false doctrine.*

"We repudiate, therefore, as a false and pernicious dogma, contrary to Christian discipline and true piety, the teaching that the law of God (in such wise as is described above) is not to be set forth before the godly and true believers, but only before the ungodly, unbelievers, and impenitent, and to be urged upon these alone."—Volume 3, pp. 130-135.

### The Scotch Confession of Faith, A.D. 1560

"Subscription [to this Confession] was required from all ministers [in Scotland] first in 1572. From that time till the Revolution of 1688 this native Confession was the only legally recognized doctrinal standard of both the Presbyterian and Episcopal Churches in Scotland. . . . Edward Irving . . . bestowed this encomium upon it: 'This document is the pillar of the Reformation Church of Scotland.' "—Volume 1, pp. 682, 684, 685. The old spelling is given, but with possibly a few exceptions the meaning can easily be understood.

"ART. XV.—OF THE PERFECTIOUN OF THE LAW, AND THE
IMPERFECTIOUN OF MAN

"The Law of God we confesse and acknawledge maist just, maist equall, maist halie, and maist perfite, commaunding thir thingis, quhilk being wrocht in perfectioun, were abill to give life, and abill to bring man to eternall felicitie. Bot our nature is sa corrupt, sa weake, and sa unperfite, that we ar never abill to fulfill the warkes of the Law in perfectioun. Zea, gif we say we have na sinne, evin after we ar regenerate, we deceive our selves, and the veritie of God is not in us. And therfore, it behovis us to apprehend Christ Jesus with His justice and satisfaction, quha is the end and accomplishment of the Law, be quhome we ar set at this liberty, that the curse and malediction of God fall not upon us, albeit we fulfill not the same in al pointes. For God the Father beholding us, in the body of His Sonne Christ Jesus, acceptis our imperfite obedience, as it were perfite, and covers our warks, quhilk ar defyled with many spots, with the justice of His Sonne. We do not meane that we ar so set at liberty, that we awe na obedience to the Law (for that before wee have plainly confessed), bot this we affirme, that na man in eird (Christ Jesus onlie except) hes given, gives, or sall give in worke, that obedience to the Law, quhilk the Law requiris. Bot when we have done all things, we must falle down and unfeinedly confess, that we are unprofitable servands. And therefore, quhosoever boastis themselves of the merits of their awin works, or put their trust in the works of super-erogation, boast themselves in that quhilk is nocht, and put their trust in damnable idolatry."—*Ibid.*, pp. 456, 457.

## The Second Helvetic Confession, A.D. 1566

This confession was written by Henry Bullinger, of Zurich, Switzerland, Zwingli's successor. "Bullinger . . . preserved and completed the work of his predecessor [Zwingli], and exerted, by his example and writings, a commanding influence throughout the Reformed Church inferior only to that of Calvin." "The Helvetic Confession is the most widely adopted, and hence the most authoritative of all the Continental Reformed symbols, with the exception of the Heidelberg Catechism. . . . Upon the whole, the Second Helvetic Confession, as to theological merit, occupies the first rank among the Reformed confessions."—Volume 1, pp. 391, 394, 395. This confession is accompanied by a number of explanatory footnotes, as is the case with various of the creeds and symbols. These footnotes have been placed in brackets in the text.

# ANSWERS TO OBJECTIONS

## "CHAPTER XII.—OF THE LAW OF GOD

"We teach that the will of God is set down unto us in the law of God; to wit, what He would have us to do, or not to do, what is good and just, or what is evil and unjust. We therefore confess that 'the law is good and holy' (Rom. 7:12); and that this law is, by the finger of God, either 'written in the hearts of men' (Rom. 2:15), and so is called the law of nature, or engraven in the two tables of stone, and more largely expounded in the books of Moses (Ex. 20:17; Deut. 5:22). For plainness' sake we divide it into the moral law, which is contained in the commandments, or the two tables expounded in the books of Moses; into the ceremonial, which does appoint ceremonies and the worship of God; and into the judicial law, which is occupied about political and domestic affairs.

"We believe that the whole will of God, and all necessary precepts, for every part of this life, are fully delivered in this law. . . .

"We teach that this law was not given to men, that we should be justified by keeping it; but that, by the knowledge thereof, we might rather acknowledge our infirmity, sin, and condemnation; and so, despairing of our strength, might turn unto Christ by faith. . . .

"The law of God [to wit, the moral law, comprehended in the ten commandments], therefore, is thus far abrogated; that is, it does not henceforth condemn us, neither work wrath in us; 'for we are under grace, and not under the law' (Rom. 6:14). Moreover, Christ did fulfill all the figures of the law; wherefore the shadow ceased when the body came, so that, in Christ, we have now all truth and fullness. Yet we do not therefore disdain or reject the law. We remember the words of the Lord, saying, 'I came not to destroy the law and the prophets, but to fulfill them' (Matt. 5:17). We know that in the law [to wit, in the moral law] are described unto us the kinds of virtues and vices. We know that the Scripture of the law [to wit, the ceremonial law], if it be expounded by the gospel, is very profitable to the church, and that therefore the reading of it is not to be banished out of the church. For although the countenance of Moses was covered with a veil, yet the apostle affirms that 'the veil is taken away and abolished by Christ' (2 Cor. 3:14). We condemn all things which the old or new heretics have taught against the law of God."—Volume 3, pp. 854-856.

### The Thirty-nine Articles of Religion of the Church of England, A.D. 1571

The official statement of doctrine of the Church of England. In 1801 the Protestant Episcopal Church in the United States of America adopted the Thirty-nine Articles with minor deletions and variations. Article IX, "Of the Resurrection of Christ," reads the same in the American Revision of 1801 as in the original English edition of 1571. To avoid the old English spelling, we quote from the 1801 revision.

#### "ARTICLE VII.—OF THE OLD TESTAMENT

"The Old Testament is not contrary to the New; for both in the Old and New Testament everlasting life is offered to mankind by Christ, who is the only Mediator between God and man. Wherefore they are not to be heard, which feign that the old fathers did look only for transitory promises. Although the law given from God by Moses, as touching ceremonies and rites, do not bind Christian men, nor the civil precepts thereof ought of necessity to be received in any commonwealth; yet notwithstanding, no Christian man whatsoever is free from the obedience of the commandments which are called moral."—*Ibid.*, pp. 491, 492.

### American Revision of the Thirty-nine Articles by the Protestant Episcopal Church, A.D. 1801

#### "ARTICLE VI.—OF THE OLD TESTAMENT

"The Old Testament is not contrary to the New; for both in the Old and New Testament everlasting life is offered to mankind by Christ, who is the only Mediator between God and man, being both God and man. Wherefore they are not to be heard, which feign that the old fathers did look only for transitory promises. Although the law given from God by Moses, as touching ceremonies and rites, do not bind Christian men, nor the civil precepts thereof ought of necessity to be received in any commonwealth; yet notwithstanding, no Christian man whatsoever is free from the obedience of the commandments which are called moral."—*Ibid.*, p. 816.

### The Anglican Catechism, A.D. 1549 and 1662

*(Church of England, and Protestant Episcopal Church in the United States of America)*

"The Catechism of the Church of England, and of the Protestant Episcopal Church in the United States of America, is found in all editions of 'The Book of Common Prayer,' between the baptismal service and the order of confirmation."—Volume 3, p. 517. The American edition contains a few minor changes. Such changes as occur in the section quoted below are indicated in parentheses.

"*Question.*—You said that your godfathers and godmothers (sponsors) did promise for you that you should keep God's commandments. Tell me how many there be.

"*Answer.*—Ten.

"*Ques.*—Which be (are) they?

"*Ans.*—The same which God spake in the twentieth chapter of Exodus. [Then follows the recital of the Decalogue.]

"*Ques.*—What dost thou chiefly learn by these Commandments.

"*Ans.*—I learn two things: my duty towards God, and my duty towards my neighbor. [Then follow two questions, one concerning the duty to God, and the other, the duty to our neighbor.]

"*Catechist.*—My good child, know this, that thou art not able to do these things of thyself, nor to walk in the commandments of God, and to serve Him, without His special grace; which thou must learn at all times to call for by diligent prayer."—*Ibid.*, pp. 518-520.

### The Irish Articles of Religion, A.D. 1615

"Probably composed by the learned Archbishop James Ussher. . . . Adopted by the . . . Irish Episcopal Church. . . . Practically superseded by the Thirty-nine Articles. . . . Important as the connecting link between the Thirty-nine Articles and the Westminster Confession, and as the chief source of the latter."—Volume 3, p. 526.

"84. Although the law given from God by Moses as touching ceremonies and rites be abolished, and the civil precepts thereof be not of necessity to be received in any commonwealth, yet, notwithstanding, no Christian man whatsoever is freed from the obedience of the commandments which are called moral."—*Ibid.*, p. 541.

## The Westminster Confession of Faith, A.D. 1647

Of the Westminster Assembly that drew up this confession, Schaff declares: "Whether we look at the extent or ability of its labors, or its influence upon future generations, it stands first among Protestant Councils."—Volume 1, p. 728. The Westminster Assembly carried on its work during that period in English history when the Puritans, who desired to reform more fully the English church from any trace of Roman Catholicism, were in the ascendancy. With minor variations, the Westminster Confession is considered authoritative by Presbyterian bodies everywhere.

Particular attention is called to the texts of Scripture given as proofs of the statements in the confession. Those texts most frequently used by the No-Law advocates, are here used in such connections by the framers of this confession as to show the difference between moral and ceremonial laws, and the perpetuity of the former, etc.

### "CHAPTER XIX.—OF THE LAW OF GOD

"I. God gave Adam a law, as a covenant of works, by which He bound him and all his posterity to personal, entire, exact, and perpetual obedience; promised life upon the fulfilling, and threatened death upon the breach of it; and endued him with power and ability to keep it.[1]

"II. This law, after his fall, continued to be a perfect rule of righteousness; and, as such, was delivered by God upon Mt. Sinai in ten commandments, and written in two tables;[2] the first four commandments containing our duty toward God, and the other six our duty to man.[3]

---

[1] Gen. 1:26, 27 with Gen. 2:17; Rom. 2:14, 15; 10:5; 5:12, 19; Gal. 3:10, 12; Eccl. 7:29; Job 28:28.
[2] James 1:25; 2:8, 10-12; Rom. 13:8, 9; Deut. 5:32; 10:4; Ex. 34:1 [Am. ed. Rom. 3:19].
[3] Matt. 22:37-40 [Am. ed. Ex. 20:3-18].

"III. Beside this law, commonly called moral, God was pleased to give to the people of Israel, as a church under age, ceremonial laws, containing several typical ordinances, partly of worship, prefiguring Christ, His graces, actions, sufferings, and benefits; [4] and partly holding forth divers instructions of moral duties.[5] All of which ceremonial laws are now abrogated under the New Testament.[6]

"IV. To them also, as a body politic, He gave sundry judicial laws, which expired together with the state of that people, not obliging any other, now, further than the general equity thereof may require.[7]

"V. The moral law doth forever bind all, as well justified persons as others, to the obedience thereof; [8] and that not only in regard of the matter contained in it, but also in respect of the authority of God the Creator who gave it.[9] Neither doth Christ in the gospel any way dissolve, but much strengthen this obligation.[10]

"VI. Although true believers be not under the law as a covenant of works, to be thereby justified or condemned; [11] yet is it of great use to them, as well as to others; in that, as a rule of life, informing them of the will of God and their duty, it directs and binds them to walk accordingly; [12] discovering also the sinful pollutions of their nature, hearts, and lives; [13] so as, examining themselves thereby, they may come to further conviction of humiliation for, and hatred against sin; [14] together with a clearer sight of the need they have of Christ, and the perfection of His obedience.[15] It is likewise of use to the regenerate, to restrain their corruptions, in that it forbids sin; [16] and the threatenings of it serve to show

---

[4] Heb. 9; 10:1; Gal. 4:1-3; Col. 2:17.
[5] 1 Cor. 5:7; 2 Cor. 6:17; Jude 23.
[6] Col. 2:14, 16, 17; Dan. 9:27; Eph. 2:15, 16.
[7] Ex. 21; 22:1-29; Gen. 49:10, with 1 Peter 2:13, 14; Matt. 5:17, with verses 38, 39; 1 Cor. 9:8-10.
[8] Rom. 13:8-10; Eph. 6:2; 1 John 2:3, 4, 7, 8 [Am. ed. Rom. 3:31, and 6:15].
[9] James 2:10, 11.
[10] Matt. 5:17-19; James 2:8; Rom. 3:31.
[11] Rom. 6:14; Gal. 2:16; 3:13; 4:4, 5; Acts 13:39; Rom. 8:1.
[12] Rom. 7:12, 22, 25; Ps. 119:4-6; 1 Cor. 7:19; Gal. 5:14, 16, 18-23.
[13] Rom. 7:7; 3:20.
[14] James 1:23-25; Rom. 7:9, 14, 24.
[15] Gal. 3:24; Rom. 7:24, 25; 8:3, 4.
[16] James 2:11; Ps. 119:101, 104, 128.

what even their sins deserve, and what afflictions in this life they may expect for them, although freed from the curse thereof threatened in the law." The promises of it, in like manner, show them God's approbation of obedience, and what blessings they may expect upon the performance thereof; [18] although not as due to them by the law as a covenant of works; [19] so as a man's doing good, and refraining from evil, because the law encourageth to the one, and deterreth from the other, is no evidence of his being under the law, and not under grace." [20]

"VII. Neither are the forementioned uses of the law contrary to the grace of the gospel, but do sweetly comply with it: [21] the Spirit of Christ subduing and enabling the will of man to do that freely and cheerfully which the will of God, revealed in the law, requireth to be done." [22]

"CHAPTER XX.—OF CHRISTIAN LIBERTY, AND LIBERTY OF CONSCIENCE

"I. The liberty which Christ hath purchased for believers under the gospel consists in their freedom from the guilt of sin, the condemning wrath of God, the curse of the moral law." [23] . . . All which were common also to believers under the law; [24] but under the New Testament the liberty of Christians is further enlarged in their freedom from the yoke of the ceremonial law, to which the Jewish Church was subjected." [25] "—Volume 3, pp. 640-644.

### The Westminster Shorter Catechism, A.D. 1647

"This catechism was prepared by the Westminster Assembly in 1647, and adopted by the General Assembly of the Church of Scotland, 1648; by the Presbyterian Synod of New York and Philadelphia, May, 1788; and by nearly all the Calvinistic Presbyterian and Congregational Churches of the English tongue. . . . It is more extensively used

---

[17] Ezra 9:13, 14; Ps. 89:30-34.
[18] Lev. 26:1, 10, 14, with 2 Cor. 6:16; Eph. 6:2, 3; Ps. 37:11, with Matt. 5:5; Ps. 19:11.
[19] Gal. 2:16; Luke 17:10.
[20] Rom. 6:12, 14; 1 Peter 3:8-12, with Ps. 34:12-16; Heb. 12:28, 29.
[21] Gal. 3:21 [Am. ed. Titus 2:11-14].
[22] Eze. 36:27; Heb. 8:10, with Jer. 31:33.
[23] Titus 2:14; 1 Thess. 1:10; Gal. 3:13.
[24] Gal. 3:9, 14.
[25] Gal. 4:1-3, 6, 7; 5:1; Acts 15:10, 11.

than any other Protestant catechism except perhaps the Small Catechism of Luther and the Heidelberg Catechism."—*Ibid.*, p. 676.

"*Question 14.*—What is sin?

"*Answer.*—Sin is any want of conformity unto, or transgression of, the law of God."

"*Ques. 39.*—What is the duty which God requireth of man?

"*Ans.*—The duty which God requireth of man is obedience to His revealed will.

"*Ques. 40.*—What did God at first reveal to man for the rule of his obedience?

"*Ans.*—The rule which God at first revealed to man for his obedience, was the moral law.

"*Ques. 41.*—Wherein is the moral law summarily comprehended?

"*Ans.*—The moral law is summarily comprehended in the ten commandments.

"*Ques. 42.*—What is the sum of the ten commandments?

"*Ans.*—The sum of the ten commandments is, to love the Lord our God with all our heart, with all our soul, with all our strength, and with all our mind; and our neighbor as ourselves.

"*Ques. 43.*—What is the preface to the ten commandments?

"*Ans.*—The preface to the ten commandments is in these words: 'I am the Lord thy God, which brought thee out of the land of Egypt, out of the house of bondage.'

"*Ques. 44.*—What doth the preface to the ten commandments teach us?

"*Ans.*—The preface to the ten commandments teacheth us, that because God is the Lord, and our God and Redeemer, therefore we are bound to keep all His commandments."

[Then follows a series of questions and answers explaining in order each of the Ten Commandments.]—*Ibid.*, pp. 678, 684, 685.

### The Savoy Declaration of the Congregational Church, A.D. 1658

Concerning the "general creeds or declarations of faith which have been approved by the Congregational Churches in England and America," Schaff declares: "They agree substantially with the Westminster

Confession, or the Calvinistic system of doctrine, but differ from Presbyterianism by rejecting the legislative and judicial authority of presbyteries and synods, and by maintaining the independence of the local churches." "The American Congregationalists have from time to time adopted the Westminster standards of doctrine [the Westminster Confession of Faith], with the exception of the sections relating to synodical church government."

"The first and fundamental Congregational confession of faith and platform of polity is the Savoy Declaration, so called from the place where it was composed and adopted [Savoy, in the Strand, London]." —Volume 1, pp. 829, 835. "The Savoy Declaration is merely a modification of the Westminster Confession to suit the Congregational polity." —Volume 3, p. 718. Schaff indicates "the principal omissions, additions, and changes." No change is noted in Chapter XIX, "Of the Law of God," or in Section 1 of Chapter XX, "Of Christian Liberty, and Liberty of Conscience," of the Westminster Confession.

## The Confession of the Society of Friends, Commonly Called Quakers, A.D. 1675

"The most authoritative summary of the principles and doctrines of the Religious Society of Friends."—*Ibid.*, p. 789.

### "THE EIGHTH PROPOSITION

### *"Concerning Perfection*

"In whom this holy and pure birth is fully brought forth [the "spiritual birth," as discussed in the seventh proposition] the body of death and sin comes to be crucified and removed, and their hearts united and subjected unto the truth, so as not to obey any suggestion or temptation of the evil one, but to be free from actual sinning and transgressing of the law of God, and in that respect perfect. Yet doth this perfection still admit of a growth; and there remaineth a possibility of sinning where the mind doth not most diligently and watchfully attend unto the Lord."—*Ibid.*, pp. 794, 795.

## The Baptist Confession of 1688
## (The Philadelphia Confession)

"This is the most generally accepted confession of the Regular or Calvinistic Baptists in England and in the Southern States of America. It appeared first in London, 1677. . . . It was adopted early in the

# ANSWERS TO OBJECTIONS

eighteenth century by the Philadelphia Association of Baptist Churches, and is hence called also the Philadelphia Confession of Faith.

"It is a slight modification of the Confession of the Westminster Assembly (1647) and the Savoy Declaration (1658), with changes to suit the Baptist views on church polity and on the subjects and mode of baptism."—*Ibid.*, p. 738. Schaff notes the specific changes made in certain chapters of the Westminster Confession. No change is noted in Chapter XIX, "Of the Law of God," or of Section I of Chapter XX, "Of Christian Liberty, and Liberty of Conscience."

## The New Hampshire Baptist Confession, A.D. 1833

"Widely accepted by the Baptists, especially in the Northern and Western States. . . . The text is taken from the 'Baptist Church Manual,' published by the American Baptist Publication Society, Philadelphia."—*Ibid.*, p. 742.

### "XII.—OF THE HARMONY OF THE LAW AND THE GOSPEL

"We believe that the law of God is the eternal and unchangeable rule of His moral government; [1] that it is holy, just, and good; [2] and that the inability which the Scriptures ascribe to fallen men to fulfill its precepts arises entirely from their love of sin; [3] to deliver them from which, and to restore them through a Mediator to unfeigned obedience to the holy law, is one great end of the gospel, and of the means of grace connected with the establishment of the visible church.[4] "—*Ibid.*, p. 746.

## The Methodist Articles of Religion, A.D. 1784

"The Twenty-five Articles of Religion were drawn up by John Wesley for the American Methodists, and adopted at a Conference in 1784. They underwent some changes, chiefly verbal. . . . They are a liberal and judicious abridgment of the Thirty-nine Articles of the Church of England. . . . The text is taken from the official manual of *The Doctrines and Discipline of the Methodist Episcopal Church,* ed. by Bishop Harris, New York, 1872."—*Ibid.*, p. 807. All the important branches of Methodism contain in their creeds the following from these Articles of Religion:

---

[1] Rom. 3:31; Matt. 5:17; Luke 16:17; Rom. 3:20; 4:15.
[2] Rom. 7:12, 7, 14, 22; Gal. 3:21; Psalms 119.
[3] Rom. 8:7, 8; Joshua 24:19; Jer. 13:23; John 6:44; 5:44.
[4] Rom. 8:2, 4; 10:4; 1 Tim. 1:5; Heb. 8:10; Jude 20, 21; Heb. 12:14; Matt. 16:17, 18; 1 Cor. 12:28.

# THE LAW OF GOD IN CHURCH CREEDS

### "VI.—OF THE OLD TESTAMENT

"The Old Testament is not contrary to the New; for both in the Old and New Testament everlasting life is offered to mankind by Christ, who is the only Mediator between God and man, being both God and man. Wherefore they are not to be heard who feign that the old fathers did look only for transitory promises. Although the law given from God by Moses, as touching ceremonies and rites, doth not bind Christians, nor ought the civil precepts thereof of necessity be received in any commonwealth, yet, notwithstanding, no Christian whatsoever is free from the obedience of the commandments which are called moral."—*Ibid.*, p. 808.

## The Longer Catechism of the Orthodox, Catholic, Eastern Church, A.D. 1839

"The most authoritative doctrinal standard of the orthodox Græco-Russian Church."—Volume 2, p. 445.

### "ON THE LAW OF GOD AND THE COMMANDMENTS

"485. What means have we to know good works from bad?

"The inward law of God, or the witness of our conscience, and the outward law of God, or God's commandments.

"486. Does Holy Scripture speak of the inward law of God?

"The apostle Paul says of the heathen: 'Which show the work of the law written in their hearts, their conscience also bearing witness, and their thoughts the meanwhile accusing or else excusing one another.' Rom. 2:15.

"487. If there is in man's heart an inward law, why was the outward given?

"It was given because men obeyed not the inward law, but led carnal and sinful lives, and stifled within themselves the voice of the spiritual law, so that it was necessary to put them in mind of it outwardly through the commandments. 'Wherefore then serveth the law? It was added because of transgressions.' Gal. 3:19.

"488. When and how was God's outward law given to men?

"When the Hebrew people, descended from Abraham, had

509

been miraculously delivered from bondage in Egypt, on their way to the Promised Land, in the desert, on Mt. Sinai, God manifested His presence in fire and clouds, and gave them the law, by the hand of Moses, their leader."

"490. You said that these commandments were given to the people of Israel: must we, then, also walk by them?

"We must; for they are in substance the same law which, in the words of St. Paul, has been 'written in the hearts' of all men, that all should walk by it.

"491. Did Jesus Christ teach men to walk by the ten commandments?

"He bade men, if they would attain to everlasting life, to 'keep the commandments;' and taught us to understand and fulfill them more perfectly than had been done before He came. Matt. 19:17; and 5."—*Ibid.*, pp. 521, 522.

Questions No. 492 to 608 deal in detail with each of the ten commands.

### D. L. Moody on the Ten Commandments

In addition to these quotations from the great Protestant creeds and confessions, it is pertinent to quote also from the writings of the evangelist D. L. Moody. He was the founder of the Moody Bible Institute, which has been followed by the creation of Bible institutes in various parts of the country. These Bible institutes today are probably the most pronounced in their declarations against the law of God, and in their denunciation of those who teach that the law has any place in the life of the saved man. The statements from D. L. Moody speak for themselves.

The book from which the following quotations are taken is entitled *Weighed and Wanting, Addresses on the Ten Commandments,* by D. L. Moody, published by Fleming H. Revell Company, Chicago, copyrighted 1898 by The Bible Institute Colportage Association. The frontispiece consists of a reproduction of the Ten Commandments as given in Exodus 20:3-17. There are twelve chapters, an introductory chapter entitled "Weighed in the Balances," then a chapter on each of the Ten Commandments, and a closing chapter entitled "The Handwriting Blotted Out." The first quotation is from the chapter entitled "Weighed in the Balances."

"It is a favorite thing with infidels to set their own standard, to measure themselves by other people. But that will not do in the day of judgment. Now we will use God's law as a balance weight. . . .

"Let me call your attention to the fact that God wrote on the tables of stone at Sinai as well as on the wall of Belshazzar's palace. . . .

"The law that was given at Sinai has lost none of its solemnity. Time cannot wear out its authority or the fact of its authorship.

"I can imagine some one saying, 'I won't be weighed by that law. I don't believe in it.'

"Now men may cavil as much as they like about other parts of the Bible, but I have never met an honest man that found fault with the ten commandments. . . .

"Now the question for you and me is, Are we keeping these commandments? Have we fulfilled all the requirements of the law? If God made us, as we know He did, He had a right to make that law; and if we don't use it aright, it would have been better for us if we had never had it, for it will condemn us. We shall be found wanting. The law is all right, but are we right? . . .

"Some people seem to think we have got beyond the commandments. What did Christ say? 'Think not that I am come to destroy the law, and the prophets: I am not come to destroy, but to fulfill. For verily I say unto you, Till heaven and earth pass, one jot or one tittle shall in no wise pass from the law, till all be fulfilled.' The commandments of God given to Moses in the mount at Horeb are as binding today as ever they have been since the time when they were proclaimed in the hearing of the people. The Jews said the law was not given in Palestine (which belonged to Israel), but in the wilderness, because the law was for all nations.

"Jesus never condemned the law and the prophets, but He did condemn those who did not obey them. Because He gave new commandments, it does not follow that He abolished the old. Christ's explanation of them made them all the more searching. . . .

"The people must be made to understand that the ten commandments are still binding, and that there is a penalty attached to their violation. We do not want a gospel of mere sentiment. The sermon on the mount did not blot out the ten commandments. . . .

"Paul said: 'Love is the fulfilling of the law.' But does this mean that the detailed precepts of the decalogue are superseded, and have become back numbers? Does a father cease to give children rules to obey because they love him? Does a nation burn its statute books because the people have become patriotic? Not at all. And yet people speak as if the commandments do not hold for Christians because they have come to love God. Paul said: 'Do we then make void the law through faith? God forbid: yea, we establish the law.' It still holds good. The commandments are necessary. So long as we obey, they do not rest heavy upon us; but as soon as we try to break away, we find they are like fences to keep us within bounds. Horses need bridles even after they have been properly broken in. . . .

"Now my friend, are you ready to be weighed by this law of God? A great many people say that if they keep the commandments, they do not need to be forgiven and saved through Christ. But have you kept them? I will admit that if you perfectly keep the commandments, you do not need to be saved by Christ; but is there a man in the wide world who can truly say that he has done this? Young lady, can you say: 'I am ready to be weighed by the law'? Can you, young man? Will you step into the scales and be weighed one by one by the ten commandments?

"Now face these ten commandments honestly and prayerfully. See if your life is right, and if you are treating God fairly. God's statutes are just, are they not? If they are right, let us see if we are right. Let us pray that the Holy Ghost may search each one of us. Let us get alone with God and read His law—read it carefully and prayerfully, and ask Him to show us our sins and what He would have us to do."— Pages 10-17.

The next quotation is from the chapter entitled "The Fourth Commandment."

"I honestly believe that this commandment is just as binding today as it ever was. I have talked with men who have said that it has been abrogated, but they have never been able to point to any place in the Bible where God repealed it. When Christ was on earth, He did nothing to set it aside; He freed it from the traces under which the scribes and Pharisees had put it, and gave it its true place. 'The Sabbath was made for man, not man for the Sabbath.' It is just as practicable and as necessary for men today as it ever was—in fact, more than ever, because we live in such an intense age.

"The Sabbath was binding in Eden, and it has been in force ever since. The fourth commandment begins with the word 'remember,' showing that the Sabbath already existed when God wrote this law on the tables of stone at Sinai. How can men claim that this one commandment has been done away with, when they will admit that the other nine are still binding? . . .

"Once when I was holding meetings in London, in my ignorance I made arrangements to preach four times in different places one Sabbath. After I had made the appointments, I found I had to walk sixteen miles; but I walked it, and I slept that night with a clear conscience. I have made it a rule never to use the cars, and if I have a private carriage, I insist that horse and man shall rest on Monday. I want no hackman to rise up in judgment against me.

"My friends, if we want to help the Sabbath, let business men and Christians never patronize cars on the Sabbath. I would hate to own stock in those companies, to be the means of taking the Sabbath from these men, and have to answer for it at the day of judgment. Let those who are Christians at any rate endeavor to keep a conscience void of offense on this point."—Pages 46-50.

The next quotation is from the closing chapter, entitled "The Handwriting Blotted Out."

"We have now considered the ten commandments, and the question for each one of us is, Are we keeping them? If God should weigh us by them, would we be found wanting or not wanting? Do we keep the law, the *whole* law? Are we obeying God with all our heart? Do we render Him a full and willing obedience?

"These ten commandments are not ten different laws; they are one law. If I am being held up in the air by a chain with ten links and I break one of them, down I come, just as surely as if I break the whole ten. If I am forbidden to go out of an inclosure, it makes no difference at what point I break through the fence. 'Whosoever shall keep the whole law, and yet offend in one point, he is guilty of all.' 'The golden chain of obedience is broken if one link is missing.' . . .

"For fifteen hundred years man was under the law, and no one was equal to it. Christ came and showed that the commandments went beyond the mere letter; and can any one since say that he has been able to keep them in his own strength? . . .

"I can imagine that you are saying to yourself, 'If we are to be judged by these laws, how are we going to be saved? Nearly every one of them has been broken by us, in spirit, if not in letter.' I almost hear you say: 'I wonder if Mr. Moody is ready to be weighed. Would he like to put those tests to himself?'

17                                    513

"With all humility I reply that if God commanded me to step into the scales now, I am ready.

" 'What!' you say, 'haven't you broken the law?'

"Yes, I have. I was a sinner before God the same as you; but forty years ago I pleaded guilty at His bar. I cried for mercy, and He forgave me. If I step into the scales, the Son of God has promised to be with me. I would not dare to step in without Him. If I did, how quickly the scales would fly up!

"Christ kept the law. If He had ever broken it, He would have had to die for Himself; but because He was a Lamb without spot or blemish, His atoning death is efficacious for you and me. He had no sin of His own to atone for, and so God accepted His sacrifice. Christ is the end of the law for righteousness to every one that believeth. We are righteous in God's sight because the righteousness of God which is by faith in Jesus Christ is unto all and upon all them that believe. . . .

"If the love of God is shed abroad in your heart, you will be able to fulfill the law."—Pages 119-124.

To all this Adventists respond fervently and without reservation: Amen, Brother Moody.

---

NOTE.—For further testimony concerning the moral law, and the difference between it and the ceremonial law, see the following chapter.

## CHAPTER 6

# Are Adventists Legalists?

THE CHARGE is repeatedly and militantly brought against us as Seventh-day Adventists that we are legalists. In other words, that we depend on a keeping of the law instead of on the keeping power of Christ, and thus point men to the law rather than to Christ.

Now, this is a grave charge indeed. If it be true that we substitute law for grace and our own frail powers for the divine power promised by Christ, then we are entitled only to condemnation by all who love our Lord and Saviour. In fact, if we substitute the law for Christ we are not really Christians

Do we plead guilty to such charge? We do not. With all the vehemence at our command we declare the charge to be false and unfounded. We insist that no fair reading of our teachings on the law warrants any indictment of us as legalists. The only way that an appearance of a case against Adventists has been produced is by taking stray passages here and there from the rather numerous denominational works and giving to them an interpretation wholly unwarranted and alien to the general tenor of Adventist writings on the subject.

What our critics do not seem to realize is that by such a method of presenting evidence the Bible writers may also be proved legalists. James declares, "By works a man is justified, and not by faith only." James 2:24. What a dreadful legalist was James! If Adventists belong outside the pale of Christendom, then where does James belong? In all our history we have never written anything quite so vigorous as this in behalf of good works. Or what shall we say of the answer that our Lord gave to the rich young man who

515

asked of Him the way to life eternal: "If thou wilt enter into life, keep the commandments"? Matt. 19:17.

But let us take the possibilities of stray passages a little further. By picking out the desired texts our critics could prove various Bible writers to be not only legalists but opponents of all sound religion! Does not Paul make reference to being baptized for the dead (1 Cor. 15:29)? and have not his words been plausibly used by those who believe in the efficacy of prayers for the dead? Does not Isaiah attribute to God the declaration, "I make peace, and create evil"? Isa. 45:7. And have not skeptics pointed to Isaiah's statement in scorn? Again, what shall we say of our Lord's word to His apostles: "Whose soever sins ye remit, they are remitted"? John 20:23. Do not Roman Catholics quote this text with great plausibility and persuasiveness in behalf of the doctrine of priestly absolution?

Now, in their zeal to ferret out false doctrine, do our critics indict these Bible authors? For illustration, do they indict James? Why let him escape the denunciation that ought to come upon the head of all legalists? Luther did not. The great Reformer, who was dazzled by the light of the doctrine of justification by faith, could see in the epistle of James only a contradiction of that doctrine and wished to dismiss the letter as "an epistle of straw." Hence, our critics would have good Protestant precedent for their attack on James.

### Inconsistent Critics

But they are not consistent. They refuse to attack any Bible writer in regard to particular passages that might seem to contradict the main tenor of Scripture and the beliefs of Christians. When skeptics point to apparently questionable texts and alleged contradictions, our critics, who generally belong to the conservative wing of Christendom, are the most vehement in crying out against what they declare are the unfair tactics of skeptics in lifting stray passages out of their context. They insist that a particular text in question shall be understood in the setting of all the Scriptures, and that other and clearer texts shall be the guide for interpreting a text that seems obscure or contradictory to the main teachings of the Bible.

## No Attack on James

Specifically, our critics refuse to indict James. They do not think that he wrote an epistle of straw. They would not thus attack a part of the canon of Holy Scripture. They would be horrified at the thought. If anything, they would attack Luther, or perhaps we should say they would explain away Luther's remark on the ground that he was just coming out of the darkness of Catholicism and had not yet discovered the higher harmony that exists between apparently contradictory Scriptures on the important subject of faith and good works.

And of course our critics would be right in taking that position with regard to the Scriptures in general and the Epistle of James in particular. Picking out stray passages in the Bible is no proper way to discover the true teachings of the Bible. And the person who does this and who goes on from this to pit one text against another, is rightly open to grave suspicion that he is approaching the Scriptures from a prejudiced viewpoint, seeking to make out a case against them.

If all this be true as regards the writings of the Scriptures—and it is—then why is it not also true as regards other writings? It is. Including even the writings of Seventh-day Adventists? Why not? But evidently our critics are not willing to concede this principle in relation to Adventist writings. If they did they would immediately have to withdraw all the charges they have made against us as legalists.

## Let Us Examine the Record

With no irreverence to the Bible writers, it may be stated as a simple matter of fact that it would be much easier for Seventh-day Adventists to prove, in terms of their writings, that they believe wholly and only in the unmerited grace of Christ for their salvation, than for James to do so from his writings. And why? Because it probably never occurred to James, after he had written his most helpful, practical epistle, to follow it with any general statement of belief, particularly on the matter of law and grace, in order to escape misunderstanding. He took for granted that the Christian believers, to whom had been preached the grace of Christ, would interpret his epistle aright. God gave him words to say in the epistle regarding the place of works, and he let the matter stand at that.

Seventh-day Adventists have not done this. We have taken care to place ourselves on record in a formal way regarding our belief as to law and grace, along with our belief on other doctrines. Besides, different Adventist authors have written whole books devoted to the theme. Those books set forth the truth that the Christian is wholly dependent on Christ. These works are easily available to all. Surely our critics must have found them, for they give evidence of having combed Adventist works with sedulous care in order to come up with a stray phrase here and there from them.

Surely they must have seen the book *Steps to Christ*, by Mrs. E. G. White, a book that has had probably a larger circulation than almost any other of our works. And it is Mrs. White that our critics desire, if possible, to quote, because they know that we view her as speaking with authority for us. How anyone could frame more clearly the doctrine of complete dependence upon Christ for forgiveness of past sins and for strength to lead a godly life until the day of our Lord's return than Mrs. White has framed in that book, we know not. This much we do know; our critics, in all their writings, have never outdone this book in ascribing to Christ all honor, all power, as the only source of the sinner's deliverance from sin and the Christian's growth in grace.

## Mrs. White's Life of Christ

Or take, for illustration, another book by Mrs. E. G. White, *The Desire of Ages*, in which she tells the story of our Lord's life on earth, of His dying for our sins, of His being raised again for our justification, and of His ascending to heaven above to minister in our behalf at the right hand of God. Have any of our critics written a work that raises Christ to greater heights or makes Him more indispensable to the sinner and to the saint in the plan of salvation than has this work? The answer is No. We say this, not out of any disparagement of the writings of our critics, but out of a calm conviction that they simply have not attained unto the heights of exultant declaration of Christ's place in the plan of salvation that Mrs. White has attained.

But Mrs. White is not the only Adventist writer on this subject. Many of our authors have written on it. And numerous times they have taken occasion to refute the false charge that we are legalists. They have been explicit in their declarations that we rely wholly and only on Christ for our salvation. It would take altogether too much space to cite the array of references that could here be given, and surely there is no need, for again we say, our critics could not have failed to find at least a portion of these writings and these explicit statements in combing our works. However, in order to keep the record straight, here are a few typical statements from Adventist authors who have also been leaders in the denomination, and thus may rightly be viewed as reflecting the theological views of the denomination.

## Testimony of Various Leaders

These statements might be viewed in the form of testimony offered by witnesses on a question at issue. The question is, What do Adventists believe to be the means of salvation? A. G. Daniells, who served as president of the General Conference for twenty-one years, will be the first to testify. He wrote a book entitled *Christ Our Righteousness.* Following are typical sentences:

"It is through faith in the blood of Christ that all the sins of the believer are canceled and the righteousness of God is put in their place to the believer's account. . . . He yields, repents, confesses, and by faith claims Christ as his Saviour. The instant that is done, he is accepted as a child of God. His sins are all forgiven, his guilt is canceled, he is accounted righteous, and stands approved, justified, before the divine law. And this amazing, miraculous change may take place in one short hour. *This is righteousness by faith.*"—Pages 22, 23.

Next is the testimony of William A. Spicer, who, first as secretary and then as president of the General Conference, served in key places in the church for many, many years. Speaking of the white raiment mentioned in the book of the Revelation, he says:

"This white raiment is the righteousness of Christ, received by faith. Not by any works that we can do to cleanse ourselves from sin, but by His own grace He cleanses us, and clothes us with His own righteousness."—*Beacon Lights of Prophecy,* p. 193.

Take now the testimony of Charles H. Watson, who was president of the General Conference for six years:

"He [Paul] also makes clear that a man, upon repentance and faith in Christ, pleading the Saviour's blood for the remission of his sins, and before he has wrought a single act of obedience to the law, is justified by his faith. . . .

"This righteousness is a gift. We cannot earn it. We cannot claim it by any natural right that we have, but, thank God, we can accept it in all its blessed fullness by faith in the atoning blood of Jesus. There is absolutely no doubt that the blood of the atonement is the means by which faith secures justification."—*The Atoning Work of Christ,* pp. 46-48.

Here is the testimony of William H. Branson, who has long held key administrative positions in the denomination and who is now its president:

"We are not asked to try to win salvation by some effort on our part but to accept it as a gift from God. We are not saved by anything we may do for God but by what He does for us. *Jesus saves,* and apart from Him there is no salvation."—*How Men Are Saved,* p. 27.

And here is the testimony of Francis M. Wilcox, for more than thirty years editor of *The Review and Herald,* which is the general church paper of Seventh-day Adventists:

"To justify is to make righteous, to make equal to the divine standard. As the penitent confesses his sins and lays hold of Christ's atoning sacrifice in his behalf, there is imputed to him, for all his past life, the righteousness of the Lord Jesus Christ, so that when God looks upon the past years of unrighteousness, He sees no longer a life filled with crime and iniquity, but He sees the spotless life of the Son of God that has been put in the place of the life of the believer. Thus the man stands in God's sight as though he had never committed iniquity."—*Review and Herald,* Centennial Issue, Oct. 19, 1944, pp. 15, 16.

For good measure here is one further quotation. This from Harold M. S. Richards, radio preacher of the Voice of Prophecy program, a nationwide broadcast that has been conducted for years under the sponsorship of the Seventh-day Adventist denomination:

"Christ died for us; Christ lives in us by His Spirit. So we belong to Him, and our salvation depends upon Him—wholly and entirely. Our obedience to God's law, then, is not to be saved, but because we are saved. It is not of our doing, but of His doing. 'Not of works, lest any man should boast. For we are His workmanship, created in Christ Jesus unto good works, which God hath before ordained that we should walk in them.' Eph. 2:9, 10."—Radio Script, "The Law and the Gospel," p. 3, broadcast Dec. 9, 1945, over Mutual network.

These testimonies hardly call for comment, unless it be the inquiry: Who is better qualified to state what Adventists believe—these witnesses or our critics?

### Official Statement of Belief

But there is even more impressive and if possible more unequivocal testimony that can be presented than that of these individual leaders and spokesmen for Seventh-day Adventists. There is the Statement of Belief that appears in the official *Yearbook* of the denomination. Adventists have never sought to formulate a creed in the historic meaning of that word. We have hesitated to crystallize in too rigid a form our understanding of the Scriptures, lest we fall into the error of refusing to go beyond our first formulated creed to any better, clearer, or more correct understanding of the Scriptures.

But we have on occasions set forth what we describe as a Statement of Belief. There have been at least two such prepared during the history of this denomination. They are in no essential point contrary one to the other. They differ rather in phrasing and thus in length. The latter one, which has appeared in the official

*Yearbook* for a number of years, and which is found unchanged in the latest edition, for all to read, devotes sections 3-8 to the subject of Christ and the sinner, the law and grace. As those sections state, we believe—

"3. That Jesus Christ is very God, being of the same nature and essence as the Eternal Father. While retaining His divine nature He took upon Himself the nature of the human family, lived on the earth as a man, exemplified in His life as our Example the principles of righteousness, attested His relationship to God by many mighty miracles, died for our sins on the cross, was raised from the dead, and ascended to the Father, where He ever lives to make intercession for us. John 1:1, 14; Heb. 2:9-18; 8:1, 2; 4:14-16; 7:25.

"4. That every person in order to obtain salvation must experience the new birth; that this comprises an entire transformation of life and character by the re-creative power of God through faith in the Lord Jesus Christ. John 3:16; Matt. 18:3; Acts 2:37-39.

"5. That baptism is an ordinance of the Christian church and should follow repentance and forgiveness of sins. By its observance faith is shown in the death, burial, and resurrection of Christ. That the proper form of baptism is by immersion. Rom. 6:1-6; Acts 16:30-33.

"6. That the will of God as it relates to moral conduct is comprehended in His law of ten commandments; that these are great moral, unchangeable precepts, binding upon all men, in every age. Ex. 20:1-17.

"7. That the fourth commandment of this unchangeable law requires the observance of the seventh day Sabbath. This holy institution is at the same time a memorial of creation and a sign of sanctification, a sign of the believer's rest from his own works of sin, and his entrance into the rest of soul which Jesus promises to those who come to Him. Gen. 2:1-3; Ex. 20:8-11; 31:12-17; Heb. 4:1-10.

"8. That the law of ten commandments points out sin, the penalty of which is death. The law cannot save the transgressor from his sin, nor impart power to keep him from sinning. In infinite love and mercy, God provides a way whereby this may be done. He furnishes a substitute, even Christ the Righteous One, to die in man's stead, making 'Him to be sin for us, who knew no sin; that we might be made the righteousness of God in Him.' 2 Cor. 5:21. That one is justified, not by obedience to the law, but by the grace that is in Christ Jesus. By accepting Christ, man is reconciled to God, justified by His blood for the sins of the past, and saved from the power of sin by His indwelling life. Thus the gospel becomes 'the power of

# ARE ADVENTISTS LEGALISTS?

God unto salvation to everyone that believeth.' Rom. 1:16. This experience is wrought by the divine agency of the Holy Spirit, who convinces of sin and leads to the Sin-Bearer, inducting the believer into the new-covenant relationship, where the law of God is written on his heart, and through the enabling power of the indwelling Christ, his life is brought into conformity to the divine precepts. The honor and merit of this wonderful transformation belong wholly to Christ. 1 John 2:1, 2; 3:4; Rom. 3:20; 5:8-10; 7:7; Eph. 2:8-10; 3:17; Gal. 2:20; Heb. 8:8-12."—*Yearbook of the Seventh-day Adventist Denomination,* 1946, p. 4.

## The Crux of the Matter

Here, then, is what we believe on the subject of law and grace, Christ and the sinner, as set forth in the writings of various of our leaders and in our Statement of Belief. In the latter we have set forth, even as other churches have set forth in their creeds, our view on this doctrine of the law in the most explicit and the most authoritative way that it is possible for us to do. And ought we not to be credited with knowing what we believe? That is finally the crux of the matter. That is the heart of the controversy that we have with our critics who accuse us of legalism.

We are certain that our critics would rise up in wrath if we charged that they really did not know what they believed, that they could not safely be allowed to interpret their own writings and resolve apparent contradictions in them, or that a statement of belief they might formulate should not be taken at face value but should be ignored in favor of stray passages in the writings of different members of their religious persuasion. If we made such a charge against them they would consider it an insult to their intelligence, an indictment of their honesty, an accusation of duplicity and hypocrisy. And well they might.

But we bring no such charge against them. We believe that our critics are able to state what their beliefs are. We grant that they should be allowed to harmonize any apparent contradictions in other of their writings with the formal, carefully phrased words in their official statement of doctrine. We would do this for any critic, any opponent. We know that the limitations of language are such that it is easily possible to create apparent contradictions where no real contradictions exist, and to make an emphasis on one doctrine appear to be a denial of another.

When we want to know what any religious body believes, we seek first to discover whether they have prepared a formal statement of belief, and if so we take that as being their official belief on doctrine. And why not? What would be the point to any religious body's formulating a creed unless it would be accepted by those who read it as being a correct statement of the doctrinal views of that religious body?

Now what we concede to others, our critics included, we claim also for ourselves. Why not? Are we less able to express our thoughts in a formal statement of belief than are all other Christian people? Do we, in contrast to all other Christian bodies, not really know what we believe and hence use words with no true meaning? Or is it possible that our critics would claim that they need not concede to us what we willingly concede to them and to all others, namely that their official statements of belief are the honest expression of their doctrines. Unless they are prepared to set forth and support the charge that we employ duplicity in words, they have no defense whatever for the tactics they follow in ignoring our Statement of Belief and citing stray passages here and there in our writings to prove a case against us.

But the charge that either we do not know what we mean by what we say or we conceal our meanings, would be a new argument indeed. We hardly think that at this late date our critics will seek to prove true such a monstrous charge as this. If the star of Adventism had appeared in the religious sky only yesterday, bursting suddenly on the vision of men with blinding light, our critics might plausibly say that Adventism was not really what it appeared to be, that the statements of its spokesmen needed to be tested against time and the outworking of the beliefs. But Adventism did not burst suddenly upon the sight of men just yesterday. Instead, it rose slowly from the New England horizon, casting ever longer rays as the years have rolled on, until today the light of Advent teachings shines in every land. We have been preaching, writing, conducting church services, in an increasing number of languages for a century. The real meaning of our teachings has been revealed in our religious services week by week, and in the lives of our members day by day, for three generations.

And what do these years reveal? Do they reveal instances of Seventh-day Adventist ministers conducting revival services in the evangelistic sense of the word, calling on men to accept Christ? Yes. In our churches and in our annual camp meetings, year after year, appeals are made directly to the hearts of men and women, young and old, to accept Jesus Christ and to accept Him as their only Saviour from sin and their only spiritual Sustainer and Source of life for the future. Strange that our critics never seem to be aware of these revival services we conduct. There is nothing secret about them. Public notices in the press invite all to come to our large camp meetings. If we conducted these revival services on a legalistic basis, if we failed to exalt Jesus Christ, is it reasonable to believe that our critics would have overlooked this contrast?

### Adventist Pastoral Visitation

And what have Adventist pastors done through the years when visiting church members? Have they carried along a scroll of the Ten Commandments and consumed the time of the pastoral visit in asking the family whether they have kept the law, assuring them that if they will keep on trying they will probably succeed in keeping those commands, but that if they fail they will be in a very sad state? This question is not posed to provoke a smile from our Adventist readers. The matter is too serious for that.

Yes, what do Adventist pastors say or do when they visit the homes of their church members? Speaking personally, I have never taken a scroll of the law to any home, nor pleaded with parishioners to try harder to keep the law, nor warned them of the terrors of ultimate hell-fire if they failed. I rather took for granted that those who have accepted Christ have the law written in their hearts, which is the promise of the new covenant. Presuming this,

I spent my time in talking of the promises of God, the goodness of the Lord, His forgiving grace for sins confessed, His proffered power for victory in the future. And I ended each pastoral visit with a prayer to God through Jesus Christ, laying claim to all these promises, most particularly to the promise that Christ will dwell in our hearts by faith and live out through us all the principles of heaven, including all His divine laws.

And has there been anything unusual in my pastoral visitation? No. I have done simply what every other Adventist minister does. Would our critics suggest some other course for us to follow in order to be in harmony with good Christian practices and beliefs? I think not.

## Our Attack on Enslaving Habits

And what do we say to someone who comes to us for freedom from slavery to an evil habit like drink or tobacco? Do we simply urge him to try to keep the law of God, adding that we trust he will secure victory over his evil habit, but that if he fails there is only damnation ahead for him? Is it possible that we say such a thing as this? Well, our critics charge that we are legalists; hence, this is what we should be expected to say. But do we really? No! We point the poor slave of evil habits to our Lord and Saviour Jesus Christ. To whom else could we point him? And we pray for his deliverance through Christ.

Now, it is a fact that tens of thousands of those who seek admittance to the Adventist Church are troubled with some such habit as tobacco or liquor. Yet they all secure victory over these habits, for no Seventh-day Adventist smokes or drinks. Here, then, is an amazing fact. The habits of smoking and drinking have a fearful grip on most of their devotees, as many of them can testify. Yet those coming into the Adventist Church gain complete and generally rather sudden victory over these habits. Have Seventh-day Adventists found an immediate and ever-dependable source of power that other Christian people through all the years have not known?

# ARE ADVENTISTS LEGALISTS?

But why press this point further? Is it not evident that we have in this amazing phenomenon of a whole membership free from the enslaving habits of drink and tobacco, and even worse habits in heathen lands, the clearest proofs that Adventists rely on the one and only Source of help, Jesus Christ our Lord?

## Why Not Take a Poll?

Here is a suggestion for you who are critics, a suggestion which, if followed out, could once and for all settle this question of whether Adventists are legalists or not. Here is a chance for you to put your charge to an honest test. Take a poll of a cross section of the rank and file of Seventh-day Adventist laymen. Exclude all Adventist preachers, who according to you either do not know what they preach and teach or else have a conspiracy to conceal the meaning of their teachings. Go instead to the homes of humble laymen, who must seek to make religion work in their everyday lives, and whose sincerity and loyalty to Seventh-day Adventist beliefs is evidenced by their amazing liberality, which is probably the highest in the religious world.

Go with your notebook in hand and ask those laymen: "Do you rely on the keeping of the law to save you?" "Do you turn your back on Christ as the one and only Saviour from past sins and the only Source of power for holy living?" Or ask any variation of these questions in order to make sure that you are framing to your satisfaction your charge that Adventists are legalists.

It is clear what the answer would be. First, there would be a look of bewilderment, then amazement, then indignation, followed probably either by a vehement denial or else a vigorous inquiry as to how you ever came to ask such a question. This would be the response whether the question was asked of an Adventist layman in America, in China, in Africa, or in the islands of the sea.

Of course our critics may wish to challenge this statement, but we shall not listen to them until they have produced the findings from their poll of Adventist homes. We know they will not risk such a poll.

On the other hand, they will hardly attempt to minimize the force of this suggestion of a poll by declaring that Adventist laymen do not really know what their denomination teaches. It is no exaggeration to state that the average Seventh-day Adventist probably has more of his church's literature in his home than members of any other Protestant body. And if our critics doubt whether he knows what Adventists believe, it must be because they have never given him an opportunity to set forth those beliefs!

Now, here is a singular phenomenon. The ordinary Adventist layman who listens to his pastor week by week and who reads Adventist literature constantly, fails entirely to discover the allegedly Christ-denying character of Adventist theology. And hence he prays to God through Christ daily and relies on the saving grace of his Lord for holy living and victory over temptation. Truly a phenomenon!

### Yes, We Magnify the Law

At this point our critics may say defensively: "But you Seventh-day Adventists have to admit you preach the law. You weave it into your whole theology in such a way that the reader meets it repeatedly. You preach on it in your lectures to the public. You extol the law. You magnify it. You even say Christians should keep the law."

Strictly speaking, it is sufficient to say in reply that whatever we may write or preach about the law, our church members who listen to such preaching return home to rely wholly on Christ. Therefore our law preaching cannot be displacing Christ. Furthermore, what we weave into our writings and sermons concerning the law is rightly to be understood in terms of our formal statement of belief.

But let us examine this statement of our critics a little further. Yes, we weave the law all through our theology. So does the Bible, from first to last. The Old Testament says much about the law and obedience to it. Everyone grants that. The New Testament also says much about obedience to the commandments of God. Indeed, the very last book of the Bible describes the company of those ready for the second coming of Christ as men and women who "keep the commandments of God, and the faith of Jesus." Rev. 14:12. And in the version of the Bible which all of us have read from childhood, there is found in the last chapter, almost as a closing benediction to Scripture, this blessing: "Blessed are they that do his commandments, that they may have right to the tree of life, and may enter in through the gates into the city." Rev. 22:14.

## The Apostles Extolled the Law

Yes, we extol the law. We magnify it. But so did the holy apostles and so did our Lord. Paul declared, "Wherefore the law is holy, and the commandment holy, and just, and good. . . . For we know that the law is spiritual: but I am carnal, sold under sin." Rom. 7:12, 14.

Wrote the apostle John: "By this we know that we love the children of God, when we love God, and keep his commandments. For this is the love of God, that we keep his commandments: and his commandments are not grievous." 1 John 5:2, 3.

Of Christ the prophet Isaiah foretold:

"The Lord is well pleased for his righteousness' sake; he will magnify the law, and make it honourable." Isa. 42:21.

The fulfillment of this prophecy we find most clearly in Christ's sermon on the mount, in which He showed how comprehensive are the commandments against murder and adultery.

Yes, we extol the law, we magnify it, believing that we have every Scriptural precedent for so doing. Indeed, we would magnify it in the very words of Scripture. Nor have we been unique in this matter. We cannot claim any distinction by comparison with great Protestant bodies in this matter of exalting the law of God. The person who reads the creeds of the great Protestant bodies would almost conclude at times that Adventists have been outdone by them in this matter of vigorous declarations concerning the significance of the law of God. But our critics, in charging us with legalism, have clearly sought to imply, when they have not openly charged, that our belief on the law is an unorthodox one, alien to the belief held by the great body of Protestant Christians. But reference to the preceding chapter, "The Law of God in Church Creeds," will reveal that this is not so.

## In What Way Do We Differ?

Will our critics please lay alongside the Protestant confessions of faith, the formal Adventist statement on law and grace that was quoted from the Adventist *Yearbook,* and tell us in what way our statement differs from the classic creedal declarations of Protestantism? We are unable to discover any difference in spirit or in doctrine taught.

More than that, we are unable to discover any practical difference between our view of the law and that of present-day spokesmen for leading Protestant bodies. In the year 1932 the International Uniform Sunday School Lessons dealt with the subject of the Ten Commandments on the Sundays of August 7 and 14. Various church papers carried these lessons and offered their own comments on them. But those comments sound wholly alien to the statements made concerning the Decalogue by our critics, who declare that the law has been abolished, and the Adventists are legalists.

### *Sunday School Times* Testifies

For example, here is what *The Sunday School Times* said in part in its comment on the Sunday school lessons on the Ten Commandments:

"To know God is to love God. The commandments were given that men might know Jehovah God, the God of love and the God of holiness. To love God is to obey Him. God's law is an expression of God's love. The fearful thunders and fire and shaking of Sinai, so dreadful that Moses said, 'I exceedingly fear and quake' (Heb. 12:21), were to reveal the greatness and glory of God, that they might truly fear and reverence Him. . . . The law is spiritual, and can be kept only in spirit and in truth. Israel 'continued not' in this covenant, and God made a new covenant, not changing the laws, but blotting out their sins, and writing these same laws on their heart. Heb. 8:8-13.

## ARE ADVENTISTS LEGALISTS?

To have faith in the God of mercy and love is to have the righteousness of Abraham, and of Moses, and the heart of love to God to keep these commandments, by His grace."—July 23, 1932.

### Presbyterian Paper Speaks

In *The Presbyterian* is found this comment:

"The ten commandments are not only precepts of God, but also a description of the nature of God, and His desire for man, that man may be like God. The Lord Jehovah, Father of our Lord Jesus Christ, is the kind of Deity described in these ten words, or oracles, or commandments. Behind them stands the Being of God, and preliminary to them stands the exodus, the Passover, the remembrance. Paul recognized the underlying connection between law and grace when he wrote: 'I beseech you therefore, by the mercies of God, that ye present your bodies a living sacrifice, holy, acceptable unto God, which is your reasonable service.' Rom. 12:1. The word 'therefore' looks backward at the great chapters before the twelfth. The law is a paragraph in a covenant of grace. It is indeed a 'law of liberty.' "—July 28, 1932.

*The Watchman-Examiner,* one of the most influential weeklies in the Baptist denomination, contains in its comments on the Sunday school lessons this statement:

"Christ taught His disciples, and all who followed His teachings, that we may have eternal life by keeping perfectly the law as given by God on Sinai, and by loving Him who is the embodiment and the fulfillment of that law."—August 4, 1932.

### The *Moody Monthly* Testifies

Church papers contain many statements on the law, in addition to those quoted in connection with the Sunday school lessons. Take, for example, a series of articles that was printed in the *Moody Bible Institute Monthly* under the head "Are Christians Freed From the Law?" The series begins with various definitions of *law* and presents three distinct codes: "the civil law," "the ceremonial law," and "the moral law." Focusing on the moral law, the writer of the series says in his first article, "Let us now see how the moral law is emphasized, enlarged, and enforced in all its details in the New Testament." He shows how Christ and the apostles dealt with it:

531

ANSWERS TO OBJECTIONS

"So far from annulling any of the Ten Commandments, He [Christ] amplified their scope, teaching that an angry thought or bitter word violated the sixth, and a lustful look the seventh. . . .

"The teaching of the apostles under the inspiration of the Holy Spirit, is even more emphatic and explicit concerning the scope and obligations of the moral law."—October, 1933.

Then follows a list of New Testament references to show how the apostles honored each of the ten commandments.

The second article deals with the "relationship between the law and the gospel," and "the Christian's true position with regard to the law of God as revealed on Sinai and his plain duty concerning it." The author explains immediately that "we must distinguish carefully and clearly between its two chief parts, the ceremonial and the moral law." A little further on he declares, "Christians are utterly to discard reliance on their observance of the moral law as any means of their justification." But he adds shortly:

"Christians are carefully to observe the moral law as the rule and method of their sanctification, and the guide of their new life. . . . The fact of their redemption does not do away with the necessity of their obedience; it only makes the obligation stronger, and heightens their responsibility."—November, 1933.

### Sunday School Times Again

An editorial in *The Sunday School Times* entitled "Are Christians Under the Law?" sets forth these clear distinctions between ceremonial and moral codes:

"Christ fulfilled and thereby canceled forever every jot and tittle of the Ceremonial Law. The Moral Law, which was given to Moses by God on the two tables of stone, . . . Christ found overlaid with traditional, legalistic rules and observances of merit-seeking. He rebuked the sham and corruption of this false system, and by His teaching and example canceled these 'commandments of men.' . . .

"Paul's argument against 'the law' was aimed at this rabbinical code; and at the continuance of the ceremonial law which Christ's redemptive work had canceled."—April 21, 1934.

Continuing the theme in the next week's issue, *The Sunday School Times* declares:

## ARE ADVENTISTS LEGALISTS?

"While obedience without the impulsion of love is servility, love that does not issue in obedience is merely nominal. 'He that saith, I know Him, and keepeth not His commandments, is a liar, and the truth is not in him' (1 John 2:4).

"Love and obedience are interchangeable, and incontrovertible ground of our assurance: 'Hereby we do know that we know Him, if we keep His commandments.' "—April 28, 1934.

### Our One Distinctive View on the Law

There is really only one difference between us and Protestants in general regarding the law. We understand the fourth commandment differently. We believe that the phrase *the seventh day* means the seventh day of the weekly cycle. And so did everyone else, until the end of the sixteenth century, when Nicholas Bownde developed the idea that the phrase meant simply one day in seven, and thus provided Puritan reformers with an apparent Scriptural support for Sundaykeeping. (See chapter 7.) If our critics wish to prefer charges against us for failure to adopt a relatively new interpretation of a Scriptural phrase, we are ready to answer the charge with this simple inquiry: Why should we be asked to accept a new interpretation when the holy prophets and the apostles all understood the words *the seventh day* to mean the seventh day of the week? The holy women who rested on the day between crucifixion Friday and resurrection Sunday "rested the Sabbath day according to the commandment." Luke 23:56.

But even though our critics have to agree that our interpretation is anchored to history and the prophets, they seem still to be sure there must be something spiritually off-color, legalistic, in our keeping of the seventh day of the week, and particularly in our calling upon others to keep the seventh-day Sabbath. We may make impassioned appeal to the licentious man to flee from the wrath to come upon the head of all who violate the seventh command. We may do the same in regard to the thief, the liar, the murderer, the covetous man, the parent-dishonoring child, the blasphemer, and the idolater. To each we may say that his life is a violation of the law of God, which is binding on all men in all ages. To each we may appeal to implore God for forgiveness and for a new heart on which is written the law by the miraculous work of the Divine Spirit. Have not all great evangelists done this? Did not Dwight L. Moody preach a whole series of revival sermons on the Decalogue? (Later printed under the title *Weighed and Wanting*.)

Yes, we may do all this and be considered orthodox in the matter of law and grace. But let us include in our appeal to men the fourth commandment, and a storm breaks around our heads. Moody included the fourth command in his fervent series on the Decalogue. But no storm broke over him. No one accused him of legalism, of setting up another standard for salvation than Jesus Christ. But then Moody did not call on men to keep the "Sabbath day according to the commandment"; he called on them to keep holy the first day of the week!

## A Strange Situation

Here is a strange situation indeed. It is even more strange when viewed in the setting of the fact that legalism is often directly involved in the urge that is put on people to keep Sunday. Have not our critics heard of Sunday laws that have been put on the statute books by ardent preachers, and vigorously invoked by them?

Just why we who invoke only the grace of God to enable man to obey the command to keep holy the seventh day, should be charged as legalists, while the hosts of Sundaykeeping ministers, who often invoke the strong arm of the law in order to compel men to rest on the first day of the week, should claim to be the exponents of grace, is surely a strange contradiction. Seventh-day Adventists have ever been vigorous opponents of the idea of approaching Sabbath rest from the legal standpoint, whereas Sunday-keeping preachers are the ones who have lobbied almost every legislative body in Christian lands into enacting strong laws to protect Sunday! We who are Seventh-day Adventists must suffer the constant strictures of a large majority of the Sundaykeeping ministry for our refusal to support their program of Sunday legislation. They declare that we are in league with the lawless element, who want an open Sunday. But whenever we urge the keeping of the seventh-day Sabbath, and invoke the law of God, some of those same ministers cry out that we are legalists! Why the difference?

## A Situation Still More Strange

To repeat the question asked earlier in this book, for it bears repeating: Just what is there about preaching first-day sacredness from the fourth commandment—as Protestant denominations in general have done through all the years—that transports such preachers to the balmy paradise of grace, whereas the preaching of seventh-day sacredness from the same fourth commandment consigns such preachers to the chill limbo of legalism? We who preach seventh-day sacredness certainly do not do so more sternly and rigorously than first-day preachers. Even a cursory acquaintance with Protestant history reveals that Sunday sacredness has quite frequently been proclaimed with a severity that frightened into conformity the majority and thrust into jail the remainder. If today there is a certain relaxation of this severity, it certainly does not reflect any fundamental difference of view toward the first day by religious leaders, for they bemoan the laxity that has crept in.

Perhaps some of our critics will say that they do not believe in this view of first-day sacredness. But that is surely not to the point. The charge of legalism is made by critics who represent a variety of Protestant bodies, which bodies have been parties to Sunday legislation. We therefore return to the question: Why is it a display of grace and faith to preach first-day sacredness from the Decalogue, but a non-Christian display of legalism to preach seventh-day sacredness from the same law?

In substance, we are charged as being "heretical" because of our beliefs on the law in general and the fourth precept in particular. The question is: Wherein does the heresy lie? In our view of the law in general, that it is God's unchangeable code for all men in all ages? No, for we declare our complete harmony with the classic confessions of faith on this point. Is it because of our view of the fourth precept in particular? And if so, why, in view of the facts presented in the preceding paragraphs?

Some time ago I fell into conversation with a Baptist minister. He deplored the Modernist-Fundamentalist controversy that was shattering his denomination. He said he judged that every denomination was thus troubled, however. I replied that ours was not. He marveled. No marvel, I said; the explanation is simple. Seventh-day Adventists could not possibly be evolutionists, for we keep the seventh day of the weekly cycle as a memorial of the completion of God's creative work in the first week of time. We keep this day holy because "in six days the Lord made heaven and earth, . . . and rested the seventh day." When we rest on the seventh day, we think of Him who rested on that day and blessed it. Ever remembering the Sabbath, we cannot forget creation. And ever believing in the Sabbath, we must ever believe in creation. We think rather of Eden than of Sinai when we keep the Sabbath.

The complete freedom from Modernism in the Seventh-day Adventist denomination, even in its colleges, is an eloquent proof of the truth of what we here claim regarding the Sabbath. Yet, behold, this Sabbath doctrine, which is our strong bulwark against Modernism, proves to be part of the reason for a withering indictment of us by Fundamentalists, in whose ranks our critics are generally found.

### How Valid Is the Testimony of an Ex-Adventist?

Have our critics any further evidence they wish to present to support their charge that Adventists are legalists? Yes, one more bit of evidence, the testimony of certain men who have gone from us. A few men after leaving us have declared that they have been "delivered from Adventism," meaning most generally and most specifically that they have been delivered from a legalistic religion and are now rejoicing in the glorious liberty of the gospel.

Now, no testimony is accepted in any court without a cross-examination of the witness. Here are some questions we, as Adventists, would like to ask an ex-Adventist witness testifying for our critics: Would you please tell us precisely what teaching of the Adventist Church in the matter of the law of God bound and fettered you, and what different view do you now hold on the law that gives you such glorious liberty? To what great Protestant creed or profession of faith do you point as containing your present view, or have you moved outside of all the historic creeds in order to find your present belief on the law?

If the witness answers that he was delivered from the Adventist teaching that the law of God is binding on all men in all ages as an expression of the great moral principles of God, then we would ask him to show us in what way this Adventist teaching is different from the Protestant creeds. This he could not do, for our teaching is identical with that of the great Protestant bodies. If the witness then declared that he had moved beyond these historic creeds, we would ask him, Who has departed from the faith? Who has turned his back on the Protestant teaching on the law—he, or Adventists?

If he answers that the Adventist teaching on the law had kept him from looking to Christ, we would ask him to be very specific in citing his proof. For reasons already stated we would not accept as valid evidence some stray phrases or sentences that appeared to support the charge of legalism that ran counter to the explicit words of the Adventist Statement of Belief and the whole tenor of our teachings. We would not do this for the same reason that we would not accept a stray statement from James or any other Bible writer that might be submitted by a Catholic in behalf of the doctrine of works. We would ask the witness whether he had ever been called upon by the Adventist Church to preach any other view of the law than that set down in our Statement of Belief. His answer would have to be No.

We would also consider it proper to call to his attention the statement he made to his employing conference when he withdrew from the Adventist ministry. I do not recall during my years of ministry of any preacher who has gone out from us declaring, as he did so, that he was leaving in order to be free from the shackles of legalism. Of course, there may have been such a case. I can only speak from memory. However, I need not strain my memory unduly, for only a few ministers have left the denomination. In most instances those who have left have done so at the request of their brethren and because of a moral fall. It is certainly disclosing no secret to say this. Adventists are still flesh and blood, and can fall before temptation the same as all others if they give ear to the tempter.

Of this sad, but fortunately very small, number who have had to leave our Adventist ministry under a cloud, I can recall two who took to preaching on their own or in some loose affiliation with another religious body, and who declared from the public platform that they had been delivered from the legalism of Adventism and now were rejoicing in the free grace of God!

This observation is made in no cynical vein and with no attempt merely to prove a case, but only to relate simple facts of history, current history that is known and can be verified. These facts are offered simply as proof that an ex-Adventist minister may not be giving the real reasons for his departure from the Adventist Church when he stands up to speak or sits down to write against us. Nothing could better illustrate the well-known fact that the reasons people offer for their actions are not necessarily the real reasons, and may, indeed, be the very opposite of the truth.

### Would Our Critics Be Willing?

Would our critics, who often are spokesmen for other religious bodies, be willing to have their religious organizations and their doctrinal teachings evaluated in terms of the testimony offered by ministers who had left their denominations for one reason or another? Then why should Adventists be indicted because of statements made by ministers who leave us? In any organization there are always a few men who, for one reason or another, fall out of step. There are occasions, of course, when a man—yes, a minister —may leave an organization because of a sincere difference of conviction. But in too many instances men leave with bitterness in their heart and thus with a distorted idea of the whole organization. The Adventist Church cannot hope to escape from this kind of personnel problem, a problem created sometimes by bad digestion, sometimes by bad nerves, and sometimes simply by a bad heart.

### A Reprehensible Course

But if it is unfair to judge a denomination by the testimony of an ex-minister, how reprehensible to make capital of testimony offered on a denomination's theology by an ex-employee who was never ordained to the ministry! But let an ex-Adventist employee, printer, businessman, or what not, cry out that he was delivered from Adventist legalism, and how quickly certain of our critics joyfully rally round him. With straight face they describe him as a former Adventist leader who held positions of great trust and who is singularly qualified to speak with authority on what that denomination believes and teaches and what its broad policies have been.

Yet the man thus lauded may have been employed in some wholly nonministerial activity, may never have attended an Adventist college or secondary school, to say nothing of a theological seminary, and thus be hardly as well qualified to speak on Adventist doctrine as the average Adventist layman. Yet somehow a lone man like this is taken as the last word on our theology. If it is a consensus of laymen's testimony that our critics sincerely desire, why do they not follow the suggestions already offered as to taking a poll of our lay members? Or is it that they wish to hear only the testimony that pleases them, even if that testimony must be a lone voice?

Surely this is a strange procedure. Would our ministerial critics ever think of exalting a businessman in their church as a spokesman on their theology? Would they not ridicule the idea that a nonministerial manager of one of their institutions, for example, should speak with authority concerning their denomination? Would they not consider it outrageous if the interpretation given to their doctrines by such a man, in opposition to that of all their authorized spokesmen, were accepted by critics as valid testimony against the teachings of their denomination? Yes, and would they not feel doubly outraged if such a man built his case against them on stray phrases from their various works, and critics promoted such an eclectic theological production as being unquestionably correct and authoritative? To ask that question is to answer it.

## Those Early Records

This discussion can hardly be closed without a word regarding early Adventist history. Some critic may even think to search for evidence of legalism in the records of the early decades of our history when doctrinal views were being slowly crystallized. But surely no fair-minded person would be much impressed by such evidence. The student of church history may remember Philip Schaff's observation regarding the beginnings of Protestantism, when the Reformers were so dominated with the glorious truth of the liberty of the gospel that some in the movement tended to mistake license for liberty. Even Calvin was ready to assert his right to bowl on the green on Sunday to show his liberty in the gospel. But no one would therefore think of charging that Presbyterianism teaches such a view.

In the first few decades of the Seventh-day Adventist Church some of its leaders were so solemnized with the truth that God's law is eternally binding that they were tempted to give it excessive and perhaps unwarranted emphasis in relation to other truths. Some of them even feared that the strong emphasis that other Adventists wished to place on righteousness by faith might blur the vital truth regarding God's law.

There is nothing mysterious about this. Good men in any developing religious movement require at least a few decades to stabilize their beliefs. Schaff provides a thoughtful sketch of how slowly there developed in Protestantism the proper realization of the doctrine of God's law. It seemed so alien at first to the idea of gospel liberty!

# ARE ADVENTISTS LEGALISTS?

Only a live and growing organization meets opposition. And the kind of opposition is the measure of the strength of the case that opponents feel they can make out against us! Surely our critics, who are neither knaves nor dolts, must have quiet moments of misgivings when they ponder this whole matter of their attacks on Adventists. They know that stray phrases can prove anything and thus prove nothing, and they know that all our formal statements on the law parallel those of the Protestant creeds. They know that they could not risk taking the poll suggested. They know that the victories gained by Adventists over liquor and tobacco, for example, cannot fit into any picture of legalism.

## Sabbath Kept Joyfully

What is more, our critics know that Adventists keep the fourth commandment—the Sabbath command—with a joyfulness and sincerity with which they (the critics) fain would have their communicants keep Sunday. They know that while they, or their fellow opponents of Adventism, seek laws to undergird Sunday, Adventists keep the Sabbath without the aid of any legal statutes by the state, and are indeed militantly opposed to any legal approach to the matter of Sabbathkeeping.

Yes, and our critics, who are generally of the Fundamentalist ranks, know that Adventists are untainted by skeptical, evolutionist doctrines, and that they are ever protected from such heresy by their weekly keeping of the Sabbath in memory of God's having created the heavens and the earth.

## Warm and Spontaneous Liberality

Our critics also know that Seventh-day Adventists give gladly and with a liberality that far outdistances the giving of virtually all other churches in Christendom, and they know that such warm liberality could not spring from cold legalism.

Besides all this, our critics know that Adventists conduct a mission program out of all proportion to their size, that they go into the heart of Africa, the recesses of Asia, and the jungles of the South Seas, and that as a result of their preaching raw savages turn from devil worship, from filthy, enslaving habits, to live circumspect, happy Christian lives. Our critics know that legalism is powerless to do this. Have they not, as good Fundamentalists, often declared that Modernists lack either the urge to go as missionaries or the power to transform lives if they went?

All this and more must trouble the thinking of our critics in their quiet moments. We think it should!

# Section III

# THE SABBATH AND THE WEEKLY CYCLE

CHAPTER 7

# The Sabbath in Church Creeds

A KNOWLEDGE of the growth of the doctrine of Sunday sacredness in the Reformation movement will enable the reader to understand better the degree to which the Protestant Reformation caused a reform in the doctrine of a divinely ordained weekly rest day. We may willingly grant that the immediate successors of Luther moved upward a great distance from the laxity of the Dark Ages when they endeavored to obey more fully the fourth commandment, even though their interpretation of it was to a greater or less degree faulty.

The most interesting fact that stands out is that the doctrine of the sanctity of a weekly rest day gained strength only as increasing emphasis was placed on the truth that the fourth commandment is morally binding on Christians. Without this emphasis Protestantism would never have had stamped upon it that measure of regard for a weekly holy day that has quite definitely distinguished Reformation churches from the Catholic Church. When religious leaders today attack the binding claims of the fourth commandment in their attempt to meet the Sabbath truth, they are attacking the foundation on which has been reared whatever degree of sanctity Protestantism has attached to a weekly rest day.

It is said that the Reformers did not move on into the full light concerning the fourth commandment; but what is to be said of their spiritual successors today who would attempt to *abolish* the command? We who are Adventists are moving on in the true path of reformation when we give increasing emphasis to the importance of the fourth commandment, and insist that this command be obeyed exactly as God gave it, and not as changed during the centuries of apostasy.

# ANSWERS TO OBJECTIONS

The following sketch from Philip Schaff, eminent church historian, places the matter of the Sabbath in proper historical perspective.

## Philip Schaff on Sabbath Reform

"Ch[apter] XXI. 'Of Religious Worship and the Sabbath Day' [of the Westminster Confession, A.D. 1647], must be mentioned as (next to the Irish Articles) the first symbolical indorsement of what may be called the Puritan theory of the Christian Sabbath which was not taught by the Reformers and the Continental Confessions, but which has taken deep root in England, Scotland, and the United States, and has become the basis of a far stricter observance of the Lord's day than exists in any other country. This observance is one of the most prominent national and social features of Anglo-American Christianity, and at once strikes the attention of every traveler.

"The way was gradually prepared for it. Calvin's view of the authority of the fourth commandment was stricter than Luther's, Knox's view stricter than Calvin's, and the Puritan view stricter than Knox's. The Prayer Book of the Church of England, by incorporating the responsive reading of the decalogue in the regular service, kept alive in the minds of the people the perpetual obligation of the fourth commandment, and helped to create a public sentiment within the Church of England favorable to the Puritan theory, although practically great desecration prevailed during Elizabeth's reign. The 'judicious' Hooker, who was no Puritan, says: 'We are bound to account the sanctification of one day in seven a duty which God's immutable *law* doth exact *forever*.'

"Towards the close of Elizabeth's reign the Sabbath question assumed the importance and dignity of a national movement, and of a practical reformation which traveled from England to Scotland and from both countries to North America. The chief impulse of this movement was given in 1595 by Dr. Nicholas Bownd (or Bound), a learned Puritan clergyman of Norton in Suffolk. He is not the originator, but the systematizer or first clear expounder, of the Puritan theory of the Christian Sabbath, namely, that the Sabbath or weekly day of holy rest is a primitive institution of the benevolent Creator for the benefit of man, and that the fourth commandment as to its substance (that is, the keeping holy one day out of seven) is as perpetual in design and as binding upon the Christians as any other of the ten commandments, of which Christ said that not 'one jot or one tittle' shall pass away till all be fulfilled.

"The work in which this theory was ably and earnestly vindicated proved to be a tract for the times. Heylin, a High Church opponent, says 'that in a very little time it grew the most bewitching error, the most popular deceit that had ever been set on foot in the Church of England.' Fuller dates from it 'the more solemn and strict observance of the Lord's day.' . . .

"The Puritan Sabbath theory was denounced and assailed by the rising school of High Churchism as a Sabbatarian heresy and a cunningly concealed attack on the authority of the Church of England, by substituting the Jewish Sabbath for the Christian Sunday and all the church festivals. Attempts were made by Archbishop Whitgift in 1599, and by Chief Justice Popham in 1600, to suppress Bownd's book and to destroy all the copies, but 'the more it was called in, the more it was called on;' its price was doubled, and 'though the book's wings were clipped from flying abroad in print, it ran the faster from friend to friend in transcribed copies, and the Lord's day, in most places, was most strictly observed. The more liberty people were offered, the less they used it. . . . It was sport for them to refrain from sports. . . . Scarce any comment, catechism, or controversy was set forth by the stricter divines, wherein this doctrine (the diamond in this ring) was not largely pressed and proved; so that, as one saith, the Sabbath itself had no rest.'

"At last King James I brought his royal authority to bear against the Puritan Sabbatarianism so called, and issued the famous 'Book of Sports,' May 24, 1618, which was afterwards republished, with an additional order, by his son, Charles I, no doubt by advice of Archbishop Laud, October 18, 1633. This curious production formally authorizes and commends the desecration of the evening of the Lord's day by dancing, leaping, fencing, and other 'lawful recreation, on condition of observing the earlier part by strict outward conformity to the worship of the Church of England. The professed object of this indulgence to the common people was to check the progress of the Papists and Puritans (or 'Precisians'), and to make 'the bodies more able for war' when his majesty should have 'occasion to use them.' The court set the example of desecration by balls, masquerades, and plays on Sunday evening; and the rustics repaired from the house of worship to the alehouse or the village green to dance around the Maypole and to shoot at butts. To complete the folly, King James ordered the book to be read to every parish church, and threatened clergymen who refused to do so with severe punishment. King Charles repeated the order. But in both cases it became the source of great trouble and confusion. Several bishops disapproved of it. Archbishop Abbott (the Puritan predecessor of Laud) flatly forbade it to be read at Croydon. . . . Those who refused to read the royal 'Book of Sports' were suspended from office and benefice, or even excommunicated by Laud and his sympathizing fellow bishops. . . .

"This persecution of conscientious ministers for obeying God rather than men gave moral strength to the cause of Sabbath observance, and rooted it deeper in the affections of the people. It was one of the potent causes which overwhelmed Charles and Laud in common ruin. The sober and serious part of the nation were struck with a kind of horror that they should be invited by the highest authorities in church and state to destroy the effect of public worship by a desecration of a portion of the day consecrated to religion.

"On the Sunday question Puritanism achieved at last a permanent triumph, and left its trace upon the Church of England and Scotland, which reappeared after the licentious period of the Restoration. For, although the Church of England, as a body, never committed itself to the Puritan Sabbath theory, it adopted at least the practice of a much stricter observance than had previously obtained under Elizabeth and the Stuarts, and would never exchange it for the Continental laxity, with its disastrous effects upon the attendance of public worship and the morals of the people.

"The Westminster Confession, without entering into details or sanctioning the incidental excesses of the Puritan practice, represents the Christian rest day under its threefold aspect: (1) as a divine law of nature (*jus divinum naturale*), rooted in the constitution of man, and hence instituted (together with marriage) at the creation, in the state of innocence, for the perpetual benefit of body and soul; (2) as a positive moral law (*jus divinum positivum*), given through Moses, with reference to the primitive institution ('Remember') and to the typical redemption of Israel from bondage; (3) as the commemoration of the new creation and finished redemption by the resurrection of Christ; hence the change from the last to the first day of the week, and its designation 'the Lord's day' (*dies Dominica*). And it requires the day to be wholly devoted to the exercises of public and private worship and the duties of necessity and mercy.

"To this doctrine and practice the Presbyterian, Congregational, and other churches in Scotland, England, and America have faithfully adhered to this day. Yea, twenty-seven years before it was formulated by the learned divine of Westminster, the Pilgrim Fathers of America had transplanted both theory and practice, first to Holland, and, finding them unsafe there, to the wild soil of New England. Two days after their landing from the 'Mayflower' (December 22, 1620), forgetting the pressing necessities of physical food and shelter, the dreary cold of winter, the danger threatening from wild beasts and roaming savages, they celebrated their first Sunday in America."—*The Creeds of Christendom*, vol. 1, pp. 776-782 (4th ed. in 3 volumes, Harper & Brothers).

## Sixteenth Century Reformers' Sabbath Views

The attitude of the sixteenth century Reformers toward the Sabbath is well illustrated by quotations from two of the most authoritative confessions of that century—the Augsburg Confession, A.D. 1530; and the Second Helvetic Confession, A.D. 1566:

## Augsburg Confession, A.D. 1530

"PART II, ARTICLE VII.—OF ECCLESIASTICAL POWER

"The Scripture, which teacheth that all the Mosaical ceremonies can be omitted after the gospel is revealed, has abrogated the Sabbath. And yet, because it was requisite to appoint a certain day, that the people might know when they ought to come together, it appears that the [Christian]* Church did for that purpose appoint the Lord's day: which for this cause also seemed to have been pleasing, that man might have an example of Christian liberty, and might know that the observation, neither of the Sabbath nor of another day, was of necessity."—*Ibid.*, vol. 3, p. 69.

## Second Helvetic Confession, A.D. 1566

"CHAPTER XXIV.—OF HOLIDAYS, FASTS, AND CHOICE OF MEATS

"Although religion be not tied unto time, yet can it not be planted and exercised without a due dividing and allotting out of time. Every church, therefore, does choose unto itself a certain time for public prayers, and for the preaching of the gospel, and for the celebration of the sacraments; and it is not lawful for any one to overthrow this appointment of the church at his own pleasure. For except some due time and leisure were allotted to the outward exercise of religion, without doubt men would be quite drawn from it by their own affairs.

---

* *Christian* is placed in brackets, Schaff explains, to indicate that the word is not in the original Latin text of the Confession, though it is in the German text.

"In regard hereof, we see that in the ancient churches there were not only certain set hours in the week appointed for meetings, but that also the Lord's day itself, ever since the apostles' time, was consecrated to religious exercises and to a holy rest; which also is now very well observed by our churches, for the worship of God and the increase of charity. Yet herein we give no place unto the Jewish observation of the day, or to any superstitions. For we do not account one day to be holier than another, nor think that mere rest is of itself acceptable to God. Besides, we do celebrate and keep the Lord's day, and not the Jewish Sabbath, and that with a free observation."—*Ibid.*, p. 899.

## Later Views Regarding the Sabbath Command

The doctrine of the Sabbath as set forth in the Irish Articles of Religion and in the Westminster Confession, to which Schaff refers in the preceding historical sketch is revealed in the following quotations from these creeds: *

### Irish Articles of Religion, A.D. 1615

"PARAGRAPHS 46-56.—OF THE SERVICE OF GOD

"56. The first day of the week, which is the *Lord's day*, is wholly to be dedicated unto the service of God; and therefore we are bound therein to rest from our common and daily business, and to bestow that leisure upon holy exercises, both public and private."—*Ibid.*, p. 536.

### Westminster Confession, A.D. 1647

"CHAPTER XXI.—OF RELIGIOUS WORSHIP AND THE SABBATH DAY

"VII. As it is of the law of nature, that, in general, a due proportion of time be set apart for the worship of God; so in His word, by a positive, moral, and perpetual commandment, binding all men in all ages, He hath particularly appointed one day in seven for a Sabbath, to be kept holy unto Him:[1] which, from the beginning of the world to the resurrection of Christ, was the last day of the week; and, from the resurrection of Christ, was changed into the first day of the week,[2] which in Scripture is called the Lord's day,[3] and is to be continued

---

* The reader is referred to pages 502 and 503 for a statement as to the importance of the Irish Articles and the Westminster Confession and the relation of one to the other.
[1] Ex. 20:8, 10, 11; Isa. 56:2, 4, 6, 7 [Am. ed. Isa. 56:6].
[2] Gen. 2:2, 3; 1 Cor. 16:1, 2; Acts 20:7.
[3] Rev. 1:10.

to the end of the world, as the Christian Sabbath.' "—*Ibid.*, pp. 648, 649.

### Schaff's Comment on the Augsburg Confession Sabbath Doctrine

The foregoing statements from Protestant creeds reveal clearly what Schaff means when he speaks of the changing views of Protestantism toward the authority of the fourth commandment. In a footnote in comment on the Sabbath doctrine statement (Article VII) in the Augsburg Confession, Schaff remarks:

"This view of the Christian Sabbath, which was held by all the Reformers, and still prevails on the Continent of Europe, overlooks the important fact that the Sabbath has a moral as well as a ceremonial [?] aspect, and is a part of the decalogue, which the Lord did not come 'to destroy, but to fulfill' (Matt. 5:17, 18; comp. 22:37-40; Rom. 3:31; 10:4). As a periodical day of rest for the body, and worship for the soul, the Sabbath is founded in the physical and moral constitution of man, and reflects the rest of God after the work of creation (Gen. 2:3). Under this view it is of primitive origin, like the institution of marriage, and of perpetual obligation, like the other commandments of the decalogue. A lax theory of the Sabbath naturally leads to a lax practice, and tends to destroy the blessing of this holy day. The Anglo-American churches have an unspeakable advantage over those of the Continent of Europe in their higher theory and practice of Sabbath observance, which dates from the close of the sixteenth century. Even Puritan rigor is better than the opposite extreme."—*Ibid.*, p. 69, footnote.

In our day in the United States that active force for Sunday sacredness, the Lord's Day Alliance, which has the blessing and endorsement of most Protestant bodies, rests its conviction as to the importance of a weekly holy day on the ground that the fourth commandment is still in force. The following quotation makes this clear:

### The Lord's Day Alliance on the Sabbath Doctrine

"The Alliance holds that the fourth commandment is still in full force and effect. It believes that the Sabbath was given, not merely

---

' Ex. 20:8, 10, with Matt. 5:17, 18.

for one nation, but for all people, and that the world needs it today more than ever, both as a day of rest from excessive activity and as a day for religious inspiration in an age of worldliness and doubt. It holds that Christ did not abolish the fourth commandment, as some have held, but rather that in freeing the Sabbath from narrow and technical interpretations He strengthened and spiritualized the holy day. He said He came not to destroy, but to fulfill the law.

"The change of the observance of the Sabbath from the seventh to the first day of the week did not end an old institution or begin a new one, but added new life and significance to the divine command. Thus not only was the day of the resurrection of Jesus celebrated, but the Sabbath was cleansed from the technicalities and traditions by which its free sanctities had been obscured."—Supplement to the January-February, 1921, *Lord's Day Leader,* official publication of the Lord's Day Alliance.

## The Proposition Narrowed Down

Thus in English-speaking countries when the Sabbath is discussed with those who subscribe to this generally accepted view of a fourth-commandment basis for Sunday, the proposition is narrowed down to this simple question: Where is the Bible text to prove that the Sabbath was changed from the seventh to the first day of the week?

When we deal with those who hold to the so-called Continental view of the Sabbath, as set forth in the Augsburg Confession, etc., the question is: Where is the Bible proof that the fourth commandment deals with merely a ceremonial requirement, when the whole Decalogue is admittedly the binding moral code for Christians?

In no case should it be logically necessary to meet a thousand and one quibbles about grace and the abolition of the law before coming to the central question of the Sabbath. The evidence from the Protestant creeds reveals beyond all controversy that a man repudiates one of the most basic beliefs of Protestantism when he discards the Decalogue.

# CHAPTER 8

# Antiquity and Unbroken Sequence
# of Weekly Cycle

THE AGITATION for calendar revision, which first became really active in the United States about the year 1928, served the useful purpose of placing eminent astronomers on record concerning the antiquity and the unbroken sequence of the weekly cycle. Never before in the Christian Era has a proposition turned so directly on the question of the validity of the week as an ancient, unbroken time cycle. Much money has been spent to promote the proposed new calendar, and arguments ranging from the sublime to the ridiculous have been employed in an attempt to break down the opposition.

The most significant fact that stands out of the whole discussion is that the proponents of calendar revision have not included in their varied arguments any claim that the weekly cycle has been broken or that time has been lost. If they could have made and supported such a claim, it would have demolished with one stroke all the appeals of Jews or Seventh-day Adventists for the preservation of the unbroken week; for why be zealous to preserve the week of today if it has been broken in the past? This silence of the calendar advocates on the question of the weekly cycle must ever stand as one of the eloquent proofs that the weekly cycle has not been broken. The fact may properly be stressed in discussing "lost time" with anyone.

But more than that, various astronomers, when asked to express their scientific opinion as to the wisdom of a new calendar which included a feature that broke the weekly cycle, opposed the change on the ground that this cycle should not be tampered with. Their comments are found in the official League of Nations document entitled *Report on the Reform of the Calendar, Submitted to the Advisory and Technical Committee for Communications and Transit of the League of Nations by the Special Committee of Enquiry Into the Reform of the Calendar*. This document was published at Geneva, August 17, 1926. The following are quotations from their statements, with the page number of this calendar report noted at the end of each quotation:

### Testimony of Astronomers

"The reform would break the division of the week which has been followed for thousands of years, and therefore has been hallowed by immemorial use."—M. Anders Donner, formerly professor of astronomy at the University of Helsingfors, p. 51.

"One essential point is that of the continuity of the week. The majority of the members of the Office of Longitudes considered that the reform of the calendar should not be based on the breaking of this continuity. They considered that it would be highly undesirable to interrupt a continuity which has existed for so many centuries."—M. Emile Picard, permanent secretary of the Academy of Sciences [France], president of the Office of Longitudes, p. 51.

"I have always hesitated to suggest breaking the continuity of the week, which is without a doubt the most ancient scientific institution bequeathed to us by antiquity."—M. Edouard Baillaud, director of the Paris Observatory, p. 52.

"It is very inadvisable to interrupt by means of blank days the absolute continuity of the weeks—the only guaranty in the past, present, and future of an efficient control of chronological facts."—Frederico Oom, director of the Astronomical Observatory of Lisbon, Portugal, p. 74.

### Testimony Before a Congressional Committee

Between December 20, 1928, and January 21, 1929, hearings were held by the Committee on Foreign Affairs of the House of Representatives at Washington, D.C., on a bill (H.J.Res. 334) that called for an international conference for the simplification of the calendar. One of the witnesses who appeared before the Committee was W. S. Eichelberger, of the U.S. Naval Observatory, whose chief work was the preparation of the annual Nautical

Almanac, the bible of all mariners. Here is a part of the testimony of Eichelberger in response to questions from Congressmen Sol Bloom and Cyrenus Cole:

"MR. BLOOM. . . . Is it not a fact that the dates are changed [in the calendar changes that have been made] but never the days? Do you know one time in the history of any calendar from the beginning of the early Egyptian calendar, that the day of the week has been changed?

"MR. EICHELBERGER. No; I do not.

"MR. BLOOM. The dates have been changed?

"MR. EICHELBERGER. Yes.

"MR. BLOOM. You can change any date of the calendar if you wish, as when Pope Gregory left off 10 days in 1582 and then the British left off 11 days in their calendar, which is the Gregorian calendar that we are operating under. The dates have been changed but never has the day been changed.

"MR. EICHELBERGER. As far as I know, that is right. . . .

"MR. COLE. . . . Is there any foundation for the idea that the Sabbath or the other days of the week have come down in unbroken continuity from the earliest times? They may have changed the dates, but Saturday, Sunday, Monday, Tuesday, Wednesday, Thursday, and Friday—those days have come in regular succession from the earliest times so far as we know.

"MR. EICHELBERGER. So far as we know they have."—"Simplification of the Calendar," a Congressional Report, pp. 68, 71.

*Nature,* the leading scientific journal of Great Britain, in an editorial department entitled "Our Astronomical Column," carried an item "Calendar Reform," in which the proposed blank-day calendar was discussed. In part it reads as follows:

"The interruption of the regular sequence of weeks, which have now been running without a break for some three thousand years, excites the antagonism of a number of people. Some of these (the Jews, and also many Christians) accept the week as a divine institution, with which it is unlawful to tamper; others, without the scruples, still feel that it is useful to maintain a time unit that, unlike all others, has proceeded in absolutely invariable manner since what may be called the dawn of history. This view found support at the meeting of the International Astronomical Union at Rome in 1922."—June 6, 1931.

## JANUARY

| Su. | Mo. | Tu. | We. | Th. | Fr. | Sa. |
|---|---|---|---|---|---|---|
| ---- | 1 | 2 | 3 | 4 | 5 | 6 |
| 7 | 8 | 9 | 10 | 11 | 12 | 13 |
| 14 | 15 | 16 | 17 | 18 | 19 | 20 |
| 21 | 22 | 23 | 24 | 25 | 26 | 27 |
| 28 | 29 | 30 | 31 | ---- | ---- | ---- |
| ---- | ---- | ---- | ---- | ---- | ---- | ---- |

## FEBRUARY

| Su. | Mo. | Tu. | We. | Th. | Fr. | Sa. |
|---|---|---|---|---|---|---|
| ---- | ---- | ---- | ---- | 1 | 2 | 3 |
| 4 | 5 | 6 | 7 | 8 | 9 | 10 |
| 11 | 12 | 13 | 14 | 15 | 16 | 17 |
| 18 | 19 | 20 | 21 | 22 | 23 | 24 |
| 25 | 26 | 27 | 28 | ---- | ---- | ---- |
| ---- | ---- | ---- | ---- | ---- | ---- | ---- |

## MARCH

| Su. | Mo. | Tu. | We. | Th. | Fr. | Sa. |
|---|---|---|---|---|---|---|
| ---- | ---- | ---- | ---- | 1 | 2 | 3 |
| 4 | 5 | 6 | 7 | 8 | 9 | 10 |
| 11 | 12 | 13 | 14 | 15 | 16 | 17 |
| 18 | 19 | 20 | 21 | 22 | 23 | 24 |
| 25 | 26 | 27 | 28 | 29 | 30 | 31 |
| ---- | ---- | ---- | ---- | ---- | ---- | ---- |

## APRIL

| Su. | Mo. | Tu. | We. | Th. | Fr. | Sa. |
|---|---|---|---|---|---|---|
| 1 | 2 | 3 | 4 | 5 | 6 | 7 |
| 8 | 9 | 10 | 11 | 12 | 13 | 14 |
| 15 | 16 | 17 | 18 | 19 | 20 | 21 |
| 22 | 23 | 24 | 25 | 26 | 27 | 28 |
| 29 | 30 | ---- | ---- | ---- | ---- | ---- |
| ---- | ---- | ---- | ---- | ---- | ---- | ---- |

## MAY

| Su. | Mo. | Tu. | We. | Th. | Fr. | Sa. |
|---|---|---|---|---|---|---|
| ---- | ---- | 1 | 2 | 3 | 4 | 5 |
| 6 | 7 | 8 | 9 | 10 | 11 | 12 |
| 13 | 14 | 15 | 16 | 17 | 18 | 19 |
| 20 | 21 | 22 | 23 | 24 | 25 | 26 |
| 27 | 28 | 29 | 30 | 31 | ---- | ---- |
| ---- | ---- | ---- | ---- | ---- | ---- | ---- |

## JUNE

| Su. | Mo. | Tu. | We. | Th. | Fr. | Sa. |
|---|---|---|---|---|---|---|
| ---- | ---- | ---- | ---- | ---- | 1 | 2 |
| 3 | 4 | 5 | 6 | 7 | 8 | 9 |
| 10 | 11 | 12 | 13 | 14 | 15 | 16 |
| 17 | 18 | 19 | 20 | 21 | 22 | 23 |
| 24 | 25 | 26 | 27 | 28 | 29 | 30 |
| ---- | ---- | ---- | ---- | ---- | ---- | ---- |

## JULY

| Su. | Mo. | Tu. | We. | Th. | Fr. | Sa. |
|---|---|---|---|---|---|---|
| 1 | 2 | 3 | 4 | 5 | 6 | 7 |
| 8 | 9 | 10 | 11 | 12 | 13 | 14 |
| 15 | 16 | 17 | 18 | 19 | 20 | 21 |
| 22 | 23 | 24 | 25 | 26 | 27 | 28 |
| 29 | 30 | 31 | ---- | ---- | ---- | ---- |
| ---- | ---- | ---- | ---- | ---- | ---- | ---- |

## AUGUST

| Su. | Mo. | Tu. | We. | Th. | Fr. | Sa. |
|---|---|---|---|---|---|---|
| ---- | ---- | ---- | 1 | 2 | 3 | 4 |
| 5 | 6 | 7 | 8 | 9 | 10 | 11 |
| 12 | 13 | 14 | 15 | 16 | 17 | 18 |
| 19 | 20 | 21 | 22 | 23 | 24 | 25 |
| 26 | 27 | 28 | 29 | 30 | 31 | ---- |
| ---- | ---- | ---- | ---- | ---- | ---- | ---- |

## SEPTEMBER

| Su. | Mo. | Tu. | We. | Th. | Fr. | Sa. |
|---|---|---|---|---|---|---|
| ---- | ---- | ---- | ---- | ---- | ---- | 1 |
| 2 | 3 | 4 | 5 | 6 | 7 | 8 |
| 9 | 10 | 11 | 12 | 13 | 14 | 15 |
| 16 | 17 | 18 | 19 | 20 | 21 | 22 |
| 23 | 24 | 25 | 26 | 27 | 28 | 29 |
| 30 | ---- | ---- | ---- | ---- | ---- | ---- |

## OCTOBER

| Su. | Mo. | Tu. | We. | Th. | Fr. | Sa. |
|---|---|---|---|---|---|---|
| ---- | 1 | 2 | 3 | 4 | 15 | 16 |
| 17 | 18 | 19 | 20 | 21 | 22 | 23 |
| 24 | 25 | 26 | 27 | 28 | 29 | 30 |
| 31 | ---- | ---- | ---- | ---- | ---- | ---- |
| ---- | ---- | ---- | ---- | ---- | ---- | ---- |

## NOVEMBER

| Su. | Mo. | Tu. | We. | Th. | Fr. | Sa. |
|---|---|---|---|---|---|---|
| ---- | 1 | 2 | 3 | 4 | 5 | 6 |
| 7 | 8 | 9 | 10 | 11 | 12 | 13 |
| 14 | 15 | 16 | 17 | 18 | 19 | 20 |
| 21 | 22 | 23 | 24 | 25 | 26 | 27 |
| 28 | 29 | 30 | ---- | ---- | ---- | ---- |
| ---- | ---- | ---- | ---- | ---- | ---- | ---- |

## DECEMBER

| Su. | Mo. | Tu. | We. | Th. | Fr. | Sa. |
|---|---|---|---|---|---|---|
| ---- | ---- | ---- | 1 | 2 | 3 | 4 |
| 5 | 6 | 7 | 8 | 9 | 10 | 11 |
| 12 | 13 | 14 | 15 | 16 | 17 | 18 |
| 19 | 20 | 21 | 22 | 23 | 24 | 25 |
| 26 | 27 | 28 | 29 | 30 | 31 | ---- |
| ---- | ---- | ---- | ---- | ---- | ---- | ---- |

THE YEAR A.D. 1582 IN SPAIN, PORTUGAL, AND ITALY

# ANTIQUITY OF WEEKLY CYCLE

## Different Calendars Agree on Week

A very strong proof that the count of the week has not been lost during the Christian Era is the fact that although Jews, Christians, and Moslems keep different calendars, they all agree on the order of the days of the week. On this point, Samuel M. Zwemer, D.D., long known as an authority on Mohammedanism, and for some years a professor at Princeton University, writing under the title "An Egyptian Government Almanac," said in part:

"Some years ago I wrote an article on 'The Clock, the Calendar, and the Koran,' showing that the religion which Mohammed founded bears everywhere the imprint of his life and character. The connection between the clock, the calendar, and the Koran may not appear obvious to the Western reader, but to those living in Egypt and the Orient the connection is perfectly evident. Both the clock and the calendar are regulated by the book of the Prophet. The Moslem calendar . . . is fixed according to the laws of the Koran and orthodox tradition, based upon the practice of Mohammed himself.

"This connection and confusion of the clock, the calendar, and the Koran brings about the result that the *only* time reckoning on which Christians, Moslems, and Jews *agree* in the Orient is that of the *days of the week*. These are numbered and called by their numbers, save Friday and Saturday, which are known as the 'day of the assembling,' and the 'day of the Sabbath.' "—*The United Presbyterian*, Sept. 26, 1929.

## Julian and Gregorian Calendars

The relation of the calendar change—Julian to Gregorian—to the weekly cycle is stated briefly in the *Catholic Encyclopedia*. It is most appropriate to quote from this Catholic work, for the calendar change was made by a pope. This is the only calendar change in the Christian Era. The quotation follows:

---

On the opposite page is a reproduction of the calendar year A.D. 1582, in Spain, Portugal, and Italy, the countries that complied immediately with the calendar-revision decree of Pope Gregory XIII. The light-face type indicates the Julian calendar, and the bold-face, the Gregorian. The calendar change called for the dropping of ten days. This was effected by causing October 4, Julian reckoning, to be followed immediately by October 15, Gregorian reckoning. But there was no break in the weekly cycle. The people retired Thursday night, October 4, Julian reckoning, and awakened next morning to find it Friday, October 15, Gregorian reckoning.

## JANUARY

| Su. | Mo. | Tu. | We. | Th. | Fr. | Sa. |
|-----|-----|-----|-----|-----|-----|-----|
| ---- | ---- | ---- | 1 | 2 | 3 | 4 |
| 5 | 6 | 7 | 8 | 9 | 10 | 11 |
| 12 | 13 | 14 | 15 | 16 | 17 | 18 |
| 19 | 20 | 21 | 22 | 23 | 24 | 25 |
| 26 | 27 | 28 | 29 | 30 | 31 | --- |

## FEBRUARY

| Su. | Mo. | Tu. | We. | Th. | Fr. | Sa. |
|-----|-----|-----|-----|-----|-----|-----|
| ---- | ---- | ---- | ---- | ---- | ---- | 1 |
| 2 | 3 | 4 | 5 | 6 | 7 | 8 |
| 9 | 10 | 11 | 12 | 13 | 14 | 15 |
| 16 | 17 | 18 | 19 | 20 | 21 | 22 |
| 23 | 24 | 25 | 26 | 27 | 28 | 29 |

## MARCH

| Su. | Mo. | Tu. | We. | Th. | Fr. | Sa. |
|-----|-----|-----|-----|-----|-----|-----|
| 1 | 2 | 3 | 4 | 5 | 6 | 7 |
| 8 | 9 | 10 | 11 | 12 | 13 | 14 |
| 15 | 16 | 17 | 18 | 19 | 20 | 21 |
| 22 | 23 | 24 | 25 | 26 | 27 | 28 |
| 29 | 30 | 31 | — | — | — | — |

## APRIL

| Su. | Mo. | Tu. | We. | Th. | Fr. | Sa. |
|-----|-----|-----|-----|-----|-----|-----|
| --- | --- | --- | 1 | 2 | 3 | 4 |
| 5 | 6 | 7 | 8 | 9 | 10 | 11 |
| 12 | 13 | 14 | 15 | 16 | 17 | 18 |
| 19 | 20 | 21 | 22 | 23 | 24 | 25 |
| 26 | 27 | 28 | 29 | 30 | — | — |

## MAY

| Su. | Mo. | Tu. | We. | Th. | Fr. | Sa. |
|-----|-----|-----|-----|-----|-----|-----|
| --- | --- | --- | --- | --- | 1 | 2 |
| 3 | 4 | 5 | 6 | 7 | 8 | 9 |
| 10 | 11 | 12 | 13 | 14 | 15 | 16 |
| 17 | 18 | 19 | 20 | 21 | 22 | 23 |
| 24 | 25 | 26 | 27 | 28 | 29 | 30 |
| 31 | — | — | — | — | — | — |

## JUNE

| Su. | Mo. | Tu. | We. | Th. | Fr. | Sa. |
|-----|-----|-----|-----|-----|-----|-----|
| --- | 1 | 2 | 3 | 4 | 5 | 6 |
| 7 | 8 | 9 | 10 | 11 | 12 | 13 |
| 14 | 15 | 16 | 17 | 18 | 19 | 20 |
| 21 | 22 | 23 | 24 | 25 | 26 | 27 |
| 28 | 29 | 30 | — | — | — | — |

## JULY

| Su. | Mo. | Tu. | We. | Th. | Fr. | Sa. |
|-----|-----|-----|-----|-----|-----|-----|
| ---- | ---- | ---- | 1 | 2 | 3 | 4 |
| 5 | 6 | 7 | 8 | 9 | 10 | 11 |
| 12 | 13 | 14 | 15 | 16 | 17 | 18 |
| 19 | 20 | 21 | 22 | 23 | 24 | 25 |
| 26 | 27 | 28 | 29 | 30 | 31 | --- |

## AUGUST

| Su. | Mo. | Tu. | We. | Th. | Fr. | Sa. |
|-----|-----|-----|-----|-----|-----|-----|
| ---- | ---- | ---- | --- | --- | --- | 1 |
| 2 | 3 | 4 | 5 | 6 | 7 | 8 |
| 9 | 10 | 11 | 12 | 13 | 14 | 15 |
| 16 | 17 | 18 | 19 | 20 | 21 | 22 |
| 23 | 24 | 25 | 26 | 27 | 28 | 29 |
| 30 | 31 | — | — | — | — | — |

## SEPTEMBER

| Su. | Mo. | Tu. | We. | Th. | Fr. | Sa. |
|-----|-----|-----|-----|-----|-----|-----|
| --- | --- | 1 | 2 | 14 | 15 | 16 |
| 17 | 18 | 19 | 20 | 21 | 22 | 23 |
| 24 | 25 | 26 | 27 | 28 | 29 | 30 |

## OCTOBER

| Su. | Mo. | Tu. | We. | Th. | Fr. | Sa. |
|-----|-----|-----|-----|-----|-----|-----|
| 1 | 2 | 3 | 4 | 5 | 6 | 7 |
| 8 | 9 | 10 | 11 | 12 | 13 | 14 |
| 15 | 16 | 17 | 18 | 19 | 20 | 21 |
| 22 | 23 | 24 | 25 | 26 | 27 | 28 |
| 29 | 30 | 31 | — | — | — | — |

## NOVEMBER

| Su. | Mo. | Tu. | We. | Th. | Fr. | Sa. |
|-----|-----|-----|-----|-----|-----|-----|
| --- | --- | --- | 1 | 2 | 3 | 4 |
| 5 | 6 | 7 | 8 | 9 | 10 | 11 |
| 12 | 13 | 14 | 15 | 16 | 17 | 18 |
| 19 | 20 | 21 | 22 | 23 | 24 | 25 |
| 26 | 27 | 28 | 29 | 30 | — | — |

## DECEMBER

| Su. | Mo. | Tu. | We. | Th. | Fr. | Sa. |
|-----|-----|-----|-----|-----|-----|-----|
| --- | --- | --- | --- | --- | 1 | 2 |
| 3 | 4 | 5 | 6 | 7 | 8 | 9 |
| 10 | 11 | 12 | 13 | 14 | 15 | 16 |
| 17 | 18 | 19 | 20 | 21 | 22 | 23 |
| 24 | 25 | 26 | 27 | 28 | 29 | 30 |
| 31 | — | — | — | — | — | — |

THE YEAR A.D. 1752 IN ENGLISH-SPEAKING COUNTRIES

# ANTIQUITY OF WEEKLY CYCLE

"It is to be noted that in the Christian period the order of days of the week has never been interrupted. Thus, when Gregory XIII reformed the calendar, in 1582, Thursday, 4 October, was followed by Friday, 15 October. So in England, in 1752, Wednesday, 2 September, was followed by Thursday, 14 September."—Volume 3, p. 740, art. "Chronology."

## Correspondence With an American Astronomer

Still further evidence that time has not been lost, and that the weekly cycle has in no way been affected by any calendar change, is contained in letters received from two eminent astronomers. Under date of February 25, 1932, a letter was sent to Dr. A. James Robertson, at that time director, American Ephemeris and Nautical Almanac, at the Naval Observatory, Washington, D.C.

The astronomer who is the director of the Nautical Almanac, or the American Ephemeris, as it is generally known, to distinguish it from the British Nautical Almanac, must always be a man in the very first rank of his profession, for it is the computations found in this weighty volume, published annually, that govern navigation for all American ships.

Following is the major part of the letter to him:

"DEAR DR. ROBERTSON:

"I have just been reading statements by various astronomers of Europe to the effect that the weekly cycle has come down to us unbroken from very ancient times; in other words, that the seventh day of our present week, for example, is identical with the seventh day of the week of Bible times. I write therefore to inquire:

"1. Do you concur in these statements regarding the antiquity and unbroken sequence of the week? Or, to state the matter negatively, Have any of your investigations of past time given you any reason to doubt these statements?

On the opposite page is a reproduction of the calendar year A.D. 1752, in English countries. England and certain other countries did not obey the pope's decree in 1582, but continued to operate under the Julian calendar until 1752. By this date it was necessary to drop out eleven days in order to adjust the reckoning. The light-face type is Julian reckoning, and the bold-face, Gregorian. Again it will be noted that there was no break in the weekly cycle. The people retired Wednesday night, September 2 of the Julian calendar, and awakened Thursday morning, September 14 of the Gregorian calendar.

# ANSWERS TO OBJECTIONS

N. N. Ob. 36

IN REPLY ADDRESS NOT THE DIRECTOR
OF THIS LETTER, BUT THE
SUPERINTENDENT, NAVAL OBSERVATORY
WASHINGTON, D. C

REFER TO NO.

EN23/H5(14)(1)

**NAVY DEPARTMENT**

**U. S. NAVAL OBSERVATORY**

**WASHINGTON, D. C.**

**12 March 1932**

<u>Inclosures. 2.</u>

Dear Sir:

Your letter of 25 February, 1932, containing questions on the continuity of the weekly cycle is at hand.

As to Question (1) - I can only state that in connection with the proposed simplification of the calendar, we have had occasion to investigate the results of the works of specialists in chronology and we have never found one of them that has ever had the slightest doubt about the continuity of the weekly cycle since long before the Christian era.

As to Question (2) - There has been no change in our calendar in past centuries that has affected in any way the cycle of the week.

As to Question (3) - The answer is implied in the answer given to question (1).

Through the courtesy of the Superintendent, Captain Hellweg, I am inclosing an article on Calendar Reform, published by Admiral Upham, that might be of interest to you.

I am also returning your very interesting debate with Mr. Eastman. It was very considerate of you, for which, I thank you.

Sincerely yours,

James Robertson,
Director American Ephemeris.

Mr. F.D.Nichol,
The Advent Review & Sabbath Herald,
Takoma Park, Washington, D. C.

"2. Have the changes in our calendar in past centuries affected in any way the cycle of the week?

"3. To make my inquiry very concrete: According to the Bible record and the universal belief of Christians, Christ was crucified on a Friday and lay in the tomb on Saturday, which was 'the Sabbath day according to the commandment' (Luke 23:56). My question is this: Is the Saturday of our present time the lineal descendant in unbroken cycles of seven from that Saturday mentioned in the record of the crucifixion?"

See opposite page for a photographic reproduction of Dr. Robertson's reply.

### Correspondence With a British Astronomer

On February 25, 1932, a letter of inquiry concerning the weekly cycle and its relation to calendar change was addressed also to Sir Frank W. Dyson, Astronomer Royal of Great Britain, who at that time was in charge of the Royal Observatory, Greenwich, London.

See following page for a photographic reproduction of his reply.

### Simplify "Lost Time" Problem

It will be noted that astronomers and others speak with certainty concerning the continuity of the weekly cycle "since long before the Christian era," to borrow the words of Dr. Robertson of the U.S. Naval Observatory. There is no need that we carry the question of "lost time" back before the beginning of our era, for the following reasons: All agree that the weekly cycle was employed in Palestine at that time, and all Sundaykeeping peoples believe that Christ arose on the first day of the week. Now, the Bible plainly states that the day preceding that first day was "the Sabbath day according to the commandment." Luke 23:56. Thus the seventh day of the weekly cycle in the first century of the Christian Era was the "seventh day" of the Sabbath command. Accordingly, it is quite unnecessary to present evidence against "lost time" for the centuries preceding Christ.

# ANSWERS TO OBJECTIONS

Communications
should be
addressed to the
ASTRONOMER ROYAL

*Royal Observatory, Greenwich,*

*London,* S.E.10.

4th.March, 1932.

F.D.Nichol Esq.,
    The Advent Review and Sabbath Herald,
        Takoma Park,
            Washington, D.C.,   U.S.A.

Dear Sir,

      As far as I know, in the various changes
of the Calendar there has been no change in the seven
day rota of the week, which has come down from very
early times.   There have been attempts in the French
revolution and in Russia to alter this cycle.

      In the Nautical Almanac for 1931, p.740, in the
last paragraph, a very learned chronologist,
Dr.Fotheringham, states - "When we come upon clear
evidence, the period of seven days was reckoned
independently of the month and in fact of all astronomical periods.   From the Jewish Church it passed into
the Christian Church".

      You will see from this statement that no
astronomical evidence connected with seven day period
can be given.

               Yours faithfully,

                F.W.Dyson

          Astronomer Royal.

# Section IV

# THE SECOND ADVENT

CHAPTER 9

# The Second Advent Doctrine in the Creeds

THE CLASSIC creeds of the early centuries, the Reformation creeds, and the creeds of post-Reformation religious bodies rather generally contain a statement regarding the Second Advent of our Lord. These statements set forth the doctrine that Christ is to return at a future time to give rewards to the righteous and mete out punishment to the wicked. The clear inference, in almost every instance, is that Christ will return as literally as He came the first time, and as literally as He ascended. The inference also seems proper that Christ will return to a world such as we dwell in today, where the righteous and wicked both inhabit the earth, and not to a world that has already enjoyed a millennium of peace and righteousness. In other words, the creeds do not support the idea of a postmillennial coming of Christ. This is an important fact. Adventists are often charged with preaching unorthodox views. Now, the Second Advent is one of our most prominent teachings. It is well for us to know what the Christian church has believed on this doctrine through the centuries. Thus can we best show that in the matter of the Advent, as in other doctrines, we are not the preachers of new, strange ideas, but the restorers of ancient truths. Here is what the creeds* say:

### The Apostles' Creed

"As to the origin of the Apostles' Creed, it no doubt, gradually grew out of the confession of Peter, Matt. 16:16. . . . It can not be traced to an individual author. It is the product of the Western Catholic Church . . . within the first four centuries." "The Apostles' Creed is the creed of creeds. . . . It is by far the best popular summary of the

---

* The creeds quoted are those given in the classic work *The Creeds of Christendom*, by the eminent church historian, Philip Schaff. All quoted comments on these creeds are likewise from this work by Schaff.

565

Christian faith ever made within so brief a space. . . . It has the fragrance of antiquity and the inestimable weight of universal consent. It is a bond of union between all ages and sections of Christendom."—Volume 1, pp. 16, 14, 15.

"I believe in God the Father Almighty . . . and in Jesus Christ His only (begotten) Son our Lord; who . . . was crucified, dead, and buried; . . . the third day He rose from the dead; He ascended into heaven; and sitteth at the right hand of God the Father Almighty; from thence He shall come to judge the quick and the dead."—Volume 2, p. 45.

### The Nicene Creed

"The Nicene Creed is the first which obtained universal authority. It rests on older forms used in different churches of the East, and has undergone again some changes. . . . The original Nicene Creed dates from the first ecumenical Council, which was held at Nicaea, A.D. 325."—Volume 1, pp. 24, 25. The text from which we quote is "the received text of the Protestant Churches."

"I believe in . . . one Lord Jesus Christ, . . . who . . . was crucified also for us under Pontius Pilate; He suffered and was buried; and the third day He rose again, according to the Scriptures; and ascended into heaven, and sitteth on the right hand of the Father; and He shall come again, with glory, to judge both the quick and the dead; whose kingdom shall have no end."—Volume 2, pp. 58, 59.

### The Athanasian Creed

"The Athanasian Creed is also called Symbolum Quicunque. . . . Its origin is involved in obscurity, like that of the Apostles' Creed, the Gloria in Excelsis, and the Te Deum. It furnishes one of the most remarkable examples of the extraordinary influence which works of unknown or doubtful authorship have exerted. . . . It appears first in its full form towards the close of the eighth or the beginning of the ninth century. . . . The Symbolum Quicunque is a remarkably clear and precise summary of the doctrinal decisions of the first four ecumenical Councils."—Volume 1, pp. 35-37.

"38. [Jesus Christ] suffered for our salvation: . . . rose again the third day from the dead.

"39. He ascended into heaven, He sitteth on the right hand of the Father God [God the Father] Almighty.

"40. From whence [thence] He shall come to judge the quick and the dead.

"41. At whose coming all men shall rise again with their bodies;

"42. And shall give account for their own works."—Volume 2, p. 69.

### The Canons and Dogmatic Creeds of the Council of Trent, A.D. 1563

"The principal source and the highest standard of the doctrine and discipline of the Roman Church are the Canons and Decrees of the Council of Trent, first published in 1564, at Rome, by authority of Pius IV."—Volume 1, p. 91.

"I believe in one God, . . . and in one Lord Jesus Christ. . . . He suffered and was buried; and He rose again on the third day, according to the Scriptures; and He ascended into heaven, sitteth at the right hand of the Father; and again He will come with glory to judge the living and the dead; of whose kingdom there shall be no end."—Volume 2, p. 79.

### The Longer Catechism of the Orthodox, Catholic, Eastern Church

"The Catechism of Philaret [after the name of its author, who was Metropolitan of Moscow], revised, authorized, and published by the Holy Synod of St. Petersburg. It is translated into several languages, and since 1839 generally used in the schools and churches of Russia. It was sent to all the Eastern Patriarchs, and unanimously approved by them. . . .

"His longer Catechism (called a *full* catechism) is, upon the whole, the ablest and clearest summary of Eastern orthodoxy."—Volume 1, pp. 71, 72.

"226. How does holy Scripture speak of Christ's coming again?

"*This Jesus, which is taken up from you into heaven, shall so come in like manner as ye have seen Him go into heaven.* Acts 1:11. This was said to the Apostles by angels at the very time of our Lord's ascension.

"227. How does it speak of His future judgment?

"*The hour is coming, in which all that are in the graves shall hear the voice of the Son of God, and shall come forth: they that have done good, unto the resurrection of life; and they that have done evil, unto the resurrection of damnation.* John 5:28, 29. These are the words of Christ Himself. . . .

"229. Will the second coming of Christ be like His first?

"No; very different. He came to suffer for us in great humility, but He shall come to judge *us in His glory, and all the holy angels with Him.* Matt. 25:31. . . .

"233. Will Jesus Christ soon come to judgment?

"We know not. Therefore we should live so as to be always ready. [2 Peter 3:9, 10 and Matt. 25:13 are then quoted.]

"234. Are there not, however, revealed to us some *signs* of the nearer approach of Christ's coming?

"In the Word of God certain signs are revealed, as the decrease of faith and love among men, the abounding of iniquity and calamities, the preaching of the Gospel to all nations, and the coming of Antichrist. Matt. 24."—Volume 2, pp. 479, 480.

### The Augsburg Confession, A.D. 1530

"The Augsburg Confession, . . . was occasioned by the German Emperor Charles V., who commanded the Lutheran Princes to present, at the Diet to be held in the Bavarian city of Augsburg, an explicit statement of their faith, that the religious controversy might be settled, and Catholics and Protestants be united in a war against the common enemies, the Turks. . . . It was prepared, on the basis of previous drafts, and with conscientious care, by Philip Melanchthon, at the request and in the name of the Lutheran States, during the months of April, May, and June, 1530, at Coburg and Augsburg, with the full approval of Luther."—Volume 1, pp. 225, 226.

"Part First," of the Confession is entitled "Chief Articles of Faith," and consists of twenty-two articles. The first article opens thus: "The churches, with common consent among us, do teach ——" The following articles simply say, "They teach," meaning the churches. Throughout, Schaff has inserted in brackets "the most important additions of the German text." The translation is from the Latin.

# ADVENT DOCTRINE IN CHURCH CREEDS

"ART. XVII.—OF CHRIST'S RETURN TO JUDGMENT

"Also they teach that, in the consummation of the world [at the last day], Christ shall appear to judge, and shall raise up all the dead, and shall give unto the godly and elect eternal life and everlasting joys; but ungodly men and the devils shall He condemn unto endless torments.

"They condemn the Anabaptists who think that to condemned men and the devils shall be an end of torments. They condemn others also, who now scatter Jewish opinions, that, before the resurrection of the dead, the godly shall occupy the kingdom of the world, the wicked being everywhere suppressed."—Volume 3, pp. 17, 18.

## The Second Helvetic Confession, A.D. 1566

For Schaff's comments on this Confession, see under the "Second Helvetic Confession" in chapter 5.

"CHAPTER XI

"We believe and teach that the same Lord Jesus Christ, in that true flesh in which He was crucified and died, rose again from the dead. . . .

"We believe that our Lord Jesus Christ, in the same flesh, did ascend above all the visible heavens in the very highest heaven. . . .

"And out of heaven the same Christ will return unto judgment, even then when wickedness shall chiefly reign in the world, and when Antichrist, having corrupted true religion, shall fill all things with superstition and impiety, and shall most cruelly waste the Church with fire and bloodshed. Now Christ shall return to redeem His, and to abolish Antichrist by His coming, and to judge the quick and the dead (Acts 17:31). For the dead shall rise, and those that shall be found alive in that day (which is unknown unto all creatures) 'shall be changed in the twinkling of an eye' (1 Cor. 15:51, 52). And all the faithful shall be taken up to meet Christ in the air (1 Thess. 4:17); that thenceforth they may enter with Him into heaven, there to live forever (2 Tim. 2:11); but the unbelievers, or ungodly, shall descend with the devils into hell, there

569

to burn forever, and never to be delivered out of torments (Matt. 25:14).

"We therefore condemn all those who deny the true resurrection of the flesh. . . .

"Moreover, we condemn the Jewish dreams, that before the day of judgment there shall be a golden age in the earth, and that the godly shall possess the kingdoms of the world, their wicked enemies being trodden under foot; for the evangelical truth (Matt. 24 and 25, Luke 21), and the apostolic doctrine (in the Second Epistle to the Thessalonians 2, and in the Second Epistle to Timothy 3 and 4) are found to teach far otherwise."—Volume 3, pp. 852, 853.

### The Belgic Confession, A.D. 1561

"The chief author of the Belgic Confession is Guido (or Guy, Wido) de Brès, a noble evangelist and martyr of the Reformed Church of the Netherlands. . . . The Belgic Confession was prepared in 1561. . . . The Confession was publicly adopted by a Synod at Antwerp (1566), . . . and again by the great Synod of Dort, April 29, 1619. . . . Since that time the Belgic Confession, together with the Heidelberg Catechism, has been the recognized symbol of the Reformed Churches in Holland and Belgium. It is also the doctrinal standard of the Reformed (Dutch) Church in America, which holds to it even more tenaciously than the mother Church in the Netherlands. . . . It is, upon the whole, the best symbolical statement of the Calvinistic system of doctrine, with the exception of the Westminster Confession."—Volume 1, pp. 504-506. The Confession contains thirty-seven articles.

#### "ART. XXXVII.—OF THE LAST JUDGMENT

"Finally we believe, according to the Word of God, when the time appointed by the Lord (which is unknown to all creatures) is come, and the number of the elect complete, that our Lord Jesus Christ will come from heaven, corporally and visibly, as He ascended with great glory and majesty, to declare Himself Judge of the quick and the dead, burning this old world with fire and flame to cleanse it. And then all men will personally appear before this great Judge, both men and women and children, that have been from the beginning of the world to the end thereof, being summoned by the voice of the archangel, and by the sound of the trumpet of God."—Volume 3, pp. 433, 434.

Then follows a statement about the resurrection of all the dead and of the judgment, with the rewards to be meted out to the wicked and to the righteous. The article, and thus the Confession, closes with the following words:

"Therefore we expect that great day with a most ardent desire, to the end that we may fully enjoy the promises of God in Christ Jesus our Lord. Amen.

"Even so, come Lord Jesus. Rev. 22:20."—*Ibid.*, p. 436.

### The Scotch Confession of Faith, A.D. 1560

For Schaff's comment on the significance of this Confession, see under "Scotch Confession" in chapter 5.

"ART. XI.—OF THE ASCENSION

"We nathing doubt, bot the self same bodie, quhilk was borne of the Virgine, was crucified, dead, and buried, and quhilk did rise againe, did ascend into the heavens, for the accomplishment of all things: Quhere in our names, and for our comfort, He hes received all power in heaven and eirth, quhere he sittes at the richt hand of the Father, inaugurate in His kingdome, Advocate and onlie Mediator for us. Quhilk glorie, honour, and prerogative, he alone amonges the brethren sal posses, till that all His Enimies be made His futestule, as that we undoubtedlie beleeve they sall be in the finall Judgment: To the Execution whereof we certainelie beleve, that the same our Lord Jesus sall visiblie returne, as that Hee was sene to ascend. And then we firmely beleve, that the time of refreshing and restitutioun of all things sall cum, in samekle that thir, that fra the beginning have suffered violence, injurie, and wrang, for richteousnes sake, sal inherit that blessed immortalitie promised fra the beginning."—Volume 3, pp. 448, 449.

### The Thirty-nine Articles of the Church of England, A.D. 1571

For Schaff's comments on the significance of the Thirty-nine Articles see chapter 5.

# ANSWERS TO OBJECTIONS

### "ART. IV.—OF THE RESURRECTION OF CHRIST

"Christ did truly *rise* again from death, and took again His body, with flesh, bones, and all things appertaining to the perfection of Man's nature; wherewith He ascended into Heaven, and there sitteth, until He return to judge all Men at the last day."
—*Ibid.*, p. 489.

## The Irish Articles of Religion, A.D. 1615

For Schaff's comment, see under "The Irish Articles" in chapter 5.

"103. At the end of this world the Lord Jesus shall come in the clouds with the glory of His Father; at which time, by the almighty power of God, the living shall be changed and the dead shall be raised; and all shall appear both in body and soul before His judgment-seat to receive according to that which they have done in their bodies, whether good or evil."

## The Westminster Confession of Faith, A.D. 1647

For Schaff's comment on this Confession, see under "The Westminster Confession" in chapter 5.

### "CHAPTER XXXIII.—OF THE LAST JUDGMENT

"I. God hath appointed a day wherein He will judge the world in righteousness by Jesus Christ, to whom all power and judgment is given of the Father. In which day, not only the apostate angels shall be judged, but likewise all persons, that have lived upon earth, shall appear before the tribunal of Christ, to give an account of their thoughts, words, and deeds; and to receive according to what they have done in the body, whether good or evil.

"II. . . . Then shall the righteous go into everlasting life, and receive that fullness of joy and refreshing which shall come from the presence of the Lord: but the wicked, who know not God, and obey not the gospel of Jesus Christ, shall be cast into eternal torments, and be punished with everlasting destruction from the presence of the Lord, and from the glory of His power.

"III. As Christ would have us to be certainly persuaded that there shall be a day of judgment, both to deter all men from sin, and for the greater consolation of the godly in their adversity: so will He have that day unknown to men, that they may shake off all carnal security, and be always watchful, because they know not at what hour the Lord will come; and may be ever prepared to say, Come, Lord Jesus, come quickly. Amen."—Volume 3, pp. 671-673.

## The Savoy Declaration of the Congregational Churches, A.D. 1658

Schaff declares: "The Savoy Declaration is merely a modification of the Westminster Confession to suit the Congregational polity." —*Ibid.*, p. 718. Schaff gives the modifications. There is none indicated for Chapter XXXIII, "Of the Last Judgment," which is quoted above. The Savoy Declaration is a doctrinal standard among American as well as among British Congregationalists.

## The Baptist Confession of A.D. 1688
### (The Philadelphia Confession)

"This is the most generally accepted Confession of the Regular or Calvinistic Baptists in England and in the Southern States of America. It appeared first in London, 1677. . . . It was adopted early in the eighteenth century by the Philadelphia Association of Baptist churches, and is hence called also the Philadelphia Confession of Faith.

"It is a slight modification of the Confession of the Westminster Assembly (1647) and the Savoy Declaration (1658), with changes to suit the Baptist views on church polity and on the subjects and mode of baptism."—*Ibid.*, p. 738.

Schaff notes the specific changes made in certain chapters of the Westminster Confession. There is no change indicated for Chapter XXXIII, "Of the Last Judgment," which is quoted above.

## The Methodist Articles of Religion, A.D. 1784

For Schaff's comments on these articles see under "The Methodist Articles" in chapter 5.

### "III.—OF THE RESURRECTION OF CHRIST

"Christ did truly rise again from the dead, and took again His body, with all things appertaining to the perfection of man's nature, wherewith He ascended into heaven, and there sitteth until He return to judge all men at the last day."

### The New Hampshire Baptist Confession, A.D. 1833

For Schaff's comment on this Confession, see under "New Hampshire Baptist Confession" in chapter 5.

#### "XVIII.—OF THE WORLD TO COME

"We believe that the end of the world is approaching;[1] that at the last day Christ will descend from heaven,[2] and raise the dead from the grave to final retribution;[3] that a solemn separation will then take place;[4] that the wicked will be adjudged to endless punishment, and the righteous to endless joy;[5] and that this judgment will fix forever the final state of men in heaven or hell, on principles of righteousness.[6]"—*Ibid.*, p. 748.

---

[1] Peter 4:7; 1 Cor. 7:29-31; Heb. 1:10-12; Matt. 24:35; 1 John 2:17; Matt. 28:20; 13:39, 40; 2 Peter 3:3-13.

[2] Acts 1:11; Rev. 1:7; Heb. 9:28; Acts 3:21; 1 Thess. 4:13-18; 5:1-11.

[3] Acts 24:15; 1 Cor. 15:12-59; Luke 14:14; Dan. 12:2; John 5:28, 29; 6:40; 11:25, 26; 2 Tim. 1:10; Acts 10:42.

[4] Matt. 13:49; 13:37-43; 24:30, 31; 25:31-33.

[5] Matt. 25:35-41; Rev. 22:11; 1 Cor. 6:9, 10; Mark 9:43-48; 2 Peter 2:9; Jude 7; Phil. 3:19; Rom. 6:32; 2 Cor. 5:10, 11; John 4:36; 2 Cor. 4:18.

[6] Rom. 3:5, 6; 2 Thess. 1:6-12; Heb. 6:1, 2; 1 Cor. 4:5; Acts 17:31; Rom. 2:2-16; Rev. 20:11, 12; 1 John 2:28; 4:17.

# CHAPTER 10

# The Prophetic Origin
# of the Seventh-day Adventist Church

SEVENTH-DAY ADVENTISTS claim that this Advent movement arose at a particular time in history to do a specific work for God in fulfillment of certain prophecies. This claim is the true and historic basis of the appeal we make to all men, in terms of the second angel's message, to "come out" and join this movement.

In view of this we need to be acquainted with the history of the beginnings of the movement. As early as 1849 James White realized this need in relation to the historical experiences of the early 1840's, which saw the rise of the Advent movement. Said he:

"In order to show the fulfillment of Prophecy, we have to refer to history. To show the fulfillment of prophecy relating to the four universal kingdoms of the second and seventh chapters of Daniel, we have to refer to the history of those kingdoms. Deny the history, and the prophecy is of no use. Just so with the prophecies relating to the second advent movement."—*Present Truth*, Dec., 1849, p. 46.

We need not only to know the history of the early 1840's as we would a period of secular history but also to see the Seventh-day Adventist movement in the setting of those times. There has been not only much ignorance among us regarding the historical rootage of Seventh-day Adventism, but also an active desire on the part of some to dissociate ourselves from the Advent movement of the early 1840's, which is generally known as Millerism. Two reasons have prompted this desire: First, the Millerites set a date for the Advent, which brought them into derision at the time and which has made them the object of ridicule ever since. Naturally we wish to escape ridicule on that score, and we are emphatic, and correct, in our declaration that Seventh-day Adventists have never set time. Second, there has grown up around the Millerites a fantastic array of stories which picture them as wildly fanatical. And of course we do not wish to be known as the spiritual children of fanatics.

## No New Attitude

It is not only an interesting but a thought-provoking fact that this desire to be dissociated from the Millerite movement that climaxed in 1844, is not something new. It was manifest almost immediately after the great disappointment of October 22, 1844, and was very active at the time James White was writing in December, 1849. The Lord had not come, as expected, and thus the prophecy of the 2300 days apparently had not been fulfilled. The result was that many nominal Adventists began to deny that God had been in the 1844 movement. They thus fell away, some of them rather relieved to be known no longer as belonging to a movement that had made a great theological blunder. Against all these James White inveighed, as he surely had to if he believed that God inspired the Advent movement.

Today, the situation is somewhat different. We, as Seventh-day Adventists, have no desire to question, for example, the basic interpretation of prophecy employed by the Millerites in measuring the limits of the 2300-day prophecy. We do not deny God's leading in the 1844 movement. We have sensed, though some of us have not clearly understood, that we need to maintain a definite connection with the 1844 movement in order to prove that Seventh-day Adventism arose in fulfillment of prophecy. Yet we rather frequently seek to blur, or at least hesitate to admit, a close and prophetic sequential relationship between the 1844 movement known as Millerism and that known today as Seventh-day Adventism. The reasons for this, as already stated, are our embarrassment over the time setting of the Millerites and the stories of fanatical acts in which they allegedly indulged.

Thus, while we have been passively willing to grant that the Millerites are our relations, though not too close, we have been wont to treat them as poor relations.

## How to Resolve the Dilemma

This unhappy dilemma disappears, and the truly prophetic origin of the Seventh-day Adventist Church stands revealed, as we establish the following seven points:

1. That the Seventh-day Adventist movement is a direct outgrowth of the Advent movement under William Miller, generally known as Millerism.

2. That it is necessary to believe in this relationship in order to find an explanation of certain prophetic passages in the Bible, and in order to prove that the Seventh-day Adventist Church is indeed God's last movement in the world.

3. That a study of Millerism will brighten our own faith in the divine origin and leadership of the Seventh-day Adventist movement, and will provide a wholly satisfactory answer to the libelous charges made by the enemies of truth for a century.

4. That the fact we are the outgrowth of the Millerite movement does not require us to subscribe to the individual views that might have been held by any Millerite preacher. Nor does it require us to minimize in any degree the significance of the distinctive teachings developed under the third angel's message, but rather the contrary.*

5. That the fact the Millerites, generally, set a certain date for the Lord's coming need not embarrass Seventh-day Adventists today.

6. That the stories of fanatical excesses by the Millerites are very largely a tissue of falsehood, and that eminent authorities in the field of history admit this.

7. That the disappointment of October 22, 1844, provides no

---

* The following discussion of the first four points originally appeared as an extra of *The Ministry,* September, 1944, which was printed by action of the General Conference Committee.

ground for the charge that God was therefore not in the Advent movement, and hence not in the Seventh-day Adventist movement that sprang from the Advent Awakening of the 1840's.

### First Point Examined

Sufficient evidence in support of the first point might be adduced simply by asking and answering a few primary questions, as follows:

*What religious movement in America came to its climax in 1844?* The great Second Advent movement under William Miller, generally known as Millerism.

*Where and when did the Seventh-day Adventist movement begin?* In America in 1844.

*Who were the first Sabbathkeeping Adventists?* A company of Millerites in Washington, New Hampshire.

*Who were the first leaders in the Seventh-day Adventist movement?* Unquestionably they were James White, Mrs. White, and Joseph Bates.

*What was their religious background?* James White had been a Millerite preacher. Ellen Harmon White accepted Millerism as a girl, and she, with her parents, was cast out of a Methodist church in Portland, Maine, because of her Millerite views. Joseph Bates was a leader in the Millerite movement, holding various offices in the general conferences of the Millerites and serving as chairman at one of the most important of these conferences.

*Who were some other very early Seventh-day Adventist pioneers?* Hiram Edson and Frederick Wheeler.

*What were their religious connections?* Both of these men were Millerites. Edson was the man who, passing through the field the morning after the disappointment, received the light on the sanctuary—that Christ had gone into the most holy place on October 22. Edson, with another Millerite brother, was on his way the morning of October 23 to "encourage some of our brethren" after their disappointment.

*For whom did our Seventh-day Adventist pioneer leaders labor quite exclusively for several years after 1844?* For their associates in the Millerite movement.

The foregoing undebatable facts of history would seem to be sufficient in themselves to settle the question of our origin. But the case becomes much stronger when we hear the testimony of the Seventh-day Adventist pioneers themselves. Did they seek to blur their relationship with Millerism and to pose as something new and different? No, they contended vigorously that they were the true spiritual successors of that Second Advent movement of the early 1840's. In 1850 we published the *Advent Review,* the forerunner of the *Review and Herald.* The first issue opens thus:

"Our design in this review is to cheer and refresh the true believer, by showing the fulfillment of prophecy in the past wonderful work of God, in calling out and separating from the world and nominal church, a people who are looking for the second advent of the dear Saviour."—*Advent Review,* vol. 1, no. 1, p. 1.

In other words, our Seventh-day Adventist pioneers in this *Advent Review* were eulogizing the so-called Millerite movement. They then proceed to chide those "Adventists" who denied the leading of God in it:

"In reviewing the past, we shall quote largely from the writings of the leaders in the advent cause [Millerism], and show that they once boldly advocated, and published to the world, the same position, relative to the fulfillment of prophecy in the great leading advent movements in our past experience, that we now occupy; and that when the advent host were all united in 1844, they looked upon these movements in the same light in which we now view them, and thus show who have 'LEFT THE ORIGINAL FAITH.' "—*Ibid.* (Capitals theirs.)

So far from seeking to blur their relationship to the Millerite movement, our pioneers boldly claimed that they were the ones who were holding to the "original faith." This issue of the *Advent Review* is almost filled with articles by Millerite leaders, reprinted from Millerite papers of the early 1840's. Two members of the "publishing committee" that brought out this *Advent Review* were James White and Hiram Edson. The cover page carries the following in display type: "The Advent Review, Containing Thrilling Testimonies, Written in the Holy Spirit, by Many of the Leaders in the Second Advent Cause, Showing Its Divine Origin and Progress." Below is a line of Scripture: "Call to Remembrance the Former Days."

### Later Leaders Speak

And what is the testimony of our Seventh-day Adventist pioneers in the years that followed? Is it clear? James White, in an editorial in the *Review and Herald* of 1853 declared: "We acknowledge that we were disappointed, and did not then understand the event to occur at the end of the days; but we do contend that this does not in the least affect the evidence of the immediate coming of Christ."—February 17, 1853, p. 156.

Our pioneers never spoke of someone else who was disappointed in 1844. They always said, "We were disappointed."

An editorial from the same pen in the *Review* of April 18, 1854, announced:

"We claim to stand on the original advent faith. . . . As to the great fundamental doctrines taught by Wm. Miller, we see no reason to change our views. . . .

"While the *Advent Review* occupies its present position, it may be expected that its columns will be enriched with spirited articles upon the second advent from the pens of Wm. Miller, Litch, Fitch, Hale, Storrs, and others, written ten or twelve years since."—Page 101.

In 1867 the *Review and Herald* contained an editorial by Uriah Smith which described one of the objectives in publishing this weekly church paper:

"One of its special objects is a review of the past great advent movement [that is, the movement before the disappointment in October, 1844]. What Adventist who shared in that movement can look back upon it but with a thrill of joy, and can but long for manifestations of the Spirit of God, in equal power, in connection with the work now? And how can a person possibly enter with any enthusiasm upon the new theories and schemes devised since 1844, which oblige him to give up all the work previous to that time, either as erroneous or premature? If God was not in the work then, will any Adventist tell us at what point He has been in it since that time? . . .

"We cannot be too thankful that we have not been left to slide from the foundation so securely laid in 1844 for the advent movement of these last days. . . . Every advent theory that has been devised, which ignores the past work, is a castle in the air, a pyramid without a base, a building without a foundation."—December 17, 1867, p. 8.

In 1877 Uriah Smith's book *The Sanctuary* was published. In this he declared:

"The present generation has seen a religious movement such as no other generation ever witnessed: a world-wide agitation of the question of Christ's immediate second coming, calling out hundreds of thousands of believers in the doctrine. Time has continued; and under the name of Millerism it now receives the flippant sneer of the careless multitudes."—*The Sanctuary*, p. 13.

"The great advent movement of 1840-1844 . . . was in the order and purpose of God. He must therefore still have a people on the earth as a result of that movement; He must still have a truth among men bearing some relation to that great work; and there must be some correct explanation of the great disappointment connected with that movement."—*Ibid.*, p. 21.

Further on in his work there is a chapter entitled "The Original Advent Faith" which discusses the point of contention that had raged between Seventh-day Adventists and first-day Adventists:

"Seventh-day Adventists are sometimes charged with being a mere off-shoot from the advent body, followers of side issues and newly created hobbies. We claim, and shall show, that we are the only ones who adhere to the original principles of interpretation on which the whole advent movement was founded, and that we are the only ones who are following out that movement to its logical results and conclusions."—*Ibid.*, p. 102.

In 1885 George I. Butler, then president of the General Conference, wrote a series of articles for the *Review and Herald* under the general title "Advent Experience." He began thus:

"The old '44 Adventists are rapidly passing away. Only a little handful remain among us. The mass of our people are not personally acquainted with the facts connected with the passing of the time [in October 22, 1844], the short period of confusion which followed before the rise of the third angel's message, and the events connected with its early history. . . . Yet there are facts of the very deepest interest connected with that interesting period, which have a vital connection with our present work. This message is connected with all that experience by indissoluble ties."—February 10, 1885, p. 89.

Late in the year 1890 Uriah Smith began a series of editorials in the *Review and Herald* under the general head "The Origin and History of the Third Angel's Message." He spoke of the "great advent movement of the present generation," which "movement has been in progress over half a century." He declared that "a movement holding so important a place in the work of God, and destined to make itself felt so deeply in the religious world, must have many interesting incidents connected with its development and progress." Then he added immediately:

"William Miller, of Low Hampton, New York, was the man who, in the providence of God, was raised up to lead out in this work. . . . It was not until 1831 that he made his views public. . . . The year 1831 may therefore be set down as the year when the first angel's message began to be proclaimed."—December 16, 1890, p. 776.

This is the testimony of the pioneers for the first half century of our movement, and is anyone better qualified to testify than they? That testimony is clear and permits of only one conclusion.

### Second Point Examined

The relationship of Seventh-day Adventists to the Millerite movement becomes even more evident, if that be possible, when we examine the second point; namely, that we must believe in a close relationship between ourselves and Millerism in order to find an explanation of certain prophetic statements and in order to prove that the Seventh-day Adventist movement is God's last movement in the world.

Very soon after 1844 some first-day Adventists began to doubt the genuineness of their 1844 experience. Our Seventh-day Adventist pioneers argued that to do this was to remove the historical facts on which certain prophecies depended for proof of their fulfillment. Said James White in 1849:

## PROPHETIC ORIGIN OF ADVENTIST CHURCH

"If we deny our holy experience in the great leading movements, in the past, such as the proclamation of the time in 1843 and 1844, then we cannot show a fulfillment of those prophecies relating to those movements. Therefore, those who deny their past experience, while following God and His Holy Word, deny or misapply a portion of the sure Word."—*Present Truth,* December, 1849.

Now, it is not possible for us today to "deny" an "experience" of 1844. We were not yet born. But when we attempt to dissociate ourselves from that "experience" do we not go as far as it is possible for us to go in denying the "experience"? And do we not thus weaken the connection between prophecy and its fulfillment? It is an interesting fact that one of the very first productions from the pen of a Seventh-day Adventist pioneer—*Second Advent Way Marks and High Heaps,* written by Joseph Bates in 1847—sought to establish the faith of "the little flock" by showing the fulfillment of certain prophecies in connection with the Millerite movement. Said he:

"The design of the author of the following pages is to strengthen and encourage the honesthearted, humble people of God, that have been, and still are, willing to keep the commandments of God and testimony of Jesus, to hold on to their past experience, in the connected chain of wonderful events and fulfillment of prophecy, which have been developed during the last seven years."—Page 2.

### Certain Prophecies Fulfilled

From that time onward Seventh-day Adventist pioneers sought to show the divine leading in the Millerite movement and the relationship of Seventh-day Adventists to that movement by making reference to certain prophecies:

1. THE VISION OF HABAKKUK 2:2, 3. This was the prophetic command to "write the vision, and make it plain upon tables"; coupled with the declaration that the "vision is yet for an appointed time," that "at the end it shall speak, and not lie: though it tarry, wait for it." The Millerites believed that the publication of their prophetic charts in 1842 fulfilled the first part of this text. They believed that the passing of the first date set for the Advent (the Jewish year 1843, which ended in the spring of A.D. 1844) was fol-

# ANSWERS TO OBJECTIONS

lowed by the "tarry" of the vision, and that the final date of
October 22, 1844, would fulfill the prediction, "At the end it shall
speak, and not lie."

Commenting on this prophecy, James White in 1850 declared:
"If the vision did not speak in the autumn of 1844, then it never
spoke, and never can speak." He firmly believed that Habakkuk
2:2, 3 was fulfilled in the way that the Millerites had preached it.
Mrs. White applies the prophecy in the same way. (See *Testimonies*, vol. 1, p. 52; *Early Writings*, p. 236.)

2. THE PARABLE OF THE TEN VIRGINS. The Millerites believed
that this parable, which is also a prophecy, had its application and
fulfillment in 1844. The "tarrying" of the bridegroom they understood to be the time between their first expectation of Christ's
coming (by the close of the Jewish year 1843, that is, in the spring
of 1844) and the true time of the fulfillment of the 2300-day
prophecy on October 22, 1844. They understood the Scriptural
statement, "At midnight there was a cry made," to be the sounding
of the true message as to the ending of the 2300-day prophecy,
which began to be heard in the summer of 1844. Indeed the very
words of the parable were used: "Behold, the bridegroom cometh;
go ye out to meet him."

The Seventh-day Adventist pioneers continued to believe that
this parable and prophecy met their fulfillment in 1844. (See,
for example, *The Great Controversy*, pp. 393-398; *Thoughts on
Daniel and the Revelation*, p. 640.) In her first vision Mrs. White
described the "bright light set up" at the "beginning of the path"
toward the kingdom, as "the midnight cry."—*Early Writings*, p. 14.

3. THE PROPHECY OF REVELATION 3:7-10. Seventh-day Adventists have consistently taken the position that the Millerite movement provides the fulfillment of this prophecy. The Philadelphia
church reached its climax in the company "who received the
advent message up to the autumn of 1844," when "every heart
beat in unison," and "selfishness and covetousness were laid aside."
—*Thoughts on Daniel and the Revelation*, p. 395. The shut door
and open door of that prophecy we understand to mean the

closing of the door of the first apartment and the opening of the door of the second apartment in the heavenly sanctuary, on October 22, 1844. (See *The Great Controversy*, p. 430.) Obviously we cannot apply this prophecy to the Philadelphia church unless we believe that the Millerite movement truly was of God and presented that state of "brotherly love" required by the symbol.

4. THE PROPHECY OF REVELATION 10: the angel with a little book in his hand. This prophecy can be understood only in terms of the Millerite disappointment. Our denominational belief is that the sweetness of hope in 1844, contrasted with the bitterness after the disappointment, fulfilled the prophecy about the little book's being sweet in the mouth but bitter in the belly. The declaration, "Thou must prophesy again," we understand to foretell the preaching of the third angel's message. (See *Thoughts on Daniel and the Revelation*, pp. 527, 528. )

5. SEQUENCE OF THREE ANGELS' MESSAGES OF REVELATION 14:6-12. This prophecy ties us to the Millerite movement in a way that no other prophecy does. In the first place, we hold that the angel of Revelation 10 is "identical with the first angel of Revelation 14."—*Thoughts on Daniel and the Revelation*, p. 521. Next, we believe that the message of the first angel of Revelation 14 "had its most direct fulfillment" in the preaching of Miller and his associates. (*The Great Controversy*, p. 368.)

Likewise we believe that the second angel's message began to be heard when Millerite preachers called on the Advent believers to come out of the churches. (*Ibid.*, p. 389.)

We believe that the third angel's message began to be heard shortly after the disappointment in 1844 under the preaching of the Seventh-day Adventist pioneers. But we also believe that the third "followed them, not to supersede them, but only to join with them."—*Thoughts on Daniel and the Revelation*, p. 664.

Hence we have properly a threefold message for the world. That is sound Seventh-day Adventist theology. But inasmuch as this is so, we are today the preachers of a message that constituted the heart and essence of the Millerite preaching, adding to it a third message and related truths. How could we be more closely tied in with Millerism? Speaking of the three angels of Revelation 14, James White said:

"The truth and work of God in this movement, commencing with the labors of William Miller, and reaching to the close of probation, is illustrated by these three angels. . . . These angels illustrate the three great divisions of the genuine movement. . . .

"Seventh-day Adventists hold fast the great advent movement [of 1844], hence have use for the messages. . . . They cannot spare these links in the golden chain of truth, that connect the past with the present and future, and show a beautiful harmony in the great whole.

"I repeat it. The three [angels'] messages symbolize the three parts of the genuine movement."—*Life Incidents*, pp. 306, 307.

This agrees with Mrs. White's statement regarding "the three angels of Revelation 14." "All are linked together," she declares. (See *Testimonies*, vol. 6, p. 17.)

The inevitable conclusion from this is best expressed in the words of George I. Butler. Comparing the Advent experience of 1844 with ours, he says:

"If that advent experience was not of God, this cannot be. If that was a fanatical movement, this must be also. But if that first message was a true prophetic movement, this surely is. The [three angels'] messages constitute but one series. They stand together or fall together."—*Review and Herald*, Feb. 10, 1885, p. 89. (See also his statement of the interlocking of three messages in *Review and Herald*, April 14, 1885, page 233.)

In the light of the foregoing historical facts and prophetic declarations, surely only one conclusion is possible: Seventh-day Adventism is the logical extension and direct development of the prophetic movement raised up of God in America in the early decades of the nineteenth century and known generally as Millerism.

### Third Point Examined

We come now to the third point: That a study of Millerism will brighten our own faith in the divine origin and leadership of the Seventh-day Adventist movement and will provide a wholly satisfactory answer to the libelous charges made by the enemies of truth for a hundred years.

As already quoted, Elder Butler declared: "If that [Millerite movement] was a fanatical movement, this must be also. But if that first message was a true prophetic movement, this surely is." This statement not only ties us to Millerism; it makes imperative that we know the truth about that movement. Our pioneers sensed this fully. That explains why the *Review and Herald* has carried many articles through the years in defense of Miller and the Advent movement of the early 1840's. These articles are militant and specific. Take this typical statement by George I. Butler:

"There were no 'ascension robes' or any such follies whatever. . . . During the night when the time passed meetings continued all night. There was a drunken, noisy rabble howling around, and making the night hideous. But the believers were praying most earnestly for God to guard, shield, and save them."—*Review and Herald*, Feb. 17, 1885, pp. 105, 106.

"The most ridiculous and foolish stories about the Adventists were set afloat, and told so confidently that many believed them true. Here was where the 'ascension robe' story originated. . . . Never was there a more ridiculous shameful lie."—*Ibid.*, Feb. 24, 1885, p. 121.

### Mrs. White Defends the Millerites

Mrs. White frequently referred to the reviving of spirit that came from recalling the early days of the Advent movement. But she even more specifically wrote in defense of the Millerites against the charges of fanaticism. She herself had suffered under those charges, for she had been a Millerite. In *The Great Controversy*, beginning with chapter 18, "An American Reformer," she devoted several chapters to a discussion of Miller and the Advent awakening in the nineteenth century, particularly the movement in America. There is no vagueness in her writing. Here is what she said, in part, to meet the charge of fanaticism leveled against Miller and his associates:

"In the days of the Reformation its enemies charged all the evils of fanaticism upon the very ones who were laboring most earnestly against it. A similar course was pursued by the opposers of the advent movement. And not content with misrepresenting and exaggerating the errors of extremists and fanatics, they circulated the unfavorable reports that had not the slightest semblance of truth. . . .

"Of all the great religious movements since the days of the apostle, none have been more free from human imperfection and the wiles of Satan than was that of the autumn of 1844. Even now, after the lapse of many years, all who shared in that movement and who have stood firm upon the platform of truth, still feel the holy influence of that blessed work, and bear witness that it was of God. . . .

"Miller and his associates fulfilled prophecy, and gave a message which Inspiration had foretold should be given to the world, but which they could not have given had they fully understood the prophecies pointing out their disappointment, and presenting another message to be preached to all nations before the Lord should come."
—*The Great Controversy*, pp. 397-405.

Mrs. White's vigorous denial of false charges against the Millerites is in full harmony with the united testimony of all the pioneers. She sensed very definitely that it would be nonsense to eulogize Miller and his work as of God, and to affirm that Seventh-day Adventists grew from Millerism, without seeking to free the reader's mind of the wild charges against the Millerites.

What Mrs. White from personal experience and through inspiration could say categorically in denial of the charges of fanaticism, we today can say if we will take the time to examine the historical sources. No truer statement was ever made than that many stories were circulated about the Millerites "that had not the slightest semblance of truth." One need not read very far into the original records without coming to the conclusion that the most conscienceless campaign of slander and misrepresentation was carried on against the Advent believers. We should have known in advance that there was little truth in the fantastic stories, for there stands the sweeping statement of Mrs. White. But almost overwhelming is the power of rumors, insinuations, and false stories. They seem so plausible. The mere repeating of them seems to give them what they originally lacked, the note of authority. And—we may as well confess—they have almost deceived some of the elect!

Doubtless it is well that we should have an answer ready for these false stories. Every encyclopedia, indeed almost every reference work, states that we sprang from the Advent movement under Miller in the 1840's, and by inference, if not directly, links us with the alleged fanaticism of the movement. But proper as it may be for us to have an answer ready, this is not the primary reason why Adventists should know the truth about Millerism. There is a more important reason. We need to know the truth about that movement in order to keep our own thinking straight and our own faith strong in the divine origin of the present movement of which we are a part.

### Fourth Point Examined

We come now to the fourth point: The fact that we are the outgrowth of the Millerite movement does not require us to subscribe to the individual views that might have been held by any Millerite. Nor does it require us to minimize in any degree the significance of the distinctive teachings developed under the third angel's message, but rather the contrary.

It would be most erroneous to think of Seventh-day Adventism as being limited in its range of doctrine because of its relationship to Millerism. Nor is any such conclusion demanded by the fact of our historical connection. An editorial in the *Review* in 1854 makes this clear:

"We have no idea that William Miller had all the light on every point. The path of the just was to shine more and more till the perfect day should come. He shed a flood of light on the prophecies; but the subject of the sanctuary was to be opened to the waiting flock, in the period of the third message. . . .

"As to the great fundamental doctrines taught by William Miller, we see no reason to change our views. We claim all the light of past time on this glorious theme, and cherish it as from Heaven. And we cheerfully let the providence of God, and plain Bible testimony correct our past view of the sanctuary, and give us a more harmonious system of truth, and a firmer basis of faith."—April 18, 1854, pp. 100, 101.

It should be remembered that Miller never sought to create a new denomination with a creedal statement on all doctrine. Rather, he viewed the Advent movement as a call to study and believe a great truth, the personal, soon coming of Christ, in the setting of certain prophecies. Millerism was not a denomination, it was not synonymous with a creed. That fact must be kept clear in our minds. The individual beliefs of different preachers or laymen— they were from virtually every religious persuasion—may have tinged the thinking of such persons, but they did not give the movement its real color. The true color of the movement was that of the golden hue of the Advent morning. It was an *Advent* move- ment—a movement whose distinctive character was due to its pro- phetic setting. We should never forget that Millerism proper was concerned primarily with the purpose, manner, and time of the Advent.

### The Essence of Millerism

As the movement drew toward its climax in 1844, the call to come out of the churches became strong and clear. This call served to make Millerism stand out more sharply from other religious groups. Thus the movement came to its climax on October 22, 1844, with one great truth distinguishing it, the judgment hour of God at hand, the first angel's message; and with a separating call to come out of Babylon, the second angel's message. Anything beyond this is not of the essence of Millerism. For example, when a prominent Millerite, George Storrs, brought forth his views on the nature of man—which views both we and the leading first-day Adventist group believe today—Miller and most of his associates opposed the views as much for their being extraneous to the single purpose of the movement as for their being, as they thought, erroneous.

If we keep in mind this easily established historical fact that the Millerite movement was a great awakening on one central truth in the setting of certain prophecies, and thus in fulfillment of prophecy, we have no difficulty in understanding how the Seventh-day Adventist pioneers could write so unqualifiedly as they did regarding our connection with it, while at the same time holding that God had given to Seventh-day Adventists certain truths not understood or preached in the Millerite movement. Our Seventh-day Adventist pioneers saw a significance in the work which was shaping under their humble preaching after 1844, first and most definitely because they believed it was the fulfillment of the *third* angel's message—the third in a divinely connected series. They saw the very distinctive doctrine of the seventh-day Sabbath, for example, in the setting of that third angel's message, and declared that only in that setting could the real force of the doctrine be realized in these last days.

### Onward in Advancing Light

The threefold message, which began as a fervent preaching of the one central truth of the personal Second Advent, and which next called on men to come out of Babylon, has assumed its full dimensions under the third angel's message, as a reform in all matters of doctrine and life in readiness for the Advent. This is consistent with the plan God has followed at all times, leading men onward in advancing light. The awakened interest in Bible study, particularly of the prophecies, under the first angel's message, placed men in an ideal position for God to give them illumination. The separation from the churches freed them of the hindrance that so often prevents men from accepting further light, the fear of what their church associates would think. Thus God prepared men for the message of the third angel. Fervently searching the Scriptures, certain that God had led them thus far, and desiring to follow on to further truth, our Seventh-day Adventist pioneers sought God with strong cryings and tears. Mrs. White tells of the many times they gathered together to study the Bible and to pray. "Sometimes the entire night was spent in solemn investigation of the Scriptures, that we might understand the truth for our time."—*Christian Experience and Teachings,* p. 193.

Light came and the truth unfolded under such study and also under the impetus of the Spirit of prophecy, a gift given in fulfillment of prophecy. Erelong the full significance of the third angel's message dawned upon our pioneers, and along with that came an understanding of other truths that had been either neglected or distorted through the centuries. The Advent movement thus developed into its final form to make ready a people prepared to meet their God. But, as the declarations of our pioneers make transparently clear, this final phase of the Advent movement for the last days was ever viewed by them as the logical, prophetical development of a work begun by God when He stirred men to preach the first angel's message.

### Stand Firm on the Record

The historical record and the testimony of our Seventh-day Adventist pioneers leave no possible doubt concerning our origin and the honorableness and prophetic significance of that origin. We must stand firmly by this record and testimony. To do otherwise—to give credence to silly stories about the Millerites, and then to attempt to sever our movement from Millerism to escape the taint of the stories—would give the lie to the testimony of our own pioneers, to say nothing of the evident facts of history. Even more importantly, it would remove from Seventh-day Adventism its prophetic validation. And—mark this well—it would also besmirch the good names of our own Seventh-day Adventist pioneers, for they were Millerites. As George I. Butler well said, "If that [Millerite movement] was a fanatical movement, this must be also."— *Review and Herald*, Feb. 10, 1885, p. 89. And as Uriah Smith emphatically declared: "Every Advent theory that has been devised, which ignores the past work ["of the once harmonious body of Advent believers," before October 22, 1844], is a castle in the air, a pyramid without a base, a building without a foundation." —*Ibid.*, Dec. 17, 1867, p. 8. And what is it but ignoring "the past work" if we seek to dissociate ourselves from it?

Surely there applies here the admonition of God's messenger, who, after "reviewing our past history" from Millerite days onward, declared, "We have nothing to fear for the future, except as we shall forget the way the Lord has led us, and His teaching in our past history."—*Life Sketches*, p. 196.

## PROPHETIC ORIGIN OF ADVENTIST CHURCH

(Proof in support of points five, six, and seven is offered under "Second Advent" objections, pages 261-275.

---

NOTE.—SEVENTH-DAY ADVENTISTS AND THE ADVENT AWAKENING IN OTHER LANDS. Someone may ask, Is it not true that the Advent awakening was a much larger thing than Millerism in America, and should we not rather place Seventh-day Adventism in the setting of that larger movement? Unquestionably, the awakening was not confined to one land. Mrs. White makes that plain in *The Great Controversy*. She describes the Advent interest that developed in various countries, in greater or less degree, and probably more in England than in other continental countries. But of this work in England she writes, "The movement here did not take so definite a form as in America; the exact time of the advent was not so generally taught."—*The Great Controversy*, p. 362. She adds that the 1844 date of the Advent was taught, explaining that an Englishman, Robert Winter, "who had received the advent faith in America, returned to his native country to herald the coming of the Lord." The Millerites often spoke of the spread of their prophetic view to far corners of the earth, chiefly through literature. After describing the Advent preaching in other lands, Mrs. White continues:

"To William Miller and his co-laborers it was given to preach the warning in America. This country became the center of the great advent movement. It was here that the prophecy of the first angel's message had its most direct fulfillment. The writings of Miller and his associates were carried to distant lands." "The second angel's message of Revelation 14 was first preached in the summer of 1844, and it then had a more direct application to the churches of the United States, where the warning of the judgment had been most widely proclaimed." —*Ibid.*, pp. 368, 389.

Furthermore, and most importantly, the preaching in other lands did not have the historical features that fit specifically into most of the prophetic statements we have been considering. For example, the prophecy of Habakkuk 2:2, 3 found its exact fulfillment only in the events of the Millerite movement. The same is true of the parable and prophecy of the ten virgins, the tarrying time, the cry at midnight. The focusing on the date, October 22, 1844, as the termination of the 2300-day prophecy, belonged to the Millerite movement. The prophecy of the little book, first sweet and then bitter, applies specifically to the Advent movement as found in America. Finally, as Mrs. White states, the first and second angels' messages found their most direct "fulfillment" and "application" in America.

It is altogether proper for us to see Seventh-day Adventism in the general setting of the Advent awakening in various lands. If God be the source of the spiritual quickening, why should we not expect that He would stir hearts in many lands as the end of all prophetic time drew near? But the fact that there is properly a general setting for the rise of Seventh-day Adventism does not minimize in any degree the fact that there is also a specific setting for our rise, and that setting is the Advent movement in America called Millerism. We have always believed and preached, as vital to the prophetic significance of our movement, that it arose at a specific time in fulfillment of specific prophecies. Only in Millerism are the specifications precisely and fully met. That is the united testimony of our Seventh-day Adventist pioneers.

CHAPTER 11

# Do Adventists Make a Real Contribution
# to World Betterment?

ONE OF the common charges against Adventists is this: That
we are so concerned about planning for another world, we
are not interested in doing our part to make the present world a
better one in which to live. Our very preaching of a soon and
certain fiery end to the world, in fulfillment of divine prediction,
has caused critics to charge that we fatalistically fold our arms in
anticipation of the event, believing that nothing man can do can
forestall or prevent the flaming catastrophe.

This indictment of Adventists, or premillennialists, as we, in
common with others who believe in the literal Advent, are often
called, has sometimes taken on added vigor in times of national
crisis, such as war. For example, a prominent divine, writing near
the close of the first world war, said this, among other things, in
condemnation:

"An hour of agony such as that through which mankind is now
passing becomes a new divine summons to the people of the twentieth
century to contribute their part toward the establishment of a better
world and the inauguration of a new day for humanity. Concretely
our special task is that of defending the sacred rights of democracy
and helping to make this ideal supreme in all international relationships.

"The premillennialist hears no imperious summons to this new
task. But that is not all. He insists on being a missionary of pessimism,
thereby dampening the enthusiasm of many whose assistance is
mightily needed for the accomplishment of the gigantic task in hand.
He still clings to the time-honored delusion of the nearness of the
end, indulging himself in this antiquated luxury of the imagination,
and vainly praying God to destroy the very world that the suppliant
himself ought to be loyally struggling to reform. In assuming this at-

titude wittingly or unwittingly he becomes a pronounced enemy of democracy and a serious menace to the nation's morale in this hour of its need."—SHIRLEY JACKSON CASE, *The Premillennial Menace*, p. 24. War and Religion Pamphlets No. 4. The American Institute of Sacred Literature.

The charge of being disloyal, of being "a pronounced enemy of democracy and a serious menace to the nation's morale," is a grave one to bring against a person and much more so against a whole company of people. But that charge well sums up the critics' attack upon Adventism in general and Seventh-day Adventists in particular, for we are the one large world-embracing body of militantly active believers in the Advent doctrine. As proof that the above charge has lost none of its force since it was published in November, 1918, listen to the following from another critic of Adventism, writing in 1941:

"Adventism is in reality defeatism. Adventism is a system of fatalism and makes such an overemphasis of the sovereignty of God as to leave no place for human co-operation in promoting the progress of the Kingdom of God."—WILLIAM P. KING, *Adventism*, p. 68.

A clergyman during the second world war took Adventists to task for what he declared was their complete absorption in the subject of the anticipated end of the world to a total forgetfulness of the immediate needs of the world. In a personal letter he inquired: "What would it matter if at the peace table the whole discussion should center around your idea of Christ's second coming, and no provision be made to treat men as human beings? To see that all men are dealt with justly? etc. Weakness of weaknesses: . . . How much does your preaching of the second advent inspire men to change their lives?"

Probably this last question is properly the one to answer first in examining the charges brought against us because of our ardent preaching of the Second Advent. If we can show that preaching the Second Advent doctrine inspires men to change their lives, then we have shown how eminently worth while it would be for the peace-table discussion to center on the Second Advent doctrine. And how shall we attempt to answer the question as to whether the preaching of the Advent inspires a change of life? First by an appeal to Scripture, for it is from the Scriptures that we draw our Advent belief.

## The Testimony of Scripture

What answer would the apostle John give to this question? He declares, "Behold, what manner of love the Father hath bestowed upon us, that we should be called the sons of God: therefore the world knoweth us not, because it knew him not. Beloved, now are we the sons of God, and it doth not yet appear what we shall be: but we know that, when he shall appear, we shall be like him; for we shall see him as he is. And every man that hath this hope in him purifieth himself, even as he is pure." 1 John 3:1-3.

John, who walked and talked with his Lord, knew that he could not contemplate meeting again his Saviour without experiencing a profound urge to holier living.

And what answer would the apostle Peter return to the objector's question? Following his description of the destruction of the world when the day of the Lord comes, Peter declares: "Seeing then that all these things shall be dissolved, what manner of persons ought ye to be in all holy conversation and godliness, looking for and hasting unto the coming of the day of God, wherein the heavens being on fire shall be dissolved, and the elements shall melt with fervent heat? Nevertheless we, according to his promise, look for new heavens and a new earth, wherein dwelleth righteousness. Wherefore, beloved, seeing that ye look for such things, be diligent that ye may be found of him in peace, without spot, and blameless." 2 Peter 3:11-14.

Evidently Peter felt that a contemplation of the broad theme of the Second Advent and all that it signifies for the world should have a most definite and chastening effect upon our lives.

And what answer would the apostle James give? We find this inspired writer painting a picture of the economic troubles of the poor in contrast to the luxury of the rich—a frequent source of revolution and bloodshed in the world's history. But does he advocate violent revolution? No. Instead he urges: "Be patient therefore, brethren, unto the coming of the Lord. . . . Be ye also patient; stablish your hearts: for the coming of the Lord draweth nigh." James 5:7, 8. Rarely are the world's troubles solved by violence and revolution. If patience can be invoked, there may be hope of ultimately working out a solution. The inspired writers preached the doctrine of patience and peaceable solution of problems. And they called upon the doctrine of the Second Advent to support their appeal to patience.

But neither James nor any other Bible writer used the Second Advent doctrine simply to produce patience and restraint from violent uprising on the part of the oppressed. The prophets thundered against the oppressor with warnings of judgment to come, when all men must meet God face to face. In the verses that precede those just quoted is found a dire warning to the rich. James reminds them: "Ye have heaped treasure together for the last days." Peter speaks in the same connection of scoffers and ungodly men, and reminds them, if they will but read, that "the heavens and the earth, which are now, . . . are kept in store, reserved unto fire against the day of judgment and perdition of ungodly men." 2 Peter 3:7.

Quite evidently Paul in his preaching to the Gentiles introduced the fact of coming judgment as a part of his appeal to holy living. He reminded the Thessalonians of how they turned from idols "to serve the living and true God; and to wait for his Son from heaven, whom he raised from the dead, even Jesus, which delivered us from the wrath to come." 1 Thess. 1:9, 10.

We do know that when the day of the Lord finally comes and men behold His flaming glory in the sky, all who have lived in rebellion against God, including very particularly "chief captains" and "mighty men," will flee in terror and cry to the mountains to fall on them and hide them from the face of God. Why? "For the great day of his wrath is come; and who shall be able to stand?" (See Rev. 6:14-17.)

We believe, and all the passages quoted support this belief, that to the extent we can now bring to the hearts of men a realization of the great day of accounting that will come at the Second Advent, to that extent we have hopes of causing men right now to cry out to God for mercy while the day of grace still lingers. We are confident that if all those who gather round a peace table ever kept before them a vivid picture of the coming day of God, when all must answer for every act, peace plans would be drawn up such as were never before seen in this poor old world of ours.

## The Paradox of the Advent Doctrine

That is the paradox of the preaching of the Second Advent. This doctrine, which turns men's minds intently to a great day ahead, causes them to make the present days better. By focusing their minds on a world to come, we cause them to make the present world a more decent place in which to live. A consuming belief in, and preparation for, the Second Advent does not blind us to a realization of the world's needs or make us passive in our relationship to those needs.

This fact seems entirely to have eluded our critics. Yet the fact is not really elusive. A visit to an average Seventh-day Adventist church would disclose a Dorcas Society busy on some form of local relief work, generally clothing the needy. Ask any one of these dexterous Dorcas ladies whether she fervently believes in the soon coming of Christ, and she will probably look at you a little perplexed as to why you should ask her. It would never occur to her that there was anything inconsistent in working to clothe the needy in the community while fervently believing in and promoting the Advent of Christ. Our Dorcas ladies see themselves as modern descendants of Dorcas, that first-century Christian who sewed for the poor while living in hope of the return of her Lord.

Indeed, we have in the first-century Christians the best historical exhibit of the relationship of Advent hope to charitable activity for the needy. Concentration of mind and heart on the Advent was never more intense than in the decades immediately following our Lord's ascension. We will let a professor in a liberal seminary testify as to these primitive Christians, for we need hardly remark that it is liberalists who have heaped ridicule on the idea of a personal coming of Christ. It is liberalists who were quoted in the opening paragraphs of this chapter. But something has happened to liberal thinking since the Atomic Era opened. There is much talk of world's end, a new examination of what the Bible has said on the matter, and some rather remarkable admissions. One liberal, a professor in Andover-Newton Theological Seminary, in discussing the sober question of world's end, seeks to show how it is possible to anticipate the end with joy. He declares:

"The early Christians had a program of action which they followed while awaiting the expected early end of the world. True, it was a spontaneous rather than a systematized program. But it was far-reaching. They not only worshipped together and strengthened one another in the belief that Jesus Christ would return and care for them while all things were being finished; they also liquidated their possessions, holding earthly goods in common and serving each person, particularly the orphan and the widow, according to need. These first-century Christians were in training for life in a new world. Joy in the Lord of heaven and earth quite overcame anxiety about the cessation of one kind of life and the beginning of another.

"The fact that these Christians were mistaken in their belief that some among them would still be alive when all things were finished is unimportant. What is of primary importance for us is the fact that they so strengthened each other in the faith that they could rejoice over the certainty they had that the world was about to end. And no less important for us is the cue which their conduct provides. Awaiting the end which they deemed a new beginning, they were constructively active, serving their fellows, putting human need foremost, and thrusting property far down the scale in value. Possessions were nothing more than means to an end, tools with which to enrich human life, tangible devices by which man could evidence his otherwise intangible love of God."—WESNER FALLOW in *The Christian Century*, Sept. 25, 1946.

Further on in his article this liberal professor observes:

"Obviously the only training adequate for global dissolution is one designed to cause men to be absorbed in worship of God and in sacrificial reapportionment of material goods, while there is time, so that Europe and Asia and all the multitudes of the world's miserable ones may have succor. Spirituality needs economic implementation. Only so will Christians attain any degree of relief—to say nothing of joy—as they contemplate the possibility of world's end. Let the local church now attend to this!"

Whether men can be persuaded by a belief in the coming of atomic bombs to share, unselfishly, their possessions with the needy, remains to be seen. But the record is clear, by the professor's own statement, that a belief in the coming of Christ caused the early Christians to share their worldly goods with the needy. That one fact in itself is an impressive answer to the charge that ardent concentration on the doctrine of the Advent makes one blind to the needs of men and women in this present world.

### Advent Action in 1844

Now, this attitude of the early Christians has been reflected in some degree in the lives of later Christians who have focused their hopes on the Advent. When the Advent pioneers in 1844 fervently believed that Christ's coming was very near, they, like the first Christians, developed a contempt for earthly possessions. Many of them sold their homes. Critics of the Advent movement have made sport of this as an evidence of fanaticism, forgetful, of course, that it paralleled the experience of the first-century Christians. Contrary to slanderous stories, Adventists in 1844 did not dispose of their property in wild abandon. The record is clear that those who sold their possessions did so for three principal reasons: To have money to pay all their debts, that they might owe no man anything when the end came; to have money to put into the Lord's treasury, so that the Advent teaching might have widest circulation; and to have money whereby they might give "alms," to borrow the old English word they used.

That they, like some early Christians, were mistaken in believing that Christ would come in their day is entirely beside the point. We are here considering the charge that concentration on the hope of the Advent results in complete apathy toward the present material needs of others. And in refutation is submitted the fact that the occasions in history when Christians have been most fervent in their belief in the Advent have also been the times when they most gladly and most thoughtfully considered the present needs of others.

Seventh-day Adventists today must confess to a lesser degree of Advent fervor than the pioneers in 1844 or the first-century Christians. But we can provide some proof—for example, the Dorcas activities in our churches—that Advent faith goes hand in hand with compassionate attention to the present needs of mankind. But we need not stop with Dorcas work. Let us go beyond that to a consideration of some of the distinctive beliefs of Seventh-day Adventists in relation to this charge that we make no contribution to the betterment of this present world.

## Our Doctrines Aid World

One of our most distinctive teachings is that good health is a part of good religion and that therefore we should seek to learn and then to obey the laws of nature as they apply to our bodily health. That is why we have published a vast amount of health literature through the years. And that is one reason also why we have established a chain of sanitariums, for these institutions seek not only to make people well but to teach them how to keep well. That, too, is why we have had cooking schools through the years.

Then came the second world war. Realizing that America would soon be drawn in, President Roosevelt called a conference of all the leading nutritionists of the country. And why? First, because nutritional studies had finally proved beyond all question that what one eats is of tremendous importance in building good health; second, because the country's defense called for healthy citizens and therefore plans must be laid to disseminate to all the citizenry instruction on proper diet.

Adventists had been endeavoring, as far as their resources permitted, to do just this. That our efforts were relatively small in relation to the whole national need of health education is beside the point. The point is that our efforts were contributing directly to the present physical health of men and women and to the defense of the country. Were our critics more active in this matter?

Closely related is the matter of activity against liquor. Through all their history Seventh-day Adventists have been militant campaigners against all forms of alcoholic beverages. It is nothing unusual for us to circulate millions of pages of temperance literature in a year. Besides, we have reinforced that literature with vigorous campaigning for legislation against liquor.

Now, our critics, who indict us for failing to do something for the betterment of the world, would undoubtedly agree that liquor is one of the greatest causes of human woe, bringing crime, vice, poverty, sickness, and death—which is another way of saying that liquor is one of the greatest enemies of the state. Evidently, then, Adventists must be making some contribution to present human welfare and toward the preservation of the state as a result of their consistent and vigorous anti-liquor campaigning. It might seem too personal, and perhaps even embarrassing, to ask our critics how much they have done, in comparison with Adventists, in the fight against liquor.

### Emphasis on Religious Liberty

Take another of the distinctive features of the Seventh-day Adventist movement, the emphasis on religious liberty. We have always believed and taught that any attack on freedom of worship is an attack on all freedom. Hence we have been preaching, writing articles, publishing a journal, and maintaining a department at our denominational headquarters for the express purpose of promoting the true principles of freedom. We have not merely paid lip service to the glorious doctrine of freedom of worship and of the separation of church and state. Instead, we have gone out and campaigned, held mass meetings, secured petitions against dangerous bills introduced into legislatures.

For our pains we have frequently been charged with seeing danger where no danger exists—with being alarmists. In reply we have called on history to witness that the majority of men rarely see the first signs of danger to their liberty and that almost invariably the most dangerous despotisms have begun as apparently harmless encroachments on the liberties of the people.

Contrary to the mistaken idea of some of our religious critics, we have not simply campaigned against Sunday laws, though we have fought such laws because we believe they clearly violate the principle of separation of church and state. For despite their present disguise as moral and health measures, Sunday laws are, in essence, religious laws, as all past generations of Sunday law advocates frankly declare. No, we have also campaigned against proposed laws that would prohibit parochial schools. We have campaigned for the right of a noncombatant to become a citizen of the United States. We have campaigned against the endeavors of those who seek to secure free school-bus transportation for parochial pupils.

Perhaps the position we have taken on these various matters might easily be questioned by some, though we think the critics considered in this chapter would agree with us on all these items except Sunday laws. But be that as it may, in several instances the Supreme Court has ruled in favor of the viewpoint we presented. Indeed, it is a simple statement of fact that we have generally found ourselves on the winning side when the final court appeal has been heard and acted upon.

Now it would be unpardonable boasting for a religious body to speak thus were it not for the fact that we must call attention to our beliefs and activities in order to meet the charge that we are unconcerned about the welfare of the country, living wholly in expectation of early entry into another world. Is it important for the present welfare of mankind that liberty be guarded? That question answers itself. How often since the draft of the Atlantic Charter have we heard men mention freedom of speech and of worship as vital to an ideal world!

Have our critics done more for such freedom than Adventists have? Have they spent more per capita on some of the campaigns just mentioned? Have they circulated more literature? We think we know the answer they would honestly have to return to these questions.

What makes our campaigning even more significant is that in the case of at least one prominent and repeating campaign, that against free school-bus travel for parochial pupils, Seventh-day Adventists would have stood to gain by the granting of such transportation. We have a whole system of parochial schools, something that most Protestant churches do not have. But we have been as militant against such transportation as we have been against Sunday laws, for illustration. And why? Because we have carried on all these campaigns in support of principle and not of denominational advantage or expediency.

If our critics believe they are doing a great service to the state in campaigning against school-bus travel, for example, will they contend that Adventists are doing a lesser service to the state when they campaign with equal or even greater fervor? Again we must observe that our interest in the Advent does not prevent us from taking an active and constructive part in serving our fellow man and defending our country.

## Adventists and Military Service

The world has just emerged from the most devastating war in all history. War presents to the state the greatest physical challenge to its stability and to its very life. Seventh-day Adventists do not believe they should strike from their minds their ardent belief in the Advent, even though a war rages. Indeed, they do not believe they should forget their belief in noncombatancy when the test of war confronts them. Obviously a belief in noncombatancy presents a real problem and embarrassment to any citizen who wishes to show that he truly loves his country in wartime. And, if our critics may be taken seriously, Adventists, with their exclusive interest in the Advent, would have no desire to do anything to aid the country in a material, practical way in connection with a war. But let us see what actually happened.

The United States is the birthplace of the Adventist Church. Here are located its headquarters, and here live a third of its members. Presumably, therefore, the course followed by these Adventists in the United States may be considered as fairly representative of the spirit and genius of Seventh-day Adventism. And what did they do when confronted with the dread challenge of war? Did they simply withdraw to their churches to contemplate, in mystical forgetfulness of a threatened land, the sublime truth of the Advent? Did they view the war in a fatalistic way, believing that it was God's judgment on sinful men, and fold their arms complacently in hope of early deliverance from this evil world? By the logic of our critics we should have done precisely this.

But what did we actually do? We freely admit that we had something to say about war as a judgment of God. We have always viewed wars in that light. But in the second world war we seem to have been quite outdone in the matter by chastened liberal leaders in Christendom, some of whom had viewed the first world conflict as a holy war to usher in a better world, and who had denounced Adventists as little better than enemies of their country.

But the important point is that although we viewed the recent war as having the quality of a judgment of God, we saw no reason, therefore, for sitting supinely by. We did not sit by even in the years preceding the war. Instead, as it became apparent that the world would soon be plunged again into war, we began to institute medical cadet training in our denominational schools in America to prepare our youth for service as soldiers in the Medical Corps of the Army. That training was specific and practical. Our youth learned the elements of military drill and organization, of giving first aid in the field, of removing the wounded on stretchers. They were trained, and in special uniforms, without any expense to the Government.

The whole medical cadet course was conducted along the most approved lines and in close cooperation with the office of the Surgeon General of the Army. The foreword to the Seventh-day Adventist Medical Cadet Manual of Instruction was written by the then Surgeon General of the United States Army, Major General James C. Magee.

# DO ADVENTISTS MAKE CONTRIBUTION?

At the graduation exercises of the first Medical Cadet Corps of the Washington (D.C.) area, held a few months before Pearl Harbor, Lieutenant Colonel J. M. Welch was present to represent the Surgeon General. In his address he said in part:

"Major General Magee, Surgeon General of the Army, whom I am here to represent, has asked me to convey his felicitations and congratulations to all your members on this occasion of the graduating exercises of the first course of field instruction completed by your corps. As an officer assigned to General Magee's office, I know that the objectives and activities of your group are very near to his heart, and that he has followed with interest and admiration the training which you have been pursuing. He feels that the aims of your organization are closely tied in with the interests and objectives of the medical department of the Army, and he has thrown open to the access of your officers the facilities of the training section of his office.

"Lieutenant Colonel Spruit, and, later, Major Wakeman, of the training section of the Surgeon General's office, have given due account and calculation to the role of the Cadet Corps project in making their plans for the requirements of a tremendously expanded medical department. Their interest in the accomplishments of this first Medical Cadet Corps of the Washington area has been a very special one. . . . I am sure also that you will not be disappointed to know that the reports on the materialization of the early results hoped for, and the results presented here by demonstration today, have been highly satisfying. . . .

"Your example of timely planning and unremitting effort against time and other obstacles illustrates the spirit so sorely needed among our people at this time. In fact, the whole conception and method of furthering the objectives of the Medical Cadet Corps movement show an insight into the needs of our time that runs far in advance of the foresight and determination of our average citizenry. . . .

"In view of your religious beliefs and ideals, it is to be regarded as highly appropriate and highly to the credit of those whose longsightedness has conceived of your organization, that you have made for the goal of these courses the development of the individual along lines that establish his value to the Army as a medical-department soldier. This aim of your organization shows that you are one with the medical department of the Army in seeking to humanize war through the alleviation of suffering; it shows also that you are one with the medical department in seeking to reduce the evil after-effects, both in the individual and to the nation, that result from sickness and injury in war; and, foremost in the rank of our humane objectives, it shows that you are one with the medical department in the fond hope that early and effective training and preparation to meet the conditions of war will greatly discourage the chance of there being any war at all. After giving you, then, these reasons for the satisfaction that you should feel in developing yourselves along lines valuable to the medical service of the Army, I should not close these remarks without saying that the medical department also has much cause for gratification in knowing that you and other young men of your moral character and beliefs are preparing themselves for duty within its ranks. We are well aware that there are important qualities quite apart from and additional to technical attainments that go toward the make-up of the ideal medical-department soldier. These indispensable qualities of uprightness in character, respect for constituted authority, and honorable devotion to duty, are characteristics that young people, reared under fixed religious principles as you yourselves have been, are very sure to have.

"And so, let me say that not only you members of the first Medical Cadet Corps, but also the military establishment itself, is indeed to be congratulated this day and at these exercises which mark the graduation of some two hundred enthusiastic young citizens—morally sound, physically fit, and suitably trained in the medical-department tasks which face the Army of our country in its hour of need.

"Gentlemen, I wish you Godspeed and like success in your further endeavors."

As already stated, these Medical Cadet Corps were created in our denominational schools and in our churches in America *before* Pearl Harbor. We anticipated our country's need. And we loyally felt we should be ready to serve. At the same time we sensed the problem created by our belief in noncombatancy. We resolved the problem by the Medical Cadet Corps that in part, at least, prepared our youth for service in the medical branch of the armed services. Now the total of 12,000 youth thus trained was not large in relation to the Army in the United States, but it was large in relation to the size of the Seventh-day Adventist Church, which had an American membership at the opening of the war of less than 200,000. Of course there were thousands of other Adventist youth besides those specially trained in our Medical Cadet Corps who served faithfully in the medical branch of the United States armed forces.

A happy sequel to all this occurred on the White House lawn on December 12, 1945, where, in the presence of the highest ranking officers of the Army and Navy, the Cabinet, and other officials, President Truman decorated Corporal Desmond T. Doss, a Seventh-day Adventist noncombatant soldier, with the coveted Congressional Medal of Honor.

### "Conscientious Cooperators"

In an interview with the press after the service of decoration, Corporal Doss declared, as Adventists have consistently declared through the years, that our noncombatant soldiers, though technically classified as conscientious objectors, should really be described as conscientious cooperators. We do not take a negative attitude toward our country in time of crisis. We display a real and an immensely practical concern for our fellow man in connection with the crisis of war.*

Seventh-day Adventist concern for the material welfare and physical needs of their fellow man is not confined to our homeland. That is evident from the medical missionary work we conduct in far lands. A vital part of our whole mission program is the medical care of the sick. Clinics and hospitals are found alongside chapels in Africa, China, the South Sea Islands—in fact, in almost every land. In some corners of the earth the only medical care the natives have ever received has been at the hands of Adventist missionaries.

### The Testimony of a Scientist

A few years ago William C. Groves, Research Fellow in Social Anthropology of the Australian Natural Research Council, made a trip to certain Seventh-day Adventist missions among the islands of the Pacific Ocean. He did not take this trip out of a love for missions, certainly not a love for Adventist missions, for he had no relation to them, and up to that time knew little about them.

---

* Many other decorations for valor and for outstanding service were given to Seventh-day Adventist noncombatant youth in the armed services during the war.

Rather, he was interested in studying the subject of the effect of European culture upon the native culture, and he simply chose certain Adventist missions because they were easy of access in the mandated Territory of New Guinea. He tells of the common criticism of missions that he had so frequently heard, and then relates how he set out on a Seventh-day Adventist schooner—for our island missions have their own boats for traveling from island to island. The first thing he noticed was that the native crew were treated decently and that there was an "atmosphere of cleanliness and quiet discipline." He continues:

"I was no friend of the Seventh-day Adventists. I mean I had no special desire to further their cause. I simply wanted to see just what was happening, and how; to evaluate the work from the point of view of present native social and economic welfare and future development.

"I knew something of the natives and the conditions of their lives —the impending disruption of their social organization, the reputation of the place for licentious living, and such things. I had gathered, too, a fairly comprehensive idea of the place ethnographically, from the published results of the very careful survey carried out by the government anthropologist in New Guinea in 1927. It seemed, on the evidence available, that the people of these islands were a decadent people—victims of that intangible malaise or inertia that comes, from causes beyond our present comprehension, upon primitive peoples, in their early contact with European cultural influences, and that frequently expresses itself in, or is associated with, a tragic condition of depopulation that may ultimately spell racial extinction. . . .

"The formula upon which the prescriptions to revive or resuscitate such peoples are based, however, is something like this: Create new wants; develop new interests; provide a new set of social-reaction stimuli; and thus bring the wavering wills back to their former strength —but with a changed, a new, field in which to work.

"With a sincere desire to see the people of Mussau, by any possible means, responding to some such prescription, and a particular interest in the precise nature of the component parts of the prescription (which was, I assumed, being offered by the Seventh-day Adventist people), I went to . . . Mussau. . . .

"From the moment we dropped anchor at Emira, where we met 'old' Naphtali, a fine, honest, hard-working, true Christian, Fijian teacher, and saw the whole of the island's population hurriedly and excitedly gathering together at the point on the beach where our dinghy was landing us—from that moment of enthusiasm and joyous welcome—I knew that the 'Seventh-day' mission 'had' these people; knew, unmistakably with my very eyes, that here was no decadent people; here no racial malaise such as I had recently seen in parts of New Ireland."

Being a good scientist, he wished to check for certain on the matter. He tells us:

"I soon got off alone amongst the natives themselves, in their settlement. . . . From every angle I approached them—trying suggestion, cajolery, ridicule, upon individuals and groups. Fast they stood, fast for the new life, with no regrets, and, as far as I could see, no possible ill-effects on their social or economic lives. In fact, in the latter connection I found that under Naphtali's leadership they had abundance of food, including varieties previously unknown."

Then he frankly relates what he had formerly thought of these particular missionaries. "I had always, without any real or genuine knowledge, fancied Seventh-day Adventism a thing of frock-coated gloom." That only made the more startling and impressive his findings as to the happiness of the natives who had been brought from heathenism into Christianity by these missionaries. But his report goes on from this to a still larger survey of Seventh-day Adventist missions as they relate to constructing a mission village and creating schools for the natives. After paying his compliments to the white missionaries who led out, he had something to say for the native teachers, who are trained as quickly as possible to give the mission work a close contact with the people. Said he:

"I was particularly struck with the faithfulness of the Solomon Island teachers—such black-skinned, joyous types as Oti, whose genuine Christian belief was apparent in his every action. Truly the S.D.A. stations will become, have become already, the focal points of new interests, the radiating centers of new life.

"And what does it all mean to the people of Mussau? For those who seek immediate spiritual results the crowded services at both stations should be sufficient.

"There is little left of the primitive culture; that, as an anthropologist, I learned. But there's nothing to be lamented in that, providing

the people have found some satisfactory new substitute forms of
life for the lost elements. And I believe that in their economic lives,
the mission is working along right lines by demonstrating the possibilities of varying their crops and making more regular and certain
their food supply. . . .

"Improved housing and village hygiene may be expected as a
result of the mission's example and teachings; what, indeed, may the
S.D.A. Mission not accomplish amongst these people, to the lasting
credit of the mission and the salvation of what was a decadent society,
if it proceeds along lines of enlightenment and understanding and
allows for continuity of policy without undue interference from
authorities outside? . . .

"What a unique opportunity has the S.D.A. Mission at Mussau—
starting in these days of educational enlightenment, to show all other
organizations the way!"

This report, which was printed in the Sydney *Morning Herald*,
August 1, 1934, speaks for itself. A like report might be made on
similar Adventist mission stations that dot hundreds of South Sea
Islands. And from there the scientist might go to other dark places
of earth and find the same hopeful results from our missions.

It hardly needs to be remarked in this connection that we sincerely believe the mission activities of other churches produce most
heartening results. But that is beside the point. The question at
issue is whether Seventh-day Adventists make any real contribution
to the material and physical needs of mankind so that the present
world may be a better one in which to live. And in partial answer
to that question is submitted the testimony here quoted.

## Our Support of Missions

And how well do we support our mission work? Do we give a
pittance in comparison to the per capita giving of great religious
bodies, many of which are dominantly liberalistic in theology, as
our critics are? Were it not for the fact that the evidence to refute
a baseless charge must be brought forth we would hesitate to make
comparisons, lest we appear boastful. The undebatable fact is
that Seventh-day Adventists contribute a per capita for missions
that is far beyond that of all the great Protestant denominations.

# DO ADVENTISTS MAKE CONTRIBUTION?

If anyone doubts this, let him consult the comparative statistical tables prepared annually by the Foreign Missions Conference of North America.

We are not rich people. Most of us are wage earners. Yet we give this very high per capita to foreign mission work. If the testimony of the anthropologist quoted may be taken at face value, then Seventh-day Adventists with their heavy per capita mission gifts are making a real contribution to the world.

Granted that we do not attempt to improve the world politically and economically by campaigning on various economic and political issues, or by seeking to tell rulers and legislators what they should do in matters of state.* But our failure to do this is not because we are blind or callous to existing social and political evils, or because, as our critics charge, we are fatalistically committed to the belief that with the Advent near, nothing need be done. Surely our critics know that through the long years there have been devout religious groups who have been as averse to direct political action for reform as Adventists ever could be, and yet who have not been distinguished by a belief in the nearness of the Advent. And why? Generally because they believed the church should make a different approach to the problems of the world. That is the position Adventists take. Whether we feel we have little or much time ere the day of God, we believe that the Christian church should make a distinctive attack upon the world's evils, using distinctive weapons.

The Christian religion teaches that the cause of all the world's troubles is the sinful heart of man. All evil activities of men and society are but sores on the surface of the body of mankind, a body that is infected with the virus of sin. Only the gospel of Christ can provide the antidote for the poison released by this dread virus. In holding this view of the world's ills, Adventists are only

---

* Our campaigning against liquor and religious legislation may perhaps be considered exceptions to this general statement. However, in the case of liquor we have put our major emphasis on an educational campaign to individual men and women, seeking above all else to secure their personal allegiance to the principle of abstinence. As regards our campaigning on religious legislation, our endeavor is not to tell government what it should do in the secular realm, but to protest its activity in the religious realm.

ANSWERS TO OBJECTIONS

holding the classic viewpoint of Protestant Christendom, and long before that, of primitive Christians.

And because we hold this view we consider that we would be recreant to our duty if we failed to focus our efforts on the heart of the trouble, the sinful heart of man. We look back to the first century and note, for example, that the apostles did not launch political campaigns to remove slavery from the Roman Empire. Though Paul twice stood before Caesar, there is nothing in the record to suggest that he capitalized the occasions for any attempt at political reform. He even wrote in his epistles as to how "servants"—our English Bible euphemism for slaves—should give obedience to their "masters." But Paul and all the early Christians drove forward with a mighty attack on sinful hearts. And as that attack succeeded, slavery had to recede. A beautiful illustration of this is suggested by Paul's letter to Philemon as to how he should receive back his runaway slave Onesimus.

### The Advent and Slavery

Speaking of slavery, it is an interesting fact that most of the leaders in the Advent awakening of the early 1840's, out of which Seventh-day Adventism grew, had been militant abolitionists. One of these men, Joseph Bates, was chided by his abolitionist friends because he was devoting all his time to promoting the Advent doctrine, and no longer took part in their antislavery activities. He replied that he was as much opposed as ever to slavery, but he believed that in calling on men to turn from all evil and make ready to meet God, he was going to the heart of all the evils that afflict society. While preaching in the slaveholding State of Maryland, Bates was accused by a slaveholder of campaigning to take his slaves from him. Bates replied that this was not so, that he had come to take both him and his slaves for the kingdom of God. This was essentially the position of all the Adventist leaders.

And did slaveholders give up their slaves as they responded to the Advent preaching? Though we have no lengthy records of Advent preaching in the South (early Adventism developed in the

Northern States), we do have the record of one campaign far south in the year 1844. The account tells, among other things, how a slaveholder, immediately upon accepting the teaching that he must be ready for the Advent, freed his slaves. There is nothing strange about this. How could a man, in sincerity, make ready to meet God face to face and continue to grind down the face of the poor in slavery!

The saintly founder of Methodism, John Wesley, is often credited with having saved England from a revolution such as overwhelmed France. A vast contribution, indeed, to the life of a nation. But did he save England by political campaigning, or anything akin to that? No. He saved England from revolution by revival—a vigorous preaching of the gospel to the hearts of men.

## Where We Differ With Liberals

Of course we realize that in the last generation or two the liberal wing of Christendom has swung far away from the ancient view of the sinfulness of man's heart as the cause of all earth's troubles. As discussed in succeeding chapters on the rise and fall of the idea of progress, every other cause except sin has been set forth as the reason for the troubles of mankind. Now, if bad housing, or poor wages, or illiteracy, for example, are the root of man's troubles, and man has inherent possibilities of improvement, then it makes sense for the church to focus first attention on these conditions and to campaign before rulers and legislators for political reforms. It always makes sense to attack prime causes by attempting to influence those who can remove the causes. If we are not too sure of a world beyond, if we doubt the reality of sin or its dread effects, and, accordingly, if we discount the significance of the gospel because it is a remedy for something we are not sure is very real, then certainly we are consistent in concentrating on the political approach to the solution of mankind's problems. We do not say that all in Christendom who invoke political action subscribe to this series of "if's," but we do say that the segment of Christendom that has been increasingly devoted to political action for a half century has been dominated by the reasoning just set forth.

Seventh-day Adventists do not believe in the inherent possibilities of perfection in man, or that his evil ways are primarily due to bad environment. We believe that something is the matter with man himself that leads him to evil as naturally as the sparks fly upward. We do not think, therefore, that men will become heavenly in their lives if only their working conditions can be made ideal and poverty be removed from their skies. We remember that the Bible describes the ancient city of Sodom as having fullness of bread and abundance of idleness. Yet with such fullness of bread and freedom from grinding toil, plus homes by a placid, sun-kissed sea, they lived in vice and bequeathed to posterity their very name as a synonym for depravity.

Adventists believe that the root of the trouble is the sinful heart. Hence we feel we are doing precisely what Christians ought to do when we concentrate our attention on applying to this malady the only remedy that we believe is effective, the grace of God as dispensed through the gospel of Jesus Christ. How could we make a better contribution to the welfare of mankind here and now? Does not the apostle Paul assure us that "godliness is profitable unto all things, having promise of the life that now is," as well as of "that which is to come"?

# CHAPTER 12

# Has a Century's Passing Invalidated Our Doctrine of the Advent?

FROM its beginning the Advent movement has been distinguished by its preaching of the nearness of the Advent. For a hundred years we have declared, in the words of Scripture, that "it is near, even at the doors." Critics have not been slow to note this fact and have reared one of their most plausible objections upon it. The objection runs thus: "You have preached for a hundred years that the Advent is near. But the Advent has not taken place. Don't you think it is about time to admit that you have been mistaken?"

First, let it be noted that the critic seeks to discredit our forecast simply because, after a century of predicting, the forecast has not yet come true. There is generally implicit, also, the thought that Adventists therefore are a fanciful lot of dreamers who have wrongly interpreted Bible prophecy, whereas the critic stands on solid ground. By his very indictment of our forecast the critic would have it appear that he is not guilty of making predictions concerning the future of the world, or that if he has made any, they have come true. But is that so? Most of our critics, or at least the most vigorous of them, are spokesmen for other religious organizations in Christendom. Is it true that religious bodies in general, with the rather notable exception of Adventists, have refrained from forecasting the future? Or if they have forecast in any degree, that the predictions have come true? The answer to both questions is No.

The facts that will be presented in chapters 13 and 14 are here anticipated a little. They deal with the rise and fall of the idea of progress, and reveal clearly that the Christian churches in general have long been forecasting a certain definite end to our present world by the coming of an earthly millennium. That forecast was old when the Advent movement began in the 1840's. Furthermore, that forecast of world regeneration was challengingly placed in opposition to the prediction of impending world conflagration as soon as the latter began to be preached by our Adventist forebears. Finally, that prediction of world regeneration, so generally believed in Christendom by the opening of the nineteenth century, was tied to Bible prophecies and given a strong flavor of time setting.

## Admissions of Critics in the 1840's

It is a fact of history, easily verified, that our critics in the 1840's did not generally question the soundness of our rules of prophetic interpretation which led us to conclude that certain great time prophecies were ending and that therefore far-reaching changes impended for the world. On the contrary, our opponents a century ago were often free to admit that they likewise believed the prophecies were ending.

One theologian, who is described on the title page of his book as "professor of ecclesiastical history in the Newton Theological Institution," wrote this in 1844, in comment on the Millerite movement:

"We need not wonder that the minds of many have, within a few years, been greatly agitated by an expectation of the speedy fulfillment of certain predictions in the book of Daniel. The way for this was prepared by some of our standard English writers on the prophecies, men of former ages, venerated for their piety and their erudition. . . . Dr. Scott, in his notes on Daniel 8:13, 14, after quoting with approbation, the remarks of Lowth and Newton, adds, 'No doubt the end of the two thousand and three hundred days, or years, is not very distant.'

"Instead, now, of being offended, or of looking scornfully at those who have only carried out and applied according to their best understanding, the principles taught by bishops and learned commentators, let each one for himself, first of all, see to it that he be prepared to meet, without dismay, whatever may occur, and to stand before his final judge; and then, let him, as his situation and circumstances may permit, endeavor, with fervent prayer, and diligent study, and holy living, to ascertain what God has revealed, and what He has enjoined."—IRAH CHASE, *Remarks on the Book of Daniel*, pp. v, vi.

The Rev. George Bush, in a series of letters to William Miller, set forth the generally held view that the world was approaching an earthly millennium. His words show how the prophetic time element was involved in the popular view, and how it was challengingly placed in opposition to the Adventist predictions. Bush, who was professor of Hebrew and Oriental literature in New York University, wrote thus to Miller:

"While I have no question that well-informed students of prophecy will admit that your calculation of *times* . . . is not materially erroneous, they will still, I believe, maintain that you have entirely mistaken *the nature of the events* which are to occur when those periods have expired. This is the head and front of your expository offending. . . .

"The great event before the world is not its *physical conflagration,* but its *moral regeneration;* and for one I am happy to think that, by your own limitation, the question is so soon to be put to the test of indisputable fact. . . . But even if years or centuries were yet to intervene, I should still be strong in my grand position, that you had mistaken *the nature of the events.*

"Although there is doubtless a sense in which Christ may be said to come, in connection with the passing away of the Fourth Empire, and of the Ottoman power, and His kingdom to be illustriously established, yet that will be found to be a *spiritual coming* in the power of His gospel. . . . Such is the dominant faith of all Christian communities at this day, and to the *tribunal of time,* as the only arbiter, they willingly refer its final decision."—GEORGE BUSH, *Reasons for Rejecting Mr. Miller's Views on the Advent*, pp. 11, 12. (Second Advent Library, No. 44, April 15, 1844.)

The evidence is clear, therefore, that the Advent movement, with its predictions on world destiny, arose at a time when the rest of Christendom held a dogmatic view concerning the future of the world, and tied that forecast to Bible prophecy, even to declaring the *nearness* of the impending world change.

But has that change, that end to our present world represented by an earthly millennium, taken place? No! And how long has this forecast of moral regeneration been made? Evidence to be presented in chapter 13 shows that the prediction began to be made early in the eighteenth century, and has been increasingly proclaimed ever since. Though the prophetic time element has been gradually drained out of it, the prediction of a better world, a really new world, has continued to be preached as an event almost at hand. Indeed, the millennium has rather generally been described as being not much farther away than the elusive prosperity of the early depression years, which was always declared to be "just around the corner." But the millennium is not here! That much is certain. In 1844 Professor Bush was very willing to refer "to the tribunal of time, as the only arbiter," the "final decision" of the controversy between Adventists and Christendom as to whether "physical conflagration" or "moral regeneration" lay ahead for the world.

If the whole matter were dealt with solely in a negative way, the indictment of Adventists, as set forth in the opening paragraph of this chapter, could therefore be dismissed merely by the remark that our critics have had no better fortune with their predictions. But the negative goal of merely silencing critics is not our chief interest. To establish positive truth is the important thing.

### Early Adventists Held Restricted View

It may be freely admitted that at the very outset most Adventists, or Millerites, as they were then called, held too narrow and restricted an idea of God's plans and purposes for the closing period of earth's history, which is known in prophecy as the "time of the end," or "the last days." The Millerites thought that the coming of Christ would follow immediately on the ending of the last of certain great time prophecies, that of Daniel 8:14. In this they were mistaken, and for two reasons: They wrongly understood the phrase "then shall the sanctuary be cleansed," and they failed to see that although the Bible speaks of the nearness of the Advent when the great time prophecies have ended, the Scriptures do not warrant, much less demand, the belief that the Advent is to take place *immediately* at the close of these time prophecies. On the contrary, the Bible makes clear that certain events are to unfold in "the time of the end" to set the stage, as it were, for the grand climax of the Advent. That the founders of the Advent movement should have failed to see all this in perspective proves only what has been proved numerous times before in Christian history—that men rarely see a new truth in its proper perspective at the very outset. The best illustration of this is found in the question the apostles put to our Lord after His resurrection: "Wilt thou at this time restore again the kingdom to Israel?"

## A Fallacy Exposed

The fallacy in the kind of reasoning that would seek to prove false our century-old preaching of the nearness of the Advent is this: The mere passage of time is not in itself the measure of the validity of the prediction we have made. Account must also be taken of what has happened during the period of time under discussion. Do those happenings give cumulative support to the prediction, or do they give the lie to it?

The question can be given an even more precise and definite quality. We have done more than simply predict, in general terms, the nearness of the Second Advent of Christ. We have diligently studied the Scriptures to learn all that they have to say about the events connected with the "last days" of earth's history. As a result we have become specific in our forecasts as to the shape of things to come. Some of these forecasts were originally made when appearances were heavy against their coming to pass. Hence, the question to be answered is this: Has the passing century provided not only general support for our basic prediction that the Advent is near, but also specific support for our definite predictions concerning developments that should take place in the days immediately preceding the Advent? What judgment does the "tribunal of time," as "the only arbiter," render?

First, as to our general prediction of the nearness of the Advent.

## ANSWERS TO OBJECTIONS

No one today will question that the world not only gives the lie to the idea of progress, but stands in such a precarious position that the end of the world, as we know it, may be only a little distance away. But what of our specific predictions regarding events that should just precede the Advent? Let us examine some of them:

### A Series of Forecasts

1. We forecast the revival of the Papacy, declaring that all the world would wonder after the beast that had the deadly wound and did live. But when we began to make such forecasts the Papacy was at low ebb. The pope lost the papal states in 1870, and made himself a voluntary prisoner in the Vatican. But today the Papacy has revived in a way that astounds the world. Diplomats of almost every country in the world are found at Vatican City.

2. We forecast increasing religious apostasy in Christendom. But at the time we began to make such dire declarations most of the churches were still firm in their orthodox beliefs regarding such primary truths as the deity of Christ and His atonement for our sins. The world mission program was just beginning to take vigorous shape. There were those who even predicted that soon the world would be evangelized. Yet we forecast increasing apostasy. And today? It is hardly necessary to present the evidence in support of the charge of apostasy. That evidence is too commonly known now. There has been nothing short of a revolution in the views of an increasing number of the clergy. The blood atonement is made of none effect, the deity of Christ denied, and the personality of God questioned.

3. We forecast troubles in the realm of capital and labor. Such a prediction hardly looked plausible, certainly not when we stressed it as a distinguishing mark of the days just ahead. There were many willing to admit that some troubles might yet lie ahead in the economic world, but that these would gradually disappear under the steadily improving conditions in the world. But today we witness a world in which one of the most prominent causes of

unrest and revolution is the tension between capital and labor. No one in the nineteenth century ever dreamed that the world would be confronted as it is today with a ferment in the economic realm so strong that it threatens to crack the very foundations of stable governments.

### Our Forecast Regarding Freedom

4. We forecast the decline of freedom. We declared that this decline, particularly in the realm of religious freedom, would find its climax in an edict that no one might buy or sell unless he conformed to certain demands of a religio-political combine. But through the latter years of the nineteenth century, and the first years of the twentieth, the idea of democracy and the rights of man was becoming more and more the accepted view in every part of the world. It was difficult even to imagine that the day would come when that tide toward democracy would be reversed. But it is not difficult to do so today.

In very recent decades we have been witnessing strange new forces at work in world thinking. We may speak of the Four Freedoms, but no one doubts that we have come to the day when the doctrine of the rights of man has suffered a serious blow. There is increasing government by edict. The very troubled state of the world seems to favor a more arbitrary kind of rule. We have even witnessed the strange phenomenon of not being able to carry on those age-old practices of buying or selling except as we conform to very rigid edicts. We do not say that this fulfills the prophecy. It does not. But it does illustrate the temper of the times and the vast change that has overtaken the world, particularly America. We have not yet come to the fulfillment of this forecast based on Revelation 13, but no one today questions an Adventist when he declares that the trend is clearly in the direction of fulfillment.

5. We forecast the coming into prominence, if not dominance, of the United States, in world affairs. We declared that the second beast of Revelation is the United States, and that that power "causeth the earth and them that dwell therein to worship the first beast," and causeth all to receive a mark, and to buy and sell

only by its permission. Hence, the time would have to come when the United States would assume a prominent, indeed, a dominant, place among the nations. But when we first began to preach on Revelation 13, the United States was very far from prominence. The latter decades of the nineteenth century were filled with civil war and painful reconstruction. Even into the early years of the twentieth century it could hardly be said that the United States had acquired a striking world prominence. But today! Yes, today, with the second world war now past, the United States stands out not only prominent but dominant in the world. The future must provide the fulfillment of the last details of Revelation 13. Here it need only be shown that the passing years have provided increasing and striking support for our forecast.

6. We forecast great wars, climaxing in a final world conflict, while at the same time we declared there would be much talk of peace and safety. The usual response of critics was that our forecasts were fantastic. Indeed, it is difficult today, even for Adventists, to realize how fantastic our forecast of world wars was considered by most people. Sometimes, if we pressed our case with vigor and showed certain evidences of preparation for wars, the evidence was brushed aside with the remark that there had always been wars, and that probably there would be some troubles in the future. In other words, there was nothing significant in our preaching.

But what could not be seen by those whose eyes were blinded by the false light of an earthly millennium was that a new approach to war was developing in Europe. Universal conscription began to be adopted in the latter years of the nineteenth century. At the same time modern science, which was making such phenomenal strides, began to be harnessed to the chariot of Mars, thus vastly increasing the potential horrors of war.

However, as late as the spring of 1914 few took seriously our forecast of world conflict. The majority were content, rather, to fix their eyes on the peace palace at The Hague. Even after the first world war there were those who still held to the fond hope that the world finally had been rid of evil forces and made safe for democracy. But the second world war followed, which brought us to the age of the atomic bomb. And that statement provides the setting for our next forecast.

### Forecasts of Fear and Confederation

7. We forecast that the time would come when men's hearts would fail them for fear, and for looking after those things that are coming on the earth. Obviously, this forecast was viewed by men in the same light as our other forecasts, as a fanciful piece of predicting. Certainly, if the world is growing better, as men believed, what possible reason could there be for a failing heart and fear of the future? Our earlier Adventist books contain meager proofs in support of this forecast. The time had not yet come. Perhaps it has not fully come today. But at least the time is here when it would be difficult to describe the state of men's minds more accurately than in the prophetic words of our Lord as to a failing of hearts for fear of what is coming. The first atomic bomb seems to have shattered not only Hiroshima but also whatever confidence and assurance of the future there remained in the souls of men. And now we read of plans for hydrogen bombs.

8. We forecast a final confederation of some kind on the part of the nations, with the Papacy very central to the confederacy. True, we have not dogmatized on this or gone into detail, for the prophecy from which we draw this forecast is confessedly difficult of full understanding. But that a confederacy involving the Papacy is mentioned in the prophecy we have been sure, and have forecast accordingly. Now, the world about us was not unwilling to entertain the idea of a parliament of the world, such as Tennyson had predicted with poetic license. But that a confederacy would be formed in the dark setting that we forecast—the very idea was ridiculed.

We admit that no such confederacy has been formed. There are still some events to take place before the end. But it is a significant fact that a great endeavor is being made today, much more earnestly than after the first world war, to create some kind of confederacy. Indeed, the cry is now raised that we must unite or perish. It would be difficult to think of the creation of an international confederacy under gloomier conditions than that. Who ever dreamed a generation or two ago that such a cry would be raised? But it is raised today, and with earnestness and hard logic.

And is the Papacy standing nearby in the shadows? Listen to this statement by the editor of the most widely quoted religious weekly in America, who was writing shortly before the close of the war and just before President Roosevelt's death:

"Sometimes it is said, by those who sense some of the foreboding realities of the days after organized fighting has ceased, that revolution is in the air. Perhaps. But more likely it is simply chaos. That, it often seems to us, is probably one reason for Mr. Roosevelt's strange attraction to the Vatican. Has he not been persisting in this diplomatic courtship in the face of widespread disapproval by the American people simply because he feels that he must find *some* factor of stability to which to attach American postwar policy in Europe, and because the Vatican seems to be about the only such stable factor short of Russia?"—*The Christian Century*, Nov. 15, 1944.

Even though the editor just quoted thinks the Vatican is hardly as stable as it "seems," this does not minimize his penetrating conclusion as to why the powerful United States seeks to maintain a close relationship. Formerly our forecast that some kind of confederacy involving the Papacy would develop in the very last hours of earth's history was considered fantastic, and we could point to no historical development that even gave plausibility to our prediction. Today, as we draw into what we believe are the last of the last days, we hear the cry raised for confederacy and we see the Papacy as one of the few rallying points around which any international group could unite. This much, certainly, is present history.

Other forecasts might be cited, but these are sufficient to let us view this Advent movement in the perspective of a century. In the setting of these predictions and their amazing fulfillment, it is pertinent to call attention to certain general conclusions that heighten the significance of the evidence presented:

# HAS CENTURY INVALIDATED DOCTRINE?

## Conclusions From the Evidence

1. No one now laughs at our most doleful predictions. Do we realize the full force of this fact? Time was when Adventist predictions of doom and destruction for the world evoked only a laugh from the great majority of people. They might have thought us sincere, but they also thought us silly; so they laughed. Some years ago a leading literary journal included in one of its articles a sketch of an Adventist preacher. The writer declared that every time this preacher opened his mouth, doom came forth through his black whiskers. It was all supposed to be funny and sophisticated. No one today is writing sketches like that about Adventist preaching. The very silence of those who formerly laughed is the loudest testimony that our preaching no longer sounds laughable.

2. To laugh at Adventist declarations of doom would be to laugh at statesmen, scientists, educators, and other eminent men, who actually outdo us in painting a dark picture of the future. The proof in support of this statement is legion.

3. Eminent men, in painting their dark picture of the future, often use language almost identical with that which Adventists have used in painting the final scene of earth's history. They speak of a new dark age, of chaos, of the end of the world as we know it, and of the complete destruction of mankind. Indeed, a listener not carefully versed in technical distinctions might almost think he was hearing an Adventist minister speak.

For example, in the official report on atomic research we find this forecast:

"Should a scheme be devised for converting to energy even as much as a few per cent of the matter of some common material, civilization would have the means to commit suicide at will."—HENRY DEWOLF SMYTH, *Atomic Energy for Military Purposes*, p. 224.

## New Meaning to Scriptures

4. Certain statements of Holy Writ take on new force and possible meaning. There are three in particular, the first of which reads thus:

627

"And the nations were angry, and thy wrath is come, and the time of the dead, that they should be judged, and that thou shouldest give reward unto thy servants the prophets, and to the saints, and them that fear thy name, small and great; and shouldest destroy them which destroy the earth." Rev. 11:18.

If there is one idea that more than any other is brought out repeatedly in all the present discussion of war, it is that of wholesale destruction. Indeed, the word *destroy*, or *destruction*, seems to be the distinguishing one in every description of the present and future nature of modern war. Never before in the history of the Christian Era could these prophetic words have had quite the force that they have today: "Destroy them which destroy the earth."

The second statement is this:

"The cities of the nations fell." Rev. 16:19. We have generally thought of this in connection with the great earthquake described in the preceding verses, and perhaps this is the full explanation for the fall of the cities of the nations. But it is not unreasonable to think of this cataclysm in the setting of the several verses preceding, which speak of the battle of Armageddon. God often uses nation against nation to bring His judgments upon men. In all the military reports of the plans for future war, in the light of improved weapons of destruction, no fact is more vigorously stressed than that the great cities of the nations are to be the chief objects of attack.

This much therefore seems sure, that when the next war comes, the chronicler of it will be able to describe one phase of it in the prophetic words: "The cities of the nations fell."

The third scripture reads thus:

"Looking for and hasting unto the coming of the day of God, wherein the heavens being on fire shall be dissolved, and the elements shall melt with fervent heat." 2 Peter 3:12. Probably no passage of Scripture has been referred to more frequently since the opening of the Atomic Era than this statement by Peter. And why? We shall let a professor in a Chicago divinity school answer. He quotes Peter's words and declares:

# HAS CENTURY INVALIDATED DOCTRINE?

"Much of the current interest in these words stems from the fact that they are so pat as a prediction of the specific manner in which the world may now be destroyed."—WINTHROP S. HUDSON, *The Christian Century,* Jan. 9, 1946.

Adventists do not believe that Peter's words will meet their fulfillment in man-released energy. We believe that God will set the fires of the last great day. But we think it is most significant that the world has come to a time when men find no better way to describe the fearsome prospects of the immediate future than in terms of a Biblical prediction of world's end in blazing fire.

## Why Should God Delay Longer?

5. The fact that the whole world is shattered and bleeding and bankrupt, with mutual suicide as the logical end of all future war planning and with no moral power sufficient to stem the tide, means that we have a new and most powerful argument in behalf of our doctrine of Christ's coming. If man reveals no power to solve the tragedy of our world by any human device, then the Adventist solution, the supernatural intervention of God by His appearing in glory, becomes the only hope. And if man's practice of iniquity has brought him to the point of completely and fully demonstrating to the universe that the wages of sin is death, even world suicide, then the Adventist belief in the nearness of Christ's coming stands revealed as the only reasonable doctrine.

6. A century ago, when the preaching of the literal soon coming of Christ began to be proclaimed, our opponents scoffed. They agreed that prophetic times were ending, but they were sure that the millennium was soon to be ushered in. They were confident that moral regeneration, not physical conflagration, was soon to transform this earth. "To the tribunal of time, as the only arbiter," they willingly referred the controversy for "final decision." Today we can say without reservation that the tribunal of time has resolved the controversy and has passed a vigorous judgment.

We do not know what the opponents of William Miller and the pioneer Adventists would say if they could rise from their graves to survey a wrecked world, and to listen to the statements of eminent men who declare that world suicide threatens us. But we do know what their spiritual successors are saying! A professor in Andover-Newton Theological Seminary writes of "global dissolution," and of the grave possibility of "planetary extinction," in view of the atomic bomb and the failure of mankind to devise a way of peace. Then he adds:

"A new heaven and a new earth, when all things that are will have passed away and old things will have been made new—these conditions are possible only after world's end. What the nature of this end will be no man can say.

"Christians normally reckon with eschatology [the doctrine of last things, world's end]. It was Christian abnormality which ignored eschatology for so long. . . . The normality which the atomic blasts over Japan brought back to Christian believers consists of the rightness, the correctness, of not only contemplating but also *expecting* world's end. . . .

"Perhaps the next few summers may lengthen into a few more summers of opportunity. Again, no man can say. But let men search the Scriptures and ponder the facts of science, the vagaries of world politics, the economic, emotional and industrial condition of the peoples—conditions pointing sharply toward *finis*, soon or a little later."—WESNER FALLAW, *The Christian Century*, Sept. 25, 1946.

Winthrop Hudson, who was quoted a few paragraphs back in comment on the statement in 2 Peter 3, concludes his discussion of the atomic bomb with this statement:

"We must stop smiling complacently at the way in which the Millerites once played upon the fears of the credulous. This time the final explosion can too easily occur. This time it is not the credulous who believe but the incredulous, not the hysterical but the coldly scientific. The task of the church is to make their fear real to the great mass of the people—to make the great mass of the people recognize the full dimensions of the peril in which they stand."—*The Christian Century*, Jan. 9, 1946.

How strangely different these statements sound from those made so confidently a century ago as to the future of the world. And these statements are typical of what a host of religious leaders are now saying with regard to the probable end of our world. True, some of them, including Winthrop Hudson, think that by some heroic endeavor we may pull the world away from the brink. But none of them are very sure.

### All World Developments Reinforce Our Belief

As already stated, Adventists do not believe that the world is to end by man-released atomic energy, though we view atomic-bomb destruction as a sign of the last days. Hence, in one sense, we think that religious leaders are today as definitely in error regarding the end of the world as they were in Miller's day. But that does not minimize the significance of their change of view concerning the future of our world. If, at the end of a century of preaching the nearness of the Advent, we can show that not only world conditions but the spiritual successors of our original opponents testify to impending destruction for this sinful earth, we need not be embarrassed by the mere passage of the years. Who knows but that God in His long-suffering may have tarried, not willing that any should perish! Suffice it to say: Every development in the world reinforces our prediction of Christ's soon coming. Every calamity in the world, and lastly the calamity of atomic power, cries out for the Advent as the only sure solution of the tragedy of a bankrupt world. We have not followed cunningly devised fables!

7. One question only remains to be answered. How did we succeed in forecasting so accurately these times? It was not a lucky guess, nor a shrewd analysis of obvious happenings. So far from being obvious, or even probable, the whole fabric of our predictions was originally held up to ridicule as the product of morbid minds that refused to see the evident proofs of world progress. The very wise men in every walk of life saw an entirely different picture of the future.

Where did we gain our prophetic insight that enabled us to foretell so accurately what is now current history? The answer is, From the Bible. We have staked our claim to being preachers of truth, to being correct interpreters of the prophecies, on the forecasts concerning last-day world conditions which we have made publicly for long years from the platform and through our numerous publications. The "tribunal of time" has passed its verdict on the accuracy of our interpretation of prophecy. Only one great prediction, the last of the series, remains unfulfilled—the Second Advent of Christ.

When the matter is placed in this setting, it becomes evident that the mere passage of the years has not weakened, but rather strengthened, our doctrine of the soon coming of Christ, because the passing years have strengthened the supporting structure on which the doctrine is reared. Those passing years have provided a kind of proof in behalf of our prophetic teachings that only the years *could* provide!

# Section V

# THE HISTORICAL SETTING
# OF THE THREEFOLD MESSAGE

CHAPTER 13

# Origin and Growth of the Idea
# of World Progress

ONE OF the points that has been in debate between Adventists and others is whether the world is growing better or
worse. The trouble, generally, with our discussion of this subject
is that we fail to deal with the matter in terms of the long perspective of history. The question of whether the world is improving or not is very much larger than a discussion, for example,
of comparative crime statistics for a decade. This question is
of the essence of the controversy that Bible-believing Christians
in general, and Adventists in particular, must wage with liberal
churchmen and secularists who have taught that the world is
improving.

If the world, by some grand law of progress, is gradually
moving toward perfection and holiness, why preach the sudden,
supernatural appearing of Christ to bring in a new heaven and
a new earth? But if the world "lieth in wickedness," even as it
lay in John's day, and is providing only increasing proofs of
wickedness in devising new war plans of mutual destruction,
then the Second Advent doctrine becomes not only eminently
meaningful but urgently necessary. The issue at stake is precisely
that.

In order to see the question in true historical perspective let
us trace through the centuries this idea that the world is growing
better.*

The idea of progress, using the term in a large and loose sense
to include both material and ethical progress, is not an ancient

* In the first part of this sketch, historical data will be repeatedly drawn from a remarkable
work entitled *The Idea of Progress*, by J. B. Bury, late regius professor of history in the University
of Cambridge.

or medieval idea, but a modern one. The ancients did not believe in any law of inevitable progress toward perfection. They held a rather pessimistic, fatalistic idea of cycles, wherein nations rise, flower, and decay. That was the best paganism could offer.

### View Held During Dark Ages

The church of the Dark Ages did not hold to any doctrine of unending progress, and for certain definite reasons. First, the medieval scholars looked to ancient Greece for wisdom. They viewed Greek culture and learning as the high point in world history. Hence they were in no mood to generate the idea of progress. They tacitly, if not explicitly, held to the doctrine of retrogression.

Again, the medieval church viewed man as a fallen creature, infected with original sin and blighted with total depravity, whose end was the grave and hell, unless the grace of God intervened. A world filled with such creatures could not be viewed as making progress toward any better level, either materially or spiritually.

Finally, the medieval church believed that the world was the object of a directly intervening Providence that had marked out the limits of man's stay upon earth, and had given an element of finality to the world by setting a day of judgment and consigning the earth to flames when that day came.

As a sure protection against any impious attempt to teach otherwise, the church required all, on pain of damnation, to accept the authority of the church in all matters of doctrine and belief. Reason, as an arbiter of truth, or as the means of discovering truth, had no standing. Men were supposed to use the faculty of faith rather than reason.

Says the historian J. B. Bury: "It may surprise many to be told that the notion of Progress, which now seems so easy to apprehend, is of comparatively recent origin."—*The Idea of Progress*, p. 6. He observes immediately that while men of former ages had some ideas of man's advancement from savagery, this does not constitute a real doctrine of progress:

"You may conceive civilisation as having gradually advanced in the past, but you have not got the idea of Progress until you go on to conceive that it is destined to advance indefinitely in the future. . . . It is not till the sixteenth century that the obstacles to its appearance definitely begin to be transcended and a favourable atmosphere to be gradually prepared."—*Ibid.*, p. 7.

In the same connection he declares:

"As time is the very condition of the possibility of Progress, it is obvious that the idea would be valueless if there were any cogent reasons for supposing that the time at the disposal of humanity is likely to reach a limit in the near future."—*Ibid.*, p. 5.

Descartes, a brilliant French mathematician and philosopher, who was born at the close of the sixteenth century, brought forth two germinal ideas that were to produce fruitage in skeptical and rational opposition to the basic medieval concepts. Descartes declared that reason is supreme and that the laws of nature are unalterable. To set up reason is to dethrone arbitrary authority, and to hold to the invariability of nature's laws is to do violence to the medieval concept of a superintending Providence. Bury observes that Descartes' views were "equivalent to a declaration of the Independence of Man."—*Ibid.*, p. 65.

## Seeds of New Ideas Planned

Thus in the first half of the seventeenth century were planted the seeds that were to bring forth a harvest of new views and theories, particularly the idea of progress.

There also began to develop, both on the Continent and in England, a school of thought that challenged the idea of the supremacy of Greek learning with its corollary that Greece provided the golden age and succeeding generations have witnessed only degeneracy. The position began to be taken that the present is equal in intellect and learning to any former era. It was only one step from this to the position that the present is superior to the past.

As the leaven of rebellion against Catholic Church authority and teaching began to work, new ideas as to the nature of man developed. Instead of being a creature born for destruction because of original sin, man began to be viewed by rationalists and skeptics as inherently good. This fundamental change of view paved the way for the idea that man is capable of improvement if only given an opportunity. Says Bury:

"With the extension of rationalism into the social domain, it came about naturally that the idea of intellectual progress was enlarged into the idea of the general Progress of man. The transition was easy. If it could be proved that social evils were due neither to innate and incorrigible disabilities of the human being nor to the nature of things, but simply to ignorance and prejudices, then the improvement of his state, and ultimately the attainment of felicity, would be only a matter of illuminating ignorance and removing errors, of increasing knowledge and diffusing light."—*Ibid.*, p. 128.

## Cornerstone of Modern Science

The centuries following Descartes saw the rapid growth of the belief in the invariable order of nature. That belief became the very cornerstone of all the developing sciences. A definitely mechanical theory of the universe took shape; it began to be viewed as a vast machine, moving in all its intricate parts in harmony with unchanging and unchangeable laws. It may be added that this so-called mechanistic view of the universe grew in popularity among scientists and skeptics until the opening years of the twentieth century. The essentially godless quality of it was its belief in the constancy of law without a belief in the constancy of a great Lawgiver who is personally planning the destiny of the universe. To discuss the factors which have operated to oppose and today to weaken the popularity of the mechanistic theory would lead us afield from our present theme. Suffice it to say that while rigid mechanism is now at a discount in many circles, the scientific belief in the invariableness of the laws of nature is stronger than ever before.

Now the growth of the idea that nature, through her unchanging laws, is really in charge, played havoc with the doctrine of a directly superintending Providence, as that doctrine was held by all Christian bodies. The Christian view that man is in the hands of God, who offers him salvation against a predetermined day of judgment, had to be abandoned by those who accepted the new views of nature and her laws. There was no longer a closed system, with man's destiny compressed into an earthly cycle of foreordained and limited length, and then world destruction. Man was not in the hands of a great and offended God, who might mercifully work miraculously to save him. Rather, he was on his own, in a world where miracles were declared to be contrary to nature's laws, his destiny dependent wholly on his own resourcefulness, his hope for betterment contingent upon his ability to master obstacles and to square with the laws of nature. And, anyway, he needed no supernatural aid, he needed no salvation, for he was essentially good at heart and needed only improvement. Indeed, the very emphasis on law, to the exclusion of the Lawgiver, increasingly tended to banish the idea of God. That tendency, ever aided by the atheistic bent of certain minds, greatly spread atheism on the Continent, and nurtured deism in England.

## Concentration on Present World

The effect of all this was to cause men to concentrate their thoughts on this world, and this world alone, where man, as the captain of his soul and the master of his fate, was to work out his own destiny. No element of finality, such as a day of judgment, was to cut short man's planning for the future. The indefinite years lay ahead. Man had made progress up to this point; why should he not continue to progress? While all who went along with the scientific and skeptical trend did not become godless or atheistic, the inevitable tendency was to minimize, increasingly, the fact and the significance of God, until He became a vague, faraway, foggy picture. As the significance of God decreased, the apparent importance of man increased. He became the center of everything, and his own endeavors and ingenuity the solution of everything.

# ANSWERS TO OBJECTIONS

The early nineteenth century saw philosophers attempting to formulate the so-called laws of progress, on the theory that "the history of civilization is subject to general laws, or, in other words, that a science of society is possible."—*Ibid.*, p. 307. Foremost in this group was Auguste Comte, a French philosopher, who is credited with having "laid the foundations of sociology." —*Ibid.* Bury thus summarizes Comte's view of history:

"The movement of history is due to the deeply rooted though complex instinct which pushes man to ameliorate his condition incessantly, to develop in all ways the sum of his physical, moral, and intellectual life. And all the phenomena of his social life are closely cohesive, as Saint-Simon had pointed out. By virtue of this cohesion, political, moral, and intellectual progress are inseparable from material progress."—*Ibid.*, p. 293.

As already stated, the doctrine of progress naturally led to the minimizing of God and the glorifying of man. It is no mere coincidence, then, that Comte, who was so prominent in promoting this doctrine, devoted his last years to writing a ponderous work on "social reorganization," which "included a new religion, in which Humanity was the object of worship."—*Ibid.*, p. 307.

## Political Movements Reflect New Views

A practical application of this philosophy of progress was the creation of such political movements as socialism, and later, of communism. By organizing the state in harmony with certain ideals of progress, the leaders of such movements naturally believed they could hasten the day of an ideal material world, and then stabilize it at that point. Others who did not endorse state-enforced speed toward perfection, but who nevertheless considered progress desirable, began to reveal their views in a school of thought known as liberalism. This term, defined politically, describes the idea that the *status quo* is not the ideal, that the slow advance of mankind up to the present should be allowed to continue without any hindering laws or customs of former days. Hence liberalism, politically, has been a ferment in modern states, urging the betterment of man's estate by providing him full liberty of opportunity and action, but eschewing state socialism. The term *liberalism* also has a religious connotation, which will be discussed later.

The nineteenth century, with its increasing developments in the field of discovery and invention, provided another impetus to the idea of progress. The wizardry of science was remaking the world and lifting man to greater comfort. Machinery was taking the place of backbreaking labor, and medical science was winning amazing victories over the ills that have long beset men and sent them to untimely graves. And ever there was the prospect of still greater wonders to be produced. Here was truly something new in the history of the world. If mankind had not already crossed into the land flowing with milk and honey, at least the Jordan had been rolled back as the feet of the scientists touched the waters. Nothing remained but to go in and possess the goodly land. It is easy to see how men could come to confuse scientific progress with the larger idea of universal progress and the perfectibility of man. Bury thus summarizes this phase of the development of the doctrine:

"The spectacular results of the advance of science and mechanical technique brought home to the mind of the average man the conception of an indefinite increase of man's power over nature as his brain penetrated her secrets. This evident material progress which has continued incessantly ever since has been the mainstay of the general belief in Progress which is prevalent to-day."—*Ibid.,* pp. 324, 325.

### Evolution Theory Provides Capstone

The capstone to the doctrine of progress and the perfectibility of man was placed by Darwin in 1859, when he published his epochal work *Origin of Species*. Before his time the idea of evolution had been held largely as a philosophical speculation, though some evidence in the scientific world had been alleged in support of it. Darwin set forth his theory as the key to unlock man's long history and to unfold his vast future. In *The Descent of Man* Darwin explored more fully the subject of evolution in relation to man, coming to this statement in the closing paragraph:

ANSWERS TO OBJECTIONS

"Man may be excused for feeling some pride at having risen, though not through his own exertions, to the very summit of the organic scale; and the fact of his having thus risen, instead of having been aboriginally placed there, may give him hope for a still higher destiny in the distant future."—Page 707.

## Evolution Principle Widely Applied

Spencer was the great philosopher of evolution, even as Huxley was its militant exponent in the arena of controversy. Spencer sought to apply the principle of evolution to all realms of life, in an attempt to prove that socially and ethically, as well as biologically, man's course is upward and onward. He had held these ideas some years before Darwin published his *Origin of Species*. Darwin's work came at the psychological moment to provide Spencer with apparent scientific support for his philosophical views. Bury declares:

"The receptive attitude of the public towards such a philosophy as Spencer's had been made possible by Darwin's discoveries, which were reinforced by the growing science of palaeontology [the study of fossil organisms] and the accumulating material evidence of the great antiquity of man. By the simultaneous advances of geology and biology man's perspective in time was revolutionized, just as the Copernican astronomy had revolutionized his perspective in space. Many thoughtful and many thoughtless people were ready to discern—as Huxley suggested—in man's 'long progress through the past, a reasonable ground of faith in his attainment of a nobler future.' "—*The Idea of Progress*, p. 342.

We need not here turn aside to discuss the fact that the theory of evolution, strictly speaking, can be used as an argument for pessimism in regard to man's future. For example, some philosophers have pointed to the increasingly complex life of highly civilized people as entailing troubles and distresses unknown to the simple savage. This is a restatement of the position of Rousseau, who long before had promoted the idea of the inherent goodness of man and the inherent badness of civilization. Bury quotes Huxley as expressing in his later years no very hopeful views as to the future of man, if even the best of modern civilization is any measure of man's development. Then Bury adds:

"I have quoted these views to illustrate that evolution lends itself to a pessimistic as well as to an optimistic interpretation. The question whether it leads in a desirable direction or not is answered according to the temperament of the inquirer. In an age of prosperity and self-complacency the affirmative answer was readily received, and the term evolution attracted to itself in common speech the implications of value which belong to Progress."—*Ibid.*, p. 345.

## Integral Part of Modern Thought

Thus has the idea of progress become a part of the thinking of modern man, a "general article of faith." Nowhere in his remarkable book, *The Idea of Progress,* does Bury reveal that he believes the idea has been proved true. He observes that in our day "indefinite Progress is generally assumed as an axiom" by all those who write on social science, but that the "law" governing it "remains still undiscovered." He places the word *law* in quotation marks to indicate, evidently, that he is not certain whether there is such a law. He even thinks that this dogma may be superseded someday by another theory of man's destiny.* But the point of interest to us is that the idea of progress became dogma for modern man. We close this survey of the secular factors that contributed to the adoption of the idea, with these words from the final paragraph of Bury's work:

"Looking back on the course of the inquiry, we note how the history of the idea has been connected with the growth of modern science, with the growth of rationalism, and with the struggle for political and religious liberty. . . . The idea took definite shape in France when the old scheme of the universe had been shattered by the victory of the new astronomy and the prestige of Providence . . . was paling before the majesty of the immutable laws of nature. There began a slow but steady reinstatement of the kingdom of this world. The otherworldly dreams of theologians, . . . which had ruled so long lost their power, and men's earthly home again insinuated itself into their affections, but with the new hope of its becoming a place fit for reasonable beings to live in. We have seen how the belief that our race is travelling towards earthly happiness was propagated by some eminent thinkers,

---

* He wrote before the gathering clouds of World War II could be seen. A new view of man's future *is* developing, as will be seen in the next chapter.

as well as by some 'not very fortunate persons who had a good deal of time on their hands.' And all these high-priests and incense-bearers to whom the creed owes its success were rationalists."—*Ibid.*, pp. 348, 349.

## Modern Paganism

The ancient pagans believed that this world was the one place on which to fasten their interests and in which to find such happiness as might be obtainable. Whether this was a good world or not, they did not know; they only knew that it was the best and only world of which they could be sure. Hence the dictum: Let us eat and drink, for tomorrow we die. The rationalists of the eighteenth and nineteenth centuries—skeptics, agnostics, deists, atheists—who were the developers of the idea of progress, simply turned men back again to this earth. They did so by undermining the Christian doctrines of Providence and heaven, and by picturing our world as a place that is in process of steadily becoming a more ideal abode.

The nineteenth century poet Swinburne shockingly reveals in the following sacrilegious lines how belief in the potentialities of material progress had in it a pagan, godless quality:

"Thou art smitten, Thou God, Thou art smitten; Thy death is upon thee, O Lord.
And the love-song of earth as Thou diest resounds through the winds of her wings—
Glory to Man in the highest! for Man is the master of things."

From this summary of secular causes that produced the earth-bound idea of progress and man's perfectibility, let us turn to consider a theological idea that has gained ascendancy in the last two centuries, paralleling and reinforcing the secular idea of progress. It is the doctrine of a temporal millennium, introduced into Protestant prophetic thinking by Daniel Whitby, an Anglican divine, in 1703. He set forth the view that the thousand years of Revelation 20 is to precede the Second Advent of Christ. During this millennium the nations will learn righteousness, the Jews will return to their own land and be converted, and all will be bliss. The resurrection that the Bible declares will take place at the beginning of the millennium, he spiritualized away, making it a spiritual resurrection of men dead in trespasses and sin. The outpouring of the Divine Spirit is to produce a kind of spiritual second coming of Christ. He is to come to this earth in spirit to abide in the hearts of men. Thus the Christian should look forward, not to a cataclysmic climax of a sinful world, but to a gradually improving society in a slowly but surely developing new heavens and a new earth freed of all sin.

### Paralleling of Two Theories

Here is a theological theory of the future of man parallel to that set forth by the rationalists. The difference is in the means by which world betterment will be brought about. How one theory may have affected the other, there is no way of telling. But this much we know, that theories, the same as men, do not live in a vacuum; they live in an interacting society. Here were two theories, having an essential point in common—that the world is headed toward improvement. The exponents of one theory of progress could hardly fail to be aided by the exponents of the other. And in the minds of many people the two theories could easily tend to blend.

This postmillennial theory made rapid headway in theological circles, so that by early nineteenth century it was quite generally accepted by Protestants. When Miller and the other Advent preachers began to stir men with their preaching of a premillennial, literal coming of Christ, theological opposition was chiefly built on the contention that world improvement, not world destruction, lay just ahead. As already quoted, the Reverend George Bush, in one of a series of letters to Miller, declared:

"The great event before the world is not its *physical conflagration,* but its *moral regeneration.* . . .

"This is the common and prevailing belief of Christendom, and I have no doubt the true one."—*Reasons for Rejecting Mr. Miller's View on the Advent,* Second Advent Library, no. 44, pp. 11, 12.

# ANSWERS TO OBJECTIONS

Bush was correct in declaring that this was the common and prevailing belief in Christendom. An examination of religious works published at that time amply supports his statement. For example, the Baptist author and preacher, John Dowling, who was a most active opponent of Millerism, wrote in a much-quoted work that was intended to expose Miller's Advent teachings:

"The doctrine I hold in relation to the millennium, and for which I think I am indebted to the Bible, is—That the reign of Christ on earth will not be a personal but a spiritual reign; that it will be preceded by the overthrow of Popery, Mahomedanism, Paganism, and all false systems; that it will consist in the universal prevalence of righteousness and true holiness, throughout the whole world; . . . that this glorious age shall pass away and be succeeded by a brief but dreadful period of wickedness [when Satan is loosed for a little time], after which the Lord Jesus shall be revealed from Heaven with His mighty angels, in flaming fire, taking vengeance on them that know not God, and that obey not the gospel of our Lord Jesus Christ."—*An Exposition of the Prophecies*, pp. 167, 168.

## New View Anchored to Bible at First

Though Whitby and the theologians of the eighteenth and nineteenth centuries, who accepted his postmillennial doctrine, drew a wrong belief from the Scriptures, they were nevertheless firm believers in the Bible. They did not even attempt to spiritualize away the whole doctrine of the Advent. They believed in a literal coming of a personal Lord and Saviour from heaven. Their error lay in placing this event at the wrong end of the thousand-year period and in declaring that during this period the world would be converted to Christ. They taught a false doctrine of world betterment that outdid even the rationalist picture of improvement, but they did it within the framework of a divinely ordained plan and with an actual, supernatural Advent of Christ as the ultimate climax.

By the opening of the twentieth century the doctrine was undergoing a significant change. Christendom quite generally continued to believe, and perhaps more ardently than ever, that the world was headed toward holiness and that the temporal millennium was not far away. But beyond that point the doctrine had become confused and blurred. The whole idea of the Advent had become spiritualized so that no clear teaching was set forth regarding events at the close of the millennium. Indeed, the very word *millennium* itself had rather become synonymous with a vague, indefinite period of time. In short, the supernatural aspects of the doctrine were quite drained out. The result was that the belief in world betterment, as the theologians set it forth, became not too sharply distinguished from the doctrine as set forth by secular philosophers and reformers.

And why had this come about? The answer is found in a trend that developed, late in the nineteenth century, in Christendom. When crystallized, this trend became a definite and finally a controlling school of thought known as Modernism, or Liberalism. The way was prepared for this by the acceptance on the part of an ever-increasing number of clergy, of the higher critical view of the Bible. In brief, this view is that the Bible is not uniquely inspired. Further, that it is largely a work of uncertain authorship, much later in composition than originally believed to be, which fades from the historical to the mythical in its earlier portions, particularly the books of Moses. This view obviously robbed the Bible of most of its divine authority. Certainly the believer in this view discovered shortly that he no longer stood on the historic Protestant platform of the supreme authority of the Bible. Instead, he found himself setting up reason as a judge of inspiration. With that transition made, almost anything could follow in the way of change in theological beliefs. And very much did follow, and almost immediately.

### Modernism Defined

As already noted, by the end of the nineteenth century the public was dazzled with the accomplishments of the scientists, who declared that they were discovering the true keys to the universe. It would have been strange, indeed, if there had not developed in the church a desire to revamp ancient beliefs to modern discoveries. That desire, expressed through those who had imbibed higher critical teachings, is what produced Modernism, or Liberalism. Probably there is no simpler way to describe theological liberalism than as a movement within the church which seeks to make religion appear intellectually respectable by adjusting it to scientific teachings.

Now, the first precept of the scientific world is the unqualified invariability of natural law. But the acceptance of that precept by theologians meant the abandonment of belief in miracles. Science has no room for miracles. The elimination of miracles from the Bible robbed it of its uniqueness and power. The wondrous things of Scripture had to be explained on naturalistic grounds. The record of Christ's life on earth began to look very different when read through Modernist spectacles.

## Man Increases, God Decreases

The major scientific pronouncement of the late nineteenth century, the evolution theory, was being exploited in secular circles as a master law governing all aspects of life. Modernism sought to harmonize the Bible with this theory. The result was that the opening chapters of Genesis were explained away as poetry, allegory, or plain myth, depending on the mood of the explainer. Genesis presents a picture of perfection at the beginning, followed by the introduction of sin and the fall, from which man can be lifted up only through the redemptive death of Christ. Therefore the Modernists, in harmonizing Genesis with science, quite completely changed their view of man. They saw him as the end result of a slow evolution upward. His undesirable qualities, hitherto attributed to sin, became simply the remnants of his brute ancestry. Furthermore, if man has made this much progress upward, why not believe that he will continue to progress toward perfection? Thus churchmen were traveling the same path in their reasoning as the rationalists had already traveled.

This idea of man's perfectibility, coupled with an acceptance of the dominance of natural law, led on logically to the idea of the increasing importance of man and the decreasing importance of God. In theological minds, even as in scientific, the classic idea of a personal God definitely and directly controlling the affairs of the universe began to fade rapidly. Now if God as a personality fades, to what can man turn? The answer is, he can turn back on himself. He can worship man.

Skeptical onlookers and some so-called advanced thinkers in Modernist circles were quick to point out that Humanism—as the worship of man is known—was the logical end of the Modernist road. And indeed to that very end came the extreme wing of Modernism in the 1920's. This was the high-water mark of the doctrine of inevitable progress for man as developed through theological channels.

A logical corollary of this whole Modernist adjustment of religion to science was the "social gospel," which began to be actively preached near the opening of the twentieth century. The pioneers of this preaching declared that their endeavor was to apply the principles of Christianity to social conditions, in the confident hope that the kingdom of God could be set up in this world.

Thus the church began to nurture a social reform movement, which though springing from a different source than socialism or political liberalism, had a not dissimilar goal in view—the creating of an ideal present world for man. However, as Modernist churchmen became increasingly earth bound in their thinking, some even moving into Humanism, the social gospel began to sound strangely like the secular doctrine of social reform. Not infrequently Modernist ministers openly allied themselves with left-wing secular reformers, feeling that they had a common goal in their reform program. This was natural if not inevitable.

### Liberalism Turns to the Left

With the supernatural quite drained out of their theology, young Modernist preachers took hold of the social gospel of a gradually idealized present world as the only gospel that really made sense for them. They could no longer preach the classic doctrine of a sure and certain heavenly home, either premillennial or postmillennial in time. From force of early training, a Modernism that finally skirted the shores of Humanism may have originally steered its bark by studying the heavens, but it soon took to determining its course by observing the earthly torches of secular philosophers and reformers, especially those lights visible from the larboard side.

It may willingly be admitted that the social gospel has been preached in sincerity by high-minded men, and that the beautiful ideals of Christ have colored the arguments for earthly reforms, without minimizing any feature of the analysis just made. The one point to be made clear is this, that the idea of earthly progress leading toward perfection developed in our modern period until, by the opening of the twentieth century, it had become a dominant belief among secularists and liberal churchmen.

### Plausible Claims of World Progress

Indeed, as the world entered the present century, these secularists, and even more so the liberal religionists, were ready to proclaim that all history, especially the history of the Christian Era, supported their boast of progress. They contrasted the present with the early centuries of the era, declaring that the Roman Empire provided a picture of decadence and dissipation never exceeded, and perhaps never equaled, in succeeding centuries. They contrasted the enlightened present with the Dark Ages, when an apostate Christianity committed millions of martyrs to the stake. Yes, and these believers in inevitable progress were particularly interested in contrasting the present with the world of the last few centuries. They pointed to the frightful squalor and lawlessness that plagued London and in lesser degree other great English cities within the last two hundred years, to say nothing of the immorality that flourished in the English court in the seventeenth century. They cited the dissoluteness of the court of Louis XIV, and the wretched condition of the populace that produced the French Revolution. They even pointed to America supposedly free from much of Europe's ills and vices, and showed that this land was formerly plagued with religious riots, including burning of churches and murder, with fatal dueling, with slave markets, and with drunkenness that was so widespread that it produced, in reaction, the temperance movement of the early nineteenth century.

All this and more the believers in world progress were presenting as proof that the world by A.D. 1900 had made great advancement. They might have been embarrassed that the progress, socially and morally, had really gotten under way only recently, but they explained this on the ground that man's possibilities of perfection awaited the improvement of the environment. And was it not in the latter part of the nineteenth century that most of the social, hygienic, and educational legislation had been enacted?

Thus both secularists and liberal religionists reasoned and exulted as they entered the twentieth century. They had no time for the Adventist minister who declared that the "whole world lieth in wickedness" and that God's judgments upon this evil world were soon to descend.

---

NOTE.—As stated at the beginning of this chapter, Bury has been followed in the main outlines of the sketch of the growth of the secular idea of progress. His viewpoint seems to be well supported. But no aspect of history is treated uniformly by historians, to say nothing of other writers who may deal with the matter. This is true regarding the history of the idea of progress. The chief difference in view as to the forces that operated to produce secularism and the theory of man's inherent worth, has to do with the part played by the Protestant Reformation.

Catholic writers, and some others, contend that Protestantism is chiefly responsible for the modern secularistic era and the erroneous idea of man's worth. This contention is quite invalid. What the Protestant Reformation did, among other things, was to break the authority of the Catholic Church over men's minds and to substitute another authority, the Bible. When the church no longer controlled men's thinking, a fraction of Europe's population turned to the Bible, the remainder responded favorably to the new voices of skeptics who were appealing to reason as the only authority for men's lives. Luther and other Reformers warned of the dangers of reason and appealed to men to turn to the Scriptures. But the Reformers, though they held on to some of the evil ideas of church and state union, never called upon the state to hold men to the church to the degree that Catholicism had done. The inevitable result was that men who formerly from fear had failed to reveal their skeptical views now began to let those views be widely known. Only in this sense may it be said that Protestantism contributed to the secularistic trend of postmedieval days. But to admit this is to bring no indictment of Protestantism; it is simply to admit that the granting of liberty of thought involves giving men the liberty to think wrongly if they desire to.

The reader who wishes to pursue further the subject of the history of the idea of progress is referred to the following works, which make significant reference to the matter.

J. B. Bury, *The Idea of Progress.* The Macmillan Company, 1932.

John Herman Randall, Jr., *The Making of the Modern Mind.* Houghton Mifflin Company, 1940.

Carl F. H. Henry, *Remaking the Modern Mind.* Wm. B. Eerdman's Publishing Company, 1946.

Arnold S. Nash, *The University and the Modern World.* The Macmillan Company, 1944.

R. G. Collingwood, *The Idea of History.* Oxford Press, 1946.

Richard Hofstadter, *Social Darwinism in American Thought, 1860-1915.* University of Pennsylvania Press, 1945.

# CHAPTER 14

# Collapse of the Idea of World Progress

SO STRONG was the idea of progress, so fully had it become an article of faith in the creed of all classes of people, that even the shadows of impending world war in 1914 did not darken the faith. We see what we wish to see, and men everywhere wished only to see proofs of progress. The mere thought of war between civilized nations was ridiculed, even as late as the spring of 1914.

So tenacious was the idea of progress that it actually maintained the control of men's minds through the four years of war. And by an easy rationalization! We are waging a war to make the world safe for democracy! It is truly unfortunate that we must engage in so horrible a strife, but it is a war to end war! Like the fabled phoenix, a new world will arise from the ashes of the old, purged of the evils of the past in the purifying fires of the great conflict! A League of Nations will make sure the brotherhood of man, and all will be well!

Here applies the cynical observation, generally attributed to Benjamin Franklin, that man is fortunately a rational being, and thus he is able to provide reasonable proofs for whatever he wishes to believe or to do. Surely a faith that was strong enough to remove a mountain of world war out of the path of the idea of progress was no mean faith!

## Peace Pacts Strengthen Idea of Progress

The will to believe that the world war of 1914-18 was only a purging fire and not a destroyer of world progress, was further strengthened by a series of peace pacts that were signed in the next decade. At Genoa, in 1922, some thirty nations adopted a resolution against engaging in war one with another. At Geneva, in 1924, the assembly of the League of Nations drew up a pact binding the League members to arbitration in the settlement of controversies. At Locarno, in 1925, France, Germany, and Belgium made a compact never to make war on one another, but to resort to arbitration. At Havana, in 1927, the Pan-American Congress adopted an antiwar resolution. And as a climax came the Pact of Paris, or the Kellogg-Briand Pact, so named from the initiators of it—America's Secretary of State, Frank B. Kellogg, and France's Premier, Aristide Briand. This pact called on the signatories to outlaw war "as an instrument of national policy in their relations with one another," and to agree that "the solution of all disputes or conflicts of whatever nature or of whatever origin they may be, which may arise among them, shall never be sought except by pacific means." This is the essence of the two short but sweeping articles that constitute the treaty.

This treaty to outlaw war was signed originally by the representatives of fifteen principal nations (and later by almost every civilized country) amid the tumultuous acclaim of the secular and religious press. The editor of *Good Housekeeping* described Secretary Kellogg as "the Man Who Ended War," and declared: "For the first time in the history of the world, world-wide and everlasting peace is to be had, if not exactly for the asking, at least by fighting for it before our treaty-ratifying bodies."—September, 1928.

### The High Point of Hope and Confidence

The editor of *The Christian Century*, who attended the treaty-signing ceremonies in Paris and wrote an eyewitness account, penned these glowing words:

"One staggers at the attempt to set forth the significance of the doings of this day. But again, the deed cannot be doubted. I saw it done. I heard the words spoken. I looked for an hour into the grave faces of the men who were empowered to sign. I handled the finished pact. I read anew the unambiguous words of renunciation. I looked at the signatures and seals. And I cannot do otherwise than command my pen to write these words:

# COLLAPSE OF IDEA OF WORLD PROGRESS

*" 'Today international war was banished from civilization.' "*

Then on prudent second thought he added:

"If this pact does not end war, it would be better for humanity had it never been signed. . . . Never did the spirit of man undertake a risk so great. It must mean a new world, a world of permanent peace on the basis of justice. And if it does not mean that, it will mean nothing less than a new epic of the fall of man."—*The Christian Century*, Sept. 6, 1928.

A fair interpretation of the widespread comment, of which the two cited are typical, permits the conclusion that the idea of world progress had not only survived the war but bid fair to flourish more abundantly than ever, under the protecting banner of universal peace. Traveling with increasing momentum for two centuries, this humanly satisfying doctrine of progress had surmounted the first great obstacle in its path, and now who would be so foolhardy as to challenge the truth of it? Had not the nations laid aside forever the weapons of war!

## The Old Order Begins to Change

But the war had shaken the structure of the world much more completely than even the most sagacious of men seemed to realize. New forces had been let loose. The old order was breaking up. The truth of this began to dawn on men when the world sank into an appalling economic depression in the early 1930's. The material good things of life were disappearing on every side, and in many instances destitution and chill penury were taking their place. The grisly side of life came increasingly to the surface. Men in all lands grew restless. The League of Nations had failed to live up to the hopes reposed in it. That failure stood out sharply against the background of economic darkness that had settled over the earth. Political and idealistic failure might be ignored if creature comforts abounded, but not if they departed. Nor had the depression more than spread its heavy pall before strange sounds were heard in the darkness, strident voices calling for new nationalistic ardor, and the clangor of armament factories.

For the roots of World War II run back at least to the early 1930's, if not to the Treaty of Versailles in 1919.

As early as the spring of 1933 a prominent religious editor, Paul Hutchinson, in discussing the forces currently operating on the church and on society at large, could make this sweeping statement of belief:

"Here, then, is my credo: I believe that we are living in a day which sees the final destruction of the illusion of inevitable progress which Herbert Spencer and the Victorian evolutionists fastened upon the prewar liberalism of the West. Even in America, where adventitious aids made a cloudless optimism seem reasonable as long after the World War as the campaign speeches of Mr. Hoover in 1928, man now finds himself confronting the possibility of chaos quite as much as of triumph, and discovering that catastrophe is much closer than either a dependable peace or a just, and therefore stable, world order."— *The Forum*, April, 1933.

## A Liberal Challenges Liberalism

Even before 1933 warning notes were sounding in church circles regarding the false heaven in which men were living. In the spring of 1931 a leading Modernist spokesman declared, in an article entitled "Let Liberal Churches Stop Fooling Themselves":

"Liberal religion has a dogma and it views the contemporary world through the eyes of this dogma. The dogma is all the more potent in coloring opinion because it is not known as a dogma. The dogma is that the world is gradually growing better and that the inevitability of gradualness guarantees our salvation. . . .

"The real fact about our civilization is that it is flirting with disaster. . . .

"Meanwhile the church lives in a comfortable world. It sees the sorry state of our civilization and yet it does not see. We can see only what our dogmas and preconceptions permit us to see. . . .

"The romanticism of the liberal church is revealed not only in its view of history but in its estimate of man. It holds, on the whole, to a Rousseau-istic view of human virtue. It has made an easy identification of this view with the Christian estimate of man as the child of God. The result is that it fails to understand the diabolical aspects of human life." —Reinhold Niebuhr, *The Christian Century*, March 25, 1931.

## How One Man's Mind Changed

Niebuhr, who has just been quoted, is unquestionably one of the most challenging figures in the contemporary religious world. The transitions in his own thinking give us an insight into the changing viewpoint of multitudes of Liberals who had been offering incense at the shrine of world progress. From a Detroit pastorate he came, in 1928, to a professorship in Union Theological Seminary, New York, easily the most prominent Modernist seminary in the United States. As a pastor he had been an ardent preacher of the social gospel. In New York, he actively gave his support to what would be described as left-wing reforms. He even ran on the socialist ticket and for a time was editor of a socialist paper. All this was incidental, of course, to his seminary teaching. In 1932 Niebuhr published a book entitled *Moral Man and Immoral Society,* and followed this, early in 1934, with another volume, *Reflections on the End of an Era.* Commenting, in 1935, on these two works, Paul Hutchinson declares:

"The two [books] have rocked Protestant church life. . . . There is no other current religious thought which has made the thought and effort of the last hundred years appear so structurally futile. . . .

"Niebuhr's very titles will suggest the direction in which his mind has traveled. He started with civilization in need of some process of cleansing—that is to say, religious socialism. Then he became oppressed with a sense of the ineradicable tendency to evil in society, so he attempted to drive a line between man who, as individual, is a pretty good chap, quite promising as a candidate for salvation, and man who, as a member of a group, is an irredeemable savage—'moral man and immoral society.' But it took him less than two years to discover that such a distinction would not stand the test, so that now we hear his voice of doom at 'the end of an era,' declaring that man is quite as immoral as the society in which he herds."—*Scribner's Magazine,* October, 1935.

In the year 1939 there appeared in *The Christian Century,* most representative of nondenominational journals in America, a series of articles entitled "How My Mind Has Changed in This Decade." Each article in the series of thirty-four was written by a different religious leader. The editor observed:

# ANSWERS TO OBJECTIONS

"We believe that there has been coming, *in the past decade,* a radical and significant change in the thinking of Christian scholarship and leadership. For many this change is in process; . . . but all of us are aware that ours is a period of intensive and profound transition. There is naturally much bewilderment. Many Christian people are walking as if in a kind of mist."—*The Christian Century,* October 4, 1939.

## Vast Changes in Decade

He asks the question, "Why was the past ten-year period taken as particularly significant?" and answers it thus:

"The answer is that it was in this period that a whole new theological outlook had emerged. The liberalism which had been for nearly a half-century the common presupposition of Christian scholarship had been for the first time effectively challenged in this decade. The earlier inferences which had been drawn from the higher criticism of the Bible had come under critical review. The New Testament presented itself in a new aspect, calling for a radical revision of the prevailing liberal conception of the origin of Christianity. It was in this decade that the optimism which had been associated with the doctrine of evolution was challenged as superficial and unwarranted. A halt had been called to the progressive capitulation of theology to the categories and presuppositions of science. The culture of Western civilization was under fire as based upon a philosophy which was now declared false.

"All this was a post-world war development. It issued from springs which began flowing in the first decade after the war, and were at first regarded as mere sporadic signs of reaction due to European chaos and despair. In the second post-war decade, however, this development assumed formidable proportions as a highly sophisticated attack on the foundations of liberal theology, and the hitherto dominant liberalism was put on the defensive."—*Ibid.*

Most of the thirty-four contributors to *The Christian Century* series expressed some degree of change of belief. The confident Liberalism of a former day is gone. The dogmatism is largely missing. Perhaps most marked is the rediscovery by many of these men of the perversity of the human heart. *Sin,* a term almost outmoded by Liberals for a generation, has come back into their vocabularies as describing a grim and grisly reality. Gone is the foolish notion that material advance implies also moral advance. Probably the most vigorous in expressing his viewpoint is Reinhold Niebuhr, whose earlier views have already been quoted. His contribution to the symposium is entitled "Ten Years That Shook My World," and contains this withering indictment of Liberalism:

"Liberal Christianity, in short, tended to follow modern culture in estimating both the stature and the virtue of man. It did not recognize that man is a spirit who can find a home neither in nature nor in reason, but only in God. . . .

"For this reason, the simple reinterpretation of the Kingdom of God into the law of progress, in the thought of liberal Christianity, is an equally serious betrayal of essential insights of the Christian faith to the prejudices of modern culture. Obviously there is progress of all kinds in human history, including progress in aerial bombing and the effective use of the radio for the dissemination of political lies. There is progress from immaturity to maturity in every field of endeavor. But there is not a single bit of evidence to prove that good triumphs over evil in this constant development of history. History points to a goal beyond itself, and not merely to an eternity which negates history." —*The Christian Century*, April 26, 1939.*

A little later, Harry Emerson Fosdick, widely quoted Modernist preacher, wrote a book entitled *Living Under Tension*. The second world war had already begun, with Liberalism as one of its victims. Fosdick set off the tragedy of our time against the bright hopes that controlled men in earlier years. Said he: "Every path that man is traveling today leads to the rediscovery of sin." He contrasts the hopes once placed in scientific inventions with the deadly war uses to which they are put. He reminds us of the confidence once placed in education: "A century ago in Boston, Horace Mann [crusader for universal common school education] believed that crime could be practically eliminated

---

* Those who wish to pursue further the subject of authoritative Modernist admissions are referred to an impressive, two-volume work by Reinhold Niebuhr entitled *The Nature and Destiny of Man*, published in 1943 by Charles Scribner's Sons. As the preface states, this work represents the two series of Gifford Lectures given at the University of Edinburgh under the general title of "The Nature and Destiny of Man: A Christian Interpretation." Probably no other present-day work has more fully or more critically examined the whole subject of man in relation to modern culture and in relation to the rosy theories of human nature that have distinguished our day.

# ANSWERS TO OBJECTIONS

in this country by increase in the size and number of our tax-supported schools."

## "High Intelligence and Low Desire"

Fosdick sorrowfully observes that today we have "a combination of high intelligence and low desires." He exclaims: "How easily some people have supposed that the human problem could be solved!" And immediately gives these two illustrations:

"In 1893 Hiram Maxim, speaking of his new and terrible gun, said: 'It will make war impossible.' That is all he knew about human nature. In 1892 Alfred Nobel, the inventor of dynamite, said that his new dynamite factories might end war sooner than peace congresses. That is all he knew about human nature. This incomprehensible monster, man, has it in him to use for wholesale destruction things a thousand times worse than dynamite and Maxim guns."

Fosdick sums up the whole matter by saying that there has been "a radical failure to see that there is something wrong in human nature itself," and that something is what earlier theologians called "original sin." (Excerpts published in *The Christian Advocate*, March 19, 1942, under the title "Today's Rediscovery of Sin.")

The ever-enlarging and ever-more-terrifying second world war brought still more admissions of disillusionment from the religious Liberals who had stood at the forefront in proclaiming the doctrine of a hopeful, sunny future. And let it be remembered in this connection that while the idea of progress was first promoted by confessedly godless skeptics, that idea was taken over and preached by Liberal ministers with a new and authoritative fervor that quite outdid the rationalists. Hence the decline of the idea in religious circles is more significant than its decline in secular ranks.

In the summer of 1945 we find Daniel Day Williams, of the Chicago Theological Seminary, writing these confessional lines:

"Today the world wears an aspect which it did not have for most men of the nineteenth century. We who thought of ourselves as men of good will creating a peaceful world are once more in the holocaust of war. . . .

"The change is not only in the outward situation but in the inward spirit of the contemporary man. Something like an unmasking of our human nature has taken place. We have thought of ourselves as men of good will building the good society. But was this not the conventional cloak for our real lack of love? Are we quite sure we can distinguish in ourselves that which is truly the spirit of unselfish giving from that which is merely the covert disguise of self-centeredness? . . .

"How, then, can we think of the world as the subject of God's redemption? For the answer to this question contemporary theology is turning back to the Reformation doctrine that this world as we now experience it is alienated from its true source and destiny. A fundamental wrongness has entered the world in the form of sin."—*The Journal of Religion*, July, 1945.

Williams admits that the basic concepts of Liberalism must be greatly revised, but he still feels that something can be done to improve our world within modest limits. Says he:

"There are, indeed, limits to the possible transformation of the world. The sober language of Christian realism will not forget the vast mystery of evil and death. It will confess the resistance to God's way in the soul of man. But no real good can come in history unless men are willing to do what they can with human problems. Hopelessness produces helplessness."—*Ibid.*

### The Primary Liberal Premise Deserted

What a chastened and subdued Liberalism those sentences reveal! A few years ago such a declaration would have been considered, for what it really is, a clear-cut desertion from the basic belief that has distinguished Liberalism, the belief in the inevitable and glorious advance of man both morally and materially in this very present world.

Willard L. Sperry, formerly dean of the Harvard Divinity School, writing at the close of the second world war, observes how the first world war did not "affect our native optimism adversely," that this optimism began to crack with the great depression of 1929 and the events that followed after. Then he adds:

# ANSWERS TO OBJECTIONS

"Nothing was farther from the thought of those of us who were already launched into our ministry before 1914 than that we should ever live to see any such event of the dimensions of the First World War, let alone two such wars. For us, let us say in the year 1910, great wars were things of the past, all fought and finished long before. We read about them in a famous book, which had been in every boy's library, called *Fifteen Decisive Battles of the World.*

"Therefore there was good warrant for devoting ourselves to the task of perfecting the social order as rapidly as possible. . . .

"Organized Christianity was wholly unprepared for the event [of two world wars], not merely because it was hopelessly divided and thus unable to speak with a single voice, but because it had not regarded any such eventuality as within the realm of historical probability."
—*Christendom*, Spring, 1946.

## Secularists Make Confession

The shock and disillusionment of two world wars, while greatest for Liberal theologians, who had buttressed their hopes of world progress with the apparent sanctions of the Christian religion, has been very great for nonchurchmen as well. Leaders of thought in every realm of life have been quite completely disenchanted. Their social planning, their confidence in the inherent qualities of man, who needs only a decent chance and a good environment in order to blossom out to perfection—all this has proved to be unfounded.

Nicholas Murray Butler made the following confession in a closing paragraph of his 1944 report as president of Columbia University:

"The history of the world's religion, philosophy, literature and science records wisdom on the highest plane and of most convincing character. Yet it is that wisdom which has shown itself unable to control the conduct of mankind. Fundamentally, the ruling force is conduct, whether that conduct be moral or immoral. If moral, there is hope for the world. If immoral, there is not only no hope, but no prospect of anything but increasing and complete destruction of all that has been accomplished for civilization during the past five thousand years."—*Columbia University, Bulletin of Information,* Forty-fifth Series, no. 5, Dec. 30, 1944, p. 52.

# COLLAPSE OF IDEA OF WORLD PROGRESS

A University of Toronto lecturer on political economy, Arnold S. Nash, makes this general statement as to the collapse of Liberalist tenets:

"According to liberalism man is fundamentally good and his inherent goodness is indicated in his increasing capacity, by using his intelligence, to solve all the problems that come his way. Such is the basis of the liberal belief in progress—the dogma that man, like the world itself, is slowly getting better so that history becomes a progressive realization of man's ideals as defects in social and economic organization are remedied and education becomes more widespread.

"Such are the essential outlines of the faith of the typical university teacher of our era in the liberal democratic countries. It is this faith which is now [1943] being shaken far more rudely by events than it ever could be by argument. The tragic happenings of the last few years have indicated not only failure of man as man but in particular the failure of thinking man."—*The University and the Modern World*, pp. 30, 31.

## The Trouble Is With Man Himself

An editorial in a learned quarterly well reveals the changed feeling and the disillusionment of secular thinkers produced by World War II. Commenting on "the starvation camps like Belsen and Buchenwald and the annihilation camps like Maidenek," the editor observes:

"It is not science that has destroyed the world, despite all the gloomy forebodings of the earlier prophets. It is man who has destroyed man. He has destroyed him face to face, with forethought and without pity. And he has not needed the newest weapons of science. He has used the oldest weapons of hunger and the bludgeon and fire.

"This will be a blow to the artist and the social thinker. . . .

"The basic assumption of twentieth-century social theory has been that mankind is caught in a tragic paradox: that man's brain creates the things his will cannot control. This has been proved true by the event. But what we must now add to it is that man's will creates the things that paralyze his brain and brutalize his heart. And we must add that man's heart has proved to be a soil in which it is possible for evil to flower.

"We are the fortunate survivors who are able to witness the crumbling of the fascist house of death. But we must not allow ourselves to

663

forget that the men who built this house of death were also men. Their impulses were our impulses, their instinctive endowments ours, their biological inheritance ours, their historical memories ours. . . .

"The axis of interest will now have to shift to man himself and his essential nature."—*The American Scholar*, Summer, 1945.

What might have been left of the doctrine of inevitable progress and the perfectibility of man was finally blasted by the atomic bomb, which not only shook the earth, but also the minds of men in a way they had never been shaken before. In comment on the bomb, Raymond B. Fosdick, president of the Rockefeller Foundation, observes:

"As modern man looks in the mirror today, the reflected image is not what he has imagined himself to be. We are apparently closer to barbarism than we fondly believed. The idea of automatic progress—the upward and onward march of the race—seems curiously unreal in the light of what we have done in these last years. . . .

"We are called upon to deal not only with the explosive power of the atomic bomb but with the equally explosive energy of human personality, and that energy can be just as devastating if released in the wrong direction. It is not the weapon so much as it is the human beings who may wish to use it that constitute the real danger. . . .

"Modern man—the end product of all the humanizing influences of sixty centuries—thus comes to the end of this war; and in the looking-glass we seem to see the image, not of a being grown kindly and tolerant with the years, but of one whose primitive emotions lie just below the surface, and who is easily capable of discarding the principles wrought out on Sinai and the Areopagus whenever they stand in his way. J. A. Hobson's characterization of twentieth-century man appears at first glance not too inaccurate: 'A naked Polynesian, parading in top hat and spats.'"—*The New York Times Magazine,* Dec. 30, 1945.

Writing in similar vein, a psychologist thus points to the real cause of terror in the Atomic Age:

"Perhaps one reason why man becomes terrified at the ominous possibilities of releasing atomic energy, is that he has so recently been confronted by the fact that there are forces just as powerful and as dangerous locked up within himself."—GRACE R. FOSTER in *The American Scholar,* Summer, 1946.

The editor of *The Christian Century,* writing under the title

"The Atomic Bomb and the Christian Faith," in this way sums up the chief significance of atomic energy for the Christian church:

"We are thus brought to the final test under which Christianity must prove itself equal to discharge its religious responsibility in a world community; namely, it must be able to do something radical about man. We are told by the scientists that the possible destroyer of the earth as the habitation of man is none other than man himself. . . . Science thus throws the whole question raised by the atomic bomb into the lap of the Christian faith. Something radical must be done about man.

"When we talk about the nature of man, we are standing on ground that has been pre-empted by Christianity. On this ground, science and Christianity now meet face to face. With one voice they declare that the future is precarious and with one voice they declare that it is precarious because of man. Christianity puts its finger upon that in man's nature which science now gravely fears may cause his destruction and the destruction of the earth with him. Science and Christianity are now looking at the same thing in man. Science has no word for it, but Christianity has. That word is *sin*."—March 13, 1946.

And now, as if two world wars, capped by the explosive discovery of the atomic bomb, were not enough, we hear dread forecasts of a greater horror, the hydrogen bomb. Though hidden behind a veil of secrecy, enough is known about the hydrogen bomb to indicate that it is a fearful advance over the atomic bomb.

### Confessions of Atomic Scientists

At the close of the second world war a group of nuclear physicists, realizing the potential destruction that resided in the product of their brains and hands, banded themselves into a society with a view to promoting plans for the control of atomic energy. They lectured to service clubs and other groups. They founded a journal, *Bulletin of the Atomic Scientists*, in which they sought further to set forth the need of controls. How poorly they succeeded in their endeavors they confess in a most revealing editorial in the January, 1951, issue of the *Bulletin*. The editor recounts the educational activities of the scientists during the preceding five years, and remarks: "Scientists—whose profession requires a recognition of facts, however unpleasant—cannot but admit the fact that their campaign has failed." This leads him to raise the morbid and self-answering question: "What then have we to show for five years of effort, except the relief of having 'spoken and saved our souls'—and the doubtful satisfaction of having been right in our gloomy predictions?"

Into the crooked and suffocating confines of this question mark may now be compressed what remains of the glory and grandeur of a world that formerly thought it needed only the operation of a law of progress, directed by the brains of scientists, to build a heaven on earth! Well has someone observed that the real problem before us today is not the new atom but the old Adam!

In the light of all this testimony, and much more that might be offered, it is not unreasonable to conclude that the doctrine of world progress is bankrupt today. To sum up—there were two pillars on which the doctrine was reared:

1. That man is inherently good or at least that he has infinite potentialities of goodness, and that he needs only better education, better environment, and better opportunities in order to bring out the best in him and cause him to slough off any remaining taint of brute inheritance.

2. That there is a deep-moving and all-pervasive law of progress that leads the whole creation onward and upward, which law finds its best scientific proof in the theory of evolution, and its best practical demonstration in the marvelous developments of the modern scientific age.

## Two Pillars of Doctrine Collapse

These two pillars that so long upheld the imposing edifice of world progress have today fallen as surely as if a modern Samson had encircled them. The figure is apt. Ancient Samson was apparently under complete control, blinded and chained by his captors, who reveled in the thought that no longer would their lives be insecure. The Samson of war, boasted modern man, is robbed of power, and chained by international laws, mutual understandings of civilized peoples, and the general progress of mankind. But two world wars, like the two hairy arms of the literal giant, Samson, have brought down the modern house of delusive progress. Beneath the ruins lie the crushed hopes, not only of modern Philistines, but of many who have paid at least lip service to the God of heaven.

Speaking literally, the so-called law of progress remains a figment of the mind of philosophers, a piece of wishful thinking. The theory of evolution, even if we were to grant for the sake of argument that it has been proved, now provides no support for the idea of progress. The latest in evolutionistic thinking departs far from the idea of early enthusiasts who saw evolution carrying us all upward as surely as an escalator lifts us up. Today, careful thinkers in that field confess they are not sure that evolution necessarily means progress. Rather, it may mean only adaptation for various forms of life, and possible annihilation for other forms that fail to adapt themselves to changing environment. Better education for the masses has resulted, not in less crime, as forecast by the public-school pioneer, Horace Mann, but in more cunning criminals. Better living conditions, symbolized often by more bathtubs in homes, have resulted in cleaner bodies, but not cleaner minds. Science, with its inventions and discoveries, stands revealed, not as the agent of progress, but as the handmaiden of destruction and chaos. Finally, man, the object of romantic eulogies by rationalists and liberal churchmen, stands exposed for what he really is, not a steadily evolving god, but a sorry creature whose good qualities, whatever they may be, are more than offset by his evil ones. With disillusionment quite complete, there are few who would question the present appropriateness of the inspired words: "The whole world lieth in wickedness."

What is the significance, for Adventists, of the rise and fall of the idea of progress? The question will be answered in the next three chapters.

# CHAPTER 15

# The First Angel's Message

IN THE two preceding chapters the rise and the decline of the idea of progress and of the perfectibility of man have been traced. The facts there set forth bear a most important relationship to the central teachings of the Advent movement, the three angels' messages.

Through the years we have often been guilty of attempting at one and the same time to prove both too little and too much in our treatment of this moot subject of the goodness or badness of the world. And to the extent we have done this, we have befogged the issue and have failed to show the full relationship of the subject to the threefold message.

And how have we been guilty, at times, of attempting to prove more than we need to prove? By seeking to prove that the very present generation is vastly worse in its morals, its practices, its gambling, its dissipation, its lawlessness, than any preceding generation. And to support this claim we offer, for example, newspaper clippings showing the appalling conditions presently existing in the world—crime, drunkenness, debauchery, and other debasing practices.

Probably no one would challenge the claim that the world today presents a black and sordid picture, and that in certain ways it undoubtedly is worse than when our fathers and grandfathers lived. But a critic of Adventism may rightly contend that proper perspective calls for a survey of centuries, not simply a generation or two. And such a critic need not be a believer in the idea of progress in order to raise a historically fortified objection that the record of former centuries could hardly be less black than that of the present. Some objectors may even remind us that Adventist teaching places the Dark Ages in the past, and glories in the spiritual enlightenment brought by the Protestant Reformation.

All this and much more can be, and often is, cited by those acquainted with history who wish to challenge the sweeping and unqualified claim sometimes made by Adventist preachers that the world today is much worse in morals and practices than it ever was in any past generation. And are Adventist critics correct in declaring that the picture of the past is black as an Egyptian night? The answer emphatically is, Yes, for all history makes most depressing reading, being one long chronicle of dark and dastardly deeds committed by sinful men. Then what is the weak spot in the argument sometimes presented by our ministers that the world is so very much worse today than it has ever been before?

### Tried to Prove More Than Necessary

The answer is, we have sought to prove more than we needed to prove. And we have been led into doing this primarily because our theological opponents have been insisting through the long years that the world is steadily improving. We set out to prove that they were dead wrong, by presenting evidence to show that the world is very, very much worse. And there is nothing more pathetic than for a man who has a good case, to weaken it by trying to prove more than he needs to. The Bible paints a picture of evil rampant in the last days, of "perilous times," of abounding iniquity. How true that picture is. We see it before our eyes. But the Bible paints an equally dark picture of the past centuries, which we describe with vigor and horror as the Dark Ages. Then it was that the Scripture was fulfilled, that he that "killeth you will think that he doeth God service." And it was during these long centuries, declare some critics, that there can be found a sufficient basis for the idea of increasing iniquity that is deduced from the text that "evil men and seducers shall wax worse and worse."

## ANSWERS TO OBJECTIONS

But someone may ask: Then what is the real point in the Biblical statements that describe the evil state of our world in the last day? The reasonable answer is: To protect us against the delusive idea of progress and man's perfectibility, that has captured and controlled the thinking of churchmen as well as secularists during all the years that the Advent movement has been in the world. From the very outset the Advent pioneers were met with the bold declaration that world betterment lay ahead. But those pioneers, and we who followed them, were not led astray by this deception. There stood the warning words from Paul: "This know also, that in the last days perilous times shall come." Our very insistence on the literal truth of such a statement protected us from the delusion of progress and placed us immediately in conflict with that prevailing view.

We took our stand on the premise that there is no Scriptural ground for believing that conditions will be better. In that we were, and are, correct. If we are able to show from Scripture and history that man is not rising to moral heights, that today it is true, even as it was nineteen hundred years ago, that "the whole world lieth in wickedness," what more need we prove?

### Secondary Reason for Unwarranted Conclusion

A secondary reason why some among us have sought to prove more than we need to prove regarding the wickedness of the world lies in the fact, already alluded to, that we make comparisons between our fathers' day and ours, and hasten to draw therefrom long-range conclusions that affect all past centuries. Furthermore, those comparisons have most frequently been made in America. In this land Adventist theological thinking was first shaped.

Now in the last generation the population of America has rapidly moved from the country to the cities, which have ever been centers of evil. It is a significant fact that Mrs. White, in her descriptions of abounding evil in the last days, focuses on the cities. (See, for example, *Testimonies for the Church*, vol. 9, pp. 89-96.) There is no debating the fact that as multitudes have moved to great cities the moral tone of the populace has been lowered.

One cannot read far into Mrs. White's descriptions of increasing evils and of the supposedly fireproof structures rising in the great cities without being impressed that her prophetic eye was most directly focused on America, the land that cradled God's Advent movement, the country so directly described by the revelator John.

But Mrs. White has left on record a description of other lands and other days. When she was transported in vision to the Dark Ages, she penned a picture before which all else, even the present, seems to pale. And well she might, for that was the time of which our Lord spoke when He said that if those days were not shortened no flesh would be saved.

It is not difficult to harmonize her fearful portrayal of the Dark Ages with her picture of the last days as wicked beyond words, and thus apparently worse than all past times. In her description of the "Conditions in the Cities" she declares:

"From age to age the Lord has made known the manner of His working. When a crisis has come, He has revealed Himself, and has interposed to hinder the working out of Satan's plans."—*Testimonies*, vol. 9, p. 91.

### Ebb and Flow of Tides of Evil

Here is clearly set forth the thought of rising tides of evil, which seek ever and anon to engulf the whole world, but which are driven back by the interposition of God. The engulfing flood at the time of the Roman Empire was driven back by our Lord's first advent. The blackness of the Dark Ages was rolled back by the Reformation. For the elect's sake the days of satanic persecution were shortened. Later, men like Wesley arose in the power of the Spirit to revive men religiously. Wesley has been credited with saving England from a frightful revolution such as overran France, where peasants cried unavailingly for bread and then arose to slay their rulers.

This view of the sorry, sinister, and so-called Christian Era gives us a true picture of the history of evil, a picture that comports with the statement quoted from Mrs. White. For us to convey the idea of a world steadily sinking, without any periods of even partial reversal of the trend, is to leave no place for the mighty workings of God upon men and nations at various times. That fact should give us pause.

We may properly make some sobering comparisons between grandfather's day and ours, and in so doing we shall find ourselves squaring with the Spirit of prophecy. But that is something quite different from those sweeping, unqualified assertions that some of us have made at times regarding the awful iniquity of the present as compared with *all* the past.

Furthermore, even in our comparisons of two closely connected generations in the setting of Mrs. White's words, we need to be restrained, and for a particular reason. We read in the Spirit of prophecy a dark picture of our day—which is our proper justification for describing it as very evil. But Spirit of prophecy descriptions of today have a way of merging into a picture of what the world will be like in the last hours of earth's history, when God's Spirit shall be completely withdrawn. Then indeed will be a state of evil without parallel, unless it be the hours just preceding the Flood. If we keep in mind that a prophet takes in the whole sweep of the future, we will be better able to make judicious use of the inspired words of the servant of God that not only describe the evils of our day but also of all the remaining days until the final hour when Satan holds complete sway over a rebellious world.

### Failed to Prove All We Might

But if we have erred at times in attempting to prove too much in regard to the iniquity of the world today, we have also erred at times in failing to see how fully and forcefully the sorry state of the world supports our preaching of the three angels' messages. In other words, we have often failed to prove all that could be proved from the facts before us regarding the secularization of the world and the apostasy in Christendom. In this and the following two chapters will be shown the relation of these facts to the first, second, and third angels' messages, which are the heart of our message to the world, and hence the chief reason for our existence as a distinctive people.

What constitutes the first angel's message? A command and an announcement. The command: "Fear God, and give glory to him; . . . and worship him that made heaven, and earth, and the sea, and the fountains of waters." The announcement: "The hour of his judgment is come." (See Rev. 14:6, 7.) The angel who gives this combined command and announcement is described as "having the everlasting gospel to preach unto them that dwell on the earth." And rightly so. The inspired explanation of the appalling depravity into which the human race sank in its early days, and in which it has continued to lie, is that men turned away from God. "Because that, when they knew God, they glorified him not as God, neither were thankful; but became vain in their imaginations, and their foolish heart was darkened. . . . Who changed the truth of God into a lie, and worshipped and served the creature more than the Creator. . . . And even as they did not like to retain God in their knowledge, God gave them over to a reprobate mind." Rom. 1:21-28. The Gentiles are described as "being alienated from the life of God," and having therefore "given themselves over unto lasciviousness, to work all uncleanness with greediness." Eph. 4:18, 19.

### The Central Message of the Prophets

The burden of the message of holy men and prophets through the long ages has been that men should turn to the true God, the God who is ready to forgive, but also who is of purer eyes than to behold iniquity. Coupled with this has been the warning that God will come in judgment upon evildoers. The sad refrain in the chronicles of Israel is that they "forgat God" and turned to idols, so that they finally did worse than the vile heathen round about them. The appeal to Israel was: "Repent, and turn yourselves from your idols." "Turn ye, turn ye from your evil ways; for why will ye die, O house of Israel?" Eze. 14:6; 33:11.

When Christ came He declared: "This is life eternal, that they might know thee the only true God, and Jesus Christ, whom thou hast sent." John 17:3. Christ came to reveal to men the Father as compassionate, but also as holy, as perfect. And His command was: "Be ye therefore perfect, even as your Father which is in heaven is perfect." With this He coupled a warning of a day of wrath and of judgment to come.

The manner in which the apostles preached is revealed in Paul's description of the results of the gospel on the Thessalonians: "Ye turned to God from idols to serve the living and true God; and to wait for his Son from heaven, whom he raised from the dead, even Jesus, which delivered us from the wrath to come." 1 Thess. 1:9, 10. Again: "God was in Christ, reconciling the world unto himself. . . . Now then we are ambassadors for Christ, as though God did beseech you by us: we pray you in Christ's stead, be ye reconciled to God." 2 Cor. 5:19, 20.

When Paul spoke to the Athenians he described the true God as the one "that made the world and all things therein," and called on them to "repent" and serve this true God "because he hath appointed a day, in the which he will judge the world." Acts 17:24, 30, 31.

### Truly the Everlasting Gospel

In the setting of these inspired passages how truly may the first angel's message be described as the preaching of the "everlasting gospel"! The fact that the words, "hour of his judgment," in the message, focus on the first part of God's great judgment work, does not set it apart from the message of coming judgment that prophets and apostles described, for the investigative judgment is the first phase of God's final judgment of all mankind. The uniqueness of the judgment message in Revelation 14:6, 7 is this: it is to be given at a certain time, in fulfillment of prophecy, and it is to be the last appeal to men to make ready for the great day of God. As Adventists we believe that message was due to be preached in 1844 and thereafter until the final climax. We have seen in this message of judgment a call to men to make ready for the second coming of Christ, for the execution of the judgment is at the coming of Christ, and is the reason for His coming.

This message of Revelation 14:6, 7, along with the two messages immediately following, is of the essence of the truth we are to preach to men from the day of the rise of the Advent movement until Christ comes. But we can preach it in its fullness and with its greatest convicting power only as we see it in the setting of events developing in the world at the time the Advent movement was due to arise. Those developing events have been described briefly in the two preceding chapters. There it was shown that the Christian world began to break away from the control of apostate Rome in the sixteenth and seventeenth centuries. While some, following the teaching of the Protestant Reformers, exchanged the authority of the Catholic Church for the authority of the Bible, a large and steadily increasing number exchanged churchly authority for the authority of reason. Rationalism led men's minds ever farther away from God, the facts and forces of nature being increasingly explained so as to leave God out of the picture. As one writer well says, "The history of the modern Western mind may be said to be the history of a gradual secularization of man."—WILHELM PAUCK in *The Church Against the World*, p. 34. The blind forces of nature were becoming a substitute for God. A prominent writer of the late nineteenth century picturesquely declared:

"Thus has gradually grown up, without our confessing it, a kind of scientific polytheism—one great Jehovah, perhaps, but with many agents or sub-gods, each independent, efficient, and doing all the real work in his own domain. The names of these, our gods, are gravity, light, heat, electricity, magnetism, chemical affinity, etc., and we are practically saying: 'These be your gods, O Israel, which brought you out of the land of Egyptian darkness and ignorance. These be the only

gods ye need fear, and serve, and study the ways of.' "—JOSEPH LE-
CONTE, *Evolution and its Relation to Religious Thought*, p. 298.

That was the picture when the Advent movement began.
How fitting the message: "Fear God, and give glory to him."
"Worship him that made heaven, and earth." When men were
declaring that the endless future held only increasing progress,
how appropriate to sound the warning of judgment at hand!

## The Existence of God Challenged

The evidence presented in the preceding chapters reveals
that the secularization so widespread at the time of the rise of
Adventism has become almost universal today, that the very
idea of God has been strongly challenged within the church itself
by a school of thought called Humanism.

How strong that challenge has become in the last few decades
is clearly revealed in the address by J. D. Jones, the moderator
at the Fifth International Congregational Council, Bournemouth,
England. Speaking on the subject "The Recovery of Our Sense
of God," he declared in part:

"The facts are that at the moment the Church is to a large extent
neglected, and religion seems to be losing its hold over vast masses
of mankind. And this neglect of the Church and decay of religion is
a symptom of something deeper and more serious still. That deeper
and more serious thing is this—the very existence of God is being
challenged and denied. The Church all down the centuries has had
to contend earnestly for the faith once for all delivered to the saints.
It is familiar with battle. But when I think of the conflicts through
which it has passed—the fight that raged around the question of the
Person of Christ, the fight which Luther fought for the freedom of
the Christian soul, the more recent disputes and controversies about
the Bible and its inspiration, and the dates and authorship of its various
books—they all seem to me to be affairs of 'outposts' and 'outworks'
compared to the fight that is upon us today. The attack today is not
upon the outworks but upon the citadel itself. It is the existence of
God that is being called in question.

"Popular writers like H. G. Wells practically repudiate the idea
of a personal God; Bernard Shaw talks about the 'life force'; others
dissolve Him into 'the sum of all ideal values'; while others like

Bertrand Russell deny Him altogether and declare that 'the individual soul must struggle alone with what of courage it can command against the whole weight of a Universe that cares nothing for its hopes and fears.' The teaching of the Scientists, backed by certain of the New Psychologists, who reduce God to a projection of the human mind, percolates through magazine and novel into the minds of the men and women of our day. It creates their intellectual atmosphere, and in that atmosphere, touched by what Mr. Walter Lippmann calls the 'acids of modernity,' belief in God, in the Christian God, has simply dissolved."—*The Congregationalist,* July 24, 1930, p. 103.

### God and Moral Standards

When God disappears from men's minds, what is the inevitable effect upon Christian ethics, that is, upon Christian standards of morality? The Congregationalist moderator immediately answers thus:

"With the dissolving of the belief in God has come a challenge to the whole Christian ethic. Huxley and Tyndall, whatever may be said of their materialistic philosophy, were men of high ethical standards. I remember hearing Dr. Fairbairn describe John Morley (as he was then) as the best Christian in the Cabinet of which he was a member, though he was a professed agnostic and spelled the word 'God' always with a small 'g'. That was the peculiarity of the agnosticism of fifty years ago—while rejecting the Christian faith, it accepted and observed Christian ethics. But that position could not for long be maintained. Flowers will not grow if they have no root, and the Christian ethic has no compulsive authority apart from the Christian belief in God. This is the point Mr. Walter Lippmann stresses in his book, *A Preface to Morals.* Men no longer believe in a Sovereign God, a God who rules this world and who by the hand of Moses issued a moral code for His subjects, and therefore that moral code has lost its binding authority."

An eminent scientist of the early twentieth century, the late Henry Fairfield Osborn, offers similar testimony in the following admission:

"It may be said without scientific or religious prejudice that the world-wide loss of the older religious and Biblical foundation of morals has been one of the chief causes of human decadence in conduct, in literature, and in art."—*The Earth Speaks to Bryan,* p. 63.

677

These quotations are typical of many that might be given in proof that the disappearance of God results in a disappearance also of Christian standards of morality. Without belief in a "Sovereign God, a God who rules this world," the "moral code" has no "binding authority." The relationship which the Bible sets up between forgetting God and falling into sin and immorality is proved true again down here in the last days of earth's history, even as it has been proved true innumerable times before.

### Present Compared With Past

The chief reason why this present-day general departure from God has not reflected itself more sharply in a lower moral level as compared with that of former generations is that a great majority of those living in earlier generations were also without God. No contradiction is stated. In the Colonial Era in America only about five per cent of the population were church members, the ninety-five per cent presumably had no clearly defined Christian idea of God to lose from their minds. In England, and certainly on the Continent, spiritual conditions were no better. Wesley's preaching to England's unchurched masses vividly illustrates this fact. But in earlier generations the clergy all held to the elementary doctrine of a personal God, and to the limited number who actually came under their influence they taught this doctrine.

In our modern times the apostles of progress have pointed with assurance to the fact that more than fifty per cent of the population in the United States are church members, as though that in itself proved that the country was far more Christian, far more moral, than in past generations. But what they forget is that the ministers who preach to this fifty per cent—or those of them that attend church—have been deeply tainted with skeptical, godless theories, some of them even to the point of accepting Humanism, which is simply a "poetic form of atheism."

In former times the uneducated and often unchurched masses might have little consciousness of God, for lack of positive training in religion. In our present day it is true that many humble church members believe sincerely the Bible. But the generally educated masses, despite their church contacts, often have an actively negative attitude toward God because of the skeptical theories they are frequently taught in church as well as in school. Thus it proves true that a day of great intellectual enlightenment does not produce a generation lighted by the truth of God. That is why darkness continues to cover the earth and gross darkness the people. And that is why the world still lieth in wickedness.

## A Most Timely Message

All this is but another way of saying that the call to men to worship the God who made heaven and earth (Rev. 14:6, 7), which was timely in 1844, has gained increasing timeliness as the years have passed by. This fact we need to realize and to stress in our preaching.

Reverting to the evidence of the preceding chapter: In view of the collapse of the idea of progress, how timely the message that the hour of God's judgment has come—judgment on a world that "lieth in wickedness"—and that a better world is soon to be set up by the Second Advent of Christ!

One of the most telling arguments set forth for the need of the Second Advent is the obvious and easily established fact that the world is no better than it was in past centuries. The edge of the blade of Second Advent preaching has been repeatedly dulled through the long generations past by the corrosive heresy that the world will gradually be improved by the efforts of man until we shall have a virtual Paradise here. The blade can be kept to razor sharpness by affirming the fact that the world still "lieth in wickedness." There are only two solutions of the tragedy of our world that have been offered by churchmen throughout the history of Christendom: (1) the improvement of the world by man's efforts, and (2) the renovation of the world by the supernatural appearing of Christ. If the former solution stands exposed as impossible of accomplishment there remains only the latter, the Biblical teaching for which we stand.

ANSWERS TO OBJECTIONS

Instead of dealing with the question of the relative wickedness of the world as simply one of a series of signs showing the *nearness* of the Advent—and attempting to prove more than we easily can —we should give to the question a more basic significance by showing that the evident failure of the world to rise from the pit of iniquity in which it has wallowed for ages, constitutes a powerful reason *why* Christ should come.

## Excellent Setting for Adventist Preaching

Let us repeat, the bankruptcy of the doctrine of world progress, because of the exposure of the innate evil of the human heart, makes a marvelous setting in which to preach the Advent. With the idea of world progress bankrupt, Adventists should take over the receivership. We can thunder forth: It is the Second Advent or nothing! We actually need not prove that the world is one whit worse than it ever was in order for that thundering challenge to echo and re-echo over the whole earth and to demand the sober attention of all men. And the thunder of our challenge is now reinforced by the roar of atomic bombs. A wicked world is today able to do what it formerly could not do—destroy itself! Thus our challenge can now ring out with irresistible power: It is the Second Advent or chaos!

If we can give so awesome a message as that to the world, while standing on the undebatable and simple premise that "the whole world lieth in wickedness," why endanger the force of that message by unnecessary, and sometimes questionable, arguments as to whether in this or that particular way the world is worse than formerly?

Undoubtedly there *are* ways in which men are worse than they were at some other periods in the past. Certain kinds of evil take on new forms and new potency at different times. Today, for example, the evils of war are the most frightful ever, and have stimulated men to depths of brutality and mass murder hardly paralleled in world history. The grisly facts of World War II neutralize quite completely such proofs of world progress as abolition of slavery, better economic conditions for the masses, and the like.

But why enter into needless debate on the relative awfulness of different forms of iniquity that sweep men down to the pit in one generation or another? There may have been a day, earlier in our history, when it seemed worth while thus to debate, because the idea of progress was dominant. But surely not today! Our erstwhile opponents in this area of discussion now quite generally make abject admission that man is not progressing, that on the contrary there is something desperately the matter with him and with the world.

### Changing Battle Lines

Lines of battle in theology, even as in literal warfare, change from time to time. To attack a deserted position is, to say the least, a sorry waste of energy and ammunition. That long-held, strategic sector of the enemy lines known as the idea of world progress is now almost completely abandoned. Those who once confidently attacked our opposing position, the supernatural Second Advent, must now spend their time reforming their lines because of having to abandon their world progress sector, from which they formerly sallied forth. We can today boldly deploy ourselves over the strategically important field known as the doctrine of man's inherently evil nature, with hardly a challenging shot's being fired. We even find joining us on that field some from the other side who frankly declare that they now believe our side in the controversy is right. Standing thus today on that strategic field, we can again sound our battle cry: The Second Advent or chaos! and go forth more successfully than ever before to win men to the banner of our soon-coming Lord.

What a day in which to preach the first angel's message!

# CHAPTER 16

# The Second Angel's Message

A ND THERE followed another angel, saying, Babylon is fallen, is fallen, that great city, because she made all nations drink of the wine of the wrath of her fornication." Rev. 14:8.

"Babylon of the Apocalypse is the professed church united with the world."—URIAH SMITH, *Thoughts on Daniel and the Revelation*, p. 648, rev. ed. The fall of Babylon is a spiritual one, and is due to two causes: (1) alliance with civil power, described in the Scriptures as fornication with the kings of the earth; and (2) teaching false doctrine. On this point Mrs. E. G. White declares:

"This cup of intoxication which she [Babylon] presents to the world, represents the false doctrines that she has accepted as the result of her unlawful connection with the great ones of the earth. Friendship with the world corrupts her faith, and in her turn she exerts a corrupting influence upon the world by teaching doctrines which are opposed to the plainest statements of Holy Writ."—*The Great Controversy*, p. 388.

Now, it is not hard to prove, as regards Roman Catholicism, that Babylon is fallen. But Babylon involves all Christendom. Protestantism can easily be proved guilty on the first count—alliance with the kings of the earth. Even from the earliest days of Protestantism there have been state churches. Nor is it difficult to show that throughout most of Protestant history there has been a distressing degree of conformity to the world and lack of godliness. But religious bodies are chiefly distinguished by the beliefs they hold. Thus in order to show that the second angel's message is truly and completely being fulfilled in our day, we must show that Protestantism has fallen away from true doctrines.

Protestantism *arose* from Rome in the sixteenth century. It did not *fall* then. True, the creeds formulated by Protestant bodies retarded the rise from the errors of Rome. But the direction, in general, was upward toward Scriptural truth and the purity of the gospel. The great Protestant bodies, as they arose, stood firmly on the high platform of the authority of the Bible, the personality of God, the deity of Christ, the blood atonement, and the Second Advent of Christ in judgment.

Although these and related primary truths of the Scripture were not always clearly and correctly held, and though they were sometimes mingled with errors of Rome, we can still truly say that the rise of Protestantism marked a rise in spiritual understanding and doctrine.

### The Timing of the Prophecy

But the prophecy being considered declares that "Babylon is fallen." And when should we look for this prophecy to be fulfilled, or at least for the message concerning its fulfillment to be proclaimed? The second cannot precede the first, and the first began to be proclaimed in a definite, organized way about the fourth decade of the nineteenth century. Mrs. White states that the second angel's message "was first preached in the summer of 1844." —*The Great Controversy*, p. 389.

And *where* was it first preached? "It then had a more direct application to the churches of the United States."—*Ibid.* And why? Because this was "where the warning of the judgment had been most widely proclaimed and most generally rejected, and where the declension of the churches had been most rapid."—*Ibid.*

Now, was the second angel's message completely fulfilled in the year 1844? No. "The message of the second angel did not reach its complete fulfillment in 1844."—*Ibid.* And why? Writing in 1888, Mrs. White declared: "The work of apostasy has not yet reached its culmination."—*Ibid.* "The change is a progressive one, and the perfect fulfillment of Rev. 14:8 is yet future."—*Ibid.*, p. 390. Commenting further on this point of progressive fulfillment, Mrs. White declares:

683

"Revelation 18 points to the time, when as a result of rejecting the threefold warning of Rev. 14:6-12, the church will have fully reached the condition foretold by the second angel, and the people of God still in Babylon will be called upon to separate from her communion. This message is the last that will ever be given to the world; and it will accomplish its work."—*Ibid.*

## The Message the Churches Rejected

What was the message preached in 1844 which the churches "rejected" and thus set in motion a "progressive" declension that would finally fulfill completely the prophecy of Revelation 14:8? The answer is that the churches rejected the doctrine of the literal, personal Second Advent of Christ to bring an end to a world of sin and to create a new heavens and a new earth wherein dwelleth righteousness.

The churches opposed the message of the literal, personal coming of Christ with the doctrine of the spiritual coming of our Lord that put into the dim future, if ever, the actual coming. Instead of teaching that Christ would come in judgment on this present evil world, they taught the doctrine of world conversion and a temporal millennium. The facts on this have already been presented in chapter 13.

## The Real Point of Controversy

There have been critics of Adventism who sought to make high sport of our doctrine of the second angel's message by declaring that we condemned the churches of 1844 and have continued to condemn them since then because they refused to believe the false teaching that the Lord would come on October 22, 1844. But from evidence already presented it is clear that this charge is false, because it fails to state the whole case. An examination of the controversy between Adventists and the various churches in 1844 leaves no possible doubt that the real point of conflict was the question of the nature of the impending event and not the time of the occurrence of that event.

The 1844 opponents of Millerism, let it be repeated here, were generally willing to admit that Adventists followed sound principles of prophetic interpretation and that the great time prophecies were probably coming to their fulfillment in the nineteenth century. In fact, some of the opponents were as definite on the matter of prophetic time as were the Adventists under William Miller. In other words, if William Miller and the Advent preachers had proclaimed that 1844 would mark the beginning of an earthly millennium which would grow more glorious for a thousand years to come, probably no opposition would have been raised.

That the real controversy dealt with the literal versus the spiritual coming of Christ becomes even more evident when we examine the article by the Millerite leader Charles Fitch entitled "Come Out of Her, My People."* This article, apparently, was the first Millerite presentation of the prophetic subject of the fall of Babylon in relation to the command: "Come out of her, my people." Fitch's thesis was this:

Catholicism, and later on, Protestantism, when preaching the doctrine of the spiritual coming of Christ and a temporal millennium, were guilty of putting off the coming of the Lord. Hence they belonged to that company of evil servants who declare, "My Lord delayeth his coming." They lulled men to sleep in a sense of false security.

Fitch also charged that the doctrine of the spiritual reign of Christ took away from our Lord His reality and that therefore the preachers of this doctrine fell under the indictment of the apostle John: "Every spirit that confesseth not that Jesus Christ is come in the flesh is not of God: and this is that spirit of antichrist, whereof ye have heard that it should come; and even now already is it in the world." 1 John 4:3. Declared Fitch:

"To confess with the lips Jesus Christ is come in the flesh, and yet to be opposed in heart and life to the objects for which He came, is

---

* This article appeared first in a Millerite paper, *The Second Advent of Christ*, published at Cleveland, Ohio, of which Fitch was the editor. The date of the issue is July 26, 1843. The article is lengthy, occupying all of the first page, and the immediately succeeding pages. Underneath the title is the display line: "A Sermon, by C. Fitch." However, this may simply mean a printed sermon, or an article in sermon form. The references to the doctrine "Come out of her, my people," as found in Millerite literature in the summer of 1843, are in terms of Fitch's article rather than of sermons he had been preaching. The quotations in the following paragraphs are from this original article. The article was later reprinted in other Millerite papers and also in leaflet form.

certainly to be Antichrist. The spirit therefore which is of God, while it confesses that Jesus Christ is come in the flesh, will cordially embrace, and heartily enter into all the objects for which he was thus manifested. All else must be Antichrist. What then was the end for which Jesus Christ was manifested in the flesh?"

## A Personal Return of Christ

After declaring that Christ came to suffer for our sins, Fitch inquires:

"But did Jesus Christ come in the flesh for no purpose but to suffer? Hear Peter on the day of Pentecost, after he had been baptized with the Holy Ghost, and fully qualified to set forth the objects of Christ's coming. Acts 2:29, 'Men and brethren, let me freely speak to you of the patriarch David, that he is both dead and buried, and his sepulchre is with us unto this day. Therefore being a prophet, and knowing that God had sworn, with an oath to him, that of the fruit of his loins, according to the flesh, He would raise up Christ to sit on his throne: he, seeing this before, spake of the resurrection of Christ,' &c. Here we are informed that God had sworn with an oath to David, that He would raise up Christ in the flesh to sit on David's throne. Christ was therefore to come in the flesh to reign on David's throne, and was raised up from the dead with flesh and bones for that purpose, and in that same body ascended to heaven, and angels declared that He would so come again, in like manner as He went into heaven. Now, as His ascension is personal, His coming must be personal. . . .

"In the new earth wherein dwelleth righteousness, therefore, Christ will sit personally and eternally on David's throne, ruling the world in righteousness, and of His kingdom there shall be no end. . . . Hence it follows, that whoever is opposed to the personal reign of Jesus Christ over this world on David's throne, is Antichrist."

Fitch then asks: "Who is opposed to the personal reign of Christ on David's throne?" and answers thus:

"1st. The entire Roman Catholic Church. The primitive church believed in the personal reign of Christ, and looked and longed for it, and waited for His appearing, and loved it as the apostles had done before them. Justin Martyr, one of the primitive Christians, declares that this was the faith in which all the orthodox in the primitive church, agreed. But when the papacy came into power, they concluded to have Christ reign, not personally, but spiritually, and hence the

Pope entered into the stead of Christ, and undertook to rule the world for Him—claiming to be God's vicegerent on earth. Inasmuch, therefore, as the Papists wish to retain their power, we find them all opposed to Christ's coming to establish a personal reign. They are willing that Christ should reign spiritually, provided they can be His acknowledged agents, and thus bring the world to bow down wholly to their dictation, and use God's authority for their own aggrandizement."

## Protestantism Indicted With Rome

After discussing at some length the Catholic Church, Fitch raises the question:

"Is the Catholic Church only, opposed to the personal reign of Christ? What shall we say of Protestant Christendom in this respect? Among all the sects into which the Protestant church is divided, where is one that is not decidedly hostile to the Bible truth that Christ has been raised up to sit personally on David's throne? Indeed, where has such a notice originated, as that Christ is to have only a spiritual reign? There is nothing in the Bible that furnishes the least shadow of a foundation for such an idea. Paul has, however, given us a clue to the origin of the very thing. (2 Tim. 4:3, 4) 'For the time will come when they will not endure sound doctrine, but after their own lusts shall they heap to themselves teachers, having itching ears, and they shall turn away their ears from the truth, and shall be turned to fables.' This is at present true of all sects in Protestant Christendom. The sound Scriptural doctrine of the personal reign of Christ on David's throne cannot now be endured, and hence the teachers which the various sects have been heaping to themselves have turned away their ears to the groundless fable of a spiritual reign of Christ, during what is called a temporal millennium, when they expect all the world will be converted; and each sect is expecting at that time to have the predominant influence. . . . But no one of them is willing to have Christ come in person to rule the world for Himself, while they take their place at His feet to do His bidding, nor are they willing to listen for a moment to what the Bible says respecting Christ's personal coming. . . . They profess to be desiring the spiritual reign of Christ, and to be living for the conversion of the world to the religion of the crucified Nazarene. Tell them, however, that Christ is coming in person, according to the oath of God, to carry out the principles of His own religion for ever, and they are ready to fight against it with all their might."

687

# ANSWERS TO OBJECTIONS

## Conflict of Belief as to Nature of Advent

These quotations make it abundantly evident that the primary controversy between our Millerite forebears and the opposing churches was over the question of whether the coming of Christ was to be literal or spiritual. It is true that the time element, the 1844 Advent date, is brought into the discussion. But this was only in a limited, minor way after the main indictment had been brought against popular churches because of their opposition to the Scriptural doctrine of the personal coming of Christ. On the time aspect, which was the chief error in the Millerite preaching of the Second Advent, Fitch declares, for example:

"All these pretended Christian sects are particularly opposed to the idea that Christ is coming *speedily* in person, to take the dominion of the world; and *especially* to the idea that there is Bible evidence for believing that He will come during the present Jewish year."

Fitch goes on to ask the question, "What is it for God's people to come out of Babylon?" and answers thus:

"To come out of Babylon is to be converted to the true Scriptural doctrine of the personal coming and kingdom of Christ; to receive the truth on this subject with all readiness of mind as you find it plainly written out on the pages of the Bible: to love Christ's appearing, and rejoice in it, and fully and faithfully to avow to the world your unshrinking belief in God's word touching this momentous subject, and to do all in your power to open the eyes of others, and influence them to a similar course, that they may be ready to meet their Lord."

## An Appeal to the Churches

Fitch then devotes a paragraph to the time element in the Advent preaching, but when he comes to making a direct appeal a little farther on "to come out of Babylon," he focuses directly and quite exclusively on the question of spiritualizing away the Advent, as the following words reveal:

"Throw away that miserable medley of ridiculous spiritualizing nonsense with which multitudes have so long been making the word of God of none effect, and dare to believe the Bible. . . .

"Away forever with your miserable transcendental philosophy, that would make the throne of David a spiritual throne, and the coming of Christ to sit upon it as a spiritual coming, and His reign a spiritual reign. Thanks be to God, His kingdom cannot be blown up into such spiritual bubbles as these, for a thousand, or even 365 thousand years, and then blown for ever away into some ethereal something, which some sneering infidel has defined, to be sitting on a cloud and singing Psalms to all eternity. No, no. Jesus Christ has been raised up in David's flesh immortalized, and He shall come in that flesh glorified."

Thus wrote Charles Fitch, the fervent Advent leader, in the summer of 1843. His view soon leavened the lump of Adventist believers, and in the summer of 1844 the cry, "Babylon is fallen," "come out of her, my people," began to be heard wherever Advent preachers held forth. To believe in the personal coming of Christ in glory to bring rewards to all, stood forth in Adventist preaching as the essence of all true Christian thinking concerning God's plan for this world. The opposing doctrine of the spiritual coming of Christ, with a temporal millennium and world conversion, stood for a denial of the doctrine of the supernatural, personal coming of our Lord and hence as a symbol of apostasy from apostolic teaching.

### Put Finger on Real Issue

We need not agree with all the reasoning set forth by Charles Fitch and other Advent preachers in what they wrote or said concerning Babylon and its fall. It may be argued that they restricted too much the meaning of the prophetic forecast concerning the fall of Babylon, and certainly they were in error to the extent that they drew in a time element. But admitting all this—and we can freely do so—still leaves valid and meaningful the heart of their preaching and of their indictment of the churches. These pioneer Adventists put their finger on the real issue when they dealt with the question of the spiritual versus the personal coming of Christ; for fundamentally different conceptions of the whole plan of God for this world grow out of those two conceptions of Christ's coming. We have already seen in an earlier chapter how the doctrine of the spiritual coming of Christ led on to a virtual denial of the whole idea of the coming of Christ and prepared the minds of religious leaders to support essentially secular ideas of world progress.

The Advent pioneers of the 1840's were also correct in declaring that the false doctrine of the spiritual coming of Christ grew out of false principles of spiritualizing Scripture that ultimately rob the Bible of any direct or literal message to the souls of men. The Reformers of the sixteenth century showed clearly that Rome by her spiritualizing of Scripture gave to it a nose of wax, as Luther declared, that could be turned in one direction or another, and hence the Bible lost its value as an authoritative spiritual guide for life. In the nineteenth century arose the Advent movement to speak out against false teachings in Protestantism concerning the primary truth of the second coming of our Lord, teachings that were the fruitage of a spiritualizing tendency that had steadily developed in Protestantism.

### Summarize Developments in Apostasy

So much for the historical record concerning the first preaching of the second angel's message in 1844 in America. We have already read the statement by Mrs. White from *The Great Controversy,* which was written in 1888, that "the work of apostasy has not yet reached its culmination," that "the change is a progressive one, and the perfect fulfillment of Rev. 14:8 is yet future." In an earlier chapter on the rise of the idea of progress we learned that the doctrine of the spiritual coming of Christ and the temporal millennium became increasingly secularized as the supernatual element disappeared, and that this was the result of an acceptance by the churches of skeptical theories and higher criticism. We also saw how Darwin supplanted Moses in the thinking of an increasing number of clergy in regard to the beginnings of Bible history. Needless to say, Protestant ministers, when confronted with the plausible arguments for evolution, discovered an easy way to harmonize evolution and the Bible by spiritualizing away the scriptures which describe the creation of our world. They had already spiritualized away scriptures concerning the end of the world.

But this acceptance of evolution by an increasing number of the clergy in the closing decades of the nineteenth century and onward produced a revolution in theological thought more complete and sudden than in any preceding period in the history of the Christian church. Let us summarize the principal Christian doctrines that were vitally affected as churchmen gave increasing ear to scientific dogmas in general and to evolution in particular.

## Doctrines Affected by Evolution

Belief in the supernatural inevitably waned. There was no place for miracles, no place for any supernatural intervention on the part of God. That would be contrary to the workings of natural law. There was no place for God. He became quite unnecessary. As one leading evolutionist years ago expressed it, "Evolution pushes the Creator out of doors." There was no place for prayer, as that term has been known throughout the history of the Christian church. For prayer is an act of communion with a personal God, and such communion has meaning only on the premise that God is free to act in response to our prayers. There was no place for the Christ of the Bible, for His virgin birth, for His miraculous deeds, for His literal resurrection, or for His bodily ascension. There was no place for the doctrine of the fall of man unless it be a fall upward through the evolutionary ages. Hence there was no place for the doctrine of sin, unless it be viewed as one of the vestigial remains of our animal heritage. But if there was no fall and no sin, then there was no place for the atonement. Nor was there a place for the law of God. The Bible statement that God wrote the Ten Commandments with His own finger was explained away, as are other miraculous statements of Scripture. But if we have no divine law, we have no divine definition of sin. There was no place for the doctrine of the Second Advent. Scientific and evolutionistic thought ruled it out altogether. A personal, supernatural coming of Christ is contrary to the orderly processes of nature. Finally, there was no place in the thinking of a rapidly increasing number of the clergy for any idea of a literal heaven. Heaven became a state and not a place.

How true was the statement of Mrs. White in 1888, that "the work of apostasy has not yet reached its culmination." The denial of the Christian doctrines just discussed has largely been subsequent to 1888. In fact, it was not until the 1920's that the Protestant apostasy came to such full fruitage that its true nature was evident to all. It was in 1928, for example, that a Modernist minister wrote two articles under the title "A Modernist's Criticism of Modernism," in which he made the most amazing admissions concerning what had taken place in the Protestant world. His confession is a startling commentary on the prophetic words, "Babylon is fallen." The author of these articles, William Henry Spence, declares:

"The losses incident to the liberalizing of religion fall naturally into two classes:

" (1) Those endured by institutional religion;

" (2) Those affecting personal religious experience."

He illustrates the first with this statement:

"The most obvious evidence of the weakening influence of liberalism on the church is the absenteeism of the educated—or one should say, many of the educated. The acquisition of the liberal viewpoint has meant, for great numbers of them, a lessening of loyalty to the church, and the forsaking of its altars."

### A Cause for "Deepest Distress"

On the second point he writes at length. Here are a few key paragraphs:

"There are some changes wrought by liberalism in the lives of men, which a pastor whose vocation is the cure of souls, observes with deepest distress. As he watches the cooling of religious ardor, the loosening of the grasp on spiritual realities, the progressive and easygoing tolerance of unethical practices, the increasing neglect of the 'means of grace' and the blurring of conviction through pride of intellect, in one after another of his parishioners, his intimate friends and his fellow clergymen, he is tempted to say now and then, adapting the words of Festus: 'Much learning hath made thee apostate.' "

This preacher has little sympathy, of course, for Fundamentalists. But he is willing to make this damaging admission concerning them:

"Certainly the Fundamentalist with his faith in the divine kinship of man is nearer right, than those liberals who, influenced by certain evolutionary theories, reduce him to a mere automaton, produced by reaction to environment."—*The Congregationalist*, Aug. 9, 1928.

As a Modernist, Spence, of course, believes that there has been great value in the "historical study of the Bible," which means the higher critical analysis of Scripture which resulted in robbing the Bible of its unique status as the infallible and inspired Word of God. But he confesses that some great and perhaps irreparable damage has been done to the Scripture and thus to the faith of the multitudes. Says he:

"The destruction of the Bible's infallibility has ruined its authority for multitudes. . . . To some liberals it has become little more than a source book of rather doubtful value for historical study. In the resulting confusion, both the man in the crowd and the liberal scholar often are like a sailor who has thrown over chart and compass, and vainly tries to steer his course under a sky whose stars are hidden by the clouds.

"When one thinks of what the old faith in the Bible did for our fathers and mothers and the kind of family life it inspired them to create, one feels less and less inclined to swagger over the fruits of the so-called modern view of the Bible. . . . With the Holy Book in their hands they felt themselves fortified by an impregnable rock. They spoke to us of duty and grace with a confidence supported by producing evidence. The printed page with its golden words gave them a sense of immediacy in their practice of the Divine Presence. When faith grew dim the opening of the Good Book brought renewal. When they were confused in any moral crisis, a quick turning to the sacred page gave them guidance. When sorrow and adversity overtook them, the precious promises gave them unspeakable comfort. When they drew near to death, the recollection of certain verses treasured in memory flung open the gates of new life to them.

"But what of us, the sons of such parents with the advantages of our higher learning, real or supposed? Must we not confess that a glory has departed from us? Has our liberalism given us an equivalent for that which we surrendered when we gave up our parents' belief in the Book? The necessity is upon us to find something to give us what the Bible gave them—the feeling of security in a trouble-ridden world, clearness and definiteness of religious convictions, the accent of authority in our testimony of religious experience and a firm, sure hold of faith in Christ—or else liberalism will yet become the great apostasy."—*Ibid.*

## A Startling Warning

Toward the close of his second article he utters this startling warning:

"Just now modernists should awake to the fact that a liberalism which tends toward a Godless humanism or rank atheism is heading toward its own destruction."—*Ibid.*, Aug. 16, 1928.

This amazing confession, written in 1928, was followed by many equally startling confessions in the 1930's, some of which have been quoted in a preceding chapter. But although Protestantism, which has fallen away from the historic doctrines of Christianity, admits its sorry state, it takes no steps in any well-defined or united way to return to these great Bible teachings. That is the present sad plight of Protestantism. It may see the weakness of the skeptical scientific assumptions it began to accept in the nineteenth century, which produced finally a loss of faith in Christian teachings. But there appears to be no evidence that Protestantism tends to return or even to see the need of returning to the basic premises or assumptions on which the Christian's faith must be built. Walter Lippmann well wrote:

"If faith is to flourish there must be a conception of how the universe is governed to support it. It is these supporting conceptions—the unconscious assumption that we are related to God as creatures to creator, as vassals to a king, as children to a father—that the acids of modernity have eaten away."—*A Preface to Morals*, p. 56.

Elsewhere in this same much-discussed work, Lippmann observes:

"This is the first age, I think, in the history of mankind when the circumstances of life have conspired with the intellectual habits of the time to render any fixed and authoritative belief incredible to large masses of men."—*Ibid.*, p. 12.

The evidence seems clear that we have finally come to the day of the complete, or virtually complete, fulfillment of the second angel's message. That means we have come to the day when we must put a new emphasis on our preaching of the second angel's message.

# CHAPTER 17

# The Third Angel's Message

THE THIRD angel's message as recorded in Revelation 14: 9-11 has two aspects, a negative and a positive. There is the warning against receiving the mark of authority of an apostate power, and by clear implication there is the call to receive the mark of divine authority, the seal of the living God, who is distinguished as the Creator of heaven and earth. In other words, the third angel's message is a warning against the keeping of Sunday and a call to men to keep God's true Sabbath day.

The true Sabbath has two distinguishing marks: (1) The mark of time. "The seventh day is the sabbath of the Lord thy God." (2) The purpose. The Sabbath was instituted as a memorial of a certain historical event, the creation of the world—"in six days the Lord made heaven and earth."

Hence, in order to understand the importance of the Sabbath and thus of the third angel's message, we must see the significance of the creation event which the Sabbath memorializes. And we must see this in the setting of the facts already presented regarding the disappearance of the very idea of God, which is the climax of the modern apostasy in Christendom.

The Genesis doctrine of creation presents the true doctrine of God, on which all other doctrines must be reared. The creation record presents God as above and apart from the things He creates. In the language of theology this is known as the doctrine of the transcendence of God. Only as we think of God as transcendent can we think of Him as personal. Either God is apart from and above all created things or else He is a part of the universe itself. There is a vast distinction. Much of the pagan world early fell into the pantheistic heresy of thinking that God is in the brook, the tree, the mountain, the river, the winds—yes, everywhere in genral but nowhere in particular. The result was that the very idea of God lost all meaning. Modern religionists who were horrified at the thought of dismissing God from the scientific processes in our modern world, largely fell into this other evil of identifying God with nature and thus destroying any idea of a personal God.

The Bible record declares: "In the beginning God created the heaven and the earth." No more primary or more important truth could have been set forth in the opening words of Holy Writ. Before all else, God. Before there was a mountain or a valley or a stream or a cloud, before even the earth itself, there is the great God. An intelligent power, apart from this earth of ours, at work to bring forth order and every kind of created thing—that is the Bible doctrine regarding God and our world.

### Bible Presents All-powerful God

The creation account presents to us not only a transcendent but also an all-powerful God. Even among those who have held to the idea of God there has often been found the heresy that God is limited by the universe in which He dwells; in other words, that He is not all-powerful. The modern skeptic scoffs at the thought that God knows all about every one of us. The creation account pictures God as being so powerful that He need only speak and even inanimate nature responds at once. "He spake, and it was done; he commanded, and it stood fast." Ps. 33:9. A majestic picture of God's absolute and immediate control of all things is given to us in the frequent refrain of the creation narrative, "and it was so." "God said, Let there be a firmament . . . : and it was so." "God said, Let the earth bring forth grass . . . : and it was so." "God said, Let there be lights in the firmament . . . : and it was so."

The prophets of old presented the fact of creation as one of the proofs that God is omnipotent. Wrote Isaiah: "Lift up your eyes on high, and behold who hath created these things, that bringeth out their host by number: he calleth them all by names by the greatness of his might, for that he is strong in power; not one faileth." Isa. 40:26. Then follows the lesson for the individual soul: "Why sayest thou, O Jacob, and speakest, O Israel, my way is hid from the Lord, and my judgment is passed over from my God? Hast thou not known? Hast thou not heard, that the everlasting God, the Lord, the Creator of the ends of the earth, fainteth not, neither is weary? There is no searching of his understanding." Verses 27, 28.

## A Personal God Set Forth

The creation story sets before us the truth of a personal God, and it is this truth that constitutes the citadel of revealed religion, the citadel so violently attacked today by secularists and liberal theologians. No blind impersonal force moves through the opening pages of Holy Writ. We hear the stately steppings of a personal God from the beginning of the record right through to the sorrowful moment when "the Lord God walking in the garden in the cool of the day" met the sinful pair and brought their Edenic residence to an end. How forcefully is the fact of a personal God brought to our minds by the declaration, "God said, Let us make man in our image, after our likeness." Gen. 1:26.

The opening chapters of Genesis set before us a moral God. One of the most seductive delusions of the devil is that right and wrong are merely relative terms to be defined in relation to changing customs and viewpoints from generation to generation in various lands. Such a view makes meaningless the whole idea of fixed and eternal standards of right, by which all men shall finally be judged. The Bible in its very opening chapters gives us a picture of a moral God who is directly concerned over absolute standards of right and wrong. In the Genesis record is the "tree of the knowledge of good and evil." There is no mistaking the primary truth that moral standards have a place in men's lives, and that the distinguishing mark of sin is that it is disobedience to the commands of a personal God. If that truth were sensed today, what a difference it might make in the attitude of many persons toward sin!

One cannot read the creation story and the comments upon it throughout the Scriptures without being profoundly impressed that God has a plan and a purpose for our world. One of the most cynical aspects of the evolution theory as generally held, and of various false views concerning God, is that our world is the result of accident and chance, that there is no purpose or destiny to life. A whole host of evils easily spring from such a hopeless view. But that dark view of life is not found in the Bible. We read that when God created living creatures He placed them in a well-ordered world. There is reason and purpose for each of His actions. Isaiah wrote, "Thus saith the Lord that created the heavens; God himself that formed the earth and made it; he hath established it, he created it not in vain, he formed it to be inhabited." Isa. 45:18. In the Genesis record man stands forth in Eden as the climax of a planned work of God, a being in God's image, designed by his Creator to live in holiness and obedience and never-ending happiness in a perfect world.

### Creation and Plans of Salvation

Not only does the creation account in Genesis give us a true conception of God, it gives us also a true setting for the plan of salvation and final restitution. Indeed, the creation story provides the only setting in which the whole plan of salvation can have real meaning. The rejection of the Genesis account makes meaningless that divine plan. *Sin, salvation, the atonement*—these and other key words of the Bible are robbed of all meaning when they are not viewed in the setting of the Bible creation. It is only when we see sin against the spotless background of Eden that we can sense the true hideousness of rebellion against God.

Finally, the creation account has meaning and purpose, in relation not only to our present world and to God's plan of salvation, but also to the world to come. A true picture of the final reward of the righteous is possible only as we know and believe in the Genesis story of the beginnings of our world. Nothing aids so greatly in forming a correct view of the nature of man as a true picture of the final abode of the righteous, and that true picture is obtained by having a right understanding of the nature of the original abode. We find that Adam dwelt in a real world as a real being, that he had a home, and that he did such real things as dressing and keeping the Garden of Eden.

When we read that God's plan is to restore the lost estate by creating a new earth, we can properly conclude that the final place of reward for the righteous will be a real place. We can take literally the words of Isaiah regarding those who will dwell on the "new earth": "They shall build houses, and inhabit them; and they shall plant vineyards, and eat the fruit of them." Isa. 65:21.

With such a view of our future abode, we are prepared to see the significance of the resurrection of the body, a truth so plainly taught in the Bible, and so little taught in the Christian churches. A real place of abode calls for real people to inhabit it. The idea of disembodied spirits forever flitting about in a heaven as misty and vague as the spirits does not square with the Bible picture of the new earth.

### Creation the Foundation Truth

The great truth of the creation stands revealed, therefore, as the foundation truth on which the whole structure of Bible doctrine is reared. How important, then, that it should ever be kept bright in the minds of men.

Hence it follows that belief in the Genesis account of creation is the distinguishing mark of a man who believes (1) in a personal God with infinite qualities and powers; (2) in the Bible as the one supreme authority; (3) and in the divine plan of salvation by which a holy God redeems His fallen children, sanctifies them, and finally places them in Eden restored.

The Sabbath is the mark, or sign, of the man who believes in creation and thus in all that creation signifies. This statement is self-evident, for the commandment is explicit that the reason for the keeping of the Sabbath is that we shall remember the great fact that in six days the Lord made heaven and earth and rested the seventh day. James G. Murphy, in his *Commentary on the Book of Exodus*, well remarks:

"The observance of the Sabbath connects man with the origin of his race, with the six days' creation, and with the Creator Himself. The connection is manifestly a historical one. He that observes the Sabbath aright holds the history of that which it celebrates to be authentic, and therefore believes in the creation of the first man, in the creation of a fair abode for man in the space of six days, in the primeval and absolute creation of the heavens and the earth, and, as a necessary antecedent to all this, in the Creator, who at the close of His latest creative effort rested on the seventh day. The Sabbath thus becomes the sign by which the believers in a historical Revelation are distinguished from those who have allowed these great facts to fade from their remembrance (Exodus 31:13). . . . The observance of the Sabbath, then, becomes the characteristic of those who cherish the recollections of the origin of their race, and who worship God not merely as Elohim, the everlasting almighty, but as Jehovah, the historical God, the Creator, who has revealed Himself to man from the dawn of his existence as the God of love, and afterwards of mercy and grace, of promise and performance."—Comments on Exodus 20:8-11, p. 230.

### Significant Facts of Bible History

In the light of all this, how meaningful, therefore, are the following facts of Bible history:

1. God established the memorial of creation at the very beginning of the history of the world. The sanctifying of the Sabbath occurred on the seventh day of the first week of time.

2. Apostasy and degeneracy began when man failed to see beyond creation to the Creator. As Paul vividly declares in the first chapter of Romans, men would not retain God in their memory; they served the creature more than the Creator. Man would not worship the true God but turned instead to idol worship, with consequent spiritual and moral pollution.

3. God declared that the Sabbath was to be kept by Israel as a sign "that ye may know that I am the Lord that doth sanctify you." The Sabbath was to be "a sign between me and the children of Israel for ever: for in six days the Lord made heaven and earth,

and on the seventh day he rested, and was refreshed." Ex. 31:13, 17. The Sabbath was a sign of the creative power of God, a sign of a personal relationship between God and man, a sign of the purity and holiness and perfection that distinguish God and all His acts. Hence the Sabbath was ever to be a sign to the children of Israel that the God whom they worshiped had lifted them above the pit of moral corruption into which the heathen round about them had fallen, that He had power to create in them clean hearts and make them new creatures.

The history of Israel as set forth, for example, by Ezekiel shows that they failed to keep holy God's Sabbath day as He had commanded. The record declares: "They . . . polluted my sabbaths: for their heart went after their idols." Eze. 20:16. The pollution of the Sabbath, that is, the failure to remember it and thus the failure to remember the true God memorialized by it, was directly related to the evil of turning to idol worship. In other words, they could not turn to idol worship without profaning the Sabbath. The Sabbath stood ever as a barrier against idolatry. The Israelite who kept the Sabbath of God provided for all men a sign that he had no part in pagan idolatry. The fearful record of man's degeneracy, as set forth in the opening chapter of the book of Romans, would never have had to be written if men had remembered always God's holy Sabbath day which He sanctified at the end of creation week.

### Facts of Post-Biblical History

In view of the great significance of creation to a true conception of Scriptural doctrines, how meaningful, also, are the following facts of post-Biblical history:

1. The rise of the mystery of iniquity in the early centuries of the Christian Era was paralleled by the decline of the Bible Sabbath. There was no one cause for the decline. Nor will church historians ever be able to agree on the relative importance of all the forces that served to bring the Sabbath into eclipse. But in the setting of the facts already presented and others to be set forth,

it is proper to conclude that there is a direct relationship between the rise of the apostasy and the decline of the Sabbath.

2. The mystical allegorizing of the early church Fathers spiritualized away the Sabbath. They talked of a new day that was to commemorate a new event, the resurrection.

3. The thin line of Sabbathkeepers through the Dark Ages was uniformly found in the ranks of Rome's opponents.

4. The decline of God's holy Sabbath day was followed by the rise of numerous holy days for saints. This is understandable. Holy days are ever the symbols of a religion, its rallying points in terms of time.

### Facts of Reformation Days and Onward

Consider, next, the significance of these historical facts of Reformation times and onward:

1. Luther and Calvin quite largely discarded the saints' days and other annual holy days because they viewed these as marks of Rome's power and apostasy. In fact, the Reformers swung so far in their first fervor over the liberty of the gospel as to question the need of keeping even a weekly holy day. Calvin declared that he could go out and bowl on the green on Sunday to show his liberty in the gospel.

2. The fact, however, that these great Reformers failed to emphasize as clearly as they might the spiritual significance of a weekly holy day resulted erelong in a lax keeping of Sunday on the Continent.

3. Puritans in England in the seventeenth century sought to purify the Church of England. They saw the laxity on the Continent in regard to Sunday. They concluded that Christians needed set times for worship if strong and consistent Christian lives were to be developed. They also realized that Sunday could not make a claim on the Christian conscience without a "Thus saith the Lord." Hence they sought to place Sunday squarely on the fourth commandment of the Decalogue. They succeeded in doing this by spiritualizing away the literal, exact meaning of the phrase "the

seventh day" and declaring that it meant simply one day in seven. That interpretation was woven into the Westminster Confession in A.D. 1647 and thus into the thinking of much of Protestantism, for the Westminster Confession is probably more widely known than any other of the great Reformation creeds. (See chapter 7.)

## Old and New Creation

Sundaykeeping theologians have not been wholly blind to the fact that the Sabbath command was specifically instituted to memorialize the historical creation recorded in Genesis. Hence, these theologians have often sought to give consistency to their belief by declaring that the seventh day of the week memorializes the "old creation," and that the first day of the week memorializes the "new creation," the re-creation in Christ Jesus.

However, there have been theologians frank enough to admit that Sunday fails to measure up fully in this matter of a memorial of creation. In a noted commentary prepared by the Church of England is found this comment on Exodus 20:8:

"The day [Sunday] which we observe, in accordance with ecclesiastical usage, holds another place in the week [than the Sabbath], and its connection with the creation of the world has thus been put into the background."—*Holy Bible With Commentary.*

But in spite of a damaging admission like this, the advocates of Sunday have generally sought to make Sunday appear as though it stood on the solid ground of the Sabbath command. In reality it has ever rested on a foundation of sand, the shifting sands of spiritualizing interpretation. And like a house built on the sand, it looked as solid as though on rock, until the storm came. Or to speak literally: The plausible proponents of Sunday as a memorial of the "new creation" did not realize, in the days before Darwin, how completely the "new creation" is dependent on the "old creation" for its significance. The only sure foundation of the "new creation" is the "old creation," the one recorded in Genesis. The same is true of all other doctrines, as we have already discovered.

When the winds of the evolution theory began to blow in the last half of the nineteenth century, churchmen were not braced against the storm by any sure footing on the weekly memorial of the creation of the world. The Bible Sabbath they had relegated to a bygone day. They thought they had greatly improved on the simple Decalogue command to keep a particular day in memory of a particular event. Most of them thought they had given an all-sufficient reason for their change by declaring that the original Sabbath was Jewish, as though there could be anything Jewish about the Garden of Eden, where the Sabbath was instituted, or Adam and Eve, to whom the Sabbath was given, or the seventh day of the week, which was the time set apart. Ah, they had something more modern—a new sabbath to honor a "new creation." Though they did not realize it, those who led out in promoting this view in the early days of Protestantism were the original Modernists in Protestant ranks. The practical effect of their exalting the first day of the week in honor of the resurrection of Christ was that the creation of the world inevitably seemed of relatively small importance. It was simply the "old creation."

Not only were churchmen not prepared to meet the evolution storm, they were actually conditioned to accept evolution, even though it contradicted the clearest statements of Genesis and other portions of the Bible. Whatever consciousness churchmen might have had of the importance of the literal creation, as recorded in Genesis, was dulled and blunted because the memorial of that creation, the seventh-day Sabbath, was not remembered. This blunted sense, coupled with the practice of spiritualizing away the literal meaning of Scripture, provides the chief reason why churchmen found themselves quite unconsciously susceptible to the claims of the evolution theory. As we have already learned, they had spiritualized away the literal statements of Holy Writ regarding the Second Advent. They had declared that the resurrection that accompanies the Advent was simply a rising from spiritual death of those dead in trespasses and sins. As regards the Sabbath, which stands in opposition to evolution, they had spiritualized away the definite seventh day and the definite historical creation, so as to make the fourth commandment actually appear to enjoin a new day in honor of a new event.

## Long Days of Genesis

Paralleling this, though not directly related, was the interpretation that was given by some churchmen to the word *day* in the creation record of Genesis. By simplest definition and by the quite unanimous agreement of Bible students through all the centuries, the word *day* there used means a literal day, a twenty-four-hour period. But one after another of Protestant divines, even before Darwin's time, began to declare that these creation days were long periods of time. When Darwin arose, this played into his hands, for time was what the evolution theory needed more than all else if it was to be viewed as even plausible. Indeed, if creation week was really the sum of seven long periods of time, what should hinder men from believing that almost any kind of slow transition of life forms might have occurred? What is more, if the concise Genesis record of that first week is expanded to countless ages, we are only one step removed from believing that Genesis is not really presenting accurate history, but only a symbolical summary of vast changes that have taken place in our earth over an interminably long and shadowy past.

Even before Darwin's day all these spiritualizing tendencies in relation to creation and the Sabbath it memorialized played a part in making churchmen susceptible to the higher critical theories of the Bible, which began to spread their baleful influence over Christian minds in the eighteenth and nineteenth centuries. Central to the higher critical theory was the claim that the books of Moses were not strictly historical, that the early records of man's life on earth are hopelessly mixed with folklore and myth.

For these and other reasons that might be given, the evolution theory gained rapid acceptance in Protestant circles. A Bible undermined by spiritualizing methods, by higher critical arguments, and by the skeptical scientific theories dominant as the nineteenth century closed, left the way fully open for a brazenly new theology. This new theology, as earlier described, climaxed in a bold attack on the central idea of a personal God. The point of departure of Modernism, it can never be too often stated, is the foundation chapters of the Bible, the creation record. When Protestant Christendom finally split asunder a few decades ago, the cleavage ran all the way back to the first chapter of the Bible, back to the beginning of the world. That cleavage presents us today with a large and steadily increasing group called Modernists, who control most church organizations. On the other hand is a group, who for lack of a more exact word may still be described as Fundamentalists, who are generally on the defensive, and are declining in numbers.

### Third Angel Fittingly Follows First and Second

In the setting of these facts, let us turn directly to the question of the preaching of the third angel's message. Both Darwinism and the Advent movement developed in the latter half of the nineteenth century. Could any message be more timely or logical as a climax to the first and second angels' messages than this third one that warns men against the keeping of a false day and by clear implication calls upon them to keep God's true day, the memorial of creation?

In the 1850's, when the third angel's message began to be definitely preached, it was impossible for the pioneers to see the full import of the message. They were not prophets. They could not foresee the vast changes that were to take place in the secular and religious world in the century that lay ahead. Hence, they preached the Sabbath largely in terms of the time factor. They stressed fervently the highly pertinent and Scriptural fact that the seventh, and not the first, day is God's Sabbath. Hence, their preaching on the Sabbath was often distinguished by an extended discussion of the meaning of the law, the perpetuity of it, and, of course, their preaching included, and rightly so, a vigorous denunciation of Sunday as a mark of apostasy.

Now the servant of the Lord, early in the history of this Advent movement, forecast that the time would come when the Sabbath would be preached more fully. It is no distortion of her words to say that they meant not only the preaching of the Sabbath over a wider area but preaching the Sabbath in greater fullness of meaning. The time has come for such preaching.

## How Preach Sabbath More Fully

And how shall the Sabbath be preached in greater fullness? By preaching the Sabbath more fully in terms of its purpose, that is, its purpose as a memorial of creation.

This means no minimizing of the significance of time, of the fact that the Sabbath is the seventh day. But the factor of time subserves the real reason for the Sabbath—the seventh day is the Sabbath because it is that day that serves with true historical accuracy as the memorial of creation. God designated a particular day, not arbitrarily, but because it is integral to the historical fact that He wished to memorialize.

We as Adventists believe fully that time subserves purpose in the Sabbath command, but in actual practice and preaching we often fail to stress as we should the purpose of the Sabbath, that it is a memorial of creation. If we refer to the creation feature of the command we too often deal with it in the negative, that is, that Sunday is not the true Sabbath because it is not a true memorial of creation. That argument is good as far as it goes, but it does not go far enough. It does not set forth the Sabbath commandment with all the force and significance with which it ought to be set forth in these days when the creation record in Genesis is the point of departure for the whole modern apostasy in Christendom.

The pioneers may be pardoned for not stressing fully the creation feature of the command, but there is no excuse for our not doing so. If we are to proclaim the Sabbath more fully we must see its full significance, that is, we must see it in the setting of conditions in the world today. Only thus will we truly have *present* truth for the world. We should never forget that all three messages of the angels were given to meet specific conditions at a specific time in the history of the world.

It is when we see the Sabbath in the setting of the modern apostasy that we can best understand the unique status of Adventists in the religious world. This Advent movement is the only religious body with a message that directly meets the key heresy of our age, the evolution theory, and calls on all who wish to come out of Babylon, out of apostasy, to accept the true sign of allegiance to the living God, the Creator. We stand revealed today as calling on men to join with us not simply in a technical dispute over the seventh or the first day of the week or to keep another day just to be different. We call on men to keep the Sabbath as a sign of allegiance to the Creator of the heavens and the earth, as a badge of loyalty to the great truths of revelation, all of which rest on the opening chapters of the Bible.

Yes, we stand unique today in the religious world. Fundamentalists, despite their devotion to Scripture and their loyalty and love toward their Lord, do not have the defense against evolution that we have, nor are they prepared to rally men and women to a great sign of allegiance to the true God as Seventh-day Adventists can. In many instances Fundamentalists hold to the long-ages view of creation days, which plays directly into the hands of the evolution theory. So, far from having a Sabbath command to set in opposition to evolution, they have actually sought to eliminate the Sabbath command from the Decalogue, while inconsistently holding that the remaining nine are binding. Yet it is the Sabbath command that reveals the Author of the law and gives to that law its binding authority.

More than any others, Fundamentalists, as we have noted, speak fervently of Sunday as a memorial of the "new creation," and claim that it is a vast improvement over what they call the "old creation." But they do not seem to realize that this "new creation" has no meaning without the "old." When Modernists rejected the Genesis record of creation, it was not long before the birth, death, resurrection, and ministry of our Lord became meaningless. When the foundation was removed, the superstructure collapsed. Fundamentalists are in the strange position of concentrating on the superstructure and minimizing the importance of the foundation.

Fundamentalists speak fervently of a personal God and of creation. In full sincerity they deplore evolutionary attacks on the Bible. They mourn the split in the churches, a result of evolution. Yet they turn about and denounce the seventh-day Sabbath that is the symbol of creation, the constant reminder of it and of a personal God, and thus of an authoritative Bible. They have only scathing denunciation for the one religious body, Seventh-day Adventists, that is wholly free of the evolution heresy. And that denunciation focuses on our distinctive Sabbath doctrine, which is our weekly protest against evolution, our weekly means of keeping fresh in our minds the fact that in six days the Lord created the heavens and the earth.

### Call Men Back to Bible

In calling men back to the Bible Sabbath we call them back to the authority of the Bible in opposition to (1) the authority of reason, which gives proof of its claims in the marvels of the scientific age, and (2) the authority of Rome, which gives Sunday as proof of its claims.

What men crave more than anything else is a note of authority in their spiritual lives. Our present age is distinguished by doubt and uncertainty. Man needs something beyond himself. Reason, despite its marvelous results in scientific discovery, does not satisfy in the spiritual realm. In fact, its deficiency is most evident in these postwar days, which dazzle us with scientific findings. Thus there are really only two claims on men's spiritual allegiance at this time—the claims of Rome and the claims of the Bible.

It is a remarkable fact that in these present times no small number of intellectuals have become converts to Rome, hoping to find in her a spiritual haven. Thus is fulfilled the remarkable statement written by Mrs. White in 1888. We quote in part her prophetic words:

# THE THIRD ANGEL'S MESSAGE

"A day of great intellectual darkness has been shown to be favorable to the success of the papacy. It will yet be demonstrated that a day of great intellectual light is equally favorable for its success. In past ages, when men were without God's word, and without the knowledge of the truth, their eyes were blindfolded, and thousands were ensnared, not seeing the net spread for their feet. In this generation there are many whose eyes become dazzled by the glare of human speculations, 'science falsely so called,' they discern not the net, and walk into it as readily as if blindfolded. God designed that man's intellectual powers should be held as a gift from his Maker, and should be employed in the service of truth and righteousness; but when pride and ambition are cherished, and men exalt their own theories above the word of God, then intelligence can accomplish greater harm than ignorance. Thus the false science of the present day, which undermines faith in the Bible, will prove as successful in preparing the way for the acceptance of the papacy, with its pleasing forms, as did the withholding of knowledge in opening the way for its aggrandizement in the Dark Ages."—*The Great Controversy*, pp. 572, 573.

We stand forth today as a people who believe in the Bible, the whole Bible, without any spiritualizing of its literal words. We believe in the Bible from the first chapter of Genesis to the last chapter of Revelation. We believe in the whole of the moral law of God and in the Sabbath command, which gives binding authority to the law. We believe in the Sabbath as the memorial of the direct relationship of a personal, moral God to this world of ours, a relationship so direct that man was made in the divine image and likeness. We keep God's holy Sabbath day because we believe literally in the historical record of the Bible from the very first chapter onward. We see in the Sabbath a bulwark against the modern apostasy in Christendom that undermines the authority of the Bible, by undermining its foundations.

Surely the time has come for us to arise and proclaim the Sabbath more fully, to see the Sabbath not only in the awesome setting of Sinai but also in the perfect setting of Eden. The Sabbath is not merely a question of days but a question of belief or disbelief in the foundation truths on which the whole Scriptures of God rest. It is for us to build up the foundations of many generations.

# Section VI

# THE SANCTUARY

18. The Scapegoat and the Atonement

CHAPTER 18

# The Scapegoat and the Atonement

THE CHARGE that Seventh-day Adventists make Satan their vicarious substitute and savior is based on the fact that we believe the scapegoat represents Satan. The Scripture passage that bears directly on this point is Leviticus 16, which gives the Atonement Day ritual.

Those who bring against us the charge of making Satan our savior hold that the scapegoat represents Christ as truly as does the slain goat. Following are the main reasons they set forth for this belief:

1. That the Hebrew word *Azazel*, which is translated "scapegoat" in our King James Version, should be translated "goat of departure," deriving Azazel from two Hebrew words meaning "goat" and "to depart."

2. That the Azazel goat is a sin offering, even as is the Lord's goat that was slain.

3. That the bearing away of the sins by the Azazel goat is a type of Christ's bearing away our sins.

4. That the slain goat represents Christ's death on Calvary, and the live goat directs attention to the risen and living Saviour (emphasis being placed on the fact that the resurrection as well as the death is needed in the plan of salvation), and that the live goat's being accompanied by someone to a desert place symbolizes the impossibility of the return of the sins.

Incidentally, those who bring against us the charge concerning the scapegoat, and who hold that this scapegoat represents a phase of Christ's work, quite generally in their attacks seem willing to allow the impression to be created that the view they hold is the practically universal orthodox belief of Christendom. Thus in the most pronounced and heinous sense of the word, Seventh-day Adventists are made to stand forth as preachers of strange, heretical doctrines.

Let us examine these four reasons:

### First Reason Examined

1. The basic claim as to the meaning of the word *Azazel* cannot be proved, as we shall discover from an examination of the etymology of the word later in this chapter.

### Second Reason Examined

2. We do not believe the Bible teaches that Azazel is a sin offering. If we were confined to the fifth verse of Leviticus 16, we might conclude that both goats were a sin offering. But the Scriptures immediately inform us that a unique procedure took place. When the two goats were brought to the door of the tabernacle, lots were cast upon them. Nowhere else in the sacrificial service is there a parallel to this. The obvious idea to be obtained from the use of the lot throughout the whole Bible is that of deciding between two or more. For example, there were two candidates selected for the office of apostleship, to fill the place of Judas. The casting of the lot determined which of the two should function in that capacity. That this is the correct understanding of the problem before us seems clearly to be borne out by the fact that after the lot was cast, the reference to the sin offering is the word *goat*— singular number. "Aaron shall bring the *goat* [not goats] upon which the Lord's lot fell, and offer *him* for a sin offering." Verse 9. Note also verses 15 and 27.

Those who hold that the scapegoat as well as the slain goat represents Christ, endeavor to find a parallel to this unusual Atonement Day procedure by reference to Leviticus 5:7-10. Here provision is made that a man who is too poor to bring a lamb may bring "two turtledoves, or two young pigeons, unto the Lord; one for a sin offering, and the other for a burnt offering." Verse 7. But:

*a.* The priest did not cast lots. Thus the most important point of comparison is lacking.

*b.* Both of the birds were for the Lord, but only one goat.

*c. Both* birds were killed by the priest.

Reference is sometimes also made to the two birds brought for the purification of a leprous man (Lev. 14:4-7), but this reference may be disposed of by comments "*a*" and "*b*" above, and by the simple statement that we have here no reference to a sin offering or to the purging of sin. Lange's commentary discusses the dual offering of the poor, and then comments on the two birds for the leprous man's purification, remarking: "These last, however, were not a sacrifice."—Comments on Leviticus 16.

The way that these two goats were brought before the Lord is without a parallel in the Levitical service. This fact in itself should at least suggest that some essentially new and added truth was to be conveyed by the service. With this general statement doubtless our critics would agree, contending that it was necessary to have these two animals in order to represent rightly the work of Christ as a sin offering. But to make such a claim as this is equivalent to saying that all the rest of the Levitical ritual of the various sin offerings, including the Passover Lamb, which the Scripture tells us is the exact type of Christ's sacrifice for us (1 Cor. 5:7), is hopelessly deficient in its symbolism.

Furthermore, how could a *live* animal properly be considered a sin offering? In every other passage dealing with the sacrificial system, the sin offering was slain. Is this to be a lone case where a sin offering lives? If so, what becomes of the very explicit scripture that underlies the whole sacrificial system, "Without shedding of blood is no remission" of sin? Heb. 9:22. Seeing that the priest does not take the life of the second goat, how can its relation to the sins of the people have any "remission" value? And if it has no "remission" value, how can it be properly described as a sin offering?

Indeed, what necessity is there for twice remitting the sins of the people? For the blood of the slain goat is taken into the sanctuary, to which the sins of the people have been transferred in type during the year, to "make an atonement for the holy place, because of the uncleanness of the children of Israel, and because of their transgressions in all their sins." Lev. 16:16. And then when the priest "hath made an *end* of reconciling the holy place, and the tabernacle of the congregation, and the altar," he turns to the live goat. The idea of having the second goat atone again for the sins seems strange even to those who hold that theory.

In an article entitled "The Meaning of 'Azazel,' " in the *Moody Bible Institute Monthly,* Grant Stroh inquires:

"Since the sins of 'all the congregation of Israel' had already been atoned for by the death of the first goat, what is the significance of confessing and placing them upon the head of the live goat that was to carry them away with him?"—March, 1932.

But he endeavors to prevent this fact from giving any aid to our view, by adding immediately:

"If these sins already had been atoned for, it certainly is incongruous to explain this ceremony as an act of judgment. This much ought to be clear."

As to whether the judgment idea is incongruous will be discussed later. But surely this much ought to be clear, that if the sins of the Israelites had already been atoned for by the death of the first goat, it is incongruous to view the second goat as a sin offering.

Mr. Stroh goes on to support his belief that the "live goat directs our attention to the risen and living Saviour," by remarking that "in the New Testament the death and resurrection of our Lord are indissolubly joined together." Paul's statement is then quoted: "If Christ be not raised, your faith is vain; ye are yet in your sins." 1 Cor. 15:17. But if "the sins of 'all the congregation of Israel' had already been atoned for by the death of the first goat," and this represented Christ's death on the cross, why must the freeing of believers from sin, in the antitype, await a further act, namely, the resurrection?

In order to have the live goat also represent Christ, those who hold this view of Azazel must blur over, if not contradict altogether, the proposition they elsewhere set forth so dogmatically, that complete atonement for sin was made on the cross.

### Third Reason Examined

3. To attempt to find a parallel between the act of the second goat in bearing away the sins, and that of Christ in bearing our sins, is to go contrary to the explicit statements of Scripture. We read of Christ, "Who his own self bare our sins in his own body *on the tree.*" 1 Peter 2:24. The margin reads, *"to the tree."* The American Revised Version reads: "Who his own self bare our sins in his body *upon the tree,"* and the margin reads, *"carried up . . . to the tree."* It is said that the live goat was needed to supply a feature that the slain goat could not, that is, the bearing away of the sins. But John the Baptist (John 1:29) used the symbol of the Lamb (which to the Jews would convey the thought of the sacrificial lamb, whose blood was poured out) to convey the truth of Christ's bearing our sins. Evidently John the Baptist viewed Christ's bearing of sins in the way Peter did (1 Peter 2:24), and not in the way these theologians do, who view the scapegoat as Christ.

Surely the Scriptures are so clear that the bearing, or carrying, or taking away, of sins is from us to the "tree," that they quite demolish the most plausible-sounding parallel between Christ and the second goat, the parallel built on the word *bear.* Evidently the live goat's bearing of sins must have a different significance from that of Christ's bearing them.

### Fourth Reason Examined

4. Those who teach that the live goat "directs our attention to the risen and living Saviour," must, to be consistent in their symbolism, believe that Christ rose from the dead loaded with the sins that He had borne up to the tree. The ritual shows very plainly that the second goat was to be regarded as a thing so unclean that the man who led it away into the wilderness must "wash his clothes, and bathe his flesh in water" (Lev. 16:26) before coming again into the camp. Do the advocates of this doctrine we are examining really believe they find in this picture of the second goat a parallel to the

glorified Christ rising from the tomb and commanding Mary, "Touch me not"?

## Biblical Authorities Cited

So much for an examination of the main reasons brought forth in behalf of the interpretation that views the live goat as well as the slain goat as representing Christ. Note now the testimony of a representative group of Biblical authorities, Jews and Christians, liberal and conservative, regarding Azazel. These quotations will reveal further evidence against the interpretation we have been examining, and will afford the reader an opportunity to judge for himself whether Seventh-day Adventists are preachers of strange and anti-Christian doctrines in holding that Azazel represents Satan.*

## M'Clintock and Strong's Cyclopaedia

"Scapegoat (Hebrew, *Azazel*) is the name given in the A.V. to one of the two goats used in the sin offering for the entire community of Israel on the great Day of Atonement, the goat which was to be sent away into the wilderness. . . . There can be no doubt that this has the appearance of being some sort of personage, or interest personified, standing over against Jehovah, or somehow contradistinguished from Him. But opinions have from early times been divided on the subject.

"1. The one followed by our translators, which regards it as a name for the goat itself, is of great antiquity, and has numbers on its side. . . .

"2. By others it has been taken as the name of a place. . . .

"3. Others, again, have taken the word as a *pealpal* form of the Arabic verb *to remove*, . . . so that the meaning comes to be for a *complete removing* or *dismissal* (Tholuck, Steudel, Winer, Bähr). Grammatically, no objection can be urged against this view; and it undoubtedly accords well with the general import of this part of the rite. 'The true expiation,' to use the words of Bähr, 'was effected by the blood of the first goat, which was set apart for Jehovah; on the

---

* Brevity demands that much of the repetitive matter in these quotations be eliminated. No attempt can be made to give the full argument for any of the views held regarding Azazel. Sufficient, however, is quoted to reveal the main reasons for the principal views. The argument based on the alleged parallel between the two goats and the dual offering for a leprous person has been omitted because it has already been noted.

other hand, the ceremony with the other goat appears as a mere addition made for special reasons, a kind of complement to the wiping away of the sins which had already been effected by means of the sacrifice.' . . .

"4. But there is still another class of writers who are disposed to claim for the word a more distinctly personal existence, and who would refer it directly to Satan. This view is certainly of high antiquity. . . .

"It was very common with the rabbins, as in later times it has the support of many authorities—Spencer, Ammon, Rosenmüller, Gesenius, etc., who hold it to be equivalent to the Roman *averruncus*, or evil demon, which was supposed to inhabit desert places, and who needed to be propitiated; but adopted also, though purged of this idolatrous connection, by Witsius, Meyer, Alting, Hengstenberg; also quite recently by Vaihinger and Kurtz. These writers hold that the view in question best preserves the contrast between the two goats— one for Jehovah, and one for the great adversary Azazel—the latter a being as well as the former, and a being who (as demons generally) was supposed to have his peculiar dwelling in the desert. The goat, however, that was sent to this evil spirit—emphatically the removed or separate one—was no sacrifice, but rather a witness that the accepted sacrifice had been made. It proclaimed, as it were, 'that the horrible wilderness, the abode of impure spirits, is alone the place to which the sins of the people, as originally foreign to human nature and society, properly belong; that Azazel, the abominable, the sinner from the beginning (John 8:44), is the one from whom they have proceeded, and to whom they must again with abhorrence be sent back, after the solemn atonement and absolution of the congregation have been accomplished' (Vaihinger). No doubt, as thus explained, the leading import of the transaction with this goat is in proper accordance with the service of the day; but it cannot appear otherwise than strange that, in the most sacred rite of the old covenant, Satan should be so formally recognized as, according to this view, he must have been."—M'CLINTOCK AND STRONG, *Cyclopaedia of Biblical, Theological, and Ecclesiastical Literature*, vol. 9, pp. 397, 398, art. "Scapegoat."

### Encyclopedic Dictionary

"*Azazel*.—1. In Scripture: A word occurring in Leviticus 16:8, 10, and 26, where it is translated 'scapegoat;' but the antithesis which makes the one goat be for Jehovah and the other for Azazel, is best preserved by supposing Azazel to be such a being as Satan or some other evil spirit."—*The Encyclopedic Dictionary*, vol. 1, p. 397.

# ANSWERS TO OBJECTIONS

## Hastings' Bible Dictionary

"Etymology, origin, and significance [of Azazel] are still matters of conjecture. The A. V. designation *scapegoat* . . . obscures the fact that the word *Azazel* is a proper name in the original, and in particular the name of a powerful spirit or demon supposed to inhabit the wilderness or 'solitary land' ([Lev.] 16:22, R.V.)."—*Hastings' Bible Dictionary,* p. 77, art. "Azazel."

## Schaff-Herzog Encyclopedia

"The meaning of the word [Azazel] has occasioned much discussion. Starting from the fact that 'for Yahweh' and 'for Azazel' stand in opposition (verse 8), many think that it is the name of a being opposed to Yahweh,—a desert monster, a demon, or directly Satan. Such as attempt an etymological interpretation then explain it as characterizing the demon or Satan as removed or apostatized from God, or a being repelled by men (*averruncus*), or one which does things apart and in secret (from *azal,* 'to go away'). Others conceive of Azazel, not as a proper name, but as an appellative noun and modified reduplicated form of a root '*azal,*' 'to remove, retire.' . . . The contrast between 'for Yahweh' and 'for Azazel,' however, in verse 8 favors the interpretation of Azazel as a proper noun, and a reference to Satan suggests itself. . . . A definite explanation, satisfactory to all, can hardly be looked for."—*The New Schaff-Herzog Encyclopedia of Religious Knowledge,* vol. 1, p. 389, art. "Azazel."

## Smith's Bible Dictionary

"In regard to the Hebrew word *Azazel* ('scapegoat,' A.V.), the opinions most worthy of notice are: 1. A designation of the goat itself. The old interpreters in general, the Vulgate, Symmachus, Aquila, Luther, the A.V., etc., supposed it to equal *the goat sent away,* or *let loose.* But the application of *Azazel* to the goat itself involves the Hebrew text in difficulty. . . . 2. The name of the place to which the goat was sent. But the place is specified in Leviticus 16:10, 21, 22 (Gesenius). 3. A personal being to whom the goat was sent. (*a*) Gesenius makes *Azazel* equal *averter, expiator,* and supposes it to be some false deity who was to be appeased by a sacrifice of the goat. (*b*) Others have regarded him as an evil spirit, or the devil himself. . . . 4. An explanation of the word which seems less objectionable, if not wholly satisfactory, would render the designation of the lot (Lev. 16:8, etc., 'for the scapegoat,' A.V.) 'for *complete* sending away.' "—*Smith's Bible Dictionary,* p. 83, art. "Atonement, the Day of."

# THE SCAPEGOAT AND THE ATONEMENT

## Jewish Encyclopedia

"Azazel (scapegoat, Leviticus 16, A.V.): The name of a supernatural being mentioned in connection with the ritual of the Day of Atonement (Leviticus 16). After Satan, for whom he was in some degree a preparation, Azazel enjoys the distinction of being the most mysterious extrahuman character in sacred literature. Unlike other Hebrew proper names, the name itself is obscure. . . . Most modern scholars . . . have accepted the opinion mysteriously hinted at by Ibn Ezra and expressly stated by Nahmanides to Leviticus 16:8, that Azazel belongs to the class of 'se'irim,' goatlike demons. . . .

"Far from involving the recognition of Azazel as a deity, the sending of the goat was, as stated by Nahmanides, a symbolic expression of the idea that the people's sins and their evil consequences were to be sent back to the spirit of desolation and ruin, the source of all impurity. The very fact that the two goats were presented before YHWH [Jehovah] before the one was sacrificed and the other sent into the wilderness, was proof that Azazel was not ranked with YHWH, but regarded simply as the personification of wickedness in contrast with the righteous government of YHWH. . . .

"Azazel would therefore appear to be the head of the supernatural beings of the desert. . . . The fact that such a ceremony as that in which he figured was instituted, is not a contravention of Leviticus 17:7, by which demon worship was suppressed. For Azazel, in the instance, played a merely passive part. Moreover, as shown, the symbolical act was really a renunciation of his authority. Such is the signification of the utter separation of the scapegoat from the people of Israel."—*The Jewish Encyclopedia,* vol. 2, pp. 365-367, art. "Azazel."

## International Standard Bible Encyclopedia

"By the use of the same preposition *le* in connection with Jehovah and Azazel, it seems natural to regard the expressions as entirely parallel and to think of some personal being. Some interpret this word as referring to a demon of the wilderness, . . . and explain the term as 'one who has separated himself from God,' or 'he who has separated himself,' or 'he who misleads others.' But a demon of this kind could not possibly be placed in contrast to Jehovah in this way. . . In later times the word *Azazel* was by many Jews and also by Christian theologians, such as Origen, regarded as that Satan himself who had fallen away from God. In this interpretation the contrast found in verse 8, in case it is to be regarded as a full parallelism, would be perfectly correct. But it must be acknowledged that in Holy Scripture, Satan is nowhere called by the name of Azazel. . . . It is accordingly advisable to interpret Azazel adjectively, i.e., to forgo finding a complete parallelism in verse 8, and to regard the preposition in connection with Jehovah as used differently from its use with Azazel. . . . With this interpretation a certain hardness yet remains for our linguistic sense, because we cannot find a good translation for the adjective. . . .

"Both goats, according to verse 5, are to be regarded as a single sin sacrifice, even should we interpret Azazel as demon or Satan, and we are accordingly not at all to understand that a sacrifice was brought to these beings. . . . In the personal interpretation, we could have, in addition to the idea of the removal of the guilt, also a second idea, namely, that Azazel can do no harm to Israel, but must be content with his claim to a goat which takes Israel's place."—*The International Standard Bible Encyclopedia*, vol. 1, pp. 343, 344, art. "Azazel."

## Kitto's Cyclopaedia

"The only difficulty here, and that is a great one, is with respect to the meaning of the word *Azazel*, which our translators, in common with a large class of modern commentators, regard as applied to the goat itself, and render it by 'scapegoat.' Others produce reasons, not easily answered, for showing that the word must be taken as a proper name. Then arises the question. What is the name? Several of the rabbinical writers regard it as the name of the *place* to which the scapegoat was conducted. . . . A step further, however, brings it more within the range of our recognition—this is, that Azazel is but a name for Satan as was the opinion of most of the Jewish writers and of the early Christian church; and that the meaning of the ceremony is, that while the remission of sin is effected by the sacrificed goat (for without shedding of blood there was no remission, Heb. 9:22), the other was laden with the sins already, through the other goat, pardoned, by way of symbolically notifying the fact of Satan, and of triumphing in his discomfiture. . . . There is another more common explanation, which, if correct, forms a very beautiful interpretation of the typical rite. This view recognizes the substantial typical identity of the two goats, and in the victim goat sees Christ dying for our sins, and in the liberated goat views Him as rising again for our justification. But it must be admitted that the whole subject forms one of the greatest difficulties of Scripture."—JOHN KITTO, *Cyclopaedia of Biblical Literature*, p. 363, art. "Goat, Scape."

# THE SCAPEGOAT AND THE ATONEMENT

## Lange's Commentary

"In regard to the meaning of Azazel: in the great variety of etymologies given for the word by scholars of the highest standing, it may be assumed as certain that nothing can be positively determined by the etymology. . . . Not only the roots themselves are varied, but their signification also, and still further the signification of the compound. Little light can be had from the ancient versions. The Sam., and the Targs. of Onk., John., and Jerus., retain the word unchanged: so also does the Syriac. . . . The Jewish authorities differ, . . . many of them explaining the word of the devil. . . . The great majority of modern commentators agree with Spencer and Rosenmüller in interpreting the word itself of the devil, although Bähr, Winer, and Tholuck contend for the sense *complete removal*."—*Lange's Commentary*, Notes on Leviticus 16.

## New Standard Bible Dictionary

"Azazel must . . . be the name either of the act of sending the goat away into the wilderness or, preferably, of the person to whom it was sent, possibly a demon in the wilderness. . . .

"In Israel it [the Atonement Day ritual] . . . was used to express the thought that sin belongs to a power or principle hostile to Jehovah, and its complete purgation must include its being sent back to its source."—*New Standard Bible Dictionary*, p. 85 (Funk and Wagnalls).

## Teachers' and Students' Bible Encyclopedia

"To determine which of the two goats was to be slain, and which sent alive into the wilderness, it was ordered that the priest should 'cast lots upon the two goats; one lot for the Lord (Jehovah), and the other lot for the scapegoat,' Lev. 16:8, but literally *for Azazel*, a word nowhere else used. There can be no doubt that this has the appearance of being some sort of personage, or interest personified, standing over against Jehovah, or somehow contradistinguished from him. But opinions have from early times been divided on the subject."—REV. PATRICK FAIRBAIRN, D.D., *Teachers' and Students' Bible Encyclopedia*, vol. 6, p. 109, art. "Scapegoat."

## Encyclopedia Biblica

"The meaning of Azazel is much disputed; it is, of course, a subject closely connected with the inquiry into the origin of the custom. It is at least certain that, as Azazel receives one goat while Yahwe [Jehovah] receives the other, both must be personal beings."—T. K. CHEYNE,

# ANSWERS TO OBJECTIONS

M. A., D. D., and J. SUTHERLAND BLACK, M. A., LL. D., *Encyclopedia Biblica,* vol. 1, p. 395, art. "Azazel."

## Eadie's Biblical Cyclopedia

"A common opinion is, that the one goat which was slain represented Christ dying and dead for the sins of man, and that the other goat, which lived and was dismissed, symbolized Christ risen and pleading our cause. But it might be objected to such a view that the sins of the Hebrew nation were laid on the live goat after its fellow had been sacrificed—an arrangement which does not harmonize with the actual atonement of the Son of God, for our sins were laid, not upon the *risen* Saviour, but upon Him *before* He died, and *in* His death. We incline to the oldest view of this subject—a view common in the church till the period of Julian the apostate, by whom it was abused and caricatured.

"The language in the original is precise and peculiar. It reads, 'And Aaron shall cast lots on the two goats—ONE FOR JEHOVAH, ONE FOR AZAZEL.' What we are to understand by Azazel has been much disputed. The language appears to us to imply the personality of Azazel—'one for Jehovah, one for Azazel.' By Azazel we venture to understand Satan, as do almost all the ancient versions, which leave the word, as they do the names of other persons, untranslated. Satan is not here, as some allege against this opinion, put on an equality with God; for the two goats were both brought 'to Jehovah,' and were His; while the very casting of lots, which was in itself a solemn appeal to God, shows that Jehovah claimed the power of disposal. Neither can it be objected that this was in any sense a sacrifice to Satan, for the animal was not slain to him; it was only sent to him in disgrace. Bearing upon it sins which God had already forgiven, it was sent to Azazel in the wilderness.

"The phrase 'scapegoat,' by which the strange term Azazel is rendered in our version, came from the *'hircus emissarius'* of the Vulgate. The term *Azazel* may mean the 'apostate one'—a name which Satan merits, and which he seems to have borne among the Jews. It was Satan that brought sin into the world; and this seduction of man adds to his guilt, and consequently to his punishment. Sin is now pardoned in God's mercy. The one goat was sacrificed as a sin offering; its blood was carried into the holy place, and the mercy seat was sprinkled with it. Guilt was therefore canceled; by this shedding of blood there was remission. But sin, though pardoned, is yet hateful to God, and it cannot dwell in His sight: it is removed away to a 'land not inhabited'

THE SCAPEGOAT AND THE ATONEMENT

—severed from God's people, and sent away to man's first seducer. The sins of a believing world are taken off them, and rolled back on Satan, their prime author and instigator. Though the penalty is remitted to believers, it is not remitted to him who brought them into apostasy and ruin. The tempted are restored, but the whole punishment is seen to fall on the archtempter."—*Eadie's Biblical Cyclopedia,* from the Original Text of John Eadie, D. D., LL. D., late professor of Biblical Literature and Exegesis to the United Presbyterian Church, art. "Scapegoat," p. 577. (Preface to the new edition written by A. H. Sayce, of Oxford, and bears date of 1901.)

### Sunday School Times

"Of the two goats, one was for Jehovah, signifying God's acceptance of the sin offering; the other was for Azazel. This is probably to be understood as a person, being parallel with Jehovah in the preceding clause. So Azazel is probably a synonym for Satan. The goat for Azazel, the scapegoat, as it is somewhat misleadingly translated, typifies God's challenge to Satan (cf. Job 1:8; Eph. 3:10)."—J. RUSSELL HOWDEN, Notes on the Sunday School Lessons in *Sunday School Times,* Jan. 15, 1927.

### Bible Translations

Following is a partial list of the translations of the Bible that retain the original word *Azazel* in the text:

English Revised Version
American Revised Version
American Baptist Improved
Rotherham's
Moulton's
Moffatt's
Darby's
Smith's (J. Powis)
Leeser's (Jewish translation of the Old Testament)
Jewish Publication Society translation, 1917. (The Old Testament by a committee of Jewish scholars. Probably the most authoritative translation among English-speaking Jews.)

### Conclusions From Quotations

From the foregoing quotations we may draw the following important conclusions:

## ANSWERS TO OBJECTIONS

1. The meaning of the word *Azazel* is so obscure that no doctrine may properly be built upon an attempted translation of the term. Special significance attaches to the fact that so many translations of the Bible, including the Jewish, leave *Azazel* untranslated. In fact, with but two or three exceptions, all our Bible translations either follow the King James Version and use the word *scapegoat*, or else leave *Azazel* untranslated. The retaining of the original term *Azazel* indicates either that the translators felt that the meaning of the word was too obscure, or else they considered *Azazel* a proper name, which would therefore not call for translation. But of course if *Azazel* is a proper name, then it must stand for some being in contrast to Jehovah.

2. A wide divergence of interpretation of the meaning of the Atonement Day ritual has existed from earliest times.

3. The view which regards Azazel as symbolizing Satan has been held through the centuries by many theologians, both Jewish and Christian. Lange's commentary, which is perhaps the most exhaustive and reliable of such works, affirms that "the great majority of modern commentators" view Azazel as Satan. (Comments on Leviticus 16.)

4. This view, which makes Azazel a personal being in antithesis to Jehovah, finds strong support in the very construction of the Hebrew itself. One goat is "for Jehovah," the other "for Azazel." To prevent the natural conclusion of opposing personalities, implied by the similar preposition ("for"), requires the doubtful expedient of understanding the preposition "in connection with Jehovah as used differently from its use with Azazel."—*The International Standard Bible Encyclopedia.* But even then, as this Bible encyclopedia admits, there remains a "linguistic" difficulty. This procedure, while technically violating no law of grammar, may properly be viewed as questionable. Certainly a heavy burden of proof rests upon those who maintain that a preposition (for) used in two apparently parallel and immediately joined phrases, should be given a different value in one phrase from the other. Evidently the proof produced has not been sufficient to convince a large part

of the theologians through the years, as is witnessed by the great number who have held that Azazel represents a personality in antithesis to Jehovah.

5. Even among theologians who do not allow Satan in the picture and who thus restrict the symbolism of both goats to Christ, the position is set forth (and by one of the most able exponents of that view, Bähr) that "the true expiation was effected by the blood of the first goat" and that the "ceremony with the other goat appears as a mere addition made for special reasons, a kind of complement to the wiping away of the sins which had already been effected by means of the sacrifice." (See quotation from M'Clintock and Strong's Cyclopaedia.) Certainly under this view of the matter, the functions of the "risen and living Saviour," if He is the Azazel goat, are reduced to a rather purposeless "mere addition."

6. The many theologians, from the ancient rabbins down to a recent contributor to the *Sunday School Times,* who have held that Azazel represents Satan, have not found it necessary to view him as a substitutionary sacrifice, a savior. On the contrary, they repudiate the thought.

7. Among the theologians who view Azazel as representing Satan, there is prominent the idea of judgment, the returning to their satanic source of the *pardoned* sins of God's children. (See quotations from M'Clintock and Strong, *Jewish Encyclopedia;* Kitto, *New Standard Bible Dictionary;* and Eadie's *Biblical Cyclopedia.*) Evidently the introducing of the thought of judgment into the Atonement Day ritual does not seem "incongruous" to a wide group of both Jewish and Christian theologians. On the contrary, the idea of judgment seems vital to many expositors.

### A Brief Survey of the Adventist Position

We would not for a moment attempt to prove that our belief concerning Azazel is correct simply because many Christian leaders through the centuries have held that belief. But when our critics endeavor to give strength to their attack on us by creating the impression that we teach strange, unchristian doctrine in this matter, we may rightly introduce as most relevant the evidence of the extent to which this doctrine about Azazel has been held from earliest times.

It is hardly within the scope of this chapter to go into an extended discussion of our teachings as to the sanctuary, which provide the proper background for our belief regarding Azazel. Extended discussions of the sanctuary doctrine are easily obtainable in various of our works. But the following brief outline may appropriately be given:

In the slaying of the Passover lamb we see Christ, our Passover, slain. (1 Cor. 5:7.) We see in the round of the Levitical service, with its priests ministering the spilled blood of the various sin offerings, our great High Priest in heaven, ministering His blood for those who accept His sacrifice. In the Atonement Day service, which was the culminating event in the Levitical cycle, and was the day when the sins that had been confessed throughout the year were finally disposed of, we see the type of the last work which Christ performs in His priestly ministry for repentant sinners.

We believe that when Christ completes this final work of cleansing the heavenly sanctuary, the fate of all is determined for eternity, and that then will go forth the edict: "He that is unjust, let him be unjust still: and he which is filthy, let him be filthy still: and he that is righteous, let him be righteous still: and he that is holy, let him be holy still." Rev. 22:11.

### Azazel Enters Picture After Atonement Is Made

In the typical high priest's coming out to the Azazel goat after having "made an atonement . . . for all the congregation of Israel," having indeed "made an *end* of reconciling," we see Christ's leaving the sanctuary after finally completing His work of atonement, and rolling back upon the head of Satan, the instigator of all sin, the primary guilt, which is his alone, for the sins of the now-pardoned and eternally saved believers.

Finally, we see in the scapegoat being led off into the wilderness, a type of Satan, the scapegoat of the universe, being taken by a strong angel and cast into the "bottomless pit." * (Rev. 20:1-3.)

We believe that this view of the sanctuary service provides an interpretation of the function of Azazel that is both rational and Scriptural.

Far from the idea of a judgment's being "incongruous" as a conclusion to the work of atonement, the very opposite is true. There is no fact more striking in the Scriptures than that Christ, when He has finished His work of pleading for men, will put on the garments of vengeance to execute judgment.

Only one objection remains to be considered. It is based on Leviticus 16:10. "The goat, on which the lot fell to be the scapegoat, shall be presented alive before the Lord, to make an atonement with him." Our critics quote this verse and declare to us, "If you believe the scapegoat typifies Satan, then you believe that Satan is your savior." We answer emphatically, "No," and add, "If you believe that the scapegoat typifies Christ, then you believe in a savior we cannot find anywhere in the Bible." Note the following facts:

1. We stand squarely on the solemn declaration that without shedding of blood there is no remission of sins. As already stated, the scapegoat's blood was not shed. Therefore this goat could not typify the work of a Being who could give to us remission of sins. Others may believe that they see the work of atonement *for our sins* typified by an animal that is not slain, whose blood is not poured out. But, standing on the Scripture, we cannot.

2. Earlier in this chapter the fact was established that only one goat, "the Lord's goat," is offered up for a *sin* offering. Therefore we must base our hope of salvation on the Being typified by the goat that was offered up for sin. That is the only kind of Saviour that the Bible describes. Those who would make a savior of one who was not offered up, teach an un-Scriptural view of salvation.

---

* The term *bottomless pit* is from the Greek word *abussos*. This is the word used in the Greek translation of the Old Testament (the Septuagint) in the sentence which describes the chaotic state of the earth at the beginning of creation week: "Darkness was upon the face of the deep [*abussos*]." Gen. 1:2. The *abussos* into which the devil is cast—the earth which has again returned to a lifeless, barren state as a result of the cataclysm of the Second Advent—may very properly be typified by the wilderness destination of the goat.

Therefore we do not, we cannot, view the live goat as typifying Christ, who saves us from our sins.

3. The blood of the slain goat made atonement "for all the congregation of Israel" for "all their sins." Verses 17, 16. And when the priest had finished ministering its blood, he had "made an *end* of reconciling." Verse 20. These statements are so plain that, as we noted at the beginning of this chapter, our critics frankly admit that "the sins of 'all the congregation of Israel' had already been atoned for by the death of the first goat" when the high priest came out to the live goat. Thus the people had already been freed from their guilt, and accordingly were no longer in need of a Saviour from their sins, when the high priest came out of the sanctuary. The Saviour described in the Bible came to our rescue "while we were yet sinners." (Rom. 5:8.) Poor sinners do not stand in need of a savior who makes no contact with their sins until *after* those sins have been atoned for. Where is the text that gives even the semblance of support for the belief that sins which have been atoned for are then laid upon Christ? Yet that is the kind of savior we would have if we viewed the scapegoat as a type of Christ. We find no such Christ in the Scriptures. Therefore, believing that Azazel represents a personal being, we are logically compelled to view the scapegoat as typifying Satan.

### Explain a Hard Passage by Simpler Ones

We willingly admit, as theologians have admitted through all the years, that Leviticus 16:10 is a perplexing passage. In dealing with it we have endeavored to follow the approved principle of Bible interpretation, that is, of understanding a difficult passage by other and clearer passages. The various other texts in Leviticus 16 regarding the function of the two goats, and the texts elsewhere that deal with the work of Christ for sinners, surely prohibit us from viewing the scapegoat as Christ. And by a parity of reasoning they prohibit us from understanding the word *atonement* in verse 10 as signifying the performance of a work similar to that performed by the slain goat.

# THE SCAPEGOAT AND THE ATONEMENT

We repeat here an illustration given under objection 98, to show the relation of Satan, the archfiend, to the plan of salvation:

A group of men have been arrested, tried, and convicted of certain crimes. A heavy fine is imposed upon them. They are in a hopeless state, for they are penniless. But their hopelessness is changed to joy; a rich philanthropist offers to pay their fine. They accept, and are free. The case is apparently settled. But no; the court, continuing its investigations, discovers that a person of fiendish cunning has really dominated these poor men, and has seduced them into their course of wrongdoing. He is captured, and judgment is meted out to him. He is made to pay a heavy fine —much heavier even than that from which the poor men have been freed by the gracious act of the philanthropist; for the court reasons that the fiend is doubly guilty.

Now, it may truly be said that the philanthropist atones, or makes satisfaction, for the crimes of these poor men. Yet in another sense we could speak of the archfiend's atoning for those very crimes. There is no confusion of meaning, even though each gives satisfaction to justice in a basically different way. Nor by declaring that the archfiend gives satisfaction for those crimes do we minimize in the slightest degree the adequacy and sufficiency of the philanthropist's gracious act toward the penniless men.

Adventists believe that this explains the statement in Leviticus 16:10. The people's sins are atoned for by a Substitute, typified by the slain goat. Then these *atoned for* sins are thrown back on the head of the archfiend, Satan, typified by the Azazel goat, who must bear the guilt of primary responsibility for their sins. In the words of Dr. John Eadie:

"The sins . . . are . . . rolled back on Satan, their prime author and instigator. Though the penalty is remitted to believers, it is not remitted to him who brought them into apostasy and ruin. The tempted are restored, but the whole punishment is seen to fall on the archtempter."—*Eadie's Bible Cyclopedia*, p. 577.

There is another objection, which is scarcely worthy of even passing notice. It is said that even if Azazel represents Satan, the goat itself did not represent Satan, that instead it was simply "for Azazel." But those who raise this quibble believe that the slain goat, chosen "for the Lord," represents the Lord Jesus Himself. Therefore it is but consistent to affirm that the goat "for Azazel" represents Satan himself.

### Why Are We Singled Out for Attack?

In view of all the evidence in this chapter, especially the evidence as to the widespread belief among stalwart Protestant theologians that Azazel represents Satan, what is to be thought of the unspeakable charge brought against us by a certain class, that we make Satan our savior, because we, along with this great company of theologians, believe that Azazel represents Satan? But those who bring these charges against us because of our views concerning Azazel, have never brought any like charges against any others who believe similarly. This is indeed the most singular fact in connection with the whole matter. We therefore decline to give further serious consideration to these indictments against us until those who bring them are willing to level the same charges against the long and impressive list of Christian leaders who have held that Azazel represents Satan.

### One Writer Retracts Charge

In fairness, it should be stated that one writer who had charged us with teaching that Satan is our savior, afterward withdrew it. In the *Moody Bible Institute Monthly* of November, 1930, Grant Stroh, editor of the "Practical and Perplexing Questions" department, made this charge. In response to a letter written to the *Moody Monthly*, Dr. Stroh published this statement in the February, 1931, issue of that journal.

"The chief exception taken to our statement concerned their doctrine of the atonement. We said: 'Seventh-day Adventism denies the atoning sacrifice of Christ as the only means of man's salvation, and declares instead that Satan is our savior, sin bearer, and vicarious substitute.'

"This seems to be an extreme statement, and having read some of the writings of the Seventh-day Adventists since it was made, we find it could be proved from them that such is not their belief. I am sure that most of these people are saved, in spite of their unscriptural teachings, and that most of them probably do not hold any such view of the atonement. It is only fair to truth, however, that we read not only a popular statement on their beliefs, such as in the booklet *Belief and Work of Seventh-day Adventists*, but also examine the way of salvation as set forth by their acknowledged prophet, Mrs. E. G. White, in *The Great Controversy*, upon which the statements in 'Heresies Exposed' were based. Even then we apologize for the baldness of the statement in our November issue, and beg forgiveness of these good people for any misstatement of their doctrines."

### Mrs. E. G. White Describes the Function of the Scapegoat

This retraction is given unique weight by the candid admission that it is the result of "having read some of the writings of the Seventh-day Adventists *since*" the charge was made. Might it not be proper to suggest to others that they likewise read carefully some of our standard works before hastening forth to broadcast the hideous charge that we make Satan our savior? It is true that Dr. Stroh further in his article expresses distress at the statements made in *The Great Controversy*, because they permit Satan to be introduced at all into the picture. But does he set forth anything from Mrs. E. G. White that warrants his withdrawing his retraction? No! How could he, when Mrs. White states unequivocally on page 658 of that work:

"Now the event takes place, foreshadowed in the last solemn service of the Day of Atonement. When the ministration in the holy of holies had been completed, and the sins of Israel had been removed from the sanctuary by virtue of the blood of the sin offering, then the scapegoat was presented alive before the Lord; and in the presence of the congregation the high priest confessed over him 'all the iniquities of the children of Israel, and all their transgressions in all their sins, putting them upon the head of the goat.' Lev. 16:21. In like manner, when the work of atonement in the heavenly sanctuary *has been completed,* then in the presence of God and heavenly angels and *the host of the redeemed,* the sins of God's people will be placed upon Satan; he will be declared guilty of all the evil which he has caused them to commit. And as the scapegoat was sent away into a land not inhabited, so Satan will be banished to the desolate earth, an uninhabited and dreary wilderness." (Italics ours.)

Our critics, who have examined so critically Mrs. White's writings in an attempt to find some stray phrase on which to base a charge, must surely have read this statement in *The Great Controversy,* for it is the climax to her description of the sanctuary service. If they had been willing to publish this quotation, the appalling indictment that we make Satan our savior would have been exposed as false. Why have they failed to do so? We must leave that question for them to answer.

# Section VII

# APOSTASY AND OFFSHOOTS

CHAPTER 19

# Six Distinguishing Marks of Apostates

THEY went out from us, but they were not of us; for if they had been of us, they would no doubt have continued with us: but they went out, that they might be made manifest that they were not all of us." 1 John 2:19.

This inspired statement was made only about seventy years after the founding of the Christian church. There were numbers still living who had witnessed the organization of this new movement in the world. Yet this short space of time sufficed for the manifestation of desertions from the church. It is not a thing to be marveled at, then, that in these last days also the church of God should be troubled with offshoots.

The Bible does not give us many details regarding the church troubles of the first century, nor is it necessary for us to know them; but it is well for us to give some thought and study to the question as it affects our own age. From time to time since the beginning of this Second Advent message there have been those who have gone out from us. Some good church members, though they may not be led away into apostasy, are not quite able to understand why such "earnest people" have gone out from us.

A good way to deal with this problem is to set down the outstanding characteristics of these offshoots, and with these before us to draw definite conclusions. Allowing for some minor exceptions, the various offshoots developed from time to time possess, or did possess while they existed, the following characteristics:

### Destructive

1. THEY ARE DESTRUCTIVE. Their message is not a new, clear, positive one, but negative. They are chiefly concerned with denouncing the movement with which they have so lately been allied.

True Protestantism, though it is a protest against the evils of the false church out of which our fathers came, is defined in terms of positive truths that were set forth by the Reformers. No great wisdom is required to be a critic or to denounce others. The evidence of wisdom, the kind that comes down from above, is in the setting forth of a new and better way in which men should walk.

## Much Ado About Nothing

2. IRRELEVANT OR UNIMPORTANT QUESTIONS ARE STRESSED. If the whole time and energy of the offshoot is not concerned with denouncing or criticizing the denomination, the "new light" given out consists of irrelevant and often ludicrous points. There are certain minds that seem possessed of the sad faculty of stressing the unimportant; they are almost ready to become martyrs for the inconsequential. We have a chronic illustration of this in the person who is ready to call down anathemas on the men of the denomination because they shave the "corner of their beard."

## Mistakes of Leaders Featured

3. THE MISTAKES OF CERTAIN LEADERS ARE HELD UP. Reduced to a syllogism, the argument runs thus: Elder Blank is a conference president. He is not what he ought to be. Therefore the whole movement is evil.

This is not a new method of attacking an organization. It is as old, and also as faulty, as the human race. The rightness or wrongness of a movement cannot thus be determined. There will always be those among the leaders who are not what God would have them to be. But the movement is not bad because of them; rather is it good in spite of them. The question of whether the Lord is leading a movement can be answered only by comparing its doctrines with the words of Scripture. "If they speak not according to this word," then we can rightly say that the organization is not of God; and, conversely, if they do speak according to the Bible, then God surely must be directing the work, for only when the Spirit of God enlightens men can they know the truth. Flesh and blood cannot reveal it unto them. Therefore this Second

Advent movement, which is teaching the true Bible doctrines, was not started by the wisdom of man nor does it thus continue.

Although it is a fact that the faulty lives of its leaders can do great damage, and cause the name of God to be blasphemed among the Gentiles; and though it is also a fact that real Christianity can be fully understood only as lived out, yet we must always remember that the question of the divine origin of Christianity must be decided by the great spiritual truths and moral standards it represents, and not by the lives of those who call themselves Christians.

Through two long world wars the so-called Christian peoples of various nations killed one another in bloody fighting, much to the bewilderment of the heathen, who thought that Christianity meant loving each other. The only explanation needed for this paradox is that these Christian peoples were not living up to what they claimed to believe. Christianity still stands as the revelation of God to man, despite the course that so-called Christian nations pursue; and, likewise, the threefold message still remains God's last message for the world, despite the course that any member or leader in the movement may take.

However, before we pass on to the next point a word of caution might well be given regarding the charges that the enemies of the denomination make against various leaders. Many of these charges are a pure tissue of falsehood, and most of the remainder are based on a gross distortion of facts.

### Extreme Position on Testimonies

4. THE WRITINGS OF MRS. E. G. WHITE ARE FREQUENTLY THE PIVOTAL POINT. The various offshoots may generally be classed in two opposing groups as regards the writings of Mrs. White. The first quote her at great length; the second denounce her as a fraud. The first use her writings because they find therein certain passages that apparently give support to their charge that the denomination is so sinful that its members should leave it. The second group denounce her writings as fraudulent in an attempt to escape their indictment against deserters from the faith.

The first group are not consistent, because the very writings of Mrs. White which declare the denomination sinful also affirm that despite this spiritual weakness, God is still with the movement, and will bring it through to a successful finish, and denounce those who raise the cry, "Come out." The second group show the weakness of their charge that Mrs. White is a fraud, by the irrelevant objections they bring forth. It is possible to bring objections against even the Bible, but they are palpably weak. Thus with the case that this second group would strive to make out against Mrs. White.

Of those who wrongly quote the Spirit of prophecy, Sister White inquires:

"Those who have proclaimed the Seventh-day Adventist Church as Babylon, have made use of the 'Testimonies' in giving their position a seeming support; but why is it that they did not present that which for years has been the burden of my message,—the unity of the church? Why did they not quote the words of the angel, 'Press together, press together, press together'? Why did they not repeat the admonition and state the principle, that 'in union there is strength, in division there is weakness'?"—*Testimonies to Ministers*, p. 56.

### Earnestness and Sincerity

5. GREAT EARNESTNESS AND SINCERITY OFTEN SEEM TO CONTROL THEM. This feature is a source of perplexity to many. "How," they ask, "can those people be so earnest and sincere if their teachings are so false?" Unfortunately, earnestness and sincerity, though they generally accompany a firm belief in anything, do not thereby prove the belief true. It is the truth of a belief that sanctifies the earnestness, and not the earnestness that sanctifies and makes true the belief.

The human mind is so constructed that a lie may ultimately be accepted as the truth if there is the will to believe. This fact is well illustrated by Scripture. "The time cometh," said Christ to His disciples, "that whosoever killeth you will think that he doeth God service." John 16:2. This is the choicest example that could be offered of wrong thinking combined with great earnestness. Further, we are told of a class of people who, "because they received not the love of the truth," finally believed "a lie." 2 Thess. 2:10, 11. A self-deceived earnest man we may appropriately pity, but we cannot believe. The Spirit of prophecy declares:

"False teachers may appear to be very zealous for the work of God, and may expend means to bring their theories before the world and the church; but as they mingle error with truth, their message is one of deception, and will lead souls into false paths. They are to be met, and opposed, not because they are bad men, but because they are teachers of falsehood, and are endeavoring to put upon falsehood the stamp of truth."—*Ibid.*, p. 55.

### Languish and Die

6. THESE OFFSHOOTS ULTIMATELY LANGUISH AND DIE. If, as they claim, they are the final "called out" of God who are to complete the great work begun by this movement, they should grow stronger and more successful as the years go by. But the reverse is true. God is not the leader of a dying movement. He is directing a growing and expanding movement in these closing days, for His last message is not to end up in a corner, but is to be proclaimed mightily in every part of the earth.

### Five Positive Facts

Whenever our minds are troubled over this question of counter movements, we should think back a moment over the characteristics that distinguish them, and then ask ourselves, Is God the author of such offshoots? To ask the question is to answer it. With that question decided in the negative, we should then remember these five great positive facts:

1. God has a church on the earth.

"God has a church upon the earth, who are His chosen people, who keep His commandments. He is leading, not stray offshoots, not one here and one there, but a people."—*Ibid.*, p. 61.

2. The remnant church is *not* Babylon.

"When anyone arises, either among us or outside of us, who is burdened with a message which declares that the people of God are numbered with Babylon, and claims that the loud cry is a call to come out of her, you may know that he is not bearing the message of truth.

Receive him not, nor bid him Godspeed; for God has not spoken by him, neither has He given a message to him, but he has run before he was sent."—*Ibid.*, p. 41.

3. This Advent movement came at exactly the right time in fulfillment of prophecy. If it had come earlier or later, it could not claim to have arisen in response to prophecy. It was no accident that this message began in the 1840's. God started it, and what is more encouraging, we have the promise that He will carry it through to a glorious conclusion.

4. The offshoots are just so many signs that the end is upon us, for the devil knows of no more effective way to hinder God's plan than to attempt to tear down this organization that Heaven has built up in these last days. Instead of being downcast by these desertions, we should lift up our heads and rejoice, for our redemption draweth nigh.

5. Despite all the weaknesses and mistakes of both leaders and lay members, God still loves and directs this Advent movement.

"God has a people in which all heaven is interested, and they are the one object on earth dear to the heart of God. Let every one who reads these words give them thorough consideration; for in the name of Jesus I would press them home upon every soul."—*Ibid.*

"The church, enfeebled and defective, needing to be reproved, warned, and counseled, is the only object upon earth upon which Christ bestows His supreme regard."—*Ibid.*, p. 49.

Let us, therefore, each one, thank God that He has called us out of darkness into this marvelous light, that He has placed us with a people who are "dear to the heart of God."

# CHAPTER 20

# An Answer to the Charge: "I Have Been Delivered From Adventism"

A N EX-ADVENTIST sometimes declares, "I have been delivered from Adventism." Evidently he means he has been freed from doctrines that blur his spiritual vision and hamper his Christian progress, and particularly from teachings that throttle his liberty and joy in the gospel. So long as he stays in the field of generalities it is difficult to answer him, for generalities are like the clouds, vaporous and constantly changing in position. But he did not come into the Advent movement on generalities. He was instructed on specific doctrines. To these he subscribed on joining the church, and from these, or some part of them, he must have been "delivered" when he left us.

A statement of these doctrines is published annually in the official *Yearbook* under the heading: "Fundamental Beliefs of Seventh-day Adventists." This statement consists of twenty-two sections. Let us examine these beliefs. For brevity's sake they are here summarized. In some instances the exact words of the formal statement are borrowed, as indicated by quotation marks.

### The Doctrines of God and Salvation

1. That the Bible is inspired and contains "an all-sufficient revelation" of God's will.

2. That "the Godhead, or Trinity" consists of Father, Son, and Holy Spirit.

3. That "Jesus Christ is very God," that He also took on Him "the nature of the human family," lived a sinless life, died for our offenses, arose, and ascended to heaven, "where He ever lives to make intercession for us."

4. That salvation is by "the new birth"; that "this comprises an entire transformation of life" by the power of God through faith in Christ.

5. That baptism "should follow repentance and forgiveness of sins." That the proper form of baptism is by immersion.

Does any Christian wish to be delivered from these doctrines? The ex-Adventist will probably say No, not from these. If he qualifies his statement by saying that he has been delivered from baptism by immersion, we need only reply that neither our Lord nor the apostles sought deliverance from it. But let us go on.

### The Law and the Sabbath

6. That the Decalogue is the moral standard for all men in all ages.

7. That the fourth command of the Decalogue "requires the observance of the seventh-day Sabbath. This holy institution is at the same time a memorial of creation and a sign of sanctification, a sign of the believer's rest from his own works of sin, and his entrance into the rest of soul which Jesus promises to those who come to Him."

8. That the Decalogue points out sin, but cannot save. That God sent His Son to save us from our sins. That "one is justified, not by obedience to the law, but by the grace that is in Christ Jesus." That "this experience is wrought by the divine agency of the Holy Spirit, who convinces of sin and leads to the Sin-Bearer, inducting the believer into the new-covenant relationship, where the law of God is written on his heart."

Does any Christian want to be delivered from these doctrines? If the ex-Adventist still wishes to be inside the circle of historic Protestantism he will have to reply, as regards the sixth and eighth points, that he is in agreement. The creeds of the Reformation churches, and all after them, are too explicit to permit debate. (See chapter 5.)

But he will say that he was delivered from that "Saturday Sabbath." Evidently there is something about the twenty-four hours at the close of the week that is fettering and confining. He was delivered from that to keep the first twenty-four hours of the week. Unquestionably, there is more laxity about Sunday. But Sunday-keeping ministers quite generally deplore it. Some of them, many of them, even campaign for civil statutes to enforce stricter Sunday rest. Perhaps the ex-Adventist wishes to be delivered from the truth of creation, which the seventh-day Sabbath memorializes. Many declare that they have been delivered from the old-fashioned, "unscientific" doctrine of creation, and proudly call themselves Modernists, or Liberalists.

Adventists do not wish deliverance from this doctrine, on which the whole Bible is reared, and so we do not wish deliverance from the Sabbath that memorializes creation. We do not wish to be freed from Genesis, from the Mosaic record that introduces the Scripture record. The record is clear, for all who believe Genesis, that God made the Sabbath at the end of creation week, in the setting of a perfect world, by resting on that day and sanctifying and blessing it. Why should we wish deliverance from a day that connects us with Eden? Why should we wish to be delivered from following the example of the great God? Why seek deliverance from that which God blessed and set apart as holy?

### Isaiah's View of the Sabbath

The prophet Isaiah seems to have held the same view. He is known as the prophet of salvation. The fifty-third chapter portrays the vicarious suffering of our Lord. The fifty-fourth chapter opens with the exultant words: "Sing, O barren, thou that didst not bear," and goes on to describe the joys of redemption. The fifty-fifth chapter calls on "every one that thirsteth" to come, buy "without money and without price." The fifty-sixth chapter declares: "Keep ye judgment, and do justice: for my salvation is near to come, and my righteousness to be revealed. Blessed is the man that doeth this, and the son of man that layeth hold on it; that keepeth the sabbath from polluting it, and keepeth his hand from doing any evil. . . . Also the sons of the stranger, that join themselves to the Lord, to serve him, and to love the name of the Lord, to be his servants, every one that keepeth the sabbath from polluting it, and taketh hold of my covenant; even them will I bring to my holy mountain, and make them joyful in my house of prayer." Isaiah did not think it incongruous to introduce the Sabbath in the midst of a grand, sweeping portrayal of salvation. And he declares that the Sabbathkeeper will be a "joyful" person.

Going onward, we find Isaiah, in the fifty-seventh chapter crying out against iniquity and declaring that God dwells with him that is of a contrite heart. The thought is continued into the fifty-eighth chapter, where the command is given to "cry aloud," and "shew my people their transgression." The true kind of fast is described, not to bow down the head, or to spread sackcloth, but to "deal thy bread to the hungry," to house the outcast, and cover the naked. Such a display of practical godliness will cause "thy light [to] break forth as the morning." "Then shalt thou call, and the Lord shall answer." "And the Lord shall guide thee continually." Then follows this statement regarding the Sabbath:

"If thou turn away thy foot from the sabbath, from doing thy pleasure on my holy day; and call the sabbath a delight, the holy of the Lord, honourable; and shalt honour him, not doing thine own ways, nor finding thine own pleasure, nor speaking thine own words: then shalt thou delight thyself in the Lord; and I will cause thee to ride upon the high places of the earth, and feed thee with the heritage of Jacob thy father: for the mouth of the Lord hath spoken it."

Isaiah, who unfolds the story of salvation, deliverance from sin, and a program of practical holiness, places the Sabbath in the midst of the picture. He describes it, not as something to be delivered from, but as something in which to "delight."

### Our Lord and the Sabbath

When our Lord walked with men He found Himself in controversy with the scribes and Pharisees concerning the Sabbath. He denounced their man-made commandments that had encrusted that holy day, but He did not denounce the Sabbath. We can imagine the ex-Adventist, if he had lived back there, announcing to Israel that they were to be delivered from the Sabbath. That would have been the time for Christ to announce deliverance from the seventh day of the week. No better setting could ever have been found. But He did not do so. Instead of preaching deliverance from the Sabbath law, He showed the people what was "lawful" to do on that day, and climaxed it by announcing: "Therefore the Son of man is Lord also of the sabbath." Mark 2:28. See also Luke 6:1-9.

Isaiah declared that the Sabbath should be considered a "delight, the holy of the Lord, honourable." Christ announced Himself Lord of the Sabbath. Adventists find "delight" in it, and seek to honor the Lord of the Sabbath by keeping His day holy. The ex-Adventist says he has been delivered from the Sabbath!

### The Nature of Man

We believe also—

9. That God "only hath immortality." That man is mortal, That immortality is a gift from God that will be "put on" at Christ's second coming.

10. That the condition of man in death is unconsciousness. That all lie in the grave till the resurrection.

11. That there is to be a resurrection of the just and the unjust.

12. That the wicked, and Satan with all his angels, will finally be destroyed by fire, and become ashes under the soles of our feet, so that every taint of sin will be blotted from the universe of God forever.

Sometimes the ex-Adventist says he has been delivered from these beliefs concerning man and his final reward. He would rather think that his righteous loved ones have enjoyed the bliss of heaven from the day of their death. But he must not permit himself to think of his unrighteous relatives, who must be writhing in torment. The thought that the wicked are to be consumed away, and be as though they had not been, causes his righteous indignation to kindle. He is happy to be delivered from any idea that the fires of hell will ever go out, the screams of the damned ever cease, the tragedy of sin ever end. And, of course, in being delivered from Adventism, he is enjoying greater freedom in Christ, greater happiness in the Christian way! We can imagine a man's thinking, as a result of reading certain texts apart from the whole context of Scripture, that he must believe in an eternally burning hell, and that unrighteous loved ones, departed, are even now writhing in it. But we cannot imagine his proclaiming that in turning to that view from the Adventist teaching he was therefore gaining greater freedom and joy in the Lord!

### The Sanctuary Doctrine

We continue our study of the tenets of our faith. We believe—

13. That the prophecy of Daniel 8:14 ended in 1844, and marked the beginning of the investigative judgment.

14. That the true sanctuary is in heaven. That Christ is our minister there, carrying on a work of which the Jewish service was a type. That the cleansing of the sanctuary is a work of judgment corresponding to the typical service on the Day of Atonement. That the close of this investigative judgment marks the close of human probation.

15. That God sent a warning message of the judgment and the nearness of the Advent in the form of three angels' messages and that these messages bring to view a work of reform to prepare men for the Advent.

16. "That the time of the cleansing of the sanctuary" is a "time of investigative judgment," first on the dead, then on the living. "This investigative judgment determines who of the myriads sleeping in the dust of the earth are worthy of a part in the first resurrection, and who of its living multitudes are worthy of translation."

The ex-Adventist may say that he has happily been delivered from such doctrines as these. He will tell us that he has no time for the idea that a special investigation must be made before anyone is accounted worthy of heaven. He speaks militantly of the "finished work of Christ" on the cross, as though the Adventist doctrine somehow minimized the sacrifice of our Lord on Golgotha. But, really, what is he delivered from? And what different view of the plan of salvation provides him greater joy and liberty?

We present Christ as having accomplished a divine work of sacrificial dying on that solemn Friday nineteen hundred years ago. We believe this has been followed by a work of high-priestly intercession by Him, that through the centuries He has been ministering His shed blood in our behalf. We are ever conscious of the price that was paid for our redemption and of the ever-present nature of the divine service instituted to provide a remedy for sin. We also believe that inasmuch as the heavenly service is the antitype of the earthly, there must come a final climax to the work of intercession and a cleansing of the sanctuary. We rejoice that God will bring the service to an orderly end and make pronouncement as to who shall be accounted worthy to receive of the reward of heaven. Surely it is reasonable to hold that God makes decisions on all cases before coming to execute judgment. That is what is involved in the idea of an investigative judgment.

But the ex-Adventist wishes to be delivered from all this. He wishes to think only of a finished work on Calvary, he declares. And how does he have greater liberty in the gospel by doing this? Why is it more joyous and soul-satisfying to restrict one's spiritual view wholly to Golgotha? The writer of Hebrews did not. He sought to carry the thoughts of the believers to the glorious ministry of our Lord after His priceless sacrifice on the cross. We would do likewise by our preaching. We would not set up artificial contrasts. We exalt the cross, and we do so partly by exalting the work of our Lord after the cross. From first to last we attribute all to Christ. We see Him in the center of the investigative judgment, for the Father has delivered all judgment into His hands. We see in Him our only hope, in His shed blood our only means of cleansing. Has the ex-Adventist found more than this by leaving Adventism?

# ANSWERS TO OBJECTIONS

## Simplicity, Modesty, Abstinence

We also believe—

17. That the child of God should stand apart from the ways of the world, particularly as regards amusements. That he should dress modestly. That he should abstain from liquor and tobacco and every practice that defiles the body and soul.

Some ex-Adventists have rejoiced in deliverance from this tenet. They do not wish to be fettered in matters of amusement, dress, or diet. This is understandable. But what is not understandable is that anyone should say that in being delivered from this doctrine of Adventism he was gaining greater joy in the Lord!

## Tithing and Spiritual Gifts

We believe, too—

18. That a tithe of our increase belongs to the Lord and that besides this we should give cheerfully of offerings, for we are but stewards of the treasures in our hands.

There are ex-Adventists who sigh a deep sigh of relief to be delivered from this tenet. They do not wish to set apart one tenth of their income for God and then add offerings thereto. This is all understandable. The Scriptures are filled with descriptions of the natural selfishness of the human heart. But we cannot understand how a person finds greater joy in the Lord by eliminating tithe and reducing his offerings. A host of Sundaykeeping ministers urge tithing on their members and assure them there is joy in such a plan. There is. Adventists know from experience.

## Spiritual Gifts

We believe, too—

19. "That God has placed in His church the gifts of the Holy Spirit, as enumerated in 1 Corinthians 12 and Ephesians 4. That these gifts operate in harmony with the divine principles of the Bible, and are given for the perfecting of the saints, the work of the ministry, the edifying of the body of Christ."

Ex-Adventists do not wish to be delivered from the general

752

belief in the gifts of the Spirit as this statement sets forth. But they often express joy over being delivered from a certain specific application of this belief. One of the gifts of the Spirit is the gift of prophecy. Adventists believe that this gift has been displayed in the life and writings of Ellen G. White. And how are those writings distinguished? Do they set forth a circumspect view of religious living, or do they advocate fanatical religious habits that lead to excesses? Do they uphold the Scriptures as the very Word of God, the supreme authority in our lives, or do they minimize the Bible or spiritualize it away? Do those writings uphold the great verities of revelation, such as the deity of our Lord and His sacrificial death and literal resurrection, or do they minimize or undermine them?

To anyone who has read Mrs. White's writings the answer is evident. Even her critics will generally agree that her writings promote the highest code of holy living in the setting of the Bible as the very voice of God to us, and that her writings call for constant sacrificial liberality in order that we may complete a task for God and be ready to meet Him in peace at His appearing. Certainly no unbiased person could make any other appraisal.

We can easily understand how an ex-Adventist might find a certain sense of relief in being "delivered" from the belief that Mrs. White's writings are a manifestation of the gift of the Spirit of prophecy—he need not live so highly, he need not sacrifice so deeply, he need not take the Scriptures of God so seriously.

But we cannot understand how that would give him a greater sense of joy in the Lord!

### The Second Advent and the New Earth

We believe, too—

20. "That the second coming of Christ is the great hope of the church, the grand climax of the gospel and plan of salvation." That this coming will be personal, and literal, and that "it is near, even at the doors," though the exact time cannot be known.

21. That for a thousand years after the Second Advent the

saints will be in heaven and the earth will lie desolate under the judgments of God. That at the end of that time the saints will return with their Lord, and fire from God destroy forever the wicked, turning them to ashes, and purging this earth.

22. "That God will make all things new. The earth, restored to its pristine beauty, will become forever the abode of the saints of the Lord."

## Ex-Adventist May Feel Relief—But

The ex-Adventist may feel relief at being delivered from the belief that Christ is soon coming to solve the tragedy of a world that seems to be headed for the third world war and mutual suicide. He may find satisfaction in the realization that he no longer believes that Heaven's purging fires will completely destroy every trace of sin and unrepentant sinners. He may feel much better pleased to think that in some segregated area of the universe the horrible thing called sin will be present never endingly in the person of its writhing, tortured, flaming devotees. He may even feel relieved that he no longer believes that God will re-create this earth a perfect and eternal abode for redeemed men and women. We can understand how he might so change his theological thinking that he would feel a sense of deliverance from these doctrines in which he no longer believed. But we do not understand how he would thereby find greater joy in the Lord!

## In Conclusion

And now this comment in conclusion. Genuine joy in religious living is not revealed by noisy amens and bodily gesticulations, but by the zest and enthusiasm with which a person engages in the religious life. The psalmist was "glad" for the invitation to go to the "house of the Lord." The genuinely joyful Christian will be found regularly in attendance at divine services. If he truly loves his Lord, he will give liberally. If he is filled with joy at the realization of what Christ has done for him, he will gladly devote hours of his time to missionary service.

## "DELIVERED FROM ADVENTISM"

Now as to church attendance, liberality, and missionary activity, how do we stand by comparison with other religious bodies? If we may judge by the way in which Adventists are often set forth by the leaders of other churches as worthy of emulation in these matters, we evidently do not suffer by comparison! But it is our doctrines that make us what we are religiously. We do not wish to be "delivered" from these beliefs; we find in them great joy in the Lord.

Section VIII

# THE FOUNDATION OF GOD
# STANDETH SURE

**21. Advent Movement Offers Certainty in Spiritual Matters**

# Advent Movement Offers Certainty
# in Spiritual Matters

A LITTLE while after the opening of the second world war the editor of *Fortune,* one of the most influential of journals in the business world, wrote a sobering analysis of the relation that spiritual values bear to the world problem. He charged that the leadership of the Christian church for the "past hundred years or so" had failed to teach "absolute spiritual values." In other words they had failed to teach that there are great truths and ideals that should be most certainly and unequivocally believed. He did not discourse on the reasons for this, though he might properly have noted that it was during the "past hundred years or so" that the Christian clergy became increasingly infected with a rationalistic, evolutionary viewpoint that inevitably resulted in their thinking of the Scriptures as something less than the voice of God speaking to men. He was concerned, rather, to challenge the clergy as to the need of a spiritually authoritative message. Note his words:

"We are asked to turn to the Church for our enlightenment, but when we do so we find that the voice of the Church is not inspired. The voice of the Church today, we find, is the echo of our own voices. And the result of this experience, already manifest, is disillusionment. . . . This is a profound and absolute spiritual disillusionment, arising from the fact that when we consult the Church we hear only what we ourselves have said. The effect of this experience upon the present generation has been profound. It is the effect of a vicious spiral, like the spiral that economists talk about that leads into depressions. But in this spiral there is at stake, not merely prosperity, but civilization.

"There is only one way out of the spiral. The way out is the sound of a voice, not our voice, but a voice coming from something not ourselves, in the existence of which we cannot disbelieve. It is the earthly task of the pastors to hear this voice, to cause us to hear it, and to tell us what it says. If they cannot hear it, or if they fail to tell us, we, as laymen, are utterly lost. Without it we are no more capable of saving the world than we were capable of creating it in the first place."—January, 1940, p. 27.

This declaration is typical of many that have been made by serious-minded men in these disillusioning years that have followed the collapse of the idea that the world is inevitably progressing onward and upward. Seventh-day Adventists find themselves in a unique relationship to this present phenomenon of disillusionment. We have never believed that the world was progressing onward and upward, but rather the contrary. We have never given ear to the higher critical, rationalistic, and evolutionary views that have so thoroughly discounted the supernatural in the thinking of a great and increasing majority of the Christian clergy.

In the setting of all this we wish to set forth certain reasons why we believe that the Advent movement provides men with that voice of authority and certainty in the spiritual realm that should ever be the distinguishing mark of a movement directed by God. To give maximum directness and vividness to them, these reasons are set forth in the first person singular as a personal testimony of a truth seeker:

## Certainty in Spiritual Realm

1. A DESIRE FOR CERTAINTY AND AUTHORITY IN THE SPIRITUAL REALM. A person cannot do any serious, intelligent thinking on the subject of religion without soon coming to the conclusion that the worth-whileness of the views held by a religious body depends upon the authority behind those views. One of the primary points of conflict between Rome and Protestantism in the Reformation days was the question of authority. The Catholic Church rested its claim first of all upon the authority of the church as set forth in the declarations of its clergy and of its councils, and upon traditions that had come down through the centuries. The Protestant Reformers declared that the valid authority for the church must be the Bible.

## CERTAINTY IN SPIRITUAL MATTERS

The tremendous need for a foundation of authority is revealed in the history of Protestantism. In modern times, as already stated, Protestant preachers have discounted the Bible, placing speculation and human reason above it. The result is that the foundations of Protestantism have been greatly weakened. An increasing number of people now view Protestant churches as having no more compelling power over their hearts than a literary society or a lodge. Men are not inclined to live, much less to die, for a religious organization that does not have behind it a compelling authority that captivates and controls their hearts. Men seek for certainty and assurance, something they can count on. That search is most marked when it comes to spiritual matters. That is one of the reasons why Rome today makes a definite appeal to many, even among intellectuals. She claims an authority that is above and beyond passing whims and theories of men.

But as a serious religious person seeking a church home, I would not take long in deciding against Rome and for the Seventh-day Adventist movement. The first and chief reason would be that I would find Adventism founded on a belief in the Bible as the supreme inspired revelation of God to man, a "Thus saith the Lord" that is free from the fallibilities and the foolishness that are often so glaringly evident in the traditions of men. I would realize that the Adventist Church was being guided the same way as was the church in the wilderness thirty-five hundred years ago, when God gave to man through Moses the first of the written revelations. I would realize that the Adventist Church has behind it the same authority and credentials possessed by the early Christian church, whose apostles declared that they preached none other things than those which Moses and the prophets declared should come, and who presented to the new believers the Bible as the true source of instruction and reproof and counsel.

As I looked further into the matter, I would find that the Seventh-day Adventist Church expounds the prophecies of the Bible, showing the evidences of their fulfillment. This would lead me, first, to an increasing confidence in the Bible as the true guide;

and, second, to a definite assurance that the Advent movement is the church I should join. The evidence of fulfilled prophecy gives one the tremendous conviction that God has a plan and a program for the world, and specifically that God foretold the rise of this Advent movement in these last days.

As I looked still further into the subject, I would find additional reason for believing that the Adventist movement could bring to my soul a sense of certainty and authority in the spiritual realm, because the gift of the Spirit of prophecy has been manifested in the movement. My study of the former dealings of God with man would show me that by a prophet the Lord brought Israel out of Egypt, and by a prophet were the Israelites preserved, guided, warned, and rebuked through the centuries. I would discover further that in the beginnings of the Christian church the gift of prophecy was definitely manifested for the guidance and the building up of the church. And then as I examined the wealth of instruction and timely counsel found in the Spirit of prophecy, I would be altogether persuaded that conversion to the Seventh-day Adventist movement would bring to me that sense of certainty and authority in the spiritual realm that I so much desired.

### The Question of Beginnings

2. A DESIRE FOR CERTAINTY REGARDING THE MOOT QUESTION OF THE BEGINNING OF OUR WORLD. For two generations the religious world has been involved in sharp controversy over the question of the beginnings of things in our world, both as to man and as to all other living things upon the earth. The advocates of the skeptical evolution theory have tried to minimize the whole discussion by declaring that it does not matter where we came from, but rather where we are going to.

But as a serious religious person who had come far enough along in his thinking to take the Bible as his source of authority, I could not be satisfied with any such rejoinder. Instead, I would be persuaded that our ultimate destination has a close relation to our beginning. In other words, even my elementary study of the

Bible would lead me to believe that the record in Genesis has a real relation to the record in the Gospels and to the description of the new earth in the book of Revelation.

I could not hope to understand rightly the trend and direction of our whole world unless I could take my bearings from the beginning of time on this earth. I could not find any satisfaction in reading the promises of an earth made new, where all would be restored to original Edenic beauty, unless I were sure of what the original was like. It would provide no thrill to my heart to be assured that the earth is to be restored to its original state, if I must believe that the original state was marked with a varied array of dank pools filled with amoebae.

Having found my source of authority in the Bible, I would naturally wish to find certainty regarding the beginnings of things in a religious body that believed what the Bible teaches concerning beginnings. And, behold, I would find it in the Advent movement. I would find my feet standing on the solid ground at the entrance to the Garden of Eden. With the aid of Bible prophecies my eyes would be directed to the new heavens and the new earth, wherein dwelleth righteousness.

And right on this very point of the importance of a clear Biblical understanding of beginnings, I would find this Advent movement observing a certain day every week in holy memory of the fact that in six days God made heaven and earth, as the Genesis record declares. I would be greatly impressed that here was a most unusual organization, one that made central in its teachings and practice a truth as vital and fundamental as the miraculous creation of our world. I would see in this practice of keeping holy the seventh day an assurance that this religious body believed with great earnestness and definiteness the truth of creation, that it was not a mere theory with them. I would be assured in my heart that when they preached to me the truth of the new creation, of the new heart and spirit which God will give to us, they were not talking some abstract theory to me, but were building their preaching upon the great historical truth that the God who promises to recreate us new creatures in Christ Jesus is the same God who originally created man perfect, and breathed into his nostrils the breath of life.

I would feel that the Sabbath gave me a sense of continuity from the very beginning of God's program for man on the earth, as if by a series of links of weeks I was anchored to that very first Sabbath, when God rested from all His works, and was refreshed. I would feel a sense of relationship right through to the new earth, when from Sabbath to Sabbath we shall all come up to worship before the Lord. Thus the doctrine of the Sabbath would stand revealed to me, not simply as a proof of the people who believe what the Bible says regarding the beginning of our world, but also as a mighty aid in generating within my heart a sense of certainty and assurance in things spiritual, a feeling of close relationship with God's great beginnings and endings for our world.

### A True Moral Standard

3. A LONGING FOR CERTAINTY REGARDING A DEFINITE MORAL STANDARD. No man can go very far in serious thinking on religious matters without coming to the conclusion that there must be a definite moral standard as a rule for life, for religious thinking immediately stirs up the moral faculties. The sense of right and wrong is quickened, conscience is aroused, the mind is filled with questionings, and all questions focus on the primary inquiry, Is there a definite moral standard by which to govern one's life? and if so, what is that standard?

Now, my acceptance of the Bible as the basis of authority for religious life would cause me soon to discover that much is said in the Scriptures concerning the moral code. I would read of the law of the Lord, which is declared to be perfect. I would read of ten holy commandments, which God spoke with His own voice, and uttered no more. I would read of how those ten commands were written also by the finger of God on tables of stone, and placed in a sacred shrine apart from all other laws. I would read that faith does not make void this law, but rather establishes it, and that this great code which is called the law of liberty will judge us in the last great day.

My longing for certainty as to a moral standard would thus have been satisfied, but where should I find a religious movement that upholds all of this law, a law that is so definitely one complete whole that to be guilty of breaking one precept means breaking the whole law? As I listened to Adventist evangelists, I would find that they stress this great truth that the Decalogue provides an infallible moral standard for all men in all ages. I would find this truth presented in Adventist literature everywhere. In neither the preaching nor the writing of the exponents of Adventism would I find any suggestion of the demoralizing doctrine that good and evil are only relative terms, that one's environment and training and the age in which one lives determine whether some act is to be considered good or bad. I would find no suggestion of the modern skeptical doctrine so often proclaimed in liberal churches, that the ten-commandment law is rather out of date, that it represents simply the best thought that Moses had long ago.

No possible doubt could be in my mind as to the belief of Adventists concerning the moral law. That, in itself, would provide me with great comfort. I would know that I could measure my life by something sure and immovable. Then as I looked at the Bible prophecy concerning a movement to arise in the last days, I would find that one of the characteristics of this movement would be its keeping of the commandments of God.

### Certainty Beyond the Grave

4. A DESIRE TO FIND AN ANSWER TO THE QUESTION THAT HAS BEEN ASKED AND REASKED THROUGH ALL THE CENTURIES, "If a man die, shall he live again?" What a vast amount of literature has been written by sages and philosophers in all ages in an endeavor to answer this question. The hopes and fears of men have revolved around it. And closely related to this has been the inquiry, What is man? is he but flesh and blood, of the earth earthy? or is that which our eyes gaze upon merely a prison house and shell for the

real being, which is ethereal and which flits away to another abode at death?

My reading of much that has been written would bring me only confusion of mind. I could not bring myself to accept the skeptical writings of even the wisest who would seek to persuade me that the grave ends all. On the other hand, I could never feel satisfied with the mysterious explanations offered by Spiritualists. I could not feel that the future of men was to be understood in the setting of the séance chamber, with mysterious mumblings and shadowy apparitions.

And even the examination of many of the Christian writings would still leave me with questionings in my mind, because having set out sincerely to search the Scriptures, I would soon find that many of the statements in so-called orthodox Christian writings did not square with the explicit declarations in the Book of God. For example, they would not square with the simple story of the creation of man, into whose nostrils God breathed the breath of life. I could not find in that creation record any account of an immortal soul being put into man. What is more, my reading of the Good Book would reveal to me that God only hath immortality, that we must seek for it, and shall not receive it until the last great day.

I would be further perplexed in my mind from reading most of the Christian writings on the nature of man, because they would not leave any reasonable, logical place for a resurrection, or for a future judgment. The teaching that man goes immediately at death either to heaven or to hell, freed from the bodily prison house, would not harmonize with what I would be reading in the Bible concerning a last great judgment day, when there is to be a literal resurrection, and all men are to receive a reward according to the deeds done in the body.

Furthermore, I would feel that there was something shadowy and uncertain about the future reward, if it dealt only with airy spirits.

But my examination of the teachings of Seventh-day Adventists concerning the nature of man would dissolve my problems and give me a sense of certainty and definiteness. I would find that the Adventist teaching presents man as a real being, standing forth perfect from the hand of God in the Garden of Eden, made animate by the breath of God breathed into him. The Adventist teaching of man is that he is one complete whole, that there is no separate entity called the soul that flits away at death, but that in some supernatural way God created a being with a physical and spiritual nature fused into one person, and that at death the animating breath from God returns to its divine source, and man —the whole man—returns to the dust. This conception of man would enable me to see why there should be a resurrection and a future day of judgment, and why God should plan to restore to us the kind of Edenic world which the original man inhabited.

At the same time I would be able to dismiss from my mind forever the disturbing claims of spiritists, for I would see in their manifestations simply a modern recital of the falsehood told to our mother Eve by the serpent in the Garden of Eden.

### Certainty as to Salvation

5. A DESIRE FOR CERTAINTY REGARDING THE SUBJECTS OF SIN AND SALVATION. Through all the centuries finite men have wrestled with these questions in an attempt to find a solution of the dark problem of sin. And those solutions have ranged all the way from the offering of one's own children in flaming, pagan sacrifice, to the bleak program of denying the reality of sin and attempting to develop a rich character by one's own individual efforts. But no one can go very far in serious religious thinking without being persuaded that there is something wrong with our innermost nature, call it by whatever name we will. We discover Paul's experience to be true to our own life, that what we would do, that we do not, and what we do not want to do, that we do. A sense of guilt and helplessness dominates the mind of a man who honestly examines his own soul. Certainly this is true if a man has gone far enough in his religious search for a church home to be a prayerful reader of the Scriptures.

ANSWERS TO OBJECTIONS

In the very heart of Seventh-day Adventist teaching is found the doctrine of the sanctuary, which portrays the whole subject of sin and salvation in such vivid figures that I would at once feel as if I were indeed watching the whole drama by which God designs to purge us of guilt and cause us to stand justified in His sight. As I studied into the typical service of the ancient sanctuary, and then listened to the truth unfolded concerning the sanctuary in heaven above, where Christ now ministers in behalf of those who call upon Him, any possible questions and uncertainties regarding God's way of dealing with the tragedy of sin in my life would disappear. I would discover in the subject of the sanctuary one of the most comforting truths that could ever be brought to the heart of a man.

## Proper Care of the Body

6. A DESIRE TO KNOW HOW PROPERLY TO CARE FOR MY BODY, WHICH THE BIBLE DESCRIBES AS THE TEMPLE OF THE HOLY GHOST. My examination of the Scriptures down to this point, in my search for a church home, would have presented to me, as discussed in a preceding section, the truth that man is one complete whole, that the spiritual is not insulated and isolated from the physical. Therefore I would realize that the care I give to my body has a vital relationship to healthy spiritual living. I would see new force in the scripture which declares that whether we eat or drink or whatever we do, we should do it to the glory of God.

In view of my discovery of the nature of man, and the inspired command to care rightly for the body, I could not feel satisfied to join a church that gave no attention to healthful living, and, in fact, permitted its members, unrebuked, to engage in many habits and practices that are altogether injurious to the body. When I turned to examine the Seventh-day Adventist movement, I would find something new and unusual, a religious organization that concerned itself not simply with theology but also with physiology, with right food for the body as well as for the spirit.

I would feel that here indeed is a church presenting a balanced

768

program for successful living, according to the Bible pattern. I would feel that I had discovered an added reason for believing in the gift of the Spirit of prophecy as manifested in the Adventist movement, because the one who made claim to the gift, I would discover from my study, is the one who presented to the Adventist Church certain distinctive outlines of the doctrine of healthful living as a vital part of the program of successful Christian life.

## The Meaning of the Times

7. A DESIRE TO KNOW WITH CERTAINTY THE MEANING OF THE TIMES IN WHICH WE LIVE, AND WHAT THE FUTURE HOLDS FOR US. All about me in the world I see confusion, men's hearts failing them for fear, and for looking after those things that are coming on the earth. I read in my daily paper of the forebodings of statesmen, the dire prophecies of general calamity and destruction throughout the earth. As a sincerely religious person seeking a church home, I naturally wish to ally myself with a religious body that will provide me with peace and assurance in my heart in these days of world unrest, and if possible with some answer concerning the questions in my mind as to the future. But as I looked about, I would find the religious bodies in general strangely troubled concerning affairs in our world. Instead of their being able to provide an answer to the question as to what the future holds, I would find them somewhat amazed that I should even ask.

Yet having started out sincerely to lead the religious life, and thus having given some study to the Bible, I would be impressed that it should be possible to know something concerning conditions in the world about me, and something also about the future. My reading of the Bible would lead me repeatedly to prophetic descriptions that seem to fit our day, and then foretell events that are connected with the end of earth's history. For example, when I read the statement of Christ in the twenty-fourth chapter of Matthew, I would find that it answers at length the question of His disciples, "What shall be the sign of thy coming, and of the end of the world?"

More than that, I would find that the various distinctive doctrines that had attracted me to the Advent movement are set in a framework of prophecy, and thus strikingly interlocked. For example, in the prophetic portions of the Bible are found declarations that the Sabbath is intended of God to be a distinguishing mark of those who in the last days are true witnesses for Him. Likewise, in the prophetic framework is found the doctrine of the nature of man, particularly his state in death, and the doctrine of the sanctuary. As already indicated, the doctrine of the Second Advent is held, not as an abstract doctrine about a distant and wholly unpredictable event; but in the pattern of prophecy as something both sure and near at hand.

Finally, as I examined further the prophetic pages of Holy Writ I would find a divine forecast that in the last days of earth's history there goes forth a call to men to "come out" of whatever organization they may find themselves in and to join the Advent movement. I would see that the purpose of this coming out is not to create one more religious body in the world but to gather together in one all those who hold the same faith and hope and objective, that they may reinforce one another's faith, and, equally important, may most effectively preach to all men everywhere the final message of the approach of the day of God.

As I examined the beliefs of Seventh-day Adventists, and particularly in the setting of prophecy, I would find what my heart was longing for—an explanation of these troubled times and a "Thus saith the Lord" concerning the future of our world. Peace would fill my heart, despite the troublous conditions about me, for I would see that all these conditions were foretold in prophecy, that despite the apparent chaos, God is working out His own plans, and soon will come the day of the return of Jesus Christ, when all the evil of this world will end. I would lift up my head and rejoice that my redemption draws nigh, and with enthusiasm would I become a convert to this Advent movement, dedicating my time and my all to the proclaiming of its truths to the world in these closing hours of earth's history.

# APPENDIXES

# How Sunday Observance Began

[The following, by Frank H. Yost, appeared as a series of articles in the *Review and Herald* in 1952, and is reprinted here with his kind permission.]

Sunday observance began in the church in Rome. Records from the dim second century show that it was the leaders of the church in Rome who put emphasis upon it.

The reason they assigned for Sunday observance was that Christ rose upon that day. The observance began under Sixtus, who was the *papa* (pope)* or leader of the church of Rome about A.D. 125 (EUSEBIUS, *Ecclesiastical History*, book 5, chap. 24, par. 14.)

But this was not at first a weekly observance, coming once each week after the Sabbath, as it was later, and as it is today. It was annual. It came once a year, at the time of the awakening of spring.

In bringing in the practice of Sunday observance the *papas* of the church in Rome brought about a change in traditional Christian practices of that day.

Very early, Christians had formed the habit of celebrating annually in the spring the memorable closing days of Christ's life. Christ was crucified on a Friday, and died about the time the Jewish Passover lamb was being slain. It was just before sunset of the fourteenth day of the Jewish month Nisan, the first month of the Jewish religious year. (Luke 23:46-56; John 18:28; 19:30-34; cf. Lev. 23:4-8.)

It became a tradition among early Christians, both Jews and Gentiles, to celebrate the crucifixion of Christ at the time the Jews were entering their Passover season. The Christians took their reckoning of the date from the Jews, and gathered in homes or in hired halls (they had no church buildings in that early day) at the same time the Jews were gathering for the celebration of the Passover. For this practice there is not a single word of authorization in the Bible.

We are told that this practice began as early as the time of the apostle John. (*Ibid.*, book 5, chap. 24.) Some Christians apparently kept only the day, the fourteenth of Nisan. Others celebrated the period

---

* The chief presbyters or bishops of all churches in the early years of Christianity were called *papa* (English "pope"). Later all heads of monasteries also were called *papa*. Still later the term was claimed as the exclusive property of the bishops of Rome.

from the crucifixion to the resurrection. Still others observed the whole time of the Jewish festival, which was the Feast of Unleavened Bread described in Exodus 12:15-20 and Leviticus 23:4-14, and lasted till the twenty-first day of Nisan. (*Ibid.*, pars. 2, 12, 13.)

But in any case the celebration centered on the day of the crucifixion, the fourteenth of Nisan, when "Christ our passover" (1 Cor. 5:7) died for sinners. It was observed without concern for which day of the week it might be, somewhat as Christmas is celebrated among Christians today, by date and not by day of the week.

It was this custom that the church of Rome undertook to change, by leading all Christians to celebrate, not the crucifixion, but the resurrection; and not on the fourteenth of Nisan, regardless of the day of the week, but always on Sunday, the first day of the week, regardless of the exact date. The church of Rome won in this endeavor, and the reasons are not hard to find.

One reason was anti-Judaism, the ancestor of the anti-Semitism of today. The Jews had always been opposed to Christianity. They rejected Jesus when He was on earth. They brought about His crucifixion at the hands of the Romans. They discredited the fact of His resurrection. They persecuted the New Testament church even to the death, as in the case of Stephen. They led the pagan Roman authorities to persecute the Christians, and indeed told such ugly tales about them that mobs in the cities were incited to bloody violence against the followers of Christ. Tertullian named the synagogues "fountains of persecution."

### The Jews and the Romans

But the Christians had cause to dread the Jews for political reasons. The Jews had always been a problem to their Roman conquerors. As the "chosen people of God" they resented deeply being ruled by despised Gentiles, and rebelled again and again. They fought against Herod when he sought to assume the kingship of the Jews granted him by the Roman Senate. They caused the removal of Archelaus, Herod's son (not without cause), as ruler in Jerusalem, and brought about the seating of a Roman procurator instead. Their bitter antagonism toward the Romans becomes clear in the Gospels.

In Acts 18:2 we learn that all Jews were expelled from Rome. In the year 68 their rebellious spirit led them into a furious revolt, which resulted, A.D. 70, in the destruction of the city of Jerusalem and the death of thousands of Jews. From then on the Jews were especially marked as a political problem in the empire. There was another outbreak about forty years later, not so serious or so widespread, but still damaging to any good relations between the empire and Judaism.

# APPENDIXES

About the time Pope Sixtus was beginning to bring about the change in the Christian spring festival, the worst revolt of all broke out. For a period of seven years and over a wide extent of the Roman Empire the Jews rebelled. Thousands upon thousands of them were killed; thousands were driven from the empire. The city of Jerusalem was again completely destroyed. A plow was symbolically dragged over its desolated site, and Roman decrees forbade any Jew again to set his foot upon the spot. The Romans then proceeded to rebuild the city under the emperor Hadrian as a strictly Gentile city.

Christians in the city of Rome especially dreaded being confused with the Jews. It was known that Christianity had sprung from the Jews and that some of the practices and observances of Christians were like those of the Jews. There was good political reason for Pope Sixtus to lead his church away from a celebration timed to the Jewish Passover, when he sought to have the spring festival fall always upon a Sunday, instead of upon the fourteenth of Nisan.

It is worth while to pause here and notice what is written in *The Great Controversy* concerning the Christians and anti-Jewish feeling and its effect in the Sabbath-Sunday controversy:

"To prepare the way for the work which he designed to accomplish, Satan had led the Jews, before the advent of Christ, to load down the Sabbath with the most rigorous exactions, making its observance a burden. Now, taking advantage of the false light in which he had thus caused it to be regarded, he cast contempt upon it as a Jewish institution. While Christians generally continued to observe the Sunday as a joyous festival, he led them, in order to show their hatred of Judaism, to make the Sabbath a fast, a day of sadness and gloom."—Pages 52, 53.

But for the pope to stress the resurrection day meant that he was stressing the day of the sun. The spring had for ages been a special time for the worship of the sun. Astrologers had named as the sun's day the one coincidental with the Jewish first day of the week, and sun worshipers on this day, as Tertullian tells us, moved their lips in adoration to the sun as they faced the east at daybreak. (*Apology*, chap. 16.)

The first hour of the day of the sun was used to reverence the sun, as the first hour of the moon's day was used to reverence the moon; and so on through the cycle of the seven days, for Mars, Mercury, Jupiter, Venus, and Saturn each had a day, with Saturn's day coinciding with the seventh-day Sabbath.

### Sunday and Sun Worshipers

A converted sun worshiper would not feel out of place at the spring festival, beginning to be urged by Pope Sixtus of Rome, for it fell both at a season and on a day familiar to him as a sun worshiper. The pope's insistence that the resurrection, and not the crucifixion, must be celebrated in spring, and not on the Jewish fourteenth of Nisan, but always on Sunday, the day of the resurrection, put Christians, by an ecclesiastical trick, as it were, in the position of honoring the sun's day.

About twenty years after the time of Pope Sixtus, when Polycarp, the head of the church of Smyrna and famous martyr, visited the church of Rome, he knew no celebration of the resurrection and no honoring of Sunday. He and Pope Anicetus of Rome discussed the question, but they avoided controversy, and each agreed to follow the custom he had been observing. Pope Anicetus declared that his practice went back to the time of Sixtus, and Polycarp said that his went back to the apostles. They agreed to disagree. (EUSEBIUS, *Ecclesiastical History*, book 5, chap. 24, pars. 16, 17.)

Not so complacent was a later pope, Victor. (About A.D. 200.) He saw that quiet pressure from Rome in favor of Sunday was not too successful. In his pride of office he ordered all bishops excommunicated who would not follow Rome's plan for the spring festival. At that early day no church recognized the authority of the pope outside of Italy; in fact, the Papal See was not always honored in Italy. But Victor, assuming a general authority which later popes were increasingly to exercise, sought to legislate for all Christendom. And it was in the interests of Sunday. He failed in his plan of excommunication, but not in the respect given to the day of the sun. (*Ibid.*, pars. 9-11.)

By then another step in Sunday reverence had taken place. Justin Martyr tells us that about A.D. 155—

"On the day called Sunday there is an assemblage of all who live in the cities or the country, and the memoirs of the apostles, or the writings of the prophets are read so long as there is time. Then the reading having ceased the leader in discourse gives the admonition and the challenge to imitate these good things. Thereupon we all rise together and offer prayer. And as we said before, when we have ceased praying, bread is brought, and wine and water. And the leader in like manner offers prayers and thanksgiving, as much as he is able, and the people express their assent, saying the 'Amen.' And there is a distribution to each one and a partaking of that over which thanks have been given, and it is sent to those absent by the deacons. And those having means and who are willing, each one according to his choice, gives whatever he wishes; and the collection is deposited at the leader's home, and he himself provides for the orphans and widows, and for those who on account of sickness or for any other reason are in want, and for those who are in prison, and for the sojourning strangers, and in a word, he is a guardian to all those who are in need. And we all in common make our assembly on Sunday, since it is the first day in which God changed the darkness and matter and made the world, and Jesus Christ our Saviour rose from the dead on the same day."—*First Apology*, chap. 67.

Justin wrote this *Apology* to the emperor, and made a point of telling him of this Christian act of worship taking place on the day of the sun. He was in Rome when he was writing, and he was describing the weekly Sundaykeeping of the church of Rome and the surrounding churches under its influence.

### Weekly Observance of Sunday Begins

Just how the step was made from the *annual observance* of Sunday to *weekly* worship on Sunday is not clear, but the step was made, and was made in *Rome*.

Under the guise of honoring the blessed resurrection of our Lord, Rome brought about the honoring of the day of the sun. Wrote E. G. White.

"I saw that God had not changed the Sabbath, for He never changes. But the pope had changed it from the seventh to the first day of the week; for he was to change times and laws."—*Early Writings*, p. 33.

"The pope has changed the day of rest from the seventh to the first day. He has thought to change the very commandment that was given to cause man to remember his Creator. He has thought to change the greatest commandment in the decalogue, and thus make himself equal with God, or even exalt himself above God. The Lord is unchangeable, therefore His law is immutable; but the pope has exalted himself above God, in seeking to change His immutable precepts of holiness, justice, and goodness. He has trampled under foot God's sanctified day, and on his own authority, put in its place one of the six laboring days."—*Ibid.*, p. 65.

"Roman Catholics acknowledge that the change of the Sabbath was made by their church, and declare that Protestants, by observing the Sunday, are recognizing her power. . . . The Roman Church has not relinquished her claim to supremacy; and when the world and the Protestant churches accept the sabbath of her creating, while they reject the Bible Sabbath, they virtually admit this assumption."—*The Great Controversy*, pp. 447, 448.

That the charge here put to the account of the Church of Rome is valid, witness Socrates, skilled historian of the church, writing about A.D. 450. He says:

777

# ANSWERS TO OBJECTIONS

"For although almost all Churches throughout the world celebrate the sacred mysteries on the sabbath of every week, yet the Christians of Alexandria and at Rome, on account of some ancient tradition, refuse to do this."—*Ecclesiastical History,* book 5, chap. 22.

In view of Rome's studied endeavor to establish Sundaykeeping and put Sabbath observance in eclipse, how displeasing it must have been, then, to Pope Gregory of Rome, A.D. 600, to find in his own territory those who were keeping the Sabbath! In book 13 of his *Epistles, Letter I,* he says, in great bitterness of soul:

"It has come to my ears that certain men of perverse spirit have sown among you some things that are wrong and opposed to the holy faith, so as to forbid any work being done on the Sabbath day. What else can I call these but preachers of Antichrist?"

We can answer Pope Gregory. These were not preachers of Antichrist. They were preachers who would obey the commandments of God and serve Christ, who is the Lord of the Sabbath. In emphasizing the Sabbath they were not advocating a compromised faith but the very truth of Scripture.

The only weekday that is identified in the Bible by a particular name is the seventh day, called the Sabbath. Numerous texts in the Bible use this name. The day is known in history.

The only other day of the week identified in the Bible is the first day of the week, known not by a name but by a number. It is called simply "the first day of the week." This English expression is used to translate a Greek phrase "first, or one, of the Sabbath, or Sabbaths." Matthew 28:1; Mark 16:2, 9; Luke 24:1; and John 20:1 are the texts that tell of the resurrection of Christ on the first day.

John 20:19 uses the expression and states that Christ came to the disciples in their fear and distress on the evening after the resurrection. Acts 20:7 and 1 Corinthians 16:2 also speak of the "first day of the week." In the first case Paul's farewell discourse to the church at Troas is mentioned. In the other the believers of Corinth are asked to lay by them, that is, in their homes, an offering on each first day of the week, so that Paul will have awaiting him when he comes to Corinth a gift to send to the needy Christian Jews at Jerusalem.

The use of the word *Sabbath* to mean "week," the total period marked off by the Sabbath day, is quite commonplace. Besides its use in the texts just given, it is used in the Hebrew for "week" in Leviticus 23:15, 16, where counting seven Sabbaths and an additional day, one is to arrive at the fifty days leading to the feast of first fruits, or *Pentecost,* which means "fiftieth." The word *Sabbaths* here must mean

APPENDIXES

"weeks" to give the full tally of the fifty days. Seven weeks, or seven times seven days, plus one day, equals fifty.

### Early Use of Sabbath for Week

This same use of *Sabbath* to mean "week" is found again and again in the writings of Christians as late as A.D. 430:

1. In the *Didache*, or *Teaching of the Twelve Apostles*, we read of fasting "on the second and fifth days of the week."—Chapter 8. The Greek reads, "second of the sabbaths and fifth." The date of this document is about A.D. 150.

2. The so-called *Constitution of the Holy Apostles*, in book 5, chapter 19, has the expression, "the first day of the week." The Greek reads, "one of the Sabbaths." The date of this document is approximately A.D. 300.

3. Gregory of Nyssa in his *Oratio II* has this: "The Hebrew nation calls the whole seven days Sabbaths. The evangelists use the expression, 'One of the Sabbaths,' indeed, for the first day of the week. The Greek reads, 'one of the Sabbaths,' for the first day of the sevens." Gregory of Nyssa wrote about A.D. 390.

4. Tertullian, a Christian Latin writer, about A.D. 225, in his treatise *On Fasting* speaks in chapter 14 of fasting on the *"fourth and sixth days* of the week." The Latin reads here, the "fourth and sixth of the Sabbath."

5. Augustine, the famous Latin theologian and bishop of North Africa, who died in the year A.D. 430, uses the word *Sabbath* to mean "week." In an *Epistle to Casulamus*, chapter 3, paragraph 10, he speaks of the "very second day of the week." The Latin reads, the "very second day of the Sabbath." In the same letter, chapter 13, paragraph 30, he speaks of the "very fourth day of the week" and the "fifth day of the week." The Latin reads, the "very fourth of the Sabbath," and the "fifth of the Sabbath." In his commentary on Psalms 80, paragraph 2, Augustine names all the days of the week, calling the first day of the week the Lord's day, and the last, the seventh day of the week, the Sabbath; the other days of the week he calls the second, third, fourth, fifth, and sixth "of the Sabbath."

Similar use of the word *Sabbath* to mean "week" is found in John Cassian's *Institutes*, book 5, chapter 19; in canon 30 of the third council of Orleans, A.D. 538; and in canon 9 of the first council of Macon, A.D. 581.

There is one other name given in the Bible for a day of the week, and that is "Lord's day." It is the usual name given for the first day of the week after about A.D. 200. But it is used only once in the Bible, in the book of Revelation, chapter 1, verse 10, written before the year A.D. 96. The term is not used in any other literature contemporary with the book of Revelation, whether Biblical or pagan, or before that time.

It was an entirely unique expression up to that time, and for many years after. But the fact that Sunday is called "Lord's day" in A.D. 200 does not mean that a hundred years before, John means Sunday when he uses the term "Lord's day" in the book of Revelation. It is not valid to force a late expression or word back into its past to name a practice or interpret a phrase.

### Possible Meanings for "Lord's Day"

There are several possible meanings for the expression "Lord's day":

1. That John was talking about the Christian Era as "the Lord's day." But it seems untenable that John would be informing his readers in indirect style that he was receiving instruction from the Spirit during the Christian Era, when there could be no mistaking that fact. Anyone who would be at all interested in reading what John had written would know that at that time Christ had already been incarnated, had lived, had died, and had ascended to heaven. The application seems without point. Furthermore, the phrase is punctiliar, dealing with specific time.

2. That he was speaking of "the Lord's day" as the day of judgment, the last time when Christ is to bring all things earthly to a close. It is argued that John's visions deal with final world events, and that therefore he was considering himself as living for the moment among those scenes.

But here again applies the same objection as under number one above. Would he not have written that he was in vision "concerning the Lord's day," or that he was being transported "into the Lord's day," had he meant the last days of judgment?

3. That he was speaking of an emperor's day as the "Lord's day." Papyri of the second century found in Egypt show that there were "Augustan," or emperor's, days, *hemerai sebastai,* which were to commemorate the anniversary of an emperor's birth, of his coronation, or of an imperial visitation to a locality. Such days were celebrated. Was John in vision on such a day?

It seems unlikely that John was using the phrase in question with this meaning. In the first place, no instance has been found of such a day being called a "Lord's day," although the emperor was called lord, and other things pertaining to him were called *kuriakos* "of the lord." In the second place, it seems extremely unlikely that John would use the word "Lord" as applying to the emperor, even when speaking of a day dedicated by others to the emperors. Christians were well known for acknowledging only one Lord and King. This place they gave to Christ alone, and were in consequence, persecuted as political enemies of the Roman state. They refused to call the emperor lord.

### True Meaning of "Lord's Day"

What day, then, is the Lord's day? No contemporary sources outside the Bible give us any help. But, as might be expected, the Bible gives us help. It does not speak of Sunday. It knows the first day of the week only as "the first day of the week," and attaches to it no sanctity.

But is there not a day of which Christ is Lord? Yes, the seventh-day Sabbath is so described all through the Bible. It is the day that belongs to the Lord. Jesus Himself so stated when He said, "For the Son of man is Lord even of the sabbath day." Matt. 12:8. What "Lord's day" could there be, of which Christ is Lord, aside from the day, the Sabbath, of which Christ declares He is Lord? None.

The Sabbath is the Lord's day of the Bible. It is, says the Lord, "my holy day." (Isa. 58:13.) It is plainly designated in the fourth commandment: "The seventh day is the sabbath of the Lord thy God."

Can we identify this Lord God to whom the Sabbath pertains? Paul says:

"Moreover, brethren, I would not that ye should be ignorant, how that all our fathers were under the cloud, and all passed through the sea; and were all baptized unto Moses in the cloud and in the sea; and did all eat the same spiritual meat; and did all drink the same spiritual drink: for they drank of that spiritual Rock that followed them: and that Rock was Christ." 1 Cor. 10:1-4.

It was Jesus Christ Himself who did all these things for His people, and who commanded that the Sabbath, the "sabbath of the Lord thy God," *His day,* should be kept.

Indeed, Christ being the Creator (John 1:1-3; Col. 1:13-17), it was He who first blessed and hallowed the Sabbath at the close of creation week (Gen. 2:1-3), and who was in "the days of his flesh" (Heb. 5:7) the Lord of the Sabbath. Because He is "Jesus Christ the same yesterday, to day, and for ever" (Heb. 13:8), He is the Lord of the Sabbath today. The seventh day is the only true Lord's day.

Why did John call it "the Lord's day," an expression not used in just that form up to his time, nor for a century after? We do not know. We are not told. But we suggest that John, knowing the expression then applied to unholy pagan observances, applied a parallel one to the day belonging to his divine Lord: the Sabbath of creation, of the commandments, and of the gospel.

# ANSWERS TO OBJECTIONS

John knew of no "Lord's day" significance for the first day of the week. In harmony with Matthew, Mark, and Luke, he mentions with significance only the seventh-day Sabbath. In nearly all the sixty times where the Sabbath is mentioned in the New Testament, there is excellent opportunity for pointing out that the seventh day is superseded by the Sunday, or that the Sunday was to be observed in addition to the Sabbath, if that had been the case, but no word is said to intimate this. Rather, the Sabbath is pointed out as a day of worship, which both Jesus Christ and Paul made use of in that way, as a matter of habit (Luke 4:16; Acts 17:2), and is called the day of which Jesus is Lord (Mark 2:28).

But was not the "first day of the week" called "the Lord's day," or given some other prominence in the writings of men who lived at the close of the apostolic age, or in the decades immediately following? The answer is No, emphatically No.

## Eight Sunday Observance "Proofs"

Sundaykeeping began in Rome as an *annual* observance of the resurrection day. By A.D. 150 *weekly* observance of Sunday had begun in Rome, as attested by Justin's *First Apology,* written in Rome to the emperor. Justin calls the day "the day of the Sun." He has no other name for it.

But what of the period between the time of the apostles and the time of Justin Martyr? We shall examine all the references that can be found in the writings of the church Fathers referring to the first day of the week, or for which any claim is made of reference to the first day of the week. We shall arrange these references in proper chronological order, beginning with the earliest and continuing our examination to about A.D. 200, when Sunday observance is fully established, and the first day of the week is referred to as the "Lord's day."

## First "Proof"

1. The first extra-Biblical reference put forth by Sundaykeepers to support the institution of Sunday is a statement by Clement, overseer of the church in Rome about A.D. 98. He wrote at that time his *Epistle to the Corinthians,* in which he urged them to "do all things in [their proper] order, which the Lord has commanded us to perform at stated times."—Chapter 40. It is argued that the expression "stated times" indicates Sunday as the proper meeting time. For this there is absolutely no basis.

# APPENDIXES

### Second "Proof"

2. Very much like it is a statement by the Latin writer, Pliny the Younger, a pagan Roman governor, in a letter to his emperor, Trajan, to be dated about A.D. 110-112. The ninety-sixth letter in Pliny's tenth book of *Letters* states that the Christians he was persecuting met for the worship of Christ early in the morning of a "stated" or "fixed" day. Pliny gives no hint as to which day of the week he understands this to be, probably because there was as yet in his day no official system of weeks among the Romans.

The identification of these "stated" days can therefore be made only from reliable Christian documents of this same time. They cannot be identified from later practices. The only inspired documents we have to use for this purpose at this date are the books of the New Testament. It is clear that the only day of worship known to New Testament Christians was the seventh-day Sabbath, observed by Christ, by the disciples, and by the apostle Paul. The "stated" days of Clement and Pliny must therefore be the seventh-day Sabbath.

### Third "Proof"

3. The next earliest reference used to bolster Sunday observance is one that is quoted so frequently that every student of the question is under ethical compulsion to examine it thoroughly and without bias. The statement referred to is in a letter by a man named Ignatius, called the overseer of the church of Antioch in Syria. According to late tradition Ignatius was taken prisoner by the Roman police during a persecution inflicted by the emperor Trajan, and transported to Rome, where the story has him put to death some time prior to the demise of that emperor, which occurred in the year A.D. 117.

The same late tradition has this martyr writing a series of letters while a prisoner on his way to Rome. The total number of letters attributed to his authorship is fifteen, but all scholars now agree in branding eight of these as gross forgeries. The remaining seven are looked upon with serious suspicion by all scholars who do not need to rely on the writings of Ignatius to support some institution of the church. Even these more complacent students accept only a short form of these seven letters.

Of these epistles of Ignatius, Dr. Philip Schaff, of the highest repute among church historians, says:

"These oldest documents of the hierarchy soon became so interpolated, curtailed, and mutilated by pious fraud, that it is today almost impossible to discover with certainty the genuine Ignatius of history under the hyper- and pseudo-Ignatius of tradition."—*History of the Christian Church*, 2d period, sec. 164, vol. 2, p. 660.

It is a statement in the so-called Ignatian *Epistle to the Magnesians*, chapter 9, that is pressed most hopefully by those who wish to find an early beginning for Sunday observance. So reputable a scholar as the late Dr. Kirsopp Lake makes Ignatius say in this epistle, "No longer living for the Sabbath, but for the Lord's *Day*."—Loeb Classical Library, *The Apostolic Fathers*, vol. 1, p. 205. (Italics ours.) But the best original Greek manuscripts contain no word "day." Actually the Greek original, in every reliable manuscript, reads, "No longer sabbatizing, but living according to the Lord's *life*, in the which also our life has risen through Him and His death."—MIGNE, *Patrologia Graeca*, vol. 5, col. 669. (Italics ours.)

To prove their point, Sundaykeeping scholars have actually gone to the length of omitting the word "life" from the original, to make possible the insertion of the word "day." But the word "life" is there, and it makes good sense when properly translated, without bias, from the original Greek. The corrupting and misinterpreting of this sentence from the supposed Ignatian epistle is now being followed by many Sundaykeeping scholars.

This interesting sentence is now before us. What does it mean? The context shows that this passage, whether truly Ignatian or not, is dealing, not with the *day* of the resurrection, but with a divine *life* which, through the risen Lord, enables the Christian to live a life of faith, free from legalism, of which traditional Jewish Sabbathkeeping was all too illustrative.

There exists a lengthy interpolation of the Magnesian letter, made perhaps between the years A.D. 300 and 400, which distorts this passage to make it apply to days of worship, and to advocate the observance of both the seventh-day Sabbath and the Sunday. It is doubtless reading back through the murkiness of this late interpolation that has forced the idea of "day" into the interpretation of this clause. It jeopardizes sound exegesis to work back to an expression from later distortions of it.

There is, as a matter of fact, no reference to a day of worship in the Magnesian letter or in any other of the early letters acknowledged as Ignatian.

### Fourth "Proof"

4. The next supposed "Lord's day" reference is from chapter 14 of an ancient document, to be dated about the middle of the second

century, called the *Didache,* or *Teaching of the Twelve Apostles.* This writing is not a product of apostolic hands; its author is not known. The sentence put forward as a support for Sundaykeeping has been translated to read, "On the Lord's Day of the Lord come together, break bread and hold Eucharist."—Loeb Classical Library, *The Apostolic Fathers,* vol. 1, p. 331.

The Greek text is obviously garbled and incomplete, but it contains no word "day." It reads literally, "according to the Lord's (?) of the Lord, coming together, break bread and hold Eucharist." There is no particular reason why the thought of "day" should be forced into this passage. A number of words, appropriate both in grammar and in meaning, could be supplied at the point of our question mark, and make as good sense as "day," or better. The form of the Greek requires a feminine word, and the Greek word *entole,* "commandment," for instance, would exactly fit both sense and grammar. In any case the word "day" does not occur in the original, and this reference in the *Didache* is certainly no true support for the institution of Sunday.

### Fifth "Proof"

5. For the next reference we turn to the church historian Eusebius, who wrote about the year A.D. 324. He was thoroughly committed to the priestly authority of the bishops of the fourth century, was a defender of the union of church and state effected by the emperor Constantine, and was a eulogizer of this emperor. He was an earnest advocate of Sunday as a substitute for the Sabbath of the Bible. He makes two references that are often quoted as supporting early Sunday-keeping. One is in a letter he quotes as proceeding from Dionysius, the overseer of the church of Corinth about the year A.D. 170, to Soter, of Rome.

The significant sentence is, " 'To-day we have passed the Lord's holy day, in which we have read your epistle.' "—EUSEBIUS, *Ecclesiastical History,* book 4, chap. 23, par. 11. There is no reference in the Bible or in any other writing up to this time showing that any other day than the Sabbath was established as the holy day of the Lord; therefore, there is no reason to apply this reference to Sunday observance, as some do. The day is not, as a matter of fact, identified in the letter.

### Sixth "Proof"

6. The other reference from Eusebius tells us that Melito, overseer of the church of Sardis, wrote about the year A.D. 175 a treatise whose title is usually translated *A Book Concerning the Lord's Day. (Ibid.,* book 4, chap. 26.) As a matter of fact, the Greek title as given by

Eusebius reads simply *A Discourse Concerning the Lord's* [?]. The word "day" does not appear in the title, and there is no information given as to what the treatise actually dealt with.

### Seventh "Proof"

7. There is also a forged second-century epistle, the so-called *Epistle of Barnabas,* which in chapter 15 quotes Old Testament condemnations of hypocritical Sabbathkeeping and pretends to make them an excuse for Sundaykeeping. It seeks further to establish Sunday by setting it forth as the eighth day of the week, and forcing it into line as a continuance of the Jewish principle of the eight-day circumcision. The inconsistency and futility of this argument, often used thereafter, must be patent to all.

It used a Jewish ceremonial requirement, occurring once in the lifetime of the male Jew, as a basis for a supposed Christian festival, expected to occur weekly in the worship experience of all believers. For all this no divine or Scriptural authorization is claimed. The date of the writing of this strange document is not known, but it cannot be earlier than mid-second century.

These are the "authorities" used to establish the observance of Sunday as the "Lord's day" in the second century. There is in none of these references the least foundation for the observance of Sunday. When the original languages are examined they give no basis for the observance of any day of the week as dedicated to God, except the seventh-day Sabbath. There is in them no claim of any authorization by the Lord of any day to take the place of the seventh-day Sabbath.

### Eighth "Proof"

8. When, then, is Sunday called the "Lord's day"? It is not until the latter part of the second century that there is a datable reference in which Sunday is indisputably called "the Lord's day." In the latter part of the second century there came into circulation a false *Gospel According to Peter.* No one today believes this document to be from the apostle Peter's hand or dictation, and even when it first appeared it received little credence. But in this false epistle the day of Christ's resurrection is for the first time clearly called "the Lord's day."

From this time on, in the writings of Clement of Alexandria, Tertullian, and others, the term "Lord's day" is consistently applied to Sunday. "Sabbath" continues to be the term for the seventh day of the week until Reformation times. After that Sunday is frequently called both "Lord's day" and "Sabbath" interchangeably.

# APPENDIXES

## How Sunday Was First Observed

Because Sunday has been observed by people in many places as a day of rest from labor and a day for worship, people are prone to think that Sunday has always been observed that way. But this is not in keeping with the facts of history.

There is no record in the New Testament of the time of day when Christians held their meetings for worship, or of the program they followed in the meetings. There are several suggestions in the epistles as to what Christians should do and not do in meeting, but that is all.

The only meeting of Christians for which the Bible has any detailed description is the farewell meeting of Paul with the church of Troas, recorded in the twentieth chapter of Acts. The meeting is said to have been on the "first day of the week," but it was a night meeting, held because Paul was leaving the next morning after having met with the church for seven days. It was obviously a special service, held at night. Since the dark part of the first day of the week, Jewish reckoning, precedes the light part of the day, this meeting must have been on what we now call Saturday night. This was certainly not a customary time for meetings of worship among Christians.

The first reference we have as to the time of day when Christians held their meetings is from a pagan source. Pliny the Younger was governor of a province in Asia Minor. In a letter he wrote about A.D. 110 he tells of interviewing some who had been Christians twenty-five years before. These people told him that Christians met early in the morning of a "stated day," to "sing hymns to Christ as to a god," to eat together food of a "harmless" kind, and to listen to admonitions to right living. Since there is no contemporary information of stated Christian meetings on any other day than Sabbath, we must conclude that what Pliny called a "stated day" was the seventh-day Sabbath.

## Why Early Morning Meetings?

The question arises, Why a meeting early in the morning? Some suppose that because Christ's resurrection took place early in the morning, the Christians were meeting at this early hour in order to celebrate that great event; therefore, this must have been a Sunday meeting of which Pliny writes. To contend this is to forget the circumstances of that time. In those early years Christians were an illegal sect. They had no standing in Roman law, and were subject to death merely for being Christians. In fact, the letter of Pliny informs the emperor Trajan that when he finds Christians he puts them to death. We have Trajan's reply approving this.

787

Here is the most rational explanation why Christians should meet early in the morning. They had no church buildings. They met in one another's homes or in hired halls. Meetings had to be carefully planned, with everything very secret. The Christians would attract the least attention going quietly to the place of meeting, doubtless dressed as though they were going to work, at the hour when others were going to their daily labor.

We have later statements as to how Christians were to keep the Sabbath. They were to be at meetings, and sing hymns, listen to the reading of the Scriptures, hear the instruction of their leaders, meditate on God's creative power and His work for men. The Lord's supper was administered on Sabbath, as later it came to be on Sunday and other days of the week. Sabbath is spoken of several times as a day of rest.

### A Description of Sunday Observance

But what of the observance of Sunday? As previously noted, Justin Martyr about A.D. 155 gives us the first description of Sunday observance by Christians. He tells of Christians gathering on the day of the sun in honor of the resurrection, listening to the Scriptures and the instruction of their leaders, partaking of communion, giving their offerings, and then adjourning. He says nothing about any abstention from labor by Christians on Sunday at that early date. They went to their daily work, apparently, at the close of the service. Justin says the worship continued "so long as there is time."

Tertullian gives us the first intimation that we have of any postponement of business from Sunday. He states that "only on the day of the Lord's Resurrection ought [Christians] to guard not only against kneeling, but every posture and office of solicitude; *deferring even our business* lest we give any place to the devil." (Italics added.)

This thought of freedom from solicitude on the day of the sun is repeated by early Christian writers, with emphasis upon the fact that there should be no kneeling or fasting on the day of the resurrection. In fact, in the West, Sundaykeeping Christians insisted that there must be fasting on the *Sabbath,* as well as kneeling.

How much is included in Tertullian's reference to deferring of business out of respect to Sunday is not clear, but even in his day there was a tendency on the part of Christians to begin to abstain from common business interests on Sunday.

A document called the *Interpolated Epistle of Ignatius to the Magnesians,* the author of which we do not know, but which can be dated probably early in the fourth century, urges Christians no longer to "sabbatize in the Jewish manner, rejoicing in holidays." "But let each of you sabbatize spiritually, rejoicing in meditation on the law, not in rest of body; admiring the artisanship of God, not eating stale things and drinking lukewarm things and walking measured distances and enjoying dancing and plaudits which do not have sense. And after the sabbatizing, let every friend of Christ keep as a festival the Lord's day, the resurrection day, the queen, the chief of all the days."—Chapter 9.

This writer is advocating an observance of Sabbath that will involve a spiritual exercise, but not the strict legalistic use of Sabbath, which was the way of the Jews.

### Constantine's Sunday Law

In A.D. 321 came Constantine's Sunday law. This decree was not a religious law, that is, it was not passed by the church. It was a civil decree. Without mentioning God, except as the sun be reckoned a god, the decree commanded that everyone abstain from common work on the "venerable day of the sun." Exception was made of farmers who, if necessary, might work on that day to save their crops.

Next the church ruled against labor on Sunday. The Council of Laodicea was a local council which met in the city of Laodicea in Asia Minor some time in the latter years of the fourth century. The exact date is not known. We have the decisions of this council. Canon 29 forbade work on Sunday and idleness on the Sabbath. This is the first official record of church legislation forbidding labor on Sunday.

But canon 16 of the same council makes provision for the reading of the Gospels on the Sabbath. This of course does not mean Bible reading in private homes, because most Christians at that time did not have the Bible in their homes. Books, then all handwritten, were too expensive. When canon 16 calls for the reading of the Gospels by Christians on the Sabbath, it must mean in meeting. Therefore, the Council of Laodicea is not legislating to do away entirely with Sabbath observance. It *is* legislating to transfer the abstention from labor from the Sabbath to the Sunday, while still allowing for public worship on the Sabbath.

What does all this mean? It means that at the beginning all Christians were keeping the seventh-day Sabbath, and refraining from common business on that day, and using it for worship and spiritual exercises.

### Growth of Sunday Observance

In the second century the weekly observance of Sunday was introduced. First it was a matter of meeting in the morning, with an evident resumption of daily occupations the rest of the day. In the third century, however, begins the tendency to refrain from common business on the Sunday, while at the same time Sabbath is still being observed. Emphasis upon Sundaykeeping, which began in Rome, becomes increasingly strong, particularly in the West, and presently both Sabbath and Sunday are being kept together on very much the same basis, except that in the West there was to be no kneeling or fasting on Sunday. In Eastern Christendom there was no kneeling in prayer or fasting on either Sabbath or Sunday.

In the beginning of the fourth century, however, Constantine forbade Sunday labor. The Council of Laodicea admonished Christians not to work on Sunday, and forbade them to be idle on the Sabbath. This is in keeping with what Eusebius writes in his *Commentary on the Psalms,* when he says, "All things whatsoever that it was duty to do on the Sabbath, these we have transferred to the Lord's day, as more appropriately belonging to it, because it has a precedence and is first in rank, and more honorable than the Jewish Sabbath."

## Character of Early Sunday Observance

But this was ineffective. Jerome, the famous translator of the Bible, writes at the end of the fourth century in commendation of women in a certain convent who returned from church on Sunday and took up their spinning and weaving. A little later Chrysostom, bishop of the great church in Constantinople, after preaching to his people on a Sunday, dismissed them to go home to resume their daily duties.

This is actually the kind of Sunday observance that has generally prevailed. Repeated Sunday laws by Christian emperors and Christian kings of the West failed to make Sunday a day of reverent idleness. When people were prevented from performing their daily tasks on the Sunday, they used the day for amusement and pleasure. It could not be otherwise when there is no Scriptural basis for the Sunday.

## Sabbathkeeping in Early Centuries

Sabbathkeeping has always been of a different nature. In the early days the Sabbath was kept by Christians either legalistically, as the Jews were keeping it, or reverently and spiritually. As the Sabbath began to go into eclipse, it must have become increasingly difficult to keep it; therefore, anyone who would go to the trouble to assert his convictions by keeping the seventh-day Sabbath, would seek to keep it in a reverent, spiritual manner.

The Sabbath is Biblical. It is Christian. It did not disappear at the

APPENDIXES

death of Christ. His followers kept "the sabbath day according to the commandment." Luke 23:56. Paul observed the Sabbath: in Antioch of Pisidia, preaching to the Jews on one Sabbath and on the next Sabbath to the Gentiles (Acts 13:14-16, 43-45); in Thessalonica, for three separate Sabbaths and it is recorded that this was according to "his manner," even as it was the "custom" of his Lord [Luke 4:16]; in Corinth, where he was for eighteen months observing the Sabbath, laboring the preceding days of each week to support himself. In Philippi he found no place open to him for worship on the Sabbath, and made his way to the riverside, where worshipers of the true God met to pray.

John was "in the Spirit on the Lord's day." And since Christ is "Lord of the sabbath" (Mark 2:28), and calls the Sabbath His holy day (Ex. 20:10; Lev. 23:37, 38; Isa. 58:13), the Lord's day must have been the seventh-day Sabbath. (See *Testimonies*, vol. 6, p. 128, and *Acts of the Apostles*, pp. 581, 582.)

### Sabbathkeeping After the Apostles

After the apostles' day, Christians still kept the Sabbath. This is attested to by many Christian writers, all of them Sundaykeepers. Tertullian, who died about A.D. 235, held that Sunday should be kept as a day of joy in commemoration of Christ's resurrection. It was his wish that there be no fasting or kneeling in prayer on Sunday. He was displeased to find Sabbathkeeping Christians insisting that they should not have to kneel in prayer on the Sabbath day. Here is what he wrote in his essay *On Prayer*, chapter 23:

"In the matter of *kneeling* also prayer is subject to diversity of observance, through the act of some few who abstain from kneeling on the Sabbath; and since this dissension is particularly on its trial before the churches, the Lord will give His grace that the dissentients may either yield, or else indulge their opinion without offence to others."

Tertullian made it plain that Sundaykeeping Christians were not kneeling on Sunday, but it is equally plain that they were going to the churches and kneeling in worship on the Sabbath. Virtually all Christians, it is evident, were worshiping, kneeling or not, on the Sabbath day.

A contemporary of Tertullian, the teacher Origen of Alexandria, though himself a Sundaykeeper, is in no doubt as to the virtue of Sabbath observance, and tells just how Christians should observe it. He meant to place this observance of the seventh day by Christians in contrast to Jewish practices when he said:

"After the festival of the unceasing sacrifice [the crucifixion] is put the second festival of the Sabbath, and it is fitting for whoever is righteous among the saints to keep also the festival of the Sabbath. Which is, indeed, the festival of the Sabbath, except that concerning which the Apostle said, 'There remaineth therefore a sabbatismus, that is, a keeping of the Sabbath, to the people of God [Hebrews 4:9]'? Forsaking therefore the Judaic observance of the Sabbath, let us see what sort of observance of the Sabbath is expected of the Christian? On the day of the Sabbath nothing of worldly acts ought to be performed. If therefore you cease from all worldly works, do nothing mundane, but are free for spiritual works, you come to the church, offer the ear for divine readings and discussions, and thoughts of heavenly things, give attention to the future life, keep before your eyes the coming judgment, do not regard present and visible things, but the invisible and the future: this is the observance of the Christian Sabbath."—*Homily on Numbers 23*, par. 4.

### *"Constitutions of the Holy Apostles"*

There is an early document describing Christian Sabbathkeeping which is called the *Constitutions of the Holy Apostles*. This document was not written by the apostles, but is evidently a product of writers, now unknown, in the Eastern Church of the third and fourth centuries. It shows that in the early centuries both the seventh-day Sabbath and Sunday were observed by Christians:

"Thou shalt observe the Sabbath, on account of Him who ceased from His work of creation, but ceased not from His work of providence: it is a rest for meditation of the law, not for idleness of the hands."—Book 2, sec. 5, chap. 36.

The *Constitutions* makes provision for Christians to worship God in His house every day, but emphasizes the need of worshiping Him, not only on Sunday, "but principally on the Sabbath-day."

"Assemble yourselves together every day, morning and evening, singing psalms and praying in the Lord's house: in the morning saying the sixty-second Psalm, and in the evening the hundred and fortieth, but principally on the Sabbath-day. And on the day of our Lord's resurrection, which is the Lord's day, meet more diligently, sending praise to God that made the universe by Jesus, and sent Him to us, and condescended to let Him suffer, and raised Him from the dead."—*Ibid.*, book 2, sec. 7, chap. 59.

In this ancient document is a prayer dedicated to God, which emphasizes both Sabbath and Sunday observance:

"O Lord Almighty, Thou hast created the world by Christ, and hast appointed the Sabbath in memory thereof, because that on that day

Thou hast made us rest from our works, for the meditation upon Thy laws. . . . He suffered for us by Thy permission, and died, and rose again by Thy power: on which account we solemnly assemble to celebrate the feast of the resurrection on the Lord's day, and rejoice on account of Him who has conquered death, and has brought life and immortality to light. . . . Thou didst give them the law or decalogue, which was pronounced by Thy voice and written with Thy hand. Thou didst enjoin the observation of the [seventh-day] Sabbath, not affording them an occasion of idleness, but an opportunity of piety, for their knowledge of Thy power, and the prohibition of evils; having limited them as within an holy circuit for the sake of doctrine, for the rejoicing upon the seventh period."—*Ibid.*, book 7, sec. 3.

At least one of the contributors to this document, who pretended falsely to write in the name of Peter and Paul, would have felt much at home with a modern five-day week:

"I Peter and Paul do make the following constitutions. Let the slaves work five days: but on the Sabbath-day and the Lord's day let them have leisure to go to church for instruction in piety. We have said that the Sabbath is on account of the creation, and the Lord's day of the resurrection."—*Ibid.*, book 8, sec. 4, chap. 33.

Evidently the writers of the *Constitutions of the Holy Apostles* believed in Sabbathkeeping. They kept the Sunday, but they did believe in keeping the Sabbath, and advocated it.

Sabbathkeeping is further illustrated by an act of the Council of Laodicea, a regional (not general) Eastern council, which met sometime between the years A.D. 343 and 381. It provided very definitely, in canon 16, for regular Sabbath worship:

" 'On Saturday [Greek, "Sabbath"], the Gospels and other portions of the Scriptures shall be read aloud.' "—JOSEPH HEFELE, *A History of the Councils of the Church*, vol. 2, p. 310.

### Sabbath Observance About A.D. 400

Around A.D. 400 Sabbath observance was also common among the monks of the church, especially in the East. Cassian tells how they observed the Sabbath. He says:

"Wherefore, except Vespers and Nocturns, there are no public services among them in the day except on Saturday [Sabbath] and Sunday, when they meet together at the third hour [nine o'clock] for the purpose of Holy Communion."—*Institutes*, book 3, chap 2.

Cassian also tells of a hermit whose religious customs show how Sabbath was still being kept:

# ANSWERS TO OBJECTIONS

"He constantly put off taking food until on Saturday [Sabbath] or Sunday he went to church for service and found some stranger whom he brought home at once to his cell."—*Ibid.*, book 5, chap. 26.

In a letter which Augustine, the great bishop of North Africa, who died in the year A.D. 430, wrote to Jerome, there is evidence of widespread Sabbath observance:

"I would esteem it a favour to be informed by your Sincerity, whether any saint, coming from the East to Rome, would be guilty of dissimulation if he fasted on the seventh day of each week, excepting the Saturday [Sabbath] before Easter. For if we say that it is wrong to fast on the seventh day, we shall condemn not only the Church of Rome, but also many other churches, both neighbouring and more remote, in which the same custom continues to be observed. If, on the other hand, we pronounce it wrong not to fast on the seventh day, how great is our presumption in censuring so many churches in the East, and by far the greater part of the Christian world!"—*Letter 82,* par. 14.

Augustine shows here that the Sabbath was observed in his day in "the greater part of the Christian world." His testimony is all the more valuable since he himself was a consistent Sundaykeeper.

### Sabbathkeeping Widespread in Christendom

A more remarkable testimony, however, concerning the observance of the Sabbath in the fifth century is that borne by two church historians, Socrates and Sozomen, who died sometime before the year A.D. 450. In his *Ecclesiastical History,* book 5, chapter 22, Socrates says:

"For although almost all Churches throughout the world celebrate the sacred mysteries on the sabbath of every week, yet the Christians of Alexandria and at Rome, on account of some ancient tradition, refuse to do this."

His contemporary Sozomen bears in his *Ecclesiastical History,* book 7, chapter 19, a similar witness:

"The people of Constantinople, and of several other cities, assemble together on the Sabbath, as well as on the next day; which custom is never observed at Rome, or at Alexandria. There are several cities and villages in Egypt where, contrary to the usage established elsewhere, the people meet together on Sabbath evenings; and although they have dined previously, partake of the mysteries."

These are revealing statements. Practically all over Christendom Christian people were still assembling, as late as A.D. 450, in the churches on the seventh day of the week.

# APPENDIXES

## No Sabbath Observance in Rome

There were two marked exceptions to this. Two churches had once observed the Sabbath, but, under pressure of tradition, had ceased to do so. Alexandria was one. Here the philosophizing teachers had once presided, and through allegorizing interpretation of Scripture these men had emphasized the keeping of Sunday, as their writings clearly indicate. We see in the defeat of Sabbathkeeping a result of their influence, which led the people of Alexandria away from the simplicity of Bible truth.

Rome also, say Socrates and Sozomen, set aside the observance of the seventh-day Sabbath. This was exactly in line with the attitude of Rome toward the commandments of God and particularly toward the Sabbath. This church has always been consistent in substituting for the commandments of God the precepts of men. It has done the very thing for which Christ condemned so severely the Pharisees of His day. (Matt. 15:9, 13.) In these two churches the people were led away from Sabbathkeeping. In almost all other churches the Sabbath was still observed.

How displeasing it must have been, then, to Pope Gregory of Rome, A.D. 600, to find in his own territory those who were keeping the Sabbath! In book 13 of his *Epistles*, Letter I, he says, in great bitterness of soul:

"It has come to my ears that certain men of perverse spirit have sown among you some things that are wrong and opposed to the holy faith, so as to forbid any work being done on the Sabbath day. What else can I call these but preachers of Antichrist?"

We answer, These were not preachers of Antichrist. They were preachers who would obey the commandments of God and serve Christ, who is the Lord of the Sabbath. In emphasizing the Sabbath they were not preaching a depraved faith but the very truth of Scripture.

# Sabbath in Matthew 28:1

[The following, from W. E. Howell, appeared in the *Review and Herald* of August 10, 1939.]

In defending the perpetuity of the Sabbath we have always had to meet certain attempted proofs of its change to the first day of the week, based on certain passages in the New Testament. One of the principal assumptions is based on Matthew 28:1, of which it is declared that since "day" is a supplied word in the phrase "the first *day* of the week," it should read "the first of the sabbaths," that is, the first sabbath in the succession of sabbaths alleged to be newly instituted and observed on the first day of the week in honor of Christ's resurrection.

For this they give two reasons: the word *day* is a supplied word, and the word *week* in Greek is literally *sabbata*, the plural of *sabbaton*, and hence may be rendered *sabbaths*. Though both these observations are true, the conclusion from them is impossible. The word *sabbaton* is *neuter* in gender, and the word *first* is *feminine*. Hence to make *first* mean first *sabbath* would violate the most fundamental and invariable rule of Greek inflection—that all modifying adjectives must agree in *gender*, as well as in case and number, with the noun modified.

As to the word translated "week" in this verse, it is true that it is in the plural form, but the word *sabbaton* is used freely in either the singular or the plural when denoting a single day. For example, in the account of the Saviour and His disciples going through the field and eating corn on the Sabbath, Matthew uses the plural in chapter 12:1, and the singular in verse 2, Mark uses the plural in both instances in chapter 2:23, 24, and Luke uses the singular in the first instance and the plural in the second, in chapter 6:1, 2 (exactly the reverse of Matthew)—and all tell the same incident. Hence the plural form does not necessarily require plural translation.

Moreover, the plural *sabbata* is the only term used in the New Testament to designate the *week*. It is so used nine times. This is very similar to the old Anglo-Saxon way of using *sennight* (seven-night; in dialect, *sennet*) for a week, just as the Anglo-Saxons did, and we do still use *fortnight* (fourteen nights) for two weeks.

The only place in the New Testament where "sabbath" is properly rendered in the plural, "sabbath days," is in Acts 17:2, where it is said that Paul reasoned in the synagogue three Sabbath days. In the Authorized Version it is put in the plural, also in Matthew 12:10; Mark 3:4; and Luke 6:2, in which texts the principle that it is lawful to do good on the Sabbath is discussed. But this is without reason, and it is put in the singular in all three places in the Revised Version, as it is also, and should be, in Colossians 2:16.

Now in Matthew 28:1, the word "week" is simply the plural of *sabbaton*, put in the genitive case, which is equivalent to our form of using *of the* or the possessive. Hence "first" being in the feminine and *sabbaton* in the neuter, and the two words being in different cases, it could not be made to read *first sabbath*. Nor could it be *first of the sabbath*, for it would make no sense with the context, and be in conflict in gender. Nor could it be *first of the sabbaths*, for that would make it mean *first sabbath of the sabbaths*, and the genders of the two words would be in utter conflict.

The true meaning of this phrase is perfectly expressed by making it read "the *first day* of the week," just as it does in the King James Version, for *first* is feminine, and *day* is feminine in the Greek, and there is harmony. In fact, Luke uses literally "the day of the sabbath" more than once for "sabbath day." It was and is the common practice in Greek up to now to omit *day* and *hour* in designating the day of the week or the hour of the day, just as we do when we say "the tenth [day] of the month" or "ten [hours] o'clock," that is, ten hours by the clock. Although we disregard gender, the Greek faithfully distinguishes the gender, making both *day* and *hour* feminine, and in this verse in Matthew *first* is also feminine; so we know beyond a doubt that *day* is understood.

Another chief difficulty in interpreting Matthew 28:1 lies in harmonizing the phrase "in the end of the sabbath" with "dawn toward the first day of the week." The Greek for "in the end" is a single adverb *opse*, meaning late. Though this word usually denotes the late or last part of the period of time in question, what Matthew intended it to mean here is made plain by the defining clause that follows, literally: "the (hour) dawning into the first (day) of the week." The base of this clause, "the dawning," is put in the dative form—the usual one for denoting *time when*. Hence we may read it: "*at the dawning of the first day of the week.*" The supplying of the word *hour* or *day* is justified by the fact that the participle *dawning* and the numeral *first* are both in the feminine gender (which shows that a feminine noun is understood); by the fact that both *hour* and *day* are feminine; and by the additional fact that the Greek commonly omits *day* or *hour* in designating a day of the week or an hour of the day.

That Matthew's use of *opse sabbaton* is intended to mean "after the sabbath" is confirmed by the three other Gospel writers in defining the time when the women came to the sepulcher. Mark says plainly, "the sabbath having passed." Luke says: "the first day of the week, at deep dawn" (the dawn scarcely breaking, very early). John says: "the first day of the week . . . in the morning, darkness yet being."

That the adverb *opse* in this connection may be properly rendered *after*, is confirmed also by the Modern Greek translation, which reads literally, "After was passed the Sabbath, about the breaking of the first day of the week, came Mary Magdalene," et cetera.

This interpretation is further supported by Friedrich Blass, Ph.D., Th.D., Litt.D., in his *Grammar of New Testament Greek*, in which he says on page 97: "*Opse sabbaton* Matthew 28:1, but not 'late on the Sabbath,' since the next clause and Mark 16:1 show that the meaning must be 'after the Sabbath.'" In his appendix, Dr. Blass cites two instances in the *Life of Apollonius*, by Philostratus, a philosopher of the Roman Imperial period (A.D. 193-211), in which *opse* with the genitive has the meaning "after"; namely, *opse musterion*, "not till after the mysteries," and *opse touton*, "after these."

From these two considerations we must conclude, either—

1. To follow blindly the literal and usual meaning of *opse*, that it denotes the last part of the Sabbath, and therefore make the passage mean that the Sabbath continued till daylight on the first day of the week, which view would be absurd; or,

2. To interpret *opse* in the light of its context and of the confirming testimony of three other Gospel writers, and give it the obvious meaning of "after the sabbath," supported also by the Modern Greek translation, by a Greek, from the original New Testament Greek, and confirmed by other scholars, which is entirely rational.

Hence the keeper of the true Sabbath may be assured that there is absolutely nothing in Matthew 28:1 that indicates a change of the Sabbath to the first day of the week, or that can disturb his confidence in the binding obligation of the fourth commandment in perpetuity.

[In the *Review and Herald* of July 4, 1940, W. E. Howell further discussed Matthew 28:1. We quote a part of his article.]

Another inquirer asks regarding the much-discussed passage in

# APPENDIXES

Matthew 28:1 concerning the Sabbath and the first day of the week. Someone has called to his attention Young's rendering of this verse, which reads, "On the eve of the sabbaths, at the dawn, toward the first of the sabbaths, came Mary."

The inquirer wants to know whether "eve of the sabbaths" and "first of the sabbaths" are justifiable translations. One hesitates to criticize the work of a finished scholar like Dr. Young, author of a well-known unabridged concordance, but I think the most kindly way of stating the matter is to say that in this case he has indulged in an interpretation instead of a translation, especially in the second phrase. I know of only one other scholar of standing who gives a similar rendering, and that by basing it on the conjunction of a yearly ceremonial sabbath with the weekly Sabbath, and concluding that the resurrection occurred on the Sabbath day. . . .

It is true that not infrequently would-be defenders of the Sunday sabbath use the interpretation "first of the sabbaths," endeavoring to make it appear that the resurrection day was the first of the new sabbaths changed to the first day of the week. No one should be confused by such a construing of this notable phrase, though it is a bit more difficult for one who does not read the Greek to expose the error in such an interpretation. It would take a book to say all that deserves to be said on this and related passages in the New Testament, but I shall endeavor to make clear in a few paragraphs the essential facts in the case.

Aside from the great preponderance of scholarly translation mentioned above, the reading of the original text itself is our safest guide, if we can accept it without bias.

The Greek word for "sabbath" in the first phrase of Matthew 28:1, and the one for "week" in the second phrase, are identical—*sabbaton*—and in the plural. By an idiom of the language, either the singular or the plural of *sabbaton* may be used for either "sabbath day" or "week." Out of sixty-eight times the word for sabbath occurs in the New Testament, it is rendered *week* nine times. In addition to the context as a guide to determining the sense of *week*, the word itself is preceded by the ordinal numeral *first* in every instance of the nine but one, in which latter the number is the cardinal "twice." Luke 18:12. It is preceded by the ordinal "first" in Matthew 28:1, and why not translate it *week* here as in the only other eight instances in which it occurs? There is no just ground for changing the translation in this one instance, from *week* to *sabbaths,* as is done in Dr. Young's and Dr. Knoch's translations.

# "The Lord's Day"

[The following is an article by W. E. Howell in the *Review and Herald* of May 9, 1940.]

This phrase, "the Lord's day," occurs but once in the Bible, in Revelation 1:10: "I was in the Spirit on *the Lord's day.*" One sees it nowadays in the public press and in the name of one or more organizations. In this use it is usually intended to mean Sunday. In the French, Spanish, Italian, and Portuguese translations of the Scriptures, it is for the most part, though not in all, rendered Sunday. Advocates of Sunday observance often employ this scripture in attempted support of the keeping of the first day of the week as the Sabbath. What is the true meaning of "the Lord's day" as used by the prophet John?

Though we may not know why John chose to use this phrase instead of one more specific, a little study of the phrase itself and of one or two kindred ones elsewhere will throw light on the question.

The word "Lord's" is a translation of an adjective used in the Greek phrase *kuriakee heemera.* The adjective *kuriakee* is derived from the regular New Testament word for Lord, *kurios,* with a suffix added to its stem. In English we have no suitable adjective form of *Lord,* since the only one we have, *lordly,* has come by usage to have a meaning not adaptable to this phrase. The nearest we can come to a proper equivalent is to say "day *of the Lord,*" or as in the text, "Lord's day," meaning a day belonging to the Lord or set apart by the Lord.

There is an interesting parallel in the use of *kuriakos* in the phrase *kuriakon deipnon,* "Lord's supper," in 1 Corinthians 11:20. As all know, this is the supper presided over by Jesus just before His betrayal and crucifixion, and ordained by Him to be observed by His followers "till he come." The adjective qualifying "supper" is exactly the same one as used to qualify "day" in Revelation 1:10, and it is not used elsewhere in the New Testament.

In the case of the supper, it was instituted by the Lord's setting the example of how to observe it, and saying to His disciples, "This do in remembrance of me." "I have given you an example, that ye should do as I have done to you."

APPENDIXES

In the case of the day, God "rested on the seventh day from all his work which he had made. And God blessed the seventh day, and sanctified it." "Remember the sabbath day, to keep it holy. . . . For in six days the Lord made heaven and earth, the sea, and all that in them is, and rested the seventh day." This is the only day God ever set apart by resting upon it Himself, and commanding us to remember to keep it holy. Numerous times after that event as recorded in the Bible, the day is called "the sabbath of the Lord thy God." In other words, it is supremely "the Lord's day," as really as the supper was and is "the Lord's supper."

Again, "the Lord's day" cannot refer to the day of His resurrection, or to a memorial of that day, for the resurrection is commemorated and symbolized by baptism—that is, baptism by immersion.

There is also another aspect of the interpretation of the phrase "the Lord's day" that should be noticed. Since the discovery of Greek writing in fragmentary papyrus documents and in inscriptions in Egypt and other dry countries, it has been found that the words *kurios* and *kuriakos* were in common use among the people at the time the New Testament was written. The word *kurios*, in fact, was then, and still is among the modern Greeks, used as equivalent to our title Mr., but by extension also to head of the house or a business concern or our common use of the word *lord* as applied to an estate or social status or even to a king or emperor.

When Jesus came in the flesh, it was the most natural and normal thing for His followers to call Him Lord, for so He was, as He Himself declared. Ever since He has been called *the* Lord without anyone's doubting who is meant. To the heathen of Christ's day, *lord* naturally applied in its highest sense to the emperor. Hence it was all the more fitting for Christians to call Jesus Lord, as He was indeed Lord of all, including kings and emperors.

Now *kuriakos* was in common use as the adjective form of *kurios*, whether applied to the head of a house or a business concern, or the emperor. So was it equally fitting for Christians to apply it to the paschal supper and to the "sabbath of the Lord thy God," especially since Jesus Himself declared that He was "Lord of the sabbath." How consistent, then, for the apostle John to write *kuriakee heemera*, "Lord's day," as a designation of the Sabbath of the Lord. How inconsistent and incompatible it would seem for him to say he was in a high state of spiritual exaltation on "the emperor's day"!

Hence, without denying that *kurios* and *kuriakos* were in common use in the speech of the day, perhaps no one has better expressed the exaltation of *kurios* from meaning Caesar to signifying Jesus the King of all kings, than has the eminent Greek scholar, Dr. A. T. Robertson, in his *Grammar of the Greek New Testament in the Light of Historical Research,* in which he says, on pages 115, 116:

"The fact that these and other terms were used in the popular language of the day gives sharper point to the new turn in the gospel message. The deification of the emperor made Christians sensitive about the words [*kurios, kuriakos,* and seven others mentioned]. . . . The Christians did not shrink from using these words in spite of the debased ideas due to the emperor cult, Mithraism, or other popular superstitions. Indeed Paul often took the very words of Gnostic or Mithra cult and filled them with the riches of Christ. . . . The mass of the New Testament vocabulary has been transfigured. . . . The new message glorified the current *koinee* [common speech], took the words from the street, and made them bear a new content, linked heaven with earth in a new sense."

Meecham, also, in his book *Light From Ancient Letters,* pages 118, 119, quoting in part from Kennedy, says of *kurios:*

" 'It was constantly used of characteristically Oriental deities, such as the Egyptian Isis, Osiris, and Serapis. In the first century it was quickly taking its place as the designation of the deified emperor, and thus becoming the central term of the imperial cult.' What Paul did, therefore, was to adopt this current title, and invest it with a deeper and more spiritual meaning. . . . Its ascription to the deified Roman ruler was anathema. There was but 'one Lord, Jesus Christ' (1 Cor. 8:6). To the writers of the New Testament the risen Christ is, above all else, 'Lord.' "

In conclusion, we may say that although the people of the day might properly say *kurios* Caesar, the Christians might most appropriately say *kurios* Jesus. Though the people might say *kuriakos logos* for Caesar's treasury, the Christians would as logically say *kuriakon deipnon* for Lord's supper, and *kuriakee heemera* for Lord's day—the only day He ever claimed as exclusively His own, "the sabbath of the Lord thy God."

# Gentiles and Sabbathkeeping—a Letter to a Fundamentalist

Some time ago a series of editorials in the *Review and Herald* commented on certain articles in a religious weekly, which declared emphatically that the Ten Commandments are still in force, but that the Sabbath command has been changed. These articles, incidentally, were Sunday school lesson helps on the Decalogue. The *Review* comments were sent to the writer of the articles, who at that time was the president of a Fundamentalist Bible school. He replied in fine Christian spirit, reaffirmed his belief in the Decalogue as the moral standard for Christians, but declared he felt that this "does not strengthen the position of Christians who keep Saturday as the Sabbath." He also restated the position taken in his articles, that it would be necessary to have the seventh-day Sabbath specifically enjoined on the Gentiles in order for us to feel duty bound to obey it. He declared that "none of the Gentiles kept the Sabbath day, but they all recognized the other commands as obligatory," and asked the question, "Is there any evidence that the Gentile Christians ever kept the seventh-day Sabbath?" Here is a portion of the letter that was sent in reply:

### The Text of the Letter

Let me open my letter with a comment on your closing paragraph. You state that though you believe Adventists are in error on various doctrines, this does not prevent your "recognizing their true faith in Christ as Saviour." This is encouraging. Various of our critics, particularly of the Bible Institute type, have, in their zeal, risen to the heights of declaring that Seventh-day Adventists turn their back on Christ, are strangers to the gospel; and as if that were not sufficient as an excoriation, they climax it by charging that we make Satan our savior and sin bearer. There is one redeeming feature about such sweeping charges as these—to anyone who knows anything at all of either Adventist theology or Adventist living, such charges collapse of their own topheaviness and absurdity.

Permit me to direct your special attention to my comments on the relation of the Sabbath to the moot question of the Genesis story of creation, which is the battlefield between Fundamentalists and Modernists.

## A Strange Silence

Though I have searched Fundamentalist literature diligently, I have never found any comment on the Seventh-day Adventist statement regarding the relation of the Sabbath to the primary tenet of Fundamentalism, the belief in the story of our world's origin as given in Genesis. All I am able to find in comment on us is merely general denunciations of us as heretics. And all the while, of course, Fundamentalists bewail the increasing tide of skeptical Modernism in their own denominations, especially in their denominational colleges and seminaries. Meanwhile, whatever else may be our sins and shortcomings, we remain absolutely free from the corrosion of Modernism, even in our colleges and seminaries. We could not become Modernists, which necessitates moving onto the platform of evolution, when every member of the church on the seventh day of every week turns aside from his ordinary labors to worship Him who in six days made heaven and earth, and rested the seventh day.

I conclude from the second paragraph of your letter that you believe that the law of God is the moral standard of life for Christians. This gives us something in common. I suppose that in your reading of anti-Sabbath literature, especially that prepared by Bible institutes, you may have noticed that the common method of meeting the argument for the seventh-day Sabbath is by declaring that the law was done away. It is this antinomian argument that we meet most frequently. Evidently you do not believe this view, which, of course, as you know, and as surely anyone who claims to have any knowledge of church history ought to know, has been denounced as a heresy in Protestantism from the days of Luther onward.

## Our Interpretation Ancient

You state that the fact that the Ten Commandments are our moral guide "does not strengthen the position of Christians who keep Saturday as the Sabbath." I conclude from this that you interpret the fourth commandment as did the drafters of the Westminster Confession, who adopted the views of Nicholas Bownde, that "the seventh day" means simply "one day in seven." The limits of a letter do not permit me to analyze what I believe are patent fallacies and irrationalities that reside in this interpretation. Suffice it to say here that such an interpretation of the plain words of the fourth command was never thought of until three thousand years after the proclaiming of that command on Mount Sinai, for Nicholas Bownde lived at the end of the sixteenth century of our Christian Era.

If the touchstone of orthodoxy be in any sense the antiquity of a belief, as Fundamentalists often suggest by the very emphasis they place on the antithetical term Modernism, then certainly Adventists are the truly orthodox ones in the matter of the Sabbath. I do not say myself that antiquity of interpretation is necessarily the proof of its correctness. But when Adventists are so often charged with preaching new and strange doctrines it is surely pertinent for me to call attention to the historical aspect of our interpretation of the Sabbath command.

Later in your letter you say: "I might add in connection with your comments on the *Sunday School Times* lesson articles that the point about a command to keep the Sabbath being necessary for the Gentiles was in view of the fact that none of the Gentiles kept the Sabbath day, while they all recognized the other commands as obligatory." Is there any evidence that the Gentile Christians never kept the seventh-day Sabbath? Why is it not just as proper for the question to be put in this form? Evidently your answer to the question would be Yes, for you have just stated that "none of the Gentiles kept the Sabbath day." How do you prove this? How are you sure what they did not do? Do you prove it by what you believe to be the silence of Scripture concerning their keeping of the Sabbath? If so, I wonder if you would be willing to allow the validity of the argument from silence in some other areas of theological discussion.

### Burden of Proof on Sunday Advocate

The whole burden of proof rests upon you in this matter. If you accept the premise that the Ten Commandments are the Christian's moral standard, then, unless you provide clear proof to the contrary, the conclusion logically follows that the early Christians did keep the Sabbath. Furthermore, even if you could produce contrary proof, which I am confident you cannot, the only logical conclusion then would be that the Gentiles from the outset broke one of the Ten Commandments.

[The matter is presented in this brief form as a logical proposition because the limits of a letter forbid the introduction of extensive historical evidence. Such evidence clearly reveals that Gentile Christians kept the Sabbath very generally for a long period after New Testament times. After apostolic days Sundaykeeping gradually came in along with other apostate practices.]

## ANSWERS TO OBJECTIONS

Let us take the matter a little further. You say that "none of the Gentiles kept the Sabbath day, while they all recognized the other commands as obligatory." This is essentially the line of reasoning of those who declare that the law was abolished at the cross, but that in some remarkable manner this law, which evidently was so faulty and unnecessary as to call for abolition, found itself nine tenths restored in the Christian dispensation. It is this process of reasoning that is employed by antinomians to escape the charge of moral anarchy which is brought against them for their doctrine that the law was done away. Now, I do not say that you subscribe to this. I simply say that your line of reasoning in this particular connection runs parallel to theirs, and so far as I can discover, is here identical with it. But this is not the teaching of the great Protestant creeds. If we are discussing the question of orthodoxy—and "heresy" is the blanket charge against Adventists —then any teaching that the ten commandment law was abolished at the cross is heresy. Accordingly, Gentiles, in order to square with Protestant creeds, must recognize all of the ten commandments "as obligatory."

I might ask further: If the Gentiles did not consider the fourth commandment as obligatory, on what, then, did they base the keeping of a weekly holy day, which you declare was Sunday? If you say they based it simply on custom and the growing practice of the church, then you admit that there is no "Thus saith the Lord" behind Sunday. If you hesitate to make this admission, and I would not blame you for so hesitating in view of the thunderings of American and English preachers through the years regarding the awful sin of Sunday desecration, then I would ask you, In what text of Holy Writ do you find a "Thus saith the Lord" for Sunday? If you can find such a text, you have done better than any theologian before you. Many theologians admit frankly that there is no command for Sundaykeeping.

### The Crux of the Matter

If you say, as you did in the Sunday school lessons, that in some way the spirit of the fourth command still holds for those who live in the Christian Era, and therefore they should keep Sunday, I would ask you to elucidate on this point. It is the crux of the discussion. What is there so elusive about this fourth command that we should be asked to view it only in some ghostly, transcendental form? Its language is as plain and as vigorous as that of any other precept of the ten, so plain indeed that men had no difficulty, and certainly no controversy, over the understanding of it for thousands of years.

Who authorized you or any other Christian minister, I ask with all good feeling, to deprive this one precept of the ten of its body and substance?

If you really do believe that the law was done away at the cross, but that nine of the ten were somehow restored, I insist that you give just as literal a resurrection to the fourth commandment if you are going to invoke it in any way in support of a weekly holy day. Why not leave wholly to the Modernists the vaporous doctrine of a spiritual resurrection? To my mind it is a curious thing, this Protestant reasoning, I am tempted almost to say casuistry, that retains on the one side, in some shadowy form, the fourth commandment, in order to have a "Thus saith the Lord" foundation for their weekly holy day; and on the other hand discards the fourth command as abolished, in order to break the force of the seventh-day Sabbath argument.

### Catholic Church More Frank

In this matter the Catholic Church is more honest, shall I say, than Protestantism; for it makes no endeavor to defend Sunday by reasoning that "the seventh" day means only one day in seven. With all its specious interpretations, Catholicism evidently thought this too unwarranted, in view of the unanimity of interpretation for thousands of years. It frankly states in its catechisms that "the seventh day" is Saturday. Then it defends Sunday on the ground that the church has a right to change laws and to institute holy days. If we accepted this view of the power of the church, we could easily accept Sunday. But we are not Catholics. We are Protestants.

I am not quite sure of your view. I concluded, from the first part of your letter, that you believed unqualifiedly that the Ten Commandments—and of course the fourth must be present in order to make the ten—are the moral standard for Gentile Christians. But the latter part of your letter, which declares that Gentiles did not keep the Sabbath, "while they all recognized the other commands as obligatory," throws me into doubt as to your view.

Therefore, to clear the air, let me ask you directly: Do you believe that the Decalogue is in full force, that it is the moral standard for us in the Christian dispensation? If you answer no, we part company right here, I standing with the great Protestant confessions and creeds, and you standing wherever you wish. If you answer that you do believe the Ten Commandments to be our moral standard, I conclude, by simple arithmetic, that you believe in the fourth along with the other nine.

# ANSWERS TO OBJECTIONS

## Two Key Questions

Then I would ask you, By what process of reasoning, or rather, by what texts of Scripture do you justify changing what was for thousands of years the one understanding of the meaning of this fourth commandment as regards the *day* of worship and the *purpose* of the worship? In other words, How do you prove that the phrase in the command, "the seventh day," which until the sixteenth century A.D., was understood by all to apply to the specific seventh day of the week, really refers to no day in particular, merely to one day in seven? And how do you prove that this fourth command, which is based on a certain historical fact, the creation, can be made to apply to another historical fact, the resurrection? Even when the minds of Christians were becoming befogged by strange doctrines and reasonings in the early centuries, the basic distinction between Sabbath and Sunday was evident to them, for the Sabbath was described as the feast of creation, and Sunday as the feast of the resurrection.

## New Creation Depends on Old

Perhaps you will say on this second point that the resurrection is the memorial of a new creation, and thus the fourth command applies; but in the articles enclosed with this letter, I have tried to show that such reasoning, though plausible on the surface, is not valid; that the Christian needs to remember and to have absolute belief in the historical creation, the event described in Genesis and quoted in the fourth commandment, before he can have any faith in, or attach any significance to, the plan of salvation and the work of Christ in the new creation. Instead of the new creation's eclipsing and taking the place of the historical creation, the simple facts are that the new creation owes its significance to the literal, historical creation. Fundamentalists have intoned sufficiently, I believe, on the primary necessity of a belief in the historical creation in Genesis as the true foundation on which all Christian doctrine must rest, to make it unnecessary for me to amplify this point here.

In asking you this series of questions I have no desire to take any unfair advantage of you by the specious procedure of asking questions which a man should not be expected to answer. Instead, I think these are the most relevant questions that could be raised. Let me repeat, the burden of proof in this whole matter must rest upon you who believe in Sunday, not upon us who believe in the seventh-day Sabbath. We represent the historic interpretation of the fourth commandment from time immemorial. We have never changed our interpretation;

we have seen no reason to do so. If words had one value and meaning in past time, we see no reason why their meaning should be basically changed today. It is for you, of course, who believe that there is a sufficient reason, and a Biblical reason at that, to produce that reason for us.

The fact that virtually the whole Christian world soon turned away from obedience to the fourth command is surely no argument in itself that such a departure is justified. I am certain you would not put it forth as a formal proposition, though it does seem to be the submerged premise in the reasoning of a great majority of first-day keepers. But knowing, as I am certain you do know, how quickly there crept into the church a great variety of false doctrines and perversions of true doctrines, which held virtually all Christendom in their control for long centuries, I am sure that you will not ask me to accept any argument for Sunday based on the early appearance of it in the church and its rapid and widespread adoption. It is not in church practice but in Bible precept that we as Protestants must find the guide for our lives.

# The Gamble Theory Examined

About the year 1900 a Methodist minister, Samuel Walter Gamble, wrote a book, *Sunday, the True Sabbath of God,* in which he brought forth a series of astounding claims regarding the nature of the ancient Jewish calendar. On these claims he built an argument against the seventh-day Sabbath and for Sunday. The book was brought forth admittedly as an attack on Seventh-day Adventists and their Sabbath preaching. We might perhaps dispose of the book with the brief observation that though it was produced for the express purpose of providing Sundaykeepers with a new and invincible argument against Sabbatarians, and though the writer of the introduction declared, "It is this or nothing," Gamble's book failed to win scholarly support. Sunday-keeping theologians ridiculed unsparingly some of the key claims of the book.

However, three reasons prompt me to examine the theory:

1. Though the Gamble book died quietly, with scarcely an obituary notice from the theologians whom it was intended to aid, the shadowy apparition of the theory is invoked quite frequently by the opponents of the Sabbath.

A choice illustration of how the ghost of the Gamble theory enters into important present-day Sabbath discussions, is found in the following quotation from the *Lord's Day Leader,* official organ of the Lord's Day Alliance:

"Nowhere did God designate the seventh day of the week [as the Sabbath]. It could not have been appointed for the seventh day of the week without interfering with the law of the Passover. The Passover was a movable feast. It was appointed to be held on the fourteenth day of the month of Abib, or Nisan. It was therefore a calendar date, and not a weekly day. This was the first great sabbath of the year, and the other sabbaths followed every seventh day. Now everybody knows that a calendar date, such as a birthday or Fourth of July, cannot fall on the same day of the week two years in succession.

"Now let us be reasonable about this matter, and admit, as all intelligent Jewish rabbis do, that the ancient sabbaths fell on the seventh

day after the Passover, and not on the seventh day of the week, and that in the course of seven years each day of the week was in turn the sabbath for a whole year. This was the law as long as the Jewish nation lasted."
—September-October, 1928.

Of course Sunday law reformers, of all people, find comfort in such a theory as Gamble's, because it enables them to invoke the Sabbath command in favor of Sunday; for is not Sunday a seventh day after six days of work?

2. Two leaders in the recent calendar-revision movement, Moses B. Cotsworth and C. F. Marvin, resurrected the Gamble theory, touched it up here and there, and sent it forth again with such publicity as they were able to command. (Of its relation to calendar revision I am not here concerned, of course.)

3. While the mere refuting of a fanciful theory may be rather profitless, though necessary, the discussion of this particular theory furnishes an excellent opportunity to set forth much positive evidence and truth regarding the Jewish annual sabbaths and the difference between them and the weekly Sabbath.

I shall not attempt to go into all the details of the theory, but confine myself to the primary claims on which it rests. If these collapse, they carry down with them the secondary claims.* I shall deal with the theory in terms of its revived form as given out by Cotsworth and Marvin in a thirty-two-page pamphlet entitled *Moses the Greatest of Calendar Reformers,* published by the International Fixed Calendar League. However, so far as the main arguments are concerned there is *no* difference between the original and the revived form. On the following page is a reproduction of the calendar which, according to this theory, was given to the Jews by Moses at the time of the Exodus. The claims made regarding it are as follows:

### Four Claims for Alleged Mosaic Calendar

1. Moses, at the time of the Exodus, established a solar calendar of 365 days. This calendar consisted of twelve thirty-day months, plus five extra days, three of which extra days were inserted at the end of the sixth month (Elul), and two at the end of the twelfth (Adar). These five extra days, though reckoned as days of the week, were not counted as days of the month.

---

* I wish to acknowledge my great indebtedness to the late Dr. Moses Hyamson, LL.D., who, at the time I interviewed him, was professor of codes at the Jewish Theological Seminary of America, New York. Rabbi Hyamson gave to me more than a whole day of his valuable time in explanation of the various customs of the ancient Israelites and in elucidation of Scriptural passages involved in this theory. He was regarded not only by his orthodox associates but also by reformed rabbis as one of the most learned of Hebrew scholars.

## ABIB (Nisan) 1st Month

| WORK DAYS | | | | | | Sabbath |
|---|---|---|---|---|---|---|
| 1st | 2d | 3d | 4th | 5th | 6th | 7th |
|  |  |  |  |  |  | 1 |
| 2 | 3 | 4 | 5 | 6 | 7 | 8 |
| 9 | 10 | 11 | 12 | 13 | 14 | 15 |
| 16 | 17 | 18 | 19 | 20 | 21 | 22 |
| 23 | 24 | 25 | 26 | 27 | 28 | 29 |
| 30 |  |  |  |  |  |  |

## TISHRI (Ethanim) 7th Month

| WORK DAYS | | | | | | Sabbath |
|---|---|---|---|---|---|---|
| 1st | 2d | 3d | 4th | 5th | 6th | 7th |
|  |  |  |  |  |  | 1 |
| 2 | 3 | 4 | 5 | 6 | 7 | 8 |
| 9 | 10 | 11 | 12 | 13 | 14 | 15 |
| 16 | 17 | 18 | 19 | 20 | 21 | 22 |
| 23 | 24 | 25 | 26 | 27 | 28 | 29 |
| 30 |  |  |  |  |  |  |

## IYAR (Ziv) 2d Month

| 1st | 2d | 3d | 4th | 5th | 6th | 7th |
|---|---|---|---|---|---|---|
|  | 1 | 2 | 3 | 4 | 5 | 6 |
| 7 | 8 | 9 | 10 | 11 | 12 | 13 |
| 14 | 15 | 16 | 17 | 18 | 19 | 20 |
| 21 | 22 | 23 | 24 | 25 | 26 | 27 |
| 28 | 29 | 30 |  |  |  |  |

## BUL (Heshvan) 8th Month

| 1st | 2d | 3d | 4th | 5th | 6th | 7th |
|---|---|---|---|---|---|---|
|  | 1 | 2 | 3 | 4 | 5 | 6 |
| 7 | 8 | 9 | 10 | 11 | 12 | 13 |
| 14 | 15 | 16 | 17 | 18 | 19 | 20 |
| 21 | 22 | 23 | 24 | 25 | 26 | 27 |
| 28 | 29 | 30 |  |  |  |  |

## SIVAN 3d Month

| 1st | 2d | 3d | 4th | 5th | 6th | 7th |
|---|---|---|---|---|---|---|
| Pentecost— ("Extra Sabbath") |  | 1 | 2 | 3 | 4 | 5 |
| 6 | 7 | 8 | 9 | 10 | 11 | 12 |
| 13 | 14 | 15 | 16 | 17 | 18 | 19 |
| 20 | 21 | 22 | 23 | 24 | 25 | 26 |
| 27 | 28 | 29 | 30 |  |  |  |

## CHISLEV (Kislev) 9th Month

| 1st | 2d | 3d | 4th | 5th | 6th | 7th |
|---|---|---|---|---|---|---|
|  |  |  | 1 | 2 | 3 | 4 |
| 5 | 6 | 7 | 8 | 9 | 10 | 11 |
| 12 | 13 | 14 | 15 | 16 | 17 | 18 |
| 19 | 20 | 21 | 22 | 23 | 24 | 25 |
| 26 | 27 | 28 | 29 | 30 |  |  |

## TAMMUZ 4th Month

| 1st | 2d | 3d | 4th | 5th | 6th | 7th |
|---|---|---|---|---|---|---|
|  |  |  |  | 1 | 2 | 3 |
| 4 | 5 | 6 | 7 | 8 | 9 | 10 |
| 11 | 12 | 13 | 14 | 15 | 16 | 17 |
| 18 | 19 | 20 | 21 | 22 | 23 | 24 |
| 25 | 26 | 27 | 28 | 29 | 30 |  |

## TEBETH 10th Month

| 1st | 2d | 3d | 4th | 5th | 6th | 7th |
|---|---|---|---|---|---|---|
|  |  |  |  |  | 1 | 2 |
| 3 | 4 | 5 | 6 | 7 | 8 | 9 |
| 10 | 11 | 12 | 13 | 14 | 15 | 16 |
| 17 | 18 | 19 | 20 | 21 | 22 | 23 |
| 24 | 25 | 26 | 27 | 28 | 29 | 30 |

## AB 5th Month

| 1st | 2d | 3d | 4th | 5th | 6th | 7th |
|---|---|---|---|---|---|---|
|  |  |  |  |  |  | 1 |
| 2 | 3 | 4 | 5 | 6 | 7 | 8 |
| 9 | 10 | 11 | 12 | 13 | 14 | 15 |
| 16 | 17 | 18 | 19 | 20 | 21 | 22 |
| 23 | 24 | 25 | 26 | 27 | 28 | 29 |
| 30 |  |  |  |  |  |  |

## SHEBAT 11th Month

| 1st | 2d | 3d | 4th | 5th | 6th | 7th |
|---|---|---|---|---|---|---|
| 1 | 2 | 3 | 4 | 5 | 6 | 7 |
| 8 | 9 | 10 | 11 | 12 | 13 | 14 |
| 15 | 16 | 17 | 18 | 19 | 20 | 21 |
| 22 | 23 | 24 | 25 | 26 | 27 | 28 |
| 29 | 30 |  |  |  |  |  |

## ELUL 6th Month

| 1st | 2d | 3d | 4th | 5th | 6th | 7th |
|---|---|---|---|---|---|---|
|  | 1 | 2 | 3 | 4 | 5 | 6 |
| 7 | 8 | 9 | 10 | 11 | 12 | 13 |
| 14 | 15 | 16 | 17 | 18 | 19 | 20 |
| 21 | 22 | 23 | 24 | 25 | 26 | 27 |
| 28 | 29 | 30 |  |  |  |  |

## ADAR 12th Month

| 1st | 2d | 3d | 4th | 5th | 6th | 7th |
|---|---|---|---|---|---|---|
|  | 1 | 2 | 3 | 4 | 5 |  |
| 6 | 7 | 8 | 9 | 10 | 11 | 12 |
| 13 | 14 | 15 | 16 | 17 | 18 | 19 |
| 20 | 21 | 22 | 23 | 24 | 25 | 26 |
| 27 | 28 | 29 | 30 | (4) | (5) |  |

THE ALLEGED MOSAIC PERPETUAL CALENDAR

APPENDIXES

2. The "seventh day" of the fourth commandment was not the "seventh day" of the week as we understand it today, but simply the seventh day after six days of labor. Therefore, to speak of the days of the Mosaic calendar as Sunday, Monday, Tuesday, et cetera, is not accurate. The specifically mentioned sabbath days in the Jewish ritual, such as Passover sabbath, give the key, and the remainder of the sabbaths in the year are located in the calendar by spacing out six working days before each of them.

3. The fifth day of the third month (Sivan), though reckoned as a day of the month, was not counted as a day of the week. This was the day of Pentecost. It was an "extra sabbath," similar to the "blank day" of the present proposed calendar. In other words, although the fourth of Sivan was sabbath, the fifth was not "Sunday," but simply a continuation of the sabbath of the fourth—a blank day so far as the reckoning of the days of the week is concerned.

4. Now, 365 days equal fifty-two weeks plus one day. But this extra day being eliminated from the count of the weeks, made the year really consist of an exact number of weeks. This caused the sabbaths always to bear a fixed relation to the month, instead of being the seventh day of a free-running week. Thus every year was an exact duplicate of every other year.

### Examine First Link in Evidence

The authors, Cotsworth and Marvin, first endeavor to prove that the Mosaic calendar was solar. This, of course, gave them their foundation for the statement that it consisted of 365 days. Most Jewish authorities hold that their ancient calendar was not solar; but let us grant, for the sake of argument, that it was. What does that prove? Nothing in particular. Our present calendar is solar, but that gives to it no unusual perpetual qualities. However, the reader of the pamphlet is led to feel that when the solar nature of the Mosaic calendar is established, the other features naturally follow. This feeling is strengthened by the fact that Dr. Julian Morgenstern and Prof. W. A. Heidel (whose views on the solar nature of the ancient Jewish calendar are mentioned in the main text of the pamphlet) are listed along with Samuel Walter Gamble, the father of the whole theory, in a footnote entitled "Some Authorities We Quote." A letter was therefore written to both these Hebrew scholars, informing them of the theory set forth in this pamphlet. The letter stated:

"The writers of this pamphlet quote you as one of the authorities in support of the major premise of their thesis, because of your contri-

## ANSWERS TO OBJECTIONS

bution on the calendar of ancient Israel. Your name and the quotations from your work, placed as they are in this pamphlet under the general head, 'Some Authorities We Quote,' lead the general reader to the impression that your researches warrant the ultimate conclusions to which the writers of the pamphlet come. I wish to inquire whether I would be correct in obtaining this impression. In other words, have your researches led you to believe, as do the writers of this pamphlet, that Moses devised a perpetual calendar that placed the Sabbath in a fixed relationship to the month, necessitating the existence each year of an extra Sabbath?"

### Hebrew Scholars Reply

The essence of Dr. Heidel's brief reply is found in this one sentence from his letter: "Messrs. Marvin and Cotsworth have quite absolutely misrepresented my views."

Dr. Morgenstern's reply is quoted in more detail:

### "THE HEBREW UNION COLLEGE

"Cincinnati, Ohio

"*Office of the President.*

"January 30, 1929.

"My dear Mr. Nichol:

"Replying to yours of the 24th inst., I am very happy to be able to assure you that Messrs. Marvin and Cotsworth have used my name in their propaganda for the new calendar entirely without my authorization and knowledge, and that the quotations from my article on 'The Three Calendars of Ancient Israel' apparently altogether misrepresent the facts with regard to the history of the calendar of ancient Israel which I have been able to establish. . . .

"Certainly I did not advance the thesis 'that the ancient Jews lived under a fixed or perpetual calendar devised by Moses, which caused the Sabbath always to recur on the same days of the month each year, instead of being an institution related only to the week, as we now have it.' On the contrary, I showed in this article that, at various times in the history of ancient Israel, different calendar systems were employed, that up to approximately 621 B.C. the old Canaanitish calendar, a purely solar calendar, taking cognizance of the days of the solar equinoxes, was employed in ancient Israel. Then from about 621 to a time somewhat later than 400 B.C., another calendar, apparently a lunisolar calendar, was employed, based apparently largely upon some

Babylonian model. It apparently took no cognizance whatever of the Sabbath, which continued as a *weekly* institution, falling upon any date in the month, regardless of any considerations other than that the Sabbath came every seventh day. At some time after 400 B.C., the calendar at present employed by the Jewish Church, also based upon Babylonian antecedents, was instituted. This also makes no effort to co-ordinate the Sabbath with any particular days or dates in the month.

"I showed likewise that at some time, probably in the third century B.C., an attempt was made to introduce into ancient Israel a calendar similar to that which Mr. Cotsworth is championing, with particular attention given to the coincidence of the Sabbath with the year divided into thirteen months of twenty-eight days, and with a particular date in each month, probably the seventh, fourteenth, twenty-first, and twenty-eighth days. This calendar is employed as the basis of reckoning in the books of Jubilees and Enoch, two pseudepigraphical writings which were never regarded as authoritative. This calendar, however, was never recognized as official by Judaism and never came into actual use. Furthermore, Moses himself had no connection whatsoever with any of these calendars. It is clear, therefore, that the above named gentlemen have either not troubled to read my article carefully, or, if they did, have not understood it or have not wanted to understand it. Certainly, the facts which they state and the conclusions which they drew from them are altogether unwarranted by my article.

"I trust that this gives you the information which you desire.
"Very sincerely yours,
"[Signed] JULIAN MORGENSTERN,
"*President.*"

Comment on this letter is superfluous. Let us therefore examine the next point.

The pamphlet authors declare that Moses inserted a leap week every twenty-eight years to serve the same purpose as our quadrennial leap day. The only "proof" cited in behalf of this is that Moses was too wise a statesman not to have done so, and that unless he *had* done so, "his wonderful calendar system" would have collapsed. The only point certain is that the "wonderful calendar system" of the *authors* will collapse without the leap-week feature. There is no proof in the world that *Moses* employed it.

### Next Link Examined

The next link in the chain is the claim that Moses divided his calendar into twelve thirty-day months, with five supplementary days that could be inserted between the months where needed. Unless he did thus divide the months, the theory could not be made to work. In other words, unless he followed the Egyptian division of months, the theory collapses. But again we are confronted with an assumption, for the authors simply *assume* that he did, and proceed to build a towering structure upon the groundless assumption, which in turn, rests upon the equally groundless assumption that Moses employed a leap week.

We come now to the examination of a passage in Exodus 19 which is brought forth as evidence for this alleged Mosaic calendar. The first text they quote, including the bracketed phrase, is: "In the third month after the children of Israel were gone forth out of the land of Egypt, the same day [that is, the third day] came they into the wilderness of Sinai. . . . And there Israel encamped before the mount." Ex. 19:1, 2, A.R.V. The bracketed phrase in this verse is inserted by the calendar authors.

They then quote a portion of the tenth and eleventh verses, which reads as follows:

"Jehovah said unto Moses, Go unto the people, and sanctify them to-day and to-morrow, and let them wash their garments, and be ready against the third day; for the third day Jehovah will come down in the sight of all the people upon mount Sinai." Verse 10.

They are endeavoring by these texts to support their contention that Pentecost came on the fifth day of the third month (Sivan), as their reconstructed calendar shows it. Their argument in brief is this:

1. That according to Jewish tradition the law was proclaimed from Mount Sinai on Pentecost; in other words, that Pentecost is a memorial of that great event.

2. That the Israelites reached Mount Sinai on the third day of the third month.

3. That the three days mentioned in verses 10 and 11 of Exodus 19 should begin with the third day of the month, thus causing the last of the three days of sanctification—the day when Jehovah came down and delivered the law, in other words, Pentecost—to come on the fifth day of the third month, as their calendar places it.

Let us now examine these three propositions. Even if it be granted that "the same day" means the third day of the month, the conclusions of the authors do not necessarily follow. They must still prove that the words of Jehovah to Moses to sanctify the people "to-day and to-morrow," as given in verses 10 and 11, were uttered the very day that the Israelites reached Mount Sinai. Unless they can do this, their third proposition collapses. But no proof can possibly be given for this claim, and every presumption is against it.

## Questionable Methods in Chronology

If the whole passage from the first verse to the eleventh is read, it will be noted that after the Israelites reached Sinai, Moses went up into the mount (verse 3), and communed for a time with God. How long, we know not. Next, that he descended from the mount (verse 7), and told the people what God had said to him. How much time this consumed, we know not. Next, that Moses reported to Jehovah what the people had said (verse 8), and that following these communications the Lord made a statement concerning the sanctifying of the people "against the third day." The Scriptures do not divulge how much time elapsed in connection with these conversations, and it is only unwarranted assumption that would declare that the whole passage must bear the date of the first verse, whatever that date may be.

If that sort of assumption is to be employed in determining the dates of events, we can quickly bring the Gamble theory into hopeless straits by turning to the sixteenth chapter of Exodus. There we read that the Israelites entered the wilderness of Sin on "the fifteenth day of the second month." Verse 1. The next two verses immediately declare that they murmured, craving the fleshpots of Egypt. Then immediately follows the statement of Jehovah (verse 4) that He "will rain bread from heaven," and that "it shall come to pass on the sixth day, that they shall prepare that which they bring in, and it shall be twice as much as they gather daily." Verse 5. Then Moses declares to the people that "in the morning" the people will have "bread to the full." Verses 7, 8. Then follows the story of how "in the morning" (verse 13) the people saw the manna lying on the ground, and gathered it up. Then, that "they gathered it morning by morning" (verse 21) until the "sixth day" arrived, when Moses informed them, "To-morrow is a solemn rest, a holy sabbath unto Jehovah" (verse 23).

## Chronology Turns Against Them

Now, if we are to date this whole passage in terms of the date given at the head of the narrative—"the fifteenth of the second month"— we would conclude that the Israelites murmured the very day they arrived in this wilderness, and that the phrase "in the morning" applied to the very next morning, namely, the sixteenth. But if the sixteenth be the first of six days of gathering manna, then the sixth day, on which they gathered twice as much, would come on the twenty-first and the Sabbath on the twenty-second day of that second month. A glance at the accompanying calendar will illustrate this clearly. But it will also reveal that the authors have listed this twenty-second day in a "work-day column." Thus according to the very rule that they have followed in trying to establish their point in the nineteenth chapter, we can bring their calendar into confusion by the incidents related in the sixteenth chapter.

Now, let it be made clear that we do not necessarily hold that on the morning immediately after the fifteenth day of the second month, the manna began to fall. The contention is that it would be as logical to maintain this as for the authors to maintain the position they take on the nineteenth chapter, and that by thus employing this principle in both chapters—for a principle of chronological interpretation ought to be able to work in more than one chapter—the theory is brought into confusion.

### Phrase Wrongly Interpreted

But we do not grant that "the same day" means the third day of that third month. Jewish scholars explain that in the Hebrew "the same day" is an indefinite phrase, and cannot properly be forced to refer back to the "third month." Unbroken Jewish tradition has understood "the same day" to mean the first day of that month.* Thus the Gamble theory advocates are in the peculiar position of *accepting* Jewish tradition in order to establish the *first* of their three propositions, namely, that the law was proclaimed on Pentecost, and *rejecting* Jewish tradition in order to establish the *second* point, namely, that the Israelites reached Sinai on the third day of the month. This is really quite an unusual situation.

Christian commentators are generally in agreement with Jewish scholars in regard to this passage, at least as regards the point that nothing definite can be understood by "the same day." One typical quotation is given. Lange, in his critical commentary on the Old Testament, thus observes:

" '*The same day.*'—According to the Jewish tradition this means on the first day of the third month, but grammatically it may be taken more indefinitely—'at this time.' "—*A Commentary on the Holy Scriptures,* by John Peter Lange, translated by Philip Schaff, vol. 2, of the Old Testament, p. 69.

---

* Rabbi Hyamson offers the following comment:
" 'In the third month.' The Hebrew word *hodesh* means also 'new moon.' Hence Exodus 19:1 might be rendered 'on the third new moon [first day of the third month] . . . on this day they came to the wilderness of Sinai.' For this rendering of *hodesh* compare 1 Samuel 20:18, 'And Jonathan said to David, Tomorrow is new moon.' "

## APPENDIXES

We come now to the main part of the Gamble theory, which may be summarized in four propositions:

1. The Sabbath command simply means six days of work followed by a seventh day of rest.

2. The annual sabbaths are decalogue Sabbaths.

3. Counting "seven sabbaths" from the Passover sabbath on the fifteenth of the first month (Abib) brings us to the fourth day of the third month (Sivan); but the "morrow after the seventh sabbath," Sivan 5, being Pentecost, which was also sabbath, gives us an extra sabbath, and this must be placed in the "Sabbath column" in the calendar.

4. Now the command to work six days is just as mandatory as the command to rest on the seventh, therefore the double sabbath of the fourth and fifth of Sivan must be followed by six days of work before the next sabbath. This results in giving us a blank day so far as the week is concerned. And this, of course, results in eliminating the one day over fifty-two full weeks in a 365-day calendar year.

### Propositions 1 and 2

Let us examine first, propositions 1 and 2. What does the Bible say concerning the nature of Pentecost? We read, "There shall be a holy convocation unto you; ye shall do no servile work." Lev. 23:21, A.R.V. It is because of this statement that the calendar authors place Pentecost in the "Sabbath column" of their calendar, "since it could not by any rational procedure, be put in any one of the work-day columns."

With this as our guide as to which days should be placed in the "Sabbath column," let us now consider some other scriptures. We read:

"In the first month [Abib], on the fourteenth day of the month at even, is Jehovah's passover. And on the fifteenth day of the same month is the feast of unleavened bread unto Jehovah: seven days ye shall eat unleavened bread. In the *first day* ye shall have a holy convocation: ye shall do *no servile work.*" Verses 5-7.

Because of this the fifteenth of Abib is placed in the "Sabbath column." But the next verse declares, "In the *seventh day* is a holy convocation; ye shall do *no servile work.*" Identical language is employed to describe the nature of the "first day" and the "seventh day" of the Feast of Unleavened Bread. Now if the fifteenth day is the "first day" of the feast, the twenty-first is the "seventh day" of it. And if the fifteenth belongs in the "Sabbath column," then the twenty-first belongs there also. But the Gamble theory does not place it there. Why? No explanation is given.

# ANSWERS TO OBJECTIONS

## Day of Atonement Destroys Theory

Come now to the seventh month. On the strength of the command that the first, fifteenth, and twenty-second days of the seventh month were to be holy convocations to the Lord, in which "no servile work" was to be done, these three days are placed in the "Sabbath column." But the tenth day of that month, the Day of Atonement—that day which was a "sabbath of sabbaths," to translate literally the original, on which not only "servile work," but "any manner of work," was forbidden under penalty of death—is placed in a "work-day column." Now if Pentecost, on which only "servile work" was prohibited, "could not, by any rational procedure, be put in any one of the work-day columns," no possible sophistry can justify placing the Day of Atonement, the tenth day of the seventh month, in "any one of the work-day columns." The endeavor to avoid this irresistible conclusion serves only to reveal more clearly the desperate plight in which this Atonement Day sabbath places the Gamble theory. The calendar authors strive to show an analogy between the choosing of the Passover lamb on the tenth of the first month and the Atonement Day on the tenth of the seventh month. Their objective is not quite clear, but their attempted analogy is absurd. When it was read to Rabbi Hyamson, he threw up his hands in a gesture of horror and disgust. For to all devout Jews Atonement Day holds a place far above all other annual sabbaths, and is above analogy to any other activity of the year.

The same Bible chapter that tells us the first, fifteenth, and twenty-second days of the seventh month are sabbaths, tells us also, and in more emphatic language, that the tenth day of the month is a *sabbath* of sabbaths.

## Must Surrender Another Claim

Furthermore, with this tenth day of the seventh month allowed to come in a "work-day column," what becomes of the interpretation that "the command to work six days is just as binding as the one to rest on the seventh"? How could a man put in six days of labor between the eighth and the fifteenth of that month, seeing he must *wholly* abstain from work on the tenth? Simple arithmetic prevents that. Now if the Sabbath commandment does not here demand six days of work following a sabbath, then how can it be made to demand it in connection with Pentecost? But if the demand be surrendered, then the whole argument based on the "extra sabbath" at Pentecost collapses. In other words, if during the seventh month a man need work only four days between the sabbath of the tenth and the sabbath of the fifteenth, why is it necessary that during the third month he must work six days following the sabbath of the fifth (Pentecost) before he can have a sabbath day's rest again?

Therefore this marvelous calendar cannot be made to operate successfully, even when we accept the premises set forth by the authors themselves. This is truly a most remarkable situation. Propositions 1 and 2 cannot be held at the same time.

Into what confusion would those ancient Israelites have been brought had they attempted to employ the premises of this Gamble theory to the understanding of the Sabbath commandment!

Yes, and what confusion is brought to the Sunday advocates who believe these annual sabbaths are decalogue Sabbaths, and that the fourth commandment simply requires rest on *a* seventh day after six days of work.

### Only One Escape From Confusion

The only escape from this confusion is to reject propositions 1 and 2 as false, and to return to the age-honored interpretation of this whole Sabbath question. This interpretation is built upon certain historical facts:

1. That "from time immemorial," as the *Encyclopaedia Britannica* phrases it,* there has existed a unit of time measurement called the "week."

2. That this time unit is distinct and altogether separate from the month or the year.

3. That the Jewish nation, throughout its history, employed this time unit, which was finally adopted by the whole civilized world.

4. That "the seventh day" of the Sabbath command has always been understood by the Jewish people to mean the seventh day of the week.

No facts of history are better substantiated than the foregoing. When we understand "the seventh day" in the commandment to mean the seventh day of the week, we have an interpretation that will harmonize with both history and the Bible.

### Propositions 3 and 4

Now, what of the claims made in propositions 3 and 4? First, let us dispose briefly of the assertion that in the Sabbath commandment,

---

* "The week is a period of seven days, having no reference whatever to the celestial motions, —a circumstance to which it owes its unalterable uniformity. . . . It has been employed from time immemorial in almost all Eastern countries; and as it forms neither an aliquot part of the year nor the lunar month, those who reject the Mosaic recital will be at a loss, as Delambre remarks, to assign it to an origin having much semblance of probability."—Article "Calendar," vol. 4 (11th ed.), p. 988.

work on the six days is as definitely commanded as rest on the seventh. If the authors conscientiously believe this to be the true interpretation, they ought to raise their voices against the trend toward a five-day work week.

We have already discovered the impossibility, during the first and seventh months, of obeying a command to work six consecutive days. But, worse still, a man who thus interpreted the commandment could never take a day's vacation during the six-day period. Happily for all concerned, the word *shalt*, in the phrase "six days shalt thou labor," does not necessarily indicate a command. It may simply indicate permission. The Hebrew word allows of either. Context and usage determine the meaning. A comparison of various scriptures, coupled with the united and uninterrupted sense in which not only Jewish but Christian scholars have understood the term, leaves no doubt that the word *shalt* is simply permissive. We are *permitted* six days in which to work.

### "Sabbath" Has Various Meanings

Applying this rule of context and usage—the proper rule to employ in examining words—to the term *sabbath*, brings us to grips with the underlying premise of this whole theory, the proper meaning of the word *sabbath*. The assumption of the Gamble theory is that the word has only one meaning, and in harmony with this belief the word *Sabbath* in the Decalogue is applied to the annual sabbaths.

But if mere similarity of words is sufficient proof of similarity of thought, then confusion would arise on every side. Take the word *day*, for example. We employ it sometimes to mean twenty-four hours, and sometimes to mean simply the light part of the twenty-four-hour period. Again, we may use it wholly in a figurative sense, as, This is the *day* of opportunity. But there rarely need be any doubt as to the meaning intended. The context, the setting, makes it clear.

As a Biblical illustration, take the word *law*. It may mean the moral, civil, and ceremonial commands contained in the books of Moses. By extension it may mean the whole of Moses' writings, as in the phrase, "the law and the prophets."

Such illustrations from either the Bible or everyday life might be multiplied indefinitely. Only confusion can result from a failure to remember that a word may have more than one rigid and restricted definition.

### Summary of Meanings

When we examine the term *sabbath* in this fashion, we discover, as might naturally be expected, that it has more than one meaning.

# APPENDIXES

The Hebrew lexicons reveal that—

1. The word *sabbath* has as its root meaning, "rest from labor."

2. The term is used primarily to denote the day of rest from labor at the close of the weekly cycle—the sense in which the word is used in the Sabbath commandment.

3. By extension, the term is used for the annual feasts, such as the Passover sabbath, etc.

4. The term is used also to mean a week, as in the phrase, "seven sabbaths shall there be complete." Lev. 23:15, A.R.V. The use of the word in this sense naturally grew out of the fact that the Sabbath coming at the end of each week marked off these seven-day units.

There are more senses in which the term may be used, but these are sufficient for the problem before us. (See page 236 for further comments on the value of the word *sabbath*.)

Just when one definition should be employed, and when another, is no more difficult to determine than with numerous other words.

With these various definitions of the word *sabbath* before us, let us examine the pivotal text of this whole theory, the text on which proposition 3 is built:

"Ye shall count unto you from the morrow after the [Passover] sabbath [the fifteenth of the first month, Abib], from the day that ye brought the sheaf of the wave-offering; seven sabbaths shall there be complete: even unto the morrow after the seventh sabbath shall ye number fifty days." "Ye shall make proclamation on the selfsame day [that is, on the fiftieth day, Pentecost]; there shall be a holy convocation unto you; ye shall do no servile work." Verses 15, 16, 21.

## View Held by Sadducees

Viewing this scripture historically, we find that two interpretations have been held. About two thousand years ago there existed for a limited period a Jewish sect called the Sadducees. They held that the word *sabbath* in these texts should be understood to mean the Sabbath of the Decalogue. This was one point of controversy between them and the Pharisees, who represented the accepted interpretation that has come down to our day. Because of this, the Sadducees contended that the count of the fifty days should not be begun on the sixteenth of Abib, which was "the morrow after the [Passover] sabbath" of the fifteenth; but that the count should begin on the day that followed the first decalogue Sabbath in Passover week. For example, if Passover sabbath came on Thursday, they held that "the morrow after the sabbath" was the following Sunday, because it was "the morrow after" the decalogue

823

Sabbath. According to their interpretation—which was held by a very limited number and for an equally limited period—Pentecost would always come on Sunday.

But the Sadducees did not therefore believe in breaking the weekly cycle; their interpretation forbade allowing even the name *sabbath* to be coupled with the Passover or any other annual sabbath. To them, the word itself as found in the fourth commandment was wholly apart from, and above, contact with annual feasts. When they came to the week end at the close of the seven-week period after the Passover, the Sadducees rested from all labor on that seventh-day Sabbath and from "servile work" the first day of the next week, which, according to their reckoning, was Pentecost. And when the seventh day of *that* week arrived, they kept Sabbath again. This was no more difficult for them to do than it is for a present-day devout Sabbathkeeper to rest from labor on Saturday of one week, take a holiday on Sunday of the next week, and then rest again from labor the next Saturday.

### How Jewish Scholars Translate the Passage

But when we turn to the now universally accepted understanding of these texts by all Jewish scholars, we find the Gamble theory demolished with equal completeness. This interpretation renders the phrases "seven sabbaths" and "the morrow after the seventh sabbath," as "seven weeks," and "the morrow after the seventh week." For Jewish authorities have never confused the decalogue Sabbath with annual sabbaths, and accordingly have understood that the term *sabbath* can have different meanings. For example, if Passover sabbath came on Wednesday, the fifty-day count would begin on Thursday of that week, and Pentecost would come on Thursday of the seventh week. Thus there would not even be a doubling up of sabbaths at Pentecost time. Therefore the passage fails to give any support to the Gamble theory.

Furthermore, let us repeat, the translation of *sabbath* as "week" in this passage is not based upon the view of some *few* Hebrew scholars who have a particular theory to maintain, but represents the translation that has been employed through all the centuries by *all* Jewish scholars—with the exception of the limited period when the small sect of Sadducees held a differing view—and is today the translation employed by both Orthodox and Reform rabbis.

In the Septuagint, the Greek translation of the Old Testament completed in the second century B.C., the word *sabbath* in Leviticus 23:15, 16 is translated by the Greek word *hebdomas*, meaning "week."

Indeed, no other meaning than "week" could consistently be understood for the word *sabbath* in the phrases "seven sabbaths" and

# APPENDIXES

"the morrow after the seventh sabbath," in Leviticus 23:15, 16, for the parallel passage in Deuteronomy 16:9, 10 reads thus: "Seven weeks shalt thou number unto thee: from the time thou beginnest to put the sickle to the standing grain shalt thou begin to number seven weeks. And thou shalt keep the feast of weeks unto Jehovah." The Hebrew word translated "week" in Deuteronomy 16 *cannot* be translated "sabbath." Therefore, the only way to make Leviticus and Deuteronomy harmonize is to give the meaning of "week" to *sabbath* in the passage in Leviticus 23. This, as we have already learned, may properly be done.

Furthermore, it is an interesting fact that the Jewish people use not only the word *Pentecost* to describe the feast day that comes fifty days after Passover, but they call it also the Feast of Weeks.

Directly bearing on this point is a letter received from Dr. Cyrus Adler, president of Dropsie College, Philadelphia, and an outstanding Hebrew scholar. It was written in response to a request for his views on this question.

"THE DROPSIE COLLEGE

"For Hebrew and Cognate Learning,
"Philadelphia,

"January 31, 1929.

"Dear Mr. Nichol:

"I am in receipt of your letter of January 25. I have not the pamphlet of Dr. Marvin and Moses Cotsworth before me, although I think I saw it some time ago. There is no warrant for their theory that there was an extra Sabbath in connection with Pentecost. If you desire to see the Jewish normal interpretation of these verses, I would refer you to the translation of the Bible issued by the Jewish Publication Society of Philadelphia in 1917. I give these verses herewith: 'And ye shall count unto you from the morrow after the day [Hebrew, sabbath] of rest, from the day that ye brought the sheaf of the waving: seven weeks shall there be complete; even unto the morrow after the seventh week shall ye number fifty days; and ye shall present a new meal offering unto the Lord.'

"This represents a very old controversy. According to the Jewish tradition, the Biblical commandment to offer the omer 'on the morrow after the sabbath' was interpreted by the rabbis to refer to Passover, so that it means that the seven weeks should begin to be counted from the first day after the beginning of Passover. There was an early interpretation that it should begin on the first day after the first Sabbath during Passover, which would make Pentecost always fall on Sunday. This sectarian view has completely disappeared.

"But what I would point out to you is that *even this sectarian view in no way favors the idea of a wandering Sabbath, it rather emphasizes the word 'Sabbath' so that it could not be used even for another holiday.* I can say to you most emphatically that whatever perturbations there have been concerning the Jewish calendar from the earliest period down, the one central feature was always to maintain the week of seven days without any interruption whatsoever.

"Very sincerely yours,
"[Signed] Cyrus Adler."

Essentially the same analysis of this passage in Leviticus is given in a long letter from Dr. H. S. Linfield, of the American Jewish Committee, New York City. After examining all the Bible texts employed by the calendar authors, he concludes his letter thus: "An examination of each passage has convinced the writer that there is not a shred of evidence in support of any of the claims made by the joint authors."

### Significance of Double Feast Days Today

One small piece of corroborative evidence on this double-sabbath argument remains to be demolished. After declaring that in ancient times the Jews kept such a double sabbath, the authors add this persuasive item of news: "The significant fact remains, that through traditional usage the Jews generally continue to observe two days at the feast of Pentecost." In reply I inquire: If at the present time a devout Jew can observe two days at Pentecost without breaking the cycle of the week, why could he not have done so anciently?

The fact is that when the Jews were dispersed from Palestine, they began the custom of keeping two days in connection with *each* annual sabbath—excepting Atonement Day—for fear that in their calculating of the new moons they might have made an error in determining the beginning of a month. (The explanation for the failure to observe the two days in connection with Atonement Day is that it would have necessitated forty-eight hours of complete fast.) By the time a calendar had been agreed upon by the "Dispersed" throughout the world—which was somewhere about the fourth century A.D.—the custom of celebrating two days for each annual sabbath had become so firmly established that it was retained by most Jews. This second day that is kept in connection with each of the annual sabbaths is described in Hebrew by a phrase which, translated literally, means: "The second day feast of the exile." This is a familiar phrase in Talmudic lore.

## An Argument for Us

Therefore, for the purposes the *authors* intended, "the significant fact" of the double sabbaths now kept by Jews in various lands has *no* significance. Instead it has a significance on *our* side of the argument. The fact that the reckoning of months presented such difficulties when the Jews moved from Palestine, reveals the absolute confusion into which the Sabbath institution would have been thrown if it had been related to the months, as this unwarranted Gamble theory contends. Only by being connected with a time cycle, the week, that runs independently of calendars, could the Sabbath of the moral code, whose precepts have worldwide application, be successfully kept in various lands. Only by connecting it with the cycle of the week could the identity of the Sabbath be retained, for the week is unique in that it has come down through the centuries independent of calendars. No matter where the "Dispersed" of Israel have been located, and no matter what their difficulties have been in keeping the reckoning of the annual feasts that are dependent on months, they have never had any uncertainty as to which day is "the seventh day" of the commandment, for the sun sets regularly each night in each land. The Jews of the Dispersion have never had any controversy with the Palestinian Jews as to which is the seventh day of the week. They have never differed in their observance of the decalogue Sabbath. And why need they, for could not the Jews in Spain, for example, count the cycles of seven sunsets as easily as the Jews in Palestine?

We discover, therefore, from an examination of Jewish history and from a study of the different senses in which the word *sabbath* may properly be understood, that the arguments built upon Leviticus 23:15, 16 have no foundation.

## Different Sabbaths Distinguished

But let us take the matter a little further. The fact that there are different senses in which the word may be employed, and that basically it means "rest from labor," demands that the phrase, "the seventh day," in the Sabbath command, possess an unmistakable definiteness.

The authors of the revived Gamble theory endeavor to give definiteness to this phrase by attempting to place the decalogue Sabbath in a fixed relationship to the months. Abundance of proof that this cannot be done has already been offered. Still further proof is offered by summarizing the command for the decalogue Sabbath alongside the commands for the annual sabbaths. When Jehovah proclaimed the Sabbath commandment, the Israelites listened to these identifying facts:

### Strong Contrasts in Sabbaths

1. Six days shall work be done.
2. The seventh day is the rest day of Jehovah—no work shall be done.
3. In six days Jehovah created the earth, and rested the seventh day.
4. Jehovah hallowed this day, that is, set it apart for a holy use.

Later, when Moses instructed the children of Israel as to the annual feast days (see Leviticus 23), they received these facts:

1. On the fifteenth and twenty-first days of the first month—first and last days, respectively, of the Feast of Unleavened Bread—"no servile work" shall be done.
2. On the fiftieth day from "the morrow after the" fifteenth of the first month—known later as Pentecost—there shall be a special ceremony of offering "two wave loaves"—"no servile work" shall be done.
3. On the first day of the seventh month there shall be a memorial of blowing of trumpets—"no servile work" shall be done.
4. On the tenth day of the seventh month there shall be the Day of Atonement—"ye shall do no manner of work."
5. On the fifteenth and twenty-second days of the seventh month—the beginning and the end of the Feast of Tabernacles—"no servile work" shall be done.

Other distinguishing characteristics might be enumerated, but these will suffice to provide more than enough material for a series of strong reasons why the decalogue Sabbath and the annual sabbaths, such as the Passover and Pentecost, are not the same:

1. If the two kinds of sabbaths are the same, and the Feast of Trumpets, for example, on the first day of the seventh month, was a decalogue Sabbath, why was it necessary for Moses solemnly to inform the hosts of Israel that the opening day of the Feast of Tabernacles, on the fifteenth of the month, was also a Sabbath? Could not even the simplest have comprehended that if the first of the month is a Sabbath, two cycles of seven would cause the fifteenth to be a Sabbath also? Or more incredible still, if the opening day of the Feast of Tabernacles on the fifteenth was a decalogue Sabbath, how utterly pointless for Moses to inform them that the closing day of that feast on the twenty-

second was a Sabbath also. Anyone capable of counting up to seven would have known that already, for is not fifteen plus seven, twenty-two? Indeed, if the Israelites were so hopelessly dull-witted as to necessitate such specific instruction as to what date in the month was seven days later than the fifteenth, would they not also need to be instructed as to what date came seven days later than the twenty-second, and so on throughout the year? Why single out one month, the seventh month at that? Why wait until the year is half over before giving them detailed information? The fact that Moses so solemnly announced the fifteenth and twenty-second days of the seventh month as sabbaths reveals clearly that these dates were not automatically sabbaths by virtue of the fourth commandment.

2. The fact has already been noted—but is so conclusive as to justify repeating it in this summary—that the annual sabbaths are not generally separated by seven-day periods, and no possible arrangement of dates can make them all come in that sequence.

3. The reasons given for observing these various sabbaths are different. The decalogue Sabbath was to be a holy rest day because "in six days Jehovah made heaven and earth, . . . and rested the seventh day." But the first day of the seventh month, for example, was to be a day of rest because it was the Feast of Trumpets; and the tenth day of that month, because it was Atonement Day; and the fifteenth and twenty-second, because they were the opening and closing dates of the Feast of Tabernacles. In the case of the decalogue Sabbath, the reason for its observance remained the same continually. But with the annual sabbaths the reason is different in each case.

Now, when the Israelites learned that they were to do no servile work on the fifteenth and twenty-second of the seventh month, *because* these dates marked the beginning and end of the Feast of Tabernacles, what possible reason was there for them to conclude that they should rest also on the eighth or the twenty-ninth of that month, for example, seeing that these dates marked neither the beginning nor the end of any feast? Rather would they reach the very opposite conclusion.

4. The fact that it was necessary to command the people to refrain from work on each of these annual feasts reveals that they were not decalogue Sabbaths, for the fourth commandment already forbade "any work" on the "seventh-day" decalogue Sabbaths.

5. The decalogue Sabbath is specifically connected with a time unit of seven days, which, according to the Bible and the best secular authorities, has been employed by the Jews and various other Eastern peoples "from time immemorial." But the annual sabbaths were

specifically connected with a time reckoning that began at the Exodus, for that was "the beginning of months" for the Israelites. It was then that their months received distinguishing titles; "first month" and "seventh month," for example. (See Ex. 12:1, 2.) Each feast was to be on a certain day of a certain *month*.

When we consider "the seventh day" Sabbath in terms of the week, then are we able to harmonize theology, philology (the science which deals with the meanings of words), and the understanding of the commandment by the Jewish race through all their history.

### The Word "Week" Analyzed

Take the word *week*. This word, when found in the Old Testament, comes from a root meaning "seven." To reveal the close relationship between these two terms, it should be explained that in ancient Hebrew only the consonants were written. The context, the setting of the word in the sentence, enabled the reader to know which of the possible variant meanings should be understood in each case. Written in this fashion without vowels, the words translated "seven" and "week" are identical. Thus the ancient scribe had to decide by the context whether to give it one pronunciation and read it as "seven" or give it a little different pronunciation and read it as "week," for in the spoken language there was a slight difference in pronunciation.

To be more exact, when the hearer listened to the word as pronounced for "week," there was really conveyed to his mind the thought of "sevenfold," "a combination of seven," or "sevened," which would be a very literal way of translating the Hebrew word for "week." Thus embedded in the roots of that ancient language is found one of the strongest proofs, not only of the existence but of the great antiquity, of a time cycle of seven days.

### A Contradiction of Terms

To an ancient Hebrew the phrase "a week of eight days" would have sounded like a contradiction of terms, for how could eight be "sevenfold"? A modern comparison would be the phrase "a fortnight of sixteen days." For how could a *fortnight,* a contraction of *"fourteen* nights," be sixteen?

This important fact as to the meaning of the Hebrew word makes altogether irrelevant the extended comments and tables in the Gamble book regarding the eight-day weeks of certain pagan peoples and the nine-day weeks of others. We are no more concerned with the many time cycles of these peoples than we are with their many gods.

# APPENDIXES

The Scriptures themselves speak of the week long before the giving of the law on Mount Sinai. Laban said to his son-in-law Jacob with regard to Leah, "Fulfill her week." (Gen. 29:27.) The history of Jewish customs reveals that this phrase refers to the week of wedding festivities which were considered a part of the ceremony, and which lasted seven days. A comparison with verse 22 shows that the feast had been called, and a comparison with various other scriptures reveals the custom of holding feasts seven days. Thus does the Bible itself corroborate strongly the undisputed understanding of this passage as given by the historians of Jewish customs. And thus does the Bible corroborate the united statements of learned authorities, that the week has been known "from time immemorial."

## What Other Conclusion?

The hosts who gathered at Sinai were a people whose ancestor Jacob was well acquainted with the time cycle called the week, and whose language employed a term meaning "a combination of seven" to describe that cycle. What, then, would be their most natural conclusion when they listened to Jehovah speak twice in the Sabbath commandment of a cycle of seven days—six days shalt thou labor, but the seventh day is the Sabbath—in six days the Lord made heaven and earth, and rested the seventh? In the absence of any declaration to the contrary, would they not most obviously conclude that "the seventh day" meant the seventh day of the week, that long-established combination of seven days? To that most natural conclusion Jews everywhere through all the centuries have come. And to what other conclusion could they rationally have been expected to come, seeing they knew nothing of the Gamble calendar! We are therefore prepared to take our leave of this revived Gamble theory. But, wait, there is one more piece of evidence that is triumphantly presented as a sort of capstone to the involved argument so confidently set forth.

## The Case Summed Up

This capstone consists of an alleged proof—independent of the main line of argument—that the second year of the Mosaic calendar began on a Sabbath. In order properly to introduce this last point, let us summarize briefly the whole series of propositions that the calendar authors have reared up:

1. If the Mosaic calendar was a 365-day solar calendar (but virtually all authorities declare it was not); and

2. If Moses divided this 365-day calendar on the basic plan of the Egyptian calendar (but for this there is not the slightest proof); and

3. If Moses placed three supplementary days at the end of the sixth month and two at the end of the twelfth (but for this there is no proof whatever); and

4. If the Sabbath commandment means simply one day of rest following six days of labor (but evidence shows it does not mean this); and

5. If the command to work six days is as compulsory as the command to rest the seventh (but it is not); and

6. If the Passover sabbath came on the fifteenth of the first month, then the first day of the first month of the first year came on a sabbath, because it was exactly two weeks earlier (but the Passover sabbath was not a decalogue Sabbath, and therefore counting back from it by sevens proves nothing); and

7. If the Israelites reached Sinai on the third day of the third month (but this is an assumption incapable of proof); and

8. If the three-day period in preparation for the giving of the law began on the third day of the third month (but this also is sheer assumption); and

9. If there was a double sabbath at Pentecost, with the extra sabbath not counted in the cycle of the week (but there was no such extra sabbath outside the week);

10. Thus and thus only could the first day of the second year begin on the same weekday as the first year.

11. Now with the point already proved that the first day of the first year began on Sabbath (but the point has been fully disproved); therefore

12. If we can prove from independent evidence that the second year began on a Sabbath, we will have provided a convincing demonstration that our argument concerning a blank day in the Mosaic calendar is correct!

### The Capstone Examined

And what is this clinching demonstration that is to give the final proof to a theory that has been refuted at every step—this evidence that the second year began on a Sabbath? Here it is: The command to set the shewbread in order every Sabbath is cited (Lev. 4:8), and then the following passage is quoted:

"It came to pass *in the first month in the second year, on the first day of the month,* that the tabernacle was reared up." "And he [Aaron] put the table in the tent of meeting, upon the side of the tabernacle northward, without the veil. *And he set the bread in order upon it before Jehovah; as Jehovah commanded Moses."* Ex. 40:17, 22, 23. (Italics theirs.)

But the authors have quoted only part of the scripture. Here is the whole passage:

"It came to pass in the first month in the second year, on the first day of the month, that the tabernacle was reared up. And Moses reared up the tabernacle, and laid its sockets, and set up the boards thereof, and put in the bars thereof, and reared up its pillars. And he spread the tent over the tabernacle, and put the covering of the tent above upon it; as Jehovah commanded Moses. And he took and put the testimony into the ark, and set the staves of the ark and put the mercy-seat above upon the ark: and he brought the ark into the tabernacle, and set up the veil of the screen, and screened the ark of the testimony; as Jehovah commanded Moses. And he put the table in the tent of meeting, upon the side of the tabernacle northward, without the veil. And he set the bread in order upon it before Jehovah; as Jehovah commanded Moses." Ex. 40:17-23.

### The Capstone Collapses

When the whole scripture is quoted, the matter assumes a very different aspect. Moses and his helpers were certainly tremendously busy that first day of the first month of the second year. The scene around the tabernacle must have been one of great physical activity, of diligent work, as the sockets were laid, the boards set up, the bars put in, the pillars reared up, the tent spread over, and the covering put above it—to recount only a part of the work that was done.

If that were proper to do on the Sabbath day, we would have an excellent precedent for building churches on the Sabbath. But then what would become of the command not to do "any work" on that holy day? And how would the Israelites be able to harmonize such labor with the warning that prefaced the whole episode of tabernacle building? For when Moses descended from the mount with the plans for the sanctuary, as recorded in the end of the thirty-fourth chapter, he assembled all the people to invite their participation in the making of the tabernacle; and from the opening of the thirty-fifth chapter to the close of the fortieth, the record deals exclusively with the construction of this center of worship. And thus is the whole narrative introduced:

"Moses assembled all the congregation of the children of Israel, and said unto them, These are the words which Jehovah hath commanded, that ye should do them. Six days shall work be done; but on the seventh day there shall be to you a holy day, a sabbath of solemn rest to Jehovah: whosoever doeth any work therein shall be put to death. Ye shall kindle no fire throughout your habitations upon the sabbath day." Ex. 35:1-3.

Then follows immediately the description of plans for the tabernacle, which, as has already been noted, must have called for an immense amount of physical labor. Jehovah left no uncertainty in the minds of the people as to the specific relationship of the Sabbath command to the task of building the house of the Lord, for He warned them immediately before they began this great task, that the seventh day should be a "sabbath of solemn rest." Therefore the passage quoted by the authors as a climax to their whole argument, and as an irrefutable proof that the first day of the second year was a Sabbath, fails utterly to aid them. In fact, it proves the opposite from what they intended—it proves that the first day of the second year was *not* a Sabbath.

### No Conflict in Commands

And now lest someone should feel that the fact this first day of the second year was not a Sabbath presents a difficulty because of the command to set the shewbread in order on the Sabbath, let us make a few observations. A command as to any feature of routine ritual cannot become operative until *after* the ritual is established. For example, the Lord declared to Abraham, "He that is eight days old shall be circumcised among you." Gen. 17:12. Then follows this statement: "Abraham took Ishmael his son, and all that were born in his house, and all that were bought with his money, every male among the men of Abraham's house; and circumcised the flesh of their foreskin in the selfsame day, as God had said unto him." Verse 23. Should we therefore conclude that there was no "male among the men of Abraham's house" who was more than an infant of eight days? The very next verses specifically declare that Abraham himself was ninety-nine years old and Ishmael thirteen at this time. Did Abraham therefore go contrary to the command of God? No. The law as to the age of circumcision applied, *not* to the *instituting* of the rite, but to the operation of it once it had been instituted.

Thus with the shewbread. The solemn rite of *changing* the bread each Sabbath could not apply until there was bread on the table to change. And in fact the whole series of instructions regarding the ritual of the tabernacle, as given in Leviticus 24, most obviously could not apply until *after* the tabernacle was completed and set in operation.

But an even more simple answer can be given by declaring that there is no proof that the shewbread was set in order on that first day. The whole passage from the seventeenth to the thirty-third verse deals with the final work of rearing up the tabernacle from the material that had been furnished. That series of verses relates to a great number of acts that might conceivably have taken several days. To declare that they must all have taken place on the one date mentioned at the beginning of the passage is to make an assumption that is impossible of proof. It is similar to the argument the authors attempted to draw out of the nineteenth chapter of Exodus. But assumption is of the essence of this Gamble theory, and it remains assumption to the end.

Cotsworth and Marvin assure us calmly that this marvelous calendar they have been describing was lost by the Jews when they went into Babylonian captivity. Just why seventy years in Babylon should cause them to abandon so vital, so remarkable, a method of time reckoning is not made clear! Indeed, the authors do not even divulge to us how the Jews lost this calendar. Therefore no attempt to pry into the matter will be made.

But Mr. Gamble, who brought forth the original form of the theory, has a very detailed theory as to the change from the alleged fixed sabbaths to free-running weekly Sabbaths. He claims that Christ kept the fixed sabbaths like other Jews until the time of His death, but that when He arose that Sunday morning, it was the beginning of a new order of Sabbaths. Mr. Gamble reaches this conclusion by translating the phrase "the first day of the week" (in Matthew 28:1 and parallel passages in the Gospels) as "the first of the Sabbaths," or "the chiefest of the Sabbaths." This translation, as fanciful as any that Gamble has presented in behalf of his theory, is answered under objection 47.

# Admissions That Charges of Fanaticism by 1844 Adventists Are Groundless

IN ·the year 1944 the Review and Herald Publishing Association printed *The Midnight Cry,* a historical study of the Millerite Movement of the 1840's, particularly as regards the false charges that the Millerites were guilty of wild fanaticism, such as wearing ascension robes. Copies of this book were sent for review to various historical and religious journals. These reviews speak for themselves. In some instances they are written by men who had earlier been guilty of repeating the false charges in their own historical writings. Hence they provide a singular kind of admission and proof that the charges should no longer be believed. Following is a representative group of such reviews:

First, from *Christendom* (American organ of the World Council of Churches), William W. Sweet, University of Chicago, reviewer:

"This book . . . has been written with the avowed purpose of defending William Miller and the Millerite movement from the calumny of historians. . . . He [the author] does lay claim to forthrightness and honesty in the presentation of his case, and the bibliography, together with the copious annotations on every page, drawn from an examination of the numerous documents of the time (many of them manuscripts hitherto unused), seems to be adequate proof that he has made a praiseworthy attempt to present the whole movement in the light of all available sources. . . .

"In refuting the 'ascension robe' stories, the author undoubtedly has proved his case, but whether or not he has made his case in regard to the charge of fanaticism depends upon what is meant by fanaticism. He has, however, shown that the leaders tried to keep the movement under control emotionally, and perhaps succeeded to a larger degree than has been generally known.

"As has already been noted, the book is forthright and honest, and deserves a careful reading."—Winter, 1946, pp. 103, 104.

*The New England Quarterly* (published at the University of Maine), Ira V. Brown, Phillips Exeter Academy, reviewer:

# APPENDIXES

"In a disarming preface the author confesses that his book does not pose as history. . . . The work is based on careful examination of original sources. . . .

"The most interesting section is that devoted to exploding the tradition that Miller's disciples garbed themselves in 'ascension robes.' Had they universally marched out to graveyards and hillsides in white muslin gowns on October 22, 1844, the final day set for the advent, it is incredible that contemporary newspapers would not have reported the fact. They are silent on this point, except for one reference describing the occasion in Cincinnati, which states that the millenarians were dressed like everyone else. It would appear that for the most part they spent the day quietly in their homes or tabernacles. Undoubtedly the movement was a much more prosaic one than the public has usually assumed.

"Many of the wilder tales regarding it do rest on contemporary newspaper evidence, but such stories were generally prefaced with 'It is reported' or 'They say.' Others were clearly facetious. Even so renowned a historian as John Bach McMaster allowed himself to fall into inaccuracies through careless reliance on journalistic sources. Independent investigation done by the reviewer two years ago confirms Mr. Nichol's conclusion as to their untrustworthy character. The book is also a valuable corrective to Clara E. Sears' popular account, *Days of Delusion,* derived chiefly from second- and third-hand family gossip."
—September, 1945, pp. 423, 424.

### *"Ascension Robes Are a Myth"*

*New York History* (quarterly journal of the New York State Historical Association), Whitney R. Cross, Connecticut College for Women, reviewer:

"As the appointed day [October 22, 1844] approached and proselytizing grew more intense, unprincipled scoffers and devoted churchmen alike persecuted the Millerites at every opportunity, distorting their preachings, questioning their motives and holding them up to hilarious ridicule. The few secular historians who have dealt with the movement utilized as sources unreliable folk traditions and hostile newspapers. Thus a seriously warped conception of this premillennial enthusiasm has prevailed for generations. . . .

"His [the author's] study of the subject is without question the most thorough and reliable ever made. It is sufficiently able to make the necessity for work along similar lines in the future extremely doubtful. He has, in my opinion, proved the lack of fanaticism in the movement, at least up to the day of reckoning. After the disappointment, when more irregular behavior occurred, he has not pursued his investigations. He has likewise proved that ascension robes are a myth, that Adventism did not drive numbers of men insane, that its leaders were sincere and courageous men, even saintly and heroic."—January, 1946, pp. 100, 101.

## Comments in Historical Association Organ

*The American Historical Review* (official organ, American Historical Association), Mary H. Mitchell, Ph.D., historical writer, reviewer:

"The author's general thesis is that Miller was an honest and sincere man who had reached his beliefs after long and careful study of the Bible, that Millerism was a part of a wide advent movement, and that it 'does not suffer by comparison with other religious awakenings.'. . .

"Newspapers printed wild and ridiculous stories about it, caricatures were issued, and mobs attacked its meetings. The followers were charged with irregularities and excesses, hysterical and fanatical behavior, and financial wrongdoing. The most serious accusation was that Millerism caused waves of insanity, suicide and murder.

"The author does not deny the presence of the 'lunatic fringe' that accompanies any movement, and cites attacks on abolitionists, among others. He asserts in defense that it should be judged by its main body of well-behaved members rather than by the actions of a few cranks and impostors. . . .

"Specific and serious charges he examines with special care. . . . He is convinced that 'Millerism was not really the cause of anyone's insanity.' His defense is so strong that hereafter if serious writers repeat the charge, it would seem to be only to illustrate the fear and hostility roused by the preaching of the end of the world.

"As to lesser charges, tales so colorful and picturesque as those of Millerites dressed in long, white robes, waiting in graveyards or in trees and on platforms for Gabriel to blow his horn, will not pass into the oblivion which he feels they deserve, but into the realm of folklore. . . .

"Mr. Nichol has done an immense amount of work, with valuable results, both in exposition and defense. His self-confessed bias is not extreme or bitter."—January, 1946, pp. 331, 332.

*Christian Advocate* (leading weekly of the Methodist Church), Roy L. Smith, editor of the *Advocate*, reviewer:

"Wild and fanciful tales were told about the Millerites, and the most scandalous charges were made against them and their doctrines. It was an age of colorful reporting on the part of newspapers, and uncertain means of communication, as a result of which gossip was made to appear as fact. Stories of ascension robes, dementia, riots, and other attendant circumstances were widely current and universally believed. That the Miller movement continues to exist as a denominational group is not widely known, though the adherents are themselves a devout body.

"One of their number, in a careful and thoroughgoing fashion, has undertaken to remove much of the stigma attached to the early movement, and in a carefully documented volume which represents an enormous amount of painstaking research he has presented a portrait of a forceful figure whose preaching created the movement. It is a good book, if for no other reason than that it explodes so many of the indefensible charges against an honest man who was proved to be also a mistaken one."—February 21, 1946, p. 26.

### University Professor Testifies

*The Christian Century* (most prominent interdenominational weekly in America), Sidney E. Mead, University of Chicago, reviewer:

"This 'defense' of the Millerites will be greeted with enthusiasm by those within the Adventist churches who have long suffered from the repetition of baseless rumors about their origins, and will receive a sympathetic welcome from people outside those churches who have an interest in historical accuracy. . . .

"The first nineteen chapters tell the story of William Miller. . . . Here the author does justice to the integrity and sincerity of Miller. . . . The exciting events of the 'year of the end of the world' (March, 1843, to March, 1844) are treated with restraint, and the 'great day of hope' (October 22, 1844), the final day set by the leaders for the second coming, is adequately dealt with.

"In the second section of the book the author argues convincingly from the evidence that common charges—for example, that the movement was fanatical and led to insanity, suicides, and murders—have been greatly exaggerated. Three of these chapters are devoted to the attempt to squelch once for all the story that the Millerites wore 'ascension robes' on *the* night. In dealing with Millerism, twentieth-century writers have frequently yielded to the temptation to dwell on the sensational, and this work will do much to balance the popularized accounts such as Clara Endicott Sears' *Days of Delusion*."—March 7, 1945, p. 304.

*Monday Morning* (a Presbyterian pastor's magazine), Rev. Alexander Mackie, D.D., president Presbyterian Ministers' Fund, reviewer:

# ANSWERS TO OBJECTIONS

"In the story of William Miller and Millerism, there is a sincerity which lifts it out of the world of fraud and deception into the land of conviction. Miller, from his studies of the Scriptures, became firmly convinced of the imminence of the end of the world and the return of our Lord, and fixed the date as some time in 1843 or 1844. . . .

"The book [*The Midnight Cry*], although apologetic in its purpose, is a welcome and kindly addition to the literature which sheds light on the religious thinking of a hundred years ago. The author is to be congratulated on a piece of thorough-going, even if purposeful, research as evidenced in his scholarly bibliography."—September 2, 1946.

### Baptist Organ Speaks

*The Watchman-Examiner* (leading Baptist weekly):

"William Miller developed a movement which emphasized the imminence of the second coming of Christ. The movement was a tremendous emphasis upon a greatly neglected truth. . . .

"In a phenomenal way, the whole country seems to have been affected, and the public press carried articles dealing with the situation. Very few of these were friendly, and the wildest rumors concerning Millerites were spread abroad. It was rumored that Millerism resulted in insanity, murder, and other extravagances. It was said that on the day appointed for our Lord to return the Millerites put on white robes and went out into the country and to hilltops to meet Him. All these reports Mr. Nichol investigated with remarkable thoroughness, and, we think, proves them false. His discussion of this historical episode is frank and factual. He seems to have left no stone unturned to get at the facts. His research is most thorough. We are glad for the appearance of this book. It corrects a great injustice done to a good, if mistaken, man in Mr. Miller and to the large company that followed his teachings. . . . Because of the widespread error concerning the Millerites, this book should have careful and thoughtful reading."—May 24, 1945, pp. 513, 514.

*The Westminster Theological Journal* (Presbyterian), A. Culver Gordon, reviewer:

"It is a safe assertion that few can read this book without a revision of their estimate of William Miller and the Millerite movement of a century ago. The author gives a history which is also a defense. . . . He does not pretend to be an impartial judge but rather the attorney for the defense. . . . Mr. Nichol is partisan, but he is also fair. . . .

"In the portion of the book which deals with an answer to various charges brought against Millerism, Mr. Nichol presents material that is of wider interest than might at first be imagined. For instance, in dealing with the question, 'Did Millerism Cause Insanity, Suicide, and Murder?' he examines the medical evidence for charges of this nature brought against evangelistic religion generally. His discussion of mental instability and religious excitement is illuminating.

"A considerable section deals with the question of fanaticism, especially on October 22, 1844, and with the wearing of 'ascension robes.' Mr. Nichol makes a good case for believing that with but few exceptions the Millerites were in their places of worship on that fateful night, that they behaved circumspectly, and that they did not wear the robes of popular legend. . . .

"Mr. Nichol in writing this book with such painstaking care has put the church in his debt. It is one that the historian, the student of prophecy, and the general reader may pursue with advantage. It is a book which, if not definitive for the Millerite movement, is the closest approach for such an ideal presently existing."—May, 1946, pp. 218-220.

New York *Herald-Tribune* (one of the most influential newspapers in America), Stewart Holbrook, author and journalist, reviewer:

"Most laymen in New England and the Midwest have been brought up on stories of the fanatical imbecilities of the Millerites—how they gathered and shouted, how they tailored ascension gowns of pure white muslin for the great day, how they climbed hills and mountains, even barns and apple trees, in order to get a good view of the event; and how many went stark mad and had to be confined. . . . These stories have long since congealed into a folklore that is as firmly believed as is Henry Longfellow's verse about Paul Revere.

"Now comes Mr. Nichol, . . . with a truly monumental and enlightening study of Millerism, with especial regard to the allegedly insane acts of its cohorts. With a self-avowed bias, but with great good humor and a vast amount of research, he has made a book that must be reckoned with. . . . He discovered—what every infidel knows—that the greatest persecutors of all were the other Christian sects. . . .

"Mr. Nichol has done a remarkably clear, fine, and important book, and it stands virtually alone in its field. Though I admire the book and found it of intense interest, I regret it must largely dissipate the more lurid of the folk tales about the Millerites, wondrous stories cherished for years."—*Weekly Book Review*, August 26, 1945, p. 26.

*Chicago Tribune* (second largest newspaper circulation in America), John Astley-Cock, M.A., (Cambridge University), religious editor of the *Tribune*, reviewer:

"Miller was an ardent and sincere evangelist of unassuming humility whose revivalism weaned many from the fleshpots and created the fruitful soil whence sprang all the adventual denominations, the most prominent today being the Seventh-day Adventists, with a world membership exceeding half a million.

"Miller, however, was jealously reviled by contemporaries, his followers accused of fanaticism, and the movement accused of causing murder, suicide, and insanity. . . . Broadsides ridiculed the ascension robes which it was alleged, entirely without foundation as it now appears, were worn in expectancy of the Rapture. All this calumny and irresponsible gossip have been so extensively copied and quoted unchecked by writers, encyclopedic and literary, during the last century that the most preposterous yarns have virtually become a part of folklore.

"This book is a defense of Millerism. Not by the apologetic method of special pleading, but solely by allowing the documentary record, either of affirmation or refutation, to speak for itself. . . . Every story is traced to its source and shown to be either fabrication or distortion and even malicious misrepresentation.

"By presenting the origin and progress of Millerism with judicial impartiality, without any of the historian's or biographer's inevitable subjectivity, the author has placed all future writers on the subject under weighty obligation."—July 29, 1945.

### Later Important Admission

William Warren Sweet, foremost American church historian of the present day, declares in a book published in 1952:

"Francis D. Nichol, *The Midnight Cry*, Washington, D.C.: 1944, is a Seventh-Day Adventist defense of William Miller and the Millerites. The author has convincingly shown that many of the stories of the excesses committed by the Millerites had little basis in fact."— *Religion in the Development of American Culture, 1765-1840*, p. 307, footnote. "Nichol's book is the most thorough piece of research that has been done on the Millerite movement in spite of its avowed purpose to defend his co-religionists against the accusations made against them."—*Ibid.*, p. 310, footnote.

"The widespread accusations that Millerism had driven people insane and caused many to commit suicide has been refuted by Nichol in a careful study of asylum records for the years involved. Nichol also has produced indisputable evidence that the numerous stories of the Millerites providing themselves with ascension robes and gathering on hilltops to await the coming had no basis in fact."—*Ibid.*, pp. 310, 311.

# How Long Is Everlasting?

[The following, by W. E. Howell, appeared in the *Review and Herald* of June 22, 1939.]

The three words *forever, everlasting,* and *eternal* are closely related in their Greek originals. Their interrelation as English words is easy to see: for-*ever,* *ever*-lasting, *ever*-ternal (contracted to *e*-ternal). They can be best studied in the order given. Then we may take them in typical passages where they occur and note the application of their individual meaning.

### *"Forever"*

This is really two words: *for* and *ever.* It is so printed in the Bible, and usually so in England even today. The word *ever* comes to us from the Anglo-Saxon *aifre,* Latin *aevum,* Greek *ai (w)on.* The last is itself from two simpler elements: *aei,* "always," "ever," and *on,* "being." From the combination of these two into *aion,* comes our direct derivative *aeon,* now usually written *eon.* Since this word is the basis of our whole study, it will pay us to notice it a bit further.

Historically *aion* is many eons old. Homer (about 800 B.C.), and in fact all the poets through the classical period to the time of Alexander, used this word in the sense of lifetime or life, which during the same period easily passed into the more general prose sense of an age or generation, the next generation being spoken of as "the coming *aion.*" From this it passed into long space of time, era, epoch, but no more definitely marked off than our corresponding terms in English. In the Byzantine period it retains the general meaning of age. Barnabas uses "the holy *aion*" to refer to the world to come. The LXX uses "from *aion*" in speaking of the giants in Genesis 6:4 as being "of old," or ancient, and in Isaiah 64:4, "from the *aion*" is used in the sense of from the beginning of the world. Modern Greek uses *aion* for century, as the "20th *aion*"; and for age, as the "golden *aion*"; also in the dialect, like our colloquial, "I have not seen him for an *aion.*"

It is easy to see that the underlying idea in this word is *continuity* (without a break), whether for a definite or an indefinite period, long or short. The New Testament usage agrees with these variations of the basic idea, as witness the following ten examples:

1. *Before the aions,* before the ages covered by this world's history (1 Cor. 2:7).

2. *From the aion* or *aions,* from the beginning of the world's history (Luke 1:70; Acts 3:21; 15:18; Col. 1:26; Eph. 3:9).

3. *In the now aion,* the present world or period of the world's history (1 Tim. 6:17; 2 Tim. 4:10).

4. *This aion,* this world, or period of the world (Rom. 12:2; Luke 16:6; 20:34).

5. *The god of this aion,* the devil now ruling men's lives during the age of sin (2 Cor. 4:4).

6. *The ends of the aions,* last part of the world's periods or ages (1 Cor. 10:11).

7. *The end of the aion,* end of the world (Matt. 13:39; 24:3).

8. *The coming aion,* the future world (Heb. 6:5).

9. *That aion,* the world to come (Luke 20:35).

10. *In the aions to come,* the successive periods of the future existence (Eph. 2:7).

Now coming back to our word *forever,* or rather two words *for* and *ever,* practically a preposition and a noun, we find their exact counterpart in the Greek, as for example:

"Let not fruit grow on thee henceforward *into the aion*" (Matt. 21:19); "he shall live *into the aion* (John 6:51; Heb. 6:20); "glory *into the aions*" (Rom. 11:36); "yesterday, to-day, and *into the aions*" (Heb. 13:8).

These simpler forms are also compounded into more emphatic expressions, as:

"Into all the generations *of the aion of the aions,*" the age embracing shorter ages (Eph. 3:21); "ascendeth up *into aions of aions,*" longer ages embracing shorter ages (Rev. 14:11); "glory *into the aions of the aions,*" seemingly more inclusive than the preceding (Gal. 1:5); "I am alive *into the aions of the aions*" (Rev. 1:18); "smoke rose up *into the aion of the aions*" (Rev. 19:3); "day and night *into the aion of the aions*" (Rev. 20:10); "shall reign *into the aions of the aions*" (Rev. 11:15; 22:5).

Now out of 123 times *aion* is used in the New Testament, it is used 55 times as the base of some phrase rendered *forever* or *forever and ever.* The conclusion on the use and meaning of *forever* may be stated as follows:

# APPENDIXES

It seems reasonable to conclude from this study that *aion*, like our *age* (which the lexicographer traces back to *aion*), denotes a period or state of undefined length, and that to determine its measure, in any given instance, even relatively, we must consider the context and other passages where it is found.

To illustrate: when it is said in Revelation 11:15 that Christ shall reign unto the *aions of the aions*, no one doubts that this means ages without end.

When it is said of the punishment of the wicked in Revelation 14:11, that "the smoke of their torment ascendeth up *into aions of aions*," we must conclude one of two things: (1) that smoke is here used as a symbol of the effect, or result, of their torment; or (2) that *aions of aions* denotes a limited, not an unlimited, period of time; for of the final destruction of the wicked it is said in Revelation 20:9 that "fire came down from God out of heaven and *devoured* them" (literally, *completely ate them up*, as the fowls did the seed by the wayside, the same word being used in Matthew 13:4).

When it says in Revelation 20:10 that the devil and the beast and the false prophet "shall be tormented day and night *into the aions of the aions*," we must not conclude that this means time without end; for they were leaders of the wicked "on the breadth of the earth," and the next scene after they were cast into the lake of fire (on the breadth of the earth) was a "new heaven and a *new earth:* for the first heaven and the first earth were *passed away.*" Rev. 21:1. The "first heaven" must refer to the atmospheric heaven (for the dwelling place of God does not pass away), and if the old atmosphere passed away, it certainly took the smoke with it; and if the old earth passed away, there must have passed with it both the wicked and the devil and the beast and the false prophet, who were tormented and *devoured* "on the breadth of the earth."

This conclusion is consistent with the testimony of Malachi concerning "all that do wickedly," that "the day that cometh shall *burn them up*" and "shall leave them *neither root nor branch,*" and the wicked "shall be *ashes* under the soles of your feet."

### *"Everlasting"*

In twenty-three out of the twenty-five times that the Greek word translated "everlasting" is found in the New Testament, it is an adjective formed on the stem of *aion*, namely *aionios*. Manifestly when this adjective form is used, we leave off the *for* and add to *ever* whatever fits best the idea of the noun which *aionios* modifies: if *life*, we say

845

*ever-continuing, ever-lasting;* if a flower, we say *ever-blooming;* if a tree, we say *ever-green;* if a certain type of person having only a "form of godliness," we say *ever-learning* and never able to come to a knowledge of the truth. In none of these instances do we understand *ever* to mean continuing without end, unless it be in the case of *life.*

Hence in the use of *ever* to render *aionios,* it is clear that it must be subject to the same interpretation as in rendering *aion* itself.

Of the twenty-five times that *aionios* is rendered *everlasting,* it is used fourteen times with *life,* every one of which fourteen no one will question means life without end. Of the remaining eleven times, two are used with *fire,* which we must understand to mean continuing unquenchable till that on which the fire feeds is consumed (see under "Forever," above). In the remaining nine times, we find *aionios* used as follows: "once with *punishment,* permanent in effect (see same comment); once with *habitations,* doubtless new earth, and without end; once with *God,* unquestionably without ceasing; once with *destruction,* in effect like punishment; once with *consolation,* unending for the saved; once with *power,* ascribed to God, hence without limit; once with *covenant,* unending in result accomplished; once with *kingdom,* ascribed to Christ, hence unceasing; once with *gospel,* which is the *power of God* (Rom. 1:16), hence limitless in duration."

In one other place (Jude 6) "everlasting" is from another word, *aidios,* always existing, which comes from the same base as *aionios;* namely, *aei,* always.

### *"Eternal"*

In every instance of its use in the New Testament, this word comes from one of the two above rendered *everlasting,* with one exception, in which it comes directly from *aion* itself. From one of the two, *aidios,* it comes but once. From the other, *aionios,* it comes forty-two times. It is applied to *life* thirty times, without question life without end; once to *damnation,* unending in result; three times to *glory* without end; once to *unseen things,* imperishable; once to *building of God,* standing without destruction; once to *salvation,* without end; once to judgment, never ending in result; once each to *redemption, Spirit,* and *inheritance,* all without limit; once to *fire,* same limit as *everlasting* (which see).

In derivation the English word *eternal* goes back through the Latin to the Greek *aion.* In use, it is a synonym of *everlasting* when applied to the future, but distinguished from it in that it may refer backward to time without a beginning, as well as without end.

# APPENDIXES

## Summary

From the study of *forever, everlasting,* and *eternal,* it is easy to see that they are subject to the same variation in interpretation, being mostly renderings of the adjective *aionios* or of the noun *aion,* which latter, in phrase, is rendered *forever.* In fact, *aionios* itself is once rendered *forever* (Philemon 15), suggesting the close relation of the three words under study here.

Thus wonderfully does the word harmonize with itself. Any unprejudiced mind can answer the question, "How long is everlasting?"

# Life, Soul, and Spirit

[The following, by W. E. Howell, appeared in the *Review and Herald* of Feb. 27, 1941.]

This article deals with a great trinity of gospel terms, "life," "soul," and "spirit." It is important to discriminate between these terms, so that we may know what it is that abides in the body during life, what it is that leaves the body at death, and what is the state of the dead.

It is a remarkable fact that in the King James Version the word "soul" always represents the same word in the original Greek, *psuchē;* but on the other hand, *psuchē* is also translated "life" forty-one different times, as compared with "soul" sixty times. It is an equally remarkable fact that "life" represents the Greek word *zōē* a total of 125 times, and *psuchē* 41 times, as stated above. This being the case, it becomes necessary to distinguish between the meaning of *zōē* and *psuchē* in the original, and of "life" and "soul" in the translation.

Each of the Greek words comes from a different verbal root meaning "breathe," but usage has established a difference in import. Thus *zōē* names the act of breathing as an *evidence* of life, while *psuchē* names it as an *act* of life, and *pneuma* (spirit) denotes the breathing as a *means* of life. From this we may deduce that *zōē* is life as an essence or principle, that *psuchē* represents life as it is possessed and lived out from day to day, and that *pneuma* denotes the medium through which life does its work, and the quality of that work.

In actual usage in the New Testament, we find:

1. That *zōē* is invariably used to denote the inherent life of God, the inherent life of Christ, imparted life, and life everlasting or eternal. But *zōē* never denotes the life that Christ gave as a ransom for sinners. The word is found in many phrases, like "bread of life," "word of life," "tree of life," "book of life," "crown of life," "water of life," "spirit of life," "gift of . . . life."

2. That *psuchē* is used to denote natural life, life as it is lived from day to day, the whole being, and especially the mental and emotional life. It is invariably used to denote the life that Christ laid down as a ransom for sinners. It is found in many phrases like: "the

young child's life," "take no thought for your life," "lose his own soul," "in exchange for his soul," "give his life a ransom for many," "is not the life more than meat?" "lay down my life for the sheep," "an anchor of the soul," "He laid down his life for us," "My soul is exceeding sorrowful," "vexed his righteous soul from day to day," "eight souls were saved," "Shepherd . . . of your souls," "every living soul died in the sea," "loved not their lives unto the death," "as thy soul prospereth."

### Terms Variously Rendered

It is easy to see that the same word *psuchē* is variously rendered "life" and "soul," according as it fits our idiom better, but that in some places in which it is rendered "soul," it could as well be rendered "life," such as, "What shall a man give in exchange for his *life* [instead of *soul*]?" "Let every *life* [not soul] be subject unto the higher powers." "An anchor of the *life* [instead of *soul*]." "Shall save a *life* from death." "Eight *lives* were saved." "Saw under altar the *lives* of them."

The thing to be noted especially in this connection is that the Greek does not confuse the words "soul" and "spirit," as we do in English. The true word "spirit" (*pneuma*) is nowhere translated "soul" in the New Testament. It is often rendered Ghost or Holy Ghost, to use an Anglo-Saxon word instead of the Latin word "spirit," but nowhere "soul," and in only one instance "life," in which instance it could as well read, "had power to give *breath* unto the image of the beast," to make it alive and active, just as God breathed breath into Adam's nostrils and he became a living being. In fact, *pneuma* is rendered "wind" in John 3:8, first part, and "Spirit" in the last part. It is this ethereal thing *pneuma* that believers in immortality of the soul confuse with *psuchē*, the true word for soul, when they talk about immortal souls or the departed spirits of the dead, which in reality are nothing more than their departed breaths. The Bible tells us that God imparted breath to Adam to make him alive, and that when he or any other man died, his breath returned to God who gave it, without being anything essentially different from what it was when God imparted it to man.

To sum up, it may truthfully be said—

1. That "soul" is a proper word to use for the *natural* life—the whole being, or especially the mind and emotional part of natural man.

2. That it cannot be properly applied to the breath or spirit that departs at death.

3. That from the human standpoint "spirit" is a proper word to use for the natural breath (the Greek uses it for even the natural air), for

the quality of man's mind and heart while he lives, and for the breath that departs at death and returns to God, who gave it.

4. That "spirit" cannot properly denote an entity that leaves the body at death, retaining its personality and continuing to live an endless life. The spirit of man is natural and mortal, as the spirit of God is divine and immortal, eternal.

5. That "life" is plainly used in two basic senses—the principle of life that gives and maintains being, and life as it is lived out in human existence. In the first instance, it may and should be called "life." In the second it may, in our idiom, be properly called either "life" (in the second sense) or "soul." The first belongs to God, and the second belongs, as a gift of God, to man. The first has no existence apart from God, and the second has no existence apart from man. There is therefore no such thing as soul distinct and apart from man, either before or after death.

What life is it, then, that sustains our physical being day by day? It is the imparted life, the zōē, breathed into our nostrils as in the case of the first man, to make and keep us alive.

How may we speak of what the zōē produces in our daily experience by stimulating us to act and think and feel? We may call it life in the sense of what experience produces, or we may call it by that wonderful word psuchē, by which we love and hate and believe and hope and aspire and achieve in our natural lives. In other words, it is the soul of living, which ceases to exist when our zōē that produces it is withdrawn, just as naturally and logically as heat stops when the gas that produces it is turned off.

What shall we say of the life that departs at death? It is nothing less and nothing more than the spirit, the pneuma, that, as the medium of life, is breathed into the body at birth and breathed out again at death. In fact, the Greek way of saying that Jesus gave up the life He had lived for us in the flesh, is "he breathed out," phrased in King James as "gave up the ghost." That is what every man does at death— merely breathes out again what was breathed into him at birth. There is absolutely no possibility here of conceiving that an "immortal soul" leaves the body at death, carrying with it a personality that goes right on thinking and feeling and never dying. The only thing that never dies is the life, the zōē of God, which He lends to us at birth and withdraws to Himself again at death. In other words, "the spirit shall return to God who gave it," and that is the end of life for us till God sees fit to breathe it in again, which He will do in the glorious resurrection morning for all those who are sleeping in Jesus.

# "Upon This Rock"

[The following, by W. E. Howell, appeared in the *Review and Herald* of June 15, 1939.]

IT is a well-known fact that the Roman Catholic Church uses Matthew 16:18, 19, as the basis of its claim that Christ made Peter the head of the church, that he was the first pope, that all the popes from his day to ours are successors to Peter, and by right of succession are vicegerents of the Son of God on earth. It is not difficult to prove the fallacy of this claim, both by the English version of the Scriptures and by the reading of the original Greek.

Through the orthodox method prescribed in the Bible itself, of comparing scripture with scripture, the meaning of this passage is made clear. A new pope has so recently been ordained in the person of Pius XII, that the procedure is fresh in mind, the acclamation of the pope reading, as in Matthew 16:18, 19, in Latin, *"Tu es Petrus,"* etc. ("Thou art Peter," etc.).

It should first be noticed how Peter came to be called by this surname. Jesus gave it to him directly at the time of his call by saying, "Thou art Simon the son of Jona: thou shalt be called Cephas [Aramaic, his mother tongue], which is by interpretation [into Greek] Peter." John 1:42, margin, and also Revised Version. The word Peter in Greek is *Petros*. The point to be established by this scripture is that Simon is named P-e-t-r-o-s. He is never called by any other etymological form of this word, though of course it is subject to all the grammatical variations common to all Greek nouns and names. He is called by this name 161 times in the Authorized Version of the New Testament, and by no other name except Simon.

Now the word *petros* is itself a masculine derivative from the feminine parent-word *petra*. The word *petra* denotes rock as a substance, rock en masse, as embedded in the everlasting hills, or as a huge boulder, or as a projecting ledge—in other words, mother rock. It therefore becomes a most fitting symbol of Christ, and is frequently applied to Him directly throughout both Old and New Testaments, often but not always written with a capital initial, Rock. Paul makes its use very clear in 1 Corinthians 10:4, in speaking of the children of Israel during the Exodus: "And did all drink the same spiritual drink: for they drank of that spiritual Rock that followed them: and that *Rock* was *Christ.*" The Greek original for Rock in both instances here is *petra*. What could be clearer than that *petra* is Christ, and that Christ is *petra* when spoken of by this symbol of *rock?*

Summing up what we learn from these two passages of Scripture, we have:

1. Peter was originally named *petros,* not *petra.*

2. In the 161 times he is mentioned by the name "Peter" (162 if we include the margin of Authorized Version and the text of Revised Version, in John 1:42), he is invariably called *petros.*

3. The word *petros* is never used for any other purpose in the New Testament than to designate Peter, including Matthew 16:18.

4. Christ is repeatedy called *petra* in both the Old and the New Testament, four times in the New, twice translated with the capital initial, Rock, as already cited, and twice with the small initial in the phrase "rock of offense."

5. Christ is never called *petros* in the Bible.

Hence we have the conclusion:

1. Peter always *petros,* and *petros* always Peter.

2. Christ always *petra,* and *petra* always Christ when used figuratively.

### Why Overthrow Established Usage?

How utterly inconsistent and self-stultifying, then, to overthrow established usage, and in the single instance of Matthew 16:18 call *petra* Peter and Peter *petra.* It illustrates with emphasis the absurd length to which a body of religionists will go to find and establish a substitute, a vicegerent, a vicar, of Christ in His church on earth— invest him with all the robes, phylacteries, crowns, on a throne, not on a cross; in pomp, not in meekness and lowliness, while tradition has it that Peter himself refused to be crucified upright on a cross, like his Master, but head downward.

But more may be said. The word *petra* has been known and used from the time of Homer and Hesiod (800 to 1000 B.C.) down through the classical period of Pericles and Demosthenes (400 B.C.), through the Koine of the time of Christ, in the patristic Greek of the Middle Ages, and in the modern Greek of today—always in the sense of rock as a substance, as bedrock.

The word *petros* also comes from a time equally early, and is defined by Liddell and Scott's unabridged Greek lexicon as "a piece of rock, a stone, and thus distinguished from *petra*, in Homer used by warriors," that is, to hurl at their enemies. It is sometimes used loosely for *petra*, but not in standard authors. The same lexicon says, "There is no example in good authors of *petra* in the significance of *petros*, for a single stone." The lexicon also says that it is used in Homer's *Odyssey* (which some of us have read with our own eyes) "as a symbol of firmness," just as by the same author *petros* is used of stones light enough and small enough for soldiers or anyone to throw.

What a striking contrast here between *petra* as a symbol of Christ, and *petros* as a symbol of Peter—of the same substance or character, but the one firm and stable as a rock, the other unstable as water, and entirely dependent upon the grace of God for firmness and strength. Hence *Petra*, Christ, is a firm foundation on which to build His church, while *Petros*, Peter, is firm only as a "lively stone" built into or upon the Chief Cornerstone of the church.

The other two words representing the substance rock in the New Testament are: *lithos*, dressed or fitted stone for building or other purposes, such as the "lively stones" mentioned by Peter; and *psephos*, a smooth pebble, used for casting a vote, as in Acts 26:10, and for inscribing a name, as in Revelation 2:17.

The reader may therefore be deeply grateful that his hope is built on nothing less than on "Christ the solid Rock," and not on a rolling, movable fragment of rock.

APPENDIX J

# How Are Prohibition Laws Related
# to Religious Liberty?

THERE are some who feel that there is a contradiction between our
Seventh-day Adventist advocacy of prohibitory liquor laws and our
insistence on liberty. That criticism comes largely from those outside
our membership. A different kind of misunderstanding in the matter
of prohibition laws reveals itself at times inside our ranks. There are
some of our members who feel that we should seek to secure prohibitory
laws because the Bible condemns liquor and drunkenness.

In these days when the crusade for prohibition is again gathering
momentum, and certain areas have prohibitory laws, we should understand clearly what kind of antiliquor laws Adventists may consistently
support, and what kind of reasoning we may properly employ in giving
our support.

### Prohibition and Personal Liberty—Letter to the Editor

First, let us examine the question of the consistency of campaigning
for prohibition laws while advocating liberty. The following letter
brings the question into focus:

"Dear Sir: Please tell me why a person has a right to enter my house
and arrest me because I have a bottle marked 'Whisky' on a shelf;
but nothing is said about the fact that on the same shelf is a bottle
marked 'Carbolic Acid,' which is as sure to kill as the whisky, if drunk
as freely? If a prohibition law is O.K. as practiced, why not have a law
to forbid the use of tobacco? 'The poison in tobacco is more subtle
than in alcohol.' 'Meat eating is doing its deadly work'—why not a
law to prohibit the use of meat? 'Drugs never cured any one'—why not
prohibit the use of drugs by law?"

The letter was answered as follows:

### Text of the Editor's Letter in Reply

The real basis on which laws prohibiting liquor rest is that the
liquor business creates a menace to the rest of society and to the
security of the community. In other words, that life, liberty, and the

854

pursuit of happiness on the part of the members of society are jeopardized by the liquor business. For example, the liquor tavern, which has been the symbol and center of the whole liquor industry through all the years and in all countries, has an unbroken record of being a public nuisance, a place where every kind of vice can breed, and where men can partake of stuff that so inflames the mind that they no longer have full possession of their faculties, and thus become a danger to their fellow men.

To call attention to the fact that all who drink do not thus become a danger is not a valid reply. It is equally a fact that not all men who might carry a revolver on their hip would use it improperly. In enacting legislation, it is obviously impossible to draw fine lines and distinguish between individuals. Instead, the principle is employed of passing a general prohibition on something which has so generally proved itself to be dangerous as to demand that sort of legislation. So today there is a law against carrying a revolver. And for anyone to contend that he would not use the revolver improperly would not avail. But surely neither you nor anyone else who is law abiding would offer objection to such curtailment of personal liberty. Yet it is obvious that in a certain sense of the word your liberty has been curtailed, for the time was that any man might carry on his person any kind of weapon he wanted.

Again, we have a prohibition on the speed we can drive our cars. Why should anyone tell us just how fast we may drive? For the simple reason that if we drive beyond that speed, we become a potential danger to society. We endanger not only our own lives but the lives of others. And it is quite pointless for any of us to argue that we can safely drive beyond such limits, and ought not to be held back because a few others cannot well control their cars at such speed. We cannot make one law for one man and another law for another. We proceed on the general principle that fast driving is dangerous to the community, and make a law against it.

Ten times over can it be established in the blood and tears of drunken brawls and broken homes that the presence of the liquor business in a country creates a real danger to the peace of society. And for that reason a prohibition upon the whole liquor business is just as rational, just as defensible, yes, a hundred times more so, as any prohibition against carrying concealed weapons or driving at an excessive rate of speed.

Now, as to your wondering why an officer may arrest you, in a prohibition area, for possessing whisky and not for possessing carbolic acid, since both are deadly. Without doubt, if a carbolic-acid beverage industry grew up in the country, and people were persuaded to get the habit, and the getting of that habit would not only work disaster upon them personally but make them dangerous to society, I believe that you, along with others, would think it quite proper to legislate against carbolic acid. But the facts are that nobody is promoting such an industry. And as is painfully obvious, if anyone got the carbolic-acid habit, he would get over it very quickly, and never prove a danger to anyone else. The situation would be automatically settled, and therefore would hardly warrant legislation. Of course, there is a prohibitory law that applies against carbolic-acid drinking. Suicide is prohibited by law!

To the extent that poisonous substances such as drugs are likely to cause men to become enemies of society or a burden upon society, we do have legislation. We have vigorous antinarcotic laws, and we all approve of them. And no rational person seems to feel that it is wrong for a prohibition to be placed on the use of such drugs, or that anyone's personal liberty is being improperly interfered with.

Your inquiry as to why tobacco should not be prohibited because it has a poison in it more subtle than that in alcohol, or why meat eating should not be prohibited inasmuch as it is unhealthful, seems to me, in view of the foregoing statements, to be wholly irrelevant. If tobacco smoking necessitated an institution like the tavern, with all its vicious atmosphere; if it caused men to maim and kill each other in tobacco brawls; if it caused them to beat or murder their wives or leave them penniless and a burden upon society, then I would say that the state had proper grounds for legislation; for the peace of society would be affected. As much as I hate even the smell of tobacco, I have never found any ground for believing that tobacco would cause men to do any of these terrible things. And much as I loathe even the sight of meat, I could never give any credence to the story of a man's rushing madly from a meal of beefsteak, or even bacon, to go out and murder his wife or his children. In fact, I have never heard such a story, have you?

### The Bible in Relation to Temperance Work

The second question, the relation of the Bible to prohibition laws, perplexes some of our Adventist Church members. When we deal with the liquor problem in terms of an appeal to men of their own free will to refrain from liquor, we should use the Bible. But when we endeavor to secure a civil statute to prohibit drinking, we should not base our appeal on religious grounds, but only on civil. A church member who had read a statement like the foregoing wrote to say that he thought we thus excluded "the Lord from a part in the temperance work," and would cause our denomination to "go the way of all other denominations. It's all right to bring forth man's strongest reasons, but they should be backed up with a 'Thus saith the Lord.' I believe if we do this, the temperance cause will win. Religious liberty will not be affected in the least. It will help religious liberty instead of harming it."

The letter was answered as follows:

### Text of the Editor's Letter in Reply

I believe as ardently as you, or any other Christian, that when we are appealing to an individual as to the relationship he personally should bear to liquor, we may properly, indeed surely ought to, use the Scriptural evidence and arguments with all the vigor we possess. We should set before him not only the fact that liquor is bad for his body and makes him an economic liability to society but that intemperance is contrary to the revealed will of God, and therefore he as an individual answerable to God should give heed to the warnings in the Good Book, and order his life accordingly.

But when we move out of the realm of the appeal to the heart of the individual to refrain from drinking over to the support of a civil statute which is intended to prevent a man's drinking whether he will or no, then we are in quite a different world. We must employ evidence, reasons, and arguments that belong properly in the civil realm: the facts that have to do with the relationship of man to man, and not man to God—the social, the economic arguments, for example.

To contend that because the Bible forbids drinking, we should have a civil statute against drink, enforced by the policeman's club, is to put ourselves essentially on the basis of the reasoning employed by the various church reform organizations. They declare, for example, that the Bible condemns Sabbathbreaking; therefore there ought to be a law on the statute books to prevent men from violating the Sabbath command. Our basic reason for taking issue with them on this attempt to enact a law is not on the ground of their error in substituting "first day" for "seventh day" in the command of God, but because we believe that the Bible, a religious book, ought not to be made the basis for civil statutes. We contend that to do so is to violate the primary principle of separation of church and state, and to do obvious injustice to a great part of the citizenry who do not view the Bible as an authority in their lives.

# ANSWERS TO OBJECTIONS

I cannot see how we, as champions of religious liberty, can safely enter into the discussion of laws at all unless we ever hold to the clear-cut principle that civil statutes must be built upon and defended by civil reasons. This, of course, does not say for a moment that various civil prohibitory laws, such as those against murder, robbery, and so forth, are not also found in the Good Book. It means that if we are going to avoid confusing the realm of the religious and the civil, we must find a sufficient justification on civil grounds for these various statutes, altogether apart from any Biblical arguments.

It is a well-known fact that almost without exception the various denominations have tied together their fight for a prohibition law with that for a Sunday law. I am afraid they would receive great consolation from the viewpoint that you apparently take, and would ask only that you be consistent, and argue also for their Sabbath law, because Sabbath desecration is as clearly condemned in the Scriptures as is intemperance. It would not relieve your situation any for you to reply to them that the Bible nowhere commands Sunday to be kept holy, for they might immediately inquire whether you were refusing your support of their Sunday law simply because you believed in a different day. You would have to answer them No, that you were against all Sabbath legislation. Such an answer would reveal, I believe, that you really could not be in agreement with them at all in appealing to Bible commands as a basis for a civil law. Therefore, to be really consistent, you would have to drop out of your antiliquor fight the Bible argument when you were focusing on the civil-statute feature of the liquor problem.

In view of this I hardly think you are quite accurate in saying that if my "theory" is adopted, "our denomination will go the way of all other denominations." The facts are that in making the distinctions between religion and the state on this liquor question we are going in the very opposite direction from other denominations. If they made the distinctions I am here expressing, they would cease to work for Sunday laws.

There was a time in the history of our country when various of the colonists, especially the Puritans, took the Bible as the basis for their code of laws. Such a procedure at first blush looks like a high and holy one to follow, but all of us know the sad results in religious intolerance that grew out of that program. As Adventists we have held up the program of the Puritans as an example of what ought not to be done. And as a denomination we have taken the position that the only escape from the dangers of religious intolerance that grow out of such a course as was followed by the Puritans, is to apply Bible commands exclusively to the hearts and the free will of men and to enact only such civil statutes as can be justified on civil grounds.

It would be very much easier for me in many ways, at least it would make it possible for me to cooperate much more largely with other religious groups, if I blurred over the distinctions that I have endeavored to set forth in this letter. But I do not feel I can do this, except at the peril of sacrificing some very primary conceptions as to religious liberty.

On the other hand, I am not willing to be viewed as behind even the most ardent Christian brother in my vigorous employment of Scriptural injunctions and commands on the matter of liquor drinking, when appealing to men's hearts to refrain from drink of their own free will. And, indeed, I believe we ought to do more of this. Such work may properly parallel our appeal on civil grounds for prohibitory laws against liquor. My contention is this: Although these two lines of activity may properly be carried on side by side, they ought never to be fused together so that we begin to declare that because the Bible says thus and so, therefore we ought to have a civil statute forcing men by pains and penalties to order their lives accordingly.

# Do Adventists Seek a "Wide Open" Sunday?

OFTEN Sunday law advocates seek to embarrass us in the matter of our opposition to Sunday laws by accusing us of aiding and abetting the disreputable elements in the country. The charge seems to have plausibility. Do not irreligious, commercial interests seek Sunday law repeal, arguing for a "wide open" Sunday for every kind of commercial amusement? And do not Adventists also urge repeal of those same laws? In fact, do not Adventists strive earnestly to liberalize such laws, even if they cannot succeed in having them repealed? And is there not already too much liberalizing in matters of religion and morality?

The fallacies in this charge are examined in an address delivered at a hearing in Annapolis, State capital of Maryland, some years ago, on a bill to liberalize the State Sunday law in certain counties. The chairman of the hearing was the then governor of Maryland, the Honorable Albert C. Ritchie. The following address sought to present the Adventist viewpoint on the matter:

### The Text of the Address

Your Excellency: I labor under an unusual handicap in attempting to speak on the Sunday Liberalization Bill that is before you. Undoubtedly the most distinctive feature of it is the permitting of movies on Sunday. My handicap is that of ignorance; I do not attend movies at all, and so I cannot speak from personal, firsthand knowledge as to the effect of movies on morals on any of the seven days of the week. Nor is my ignorance relieved by inquiry of my parishioners, for they do not attend. It is one of the requirements of Seventh-day Adventist church fellowship that the members do not attend movies, the theater, or any similar places of amusement.

It is necessary to make my position clear at the outset, that my attitude may not possibly be misunderstood. For someone to say, as has been repeatedly said because of my public statements on this matter in the past, that "Mr. Nichol wants the movies opened on Sunday," is to put the matter in an altogether wrong light. It would be as accurate to say that I want the grocery stores, the bank, the bakery, opened on Sunday. But my real interest would be revealed by saying that I want the theater man, the banker, the grocer, and the baker to have the *right* to open if they *wish*. As a citizen, I do not care which day any one of them opens or closes—least of all the moving-picture theater. I might even go so far as to express the wish that some places of amusement, including some theaters—if well-authenticated reports may be believed—were not open any day in the week. Yes, I would go even further, and say that without doubt some of these places of amusement ought properly to be the object of vigorous legislation, and compelled to close their doors forever.

### Sunday Law Wrong Solution of Problem

But, Your Excellency, the point that I wish to make clear is this: That Sunday legislation is not the proper way to deal with any business or industry or institution inimical to society. The state can know no distinction of days in determining the question of the propriety of acts either of an individual or of a business. To contend that what is proper on one day is wrong on another is most certainly to contend that there is an essential difference in the two days. This is the logic of all Sunday legislation. It is the logic of the Maryland Sunday law, which the bill before you proposes to liberalize.

I cannot consistently restrict my remarks to the question of liberalizing this law. To work simply for the liberalization of a law is to admit tacitly that the law is right and just in principle, and needs only revision. Believing, as I do, that Sunday legislation is wrong in principle, I appeal, not for liberalization, but for absolute repeal.

Let no member of the clergy gasp at this statement and hasten to charge that I would have the state remove all restraint and give license to any conduct. My appeal is only for repeal of the Sunday law, and not of the criminal statutes under which evil deeds or evil amusement may be prosecuted seven days in the week. To say that the Sunday law must be retained in order to protect the morals of the citizenry is to state a fallacy, for we have a surplus of laws touching on every conceivable question of morals and our relation to one another as citizens.

### Sunday Laws and the Laboring Man

Or to say that Sunday laws must be maintained in order to protect the workingman is also to state a fallacy. The advocates of Sunday laws deplore the laxity in enforcement in recent years compared with former generations. Yet the condition of the workingman in this present generation is vastly better than in any former time. In fact, in States where there is no Sunday law, the workingman does not suffer. There are civil statutes which protect him from oppressive hours of labor.

There is only one ground on which Sunday laws can be urged. It is the historical ground on which such laws in all former centuries have been promoted, and that is to protect a day which many devout persons consider holy. That Sunday legislation is primarily and essentially religious legislation, and only secondarily and indirectly social and moral legislation, is surely not open to question. The reading of the texts of the Sunday laws of past generations makes abundantly evident their religious nature, without the necessity of my entering into any extended historical discussion. Let me be specific, and quote the opening words of the first Sunday law in Maryland: "Forasmuch as the sanctification and keeping holy the Lord's day commonly called Sunday, hath been and is esteemed by the present and all the primitive Christians and people, to be a principal part of the worship of Almighty God, and the honor due to His holy name; Be it enacted," etc. This is typical of other Sunday laws of the colonies and of the old country. It is certain that if we had lived in those days, we would not have thought to ask a colonial whether Sunday laws were religious laws, for the question would have found its unequivocal answer in the texts of the statutes. The fact that the revised codes of postcolonial times have dropped out certain religious phrases from the texts of the Sunday laws in no way affects the essential nature of such laws or their definite historical connection.

### Why We Plead for Repeal

Your Excellency, it is because Sunday legislation is religious legislation that I plead not simply for its liberalization but for its repeal. And my plea grows out of the fact that I am a believer in the Bible and also in the principles set forth by the founding fathers regarding separation of church and state. In matters of religion and our duties and relationship to God, I believe that the state should play no part. Religious beliefs and our sense of religious duties proceed from the depths of the conscience and from our interpretation of God's Word. Therefore, to make such beliefs and duties the objects of cold civil legislation is to change the basis of our relationship to God from that of free will and loving obedience to that of coercion and necessity. There is doubtless no one in this fair State of Maryland but would declare that he believed in religious liberty. Indeed, many of our forefathers came to America for the express purpose of securing religious liberty. Yet so steeped were they in the Old World idea that religion is properly a subject for legislation that they immediately formulated laws reflecting their religious viewpoint. The result was that even in this new land dissenting religious minorites suffered various degrees of hardship and even persecution. The early colonists did not immediately see that religious liberty meant liberty not only for themselves but for all others no matter how differing their religious views. It was not until the founding of the Federal Government that the principle of the separation of church and state was fully and clearly enunciated and applied.

### A New Principle in Political World

It was indeed a new thing for the rest of the world, accustomed from time immemorial to the fusion of church and state, to see a new nation created on the principle that the state has no proper jurisdiction over the church, nor the church over the state, but that each has an individual sphere of its own. An amazed world heard proclaimed the doctrine that conscience and religious beliefs are not amenable to civil legislation. It is in this vital particular that our nation is different from all others. There have been republics since the days of Rome. Democracy was a form of government that flourished in ancient Greece, and confederacies of states were known long before our day. But a state with no state god, no national church, and repudiating the very principle upon which any fusion of religion with the state might be built—ah, that was something new!

On this clear principle of the separation of church and state our Federal Government was built. It is America's distinctive contribution to political history. It is to this principle above all else that we owe the vitality and reality of our boasted liberty, especially religious liberty.

### Slow Deletion of Religious Laws

But the various States of the Union were founded in an earlier century, when this principle of church and state separation was only dimly understood. Gradually, as the leaven of this revolutionary principle began to work, religious laws were deleted from the statute books, until today they are virtually all gone—all but the Sunday laws. True, the strongly religious language of the Sunday statutes is tempered, as are also their penalties, but the laws still remain. They are a relic from a former age, reminders of a day when legislation on religious duties was as common, and considered as proper, as legislation on civil ones.

# ANSWERS TO OBJECTIONS

### *Ever-present Threat to Liberty*

But modified though they are, these Sunday laws are strangely out of harmony with true American principles. And though no longer consistently enforced, even in their present form, nevertheless these laws restrict in a real way the liberties of those who do not desire to rest on Sunday. Specifically, right here in Maryland the law operates to compel the man who believes in no day to give passive homage to a certain day because the majority in the State happen to believe in that day. What is even more unfair, this Sunday law compels a man who has already rested on a day which he believes holy to rest an additional day in the week, and all because he happens to be in the minority.

But here is where Sunday-law proponents endeavor to make a bold defense of their course by employing the language of democracy. They declare that the majority of the people wish a Sunday law, and should not the majority rule? But, Your Excellency, if the majority have a right to enforce their will on the minority in this one particular area of religion, who can logically deny their right to enforce their will in other areas of religion? Is not the fallacy evident? Their argument proves too much.

### *What if Adventists Were in Majority?*

But to make certain that the advocates of Sunday legislation do not fail to see the untenability of the majority argument in religious questions, let us suppose that Seventh-day Adventists became in the majority in Maryland—stranger things have happened in the history of religion. And suppose we should have enacted a law to compel all to rest on Saturday, no matter what their religious beliefs might be. Suppose, further, that various of our members took occasion at times to report to the police even such a minor infraction of the law as the doing of a little work around one's house on Saturday. How quickly —yes, and how properly—would our Sundaykeeping friends cry out that they were being oppressed by religious legislation, that their rights were invaded! And how altogether unconvincing to them would sound our argument that the majority wish a Saturday law! With vigor would they insist that matters of religion cannot be settled by majorities.

But today they are in the majority, we in the minority. And, accordingly, we suffer handicaps, and not infrequently hardships. Only a short time ago a member of my church was spied upon while doing a little painting on a window inside his home on Sunday, and suffered five days' imprisonment. His only offense was that he had violated a religious law.

And yet, Your Excellency, we are made the objects of scorn, and charged with being enemies of religion, of society, and of the state, because we raise our voices against such a law. I contend that the facts warrant the conclusion that ours must be a real religion to continue active under such handicaps, and that we are friends, not enemies, of the state in pleading for the complete repeal of all religious legislation.

### Religion Too Holy to Mix With State

To extol the glories and the divine origin of religion or religious days is not therefore to furnish a valid reason for state legislation in behalf of religion, but rather the contrary. Something so holy as religion should be freed from alliance with something so secular as the state. Christianity displayed its greatest purity and its greatest growth in the early centuries, when it not only lacked the support of the state but was the object of bitter attack.

I am not a party to the framing of this present bill for liberalization, and have no conceivable interest in it personally. But I am vitally concerned with the primary question that is raised by any bill that deals with Sunday. And it is with the primary principle alone that I am concerned.

Doubtless it will be charged, in conclusion, that the adoption of this principle of the absolute repeal of all religious laws would make for a "wide open" Sunday. Your Excellency, the state should know no widths to days; certainly it should not attempt to determine widths by the varying yardsticks of different creeds. The state should not be in the business of enforcing religious tenets; the church should not seek such aid. The arm of the Lord, not the arm of the law, should be the strength of religion.

# How to Meet the "Christian Nation" Argument

IN America one of the premises on which Sunday law advocates build is that this is a Christian nation, and therefore Sunday legislation is not only defensible but imperative if Christian standards are to be reflected through the activities of the government. At first the argument in support of the Christian-nation claim was rather vague and of this order: Christian people founded the country, some of them coming here for religious reasons. The moral principles of Christianity are woven into our customs and laws. The oath is administered in the name of God. Sunday is excluded from the count of days in determining certain judicial matters, cognizance thus being taken of its distinctive character.

These and like reasons were originally offered in proof that this is a Christian nation, and hence should protect Sunday with legislation. Then came the decision of the Supreme Court of the United States in 1892, in what is known as the Holy Trinity Church case, in which the statement is made that "this is a Christian nation." The case dealt with the right of that church to import a minister from abroad. Lower courts had ruled that this violated a law forbidding the import of foreign labor.

## Supreme Court's Reasoning in 1892

The Supreme Court reasoned that the legislators never intended to include religious groups or individuals in the restrictive law, and supported this reasoning by showing that from earliest days the people of this country had acknowledged God as supreme and had sought to do His will. After citing declarations as far back as the commission of Ferdinand and Isabella to Columbus, the court declared:

"These, and many other matters, which might be noticed, add a volume of unofficial declarations to the mass of organic utterances that this is a Christian nation.''—143 U.S., 457.

How far the justices intended the logic of their statement to be carried is not evident from that decision. They there invoked the

"Christian nation" claim only to create a reasonable presumption that the legislators never intended to include ministers in their law against foreign labor. Thus, strictly speaking, the reasoning that climaxed in the conclusion that this is a Christian nation, is really not the decision of the court, but is, in legal parlance, an obiter dictum, a kind of parenthetical observation. The court was not ruling on the question of whether this is or is not a Christian nation, but on whether the Church of the Holy Trinity had violated a labor law.

### Reformers Comment on Court's Words

However, Sunday-law reformers did not trouble themselves over legal niceties. They had their own convictions as to the implications of the Christian-nation statement. In the organ of the National Reform Association appeared this exuberant comment:

" 'This is a Christian nation.' That means Christian government, Christian laws, Christian institutions, Christian practices, Christian citizenship. And this is not an outburst of popular passion or prejudice. Christ did not lay His guiding hand there, but upon the calm, dispassionate, supreme judicial tribunal of our government. It is the weightiest, the noblest, the most tremendously far-reaching in its consequences of all the utterances of that sovereign tribunal. And that utterance is for Christianity, for Christ. 'A Christian nation!' Then this nation is Christ's nation, for nothing can be Christian that does not belong to Him. Then His word is its sovereign law. Then the nation is Christ's servant. Then it ought to, and must, confess, love, and obey Christ."—*The Christian Statesman*, Nov. 19, 1892.

This quotation reveals how far reaching were the conclusions that the reformers drew from the words of the Supreme Court. Of course, these reformers were chiefly and immediately concerned to find support for Sunday laws. Charity toward them requires us to believe that they did not truly see what their bubbling rhetoric could lead to. Zealots and reformers are rarely given to dispassionate, calm, and logical analysis. They are inclined, rather, to seize with fervor whatever appears to support their cause, without troubling to inquire whether it may prove to be a broken reed that will pierce them.

### Our Analysis of Reformers' Position

Seventh-day Adventists have consistently argued that the National Reformers, in reasoning as they did, logically gave to the state a religious character, and caused its statutes to appear as springing from the mind of God and a holy people. Hence, to rebel against the state or against any of its laws would be tantamount to rebelling against the will of God. But if that be so, it is pointless for a citizen to set up his individual conscience against *any* mandate of the state. Is it not presumptuous for anyone to say that God, speaking to him through his conscience, forbids him to obey a law of a *Christian* nation? Does God contradict Himself?

In other words, we have consistently held that the logic of the Christian-nation premise leads inevitably to a revival of the medieval doctrine that the king can do no wrong. How plausibly, in bygone centuries, that claim was made! Did not God set up the king? Does not the Bible declare that he is the minister of God? The peasant in those days of the divine right of kings could not hope to make a case in court by arguing that his conscience forbade his obeying a law of the king. The argument had no standing.

### Supreme Court Speaks in 1931

Adventists have often wondered whether the Supreme Court might someday interpret its own words and reveal what are the logical conclusions that follow from the loose, though sweeping, observation that "this is a Christian nation." The Holy Trinity Church case was decided in 1892. In the year 1931 the Supreme Court handed down a decision in the case of Dr. Douglas Clyde MacIntosh, who had applied for citizenship, with a reservation regarding the bearing of arms. Dr. MacIntosh reserved the right to let his conscience tell him whether he ought to bear arms in a particular war that might be fought. In ruling against his application, the court reasoned in the following manner:

"When he speaks of putting his allegiance to the will of God above his allegiance to the Government, it is evident, in the light of his entire statement, that he means to make his own interpretation of the will of God the decisive test which shall conclude the Government and stay its hand. We are a Christian people (Holy Trinity Church *vs.* United States, 143 U.S. 457, 470, 471), according to one another the equal right of religious freedom, and acknowledging with reverence the duty of obedience to the will of God.

"But, also, we are a nation with the duty to survive; a nation whose Constitution contemplates war as well as peace; whose Government must go forward upon the assumption, and safely can proceed upon no other, that unqualified allegiance to the nation and submission and obedience to the laws of the land, as well those made for war as those made for peace, are not inconsistent with the will of God."

# APPENDIXES

## Reformers Comment on Court's Decision

The same *Christian Statesman* that in 1892 had given such fulsome praise to the Supreme Court for its declaration that this is a Christian nation, joined the chorus of the religious press in denunciation of the court in 1931, with these scathing words:

"Just now the American people have been rudely awakened to the fact that this liberty of the conscience for the individual citizen is threatened at least, by making its surrender one of the conditions for becoming a citizen by naturalization. . . .

"In this case the Federal Government has officially declared that it has the power to decide when and in what circumstances it may, under the plea of necessity, override the conscience of the individual citizen. Carried into the realm of actual citizenship, this would abolish the right of the individual to judge of the righteousness of the acts of the government he has helped to create and of his own active participation in them. It requires but logic and the ruthlessness born of excitement, to march from this premise straight to all the conclusions of the state sovereignty of Soviet Russia."—*The Christian Statesman*, July-August, 1931.

Nowhere in this fervent defense of the individual conscience does *The Christian Statesman* reveal that it is aware that the court had used the National Reformers' favorite Christian-nation * phrase as the basis for its decision against MacIntosh. The reformers observed that the court's decision gave the government the "power" to "override the conscience of the individual citizen." But the court contended not only that the state has the power but also the *right,* and that this right rests upon the premise that "unqualified allegiance to the nation and submission and obedience to the laws of the land . . . are not inconsistent with the will of God." This is but another way of saying that the laws of the land are not inconsistent with the will of God. And of course this leads on to the far-reaching but inevitable conclusion that the citizen is to discover what is the will of God for him, not by searching his heart and conscience, but by examining the laws and statute books of the state.

## Reasoning Valid if Premise Correct

And why may not the court thus reason if it really believes that this is a "Christian people"? If this or any other nation is truly Christian; if, as a state, it possesses not only a political but a religious character, the Christian religion at that, then it may plausibly be argued

---

* In the Trinity Church case the phrases "Christian nation," "Christian people," and "religious people" are used interchangeably as virtually synonymous.

that the laws of the land are not inconsistent with the will of God. Indeed, only on the premise that this is a *Christian* nation, and thus guiding its course by the standards of Heaven, could it possibly be contended that the laws of the land are not inconsistent with the will of God.

The National Reformers were happy to declare that the Supreme Court acted under the guiding hand of Christ when it said in the Holy Trinity Church case that this is a Christian nation. In fact, they declared at the time that the court's statement in that case actually established that this *is* a Christian nation. But when this same supreme tribunal later quoted the Trinity Church case and went on to reason that citizens should give unquestioning obedience to the laws of the state, the reformers were ready to pillory the court. But how did the reformers know that Christ guided the court in the first instance but not in the second? Are the National Reformers better able to decide what are the ultimate conclusions that may logically be drawn from a statement of the Supreme Court than is the court itself?

It is evident that the only way to escape the conclusion reached by the court in the MacIntosh case is to set down the counter view that "unqualified allegiance to the nation and submission and obedience to the laws of the land" may, in certain instances, be wholly "inconsistent with the will of God." But to maintain this position we must surrender the view that the nation is Christian. That is the dilemma that has confronted the National Reformers ever since the Supreme Court decision in the MacIntosh case.

### Other Fallacies in Reformers' Claims

Turning aside, now, from this devastating Supreme Court commentary on the famous Christian-nation phrase, let us explore a little further the statements made by the National Reformers in their historic pronouncement of 1892. We shall see that their reasoning contains other fallacies than those exposed by the Supreme Court decision in the MacIntosh case. In 1892 they came to the sweeping conclusion that because this is a Christian nation "this nation is Christ's nation, for nothing can be Christian that does not belong to Him. Then His word is its sovereign law. Then the nation is Christ's servant. Then it ought to, and must, confess, love, and obey Christ."

The National Reformers appear to have made this statement to protect themselves against the question that clamors for expression: Why call this country Christian when its citizenry in general are anything but Christian? Let us examine the statement. If we should say to a man, "You are now a Christian, therefore you 'ought to, and must, confess, love, and obey Christ,'" our words would need explaining, to avoid most serious error. If we meant simply that the man was to *continue* such a relationship to Christ, well and good. But if we meant that because he had been pronounced a Christian, he must therefore *begin* to relate himself thus to Christ, we would be guilty of turning the Christian program upside down. It is because a man confesses, loves, and is willing to obey Christ that he *becomes* a Christian.

Now the National Reformers were unable to say in 1892 that the nation could be pronounced "Christian" on the ground that it had been confessing, loving, and obeying Christ. So they were obliged to work from the opposite end, affirming, first, that the nation *is* Christian, and then telling it that it "ought to, and must," act Christian.

## What Will They Say Today?

The reformers made that statement more than half a century ago. Will they contend that the nation has, during those years, changed its ways as "it ought to," and justified the pronouncement as to its national Christianity? I hardly think they would have the hardihood to attempt to prove this. The fact of the increasing problem of crime, and of disregard for law on the part of the citizenry at large, is too generally known. Those who sought to give spiritual guidance to millions of men in two world wars declare that the nation is largely pagan.

If, after half a century, the nation has failed to conform to Christianity as "it ought to," but instead has become only worse, is it not about time that all those who truly love the name Christian protest against the hypocrisy of the phrase "Christian nation"? The nation has not been improved by the magic of the famous phrase. And certainly the beautiful word "Christian" has received no added richness of meaning from being thus combined with "nation."

But perhaps the National Reformers may contend that although it is true that national conditions have become only worse during the years, nevertheless the title "Christian nation" should still be retained, because as a result of reforms that they will launch, the nation will finally do what "it ought to." In reply it might be said that the title never should have been given in the first place, not only because as a matter of fact the nation is not Christian in its conduct, but because the state cannot properly have a religious character. Nevertheless, let us consider this final argument in defense of the notable phrase. Can the National Reformers point to any nation that has been nationally reformed? We read much of the decline and fall of empires, morally as well as politically, but scarcely a word of their reformation.

And if, after a half century and more of active endeavor by the National Reformers, the country has gone only downward morally, what reason can they offer as to why we should believe they can reform it, throughout, in the future? Can they do what earnest contenders for Christian principles have been unable to do in any other nation or century?

Surely history does not warrant the belief that the nation at large will ever do what "it ought to." Should we, nevertheless, continue to describe it as "Christian," solely because "it ought to" do that which it never has and never may be expected to do as a nation? If so, then words have lost their distinctive meaning, and we can properly call a man "Christian" who for half a century has steadily sunk lower morally —not because we believe he is confessing, loving, and obeying Christ, but because we believe he "ought to."

APPENDIX M

# The Remission of Sins

[Under the above title Mrs. E. G. White discusses in the *Review and Herald,* June 13, 1899, the difficult question of remission of sins in terms of Christ's statement in Matthew 16:19. Because this text is so frequently quoted by Catholics in their discussions with Adventist workers, Mrs. White's article is here reprinted in full. See also *The Desire of Ages,* pp. 414, 805, 806.]

BEFORE His death Jesus told His disciples what the priests and rulers would do to Him, but the disciples could not understand His words. Now, after they had been verified, after Christ had been rejected, condemned, scourged, crucified, buried, and had risen from the dead on the third day, the disciples believed. They had gained a valuable experience. All the sophistry and reasoning of the scribes and Pharisees could not now turn them from Christ. They could say, as did Paul, "I know whom I have believed." Their faith in Christ was rewarded by a most remarkable experience. They saw their beloved Master. They heard His voice and He opened to them the Scriptures; and from this they obtained much knowledge.

The lessons given by Christ to His disciples after His resurrection were with reference to the Old Testament Scriptures. He could now explain to them the prophecies concerning Himself. They were surprised that they had not discerned the meaning of the inspired record of Christ's work and the reception that would be given Him by the Jewish dignitaries. While the poor heard Him gladly, those to whom had been committed the sacred oracles closed the eyes of their understanding, that they might not see Christ. And by misapplying the Scriptures, substituting their own traditions and fables for truth, and upholding their words as the commandments of God, they so bewildered the minds of the people that they could not see Christ.

Christ rebuked these false teachers. "In vain they do worship me," He said, "teaching for doctrines the commandments of men." "Thus have ye made the commandment of God of none effect by your tradition." This is the work of many of the teachers of this time. They make void the law of God by teaching the commandments of men.

# ANSWERS TO OBJECTIONS

"Ye do err, not knowing the Scriptures, nor the power of God," Christ said to the teachers of His day; and His words apply to all who claim to know the truth, yet who make void the law of God by their traditions.

"Then the same day at evening, being the first day of the week, when the doors were shut where the disciples were assembled for fear of the Jews, came Jesus and stood in the midst, and saith unto them, Peace be unto you. And when he had so said, he showed unto them his hands and his side." He gave them evidence that He was the same Jesus who had been crucified. "Then were the disciples glad, when they saw the Lord. Then said Jesus to them again, Peace be unto you: as my Father hath sent me, even so send I you. And when he had said this, he breathed on them, and saith unto them, Receive ye the Holy Ghost: whosesoever sins ye remit, they are remitted unto them; and whosesoever sins ye retain, they are retained."

Thus the disciples received their commission. They were to teach and to preach in Christ's name. The instruction given them had in it the vital, spiritual breath that is in Christ. He alone could give them the oil which they must have in order to work successfully. Christ's likeness must appear in them. They could be successful only as they studied their Master's character and followed His example.

The Holy Spirit is the breath of life in the soul. The breathing of Christ upon His disciples was the breath of true spiritual life. The disciples were to interpret this as imbuing them with the attributes of their Saviour, that in purity, faith, and obedience, they might exalt the law, and make it honorable. God's law is the expression of His character. By obedience to its requirements we meet God's standard of character. Thus the disciples were to witness for Christ.

The impartation of the Spirit was the impartation of the very life of Christ, which was to qualify the disciples for their mission. Without this qualificatior. their work could not be accomplished. Thus they were to fulfil the official duties connected with the church. But the Holy Spirit was not yet fully manifested, because Christ had not yet been glorified. The more abundant impartation of the Holy Spirit did not take place till after Christ's ascension.

"Whosesoever sins ye remit, they are remitted unto them; and whosesoever sins ye retain, they are retained." The lesson here given to the disciples means that wise men, truly taught of God, possessing the inward working of the Holy Spirit, are to act as representative men, samples of the whole body of believers. These are to show themselves capable of preserving due order in the church; and the Holy

Spirit will convince of sin, of righteousness, and of judgment. But the remission of sins is to be understood as the prerogative of God alone. The warnings in the seventh chapter of Matthew forbid men to pronounce judgment on their fellow men. God has not given His servants power to cast down or to destroy. The apostles were unable to remove the guilt from any soul. They were to give the message from God: It is written—the Lord has said—thus and thus in regard to lying, Sabbath-breaking, bearing false witness, stealing, idolatry.

Christ has given rules for the guidance of His church. "If thy brother shall trespass against thee," He said, "go and tell him his fault between thee and him alone: if he shall hear thee, thou hast gained thy brother. But if he will not hear thee, then take with thee one or two more, that in the mouth of two or three witnesses every word may be established. And if he shall neglect to hear them, tell it unto the church: but if he neglect to hear the church, let him be unto thee as an heathen man and a publican. Verily I say unto you, Whatsoever ye shall bind on earth shall be bound in heaven: and whatsoever ye shall loose on earth shall be loosed in heaven."

Remitting sins or retaining applies to the church in her organized capacity. God has given directions to reprove, rebuke, exhort, with all long-suffering and doctrine. Censure is to be given. This censure is to be removed when the one in error repents and confesses his sin. This solemn commission is given to men who have in them the breath of the Holy Spirit, in whose lives the Christ-life is manifested. They are to be men who have spiritual eyesight, who can discern spiritual things, whose actions in dealing with the members of the church are such as can receive the indorsement of the great Head of the church. If this is not so, in their human judgment they will censure those who should be commended, and sustain those who are controlled by a power from beneath.

The gospel commission is to be carried out by men who know the inward working of the Spirit of God, who have the attributes of Christ. Christ's breath is breathed upon them, and He says to them, "Receive ye the Holy Ghost." All who are thus inspired by God have a work to do for the churches. As Christ's representatives, the ministers of the grace of God, they may say to others, It is written, "If we confess our sins, he is faithful and just to forgive us our sins, and to cleanse us from all unrighteousness." This is remission of sins in accordance with the word of God.

In all labor with the members of the church, every eye is to be directed to Christ. Those in the wrong are to confess their sins to the sin-pardoning Saviour; and the servants of the Lord Jesus are not to strive, but to minister in word and doctrine. The shepherds are to take a kindly interest in the flock of the Lord's pasture. They are to present the grace of Christ, comforting the erring by speaking of the divine tenderness of the Saviour, encouraging those who have fallen to repent and believe in Him who alone can pardon transgression.

Let the tenderness of Christ find a place in the hearts of His ministers. Watch for souls as they that must give an account. Watch constantly, vigilantly, and pray earnestly. Faithfully warn every soul that is in danger. Encourage the sinner to go to Christ. If he repents of his sin, he will find abundant pardon. He has assurance that his sins will be remitted; for thus it is written. Bear in mind that first the Lord gave His disciples the Holy Spirit. Those to-day who would do the work of the disciples must receive the presence of the Holy Spirit, and work under its influence.

Remission of sins can be obtained only through the merits of Christ. On no man, priest or pope, but on God alone, rests the power to forgive sins. "Behold the Lamb of God, which taketh away the sin of the world." "As many as received him, to them gave he power to become the sons of God." "If we say we have fellowship with him, and walk in darkness, we lie, and do not the truth. . . . But whoso keepeth his word, in him verily is the love of God perfected." This is the message that is to be borne. On this basis Christians are free. Give encouragement of sins remitted. "If we walk in the light, as he is in the light, we have fellowship one with another, and the blood of Jesus Christ his Son cleanseth us from all sin. . . . If we confess our sins, he is faithful and just to forgive us our sins, and to cleanse us from all unrighteousness." "These things write I unto you, that ye sin not. And if any man sin, we have an advocate with the Father, Jesus Christ the righteous: and he is the propitiation for our sins: and not for ours only, but also for the sins of the whole world."

# Rome's Claim to Unity in Contrast to Protestantism's Divisions

ONE of the historic differences between Catholicism and Protestantism is that regarding the right of private judgment or private interpretation of the Scriptures. Catholicism holds that the individual, devout Christian though he may be, is not capable, alone, of understanding the Bible; that his private judgment is so faulty and erring that only confusion can result from permitting him to determine his spiritual life by what he reads in the book of God. Rome holds that the church—and by the church is meant the Catholic clergy in general and the pope in particular—is the only safe and true interpreter of Scripture. This view naturally explains why, as a general rule, the Catholic laity are not students of the Scriptures; in fact, in many instances, are not encouraged and sometimes not even permitted to have the Scriptures.

Inasmuch as the Protestant movement was reared on the foundation principle of the Bible and the Bible only, it was both natural and logical that this Catholic view should be challenged and repudiated. Many have been the disputes that have raged over this question.

### Argument From Diversity of Sects

The very diversity of Protestant sects provides Rome with what it believes to be an absolute demonstration of the truth of its teaching that private judgment is a dangerous heresy; for, "See," it declares, "what confusion and disintegration have come to Protestantism!" And whenever a sharp religious dispute occurs within a Protestant denomination, Rome considers it simply an added proof.

For example, the controversy that occurred some years ago in the Presbyterian ranks, provided a concrete illustration on the question at issue between Rome and Protestantism. Note these lines that appeared on the editorial page of the *Pilot*, a leading Catholic weekly newspaper published in Boston:

"Once again communions outside the [Catholic] church are given opportunity, in the controversy which has been aired in the press between the Presbyterian Board of Foreign Missions and one of its missionaries, to see more clearly the desperate plight to which 'private judgment' has reduced the religious groups outside the Catholic Church. In that is the sole value of the incident. The prominence of the offending missionary has inspired a publicity doctrinal differences are rarely accorded by a secular press. For all that, the only permanent and real value the matter possesses is that it draws clearly issues all sincere people must sometimes face."—June 10, 1933.

The editorial is referring, of course, to the stir that was created by the statements of a certain well-known woman missionary of the Presbyterian Church, in connection with the much-discussed laymen's foreign mission report. She expressed ideas so alien to the historic position of Protestant Christianity, and so ultra-modernistic, as to necessitate her resignation. According to her view, it matters not really whether our Lord Jesus Christ ever actually lived, because, to give her words, as quoted in the *Pilot:*

"If there existed mind or minds, dreams, hopes, imaginations, sensitive enough to the human soul and its needs, perceptive enough to receive such a heavenly imprint on the spirit as to be able to conceive a personality like Christ's and portray Him for us with such matchless simplicity as He is portrayed, then Christ lived and lives, whether He was once one body and one soul, or whether He is the essence of man's highest dreams."

### Not Heresy, but Apostasy

The Catholic editorial immediately adds, and most appropriately: "To lodge the accusation of 'heresy' against the author of this sentence is to err seriously regarding the nature of the offense. These sonorous platitudes constitute a total apostasy."

Then follow the conclusions which Rome believes must necessarily be drawn from such an incident as this:

"Yet, given the principle of private judgment, how can one quarrel with any conclusion, however fantastic? The Scriptures, variously understood, have split Christendom into countless fragments. It was inherent in the principle that some erratic intelligence should at last conceive a Christ who never lived, but who is real because 'He is the essence of men's highest dreams.'

"It is a chaotic world in about every field of human activity. But, by the grace of God, we are spared uncertainty in that sphere of life which is paramount above all others. The Catholic Church, protected by the abiding presence of the Spirit of truth, teaches at this hour the faith delivered to the apostles.

# APPENDIXES

"She teaches, not speculatively, or with mere probability, but with an assurance which is altogether divine. Her credentials entitle her to the allegiance of every reasonable intelligence. The day draws nearer when the simplest of minds must perceive that their choice lies between her or nothing."

But a very vital point is overlooked in this Catholic editorial, and that is that this Protestant missionary under discussion found it necessary to resign because of her views. And why?—Because those views were so clearly at variance with the teachings of Scripture that she could not continue her work with the Presbyterian Board. The second fact overlooked is this: That the reason why such views as those of this missionary are held by an increasing number in Protestant communions is not so much because of a new interpretation of the Scriptures, as because of a repudiation of them.

## Changed Basis of Comparison

It is one thing to deal with the centuries-old controversy of private judgment in terms of the historic attitude of Protestantism, that the Bible is the infallible, inerrant word of God from cover to cover, and therefore to be accepted and followed implicitly as its teachings are revealed to the heart through prayer; it is an altogether different thing to deal with this doctrine of private judgment in terms of what is now becoming the widely accepted view of Protestantism—that the Bible is not the infallible, inerrant guide for our lives, and that prayer does not bring enlightenment and understanding of God's will. There is really little if any comparison between the two positions, and it brings only confusion of thought to attempt to test the validity of the Reformers' beliefs regarding the Bible and private judgment by the deplorable situation now existing, of which this Presbyterian missionary incident is a striking illustration.

As already remarked, the Catholic *Pilot* spoke accurately when it declared that "to lodge a charge of 'heresy' against" this missionary is "to err seriously regarding the nature of the offense," that, instead, her utterances "constitute a total apostasy." Why should the views of one who, it is admitted, has apostatized, be used as evidence of the dangerous beliefs held by those from whom she has apostatized? Rome answers: "Because her apostate views grew naturally from the Protestant premises of private judgment." To which we reply that this apostasy from historic Christian teaching regarding Christ, involves *also* an apostasy from basic Protestant beliefs regarding the Bible, the Spirit of God, and prayer—beliefs which dominate and control the

879

principle of private judgment. Therefore we inquire again, Why present as evidence against Protestantism the views of one who has apostatized from the primary tenets on which historic Protestantism was built?

It was not the teaching of the Reformers that everyone's private views on religion are equally valid, but simply that there is no tribunal that God has set up in this world before which those views are to be judged; and the *Pilot* therefore caricatures the basic idea in the Reformers' teaching by declaring that, "given the principle of private judgment, how can one quarrel with any conclusion, however fantastic?" In other words, the essence of the Reformers' position in this matter was not that private judgment is infallible, or even good in various cases, but that the claim of the Catholic Church to the right of domination over the private judgment and beliefs of men, is altogether wrong.

The application of the principle of private judgment to the interpretation of Scripture was based, by the Reformers, on the following beliefs: That God has revealed His will to men in an infallible Book; that Christians are enjoined in the Scriptures to study this Book; that we are promised God's Spirit to enlighten our minds, that we may discern spiritual things and may be led into all truth; that nowhere does the Bible declare that God has set up any human institution to stand between the Christian and the understanding of the Bible.

It may be freely granted that the application of these principles has permitted a certain divergence in Protestantism through the centuries. But such divergence, contrasted with the seeming unity of Rome, does not in itself provide the proof that the Protestant attitude toward the Scriptures is wrong and the Catholic one right. It is possible to maintain quite a definite measure of unity of utterance in an organization without possession of any supernatural or infallible powers. It is also possible, on the other hand, in various branches of an organization, to have a considerable amount of divergence on secondary questions, while maintaining a remarkable unity on vital matters.

### Remarkable Unity

A reading of the great Reformation creeds reveals a singular measure of unity on the vital doctrines of salvation, a measure of unity, indeed, that can be explained only on the ground that the Divine Spirit has exercised a manifested degree of control over the hearts and minds of all. An examination, on the other hand, of beliefs that have been held inside the circle of the Catholic Church, indicates that a wide variation has been present there, despite the closely knit nature of the organization—divergences and controversies so sharp that if equivalent ones had occurred in Protestant ranks, Catholic writers would have made capital of them.

## *Wylie's Critical Comments*

On this very point Wylie, in his notable essay, "The Papacy," observes:

"When one man only in the world is permitted to think, and the rest are compelled to agree with him, unity should be of as easy attainment as it is worthless when attained. Yet despite the despotism of force and the despotism of ignorance, which have been employed in all ages to crush free inquiry and open discussion in the Church of Rome, serious differences and furious disputes have broken out in her. When we name the pope, we indicate the whole extent of her unity. Here she is at one, or has usually been so; on every other point she is disagreed. The theology of Rome has differed materially in different ages; so that her members have believed one set of opinions in one age, and another set of opinions in another age. What was sound doctrine in the sixth century, was heresy in the twelfth; and what was sufficient for salvation in the twelfth century, is altogether insufficient for it in our day.

"Transubstantiation was invented in the thirteenth century; it was followed, at the distance of three centuries, by the sacrifice of the mass; and that again, in our day, by the immaculate conception of the virgin. In the twelfth century, the Lombardic (so called from Peter Lombard, who collected the opinions of the fathers into one volume; the differences he had hoped to reconcile he but succeeded, from their proximity, in making more apparent) theology, which mingled faith and works in the justification of the sinner, was in repute. This had its day, and was succeeded in about a hundred years after by the scholastic theology. The schoolmen discarded faith, and gave works alone a place in the important matter of justification. On the ruins of the scholastic divinity flourished the monastic theology. This system extolled papal indulgences, adoration of images, prayers to saints, and works of supererogation; and on these grounds rested the sinner's justification. The Reformation came, and a modified theology next became fashionable, in which the grosser errors were abandoned to suit the newly risen light.

"But now all these systems have given place to the theology of the Jesuits, whose system differs in several important points from all that went before it. On the head of justification the Jesuitical theology teaches that habitual righteousness is an infused grace, but that actual righteousness consists in the merit of good works. Here are five theologies which have successively been in vogue in the Church of Rome. Which of these five systems is the orthodox one? Or are they all orthodox?

"But not only do we desiderate unity between the successive ages of the Romish Church; we desiderate unity among her contemporary doctors and councils. They have differed on questions of ceremonies, on questions of morals, and they have differed not less on the questions of the supremacy and infallibility. Contrariety of opinion has been the rule; agreement the exception. Council has contended with council; pope has excommunicated pope; Dominican has warred with Franciscan; and the Jesuits have carried on ceaseless and furious battles with the Benedictines and other orders. What, indeed, are these various orders, but ingenious contrivances to allay heats and divisions which Rome could not heal, and to allow of differences of opinion which she could neither prevent nor remove? What one infallible bull has upheld as sound doctrine, another infallible bull has branded as heresy. Europe has been edified with the spectacle of two rival vicars of Christ playing at football with the spiritual thunder; and what we find one holy Father, Nicholas, commending as an assembly of men filled with the Holy Ghost, namely, the Council of Basil, we find another holy father, Eugenius, depicting as 'madmen, barbarians, wild beasts, heretics, miscreants, monsters, and a pandemonium.'—*Elliott's 'Delineation of Romanism,'* p. 463. But there is no end of the illustrations of papal unity. The wars of the Romanists have filled history and shaken the world. The loud and discordant clatter which rose of old around Babel is but a faint type of the interminable din and furious strife which at all times have raged within the modern Babel,—the Church of Rome.

"Such is the unity which the Romish Church so often and so tauntingly contrasts with what she is pleased to term 'Protestant disunion.' As a corporation, having its head at Rome, and stretching its limbs to the extremities of the earth, she is of gigantic bulk and imposing appearance; but, closely examined, she is seen to be an assemblage of heterogeneous materials, held together simply by the compression of force. It is a coercive power from without, not an attractive influence from within, that gives her being and form. The appearance of union and compactness which she puts on at a distance is altogether owing to her organization, which is of the most perfect kind, and of the most despotic character, and not to any spiritual and vivifying principle, whose influence, descending from the head, moves the members, and results in harmony of feeling, unanimity of mind, and unity of action.

It is combination, not incorporation; union, not unity, that characterizes the Church of Rome. It is the unity of dead matter, not the unity of a living body, whose several members, though performing various functions, obey one will and form one whole. It is not the spiritual and living unity promised to the Church of God, which preserves the liberty of all, at the same time that it makes all ONE: it is a unity that degrades the understanding, supersedes rational inquiry, and annihilates private judgment. It leaves no room for conviction, and therefore no room for faith. It is a unity that extorts from all submission to one infallible head, that compels all to a participation in one monstrous and idolatrous rite, and that enchains the intellect of all to a farrago of contradictory, absurd, and blasphemous opinions. This is the unity of Rome. Men must be free agents before it can be shown that they are voluntary agents. In like manner, the members of the Church must have liberty to differ before it can be shown that they really are agreed. But Rome denies her people this liberty, and thus renders it impossible that it can ever be shown that they are united. She resolves all into absolute authority, which in no case may either be questioned or opposed. Dr. Milner, after striving hard, in one of his letters [End of Controversy, let. xvi.], to show that all Catholics are agreed as regards the 'fundamental articles of Christianity,' is forced to conclude with the admission, that they are only so far agreed as that they all implicitly submit to the infallible teaching of the Church. 'At all events,' says he, 'the Catholics, if properly interrogated, will confess their belief in one comprehensive article, namely this, *'I believe whatever the Holy Catholic Church believes and teaches.'* So, then, this renowned champion of Roman Catholicism, forced to abandon all other positions as untenable, comes at last to rest the argument in behalf of his Church's unity upon this, even the unreasoning and unquestioning submission of the conscience to the teaching of the Church. In point of fact, this 'one comprehensive article' sums up the entire creed of the Papist: the Church inquires for him, thinks for him, reasons for him, and believes for him; or, as it was expressed by a plain-speaking Hibernian, who, making his last speech and dying confession at the place of execution, and resolved not to expose himself to purgatory for want of not believing enough, declared, 'that he was a Roman Catholic, and died in the communion of that Church, and believed as the Catholic Church ever did believe, now doth believe, or ever shall believe.' Put out the eyes of men, and there will be only one opinion about colour; extinguish the understandings of men, and there will be but one opinion regarding religion. This is what Rome does. With her rod of infallibility she touches the intellect and the conscience, and benumbs them into torpor. There comes thus to reign within her pale a deep stillness, broken at times by ridiculous disputes, furious quarrels, and serious differences, on points termed fundamental, which remain unsettled from age to age,—the famous question, for instance, touching the seat of infallibility; and this profound quiescence, so like the repose of the tomb, accomplished by the waving of her mystic rod, she calls unity."—*The Papacy*, by J. A. Wylie, pp. 194-198.

### The Answer to the Problem

The answer to the distressing problem of divergence of belief on the part of those who hold to the Bible as their one guide, is not to surrender their minds to the Catholic Church, but to pray the more earnestly for divine enlightenment by the Spirit of God, "till we all come in the unity of the faith, and of the knowledge of the Son of God, unto a perfect man, unto the measure of the stature of the fulness of Christ." Eph. 4:13. Quite evidently in Paul's day there were some divergences, or else there would have been no point to the statement about coming into "the unity of the faith."

Of course, it must not be forgotten that one of the handicaps that belong to the Protestant position is that a man who for some selfish or stubborn reason desires to hold to some diverse view, can do so on the declaration that he sees the matter thus and so, even though his mind may have been clearly convinced to the contrary by the Scriptural evidence and God's Spirit. The Protestant view sets up no tribunal to judge the hearts of men, no confessional to probe the innermost thoughts of the soul, and thus a man's hypocrisy cannot be uncloaked; yet the differences of view that grow out of such a situation as this, and doubtless there are numbers of them, when we remember the willfullness of the human heart, provide no proper indictment of the Reformers' principle of private judgment in relation to the Bible. God alone can reveal hypocrisy, and we must await the day of judgment for that.

### Cannot Accept Catholic Conclusion

We cannot agree with the conclusion of the *Pilot* editorial: "The day draws nearer when the simplest of minds must perceive that their choice lies between her [the Catholic Church] or nothing." The choice is not that of the Catholic Church or nothing. Rome offers us the Bible plus tradition, with tradition taking precedence over the Bible, and with both interpreted by the Catholic Church. Historic Protestantism offers us the Bible alone, and as interpreted to our hearts by the Spirit of God, who will guide the believer "into all truth." John 16:13.

The question is really three sided, for there are not only the Catholic and Protestant views, but also that of a large number today who have discarded both the Bible and tradition, who have faith neither in the Catholic Church's interpretation nor in the supernatural operation of the Spirit of God on the human heart and mind. This third group, known loosely as Modernists, or Liberals, offer the Bible plus scientific works, with the latter given precedence over the former, and with both interpreted by human reason. The presence of this third group today makes the religious problem much more complex than formerly, when the question was simply one between the Catholic Church and historic Protestantism. There is a new need for those who stand on the platform of the Bible and the Bible only, to provide strong reasons for their stand. They are beset today, not alone by their traditional opponent, Rome, but by a new and even more subtle one, Modernism.

# SCRIPTURE INDEX

# Scripture Index

# SCRIPTURE INDEX

# ANSWERS TO OBJECTIONS

# SCRIPTURE INDEX

We invite you to view the complete
selection of titles we publish at:

**www.TEACHServices.com**

Scan with your mobile
device to go directly
to our website.

Please write or e-mail us your praises, reactions, or
thoughts about this or any other book we publish at:

P.O. Box 954
Ringgold, GA 30736

**info@TEACHServices.com**

TEACH Services, Inc., titles may be purchased in bulk for
educational, business, fund-raising, or sales promotional use.
For information, please e-mail:

**BulkSales@TEACHServices.com**

Finally, if you are interested in seeing
your own book in print, please contact us at

**publishing@TEACHServices.com**

We would be happy to review your manuscript for free.

CPSIA information can be obtained
at www.ICGtesting.com
Printed in the USA
FFHW010708111119
56014928-61902FF